Share Investing

4th Australian Edition

by James Dunn

for dummies®

A Wiley Brand

Share Investing For Dummies®, 4th Australian Edition

Published by
John Wiley & Sons Australia, Ltd
Level 1, 155 Cremorne Street
Richmond, Vic 3121
www.dummies.com

ISBN: 978-0-730-39653-6

 A catalogue record for this
book is available from the
National Library of Australia

Cover image: © WHYFRAME/Shutterstock

Typeset by SPi

 M WEP338875 160125

Contents at a Glance

Table of Contents

Introduction

I said these important words in the first three editions of this book, and now I'm saying them again — thanks for choosing *Share Investing For Dummies*. In this fourth edition, I bring you up to date on how the Australian sharemarket is dealing with the massive societal and economic changes wrought by the global COVID-19 pandemic; as it happens, in the introduction to the third edition I talked about bringing readers up to date on how the market was recovering from the massive financial storm that hit it (and all its global peers!) between 2007 and 2009, during the global financial crisis (GFC). Just as the GFC and the market slump that ensued eventually receded into history — despite denting many investors' faith in investing in shares — I'm reasonably confident that COVID-19 will do the same.

In any case, just as in the preceding editions, such changes in the sharemarket give me a backdrop to set out how, despite the scary headlines and the ever-present possibility of a market fall, profitable companies continue to generate capital growth for their shareholders over the long term. The great paradox of the sharemarket is that while it is the most volatile of the asset classes, it is also the one most capable of reliably building wealth over the long term for the individual investor; I show you how in this book.

I've attempted to describe some of the wondrous investment stories that have played out on the corporate paddock since the first edition of the book was published 21 years ago — as well as some of the less luminous stories that are always possible when you're investing in shares. This fourth edition also updates my advice on where to start if you're a first-time investor, some of the newer tools that are available to you, some of the pitfalls to avoid and how to have fun (and not take too many risks) while your money goes to work for you.

Australia has grown and developed in many directions since the first edition of *Share Investing For Dummies* welcomed investors taking their first steps into the sharemarket. If you followed the first three editions, you're hopefully now managing a portfolio, researching stocks that interest you, keeping abreast of the daily market play and boosting your initial investment to something that'll at least pay for your dream holiday and at best see you comfortably through the years.

In many of the speeches and presentations that I've made around the country in 33 years as a finance journalist, I've tried to present the sharemarket as a hugely interesting institution. Because it is! And, moreover, this market, which touches everyone's lives in one way or another, doesn't have to be daunting. The sharemarket is not a hard concept to understand. When people say to me that I make the idea of buying and selling shares understandable for them, I curse whatever it was they'd been reading or hearing that made it appear the opposite.

About This Book

Share Investing For Dummies explains the sharemarket's intricacies in terms that anyone can understand. Although the sharemarket looks like a high-tech computer game, with its flashing lights and scrolling letters and numbers on the trading screens, the sharemarket is actually based on a very simple concept. Companies divide their capital into tiny units called *shares*, and anyone can buy or sell these units in a free market at any time. Companies use the sharemarket to raise funds from the public, and the public — meaning you — invests in the companies' shares. You invest your money in shares because you expect to get a better return in earnings than with other investments.

Most of the time the sharemarket is profitable for investors. Despite the occasional spectacular market fall, such as the great 'bear market' of 2007 to 2009 — or even the odd collapse of one of its constituent companies — the sharemarket generally plods along making money for its investors. The sharemarket revolves around money, but it is also very much a human institution. The sharemarket is sometimes described as a living entity (for which we finance journalists are often mocked). Oddly, the sharemarket does have human moods because it reflects the greed or fear of its users, who are sometimes *very* human.

Greed is a powerful influence on the sharemarket, and so is fear. A saying on Wall Street suggests that these two emotions are the only influences ever at work on the sharemarket, and they fight a daily battle for supremacy. On a day-to-day basis, the sharemarket wavers between the two. The 2000s began with the fear of the 'tech bust', then switched firmly to greed for the middle part of the decade, only for fear to come roaring back into the spotlight in late 2007. Greed regained its primacy in early 2009 and — despite a major interruption in 2020 as COVID-19 reared its ugly head — the 'risk-on' approach of viewing the sharemarket as a money-making machine has prevailed virtually right through until the time of writing. All of which goes to ensure that fear will have its day again, and sooner rather than later.

The sheer range of activities of the companies listed on the Australian Securities Exchange (formerly the Australian Stock Exchange) makes it a very interesting place — if a trading system that you can see only on computer screens all over the nation can be called a place. The number of different types of shares you can invest in is mind-boggling — perhaps there is too much choice. As an individual investor, you can't own every type of share so the solution is to come up with an investment strategy.

As you will discover, of the 2,200 or so stocks listed on the Australian Securities Exchange (ASX), most investment professionals confine their activity to about one-sixth of them. Even in the 500 stocks that comprise the S&P/ASX All Ordinaries index (one of the Australian sharemarket's main indicators), the last 1,900 or so don't hold much interest to Australian fund managers. This is where a self-reliant investor like you can find some undiscovered gems caught in that bind of being too small to attract the fund managers' and brokers' attention, and then remaining small because they can't get this attention. Some of the sharemarket's acorns really do become great oaks. As a self-reliant investor, with the knowledge and the time to thoroughly research potential stock purchases, you can really steal a march on the pros.

It gets harder and potentially more rewarding the deeper you delve into the sharemarket. In the bottom 1,900 or so stocks, you may find some real dogs that should not be listed (and probably won't be for much longer), but you can also discover wonderful companies that are about to flourish. This kind of investing is called bottom-fishing. You need to be wary and know how to back up your discoveries with solid research. At these depths of the market, you can make some very wrong moves.

You don't actually have to own some of the 2,200 stocks in order to experience the ups and downs of the sharemarket; one of the big changes in the market in the last two decades has been the introduction of (and growth in) simple and cheap listed instruments that give you instant, diversified exposure to the sharemarket (whether you choose the Australian, US, global or other country markets) and asset classes in general. Access to the sharemarket has never been easier, and I take you through that, whether you want to invest at the individual stock (company) level or the index (sharemarket itself) level. The tools that enable you to get into the market intelligently are right here in this book.

The sharemarket should be an essential part of everybody's investment strategy. Sharemarket participation in Australia is among the highest in the world, but too many people still don't understand its benefits. As the nation's population ages and superannuation grows in importance, the amount of Australians' investment assets (and retirement nest eggs) going into Australian shares is set to rise dramatically. My aim in this book is to help you understand the sharemarket so that you can control your future financial security.

Foolish Assumptions

This book doesn't require you to have any prior knowledge of investing in shares — that's my job. However, I do make a few assumptions about you — I assume you're interested in the sharemarket and you want to find out a bit more. Perhaps you've read a few blogs, watched a few YouTube videos or read other books that piece together various aspects of share investing, and you're looking for something to help you turn the theory into reality. Perhaps you've already traded shares online at some stage, or maybe you've realised that the bulk of your superannuation is held in shares, and you want to know why — and how that works.

Wherever you're starting from, this book is designed to help you build on your existing knowledge and develop your understanding of the sharemarket and the things that influence it — for good and bad.

Icons Used in This Book

Throughout this book you see friendly and useful icons to enhance your reading pleasure and highlight special kinds of information. The icons give added emphasis to the details that I think are extra important.

REMEMBER

Take extra special notice of this piece of information. You may find this detail is something to store away for future use.

TECHNICAL STUFF

It's not vital that you read this stuff as you'll get a good understanding of the subject matter anyway. But it's often interesting and sometimes an entertaining diversion.

TIP

This is information I think you can profit from, so I've pre-highlighted it for you (I'm trying to save you from getting highlighter ink on the opposite page when you close the book).

WARNING

Uh-oh! Wealth hazard ahead! Manoeuvre carefully around this obstacle, and mark it down in the memory bank.

Where to Go from Here

In this book, I set out the risks and the rewards of share investing, explain where the returns come from that can make share investing a rewarding and lucrative experience, and outline the many things that influence the prices of shares. I follow a logical order so that you can easily navigate to the correct chapter to find out more about particular aspects of share investing. For example, you may be itching to explore investment strategy ideas (which I cover in Part 2) or prefer to start with the basics in Part 1. Alternatively, you may be looking for inspiration when picking the stocks that suit your risk 'comfort zone' (Part 3), or you might want to contemplate looking further afield at overseas shares and derivatives (Part 5). And if you're feeling particularly keen, you may find yourself drawn to the number-crunching involved when making sense of fundamental and technical analysis techniques (Part 4) — just don't forget your calculator!

I hope that after you go through this book, you'll want to take the next steps to starting your first portfolio of shares. And if you're already an investor — great! You'll be ready to become a better-informed and more effective investor. Work out what financial security means to you, sit down with a financial adviser (or not; but it is advisable) and decide how shares can help you achieve your goals. Then, get started. Today!

Thanks for allowing me to play a small part in your journey — I'm excited for you too, as I know what an adventure it can be.

1

Putting the Share in Sharemarket

IN THIS CHAPTER

» **Timing your investments**

» **Defining a share**

» **Buying for profit**

» **Discovering the five big pluses**

» **Reducing risk**

Chapter **1**

So, You Want to Invest in Shares

I f you've been hearing about the sharemarket for a long time, but you're only now taking the plunge, welcome aboard. There simply isn't a better place to invest money.

You're probably already familiar with shares and how they generate long-term wealth. In that case, you may want to skim through Chapter 1 and Chapter 2 quickly and then move on to Chapter 3 for an in-depth view of investment strategies. If that isn't the case, then you're in the right spot to get started.

Investing Is All about Timing

Australians are among the world's most avid share investors, with the Australian Securities Exchange (ASX) reporting in its 2020 *Australian Investor Study* that 35 per cent of the adult population, or 6.6 million people, directly own listed investments — a term that covers shares, real estate investment trusts (REITs), exchange-traded funds (ETFs), listed investment companies (LICs), listed hybrid securities and anything quoted on an exchange (the ASX and international exchanges). The figure is slightly lower than the 37 per cent of adult investors who owned on-exchange investments in the 2017 *Australian Investor Study*.

While this proportion has fallen from the 55 per cent that owned shares in the ASX *Share Ownership Study* in 2004, the ASX now looks more broadly at investing. The ASX used to compare Australia's share ownership levels with its overseas peer-group of markets, but differences in methodology mean that it no longer does so. For example, official US data measures share ownership — directly or indirectly — by households. A survey released by polling group Gallup in April 2020 found that 55 per cent of American households reported having money invested in the share-market, either in an individual stock, a mutual fund or a retirement account. That figure was down from 60 per cent before the 'Great Recession' (what Australians would call the global financial crisis, or GFC) of December 2007 to June 2009.

The ASX's 2020 *Australian Investor Study* found that:

>> 9 million adult Australians own investments outside of superannuation and their primary residence.

>> Of those 9 million, 6.6 million own on-exchange investments, making them the most widely used type of investment. Other options invested in included investment properties (residential or commercial), unlisted managed funds and term deposits.

>> Of the 6.6 million who own on-exchange investments, 58 per cent own shares listed on an Australian exchange and 15 per cent own shares listed on an international exchange.

>> 15 per cent of Australian investors own ETFs.

>> Close to a quarter of all investors had started investing in the two years leading up to the study.

>> Women now make up 45 per cent of all new investors.

In addition to this data, Australian investors own a further $1.2 trillion worth of shares (domestic shares of $595 billion and international shares of $610 billion), which are managed for them in their superannuation accounts.

Furthermore, a 2021 report from investment research firm Investment Trends, the *2021 1H Online Investing Report*, found that during 2020, 435,000 Australians began trading listed investments for the very first time amid the pandemic-induced lockdown. The report said this took the population of *active retail online investors* (defined as those buying or selling shares at least once over the 2020 calendar year) in Australia to a new high of 1.2 million.

Of these new-to-market traders, 18 per cent were younger than 25 years of age and 49 per cent were aged between 25 and 39, indicating what Investment Trends called an 'unprecedented' spike in activity by Millennial (born between 1981 and

1996) and Generation Z (born after 1997) Australians. This increase in active traders represents a 135 per cent jump since June 2013 and a 66 per cent increase year-on-year from December 2019.

The Investment Trends research also found that the number of Australians actively trading international shares (as opposed to ASX-listed investments) doubled from 54,000 to 109,000 over the course of 2020. The report suggested that growth in the supply of low-cost digital investing and stockbroking products, many of which provide easy access to the US and other offshore markets, was supporting the influx of new sharemarket participants.

So, chances are you've dipped your toes in the sharemarket pond (at least indirectly) before picking up this book.

Figure 1-1 shows share investing trends in Australia from 1986 to 2020.

Ownership of on-exchange investments, proportion of adult population

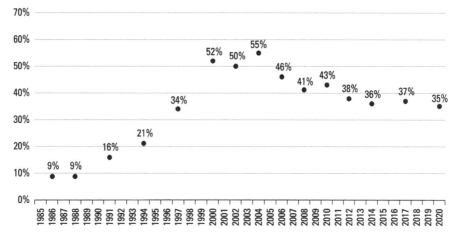

FIGURE 1-1: Ownership of on-exchange investments in Australia 1986–2020.

Source: 2020 Australian Investment Study, Australian Securities Exchange

Note: Where earlier data relies on ownership of shares, the studies since 2014 have used ownership of all listed investment products offered at ASX, which includes shares.

'Hang on,' you say, 'doesn't the sharemarket crash and correct regularly? What about the headlines that talk of billions of dollars of investors' savings being wiped off the value of the sharemarket in a day?' (For one example among many, see the sidebar 'Just another (crazy) year on the sharemarket', later in this chapter.)

Occasionally, that happens. No-one who goes into the sharemarket can afford to ignore the fact that, from time to time, share prices can suddenly move in an extreme fashion — sometimes up, sometimes down. When share prices move down, they attract media headlines. However, what the headlines don't tell you is that on many other days, the sharemarket is quietly adding billions — or even just millions — of dollars in value to investors' savings (I expand upon this in Chapter 3).

People want to invest in the sharemarket because the unique qualities of shares or stocks (the terms are used interchangeably in Australia) as financial assets make the sharemarket the best and most reliable long-term generator of personal wealth available to investors. Since 1900, according to AMP Capital, Australian shares have earned a return of approximately 11.8 per cent a year, split fairly evenly (49 per cent to 51 per cent) between capital growth and dividend income respectively.

And since 1950, according to research house Andex Charts, the All Ordinaries Accumulation Index (which counts dividends reinvested, as well as capital gain) has delivered an average return of 11.7 per cent a year up to 31 December 2020, which is enough to turn an investment of $100 in 1950 into $260,786 (see Figure 1-2). That compares to 7.5 per cent a year for bonds, 6.1 per cent a year for cash, and inflation at 4.8 per cent a year (making the sharemarket's real or *after-inflation* return 6.9 per cent a year). In the 30 years to 31 December 2020, says Andex Charts, the same index earned 10.1 per cent a year, for a real return of 7.8 per cent a year.

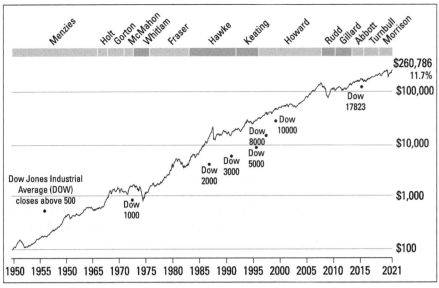

FIGURE 1-2:
The growth of a $100 investment in the sharemarket over 70 years.

Source: Andex Charts Pty Ltd

This performance track record makes the sharemarket a serious money-making machine, with one important caveat: not all shares make money (see Chapter 3).

In 1985, the Australian stock market was valued at $76 billion, about one-third of Australia's *gross domestic product* (GDP — the amount of goods and services produced in the Australian economy). In May 2021, the stock market was valued at $2,400 billion, while GDP was about $2,000 billion. Although the nation's economic output has grown almost nine times since 1985, the value of the stock market has grown by almost 32 times.

Investing is about building wealth for yourself, to help you have the lifestyle you want, educate and give your children a start in life and ensure that you have a well-funded, carefree retirement.

When you invest in shares, you get a number of advantages, such as:

» The opportunity to buy a part of the company for a small outlay of cash

» A share of the company's profit through the payment of dividends (a portion of company profits distributed to shareholders)

» The company's retained earnings working for you as well

» The possibility of capital gains as the share price rises over time

» An easy way to buy and sell assets.

The sharemarket is virtually unbeatable as a place for individuals to build long-term wealth. Shares can provide long-term capital growth as well as an income through dividends: just over half of the long-term return from the sharemarket comes from dividends.

The sharemarket has an exaggerated reputation as a sort of Wild West for money and therefore it can be a daunting place for a new investor. The sharemarket is a huge and impersonal financial institution; yet paradoxically, it's also a market that's alive with every human emotion — greed, and fear, hope and defeat, elation and despair. The sharemarket can be a trap for fools or a place to create enormous wealth. Those who work in the industry see daily the best and worst of human behaviour. And you thought the sharemarket was simply a market in which shares were bought and sold!

The sharemarket is precisely that: a place for buying and selling shares. Approximately $7 billion worth of shares change hands every trading day. Shares are revalued in price every minute, reacting to supply, demand, news and sentiment, or the way that investors collectively feel about the likely direction of the market. The sharemarket also works to mobilise your money and channel your hard-earned funds to the companies that put those funds at risk for the possibility of gain. That ever-present element of risk, which can't be neutralised, makes the sharemarket a dangerous place for the unwary. Although you take a risk with any kind of investment, being forearmed with sound knowledge of what you're getting into and forewarned about potential traps are absolutely essential for your survival in the market.

Finding Out What a Share Is

Companies divide their capital into millions (sometimes billions) of units known as shares. Each share is a unit of ownership in the company, in its assets and in its profits. Companies issues shares through the sharemarket to raise funds for their operating needs; investors buy those shares, expecting capital gains and dividends. If the company fails, a share is also an entitlement to a portion of whatever assets remain after all of the company's liabilities are paid.

A share is

>> Technically a loan to a company, although the loan is never repaid. The loan is borrowed permanently — like the car keys, if you have teenagers.

>> A financial asset that the shareholders of a company own, as opposed to the real assets of the company — its land, buildings and the machines, computers and equipment that its workers use to produce goods and services. Assets (both tangible and intangible) generate income; financial assets allocate that income. When you buy a share, what you are really buying is a share of the future flow of profits.

>> A right to part ownership, proportional to the number of shares owned. In law, the part of the assets of a company owned by shareholders is called equity (the shareholders' funds). Shares are sometimes called equities. They are also called securities because they signify ownership with certain rights.

Now you know what you're getting when you buy shares. You become a part-owner of the company. As a shareholder, you have the right to vote on the company's major decisions. Saying 'I'm a part-owner of Qantas' sounds so much more impressive than 'I'm a Qantas Frequent Flyer member.' Just remember not to insist on sitting in with the pilots; as a shareholder, your ownership of Qantas is a bit more arm's-length than that. That's what shares were invented to do — separate the ownership of the company from those who manage and run it.

Sharing the profit, not the loss

When you're a shareholder in a company you can sit back and watch as the company earns, hopefully, a profit on its activities. After paying the costs of doing business — raw materials, wages, interest on any loans and other items — the company distributes a portion of the profit to you and other shareholders; the rest is retained for reinvestment. This profit share is called a dividend, which is a specified amount paid every six months on each share issued by the company. Shareholders receive a dividend payment for the total amount earned on their shareholding.

If the company makes a loss, shareholders are not required to make up the difference. All this means is that they won't receive a dividend payment that year, unless the company dips into its reserves to pay (for more on dividends, see the section, 'Dividend income'). However, too many non-profitable years and the company can go under, taking both its original investment and its chances of capital growth with it.

Companies that offer shares to the public are traded on the sharemarket as limited companies, which means the liability of the shareholders is limited to their original investment. This original investment is all they can lose. Suits for damages come out of shareholders' equity, which may lower profits, but individual investors aren't liable. Again, shareholders won't be happy if the company continues to lose money this way.

Understanding the market in sharemarket

Shares aren't much good to you without a market in which to trade them. The sharemarket brings together everybody who owns shares — or would like to own shares — and lets them trade among themselves. At any time, anybody with money can buy some shares.

The sharemarket is a matchmaker for money and shares. If you want to buy some shares, you place a buying order on the market and wait for someone to sell you the amount you want. If you want to sell, you put your shares up for sale and wait for interested buyers to beat a path to your door.

The trouble with the matchmaker analogy is that some people really do fall in love with their shares. (I talk about this more in Chapter 7.) Just as in real love, their feelings can blind them to the imperfections of the loved one.

REMEMBER

Shares are assets that are meant to do a job — to make money for you as the investor and your family. Making money is what the right shares do, given time.

Because shares are revalued constantly, the total value of a portfolio of shares, which is a collection of shares in different companies, fluctuates from day to day. Some days the portfolio loses value. But over time, a good share portfolio (or, more correctly, a portfolio of good-quality shares) shrugs off the volatility in prices and begins to create wealth for its owner. The more time you give the sharemarket to perform this task, the more wealth the sharemarket can create.

Buying Shares to Get a Return

Shares in successful companies create wealth. As companies issue shares and prosper, their profits increase and so does the value of their shares. Because the price of a share is tied to a company's profitability, the value of the share is expected to rise when the company is successful. In other words, higher quality shares usually cost more.

Earning a profit

Successful companies have successful shares because investors want them. In the sharemarket, buyers of sought-after shares pay higher prices to tempt the people who own the shares to part with them. Increasing prices is the main way in which shares create wealth. The other way is by paying an income or dividend, although not all shares do this. A share can be a successful wealth creator without paying an income.

As a company earns a profit, some of the profit is paid to the company's owners in the form of dividends. The company also retains some of the profit. Assuming that the company's earnings grow, the principle of compound interest starts to apply (see Chapter 3 for more on how compound interest works). The retained earnings grow and the return on the invested capital grows as well. That's how companies grow in value.

Ideally, you buy a share because you believe that share is going to rise in price. If the share does rise in price and you sell the share for more than you paid, you have made a capital gain. Of course, the opposite situation, a capital loss, can and does occur — if you've chosen badly, or had bad luck. These bad-luck shares, in the technical jargon of the sharemarket, are known as dogs. The simple trick to succeeding on the sharemarket is to make sure that you have more of the former experience than the latter!

When creating wealth, shares consistently outperform many other investments. Occasionally you may see comparisons with esoteric assets, such as thoroughbred horses, art or wine, which imply that these assets are better earners than shares. However, these are not mainstream assets, and the comparison is usually misleading. The original investment was probably extremely hard to secure and not as accessible, and not as *liquid* (easily bought and sold) as shares.

Of the mainstream asset classes (in terms of creating wealth over the long term), shares usually outdo property and outperform *bonds* (loan investments bearing a fixed rate of interest) — especially once the impact of franking credits (see Chapter 18) is taken into account.

Investing carefully to avoid a loss

Shares offer a higher return compared to other investments, but they also have a correspondingly higher risk. Risk and return always go together — an inescapable fact of investment, as I discuss in Chapter 4. The prices of shares fluctuate much more than those of property, while bonds are relatively stable in price. The major risk with shares is that, if you have to sell your shares for whatever reason, they may, at that time, be selling for less than you bought them. Or they may be selling for a lot more. This is the gamble you take.

Everybody who has money faces the decision of what to do with it. The unavoidable fact is that anywhere you place money, you face a risk that all or part of that money may be lost, either physically or hypothetically, in terms of its value. The simplest strategy is to deposit your money in a bank and leave it there. However, when you take the money out in the future, inflation (the rate of change in the price of everyday items) may decrease its buying power.

Risk is merely the other side of performance. You can't have high returns without running some risk. You can lower risk through the use of *diversification* — the spreading of your invested funds across a range of assets, as explained in Chapter 5.

REMEMBER

Trying to avoid risk is self-defeating because you're passing up the chance of any return, which is why you invest in the first place. So, accept risk, manage your level of risk and don't lose any sleep.

Making the Most of Share Investing

Investing in shares offers five big pluses. The first two pluses that I discuss in this section are the most critically important. The other three pluses are bonuses, one literally so.

Capital growth

As a company's revenue, profits and the value of its assets rise, so does the market price of its shares. Subjective factors, such as the market's perception of the company's prospects, also play a part in this process. After you've looked through this book, you'll know how to put together a share portfolio that makes the most of this crucial ingredient — capital growth.

REMEMBER

Shares are the undisputed champion of long-term capital growth (which I talk about further in Chapter 3). As the magic of compounding interest gets to work on the higher returns generated by shares, your portfolio starts to build wealth at an unmatched rate. The longer you hold your sharemarket investment, the better its performance over any other investment. By following a few basic rules (see the strategies for investment, also in Chapter 3), you can be confident your investment can keep on growing.

Dividend income

Shares may generate for their owners an income, which is called a *dividend* (a portion of company profits distributed to investors). The dividend is another important method for generating investor wealth — it accounts for just over half (51 per cent) of the long-term return of the sharemarket index. A company dividend is paid in two portions: an interim dividend for the first six months of the financial year, and a final dividend for the second half. The two amounts make up the annual dividend. Not every company pays a dividend, but the paying of dividends is a vital part of becoming a member of that elite group of shares known as blue chips.

TECHNICAL STUFF

Franking credits are not dividends paid directly to an investor but arise through the system of dividend imputation, in which shareholders receive a rebate for the tax the company has already paid on its profit. The flow of franking credits from a share portfolio can reduce, and in some cases abolish, your tax liability. (I look at dividend imputation in detail in Chapter 18.)

Shareholder discounts

Recently, another reason for owning shares — or, more correctly, a bonus for shareholders — has emerged in the form of the discounts companies offer to shareholders on their goods and services. Many companies offer some form of discount, and the number of companies making these offers is growing. These businesses realise that any inducement they can give people to buy their shares makes good marketing sense. Shareholder perks range from holiday deals to wine, shopping and banking discounts. For example, vitamins and supplements maker

Blackmores offers shareholders a 30 per cent discount on purchases of some of its range; Domino's Pizza Enterprises shareholders get discount codes on pizzas; and Event Hospitality & Entertainment shareholders can get discounted accommodation and dining at some of its Rydges, Atura or QT hotels, as well as discounts at Thredbo Alpine Resort and at the company's Event Cinemas, Greater Union, BCC and GU Film House cinemas.

Liquidity

A major attraction of shares as an asset class is that they are extremely liquid, meaning that you can easily buy and sell them. Through your broker's interface to the stock exchange's trading system, ASX Trade, virtually any number of shares put on the market by a seller can be matched with a buyer for that number of shares. Some shares are less liquid than others; therefore, if you buy unpopular shares, they may be hard to sell.

Divisibility

A share portfolio is easily divisible. If you, the shareholder, need to raise money by selling some shares, you can sell any number to raise any amount. Divisibility is a major attraction of shares as compared to property. You can't saw off your lounge room to sell it, but you can sell 500 Telstra shares with one phone call — or at the click of a mouse or a tap on a screen.

Guarding Against Risk

Shares are the riskiest of the major asset classes because no guarantees exist as to the likelihood of capital gains. Any investor approaching the sharemarket must accept this higher degree of risk.

REMEMBER

Share prices fluctuate continually and can move in a downward direction for extended periods of time. You can't get a signed, sealed and delivered guarantee that a share's price will rise at all after you buy it.

You can minimise but never avoid the risk that accompanies investing in shares. Share investment is riskier than alternative investments, but after you discover how to keep that risk under control, you can use this knowledge to build wealth for you and your family. I discuss the possible risks you can encounter and how to minimise their effects in Chapter 4.

JUST ANOTHER (CRAZY) YEAR ON THE SHAREMARKET

Sharemarket slumps are an occupational hazard to investors, but the COVID-19 crash of February–March 2020 was a doozy, mostly because of its unexpected source — the outbreak of a mysterious disease.

Coming into 2020, all was looking fine on the sharemarket front. By 19 February, the S&P 500 index was already 4.8 per cent to the good for 2020 so far; the S&P/ASX 200 was doing even better, up 6.8 per cent.

And then . . .

The sharemarket began to realise that the world was potentially dealing with the most lethal global pandemic in decades — the fast-spreading COVID-19.

The initial downward moves on the sharemarket did not seem too worrying. A succession of minor falls from 20 February took the slide to 12 per cent — officially into 'correction' territory (a fall of 10 per cent or more). But alarm was mounting, and as the cases and deaths increased, international travel began to slow down and companies worldwide began asking staff to work from home where they could. Airline and travel stocks started to feel the hit.

Monday 9 March 2020 was the day when COVID-19 — helped by a slump in the price of oil following news of the demise of a Russia–Saudi Arabian agreement to keep a curb on production to maintain oil prices — caught up with the global sharemarkets with a vengeance. The price of oil fell by more than 30 per cent. 'Black Monday' saw the S&P 500 lose 7.6 per cent, and the Dow Jones Industrial Average dropped by more than 2,000 points in a day for the first time ever, a decline of 7.8 per cent. In London, the FTSE 100 index lodged its fifth-worst day in history, plummeting by 7.7 per cent. France, Germany and Spain all lost about 8 per cent, outstripping the depths of the Eurozone sovereign debt crisis. The biggest sell-off came in Italy, with stocks in Milan collapsing by more than 11 per cent. The Australian market fell 7.3 per cent — a $155 billion loss.

In the space of just 22 trading days, the US market (the S&P 500) lost 30 per cent of its value, from its record high reached on 19 February 2020. That represented the fastest drop of such magnitude in sharemarket history. Scared by the potential fall-out of the COVID-19 crisis, investors dumped their shares, despite the massive stimulus and rescue packages being thrown at economies by governments and central banks. Investors were appalled at the job losses and welfare claims surged around the world, while economies and borders were deliberately shut down in an effort to contain the spread of the virus. Countries all over the world braced themselves for the deepest peacetime recession since the Great Depression of the 1930s.

The Australian market was not far behind its US peer, with the S&P/ASX 200 plunging 20.5 per cent in just 14 days — the sharpest fall in the local market since the historic 25 per cent slump on 'Black Tuesday' in October 1987 (which was the day after the US market lost 23 per cent in one day) — on its way to a 38.8 per cent slide to its lowest point, in just 22 trading days, during which the Australian market shed $680 billion in value.

During this early response to the pandemic, the global stock market plunged 30 per cent in just 40 trading days. By then, the sharemarket falls had gone well past a correction and they had moved beyond a bear market, too (for more on bear markets and periods of sharemarket volatility, turn to Chapter 3). This slump had officially become a market crash.

But somehow, although no-one knew it at the time, a temporary floor had been established as of 23 March.

While the sharemarket has never failed to recover from a loss, falls of such a severe extent usually take years to recover from. However, 2020 produced a stunning recovery. The US market (S&P 500 index) took just six months — 126 trading sessions — to return to the point from which it fell: an amazing 65 per cent rebound. In previous downturns, the index had taken an average of more than 1,500 sessions — equivalent to about six years — to return to its previous high.

In contrast, the local S&P/ASX 200 was positively pedestrian in recovery, taking almost a year and a half (until May 2021) to regain the lost ground and reach a new record high, with a 63.5 per cent recovery.

Despite COVID-19's depredations, investors responded positively to the unparalleled financial support that governments and central banks poured into the economy. Governments underwrote loans to companies and paid stood-down workers' wages. Central banks injected stupendous amounts of liquidity into the financial system. Because the sharemarket is a forward-looking beast, investors focused on the eventual rebound in activity and pushed indexes higher as the world got on top of COVID-19.

At the end of 2020, the US S&P 500 index was up 16.1 per cent for the year. The Australian S&P/ASX 200 index was down, but only by 2.2 per cent — the same degree of loss as the global sharemarket. If a person had been in a year-long coma and woke up to see those figures on New Year's Eve in 2020, they would have been forgiven for remarking, 'I see it was a pretty boring year on the sharemarket.' Instead, when investors caught their breath at the end of the year, they realised they had witnessed the

(continued)

(continued)

extremes of fear and greed of which a sharemarket is capable, all compressed into one unforgettable year. The fear caused the crash, in February–March; the greed drove the rebound, from late March onwards, as investors realised just how suddenly cheap many great companies were.

At time of writing, the US sharemarket is up 84 per cent on its 2020 low, the S&P/ASX 200 is up 66 per cent and the global sharemarket (MSCI World Index) is up 77 per cent. No-one ever knows when another crash will happen.

The February–March 2020 'COVID crash' was very quick in its onset, and very rapid in its recovery — seeing market behaviour as unpredictable as the pandemic's impact. But as Figure 1-2 shows, even the direst scenario has never stopped the sharemarket index from regaining its previous high-point and moving even higher.

IN THIS CHAPTER

» Obtaining shares through a float

» Perusing a prospectus

» Trading, buying and selling

» Meeting the major markets

» Introducing the futures market

Chapter 2

Watching the market operate

This chapter is about the two different types of market that make up the Australian sharemarket. The *primary* market is where companies, new or old, offer their shares to investors for the first time. This offer is called a *float*. Primary refers to the initial issuing of shares, not whether this particular type of market is more important. The *secondary* market is the day-to-day trading of all shares listed. Both of these markets make up the activity of the Australian stock market.

Floating of new companies is an important part of sharemarket activity, but small in terms of dollar value. Although floats of companies that are worth more than $1 billion are still relatively rare on the sharemarket, a typical day sees just over $7.2 billion traded on the secondary market ($5.8 billion through the Australian Securities Exchange (ASX), and $1.4 billion transacted through the second exchange, Cboe Australia, formerly known as Chi-X.)

Floating: The Primary Market

The primary market is where companies raise money to fund their enterprises. Companies offer shares for sale through a prospectus (see more on the function of a prospectus in the later section 'Planning the Prospectus'). A *prospectus* is a legal document that invites the public to subscribe to a share issue, or *initial public offering* (IPO). As the name suggests, an IPO signifies the first public offering of shares. Investors provide capital for a company by buying shares in the IPO. A company *floats* on the sharemarket when it lists or quotes its shares for trade. As soon as the first trade takes place, the shares join the secondary market, which is where listed shares are bought and sold, all day on every trading day.

TIP

Actually, describing all new companies that come to the sharemarket as floats isn't strictly accurate because some sink like a stone and don't get back to the surface without a pretty exhaustive salvage effort.

According to the ASX, more than 2,500 companies have listed on the exchange through an IPO since October 1988, raising about $170 billion from large and small investors, for an average IPO size of $68 million. The ASX is one of the world's most active exchanges by listing volumes — there are more than 120 listings a year, on average, which raise about $10 billion a year. Another $45 billion of follow-up (or 'secondary') capital — vital to help newly listed companies keep growing — is typically raised on the ASX annually. In 2020–21, there were 199 listings on the ASX, and $102.5 billion raised (counting all IPOs, debt listings, compliance listings, spin-offs and dual listings — see Chapter 13 for what these are — and $64.1 billion in secondary capital).

Understanding why companies float

Companies float to raise money from investors. Like anybody selling anything, companies try to convince you that buying their shares is the greatest thing since sliced bread.

Occasionally you hear a lot of noble-sounding guff about the primary market being the great engine of the capitalist economy, mobilising the funds of the savers in the economy and channelling these funds to the enterprises that can make best use of them. All that may be true, but it's still guff. Vendors still want your money. However, you can make their need for funds work for you.

A company that floats is seeking private investment capital, whether from ordinary individual investors or professional investors such as *fund managers* — the people who manage the big investment companies. The company uses the money raised from the float in its commercial ventures, literally putting the money at risk. The risk is high because you have no guarantee the company is going to be successful. Some companies fail. For this higher risk, investors expect their capital to earn more than it can with less risky investments. In many cases, they also expect an ongoing income from the company in the form of dividends (for more on dividends, refer to Chapter 1).

WHO INVENTED THE SHAREMARKET?

In post-Renaissance Europe, economic activity moved from feudalism to mercantilism, and the burgeoning of trade that accompanied this shift required an infusion of capital that traditional banking sources couldn't supply. The great breakthrough came in 16th century London, with the invention of the joint stock company.

Formed as trading companies, the first joint stock ventures were the Muscovy (1555), Levant (1581), East India (1600) and Dutch East India (1602). These early trading companies were the ancestors of today's public companies. For the first time, individuals were able to invest their capital in an entity that transacted business on their behalf, and the investors shared in the profits. More importantly, investors were able to buy and sell their interest in these ventures.

The joint stock company concept was further refined with the legal definition of *limited liability*, which restricts the liability of the members for the company's debts.

When the Muscovy Company — or the Mystery and Company of Merchant Adventurers for the Discovery of Regions, Dominions, Islands and Places Unknown — was formed, each of its investors received an individual deed of title, considered to be the first share certificates.

The trading companies grew in number with colonisation and expansion, and consequently the means to trade the shares had to grow as well. Intermediaries, the first stockbrokers, sprang up. In 1760, after being kicked out of the Royal Exchange because of their rowdiness, a group of 150 brokers formed a club at Jonathan's Coffee House where they met to buy and sell shares. In 1773, the members of this club voted to change the name of Jonathan's to the Stock Exchange. By the 1790s, securities dealers were also operating in New York, again from a coffee house. In 1817, the New York Stock Exchange (NYSE) was formed.

In Australia, share trading sprang up in the 1850s, following the big gold discoveries. Virtually all of the major goldfields had their own stock exchanges. Ballarat, Bendigo, Gympie, Charters Towers, Zeehan, Queenstown, Kalgoorlie, Coolgardie and Cobar had their own exchanges. Even Broad Arrow — a gold boom town that is now nothing more than a pub in the desert north of Kalgoorlie — had a stock exchange.

The unofficial trading spread to Melbourne and Sydney, where formal exchanges were set up in the 1860s and 1870s respectively. The Hobart exchange was formed in 1882, followed by Brisbane (1884), Adelaide (1887) and Perth (1889). In 1937, the six exchanges formed the Australian Associated Stock Exchanges.

(continued)

(continued)

The Australian Stock Exchange (ASX) was formed in 1987, and computerised screen trading took over from the trading floors soon after. In 1998 the ASX completed a remarkable 150 years when it transformed itself from a member-owned cooperative to a company limited by shares and listed on its own exchange, only the second stock exchange (after Stockholm) to do so. Most major exchanges are listed companies in their own right, including NYSE Euronext, Deutsche Boerse AG, Nasdaq OMX Group and the Hong Kong Stock Exchange.

In July 2006, the Sydney Futures Exchange (SFE Corporation Limited) merged with the ASX. Later that year, the Australian Stock Exchange changed its name to become the Australian Securities Exchange (which is also known as the ASX).

Australia's second stock exchange, the local arm of global exchange business Chi-X, opened in October 2011, ending ASX's monopoly; however, Cboe Australia (as it is now known) is a trading venue rather than a listings exchange. Cboe Australia currently handles around 18 per cent of the average daily trading volume and 35 per cent of the exchange-traded fund (ETF) volume. ASX and Cboe Australia compete for trades — brokers connected to Cboe Australia can send all or part of an order to Cboe Australia to be executed, allowing them to seek the best possible price.

In fact, Cboe Australia is the third exchange if you count the National Stock Exchange of Australia (NSX). Founded in 1937 as the Newcastle Stock Exchange, the NSX lists over 60 companies, for a total capitalisation of $2.2 billion. The NSX is viewed as a secondary exchange, mainly used by private companies with a market value of up to $50 million. Its operating company, NSX Limited, is listed on the ASX.

Raising money

Suppose you want to start a business making furniture. To do this, you employ managers to buy raw materials and you put together a workforce to make and sell the furniture.

Unless you already have capital set aside to fund the business, you need to find a way to finance your business. Your investment, allowing you to buy the raw materials and to pay the people who make and sell your furniture, probably has to be made with borrowed capital; for example, a normal commercial loan. As you sell the furniture that your company makes, you generate cash, which pays the cost of those sales — your wages, factory rental, marketing and advertising sales. Then, you must pay off the loans that enabled you to get started. Any money left after that is your *profit*.

The profit that your firm generates is the basis of wealth creation. How this wealth is shared depends on what corporate structure you choose for your furniture-making company. You can be a *sole proprietor* (own your own business), you can form a *partnership* (own a business with others), or you can form a *company* (own a formal legal entity). If your company decides that it wants to tap the private capital market, it may offer shares in itself and float on the stock exchange.

Offering shares to the investing public is a straight swap of capital for the privileges of ownership. Obviously, you, as the company's owner/founder, are giving up some control, allowing others to have a say in the running of your company. The shareholders of a company limited by shares own the company by law. Some shareholders aren't shy in expressing this fact. The dilution of control can be disconcerting to the owners of private businesses that have floated, because management's aims are often different from those of the shareholders — who want to see returns, and pronto!

Often the owners of a business float the company to sell some (or all) of their holding. The instant *liquidity* of the sharemarket — that is, the ability to sell shares when a company needs money — is attractive to owners. Selling a stake in a business or partnership can be as time-consuming as selling a house — offers are made, haggled over and refused. However, on the sharemarket, the business is priced to the cent at any second.

Planning the Prospectus

The document that invites the public to invest in a company is called the *prospectus*. A prospectus (see Chapter 13 for more detail) sets out in great detail the company's background, business, financial accounts, management and prospects. You can make an application for the shares only through the application form contained in the prospectus. The prospectus is a legal document and may read like the very worst of that breed, but the prospectus also contains all the necessary facts to inform and persuade a buyer.

WARNING

Under the Corporations Law, the requirements of what to include in a prospectus are strict. Unfortunately, this means that a prospectus is a very bulky document, with many pages of material in small, closely packed type. For investors who aren't also accountants, a prospectus can be a daunting read. However, it's a vital document. You can find everything you need to know about a company inside the prospectus. Too many investors don't read it. Don't make that mistake.

REMEMBER

For companies listing on the sharemarket, the prospectus is a marketing document too. The design, artwork and photography are all part of the effect. Many prospectuses resemble an edition of *National Geographic*. Visually impressive documents they may be, but don't let that distract you from reading the difficult bits because the difficult bits are where you find the nitty-gritty that tells you whether the shares are worth buying.

A SOUTH SEA DREAM — THEN THE BUBBLE BURST

Promoters of companies listing on the sharemarket have never been guilty of overestimating the avidity with which the investing public scours every paragraph of a prospectus. No-one has ever made this assumption as blatantly as the chap who, at the height of the South Sea Bubble investment mania of the 1720s, hawked a prospectus around London seeking subscriptions to 'an undertaking of great advantage, but nobody to know what it is'. He decamped to the Continent with several thousand pounds. Obviously, no-one read his brief prospectus.

Nowadays the Australian Securities and Investments Commission (ASIC), which regulates the fairness of the securities markets, wouldn't let anything as crass as that happen. Unfortunately, floats that rely more on the gullibility of investors than the intrinsic merits of the company still occur.

Trading: The Secondary Market

The Australian Securities Exchange is the operator of the main Australian sharemarket. The 2,200 companies listed on the Australian market had a total value of $2,500 billion at May 2021, which makes Australia one of the top 15 world sharemarkets.

After a company floats, it joins the secondary market, which is hosted on the Australian Securities Exchange (which is abbreviated to and known colloquially as the ASX) and Cboe Australia. Every day on these exchanges, about $7.2 billion worth of these shares are bought and sold. No restriction exists on the number of shares that can change hands during trading hours. *Stockbrokers*, who are employees of stockbroking firms that are participants of the ASX, do the buying and selling of transactions.

Finding the market action at ASX Trade

All transactions in shares are conducted on the trading screens of the ASX and Cboe Australia. If a bid is the one that matches the offer, the bid gets transacted immediately. Every user can see the prices of all transactions and the number of shares involved.

Most trading goes through the ASX's trading system, ASX Trade, to which only authorised stockbroking firms are permitted access. ASX Trade provides individual share information from the Australian sharemarket, and access to the trading venues, even those not operated by the ASX. Launched in 2010 — and overhauled in 2020 — ASX Trade provides for the cash market and for every one of the approximately 2,200 stocks listed on the market, among other data, such vital statistics as the last sale price, the buy quote (*bid*) and the sell quote (*offer* or *ask*). ASX Trade places all bids (the prices that buyers are prepared to pay) and offers (the prices that sellers are prepared to accept) on the computer screens of brokers' clients.

ASX Trade hosts two trading services, or 'order books':

>> **TradeMatch** is the main market, and handles retail orders. It handles about 80 per cent of all trading. TradeMatch is a 'lit' market, meaning the bids, offers and volumes are displayed, and the market sees each transaction as it is struck.

>> **Centre Point** is a 'dark' market, meaning that buyers and sellers are matched anonymously. Centre Point participants do not see the bids and offers before the trade, but all trades are then published immediately. Institutional investors strike 'block' trades (trades involving large numbers of shares) in Centre Point to lessen the impact of such large orders hitting the market. But brokers also route retail orders through Centre Point, which is effectively a price improvement service. Retail investors can request that their broker use Centre Point because of the possibility that retail investors will get a better price than in the lit market. Using ASX Sweep, Centre Point users can be seamlessly routed between the two liquidity venues, increasing execution certainty.

Another advantage of Centre Point is that fewer high-frequency traders are present, who use complex algorithms to analyse trading patterns and execute orders based on market conditions in that market.

Cboe Australia has an 'integrated order book', which means its lit and dark markets work together. So when you place a trade on Cboe Australia, the trading system will look at both its lit and dark markets (its Mid-Point) to fill your trade. Having two exchanges means you can trade on Cboe Australia if it has a better price, and vice versa — within broking firms, sophisticated smart order router technology sends the order that the investor places to the best place to execute that order (ASX or Cboe Australia), based on factors such as best price and liquidity. Virtually every broker these days uses such routers.

Brokers access ASX Trade through a range of interfaces. Brokers and market participants either have their own proprietary systems or rely on third-party interface providers (such as IRESS Trader, provided by ASX-listed financial software company, IRESS Limited). No end-customer connects directly to an ASX product — any functionality that end-customers see is provided by their broker.

Through whichever interface they use, every stockbroker has direct access to the raw sharemarket data from his or her desktop. Investors don't see or interact with ASX Trade — only brokers do. Clients of online brokers see a re-presented version of ASX Trade based on direct feeds from the ASX when they log in to their broking account, and how these brokers present the market graphically is up to each broker. I discuss the operation of the market in more detail in Chapter 6.

Buying and selling for everyone

Two kinds of investors use the sharemarket: institutional and private investors. Institutions, such as superannuation and pension funds, insurance companies, fund managers and investment companies, trustee companies, banks and other financial institutions, buy shares with other people's money. Private investors are individuals, like you and me, who buy shares with their own money.

REMEMBER

Anyone who has insurance cover, a superannuation plan or a managed investment portfolio is indirectly a sharemarket investor. This means that institutional investors dominate the ownership of the Australian sharemarket and, within that category, the superannuation funds and life insurance companies dominate the institutional investment industry. Because of this, even those people who shun the sharemarket are likely to be involved in share trading indirectly.

When you buy shares as a private investor, you don't know the identity of the person selling them to you. It may be an institution selling the shares you're buying, or a cane farmer in Queensland. Your bid (buying) and offer (selling) prices are matched, but you don't have any contact with the person on the other side of the transaction.

Institutions occasionally trade shares among themselves in transactions called *block trades*, which are conducted away from the open market so as to avoid volatile movements in the share price and minimise any alarm bells. However, even these transactions must be struck through a stockbroking firm, and they are sometimes underwritten. The stockbrokers have a monopoly, which so far has avoided the scrutiny of the Australian Competition and Consumer Commission (ACCC).

Working with a go-between

Every transaction on the stock exchange must be conducted by a stockbroking firm that is a corporate member of the ASX. About 70 firms are registered as stockbrokers in Australia, although some of those deal only with institutional or professional investors.

TIP

Before you walk into a stockbroking firm with that $4,000 you saved to start your investing career, check with the ASX whether your broker deals with the retail or private investor market.

Stockbroking is now a buyers' market and brokers are engaged in a price war over fees, helped by the easy access the internet provides. What was once regarded as the model stockbroker–client relationship, where the broker advised the client and provided research and access to floats, was exploded by the cost-cutting brought by the internet. Online brokers have had to lower their transaction fees dramatically. You can get more details on stockbroking in Chapter 12.

Using the Index

Every sharemarket has a major *index*, a notional portfolio designed to reflect the wider sharemarket as accurately as possible. The index gives investors a means of tracking market performance. The index is also a shorthand way of assessing the performance of the sharemarket on a given day. However, an index is only an indicative number. The index may not tell you whether a share you own has risen or fallen, but only the general trend in the market. Sometimes, some shares rise in price although the index itself has fallen, or vice versa.

In June 2021, the Australian sharemarket was the 15th-largest national sharemarket (but the 17th-largest exchange, because some nations have two main exchanges) in the world, but it accounted for only about 1.6 per cent of the total value of world sharemarkets. To put the size of the Australian market in perspective, the two largest US stocks, Apple and Microsoft, were each valued at the time of writing at more than the entire ASX market capitalisation — at US$2,125 billion (A$2,760 billion) and US$1,942 billion (A$2,520 billion), respectively.

Table 2-1 shows the world's top 20 sharemarkets by value as at June 2021.

TABLE 2-1

The Top 20 Sharemarkets by Value

Sharemarket	Market Value (US$ trillion)
1. New York Stock Exchange	24.67
2. Nasdaq	20.99
3. Shanghai Stock Exchange	7.07
4. Hong Kong Exchanges	6.87

(continued)

TABLE 2-1 *(continued)*

Sharemarket	Market Value (US$ trillion)
5. Japan Exchange Group	6.67
6. Euronext*	5.91
7. Shenzhen Stock Exchange	5.34
8. LSE (London Stock Exchange Group)	3.69
9. TMX Group (Canada)	3.00
10. National Stock Exchange of India	2.78
11. Saudi Stock Exchange	2.58
12. Deutsche Boerse (Germany)	2.54
13. Nasdaq Nordic & Baltics#	2.33
14. Korea Exchange (Seoul)	2.32
15. SIX Swiss Exchange	2.02
16. Taiwan Stock Exchange	1.92
17. Australian Securities Exchange (ASX)	1.86
18. Johannesburg Stock Exchange	1.15
19. Tehran Stock Exchange	1.06
20. Brasil Bolsa Balcão	0.98

* Paris, Amsterdam, Brussels, Lisbon, Milan, Dublin and Oslo stock exchanges
 # Stockholm, Copenhagen, Helsinki, Iceland, Tallinn, Riga and Vilnius stock exchanges
Source: International Federation of Stock Exchanges

The All Ordinaries index

The long-standing indicator of the ASX is the S&P/ASX All Ordinaries index, which contains the 500 largest companies by market capitalisation or value. The All Ordinaries index covers more than 95 per cent of the value of the Australian market, making it relatively broad in scope when compared to its international peers.

As a junior market, the ASX barely cracks a mention in the world's financial press, but its international peers make headlines over here. The global indices are the equivalents of the All Ordinaries in the overseas markets. However, not many international indices have market coverage that is as broad as the Australian index, which gives you, as an Australian investor, a decided leg-up.

The S&P/ASX 200 index

In 2000, the S&P/ASX 200 index was introduced as a replacement benchmark index for the Australian market, and is now more widely followed than the All Ordinaries. It comprises the 200 largest companies by market value and is used by investment managers as a proxy for the Australian market to build portfolios and compare performance. The S&P/ASX 200 index is a subset of the All Ordinaries and covers about 80 per cent of the Australian market by value. You can follow the ups and downs of the S&P/ASX 200 index in newspapers and media reports.

The Dow Jones

The venerable Dow Jones Industrial Average has been tracking the industrial heavyweights of the New York Stock Exchange (NYSE) since Charles Dow first calculated it in May 1896. Since then, the index has chopped and changed many times, with the last original constituent, General Electric, dropping out in June 2018. The top ten of the Dow Jones in June 2021, by market value, were Apple, Microsoft, Visa, JP Morgan Chase & Co., Johnson & Johnson, Walmart, United-Health, Home Depot, Procter & Gamble and Disney.

REMEMBER

The Dow Jones is, unfortunately, an unrepresentative index, comprising only 30 industrial stocks at any time. It was criticised in the late 1990s for not adequately reflecting the technology-based new economy. The only technology-related companies in the Dow Jones at the time were Hewlett-Packard (now split into HP Inc. and Hewlett Packard Enterprise) and IBM because they were the only tech stocks old enough to qualify, having been established in 1939 and 1911, respectively. In the famous 'new economy' shake-up of November 1999, stalwarts Goodyear, Sears Roebuck, Union Carbide and Chevron were ditched and Microsoft, Intel, SBC Communications and Home Depot added. Apple wasn't invited in until 2015!

Three companies in the Dow Jones — Cisco Systems, Microsoft and Intel — actually trade on the Nasdaq (see the next section), not the NYSE. The third-largest US stock by market value, Amazon (worth US$1.7 trillion), is not a Dow Jones member, and nor are the fourth-largest (Alphabet, Google's parent company, worth US$1.6 trillion), the fifth-largest (Facebook, worth US$939 billion) or the sixth-largest (Warren Buffett's investment company Berkshire Hathaway, worth US$655 billion). The main reason these companies are not included in the Dow Jones is that their share prices are just too high for an index that is calculated based on share price — including them would mean that their price changes would swing the index up or down, no matter how the other stocks performed.

The Nasdaq

The *Nasdaq* is the acronym for the National Association of Securities Dealers Automated Quotation, the other US sharemarket. Today it's known as the Nasdaq Stock Market.

The Nasdaq was formed in 1971 to provide a screen-based marketplace for shares that didn't meet the listing requirements of the NYSE but were widely owned and had outgrown the smaller, local markets on which they traded.

From the beginning, the Nasdaq hosted the technology start-ups that have gone on to become well known and larger, in some cases, than the industrial giants that make up the Dow Jones. The tech giants dominate the Nasdaq — that's where Amazon, Alphabet and Facebook hang out. Valued at US$21 trillion, the Nasdaq has become known as the technology market, and its major index, the Nasdaq Composite, as the prime technology indicator and most widely followed indicator of the US 'tech' stock market.

Based at Times Square in New York, the Nasdaq Stock Market trades about the same dollar value in shares as its cross-town rival, the NYSE (valued at US$24.7 trillion) — each trading about US$90 billion a day — but the NYSE trades more shares, at about 1.8 billion a day to the Nasdaq's 1.5 billion. The pair share 36 per cent of US share volume and 41.7 per cent of US trade value.

The S&P

The S&P 500 index, calculated using the value of the top 500 US stocks by market value, is the broadest of the big three US indices — and has recently elbowed the Dow Jones aside to assume 'star index' status with the Nasdaq. The S&P 500 is the main proxy for the US sharemarket when fund managers need a benchmark against which to compare the performance of their portfolios. Calculated by Standard & Poor's, a 160-year-old financial data and analysis firm, the S&P 500 was introduced in 1957. Only 60 of the original companies still remain in the index, which actually contains 505 stocks, because some of the constituent companies have multiple share classes. For example, Berkshire Hathaway has Class A and Class B shares, which have different prices (Class B has had a share split) and different voting rights.

The Footsie and the rest

The Financial Times Stock Exchange 100 (FTSE 100), better known as the Footsie, is the major indicator of the London Stock Exchange, representing about 81 per cent of total market value. The Footsie, which comprises the 100 largest British stocks by market value, was introduced in 1984. Only 27 of the original 100 constituents remain members.

All sharemarkets have a major index. Here are some of the other global heavyweights:

>> Shanghai Composite for the Shanghai Stock Exchange

>> EURO STOXX 50 for the European stock market

>> Nikkei Index for the Tokyo Stock Exchange

>> Hang Seng Index for the Hong Kong Stock Exchange

These indices operate in the same way as the S&P/ASX 200 index. Anywhere a stock market exists, somebody has developed an index to track it.

The mighty MSCI

Now that you have the basics of the market covered, you can move on to how to use it. Before the rise of index funds, which put together portfolios to follow or track a particular index and mirror its performance faithfully, the major indices were merely indicators of the sharemarket. Now these indices represent guaranteed buying on the part of the index funds. If a company is included in one of the major indices, its shares will find instant buyers. If they leave that index, the index funds will sell them. For smaller companies, graduation into the major indices is a rite of passage and exclusion sends their share price plunging.

In Australia, we think of our own benchmark index, the S&P/ASX 200, as the ultimate in status, but it's not. Global fund managers want to know whether an Australian stock is part of the Morgan Stanley Capital International (MSCI) World Index, which is market capitalisation-weighted, meaning bigger companies have more clout. The MSCI World Index comprises the 1,562 largest companies in the world's 23 most developed economies — and 63 ASX-listed stocks make the grade. MSCI calculates more than 225,000 sharemarket indices every day, and it estimates that more than US$14.5 trillion is benchmarked to its indices on a worldwide basis.

Indices started out as simple gauges that helped investors measure sharemarket performance, and they continue to perform this function. But indices have also become embroiled in the debate between 'active' and 'passive' investing (see Chapter 5 for more on this) and, by extension, the exchange-traded fund (ETF) sector (see chapters 5 and 9 for more on ETFs). In essence, many investors now view the main index for a particular asset class — for example, the S&P/ASX 200 index for Australian shares, whether the price index or the accumulation index, which counts dividends — as the return from that asset class to which they are entitled, and they judge active fund managers as successes or failures according to whether they outperform this index. The feeling is one of, 'I can get this index performance through an ETF, so I don't want to pay an active manager fees and end up not beating the index.'

The other big change in the index world is that providing indices has become a big business. For example, if a new ETF is developed that is based around an investment 'theme' (such as cyber-security), someone has to construct the index that the ETF follows — which is where index providers come in. An ETF has to track (attempt to replicate the performance of) something, and many of the larger ETFs track established indices; however, many more track new niche indices, which are developed by specialist index providers to fit the investment focus of a particular ETF.

Stepping into the Futures Market

The sharemarket has a double that exists in future time, although this sharemarket, the futures market, trades in the present. *Futures markets* are a long-established and legal way to buy or sell a specified commodity at a fixed time in the future. Futures markets began in the agricultural commodities markets of medieval Europe and have grown in sophistication since then.

Futures markets allow producers and consumers of commodities to lock in their prices. Producers like to know what price they will get for their product in six months' time. Users like to know what they will have to pay for that product in six months' time so they can plan their budget accordingly. Speculators want to make money either way, by picking which way the price will go. These three players are the essential oil that lubricates the futures market.

Late last century, the technique of trading commodities was applied to the sharemarket. In this situation, a certain value of shares becomes the commodity being traded. This value is the notional value of a market index, multiplied by a certain dollar value per point on the index. In the US, the main index on which futures contracts are traded is the S&P 500. In Australia, it's the Share Price Index 200, or SPI 200, which is the S&P/ASX 200 index's futures market twin. The actual sharemarket represents the *spot market*, the term used in the commodity markets to denote today's price. The futures market anticipates what that spot value will be in the future. If investors expect the spot price of the S&P/ASX 200 to rise, they will pay a premium for the future value. If, on the other hand, they expect the S&P/ASX 200 to fall, the SPI will trade at a discount to its actual twin.

KEEPING UP WITH THE SHAREMARKET MENAGERIE

The sharemarket also contains some forms of animal life — that is, in the descriptions given to different kinds of investors.

First come the bulls, who are hoping that share prices will charge upward and are trying to propel them that way. The bulls are as impetuous as their namesake and charge through the market as though they're being run through the streets of Pamplona. However, if these sharemarket creatures lose their nerve, they can just as likely resemble the tourists running from the bulls at Pamplona.

Then come the bears, who are expecting prices to bear downward. The bears are not as swift as the bulls, being a more lumbering type of animal. Although habitually slow and ponderous, bears can occasionally act with frightening speed, tearing at share prices with their sharp claws.

The battle between the bulls and the bears for influence over the sharemarket doesn't really faze the third member of the menagerie, the stag. Stags are concerned solely with how new floats perform on debut. Sometimes the stags are allied with the bulls because they're looking to sell out of a float as soon as the shares list, banking on a good reception for the shares and a nice instant capital gain. Stags aren't happy to see the bears take over the market because it limits their opportunities severely.

After any sharemarket boom, a fourth member of the menagerie appears — the dogs. Dogs sit accusingly in an investor's portfolio at prices far below what was paid for them. A dog is a stark reminder of what happens when you leave the sharemarket to animal instincts.

WARNING

The futures market is a specialised area, and you need a lot of experience and information before you venture into it. The futures market is also a *leveraged investment*, meaning that losses as well as profits are magnified, and you can lose more than you invest.

2

Investing Strategies for Success

Develop a strategy for building wealth while riding out volatility.

Get a handle on assessing different types of risk and identifying dud shares.

Diversify your share portfolio as widely as possible for a smoother sharemarket ride.

Chapter **3**

Developing an Investment Strategy

D evising a sharemarket investment strategy means asking a basic question: 'Why am I buying this share?' If the answer to the question is 'My brother-in-law told me at a barbecue on the weekend that this share was about to go through the roof' . . . then you're gambling.

But if the answer to the question is

» I've researched this unloved stock pretty thoroughly and I think the company is making a good product that doesn't have much competition.

» I'm fairly confident the company has solved the problems that caused the share price to fall and I believe its earnings are going to grow.

» This share fits all my criteria for buying and I'm happy to buy it at this price . . .

. . . then you're investing, and developing your investment strategy is what this chapter is about.

Investing is a simple concept. You store buying power in the form of money today for future use. What you're trying to do when you invest is to conserve the capital that you've earned and saved, and to make it grow. To invest successfully, you need to put your money where your investment can generate a return ahead of inflation (the rate of change in the cost of living), so that the purchasing power of your capital is at least conserved. Naturally, you want to earn a return above the inflation rate so that your invested money is actually growing in value.

Getting Rich Slowly

Investing in shares requires patience. If you attempt to compress the wealth-creating power of the sharemarket into weeks or even days, you're asking for trouble. Occasionally — for example, amid the technology boom of 1999 to 2000 or, more recently, the over-confident market of 2019 or the spectacular recovery from the 'COVID crash' of 2020–2021 — Australians forget this rule and try to participate in the spectacular short-term capital gains available on the sharemarket.

Giving yourself time in the market

Only after one of these periodic bouts of insanity do investors remember how the sharemarket really creates wealth — slowly, over years. Since 1900, according to AMP Capital, the All Ordinaries Accumulation index has delivered a total return of 11.8 per cent a year; much better than Australian bonds (5.8 per cent a year) or cash (4.6 per cent a year). If you'd had an astute investor in your family tree who'd put $100 in the sharemarket on your behalf in 1900 (in the equivalent of the All Ordinaries index) and left it to accumulate, with all dividends reinvested, that investment would have grown to more than $70 million by now.

Since 1950, says research house Andex Charts, the S&P/ASX All Ordinaries Accumulation index has delivered a return of 11.7 per cent a year, enough to turn an investment of $100 in 1950 into $260,786 (I share a graph showing this in Chapter 1).

Not many people have an investment term of 100 years, or even 50 years. Most investors are active for 20 or 30 years. Over the 30 years to the end of 2020, says Andex Charts, the S&P/ASX All Ordinaries Accumulation index has earned investors 10.1 per cent a year; over 20 years the return is 8.3 per cent a year. Although both the 20-year and 30-year periods bear the scars of the Global Financial Crisis (GFC) — which more than halved the value of the index between November 2007 and February 2009 — this steady rise in shares over time is the key to sharemarket investing.

Although share prices are extremely volatile, share dividends are far less so. When you buy a share, you're buying a portion of the future earnings of that company, part of which comes to you as a dividend, and part of which goes into retained earnings. Over time, this process of building equity also results in capital gain.

You can't expect a return of 11.7 per cent on your share portfolio next year or the year after that, but the pattern of growth should remain similar even though the market may lose value during any given year. Those downward blips on the graph in Chapter 1 (showing the growth of a $100 investment over 70 years) represent risk.

REMEMBER

These numbers reflect the performance of the sharemarket index — not that of individual companies. Over the years, some companies perform much better than the index; however, an awful lot don't.

Any sharemarket index has a very high degree of 'survivor bias'. In 2019, advisory firm Stanford Brown crunched the Australian numbers and estimated that the 2,300 companies listed on the ASX represented just 6 per cent of the companies that had raised money from investors and listed on an Australian stock exchange since the early 1800s. Moreover, only an estimated 580 of those listed companies were making money — meaning that only about 1.5 per cent of all the companies that have ever listed in Australia managed to survive and build a profitable business.

Where did the 94 per cent of companies that had not survived go? Stanford Brown estimated that up to 1,000 of them, or about 3 per cent, were taken over by other local companies. Another 200 or so were taken over by foreign companies. The rest simply failed and disappeared, or were mopped up at very low prices.

It's a similar story in the US, where a 2018 study by Hendrik Bessembinder of the Department of Finance at the WP Carey School of Business at Arizona State University looked at the US stock market between 1926 and 2016 in terms of shareholder wealth creation (which the study defined as generating a return above that which could have been achieved by investing in US Treasury bills, which are short-term bonds). The study found that the top-performing 1,092 listed US companies (or 4.31 per cent of the total number of listed stocks during this time period) accounted for all the wealth creation from investing in equities (that is, excess equity returns relative to treasury bills). In 2019, Bessembinder replicated this study across 42 countries over the 1990 to 2018 period, and he found that the returns globally were even narrower — the best-performing 811 firms (or 1.33 per cent) accounted for all the net global wealth creation in shares.

It gets worse — in a 2020 update, Bessembinder found that just 83 companies (0.32 per cent of the total) accounted for half of the lifetime shareholder wealth creation of US$47.4 trillion ($61.5 trillion) in the US stock market between 1926 and 2019. A mere five companies (Apple, Microsoft, Exxon Mobil, Amazon and Alphabet, Google's parent company) accounted for 11.9 per cent of the total gain.

It's a sobering thought — an extremely narrow group of stocks drove all the equity market returns. The 'survivor bias' is huge.

REMEMBER

This data indicates that many — if not most — of the 2,200 companies listed on the ASX in 2021 will probably end up worthless. When investors talk about indices, they're talking about indices made up of the listed companies that are investment-grade, which are a minority. But the survivors can do amazing things, as you can find out more about later in this chapter.

Compounding magic

You're taught about compound interest at secondary school, but you probably didn't pay too much attention to it. A quote commonly misattributed to Einstein is that compound interest is 'the greatest mathematical discovery of all time'.

REMEMBER

The longer you maintain an investment, the greater will be your financial gain. This gain happens because of the magic of compound interest, which is the investor's major ally in achieving all financial goals.

Here's how compound interest works:

>> Interest is earned on the original sum invested.

>> Next, interest is earned on both the original sum invested plus the first round of interest.

>> Then, interest is earned on the original sum and all the interest so far accumulated, and so on over the period of the investment.

Over time, compound interest produces impressive growth. An investment earning 7 per cent a year will almost double in ten years. When the time required for compound interest to really get cracking is not available — for example, you want your investment to double in less than ten years — then you need to be a less conservative investor. If you want to shorten the time for your investment strategy and still double your money, you need to draw a deep breath and take more risk.

Starting with Strategy

Self-knowledge is the key to setting up your investment strategy. You have to know where you're going before you set out on the journey. You already know that time, patience and diversification load the dice in your favour when approaching sharemarket investment.

Before you start, you need to determine what kind of investor you are:

>> **Income investor:** Someone looking for share investments that can pay a wage

>> **Retiree:** The most conservative and risk-averse income investor

>> **Straight investor:** A wealth builder

>> **Speculator:** An impatient wealth builder willing to take risks

>> **Trader:** An impatient wealth builder, prepared to spend a lot of time watching the market for opportunities

Each of these types of investor faces different challenges. You can determine which type of investor you are and then choose the strategy that serves your needs. Retirees invest their money conservatively in order to guarantee returns. Gamblers — speculators — take very risky short-term bets to make a quick capital gain. Straight investors stick to the higher quality industrial stocks, the blue chips, for long-term growth.

Spreading the risk

Diversification, which you can read more about in Chapter 5, is a popular investment strategy. The idea is to spread the funds you have available for investment among different assets in order to distribute and hopefully contain the risk.

TIP

Although diversification is a fundamental law of investment, the concept of diversification can easily be misunderstood. Spreading invested funds across a number of different assets reduces the overall risk for your portfolio because you're not relying on only one asset as your investment.

The other side of diversification is that it can lower performance because it introduces more elements; but for many investors, containing the risk of sharemarket investment is more important.

Diversification isn't just a protective measure; it also allows you to generate a higher rate of return for a given level of risk. You can achieve reasonable diversification of a share portfolio with as few as ten stocks. Buying up to 15 different stocks adds to the diversification, but beyond that number, monitoring your portfolio of stocks properly is difficult. A good diversification strategy for ten stocks means not having more than 15 per cent of your portfolio by value in any one stock.

A share portfolio can be spread around and still not be properly diversified. You need to buy shares from market sectors that balance each other, so if one part of the portfolio is performing poorly, other shares will be doing better. For example, an investor who bought shares in CSL and subsequently in REA Group balanced global healthcare with an investment in real estate websites in Australia, Europe, Asia and the US. The same investor buying shares in iron ore producer Fortescue Metals Group would give the portfolio an interest in industries unrelated to the other two. Adding an investment in Australia's biggest grain handler, GrainCorp, which exports to more than 30 countries, widens the investor's diversification further — and so on.

TIP

Generally, buying shares in similar companies isn't a good idea. If one of the big four banks has done well for you, don't buy the other three as well. You'll find that your portfolio is too heavily weighted to banks. Be comfortable in the choice you've made and stick with your choice unless circumstances change and you find you have to sell shares.

REMEMBER

Diversification within a share portfolio isn't much use if a major correction (or worse, a bear market) hits the market. In that case, you hope to have a diversified portfolio of investments across a range of asset classes, not just a diversified share portfolio.

Setting your goals

What are you hoping to do with your share investments? Are you saving for a deposit on a house? Your children's school fees? Retirement income? Or, are you simply trying to maximise capital growth? All these goals pose different time constraints and risks. After you've settled on the type of return you're after — a decision that also helps you decide what type of investor you are — you can decide which shares can deliver the results and which shares you can rule out. If you're a straight investor, look for companies that promise long-term capital growth. If you're a retiree, you may be interested in a strong and sustainable flow of fully franked dividends.

Setting your time frame

How long can you give the investment? The longer you give your investments, the better. However, if you need short-term income, you have to be more aggressive in your wealth creation strategy. You may have to take on some speculative shares that carry more risk but promise greater return. This means, unfortunately, that you're in for some scary periods because you're unable to use the great risk minimiser — time. Deciding how much time you have helps you determine what type of investment strategy, and therefore shares, you require.

Setting your risk tolerance

After you know your goal and your time period for investing, you can begin to understand your risk profile. What is the maximum level of risk that's acceptable? How comfortable will you be if your investment loses 20 per cent of its value — or half? If you can't handle that sort of volatility, you may need to adjust your goals and the time frame. Unfortunately, risk comes with the territory. If you want to invest in the sharemarket, as opposed to other asset classes, it pays to be realistic about the level of risk that you can tolerate.

If you want your share investments to fund your children's education, or your own retirement, you have to be reasonably risk-averse. That doesn't mean sticking to government bonds or term deposits, because those assets simply wouldn't create the capital growth that you need. Being risk-averse as a share investor means concentrating on those companies with the most reliable long-term track record of earnings and dividend growth, rather than speculating on a technology company, drug-development hopeful or minerals explorer that has not yet made a profit. Those kind of stocks *may* make a lot of money, but as a risk-averse investor you can't afford to take that bet. You need to be in stocks where the compounding of a growing earnings stream is a much surer driver of capital growth.

Setting your financial needs

Do you have tax and liquidity issues? If you have short-term financial needs, you may have to face the prospect of unravelling your strategy. If the money you plan to invest in the sharemarket is money that you really can't afford to lose, maybe you need to rethink what you're doing in the first place.

Although the sharemarket offers a better prospect of capital growth than a term deposit in a bank or a government bond, it's not as safe a place to put money that you can't afford to lose. The sharemarket is much better suited as a place to invest money that you can afford to lose — and leave for a long time — to give your investment the best possible chance to make money for you.

Buying and Holding

A straightforward strategy for share investment is to buy and hold. You buy a portfolio of stocks and hold on to them for the long term.

REMEMBER

If you stay in the market long enough, you minimise the risk that your portfolio may lose its value and you allow the value of your portfolio to increase through compound interest. You also pay transaction costs only once.

One more element to the buy-and-hold strategy exists and that is 'sell' (although the strategy would then become buy, hold and sell). If you never sell a stock, the wealth the stock creates exists only on paper.

Philip Fisher, in his classic book *Common Stocks and Uncommon Profits*, states: 'If the job has been done correctly when a common stock is purchased, the time to sell it is — almost never.' This approach is fine if you want the value of your shares to be part of your estate, to be passed on to your heirs, but plenty of people look at successful buy-and-hold share investing as a way to fund a happy and fulfilling retirement, free of financial worry. If that's what you've decided, selling shares to raise money is fine if you plan carefully.

For the buy-and-hold strategy to work, you have to choose your stocks wisely. Obviously, you want more stocks in your portfolio to be like Westfield (sadly, gone from the Australian sharemarket, apart from a lingering representation) or CSL. (If you manage to pick the next Westfield or CSL, you don't have to worry about the rest of your portfolio. See the sidebar 'The miracle of Westfield' for more information on this stock, and the later section 'Timing for the long run' for more on CSL.) But buy and hold doesn't work with every stock. For example, it doesn't make sense to buy shares in building materials companies, such as CSR, Boral, James Hardie Industries and Adbri, and just put them in your bottom drawer. The Australian building industry is highly cyclical because it's based on the ups and downs of the economic cycle. The industry has taken steps to rectify this by moving into other countries, but it remains vulnerable to Australian construction cycles.

A range of shares exists that's too volatile to be part of a stable portfolio that doesn't change over a long period. For example, property developers and contractors don't really suit this purpose because their activities depend on interest rates, which can fluctuate. The same used to be said for the big mining shares, such as Rio Tinto, BHP, Fortescue Metals and Alumina, because they are linked to the ups and downs of commodity prices, which are linked to the economic cycle of the major Western economies. However, this perception prevailed before the Chinese economy, with its huge appetite for raw materials, took off in the late 1990s to early 2000s, on its way to becoming the second-largest economy in the world. Australia's miners are still exposed to the global economy, but the driver of the global economy is China. As the world comes out of the COVID-19 pandemic, the International Monetary Fund (IMF) forecasts that China will contribute more than one-fifth of the total increase in the world's gross domestic product (GDP) in the five years to 2026.

THE MIRACLE OF WESTFIELD

If you'd invested the equivalent of $1,000 in the float of Westfield Holdings in September 1960 — an amount that inflation has turned into about $15,800 — and reinvested every dividend and bonus that Westfield paid, your investment in the Westfield Group was, by December 2017, worth $440 million. That original investment had compounded at a rate of 25.6 per cent a year, for 57 years.

The Australian Securities Exchange believes the Westfield experience is the best example of long-term wealth creation of any stock. Sure, this figure is a gross calculation and doesn't take into account how much money has been reinvested. However, the point is that our original investor didn't need to contribute any other money to achieve that outcome. That amount of $440 million — almost enough to gain you a place in the Australian Financial Review Rich List — was all generated by that fortunate original investment.

From its original small shopping centre in the western Sydney suburb of Blacktown, Westfield built a global portfolio of shopping centres, with a list of iconic properties that included Westfield London, Westfield World Trade Centre in New York and Westfield Stratford City, in a portfolio of 35 properties widely recognised as the world's highest quality shopping centre portfolio.

Unfortunately, December 2017 was the end of the line, as the Lowy family sold Westfield into a takeover by French–Dutch commercial real estate company Unibail-Rodamco, which has added Westfield to its name. Unibail-Rodamco-Westfield (URW) is the largest commercial real estate company in Europe and owns properties in 12 countries. (Westfield's Australian and New Zealand shopping centre portfolio is owned and operated by Scentre Group, which was spun-off by Westfield in June 2014.) Because part of the $33 billion payment for the takeover was shares in Unibail-Rodamco, that entity still trades on the ASX, where it's known as Unibail-Rodamco-Westfield, so a small part of the Westfield wealth creation story carries on.

Of course, not every stock does what Westfield did. Many companies fail and their stocks disappear from the market and take their investors' money as well. Plucking one exceptional stock story out of the many that have been part of the Australian sharemarket may distort what is possible. But the beauty of ordinary equity is that while losses are limited to 100 per cent, the gains that can be made in a successful stock — such as Westfield — are not.

TIP

With a buy-and-hold strategy, you're buying growth, such as shares in the banking and finance sectors. You're also buying compounding interest and you're also buying time. If done well, buy and hold is as close as you can get to worry-free investing on the sharemarket. But, as investors saw in 2007–09, and again in 2020, when a major bear market hits, you may have to hold your buy-and-hold investment a bit longer than you thought!

Timing your strategies

With the right timing, you can make money on the sharemarket. You can buy a share, sell it for a gain, watch it fall all the way back and buy it again, and then begin the whole process over. However, this sort of transaction is hard to do because it involves forecasting. Predicting the points in the sharemarket at which a top or a bottom is reached is virtually impossible.

Nobody rings a bell at the top, or the bottom, of the market; these highs and lows can usually only be seen in hindsight. For example, in March 2009 when the Australian market finally found a bottom after 15 months of falling — or even after a much quicker fall such as in February to March 2020 — going back into the market seemed the worst thing to do, because the headlines were uniformly gloomy and the prevailing sentiment was terrible.

Studies from the USA, Canada and Australia show that professional investors and fund managers don't always make money from attempting to correctly time their moves (see Chapter 5). In fact, some of these experts can make big mistakes. Knowing when to time risk can be a big problem for market timers; they often fail to predict a turning point. An example is when market timers pull their investments out of the market, believing that the market will fall, and then a sudden rally leaves them little time to get back in. The problem for aspiring market-timers is that very few investors, even professional ones, can accurately predict the behaviour of the market.

A further problem is that if you buy and sell an investment several times, you have to take this activity into account when adding up your profit. Your profit can be eroded by transaction costs — if you sell the shares and remake the initial investment several times, your capital gain may not be as good as that made by the investor who buys once, holds and sells.

Trading on your portfolio

Even if you invest with a long-term view, you can also act in the short term. You may think that, having chosen 10 to 12 stocks for a portfolio, you'll still be holding them at the end of your predetermined investment period. Sometimes, however, you have to change your strategy.

If some of the shares in your portfolio are performing poorly, or if you change your view on the quality of the business, don't hesitate to turf them. The shares in your portfolio are there to do a job, which is to make money for you. If circumstances change and they can't do the job, cut them loose. Set a level of loss beyond which you're not prepared to follow — say, 15 per cent. Set a profit limit, too, beyond which you're not prepared to follow. Be ruthless with yourself and don't regret the profits you didn't get. As the saying goes, you don't go broke taking a profit. Of course, long-term investors may choose to use a short-term price fall to buy more shares.

TIP

If you're lucky enough to double your investment in a stock, consider selling half the holding. You keep the rest for free. You've eliminated your downside but kept the upside open.

Whatever strategy you choose, stick to it. If you adopt the buy-and-hold approach, don't allow yourself to be panicked out of a shareholding. If your strategy is to maximise your returns through active trading, make sure you have your ground rules in place on when to buy and sell. Don't be seduced by emotion — whether it be fear or greed!

Timing for the long run

Time works to minimise risk. In the short term, shares are the most likely of the asset classes to fall in price — in the words of the pros, to 'generate a negative return'. Statistically, the sharemarket is more likely to record a negative return in a given year than any other asset class. In the longer term, however, shares are the most likely to generate a positive return.

TIP

Investing in the sharemarket requires patience. You need to give your share portfolio investment at least five years to see positive growth. That's enough time to smooth out the volatility of the sharemarket and allow you to get the kind of returns that a balanced and diversified portfolio of shares can achieve.

Andex Charts has calculated the risk and return from the Australian sharemarket (as measured by the S&P/ASX All Ordinaries Accumulation index) over the period 1 January 1950 to 31 December 2020, measured over one, three, five, ten and 20 years, with investments made at month ends. Andex measured 841 one-year periods, 817 three-year periods, 793 five-year periods, 733 ten-year periods and 613 20-year periods (see Figure 3-1).

The one-year investments showed great volatility, with a best return of 86.1 per cent (year to 31 July 1987) and a worst performance of minus 41.7 per cent (year to 30 November 2008). The average gain was 13.3 per cent, but more than one in five (23.2 per cent) of the short-term investments showed a loss.

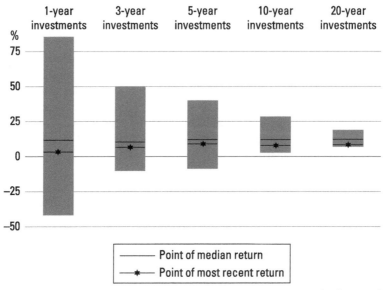

FIGURE 3-1:
How time
tempers the risk
and return on
shares.

Source: Andex Charts Pty Ltd

When the investment period was extended to three years, the probability of success rose to more than 90 per cent. The best return was 50.3 per cent a year (in the three years to 30 September 1987), while the worst performance was minus 10.9 per cent a year (in the three years to 31 December 1974). The average gain was 12.1 per cent a year.

The average return over five years was 12.1 per cent a year, with a best return of 40.4 per cent a year (in the five years to 31 August 1987) and the worst performance being a loss of 9.2 per cent a year (in the five years to 31 December 1974). The risk of loss in the five-year periods was still present, though, with a handful of the periods (4.3 per cent) failing to make a positive return.

By the time the investment term was extended to ten years, all investment periods showed a positive return (even if, sometimes, dividends were needed to get the result into the black). The best result was 28.7 per cent a year (in the ten years to 30 September 1987), the worst was 2.9 per cent a year (in the ten years to 30 September 1974) and the average gain was 12.1 per cent a year.

Over 20 years, the average investment in the sharemarket showed a gain of 12.3 per cent a year. The best was 18.9 per cent a year (in the 20 years to 30 September 1994), while the worst came in at 7.9 per cent a year (in the 20 years to 31 December 2018). The sharemarket doesn't come with a capital guarantee, but on the statistical evidence gleaned from seven decades, a ten-year investment in the sharemarket is as good as guaranteed.

DON'T BE SCARED OF VOLATILITY

The sharemarket is the most volatile of the asset classes, which means that its returns can fluctuate more than those from other asset classes.

Using accumulation data from 1950 through to 2020, research house Andex Charts calculates that Australian shares generated an average 12-month rolling (from month-ends) return of 13.3 per cent a year, but investors often had to endure years of negative returns (more than one in five 12-month periods, on average), and periods of great volatility. Of the returns observed, 90 per cent fell within a band of 49.4 per cent to minus 19.6 per cent.

Sharemarket investors simply must accept that along the way to these strong long-term average returns, deep and long-lasting falls may need to be endured. A correction in a sharemarket (usually a reversal after a sustained rise) is defined as a fall of 10 per cent or more in the market's main index. According to AMP Capital Investors, 19 falls of 10 per cent or worse have occurred on the Australian sharemarket since 1989.

Worse than a correction is a bear market, the term used if the index falls by more than 20 per cent. In one of the worst of them, the bear market that followed the GFC crash — the period between 1 November 2007 and 6 March 2009 — the S&P/ASX All Ordinaries Accumulation index lost 52 per cent of its value.

There have been 19 bear markets on the Australian sharemarket since 1900. According to investment company AMP Capital, these bear markets experienced an average fall of 32.7 per cent and took an average of 16 months to reach a trough (the longest trough, in 1937–42, taking 61 months to plumb its lowest depth, with the shortest trough being the one-month plunge during the 2020 COVID-19 crash). But the index has never failed to regain its previous high point and continue to push higher.

Not all bear markets are the same. Broking firm Credit Suisse coined the distinction between a 'gummy bear', where the market rebounds fully within about a year, and a 'grizzly bear', where the plunge is usually associated with economic recession, so it is deeper and usually longer-lived — for example, the GFC-inspired fall, which took 55 months to recover from on the Australian market.

The grandaddy of grizzly bears was the two-decade slump in Japan's Nikkei index from 38,916 in December 1989 to 7,173 in March 2009 — a horror-show of a plunge that sent more than four-fifths of the sharemarket's value up in flames. Despite quadrupling since that low point (to around 29,000 at the time of writing), the Japanese index remains 25.5 per cent below its 1989 record high.

(continued)

(continued)

Alongside these alarming tales of bear markets, grizzly or otherwise, the sharemarket also corrects regularly. For example, AMP Capital says the Australian sharemarket saw a 10 per cent pullback in 2012, an 11 per cent fall in 2013 (sparked by the so-called 'taper tantrum', when the US market thought the Federal Reserve was going to put the brakes on its huge economic stimulus program), an 8 per cent drop in 2014, a 20 per cent slide between April 2015 and February 2016, a 7 per cent fall early in 2018, a 14 per cent fall between August and December in 2018, and a 7 per cent fall in August 2019 — all occurring during an overall gradual rising trend. So no investor, when the market plunged in February 2020, could really have claimed to be shocked.

The sharemarket has shown that it always regains and exceeds its previous peak after a fall, but the big question is how long that takes. Those willing and able to ride out the bad times are usually rewarded. During the 2007 to 2009 slump, many investors discovered that they didn't have the nerve, or the resources, to stay in the game, and it is true that some stocks went under; however, those investors who were able to hang on to their good-quality stocks saw their portfolios largely recover. In early 2020, they were facing the same situation — and the recovery was surprisingly swift.

Ultimately, sharemarket corrections are often healthy because they puncture complacency and excessive risk-taking, and return investor attention to market and company fundamentals. In fact, corrections give investors a chance to get into good-quality shares at suddenly much cheaper prices. Professional investors in particular see the panic after corrections and crashes as rich in opportunities to buy bargains. When department stores have sales, people rush the doors down; when something similar happens on the sharemarket, investors often panic.

The Australian market — in the form of the S&P/ASX 200 index — was viewed critically after the GFC crash, because it did not surpass its November 2007 high for 2,974 days, until July 2019. But in its accumulation form (with dividends reinvested), the Australian index made it back to a new record in September 2013, just a few months after the US S&P 500 recovered to its total return high. Given that Australian investors get just over half (51 per cent) of their long-term sharemarket return from dividends, that is arguably a better comparison.

Share prices can and do fluctuate alarmingly. In the COVID-19 crash of February to March 2020, some of the price falls in the S&P/ASX 200 included the following:

» Flight Centre –74.9%

» Afterpay (this is now part of Block, Inc.) –74.8%

- ⟫ Credit Corp –73%

- ⟫ Webjet –72.2%

- ⟫ oOh! Media –70.4%

- ⟫ Corporate Travel Management –69.5%

- ⟫ EML Payments –69.5%

- ⟫ Challenger –67.8%

- ⟫ Oil Search (which has subsequently merged with Santos) –67.8%

- ⟫ Qantas –67.1%

In that kind of heightened volatility and extreme nervousness, shares can plunge alarmingly — and indiscriminately. Even the market's top ten behemoths by market value were pounded mercilessly in February to March 2020:

- ⟫ CSL –29.2%

- ⟫ Commonwealth Bank –41.3%

- ⟫ BHP –43.2%

- ⟫ Westpac –55.2%

- ⟫ National Australia Bank –56.0%

- ⟫ ANZ Banking Group –51.9%

- ⟫ Wesfarmers –37.3%

- ⟫ Macquarie Group –53.8%

- ⟫ Transurban Group –44.7%

Those are the kinds of falls that can immolate several years of patient appreciation. On the plus side, however, news of a takeover bid, a mineral discovery or a successful drug test result can send a share rocketing. Any share that you own can jump by 25 per cent tomorrow (less likely for a larger stock), but it can just as easily suffer a drop of the same proportion.

REMEMBER

Successful investing on the sharemarket isn't easy — but it is straightforward. All that an investor has to do is to find well-run and profitable companies, and wait for the dividend flow and the compounding of retained earnings to create wealth.

If you get in on the ground floor, the rewards can be spectacular. For example, the former Commonwealth Serum Laboratories (now CSL Limited) — the largest Australian stock by value — is one of the all-time great stories of the Australian stock market. When the Australian government floated CSL on the stock market in June 1994, it clearly had no idea what it owned.

CSL was floated at $2.30, raising $300 million for the government (it is now valued at $139.6 billion.) After a three-for-one share split in 2007, the float price was effectively 77 cents a share. Each of those shares now trades at a staggering $306.00. Add the $24.90 that has been paid in dividends to the share price, and the original shareholders have made almost 430 times their investment. To have generated $1 million out of CSL, all that an investor buying in the float had to put in was $2,327.

Commonwealth Bank was also sold onto the sharemarket by the Australian government, in its case for $5.40 a share, back in September 1991 (subsequent tranches sold for $9.50 and $10.00). Investors who backed the original float now have shares that trade for $105, meaning they have multiplied their investment by more than 19 times. But they have also received $68.47 in dividends along the way, which takes their gain to more than 32 times. Financial newsletter *The Motley Fool* takes this even further, calculating in 2020 that an initial investor who reinvested every dividend in more CBA shares would have made 73 times their money.

Property websites operator REA Group was floated (as realestate.com.au) in December 1999 at 50 cents; at $172, shareholders have made 344 times their money. And if you were one of the prescient investors who snapped REA up for 4.9 cents a share in September 2001, when the sharemarket in its wisdom judged that the business wasn't going so well — you've multiplied your investment by 3,510 times! To make $1 million, all you had to do was chip in $285 when the stock was going for 4.9 cents.

The sharemarket is full of these kinds of stories. Indeed, investors often talk about the hunt for the almost-mythical 'ten-bagger' — a stock that returns ten times the investment — but 20-, 30-, 40-, even 50-baggers are everywhere, with the important caveat that investors only know this with the benefit of hindsight. And 'baggerhood' of any multiplication, once achieved, is not necessarily permanent.

Macquarie Bank (now called Macquarie Group) came to the sharemarket in 1996 at $6.50 a share. It went as high as $98.64 in May 2007 — becoming a 15-bagger — but the GFC knocked it back to $15 in March 2009. Amazingly, investors got another chance: the company's impressive post-GFC turnaround has seen it reach $154, becoming a ten-bagger for the second time. And that's just on the share price, without counting the dividends.

The sharemarket's lightning-quick plunge of 38.8 per cent in February–March 2020 threw up some opportunities that (with the benefit of hindsight!) were certainly attractive. Buy-now-pay-later (BNPL) pioneer Afterpay (which was taken over by Square, Inc. in January 2022; Square, Inc. is now known as

Block, Inc.) became a 12-bagger, rising from $1.40 at its March 2020 low to $13.92 11 months later. Fellow BNPL stock Sezzle went even better, increasing its price by more than 20 times over the same period (from 58 cents to $20.30). Online goods marketplace Redbubble became a 14-bagger during that time, while online bookmaker PointsBet turned into a 13-bagger. (Of course, these upper valuations are at a snapshot in time — the subsequent performance of some of these stocks may give back a lot of this paper gain.)

But, sadly, at any time some companies are always heading in the other direction. In May 2007, law firm Slater and Gordon floated on the stock exchange at $1.00, as the world's first legal practice to list. At its peak in April 2015, the shares were $8.00; however, the company blew up through over-expansion and the shares fell to be virtually worthless — after a one-for-100 consolidation, the still-trading shares are down by 99.9 per cent from the high. (See Chapter 4 for more on the rise and fall of Slater and Gordon.)

Surfwear group Billabong International was floated in August 2000 at $3.15 a share, raising $295 million. Seven years later, when Billabong's shares touched $18.51, the company was worth $4 billion. But problems with expansion and mounting losses saw Billabong hit the skids. In June 2013, the shares hit a record low of 13 cents. In other words, in May 2007, a buyer was willing to pay $18.51 for Billabong; however, in June 2013, a seller was willing to accept 13 cents. Let's hope it wasn't the same person, because that 99.3 per cent potential loss is about as bad as it gets on the sharemarket.

Billabong was a growth story in the 2000s, and the sharemarket loved the notion of the Australian brand going global. But it eventually left the sharemarket after being taken over in April 2018, at the equivalent of 21 cents a share, by US sports and lifestyle company Boardriders.

REMEMBER

A company's price on the stock market at any time, or any point in its history, is a record of transactions. No 'price' exists without a transaction — at any time, the market is made of bids (the prices that buyers are prepared to pay) and asks (the prices that sellers are prepared to accept). Over time, a profitable, well-run company tends to get 'bid' higher.

However, as Stanford Brown's research (refer to the earlier section 'Giving yourself time in the market') discovered, traffic towards the corporate knackery is constant. The trick to successful investing on the sharemarket is to have more of the stocks in their portfolios heading in the CSL or CBA kind of direction, rather than the Slater and Gordon or Billabong one.

REMEMBER

The gains on a successful company have no upper limit, but at least your loss on an unsuccessful stock tops out at 100 per cent (unless you've borrowed money to buy your stocks — for more on this, see Chapter 21).

Chapter **4**

Assessing Your Risk

once studied English literature and language and thought myself a traditional-ist, particularly when watching Shakespeare's plays. That perception changed when I saw the Bell Shakespeare Company's version of *The Merchant of Venice*, with the characters dressed in snappy suits and sunglasses with mobile tele-phones glued to their ears. Antonio and his friends looked like stockbrokers — the Venetian equivalent. I was hooked on this modern interpretation. I found out that Antonio, like any finance professional, understood that diversification helps to spread the risk.

My ventures are not in one bottom trusted

Nor to one place; nor is my whole estate

Upon the fortune of this present year:

Therefore my merchandise makes me not sad.

Well, he thought he was protected by diversification, until all his ships hit bad weather and were wrecked. The problem for Antonio was that, although his ven-tures were all seemingly well diversified, and his ships sailed from different places, his investments were all the same asset class — trading ships. In this chapter, I discuss how many investors think they've covered their risk through diversification or hedging until some unforeseen event changes everything.

Gambling or Investing?

Risk is the chance of an unexpected event happening or a particular objective or outcome not being attained; its basis is the unpredictability of the future. Risk is a relative concept that alters with circumstances and personalities. In the context of finance, risk means the possibility of losing invested capital. However, an investment doesn't have to be unprofitable to be an unacceptable risk; the major aim of investing is to generate a financial return above inflation.

REMEMBER

The highest risks bring the highest rewards. If you place your money on a single number at the roulette table, you have a 1 in 36 chance of your number coming up. That's why the table pays $35 for every dollar you put on it. As anyone who plays roulette can tell you, the 35 to 1 payout is a wonderful win to have early in the night. However, if the hour is late and you're chasing a win to get out of trouble, your odds may seem more like a 1 in 360 chance.

Like successful roulette players — if such people exist — successful investors understand that risk is merely the other side of gain, and you can't have gain without risk. An experienced investor knows that the promise of high percentage returns usually means increased risk. Sometimes, people new to investing don't make the proper connection between risk and return.

Measuring risk mathematically is possible. The statistical terms of variance and standard deviation measure the volatility of a security's actual return from its expected return, but that's a discussion that belongs in another book. However, in discussing the risk of a particular stock, standard deviation of return is a useful concept. The *standard deviation* measures the spread of a sample of numbers and the extent to which each of the numbers in the sample varies from the average. A *low standard deviation* of return in a stock means that it's a relatively less risky investment.

Another way of measuring risk uses the *beta factor*, a statistical measure of a share's volatility (see the sidebar 'Measuring volatility') compared with the overall market. The beta factor measures a share price's movement against that of the market as a whole (for example, the S&P/All Ordinaries index). The index has a beta factor of 1.0. If the share has a beta factor of less than 1.0, you can expect its price to move proportionately less than the index. If the share has a beta factor greater than 1.0, you can expect the share price to rise or fall to a greater extent than the index. The higher the beta factor, the more volatile is a share's price.

MEASURING VOLATILITY

Don't confuse volatility with risk because volatility is only one measure of risk. *Volatility* is the statistical term for the extent to which any series of numbers (such as a share price history) fluctuates. The higher the volatility of the price of an asset, the less certain is the return from that asset.

For example, research firm Andex Charts looked at 841 12-month investments in the S&P/ASX All Ordinaries Accumulation index (with dividends included), and its forebears, from January 1950 to December 2020 (that is, investments made at each month-end, and held for 12 months). The average 12-month return was 13.3 per cent and the standard deviation was 20.1 per cent. Of the 841 12-month periods examined, 90 per cent of the returns fell within a band of between −19.6 per cent and 49.4 per cent.

So, in a given 12-month period, an investor could reasonably expect a range of returns from 49.4 per cent to minus 19.6 per cent. The remaining 10 per cent of the 12-month returns fell outside this range. To benefit from that average 12-month return of the sharemarket, investors had to put up with the possibility of taking a 19.6 per cent loss (with an absolute worst-case in the sample of a 41.7 per cent loss, which occurred over the 12 months to 30 November 2008).

The good news is that, over the long term, returns tend towards the market average, and volatility is greatly reduced over longer periods.

The most famous volatility measure is the Market Volatility Index (VIX) of the Chicago Board Options Exchange (CBOE). Introduced in 1993, the VIX measures the implied volatility of options contracts traded over the value of the S&P 500 index on the CBOE. It has become the benchmark for short-term (30 days) expectations of stock market volatility, and goes by the nickname of the 'Fear Index'.

When the VIX is at high levels, the market expects a large change over the next 30 days. A low VIX implies a market expectation of very little change. Up until 2008, US investors believed that any time the VIX approached 48, it was a time to buy stocks. It was this kind of thinking that had investors buying back into the US market in mid-2008, because accepted VIX wisdom told them that was the right thing to do. But what nobody had envisaged was the sheer turmoil of the GFC. When the VIX peaked at 89.53 in October 2008, in the wake of the collapse of Lehman Brothers, the fear was no longer whether the US stock market was going to recover — it was whether the global economy financial system still functioned.

The VIX spent long periods since that peak trading around the 10–20 range — spiking up towards 30 on the back of events such as the credit rating downgrade of US

(continued)

(continued)

sovereign debt in August 2011, the US and Chinese 'flash' market crashes in August 2015, and the reaction to Donald Trump's election victory in November 2016 — but if anyone thought volatility levels would never surge back to GFC levels, the COVID-19 crash removed that notion very quickly. At the time of the first wobbles in the US share-market on 19 February 2020, the VIX was snoozing at 14.38. Less than a month later, on 16 March 2020, the VIX had rocketed to 83 and volatility was back with a vengeance, as the sharemarket got used to its new reality, digesting COVID-19 death, infection and hospitalisation numbers as thoroughly as it tried to factor in the effects of the pandemic on the global economy and corporate earnings. But as 2020 wore on, the VIX slowly subsided — and by June 2021, with the world seemingly making progress on the long journey out of COVID, the measure was back inside its old range, at 17.05.

In September 2010, the ASX introduced the S&P/ASX 200 VIX, constructed using the same methodology as the US VIX. Like its US counterpart, ASX back-testing shows that the Australian VIX surged to a high of 66.72 points when Lehman Brothers collapsed, but an improved outlook saw it fall to trade mostly in a 10–20-point range for most of the 2010s, with a couple of spikes to the 30s in September 2015 and February 2016, the latter of which saw the Australian VIX reach a record of 30.3 points. Like its US counter-part, the Australian VIX was sitting at a very unremarkable level just prior to the COVID-19 crash — at 12.3 points on 14 February 2020 — but by 18 March, was perched at a new record of 53.1 points. As with its big American brother, the Australian volatility gauge has slowly retreated over the rest of 2020 and into 2021, and by June 2021 it was back at 11.39.

In intra-day terms, funds management company Allan Gray says volatility on the S&P/ASX 200 surged from 2 per cent to 15 per cent in March 2020, on the back of increased uncertainty, fear, forced and panic selling, as well as reduced liquidity. Intra-day volatility has fallen and is now running close to its 20-year trend of 2–3 per cent. While elevated volatility can be highly alarming for investors, Allan Gray makes the point that volatility can often be the friend of the long-term investor — extreme fluctuations in price usually present excellent buying opportunities for long-term, patient investors.

The bad news: Risk is inescapable

All investors store money for future use. What most concerns you is the possibility of losing the money you're saving. Now you're talking risk! However, some pro-fessional investors set even higher risk levels than the average individual investor. For example, a fund manager may decide that her fund will outperform the S&P/ASX 200 index. The manager's main risk is not achieving this goal. Even if the fund's investments make money, if they don't exceed the return of the index, the portfolio has had a bad year. Investors know the fund failed to reach its benchmark, which can cause some fund investors to take their money elsewhere.

Wary investors associate risk with cataclysmic events, such as the great sharemarket crashes of 1929, 1987, 2007–09 and 2020, the bond market downturn in 1994, and the tech wreck of 2000. These events spark memories of collapsing companies, bankruptcies and share certificates made worthless overnight.

All assets offer a different reward and a different level of risk. They range from government bonds, which are considered a risk-free asset because they're guaranteed by the government, to futures contracts and options, and bitcoin (and other cryptocurrencies), where you can easily lose all of your money. With futures assets, you're taking on higher risk than if you buy an Australian government ten-year Treasury bond, but you're entitled to expect a far greater return. Successful investing means balancing the return against the risk.

The good news: Risk is manageable

You can offset risk either by hedging or diversification. *Hedging* is investing in one asset to offset the risk to another. *Diversification* is the spreading of funds across a variety of investments to soften the impact on your portfolio return if one investment performs badly. You can also include a few individual risk shares in a portfolio that's otherwise well balanced.

REMEMBER

Because returns from different assets aren't perfectly correlated, by diversifying your portfolio you decrease your overall risk. But you can't eliminate all risk. A well-diversified portfolio gives the best risk–return trade-off over the longer term.

Hedging is a form of insurance in which you try to make two opposite investments, so that if one goes wrong, the other can nullify or lessen the blow. When buying or selling shares, you can use the derivatives markets (exchange-traded options or warrants) to take the opposite position to an investment in the sharemarket. You may own shares in National Australia Bank (NAB), but also own a *put option* (the right to sell the shares at a predetermined price; for more on this, see Chapter 21) in NAB that will increase in value if the share price falls.

TIP

Time also manages risk by minimising it psychologically. As you come to understand the returns a share portfolio can generate over time, you begin to relax about short-term fluctuations.

THE ELUSIVE RISK-FREE ASSET

In every market, an investment considered a 'risk-free' asset exists, against which all other investment returns are compared. In Australia, it's the Australian government ten-year Treasury bond, because the Australian government guarantees to pay the holder of that bond the interest payment on the due dates, and the amount of the bond in full on maturity. You can't lend money to a better or more reliable debtor.

The ten-year bond is risk-free only if the buyer holds it to maturity. You can buy and sell bonds, just like shares, on the market, five business days a week. Bond prices move up or down based on how the market assesses the likely movement in interest rates. If interest rates rise, bonds issued at lower interest rates aren't as attractive as higher-yielding newer bonds. Naturally, the opposite is true if interest rates fall. When you're unable to hold the bond to maturity and have to sell it, you may have to sell it at a loss. The world bond markets fell dramatically in 1994 when interest rates spiked upward and caused the prices of lower-yielding bonds to slump. More recently, the bond markets experienced a 'bondcano' in February–March 2021, when US ten-year Treasury bond yields surged from 1.02 per cent to 1.75 per cent, giving rise to price falls of about 7 per cent in the bonds — that's a rare and significant kind of fall in the less-volatile bond market.

The difference between the risk-free return and the much riskier return on shares is called the *equity risk premium*, or ERP. Share investors demand a risk premium *over bonds* and they generally get it. Over the period 1900–2020, according to *Global Investment Returns Yearbook* (Credit Suisse, 2021), the Australian sharemarket generated one of the highest ERPs in the world — a 4.9 per cent gap in the annualised returns between shares and bonds. This compares to a premium over bonds for the world as a whole of 3.1 per cent a year. Only Japan and Germany had a higher ERP than Australia. (For more information see *Triumph of the Optimists* by Elroy Dimson, Paul Marsh and Mike Staunton, and the *Global Investment Returns Yearbook*, Credit Suisse, 2021.)

But the ERP does have one major drawback — it's not valid for any and all time periods. Someone who bought shares in October 2007, for example, has struggled to achieve a premium. Circumstances can exist when the premium disappears for long periods.

Generally speaking, because of the ERP, low-risk assets such as the Australian government ten-year Treasury bond, which generates low returns, may actually be too risky in the context of building capital wealth because the bond doesn't generate the returns of a long-term equity investment.

Spreading the news: Risk increases your return

The mathematics involved in *risk-and-return* theory are mind-boggling. In taking your first steps into share investing, you may come across terms such as 'modern portfolio theory' and the 'capital-asset pricing model'. These are complicated theories for money nerds to play around with and are far beyond the scope of this book — and far beyond your humble author, too! Simpler ways exist to understand how risk increases your return. For example, when you have an asset that earns a rate of return every year, you end up with a sample of yearly returns. When you've owned the asset for two years, you can calculate the average return that the asset has earned. However, the share return at any given time may fluctuate a good deal more than your calculated average. The wider the variance of the extremes, the more volatile the asset and the higher its standard deviation.

TIP

To reduce the standard deviation of your portfolio and increase its return, you can increase the proportion of more risky assets. Adding a new asset to the portfolio acts as a hedge to the other shares. With careful portfolio selection, you can achieve such a result, but it's necessary for you to bring in assets other than shares.

Assessing Your Risk

As an investor, you have to deal with different kinds of risk. In some instances, you may be able to lessen the risk, but in other situations, the degree of risk may be unchangeable. Some investments are like a cocktail of several kinds of risk. Understanding how each type operates helps you put together a balanced portfolio.

Market risk

Market risk is the risk you take by being in the sharemarket, trying to capture the higher return generated by shares (which, with dividends included, has run at 11.7 per cent a year since 1950). As the market fluctuates, the price of a company's shares varies too, independent of factors specific to the company. The higher prices rise and the more the market moves away from its long-term trendline, the more likely a correction will take place (when a share price or market index falls by 10 per cent or more).

The crash of 1987 stripped 25 per cent from the value of the All Ordinaries index in one day. The slump knocked the very best stocks off their perch for a year to

18 months. Many others in the top 100 took three years to get above their pre-crash highs and some stocks never recovered. The massive bear market of November 2007 to February 2009 stripped 54 per cent from the value of the Australian sharemarket — once again, setting many companies a long and difficult task to regain and surpass their previous share-price high-points.

In February–March 2020, the damage to the index was 38 per cent, and considerably more than that to the share prices and market valuations of many individual stocks (refer to Chapter 3 for some examples).

REMEMBER

That is the impact of market risk. In a market fall of that magnitude, it doesn't matter how well diversified your share portfolio is; all stocks fall. The good ones eventually regain and surpass their pre-crash peak prices — and the really good ones leave those once-amazing levels for dead.

CSL, for example, was trading at $34.50 before the market slump started in November 2007 — fast-forward to February 2020, just before another big slump, and it was trading almost ten times higher, at $341.00. It fell as low as $270.88 in March 2020, but by June 2021 it was back at $305.00. But it must be said, not every stock has done that well.

REMEMBER

Economic data, such as inflation, interest rates and gross domestic product (GDP), all contribute to the risk of being part of the market. If the market falls by a marked amount, most shares fall as well. You can't lessen market risk by diversifying within your share portfolio. To offset the systemic risk of the sharemarket, your portfolio needs to contain other asset classes, such as property or bonds. Ideally, your portfolio features overseas assets as well, to lessen the reliance on the Australian economy. That's diversification, which I cover in Chapter 5.

Every sharemarket company incurs a cocktail of risks, daily, in going about its business. That's part and parcel of business — running risk to generate return.

Financial risk

Every company has *financial risk*; that is, the possibility of the company getting into financial difficulties. Managing the finances of a publicly listed company isn't an easy task. The company may have borrowed too heavily and exposed itself to danger from rising interest rates, a recession or, worst of all, a *credit crunch* — when banks stop lending. That's what happened in the GFC, particularly after Lehman Brothers collapsed and the global banking system temporarily froze. Suddenly, after years of cheap credit, debt was a dirty word. Over-borrowed companies' share prices simply sank like stones on the sharemarket when they couldn't roll over their debt.

Structured finance specialist Allco Finance Group, which was valued at $5 billion at its peak in February 2007 — shortly before it was the key player in a consortium that tried to take over Qantas — fell 98.9 per cent on the way to administration in November 2008, owing more than $1 billion. Investment bank Babcock & Brown, which floated at $5 in 2004 and reached a peak of $33.90 in mid-2007 (when it was valued at $10 billion on the ASX), fell 99.6 per cent — 45 per cent of that in two days, in June 2008 — before it limped into administration in March 2009.

In January 2008, financial services and property group MFS lost almost 70 per cent of its value during a phone call — a conference call with analysts in which chief executive Michael King revealed a shock $550 million capital raising, almost three times larger than the analysts were expecting. MFS changed its name to Octaviar, but went into liquidation in July 2009.

Shopping centre owner Centro Properties lost 99.4 per cent between February 2007 and April 2009; 84.5 per cent of that value was lost in two trading days, in December 2007, after it revealed that it couldn't roll over $4 billion in short-term debt. (Centro did not go into administration; in fact, it never missed an interest payment. Its banks sold the debt to the bondholders, who ultimately swapped the debt for equity in a new company, Federation Centres, which in 2015 merged with Novion Property Group to form Vicinity Centres.)

Childcare centre operator ABC Learning plunged 92 per cent on its way into receivership, and infrastructure operator Asciano fell 96.5 per cent, from $11.64 in June 2007 to 40.8 cents in February 2009. (Asciano was taken over at $9.13 a share in mid-2016 by logistics group Qube, Canada's Brookfield Infrastructure and a group of international pension funds.) The end of the road in share price terms for Allco Finance Group, Babcock & Brown, MFS/Octaviar, Centro Properties and ABC Learning is shown in Figure 4-1.

Real estate investment trusts (REITs) with high debt levels were hammered just as badly. FKP Property, Goodman Group and ING Industrial Fund all fell more than 95 per cent; GPT lost just less than that. Abacus Property and Australand both lost 91 per cent. Anywhere the market saw short-term refinancing risk, or simply too much debt, it was much the same. (Although still well short of their pre-GFC unit-price highs, Goodman Group and GPT remain pillars of the A-REIT sector.)

The worst slump of all was toll road company BrisConnections, which was floated by Macquarie Group and Deutsche Bank with awful timing — in July 2008, when over-geared infrastructure stocks were badly on the nose. BrisConnections' $1 partly paid units fell 59 per cent on their first day of trading, and by May 2009 they were trading at 0.1 cent (the lowest tradeable price on the ASX), for a fall of 99.9 per cent.

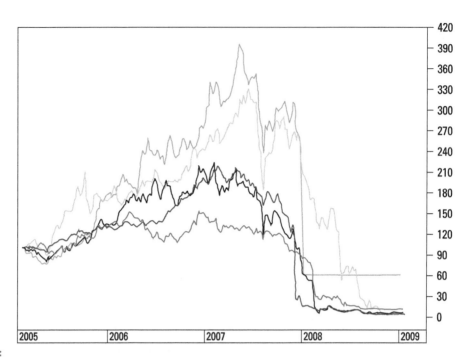

FIGURE 4-1:
Allco Finance
Group, Babcock &
Brown, MFS,
Centro Properties
and ABC Learning
share prices,
2005–09.

—— Allco Finance Group

—— Babcock & Brown

—— MFS/Octaviar

—— Centro Properties

—— ABC Learning Centres

Data source: © IRESS Market Technology

At the time, holders of the units were still obliged to pay the second and third instalments of the purchase price, of $1 each; naturally, they didn't want to do so. Many decided not to, amid threats of legal action. Eventually Macquarie Group and Deutsche Bank took up the unwanted units, leaving them owning 79 per cent of the company. The fully paid (to $3) units returned to trading in January 2010, at $1.30; the company's toll road in Brisbane, the Airport Link, opened in July 2012 but failed to meet its traffic targets, and the units were suspended for good in November 2012, at 40 cents.

Another example of financial risk involved the mining group Sons of Gwalia, which collapsed in 2004. Better known as a gold miner, Sons of Gwalia was also the world's largest producer of tantalum, a metal widely used in the electronics industry, and lithium, a metal used in aerospace and healthcare (and, these days, a crucial component of batteries for renewable energy, such as solar and wind power, and electric vehicles). In 2001, Sons of Gwalia was valued at more than $1 billion. Three years later it collapsed, taking about $250 million of shareholders' funds with it. Sons of Gwalia got its gold hedging wrong. It had forward sales agreements that committed it to deliver gold, but the reserves that it had to mine were insufficient to meet those commitments. A $500 million liability on its gold and foreign exchange hedging 'book' brought it down.

REMEMBER

Mining is a risky business, but the financial engineering that the miners' treasuries sometimes indulge in can be even riskier when it involves effectively making bets. Sons of Gwalia's fall (see Figure 4-2) came only four years after zinc and lead miner Pasminco imploded after getting its foreign exchange hedging wrong. Pasminco was refinanced in 2002 and returned to the sharemarket in April 2004 as Zinifex, which in 2008 merged with Oxiana in an $11.6 billion merger that created Australia's fourth-largest miner, called Oz Minerals. Bad timing — the credit crunch hit, and Oz had to make massive write-downs and sell its refinery and smelting operations, on the way to a $509 million loss in 2008–09. The share price fell 80 per cent, and in mid-2021 was still 45 per cent below its pre-GFC peak, trading at the same price it was in June 2008. Two of that company's three incarnations have given shareholders a tough time! (However, Oz Minerals has been an excellent performer for most people who've bought it since the GFC.)

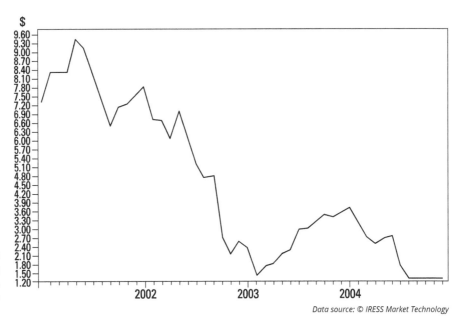

FIGURE 4-2:
Sons of Gwalia
share price,
2001–04.

Data source: © IRESS Market Technology

Another kind of financial risk is when the price of a company's product drops for reasons beyond its control. Agrichemical company Nufarm encountered this problem between 2008 and 2010 when prices for its main weedkiller product, glyphosate, slumped as cheaper Chinese products and weak demand hit the market. Nufarm's margins more than halved over the period, forcing the company into a loss in the 2009–10 financial year, its first loss in more than a decade. Nufarm was forced to slash its earnings forecasts in half in July 2010, triggering breaches of debt covenants (agreements between a company and its bankers that the company should operate within certain limits) that left it at the mercy of its banks. Nufarm shares slumped by 70 per cent in 2010, and by mid-2021, the share price remained 73 per cent below its 2008 peak.

Commodity risk

A *commodity* is a tradeable good; the word is generally used in the context of physical commodities — basic resources and agricultural products — that are bought and sold all over the world, and have actively traded markets. 'Hard' commodities are those extracted by mining, while 'soft' commodities are agricultural goods that are grown. You also get 'energy' commodities, such as oil and gas. Companies that produce commodities are exposed to *commodity risk*, which refers to the uncertainty caused by the fluctuation of the price of commodities in the market, and thus the income derived from producing them.

The surge in Chinese economic growth through the 2000s — peaking at an exhilarating 14 per cent in 2007 — sent the price of iron ore rocketing, from US$12.45 a tonne in June 2000 to US$187.18 in February 2011. This was fabulous news for Australian iron ore miners, who dug up as much ore as they could and shipped it to China. Moreover, any mining company that could do so committed to huge volume expansions to take advantage of the higher prices. BHP, Rio Tinto and Fortescue Metals Group all forged ahead with big expansion plans, as did the other major iron ore player, Valé of Brazil. New players also entered the market. But, as is typical with supply responses to high prices, the extra tonnes began to arrive just as the demand from China began to slow on the back of a weakening economic growth rate. (This was to be expected, because China had moved slowly towards a more consumer-spending and services-oriented economy, and relied less on massive infrastructure projects to boost its growth.)

By 2015, China's GDP growth rate had fallen to 7 per cent a year, and although this is still massive growth, given the sheer size of the Chinese economy, it meant that iron ore was less in demand. Sure enough, by December 2015, the iron ore price was under US$50 a tonne.

This was bad enough for the major producers, BHP and Rio Tinto, but at least they were diversified commodity producers. For the miners that only produced iron ore, however, it was a disaster, as the sagging iron ore price threatened to fall below their cost of production.

The largest of the single-focus iron ore miners, Fortescue Metals Group, dropped 71 per cent on the ASX. The smaller iron ore 'juniors' fared even worse: Gindalbie

Metals slumped 98.5 per cent, Atlas Iron lost 99 per cent, BC Iron plunged 94.5 per cent and Mount Gibson Iron fell 91 per cent. Gindalbie and Atlas Iron bit the bullet and stopped mining temporarily. Gindalbie was eventually taken over by a Chinese company in 2019, Atlas Iron was taken over by Gina Rinehart's Hancock Prospecting in 2018, and BC Iron got out of the iron ore business and changed its name to BCI Minerals. Only Mount Gibson Iron is still producing (after an unfortunate hiatus — see the section 'Engineering risk', later in this chapter, for further details).

However, from the low point mid-decade, iron ore kicked off again, helped by a catastrophic tailings dam failure in Brazil, to reach US$120 by July 2019. The tragedy in Brazil cut the production of the dam's owner, Valé, by one-fifth in 2019, to 302 million tonnes (allowing Rio Tinto to topple Valé as the world's largest producer). Continued production difficulties at Valé — and China's determination to re-stimulate its economy after the economic impact of the COVID-19 pandemic — have seen iron ore push through US$150 a tonne (in December 2020) and then US$200 a tonne (May 2021), to arrive at US$212 a tonne at the time of writing.

Chinese steel manufacturers would have been grinding their teeth paying these kinds of prices, but they've had little choice. China's own iron production has fallen from its depleted mines, and at the time of writing, Valé's production was still curtailed by order of the Brazilian courts — its 2021 production is expected to be just over 81 per cent of production before its most recent dam accident. While new supply is expected from African mines, the market expects increasing demand from steelmakers; however, in the long term, iron ore prices are not expected to remain at the current elevated levels.

Miners don't just sit on their hands and hope for strong prices and favourable exchange rates; they work hard to control what they can control, which is the cost at which they produce, given the orebodies they work with. As at mid-2021, Australian miners continue to drive their cost of production ever lower, while their margins continue to balloon on the back of the iron ore price. Take Fortescue Metals Group as an example. Having brought its cost of producing a tonne of iron ore down from US$48 a tonne in 2011–12 to US$13.45 as at March 2021, it has put itself in a good position to handle much lower iron ore prices in the future. It's no surprise that the dark days of a share price of $1.50 in January 2016 seem a long way away for Fortescue — it became a 16-bagger from there, at $25.

Liquidity risk

Liquidity risk is the possibility that you'll be unable to get out of an investment because no-one will buy your shares. Holders of internet stocks after the April 2000 tech wreck know all about liquidity risk, as do owners of small company stocks during the GFC. You can't sell shares if no-one wants to buy them. If liquidity risk bothers you, don't stray out of the top 100 stocks. Even then, liquidity cannot be guaranteed.

TECHNICAL STUFF

As Howard Marks, chairman of US global investment house Oaktree Capital Management, puts it: 'The liquidity of an asset often depends on which way you want to go . . . and which way everyone else wants to go. If you want to sell when everyone else wants to buy, you're likely to find your position is highly liquid: You can sell it quickly, and at a price equal to or above the last transaction. But if you want to sell when everyone else wants to sell, you may find your position is totally illiquid: Selling may take a long time, or require accepting a big discount, or both.' If that is the case, says Marks, then the asset can't be described as being either liquid or illiquid: it's 'entirely situational' as to which it is.

Given that Oaktree is the largest investor in *distressed securities* — securities in companies or entities that are experiencing financial or operational distress — in the world and also specialises in 'alternative' investment strategies (see Chapter 5), he could be describing situations more exotic than the sharemarket. But Marks' explanation is as good a summary of liquidity risk as you could hope to find.

Business risk

Each share carries *business risk* — that is, the possibility that the company will make a mistake in its business. Business risk is part and parcel of the capitalist system. But business risk can very soon become financial risk — a very good reason to have a well-diversified share portfolio.

REMEMBER

Company collapses do happen — and they come in all shapes and sizes. Electronics retailer Dick Smith Holdings Limited (no longer connected to the eponymous 1968 founder, Dick Smith, who sold his entire interest to Woolworths in 1982) was floated by its owner, private equity group Anchorage Capital in December 2013, a little over a year after Anchorage bought the business from Woolworths. Dick Smith shares were offered in the prospectus at $2.20 and closed their first day of trading at that price. That valued the company at $520.3 million — just over a year after Anchorage had paid $20 million to buy it.

In the IPO, 66.2 per cent of Dick Smith was sold, with Anchorage holding on to 47.3 million shares or 20 per cent. However, Anchorage had fully sold out by September 2014.

By January 2016, Dick Smith Holdings was in receivership, with 393 stores and 3,300 employees. The appointment of administrators and receivers came after two painful earnings downgrades in its last six months and a $60 million inventory write-off that sent the shares plunging by as much as 70 per cent, hitting 20 cents at one point. By the time Dick Smith shares went under, the shares had slumped by 84 per cent.

What blew the company up were inventory problems — it bought too much inventory in anticipation of certain sales levels, and then didn't achieve those levels. Court hearings into the collapse heard that Dick Smith's management chose its products to maximise rebates (the money that retailers get from suppliers to stock and promote their goods), rather than on what its customers actually wanted to buy. Worse, the receivers alleged that the company breached accounting standards by booking those rebates as profit before it actually sold the products and was paid. As rebate-carrying inventory built up, the company had difficulties securing finance to purchase new stock.

This became a vicious circle — the reliance on rebates ultimately led to slowing of inventory turnover rates, because the products were generally less popular with customers. Eventually, reported the company's administrator, 'heavy discounts were needed to sell the rebated stock, destroying the margin uplift that the rebate sought to achieve and, in some cases, the stock could not be sold at all and became obsolete.'

The company committed some of the cardinal sins — it grew too fast, used short-term working capital to fund long-term assets and (after stock write-downs) wasn't profitable. The bottom line is that there was insufficient profitability or insufficient access to funding for growth, and its executive remuneration appeared to be too focused on the short term. In November 2015, the company revealed it would write-down the value of its inventories by 20 per cent, or $60 million. Dick Smith became insolvent because it was unable to make scheduled payments to its financiers, and it breached its banking facility agreements in December 2015. The company tried a last-ditch '70 per cent off everything' sale just before Christmas 2015, but it didn't work.

In the end, Dick Smith had $1.3 billion in sales but collapsed owing its creditors $260 million. The retailer's staff received their full entitlements, but shareholders lost their dough.

Figure 4-3 shows Dick Smith Holdings' share price over its life as a listed company.

Product risk

Similar to business risk, some companies carry *product risk* — that is, the possibility that their products may fail. This is a particular concern for biotech shareholders because a failed clinical trial can make a major dent in their investment.

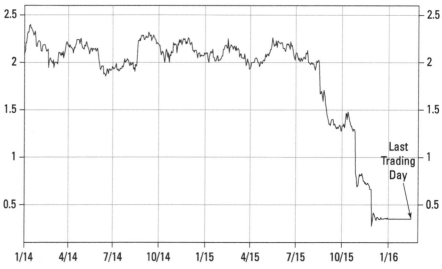

Dick Smith Holdings Ltd (DSH-AU)

Last Trading Day

Source: FactSet Financial Data and Analytics

FIGURE 4-3: Dick Smith Holdings' share price, 2013–16.

Just ask the shareholders of Factor Therapeutics, which in November 2018 was testing its wound-dressing drug VF001 to treat venous leg ulcers. But the trial failed — or, in the precise language of biotech, 'analysis demonstrated no clinically meaningful or statistically significant difference in measures of wound healing compared to placebo' — and the shares were virtually wiped out, closing that fateful day down 97 per cent at 0.2 cents. Ongoing development of VF001 for all indications was halted.

'We started with hope and belief based on the evidence we had that it would be effective and we could take it to market,' Factor Therapeutics chair Dr Cherrell Hirst told a conference call with investors on the day it reported the trial result. 'But the results were strongly negative and there was no ambiguity.'

After that, the company said it was still looking for a new business opportunity that involves clinical-stage (or near to clinical-stage) assets with sufficient data to support a high likelihood of successful commercialisation. In 2021, Factor Therapeutics changed its name to Dominion Minerals, shifting its focus to copper and gold exploration.

It was an even worse story for shareholders of Innate Immunotherapeutics in June 2017. Innate was developing a drug called MIS416 for the treatment of multiple sclerosis (MS), specifically the secondary progressive stage of the disease. MIS416 looked to stimulate the body's immune system to reduce inflammation, and protect against — and even repair —some of the damage the disease causes to the central nervous system. No approved drugs for the effective treatment of secondary progressive MS were yet available, so the drug had blockbuster (US$1 billion-plus) sales potential.

Innate shareholders would have gained confidence from the data from an earlier clinical trial, as well as the fact that the drug had 'investigational new drug' (IND) status from the US Food & Drug Administration (FDA). Anecdotal evidence was also coming from New Zealand, where it was being used under a 'compassionate' patient program, because patients had no other effective treatment options. This indicated the drug actually reversed some of the disabilities that came with MS, and looked to be particularly effective at improving physical strength, energy levels and lessening pain.

That's what makes it even worse for Innate shareholders — the drug looked good. But again came the dread words — 'no clinically meaningful or statistically significant difference in measures of neuro-muscular function or patient-reported outcomes.' The shares fell 90 per cent in a matter of minutes. (Incidentally, the slump in Innate Immunotherapeutics shares claimed the job of a US congressman, who was a director of the company and its largest shareholder: Chris Collins resigned from Congress after being charged with insider trading in Innate shares, of which he was found guilty. He was jailed in 2020.)

Innate Immunotherapeutics is now known as Amplia Therapeutics (see Chapter 8), which has a drug candidate that has received two 'orphan drug' designations from the FDA. This status is given to drugs intended to treat, prevent or diagnose a rare disease. In June 2021, positive clinical trial news on one of these drugs sent the share price jumping nearly 50 per cent in a day: although welcome, the share price was still down 80 per cent on where it was before that fateful 2017 day.

Not even Australia's world-leading medical device makers — hearing aid maker Cochlear and sleep-breathing product developer ResMed — have been immune from this kind of issue. In September 2011, Cochlear issued a global recall of its bestselling product line after noticing a mysterious rise in the number of its hearing implants that had suddenly stopped working. The share price fell 25 per cent in a morning. And in May 2015, ResMed shocked the market with the results of a clinical trial that it hoped would show that its sleep therapy products protected heart attack victims; instead, the trial result showed that a group of patients were put at increased risk of dying. The sharemarket reacted by cutting 27 per cent from ResMed's share price.

REMEMBER

Both medical device companies have had periods of flat sales and profits as competitive pressure intensified — when analysts could have been forgiven for being bearish. But they have been tremendous long-term performers, because when product problems have emerged, they have solved them quickly. ResMed listed on the ASX in November 1999 at the equivalent of 88 cents (it was already listed in the US). It is now trading at $32. Global hearing-implant specialist Cochlear was floated at $2.50 in December 1995 by its owner, the Pacific Dunlop group. Seven years later, Pacific Dunlop was no more, but 25 years later, Cochlear became a '100-bagger', trading at $251.55 just before the COVID-19 crash (in June 2021, Cochlear was trading at $246.85).

Legislative risk

Another form of specific risk is *legislative risk*, which is the possibility that a change in legislation may adversely affect a company in which you own shares. (This is also known as *regulatory risk*.) No better example of this exists than the experience of salary packaging and vehicle fleet management services company McMillan Shakespeare in July 2013. McMillan Shakespeare was blindsided by the then Labor Government's proposed changes to fringe benefits tax (FBT) laws in relation to car use for business. As a major player in the car-leasing market, McMillan Shakespeare immediately stood to lose up to 40 per cent of its earnings. The shares promptly fell 55 per cent.

Until then, McMillan Shakespeare had been a market darling, rising from a post-GFC low of $2 to $18. What most angered McMillan Shakespeare and its fellow car-leasing companies was the lack of consultation. The change was sprung on the industry by the government, out of the blue — hence the dramatic share price fall. Even though the incoming Coalition government overturned Labor's changes later that year, the shares took five years to recover the lost ground. Complicating matters were also involved — competition intensified in McMillan Shakespeare's business areas in Australia, New Zealand and the UK; the company's efforts to diversify resulted in a class action over its extended car warranty business NWC; and a planned merger with fellow auto-leasing company Eclipx fell through. The bottom line, however, is that McMillan Shakespeare was badly bruised by a government decision that it didn't see coming — see Figure 4-4. (The COVID-19 crash took 58 per cent off the McMillan Shakespeare share price, but that's a different kind of risk.)

McMillan Shakespeare did eventually surpass its 2013 peak in August 2018; however, at $12.70 in mid-2021 (at the time of writing), the stock is once again well short of clear water.

As mentioned, a close relative of legislative risk is regulatory risk. In September 2018, life-insurance distributor Freedom Insurance experienced a gruelling appearance at the Royal Commission into Misconduct in the Banking, Superannuation and Financial Services Industry, in which its business model of directly selling insurance through cold-calling (unsolicited phone calls) was exposed as having involved high-pressure sales tactics, and high commission payments. As a result of the Royal Commission hearings, in December 2018, the Australian Securities and Investments Commission (ASIC) banned insurers from cold-calling customers to sell life and consumer credit products. At a stroke, that ban took away Freedom Insurance's business model. Between them, the Royal Commission hearings and the ASIC ban stripped 95 per cent from Freedom Insurance's market value — and left the company no option but to voluntarily put itself into receivership.

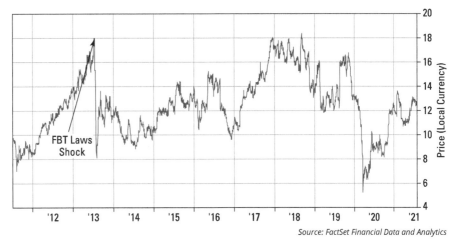

FIGURE 4-4: McMillan Shakespeare share price, 2011–21.

Source: FactSet Financial Data and Analytics

Technical risk

Occasionally, companies developing ambitious new projects using new technology can come unstuck on *technical risk*, when the technology proves difficult to bed down or simply doesn't work.

Anaconda Nickel was a Western Australian nickel company that in the mid-1990s, saw the potential of large, already-discovered laterite deposits in the northern goldfields of WA. These deposits were discovered in the nickel boom of the early 1970s but were left untouched because they were considered to be uneconomic. But with the development of a new process called pressure-acid-leach, suddenly these deposits became viable.

Anaconda embarked on an ambitious $1 billion world-scale 45,000 tonnes-a-year nickel plant at Murrin Murrin, near Leonora in Western Australia. Anaconda had no difficulty raising the money, with mining giant Anglo American and Swiss metal trader Glencore among the project backers. The plan was to expand production at Murrin Murrin to 100,000 tonnes of nickel and become one of the world's biggest producers. In 1999, Anaconda was a top 100 company, valued at $1.5 billion. However, the cracks in the plan were emerging.

Anaconda was in a hurry to get into production, so it skipped the demonstration plant stage and went straight from the laboratory to full-scale production. The plant couldn't handle it. The ore proved more difficult to process than first thought, and construction design flaws and engineering problems rose aplenty. In March 2002, Anaconda — now out of the top 100 — defaulted on its debt, and in September 2002 the company posted a net loss of $919 million, then the largest loss from a company ranked outside the top 100. As the company's flagship project stalled and the share price plummeted, in 2001 Anglo American led a bid to oust Anaconda's chief executive — one Andrew Forrest, who soon after moved on to another, more successful career as an iron ore magnate, with Fortescue Metals Group. Anglo American sold out of its disastrous Anaconda investment in 2003, leaving Glencore to take full control. In the same year, the company was renamed Minara Resources, which Glencore ultimately took over in 2011.

Engineering risk

Closely related to technical risk is *engineering risk*, of which Mount Gibson Iron fell foul. The company has the distinction of producing Australia's highest grade of direct shipping ore, at 65.5 per cent iron. But that didn't do it much good between 2014 and 2019, when its open-cut mine on Western Australia's Koolan Island was not only filled with water, but even hosted sharks and crocodiles.

Koolan Island is on the remote Kimberley Coast, 2,000 kilometres north of Perth, and the mine there (first developed by BHP in the 1950s) lies below sea level, separated from the sea by a wall. In 2014, its seawall collapsed, flooding the mine's main pit. Mining stopped for five years, but insurance payments, plus ongoing cash from its Iron Hill mine inland from Geraldton, kept Mount Gibson in a healthy financial position, and after two years of cleaning up the site, a new seawall was built, enabling mining to recommence. In April 2019, Mount Gibson Iron was back in business, shipping ore. Mine life is a problem at Koolan Island, but at current iron ore prices its high-grade ore is raking it in: Mount Gibson made a net profit of $84 million in 2019–20 and paid a 3 cent fully franked dividend. At the time of writing in mid-2021, Mount Gibson shares were trading at 95 cents, only 19 per cent short of where they were prior to the mine closure in 2014 (and up almost five-and-a-half times on their 2015 low point).

Project risk

Similar to technical and engineering risk is *project risk*, when a project runs into problems that end up being terminal.

Mining services company Forge Group floated in 2007 at 64 cents a share, and peaked at $6.80 in 2011. But the company collapsed in March 2014, with the shares back down to 82 cents and under the weight of more than $500 million in debt.

Forge's problems began when it bought power station builder CTEC in 2012. Two power stations that CTEC was building ran into construction problems and cost blow-outs, and Forge Group had to make major write-downs. The power station issues couldn't be solved and Forge Group had to go into administration.

The administrator's report was not enjoyable reading for Forge shareholders. It found that Forge over-estimated its income, and its labour costs, material costs and work overheads were much higher than budgeted. The administrator said Forge had collapsed for a combination of reasons, including a reliance on debt for capital funding, an aggressive approach to acquisitions, insufficient risk control measures and failed restructuring.

The administrator's report also revealed to shareholders that Forge's largest shareholder, engineering group Clough, raised its concerns that at the time Forge bought CTEC, Forge had not conducted its due diligence on the acquisition properly.

Figure 4-5 shows Forge Group's share price over its life as a listed company.

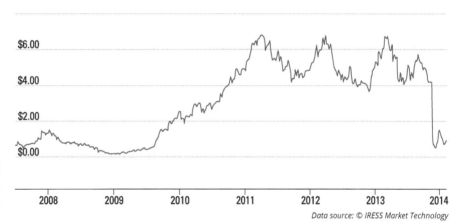

FIGURE 4-5:
Forge Group
share price,
2007–14.

Data source: © IRESS Market Technology

Engineering group RCR Tomlinson, founded in Perth in 1898 and listed in 1951, also fell victim to project risk, which saw it enter voluntary administration in November 2018. The problems began when the company — which specialised in the mining and resources industry — moved aggressively into the solar power arena from 2016 onward. By mid-2017, RCR was telling shareholders that it was 'positioned for major spend in solar' and when it announced its interim results in February 2018, it boasted its group revenues had doubled to $940 million with help from its expanding renewable energy portfolio. At that stage, RCR controlled 20 per cent of the market for building solar power farms.

But later that year, it started to emerge just how ultra-competitive that construction market was, as intensifying rivalry for new projects squeezed profit margins. RCR's strategy of bidding aggressively for solar farms and undercutting its competitors was causing problems. Although its solar portfolio had grown to include more than $1 billion worth of projects, several of them were behind schedule, forcing RCR Tomlinson to pay damages to solar farm developers at the same time it was trying to pay workers and suppliers, draining its available cash.

In August 2018, RCR shocked the sharemarket by announcing a $57 million write-down on two Queensland solar farms and launching a $100 million capital raising. Ground conditions had been misjudged, along with procurement issues and poor information flow to management; more importantly, however, costs had blown out on the fixed-price contracts RCR had signed to build the solar farms. RCR did raise the $100 million — assuring investors that its business was secure — but the write-down was the beginning of the end. In November 2018, the company collapsed when its banks refused to lend it any more money. In December 2018, the administrators reported that RCR had debts of up to $630 million. At its peak in August 2017, shares were trading at $3.50, and the company was valued at almost $1 billion. The shares were trading at 87 cents when the company collapsed; shareholders got nothing. Figure 4-6 shows the share price fall.

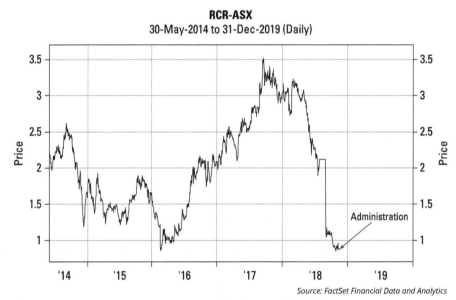

FIGURE 4-6: RCR Tomlinson share price, 2014–19.

Source: FactSet Financial Data and Analytics

Valuation risk

Valuation risk is tied to the price of a share. A company may be well run, profitable and part of a stable industry, with a conservative balance sheet, but the shares can be too expensive to buy. The shares are *overvalued*.

Valuation risk usually isn't a problem for investors with a long-term investment strategy because they can afford to wait for the quality of the stock to push the stock past its over-stated value, although a major market slump can force them to extend their holding period beyond what they had expected.

However, short-term investors have to wait for the *price/earnings ratio* (P/E) to come back down to earth, which may not fit their investment strategy.

A good example is Commonwealth Bank (CBA), which in June 2021 was trading at $100.23. The consensus view of financial research firm FNArena's analysts at this time was that their price targets for CBA shares were below the prevailing share price, at discounts ranging from 5 per cent to 27 per cent, with a consensus price target of 12 per cent below the share price (a *price target* is the price that an analyst who follows CBA believes it will reach; the consensus price target is the average of the price targets in the market). Over at fellow financial research firm Stock Doctor, the consensus price target is below the share price by a similar percentage. The consensus of the analysts that follow CBA was that in June 2021, the share price was overvalued — meaning that in the view of the professionals, the stock was more likely to fall in the near future (usually, the next six to 12 months) than rise.

Political risk

Political risk refers to the uncertainty of return from a foreign investment because political or legislative changes in that country may be detrimental to investors' interests; or, in less stable countries, that coups and political violence can affect companies.

Australian companies, particularly mining and petroleum exploration companies, operate in some of the furthest-flung reaches of the planet, in some cases under regimes considered highly unsavoury and in countries considered unsafe for Westerners.

In November 2019, for example, a convoy of buses containing hundreds of workers at a Canadian-owned mine in the African nation of Burkina Faso — some of them employees of Australian engineering company Perenti Global — was attacked by jihadi terrorists. In the attack, 37 people were killed, 19 of them Perenti employees, and 20 of the company's employees were wounded. It was a sobering reminder of the risks of operating in unstable regions, and Perenti would hardly have cared about the 11 per cent fall in its share price. The company exited that mining services work contract immediately and has since quit two other work contracts in Burkina Faso, leaving just one active contract in the country. Perenti operates in 11 other countries around the world, and in 2021 it won a large contract in the more politically stable African country of Botswana, working with Australian copper mining company Sandfire Resources (see Chapter 8).

Africa-focused Australian gold miner Resolute owns and operates three gold mines in Africa — Syama in Mali, Mako in Senegal and Bibiani in Ghana — and concedes that the jihadi terrorist risk has increased in Mali in recent years. While the French Army is working with the Malian government to pacify the country, Resolute says it is taking all the safety measures that it can, including building refuges at the Syama mine.

A more traditional case of political risk involved Australian mining company St Barbara, which operated the Gold Ridge gold mine in the Solomon Islands. Gold Ridge had already been abandoned by its Australian owners once before (in 2000) due to civil unrest, and St Barbara took it over in 2012. The mine experienced incursions into the site, attacks on company vehicles, and vandalism and fire damage to mine infrastructure, only for the workers doing the repair work to then be attacked by locals. Then in 2014, deadly floods shut the mine and threatened its tailings dam, stretching St Barbara's relationship with the Solomon Islands' government to breaking point. In 2015, St Barbara sold the mining operation to local landowners for just $100, but not before the problems at Gold Ridge had slashed the company's value by 96 per cent. (At the time of writing, St Barbara has put its Solomon Islands problems well behind it by concentrating on its mines in Australia, Papua New Guinea and Canada.)

In early 2016, Australian miner Kingsgate Resources was happily mining its Chatree gold mine in Thailand, which it had discovered in 1995 and started mining in 2001. But in May 2016, the Thai government announced that all gold mining in Thailand would cease by 31 December 2016 — and Chatree was the only operating gold mine. Kingsgate put the mine on 'care and maintenance' in January 2017.

The Thai government's stated reason for its decision was that the local community was being affected by elevated levels of arsenic and manganese, leading to sickness. Kingsgate countered that extensive testing had shown levels of the naturally occurring toxins to be similar to other provinces in Thailand. That did not help — the mine was not only closed, but was also expropriated by the Thai government.

Kingsgate had specific 'political risk' insurance, but when it tried to claim on this policy in May 2016, the claim was denied. Kingsgate commenced international arbitration proceedings against its insurers in October 2017. In March 2019, the company settled a New South Wales Supreme Court case against its political risk insurers for more than $82 million.

Eventually, relations between Kingsgate and the Thai government thawed a little, with a Kingsgate subsidiary allowed late in 2020 to sell about $14 million worth of gold and silver 'sludge' left over from the decommissioning of the Chatree mine, as well as being granted a fresh set of mineral prospecting licences for the country. In September 2021, Kingsgate announced that it was in 'advanced stages' of negotiation with the Thai government and that an arbitral tribunal was 'ready to issue all operating licences and permit applications required to restart the mine'.

Political risk can also affect companies selling their wares abroad. This was the case for Treasury Wine Estates, Australia's largest wine company and the maker of well-known brands such as Penfolds (and its iconic Grange label), Wynns, Seppelt, Wolf Blass, Pepperjack and Lindeman's, in late 2020.

After starting the year at a share price of just over $16, Treasury Wine Estates had moved nicely to $17.70 — then the COVID-19 pandemic stripped its market value in half, taking the share price to $8.61. Then, having painstakingly rebuilt its value back to $10.57, Treasury was blindsided by an announcement from China's Ministry of Commerce in November 2020 that applied tariffs on Australian wines ranging from 107 per cent to 212 per cent, which doubled and even tripled the price of its wines in the Chinese marketplace.

The move was ostensibly the result of the findings of an anti-dumping investigation, in which China claimed that Australian winemakers were selling wine below the cost of production and causing China's winemakers 'substantial harm'. But everyone knew it was not about 'dumping', as this trade practice is known: Australia had annoyed China on the geopolitical front, on several matters. It did so most notably in May 2020, when the Australian government called for an independent international inquiry into the origins of the outbreak of COVID-19. Wine was just one of a number of commodities through which China took punitive action against Australia.

Overnight, Treasury Wine Estates' business in China was rendered unprofitable. At the time, Treasury was selling about $500 million worth of wine into China a year (nearly half of the $1.3 billion in total that Australian winemakers were sending) and generating about 30 per cent of its profit there; in other terms, about 25 per cent of the top-quality Penfolds range had been going to China. Treasury told the stock exchange that it expected demand for its wine in China to be 'extremely limited' from now on. Broker Morgan Stanley put it more bluntly. It said the company's sales into China would 'essentially cease'.

Treasury reacted by reallocating the wine it sold into China to other markets, re-organising its structure, and stepping-up its marketing efforts in other countries, in particular the US, Europe and other markets throughout Asia, to strengthen Penfolds as a 'global luxury icon' brand in the 60 countries where it was being sold. While the China earnings hole was unlikely to be filled completely during the 2020–21 period, the company is doing its best to show the market that it has sustainable long-term growth prospects that are not reliant on China.

As at March 2021, Treasury's wine exports were up 7 per cent in 12 months, excluding China; however, this was only enough to offset about 18 per cent of the lost Chinese exports. Figure 4-7 shows how China's move slammed the Treasury Wine Estates share price.

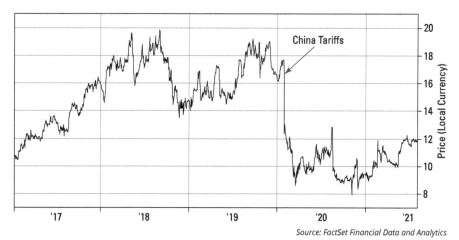

FIGURE 4-7:
Treasury Wine Estates share price, 2017–21.

Source: FactSet Financial Data and Analytics

Expansion risk

Many companies come awry when they attempt to expand, particularly when moving into another country. Obviously, companies can outgrow the small Australian market, and companies such as CSL, Sonic Healthcare, Ramsay Health Care, IRESS, Computershare, Amcor, Macquarie Group, James Hardie Industries, Cochlear, ResMed and Aristocrat Leisure, to name just a few, have made a very good fist of expanding overseas. Geographic diversification is a good thing.

But many companies have failed.

Examples abound. Casino operator Crown Resorts' push overseas, from 2004 to 2016, is a case in point. In the heady pre-GFC times, then Crown boss James Packer decided to expand into the gambling hub of Macau. In 2004, Crown entered a joint venture with Melco International Development — the company of Hong

Kong and Macau billionaire Stanley Ho — to develop the City of Dreams casino complex in Macau. The joint venture, Melco Crown Entertainment, in which Crown invested $770 million, opened the City of Dreams, Studio City and Altria casino resorts in Macau.

Then, in 2011, Crown bought the Aspinall's Club in London, a private Mayfair gambling club that it rebranded to Crown London Aspinalls. In 2014, Crown decided to enter the Las Vegas gambling market, buying a prime 7.4-hectare site (and leasing the remaining 6.5 hectares), where Packer planned to build the $2.5 billion Alon casino and hotel project. Then, in 2014, Melco Crown applied for a licence to build a new $US5 billion ($5.4 billion) casino complex in Japan, in time for the 2020 Tokyo Olympics.

This expansion was too much. It turned out that competing in Las Vegas and Macau was a bit different from owning an exclusive casino in Melbourne. In October 2016, 17 Crown employees (and two former employees) were arrested in China and charged with illegally promoting gambling; ten (including two Australians) were jailed for nine months. Crown had legitimate fears that it might lose its licence, so it sold out of Macau, halted its development plans in Las Vegas, and shrank the business back to Australia and its three casinos. In November 2013, Crown announced it had received approval for a second Sydney casino licence at the Sydney precinct of Barangaroo, where it has built Crown Sydney.

Even returning to a domestic business has not been easy, with the company encountering difficulties in both Victoria and New South Wales regarding its suitability for holding a casino licence (in the wake of damaging governance allegations and revelations of criminal infiltration and money laundering at its Melbourne and Perth casinos). In 2021, Crown was found unsuitable to retain its casino licences for both Crown Melbourne and the built-but-not-yet-operating Crown Sydney, but the company avoided suspension of its Melbourne licence subject to a two-year probation under the supervision of a special manager and is working with the New South Wales gaming regulator on arrangements to open the casino at Crown Sydney. In April 2021, the New South Wales gambling regulator forced James Packer to sever all management influence at the company; now, he simply has a passive interest in the business as its largest shareholder, owning 37 per cent of the company's shareholding. The company had fixed its expansion-risk problems — but not its reputation-risk ones (for more on reputation risk, see the later section 'Reputation risk' in this chapter).

In 2016, Wesfarmers bought the UK/Ireland hardware business Homebase for $700 million, hoping to clone its successful Australian Bunnings concept offshore. Wesfarmers initially told Australian fund managers that it would expand into the British Isles incrementally — but it seemed to get impatient, and changed all the Homebase stores to the Bunnings Australian format straightaway. The business lost sales, key staff and, most importantly, customers, too quickly. In February 2018, Wesfarmers wrote off $1 billion from its investment in Homebase; three months later, it sold the Homebase business for £1, to restructuring firm Hilco Capital.

Another of the biggest bonfires of shareholder value in recent years also took place in the UK. As mentioned in Chapter 3, Melbourne-based law firm Slater and Gordon listed in May 2007, the first legal firm to list in the world, and floated at $1. The stock was welcomed onto the ASX, rising to $1.40 on its first day of trading. With the capital contributed by external shareholders, Slater and Gordon was able to accelerate its acquisition of competitors and consolidation of the Australia market. The firm made progressively larger acquisitions, and in the process consolidated its position as Australia's largest personal injury law firm, with a market share of about 30 per cent.

These acquisitions grew earnings per share (EPS) significantly, as Slater and Gordon was generally able to buy smaller law firms at attractive prices. In 2015, Slater and Gordon saw an opportunity in the UK, where the personal injury law market was up to five times the size of that in Australia. Slater and Gordon could increase the size of its business many times over by snatching a 10 per cent or 15 per cent share of that market.

In early 2015, the Australian firm swooped on the professional services division of British law firm Quindells, buying it for $1.3 billion. The debt-funded acquisition, which management hoped to be transformational, very quickly turned into large losses. Quindells was a basket case, in a cash crisis, and its aggressive accounting tactics had been questioned by analysts. In February 2016, Slater and Gordon wrote down the value of this investment by $800 million. By August 2016, the investment had been completely written down, plunging Slater and Gordon to a $1 billion loss for 2015–16, and forcing it to restate its 2014–15 profit from $82 million to $62 million.

The company could not recover from the disastrous acquisition. By March 2017, its banks — including Westpac, National Australia Bank, Barclays and Royal Bank of Scotland, which were collectively owed about $700 billion — sold their debt to distressed debt-buyers (mainly hedge funds), and recapitalised with a one-for-100 share consolidation, virtually wiping out the existing shareholders.

These shareholders had seen their shares peak at $8 a share in July 2015, which valued the company at $2.8 billion. Between July 2015 and April 2017, the share price fell 99 per cent, to 6.8 cents. In its independent expert's report for the recapitalisation, accounting firm KPMG estimated an implied pre-recapitalisation value for the shares of *negative* $1.19 to *negative* $1.65. The shares are still listed in 2021, trading at 68 cents, or 0.68 cents in the pre-recapitalisation currency (see Figure 4-8).

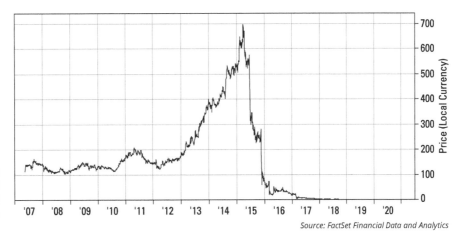

FIGURE 4-8:
Slater and
Gordon share
price, 2007–21.

Source: FactSet Financial Data and Analytics

Currency risk

If a company operates in any currencies other than the Australian dollar, that company has *currency risk*. Currency risk is a bet that can have a number of outcomes. If the price of your foreign assets rises, you get a capital gain. The important question then concerns the value of those assets in their local currency. Here's what can happen:

» If the foreign currency strengthens against the Australian dollar (A$), your capital gain is magnified.

» If the foreign currency loses ground against the A$, your capital gain is reduced.

» Conversely, if your foreign assets fall in value, you don't want the foreign currency to weaken against the A$ because that increases your loss.

» With a falling asset price, you want the foreign currency to strengthen against the A$ to offset some of your capital loss.

Companies try to lessen or negate their currency risk by using the derivatives markets to lock in future receipts or amounts to be spent, at a predetermined rate. This practice of hedging is a form of insurance that can cost money. Hedging doesn't always work, as with the Sons of Gwalia example, which I discuss in the section 'Financial risk', earlier in this chapter.

Specific risk

Risk that is particular to a certain stock is called *specific risk*. A good example is the biological risk that has affected several listed aquaculture businesses. The first example is Western Kingfish, which was floated on the ASX in July 2007. Western

Kingfish operated fish farms at Jurien Bay in Western Australia, where it produced yellow-tailed kingfish. In November 2008, a bacterial infection wiped out 75 per cent of the company's fish, plunging it into administration.

Fellow fish farmer Clean Seas Seafood had a similar issue. It endured a disastrous period in 2008 to 2012, when it saw fish deaths increase from a normal rate of 15 per cent to about 80 per cent, and it lost 4,000 tonnes of biomass. The company had to liquidate assets, cut workforce numbers in half and withdraw from international markets (Europe and USA) to survive. It was discovered that the fish-feed was defective in levels of a critical sulphonic acid, taurine, and restocking biomass and slowly re-entering international markets took two years. Death rates have since returned to pre-feed crisis levels of about 15 per cent — and Clean Seas successfully sued its feed supplier, receiving a $15 million payout in January 2020. At least Clean Seas Seafood survived — it specialises in yellowtail kingfish and is Australia's only commercial producer of the species, and the largest breeder outside Japan, where the 'hiramasa' (as the species is known) is prized eating.

Tasmanian-based Atlantic salmon producer Tassal has also been plagued by environmental issues. As with all animal husbandry, aquaculture has inherent challenges with managing disease and environmental impact, and these challenges have certainly been encountered in Australian aquaculture.

On land, the share price of Australia's biggest beef producer, the Australian Agricultural Company (AAC), was hammered by Australia's climatic extremes of weather, from droughts to floods (as immortalised in Dorothea McKellar's 1904 poem, *My Country*). For the AAC, damaging drought periods through the 2000s and 2010s in its south-western Queensland and Northern Territory areas hurt operations, only for 'once-in-a-century' heavy rains and flooding in Queensland to strip its share price to a 15-year low in early 2019 when livestock and infrastructure suffered from the extremes of weather. The AAC experienced lower calving in 2018–20 due to the prolonged drought and then the flood event; next, the company's food export markets were slammed by the COVID-19 pandemic. But the AAC's shares have been on a slow-burn recovery since early 2019, when agricultural conditions began to improve in its operating areas. Figure 4-9 shows how drought and then floods slammed the AAC's share price.

REMEMBER

Stories such as these are a good reminder why, when building your portfolio, you shouldn't put all your eggs in one basket (turn to Chapter 5 for more on diversifying risk).

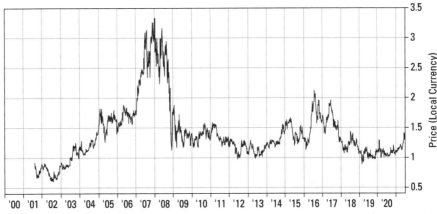

Source: FactSet Financial Data and Analytics

FIGURE 4-9:
The Australian
Agricultural
Company's share
price, 2000–21.

Sector risk

A risk not shared by the market as a whole, but affecting representatives of only one industry, is called *sector risk*. The mining companies' health, for example, is dominated by overseas news (especially from emerging markets) and movements in commodity prices and exchange rate movements, requiring investors to keep a close eye on global macroeconomic and geopolitical events.

Fraud risk

Any company with inadequate internal financial controls runs the risk of falling victim to *fraud* (an economic crime perpetrated against a company, whether by an insider or outsider).

In August 2009, electrical retailer Clive Peeters' senior accountant defrauded the company of $20 million. She was caught and jailed for five years, while Clive Peeters went into receivership in May 2010, after falling sales and crippling debt of $140 million forced the board to pull the plug. Harvey Norman bought the business in July 2010. The fraud wasn't responsible on its own for the demise of Clive Peeters, but it certainly contributed.

In 2014, the high-flying chief executive officer of biotech company Phosphagenics, Esra Ogru, was sentenced to six years in jail for creating an elaborate system of fake invoices and credit-card claims to defraud the company of $6 million in a fraud that took place over nine years between 2004 and 2013. After Phosphagenics (which changed its name to Avecho Biotechnology in May 2019) alerted the ASX in July 2013 that 'invoicing and accounting irregularities' had occurred, the share price lost 82 per cent.

In 2015, the former chief executive and former chief financial officer of generic drug maker Sigma Pharmaceuticals (which changed its name to Sigma Healthcare in March 2017) pleaded guilty to falsifying the company's accounts in 2009 and 2010. The court heard that Sigma's accounts overstated the company's income and revenue by $15.5 million, inventories by $11.3 million, and net profit by $9.6 million.

Sigma's financial difficulties during 2009 and 2010 had already resulted in the company agreeing to pay shareholders almost $60 million in 2012, to settle a class action brought by disgruntled investors. The class action rested on the company predicting that it would record modest profit growth when it was conducting a $300 million capital raising in September 2009; six months later, Sigma shocked the market by revealing a $424 million write-down that led to a $389 million loss for the 2009–10 financial year (ending 31 January 2010).

That unexpected loss — announced in March 2010 — saw the sharemarket halve Sigma's market value in a day.

Fraud can even come from outside the company. In January 2013, coal miner Whitehaven Coal lost 9 per cent of its market value after an anti-coal activist issued a fake press release stating that ANZ Bank had withdrawn its $1.2 billion loan to help Whitehaven build a new coal mine because of environmental concerns. Whitehaven shares lost about $280 million in market value in a matter of minutes.

Agency risk

Agency risk refers to the risk that management and the board (the investors' 'agent') may act in the best interests of the agent rather than the investors. An obvious example is when boards approve ridiculous salary packages for managers, but agency risk can manifest itself in quite a number of areas:

>> Senior management paying themselves disproportionately to the earnings of the business, and their own performance

>> Management making investment decisions that might maximise the short-term earnings and/or share price performance to realise incentive payments, even if those investment decisions are not in the long-term interests of shareholders

>> Management increasing corporate expenses, including significant employee perks

>> Management focusing on growing the size of the business, rather than its profitability

Less obvious examples of agency risk include:

>> New management tossing out the garbage early in their term of office — for example, booking big provisions and write-downs in the early years, so as to demonstrate improved performance and make earnings targets easier to reach in later years, thus achieving bonuses

>> Management making decisions on mergers and/or acquisitions (either as the target or the acquirer) that result in significant personal benefits, when the benefit for shareholders is far less apparent.

An increasing trend in recent years has been professional fund managers looking to lessen agency risk by tilting toward businesses where the agency risk is naturally lessened; typically, where the business (although listed) is still largely founder-led, or where the CEO and/or board members have significant ownership of shares. These investors are voting with their feet by seeking out companies with much tighter alignment between management's and investors' interests.

Examples of companies where the founders — or their families — are still heavily involved at management level include plumbing supplies group Reece (the Wilson family), retail business owner Premier Investments (Solomon Lew), Flight Centre (chief executive Graham Turner is one of the three founders, and the other two founders, Bill James and Geo Harris, are still major shareholders), enterprise software group TechnologyOne (founder and executive chairman Adrian Di Marco), Nick Scali Limited (the Scali family) and Event Hospitality (the Rydge family). Other companies where the founders remain big shareholders include Fortescue Metals Group, TPG Telecom, Computershare, Magellan Financial, Mineral Resources and Pro Medicus.

Non-financial risk

Non-financial risk can come from such areas as product liability, occupational health and safety, human resources and security issues. Political, environmental and market changes can also be termed non-financial risk. Although these elements don't have specific dollar values, they eventually have a direct impact on financial risk.

Just because many of these newer risks are termed 'non-financial' risk doesn't mean companies can take any comfort from that, because such risks broadly flow back to financial outcomes. Where companies once thought that they answered only to their shareholders, creditors, regulators and governments, they now understand that they have a broad range of 'stakeholders' that can affect or be affected by the company's actions, objectives and policies. Examples of crucial stakeholders are employees, suppliers, vendors, partners, unions, customers, visitors to the company's premises and sites, and the community from which the business draws its resources.

Climate-change risk

These days, companies are expected to monitor and report to shareholders on their exposure to material economic, environmental and social sustainability risks, and what they are doing to manage these risks. In particular, *climate-change risk* — the risk that modelled and projected changes in the world's climate will negatively affect society, asset values, the operations of companies and human life in general — has become an important risk to be disclosed, and every regulator with which Australian listed companies deal has spelled out for them what is expected.

In the last five years, listed companies have had the Australian Securities and Investments Commission (ASIC), the Australian Prudential Regulation Authority (APRA), the Australian Accounting Standards Board (AASB), the Auditing and Assurance Standards Board (AUASB), the Council of Financial Regulators (CFR) and the ASX — and even the Reserve Bank of Australia (RBA) — all emphasise the need to improve climate-change risk disclosure.

The framework that has become increasingly prominent globally — and has been adopted by Australian regulators — is that of the Taskforce on Climate-Related Financial Disclosures (TCFD), a body established by the Financial Stability Board of the G20 nations.

The TCFD recommendations set out the kind of information that must be analysed and disclosed in order to truly and fairly represent (and enable assessment of) the impact of climate-related risks on companies' financial positions and prospects, in a consistent form, such that investors, lenders and insurers can base decisions on it. The TCFD contemplates not only the disclosures themselves, but also the risk metrics and targets, strategy and governance processes within which climate-change risk issues are managed.

For example, the TCFD recommendations require companies to report on 'Scope 1' greenhouse gas emissions, which are the emissions directly emanating from their own business activities; 'Scope 2' emissions, which are the emissions arising from the energy that businesses buy from suppliers for their own use (such as for heating or lighting); and 'Scope 3' emissions, which are the emissions of the company's customers and the end-users of its products.

In August 2019, ASIC rewrote its Regulatory Guidance on market disclosures for both prospectuses (RG228) and annual report operating and financial reviews (RG247), describing climate change as 'a systemic risk that could have a material impact on the future financial position, performance or prospects of entities'.

ASIC also now includes climate risk in its list of factors that may result in non-financial impairment.

In the fourth edition of the ASX's Corporate Governance Council's Principles and Recommendations — which took effect for an entity's first full financial year commencing on or after 1 January 2020 — the ASX explicitly referred companies to climate-change risk as part of Recommendation 7.4, which deals with material exposure to 'economic, environmental and social sustainability risks'.

Recommendation 7.4 encourages entities to consider whether they have material exposure to climate-change risk by reference to the TCFD recommendations and, if they do, make the disclosures recommended by the TCFD.

REMEMBER

While the ASX recommendations are not mandatory, the broad view in the market is that investors and other stakeholders expect listed companies to demonstrate how they have considered climate change as a risk for their business, and what they are doing to respond to it — and if they're not, they're expected to explain why not. This pressure can only increase dramatically in the coming years, and investors can expect even tighter mandatory reporting regulations to be instituted over time.

Reputation risk

Climate-change risk is just one risk that comes under the environmental, social and governance (ESG) umbrella, which refers to how a company is performing in terms of the environmental, social and governance aspects of its operations — and how seriously it takes those aspects. ESG is a broad topic, but it covers areas such as environmental impact; 'human capital' issues, such as gender and ethnic diversity in the composition of board, management and staff; the social and health impact of the company's operations; and the quality of the governance by which the company is structured and operates.

ESG risk is an example of risk that is incurred by the company's conduct, which can affect its reputation. *Reputation risk* directly affects a company's standing in the broader community, and in the eyes of its investors, lenders, staff, suppliers, customers and other organisations with which it works. And with the rise of social media, companies have had to get used to the idea that any reputational risk is likely to be on social media within minutes. *Cyber-risk* (the risk of having data compromised) and *supply-chain risk* (the risk that other companies in the supply chain have practices they may not know about, such as modern slavery) are other, newer risks that companies run; *terrorism risk* (the risk of terrorist attacks on companies' assets, sites or operations, causing damage and loss of life) is another.

How good a corporate citizen a company is — with respect to all of its stakeholders, and measured by ESG factors — now ranks as one of the most important ongoing tasks for management. Being measured solely on financial metrics and praised as a good investment that rewards shareholders is no longer good enough; companies are now seen as having a 'social licence to operate', that they must maintain, and which, by implication, can be withdrawn at any time if the community feels let down by the company's actions.

TECHNICAL STUFF

Companies may feel that the concept of a 'social licence to operate' is highly subjective, and the ASX seemed to tacitly concede this in 2019 when — to the surprise of some — it dumped a proposal to include reference to a social licence to operate in its updated corporate governance guidelines (referred to in the preceding section). The new guidelines did refer to a company's need to maintain its 'reputation' and 'standing in the community', however.

The problem of subjectivity is shown by the case of coal miner Whitehaven Coal, which, as a producer of coal, is accused by environmental groups of not having a social licence to operate. But Whitehaven Coal turns that around by arguing that hundreds of millions of people in Asia and other parts of the world do not have electricity, and that it supplies the coal that brings electricity — and thus, the ability to function better economically — to some of these people (who, if they didn't use high-energy-content Australian coal, would use inferior coal from other countries, actually increasing carbon dioxide emissions). That argument shows that the social licence to operate is in the eye of the beholder.

REMEMBER

The social licence to operate is now broadly seen as one of the most (if not the most) valuable intangible assets a company has. That licence can be lost if the company or any of its directors, officers or employees is perceived to have acted unlawfully, unethically or in a socially irresponsible manner.

Some companies have been slow to respond to ESG allegations, believing that it does not pay to rock the boat. When copper miner Sandfire Resources read in the media in 2014 that Australian National University (ANU) was selling out of its shares in the miner (and six other resources companies) because they were 'not socially responsible, and doing harm', according to the university's then vice-chancellor, it was at first annoyed, and then — when the ANU's decision was reported on the front page of the *Wall Street Journal* — it was angry.

Research firm the Centre for Australian Ethical Research (CAER) had been commissioned by the ANU to do proprietary research into the environmental, social, governance and ethical performance of the companies in its portfolio, and it recommended that Sandfire be dropped. Sandfire believed that what CAER had said about it was incorrect, out of date and misleading.

Sandfire brought a case against CAER in the Federal Court, which it discontinued in April 2015 after CAER issued a statement saying that the ESG ratings and reports on Sandfire it had provided to the ANU were 'deficient and inaccurate' and that 'significant aspects of the research, conclusions and ratings were drawn from incomplete and out-of-date information'.

Sandfire's CEO said that the stakes were too high to let the allegations slide. At the time, the company was trying to gain permits for a copper project in the US — and letting the allegations stay on the public record could have prejudiced that. But more worrying to the company was that it did not want the rest of its shareholders and stakeholders to believe that it was not prepared to defend its ESG record.

On the other hand, clear cases of companies not adhering to ESG factors can greatly cost them. One of the highest-profile examples is German car giant Volkswagen, which was discovered in 2015 to have cheated on its cars' pollution emission tests. The scandal cost Volkswagen US$33.3 billion (A$51 billion) in fines, penalties, financial settlements and buyback costs, but what would have hurt the company more was that it halved the share price — and trashed its reputation.

Closer to home, financial services heavyweight AMP had a horror time in the Australian government's Royal Commission into Misconduct in the Banking, Superannuation and Financial Services Industry in 2018. As if two decades of poor performance were not enough, AMP shareholders had to endure the painful sight of a string of executives, including then-chief executive officer, Craig Meller, and head of wealth solutions, Paul Sainsbury, admitting to various kinds of corporate misconduct, including charging customers fees where no service had been pro- vided, and even continuing to charge deceased customers despite knowing they had died; breaching criminal provisions in the Corporations Act; and intentionally misleading the corporate regulator, ASIC, for almost a decade.

Figure 4-10 shows what the sharemarket thought of AMP's appearances at the Royal Commission — the company's already poor reputation headed to the toilet. (Mr Meller's and Mr Sainsbury's appearances before the Royal Commission are indicated at points (1) and (2).) At the time of writing in mid-2021, the share price had fallen even lower than after those events.

Information risk

Information risk is when investors who are buying shares rely on such published information as a company's prospectus, announcements to the stock exchange, annual reports and brokers' research documents. All of these documents carry legal disclaimers that say, in a variety of ways, that they can't be relied upon, even if audited. As a wary investor, you need to research information from different sources to lessen the impact of information risk.

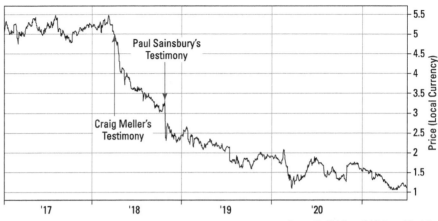

FIGURE 4-10:
AMP share price,
2017–21.

Source: FactSet Financial Data and Analytics

Avoiding the Turkeys

You can use a variety of techniques to assess whether any of the shares in your portfolio are at risk. The health checks you can apply to shares can be either fundamental or technical. *Technical analysis* (see Chapter 16) involves charting share prices and trying to extrapolate from past trends. *Fundamental analysis* (see Chapter 15) looks at a company's financial performance — cash flow, balance sheet, revenue, earnings and dividends.

Using technical analysis

Investors who follow charts like to identify support levels for stocks — that is, prices at which, in the past, the stock has turned upward. A stock falling through a support level on a chart is enough for most technically oriented traders to pull out of a company's shares. Even if you don't wholly trust technical analysis, you'll find that often — especially with the aid of that precious investment tool, hindsight — the charts tell a story of trouble before the news gets out to the market.

Watching cash flow

When you review a company's performance, always reconcile *cash flow* — the difference between revenue and outgoings as depicted in the cash flow statement — with reported profit. Those are the only earnings that matter. If you do this annually, you need to look beyond the company's reported result to the improvement in its balance sheet. Deterioration in cash flow (or, worse, cash inflow becoming cash outflow) is a signal that the risk has become higher.

Charting dividend changes

A lowered dividend, or a dividend that is only maintained at the previous year's level, is also a danger signal. Companies that pay a dividend go to almost any lengths, including borrowing, or dipping into their reserves, to maintain that dividend.

WARNING

A company cuts or suspends its dividend only under extreme financial duress. You need to follow the dividend returns of companies in your portfolio and know when your dividend is under threat, despite the spin-doctoring in company announcements.

Gauging who's selling — or buying

Heavy *institutional selling* (when the super and managed funds sell their shares) is an indication that something isn't right with a company. The institutions follow a stock more closely than you do and know more than you do. If they're queuing up to sell shares, it isn't a good sign.

The exit of institutional investors from the share register of Sons of Gwalia after a profit warning in July 2004 was a sign that the market was concerned at the company's direction — concerns that were borne out. Your broker is able to provide this kind of information so you can protect your portfolio.

The directors of a company know its prospects better than anyone. These days, following all the announcements a company makes is relatively easy and directors must notify the sharemarket if they sell shares. Change of Director's Interest Notices announced to the ASX disclose when directors are selling securities in a company. This will be a signal for institutional investors to at least investigate the reason for the sale.

REMEMBER

Normally, if directors sell small amounts of shares, you needn't worry. Like all Australians, the directors need cash occasionally. However, large sales by directors, such as 50 per cent or more of their holding, is a warning sign.

Insider selling is quite common, and investors often notice that it can precede company problems and steep share price declines. In recent years, examples include selling at Aconex and Bellamy's Australia (when both were listed), Brambles, Healthscope, Sirtex Medical, Vita Group and Vocus Communications.

TECHNICAL STUFF

Company directors selling some of their shares isn't always a bad sign; in fact, the ASX specifically cautions against assuming as much. In ASX Guidance Note 22, it states: 'ASX does not believe that directors' securities trading is necessarily an indicator of an entity's prospects and discourages any perception that investors should rely on such information in making investment decisions.'

Insider selling can also occur in the best-performing companies, and at prices where the insiders forego considerable upside. Qantas CEO Alan Joyce sold $7 million worth of shares in August 2016, at $3.29 — prior to the COVID-19 crash, Qantas shares were trading at twice that price. Outgoing Aristocrat Leisure CEO Jamie Odell sold $12.6 million worth of shares in December 2016, at $11.94 — in that case, prior to the COVID-19 crash, Aristocrat shares were trading at more than triple that share price.

Insider share movements can also go the other way. Late in 2019, the new NAB CEO, Ross McEwan, showed his commitment to his new employer through an on-market purchase of 5,000 shares at $25.459. Spending $127,295 of his own coin would have come as a welcome vote of confidence for NAB shareholders, who had watched their company's share price slide from $41.46 in 2007. Sadly for McEwan, after the COVID-19 crash, his investment was soon 35 per cent under-water. At least the shareholders knew that their CEO was hurting, too — and that he had a strong incentive to work hard to drive the share price higher.

REMEMBER

A shareholder owning more than 5 per cent of a company must notify the market if they cease being a substantial shareholder (defined as a person or entity that owns 5 per cent or more of a company). Watching substantial shareholder notices announced on the ASX can identify if large investors are entering or exiting a company. One of these large investors announcing that it is no longer a substantial shareholder may indicate they are planning to completely exit their holding.

In contrast, a new shareholder becoming a substantial shareholder is a sign that someone likes the company — whether as an investment or, in some cases, as a potential acquisition. Once an entity is a substantial shareholder, any subsequent increase of 1 per cent in its stake must be disclosed to the ASX. (They must also announce each 1 per cent decrease in their holdings.) The law prevents individuals or entities from acquiring over 20 per cent in a company without a formal takeover bid, but the 'creep rule' provision of the Corporations Act is an exemption — it states that an investor that has moved to holding 19 per cent of a company is allowed to buy an extra 3 per cent of the company every six months (even if they creep to holding 20 per cent or more). However, they have to wait another six months before making any formal acquisitions.

TIP

A sharp-eyed investor can read the play through the ASX announcements, and see which players are moving up the list of top 20 shareholders in companies. If you conclude that the smart money is buying a stock, it's often a good signal that the share price could be going up.

IN THIS CHAPTER

» **Building a strategy for diversification**

» **Selecting a variety of shares**

» **Managing a balanced portfolio**

» **Relying on managed funds**

» **Investing overseas with managed funds**

» **Looking at some non-traditional options**

Chapter **5**

Eggs and Baskets

iversification means using your investment money to buy different assets. Your goal in diversifying is to benefit from the performance of different assets that are usually not synchronised. If shares, for example, are performing poorly, property or bonds may be performing well. You want to include one or both of these in your portfolio in order to diversify across a range of investment options. You also want to diversify within an asset class. Say you already own mining shares — if you then buy a bank stock, a portion of your portfolio isn't dependent on commodity prices for growth. The aim of diversification is to ensure that, at any time, part if not all of your investment portfolio is performing well.

These days, an Australian investor's portfolio may contain any of the following:

» Australian shares, property and bonds

» Foreign shares, property and bonds

» Managed funds

» Hybrid securities

» Exchange-traded funds (ETFs), exchange-traded products (ETPs) and quoted managed funds

>> Listed investment companies and trusts (LICs and LITs)

>> Warrants, options and derivatives

>> Digital assets (assets created using blockchain technology and secured by advanced encryption techniques), including cryptocurrencies (for example, Bitcoin and Ethereum), *stablecoins* (a cryptocurrency pegged to a real-world asset, such as gold or a fiat [official government] currency) and *tokens* (digital representations of a particular asset on a blockchain).

Keep in mind that diversification is a good strategy for all types of investing. If you think of diversification in terms of the adage about eggs and baskets, then you have more baskets than ever before to accommodate your precious eggs.

In this book, I talk mainly about diversification within a single asset class, shares. In this chapter, I cover risk versus return, growth and value stocks, investing overseas, using managed funds and considering alternative options such as hedge funds, commodities and collectables.

Spreading the Risk

Diversification is an essential strategy for protecting your investments over the long term. The second share you buy diversifies your portfolio, at least a little. Understanding how diversification works is a necessary step in acquiring a balanced portfolio. Three levels of diversification exist:

>> You can own different asset classes, such as shares, government bonds and property.

>> You can acquire different investments within one asset class, such as owning shares in BHP, CSL, Altium, Australian Agricultural Company and Woolworths.

>> You can use geographical diversification, such as making an investment in overseas assets.

As an Australian investor, you can choose from about 2,200 stocks listed on the Australian Securities Exchange (ASX), which allows you to put together a highly diversified portfolio. You can put together a portfolio that includes higher-risk, higher-reward opportunities, as well as conservative investments. You can place a small proportion of your total investment funds in higher-risk speculative shares — perhaps 5 to 10 per cent, depending on your appetite for risk. (Refer to Chapter 4 if you need help in quantifying just what your risk level is.) However, high-risk investments need good research to ensure that those investments are more of a calculated risk rather than a wild stab in the dark.

Unfortunately, Australian investors have a poor record with diversification when buying shares. A total of 35 per cent of Australian adults — or 6.6 million people — own listed investments outright, according to the ASX *Australian Investor Study* for 2020. Of course, many more people own listed investments indirectly, through their superannuation accounts.

The likelihood of share ownership increases with age. In 2020, only 40 per cent of 'next generation' investors (those aged 18 to 24) hold domestic shares directly, compared to 62 per cent among 'wealth accumulators' (25 to 59 years) and 84 per cent among retirees (60+ years).

However, adequate diversification remains a problem. In the 2017 ASX *Australian Investor Study*, 46 per cent of investors said they had a diversified portfolio, yet on average, they owned only 2.7 investment products. In 2020, 54 per cent believed their portfolio was diversified. Of these, however, 58 per cent were only invested in one to two products, with the average holding 2.6 investment products. Only around 5 per cent held six or more investment products. Investors who believe they have diversified portfolios are significantly more likely to hold ETFs, international direct shares, LICs and managed funds, all of which help a lot with their portfolio diversification.

REMEMBER

Over the past four decades, the need for diversification has been clearly demonstrated as, repeatedly, all the asset classes took their turn suffering big slumps. The sharemarket crashed in October 1987 and fell badly again in 1990, 2000, 2001, the GFC crash of 2007–2009, 2018 and 2020. The bond market had its version of a crash in 1994. (US 30-year Treasury bond yields spiked from below 6 per cent to above 8 per cent, a massive move for that market. *Remember:* Bond prices fall as yields rise.) Australian cash rates fell by two-thirds from 1989 to 1994, and later traced an even deeper decline — from 7.25 per cent in August 2008, the cash rate fell to 3 per cent in just nine months and has since been in a slow slide to a record low of 0.10 per cent (at the time of writing; it was last altered in November 2020). That 99 per cent slide caused the average three-year term deposit rate in Australia to plunge from 7 per cent to 0.54 per cent at present — a 92 per cent decline.

The unlisted property sector collapsed at the start of the 1990s, as regulators were forced to impose a freeze on every unlisted property trust in the country. The sector slowly returned to favour, only to blow up again in the GFC. Once again, many unlisted property structures were frozen as they struggled with excessive debt, and some were forced to cease distributions. And once again, the liquidity risks inherent in having investment vehicles that offered ready redemptions despite their underlying assets being illiquid made themselves felt. Structures were cleaned up following the GFC slump, and unlisted property recovered its place in a portfolio. Over the ten years to December 2020, as interest rates plumbed new lows, Australian unlisted property generated 9.4 per cent a year for investors, according to global index provider MSCI and the Property Council of Australia (PCA).

REMEMBER

Each of these slumps was preceded by large flows of money to a different asset class. A market that's running hot tends to pull funds from other markets showing relatively low returns. This situation also happens in the sharemarket when *herd mentality* drives investor buying. Diversification of your portfolio is the best protection in this situation. Having a spread of investments reduces your risk and the volatility of returns.

Table 5-1 shows the historical total returns (meaning income is included) from different asset classes available to an Australian investor in the financial years between 1992 and 2021. Each of these asset classes has enjoyed at least one year in which it was the best performer — except cash, which is very rarely the winner. A portfolio that was wholly invested in US shares would have been the best performer, on average, with 12.3 per cent a year, followed by international listed property, on 11.2 per cent a year, and Australian shares, with 10.4 per cent a year. Volatility was similar in terms of negative years: US shares had six, and so did Australian shares. US shares were the best-performing investment in seven of the 30 financial years, and the worst in three; Australian shares scooped the pool in three of the years, and were the weakest performer in two. On average, unhedged international shares — taking full 'currency risk' (refer to Chapter 4) — beat international shares hedged into A\$, by 9.5 per cent a year to 9 per cent a year.

At the other end of the risk–return scale, cash isn't capable of consistently generating the return of a growth asset like shares. However, cash never returns a loss.

Building a Portfolio

Before you start buying shares, decide your level of risk, what income you want from shares and your time frame for investing. With a well-diversified portfolio and a medium- to long-term horizon — at least five to ten years — you're giving your sharemarket investment the best chance to come out ahead of the other asset classes. Choosing your stocks well is the hard part. You need to follow a logical method in deciding on the stocks you buy.

REMEMBER

Some investors use the *top–down approach*, which means that they take an overview of the state of the economy, determine which sectors are likely to do well and then examine the companies in those industries for the best candidates for investment. This strategy is sound because the economy drives the sharemarket. Other investors choose stocks by a *bottom-up approach*, which concentrates on the attributes of individual stocks rather than economic factors. This approach seeks to pick winners on their merits. Two popular approaches to choosing stocks involve buying growth shares or buying value shares.

TABLE 5-1: Asset Class Returns, 1992–2021

Year	Australian Shares	International Shares	International Shares (Hedged)[1]	US Shares	Australian Bonds	International Bonds (Hedged)[2]	Cash	Australian Listed Property	International Listed Property[3]
1992	13.0	7.1	−3.0	16.5	22.0	15.8	9.0	14.7	6.9
1993	8.7	31.8	17.3	27.9	13.9	14.7	5.9	17.1	28.3
1994	15.5	0.0	6.7	−7.8	−1.1	2.1	4.9	9.8	8.4
1995	6.4	14.2	3.7	29.9	11.9	13.1	7.1	7.9	7.5
1996	14.3	6.7	27.7	13.5	9.5	11.2	7.8	3.6	2.4
1997	26.8	28.6	26.0	41.5	16.8	12.1	6.8	28.5	35.7
1998	1.0	42.2	22.1	57.5	10.9	11.0	5.1	10.0	25.0
1999	14.1	8.2	15.9	14.9	3.3	5.5	5.0	4.3	−6.8
2000	16.8	23.8	12.6	18.2	6.2	5.0	5.6	12.1	14.1
2001	8.8	−6.0	−16.0	0.6	7.4	9.0	6.1	14.1	38.2
2002	−4.5	−23.5	−19.3	−25.8	6.2	8.0	4.7	15.5	7.5
2003	−1.1	−18.5	−6.2	−16.1	9.8	12.2	5.0	12.1	−5.2
2004	22.4	19.4	20.2	14.7	2.3	3.5	5.3	17.2	28.7
2005	24.7	0.1	9.8	−2.8	7.8	12.3	5.6	18.1	21.2
2006	24.2	19.9	15.0	11.5	3.4	1.2	5.8	18.0	24.2
2007	30.3	7.8	21.4	5.6	4.0	5.2	6.4	25.9	3.0
2008	−12.1	−21.3	−15.7	−23.2	4.4	8.6	7.3	−36.3	−28.6
2009	−22.1	−16.3	−26.6	−12.4	10.8	11.5	5.5	−42.3	−31.2

(continued)

TABLE 5-1: *(continued)*

Year	Australian Shares	International Shares	International Shares (Hedged)¹	US Shares	Australian Bonds	International Bonds (Hedged)²	Cash	Australian Listed Property	International Listed Property³
2010	13.8	5.2	11.5	9.5	7.9	9.3	3.9	20.4	31.3
2011	12.2	2.7	22.3	3.1	5.5	5.7	5.0	5.8	9.2
2012	–7.0	–0.5	–2.1	10.1	12.4	11.9	4.7	11.0	7.5
2013	20.7	33.1	21.3	35.0	2.8	4.4	3.3	24.2	24.3
2014	17.6	20.4	21.9	20.8	6.1	7.2	2.7	11.1	11.8
2015	5.7	25.2	8.5	31.9	5.6	6.3	2.6	20.3	23.1
2016	2.0	0.4	–2.7	7.3	7.0	10.8	2.2	24.6	20.4
2017	13.1	14.7	18.9	14.4	0.2	–1.0	1.8	–6.3	–4.8
2018	13.7	15.4	10.8	18.7	3.1	2.5	1.8	13.0	9.0
2019	11.0	11.9	6.6	16.3	9.6	7.0	2.0	19.3	13.5
2020	–7.2	5.2	3.6	9.6	4.2	5.4	0.8	–21.3	–13.4
2021	30.2	27.5	37.1	29.1	–0.8	–1.5	0.1	33.2	23.3
Ave.	10.4	9.5	9.0	12.3	7.1	7.7	4.7	10.2	11.2
Best	30.3 (3)	42.2 (2)	37.1 (6)	57.5 (7)	22.0 (2)	15.8 (3)	9.0 (0)	33.2 (3)	38.2 (4)
Worst	–22.1 (2)	–23.5 (2)	–26.6 (4)	–25.8 (3)	–1.1 (2)	–1.5 (3)	0.1 (7)	–42.3 (4)	–31.2 (2)

(X) denotes the number of times each asset class was the best/worst performer during a financial year ending between 1990 and 2019.
Source: Andex Charts Pty Ltd.
Notes: 1. MSCI World ex-Australia Net Total Return Index (Local Currency) – represents a continuously hedged portfolio without any impact from foreign exchange fluctuations. 2. Index prior to 30 June 2008 is the Citigroup World Government Bond Index AUD hedged, from 30 June 2008 the index is the Bloomberg Barclays Global Treasury Index in $A (Hedged). 3. Prior to 1 May 2013, index is the UBS Global Real Estate Investors Index ex-Australia with net dividends reinvested. From May 2013 the index is the FTSE EPRA/NAREIT Developed ex AUS Rental Index with net dividends reinvested. Past perfor- mance is not an indicator of future performance.

Professional investors who are active managers of a share portfolio (those who try to add value to the portfolio by choosing stocks that can outperform the market) are usually either growth-oriented or value-oriented. As the name suggests, *growth* investors are trying to buy companies that are still expanding, have plenty of room to grow and are expected to show huge revenue growth over the medium term. *Value* investors, on the other hand, specialise in picking out-of-favour companies that they believe to be undervalued by the sharemarket.

Growth investors loved the tech boom of 1999 to 2000 because it briefly fulfilled their wildest dreams. Value investors hated it because the market paid no attention to their carefully chosen bargains. The market of the value investors' dreams was the one that came about after the market had halved, from March 2009 onwards. The 'COVID crash' of February–March 2020 was also a great time for value investors.

TIP

Growth outperformed value in the second half of the 2010s — and then another crash in 2020 brought great pickings for the value investors. As a non-professional investor, if you can identify an undervalued bargain, by all means buy it, and if you're satisfied that you've identified a standout growth candidate, buy it too. Your portfolio can benefit from both approaches.

Buying growth stocks

Growth stocks are typically shares that are expected to increase their revenue and earnings at a faster rate than the average business in their industry — or the market as a whole. However, often they don't have earnings; they have rising sales and high margins (60 per cent or above), which shows investors that they are in good shape to generate profits at a future point and then over the long term.

REMEMBER

Growth stocks tend to reinvest the majority of their profits back into the company, meaning that they rarely pay out dividends. They also tend to have a much higher return on equity (ROE) than their sector's average. *ROE* is a measure that shows a company's profitability in relation to the money shareholders have invested, calculated by dividing a company's net income by shareholder equity. A high ROE — as a rough guide, anything above 10 per cent is good, while 20 per cent or above is top-shelf — indicates that the company is efficient at generating returns using shareholder capital; it shows, in effect, that the company has a competitive advantage. That's exactly what investors hoping to compound stock returns over time want to see.

When you buy a growth stock, you're usually relying solely on capital gain for the return on your investment. They usually have innovative products, unique technology or a business model that is able to 'disrupt' the incumbent companies in that field, and a large (and expanding) market opportunity. Growth companies have been the perennial winners over their value counterparts through the past decade as tech companies have swelled larger, spurred on by the uptake of digital services.

The rise of the technology stocks has put a lot of stress on 20th-century investment truisms — such as the Warren Buffett (see Chapter 23) Paradigm — which hold that a stock's value is based on hard assets and reliable earnings. For many of the big tech growth stocks, value is based on the future revenue from the technology they've developed — and value investors struggle to reconcile this with their precepts, because that value is usually not captured by the measures that value investors use.

In many cases, growth stocks have a high total addressable market (TAM) value, which means the total value of the global markets in which their products or services will be sold. For growth fund managers, the 'survivor bias' of the stock market (refer to Chapter 3) is front of mind — they want to own the stocks that can 'win' their markets and create wealth.

REMEMBER

Investors expect growth stocks' earnings to increase rapidly. Usually these stocks are market leaders and innovators, with a unique and compelling investment history. They capture the admiration of the market, which is prepared to pay a large premium (measured by the price/earnings (P/E) ratio) to own them. The downside to this strategy is that any interruption to the expected growth pattern means an instant price reduction. However, many growth stocks that are perfectly realistic investments for a growth fund manager don't even have a P/E ratio — because they don't yet have earnings. Therefore, they won't have a dividend, and thus dividend yield, either — but that doesn't necessarily matter to the growth investor.

Over the latter part of the 2010s, as growth investors took the upper hand, a new generation of market darlings began to command P/E ratios of 40, 70 and even 100-plus times forecast earnings. (The general rule for P/E ratios was traditionally that a value of 10 or lower was cheap and 20 or above was expensive — see Chapter 7 for more information.) This group was led by the ASX's cohort of technology stars, the so-called 'WAAAX' stocks: cloud-based logistics software provider WiseTech Global; buy now, pay later (BNPL) pioneer Afterpay (taken over in 2021 in a scrip — that is, shares-based — deal by US payments giant Square, Inc. in a $39 billion deal that settled in March 2022; Square, Inc. subsequently changed its name to Block, Inc.); electronic printed circuit board design software company Altium; Appen, which provides annotated data to train the 'machine learning' processes that drive artificial intelligence (AI) applications; and cloud-based business accounting developer Xero. Construction software company Aconex was also a tech growth star until it was bought by Oracle for $1.6 billion in early 2018; data centre owner operator NEXT DC was another one, as were specialist dairy company the A2 Milk Company and Domino's Pizza.

ANATOMY OF A GROWTH STOCK

Xero is a great example of a 'growth' stock. The Kiwi cloud-based accounting software impressively conquered the small-to-medium-sized enterprise — or small business — accounting market in Australia and New Zealand, and springboarded from that base into North America and Europe. Although there were (and still are) competitors — for example, Intuit and its QuickBooks product is a formidable foe for Xero in North America — the company has demonstrated most of the classic traits of a growth stock.

Xero offered its small business customers software hosted 'in the cloud' — accessible at any time, on any internet-connected device, and paid for through a monthly subscription fee (rather than the usual software licence that could be installed on physical computers). At a stroke, this model — known as 'software-as-a-service', or SaaS — lowered the upfront cost to customers, while creating a more predictable earnings stream for Xero and a higher total lifetime value (LTV) per customer.

Instead of customers buying licences for software that went out of date quickly, inducing them into expensive upgrades, the SaaS model allows customers to subscribe to a software product that's continually being updated. The software company gets a reliable stream of recurring revenue, while the customer gains flexibility and always-up-to-date software. It is a largely win–win model in which the costs to subscribe are comparatively low, customers are very 'sticky' (assuming the product meets their needs), and the software providers build up strong recurring revenue and high gross margins.

Xero has continued to expand the features, tools and functionality it offers its SME customers, and along the way, the product has become something that many of them cannot do without — despite it still being quite cheap. In fact, Xero has become for many customers not simply an accounting software package but a complete SME business platform — or even an 'ecosystem', as some call it.

The company has hit upon one of the holy grails for the growth investor — the *network effect*, the phenomenon in which a product or service gains additional value as more people use it. Xero has also created an open-source system for third-party developers to build handy apps on its platform. This allows accountants to offer broader and higher-valued services for their clients, which all results in the end-user receiving better value from the product they're paying for.

Partners (accounting and finance app developers) want to connect to Xero's 2.7 million customers (especially as it grows North American subscriber numbers). In return, these customers benefit from all the new tools they're being offered. Because all the tools integrate, vendors selling digital products via the Xero platform can share customers.

(continued)

(continued)

No matter how small a vendor is, all it needs to succeed on the Xero platform is to offer something innovative — all of which adds to the network effect.

Xero achieved its first net profit in the year to 30 March 2020, delivering on the promise of chief executive Steve Vamos to keep investing for growth, but in a disciplined fashion. Xero added 467,000 new subscribers in that same period and had a total subscriber base of 2.29 million worldwide, with its biggest markets being Australia, the UK, New Zealand and the US. It increased its revenue by 30 per cent to NZ$718.2 million (A$668.1 million) in FY20, while achieving a net profit of NZ$3.3 million (A$3.07 million). In earnings per share (EPS) terms, that came to 2 Kiwi cents (1.94 Aussie cents) a share.

That was good news for the P/E — because one could finally be calculated. On actual FY20 numbers, Xero was trading on 4,381 times earnings. Clearly, that was ridiculous. At the time, having become profitable, analysts' consensus was that Xero would earn 25.3 Australian cents a share in FY21, and 50.3 cents in FY22, which at a share price of $85.00 at the time, put it on forward P/E multiples of 336 times FY21 earnings and 169 times FY22 earnings. There was simply no way that a value-oriented investor would consider paying such multiples.

In the year to 30 March 2021, a year hit by COVID-19, Xero reported a net profit of NZ$19.8 million, which came to a statutory 14 cents a share. While that looked good compared to 2 Kiwi cents the year before, it fell short of analysts' consensus by about 65 per cent — and the shares fell by 16 per cent in a week.

But growth managers would hardly even have noticed the earnings 'miss'. To them, Xero's FY21 results were full of good news. They notice things like the 18 per cent increase in revenue to NZ$848.8 million, which was driven by a 20 per cent increase in subscribers, to 2.74 million — including an 18 per cent rise in the North American market (which is crucial to Xero's future) to 285,000 subscribers. To attract subscribers, Xero has to add more tools and functionality to its platform — growth managers would have noticed that Xero spent NZ$311.7 million on product design and development in FY21, up 38 per cent, and consuming almost 37 per cent of revenue.

Annualised monthly recurring revenue (AMRR) rose by 17 per cent to NZ$963.6 million and total subscriber LTV — the revenue that an average subscriber represents to Xero over the subscriber's lifetime — surged by 38 per cent to NZ$7.65 billion. Just four years ago, that figure was NZ$2.2 billion. At March 2021, Xero's 'churn' rate — the rate at which it loses customers — was running at just over 1 per cent a year. In other words, almost 99 per cent of Xero's customers keep using its services, month after month. And while Xero's accounting software is an incredibly 'sticky' product, the company continues to attract more subscribers. The power of customer retention works for Xero because it can extract more revenue from those subscribers over time.

The customer acquisition cost (CAC), as a percentage of revenue, declined from 43.6 per cent in FY20 to 36.3 per cent in FY21. In FY21, it cost Xero NZ$433 to acquire a subscriber; based on an average revenue per user per month (ARPU) of NZ$29.30 (this figure was down 2 per cent in FY21), payback occurs after just 15 months. Combined with the churn rate, this gives an LTV of NZ$2,789 per customer and an LTV/CAC ratio of 6.4 — meaning the average lifetime value of a subscriber is 6.4 times the cost of acquiring that subscriber. (In its dominant markets of Australia and New Zealand, this ratio is over 13 times.) For an SaaS company like Xero, these are the crucial numbers.

Operating earnings — earnings before interest, tax, depreciation and amortisation (EBITDA) — gained 39 per cent, to NZ$191 million, while free cash flow doubled, to NZ$56.9 million. *Free cash flow* is the company's true operating cash flow — it is the cash flow generated from operating activities minus cash used for investing (for example, capital expenditure) and paying interest and dividends, but excluding any cash used for acquisitions. Free cash flow is a company's true operating cash flow and provides the business with a lot of capital to deploy. Xero only broke through to positive free cash flow in FY19, with NZ$6.5 million — now its free cash flow is NZ$56.9 million. To top it off, at the end of FY21, Xero had more than doubled its net cash position over the year, to NZ$256.6 million.

Xero's net profit of NZ$19.8 million in FY21, up from NZ$3.3 million the year before, equated to 14 NZ cents a share: those investors who want to can calculate a P/E, and at $132.80 (NZ$142.10) a share, it's 1,015 times 2020–21 earnings. With analysts expecting profit to come down to about 9.1 Australian cents a share in 2021–22, the one-year forward P/E is 1,460 times earnings; but with EPS expected to rise to about 43 Australian cents in 2022–23, the two-year forward P/E stood at 308 times.

But Xero's gross margin in FY21 was 86 per cent, compared to 65 per cent in FY14. For growth investors, this margin is the key — with a margin of that size, Xero could come up with any net profit after tax (NPAT) number it wished, had it wanted to do so. In other words, if Xero wanted a P/E that was more acceptable to value investors, it could easily bank more of its revenue as profit. Instead, it prioritises reinvesting its revenue in its product to improve its features, and marketing it and advertising it so as to attract more subscribers, which then attracts more Xero partners and strengthens the Xero ecosystem and Xero's network effect.

While Xero has 2.74 million SME subscribers at the time of writing, the company estimates its total addressable market (TAM) in the English-speaking cloud accounting market to be more than 45 million potential customers. Some analysts see this TAM as worth close to NZ$75 billion ($70 billion) a year — and Xero has only snared about 6.1 per cent of it. That gives it a huge potential runway for growth, and for the ability to compound. That is what growth investors are buying when they invest in Xero.

(continued)

(continued)

Xero is obviously trading on huge expectations that its aggressive growth strategy pays off in the long run as tax and compliance for its SME market increasingly goes digital, and it gets the same kind of take-up in markets like the UK and North America that it has notched up in Australia and New Zealand. Its success will depend on the company's ability to continue to innovate and provide a product to customers that they find superior, for their purposes, to the offerings from Xero's competitors — of which there are plenty.

Xero's challenge is to keep growing customers and revenue; while it continues to dominate the Australasian market, it has to move offshore. Growth investors buying companies like Xero at these valuations simply believe that the market undervalues the leverage coming through the business as it gradually builds market share in large overseas markets.

Value investors wouldn't consider these stocks, believing such P/Es to be ridiculous. Afterpay didn't even own a P/E, because it hadn't made a net profit (and still hasn't — at the time that Square, Inc. made its bid, analysts didn't expect the company to make a net profit until 2022). Xero, at $130.07 in June 2021, was priced at 770 times its historical earnings (it earned 16.9 cents a share in the financial year to March 2021) and at 250 times its forward earnings (the consensus among analysts is that it will earn 52 cents a share in FY23). Glumly, value investors watched the growth superstars rise ever-higher, made worse by the fact that not owning them pummelled the value managers' performance figures relative to growth managers — making value investing look like a mug's game.

The growth fund managers, on the other hand, were — as you'd expect — focused on the growth.

Like Xero (see the nearby sidebar 'Anatomy of a growth stock'), the big three original Australian internet businesses — REA Group (which operates the realestate.com.au website), Carsales.com (which operates the carsales.com.au website) and jobs website Seek — all show the network effect (this is the trio that in the late 1990s/early 2000s ripped away from the venerable Fairfax its 'rivers of gold' classified advertising business, taking about 90 per cent of its advertising revenue with it, in one of the most comprehensive examples of disruption that the Australian sharemarket has ever seen).

In REA's case, the more properties listed for sale, the more buyers use realestate.com.au — which in turn results in more reasons for sellers to advertise on realestate.com.au and fewer reasons to advertise on a competing website. As for Seek, it dominates the Australian job search market — job seekers spend an incredible 90 per cent of time online on seek.com.au when searching for a job, so that's where employers want to advertise. Similarly, Carsales.com has the network effect, because car sellers want the platform with the most buyers, and buyers only bother browsing platforms that have the most sellers. Even if the network effect doesn't always guarantee winner-takes-all, it certainly gives its holders very strong market positions.

Modern-day growth managers are very mindful of the survivor bias of companies (Chapter 3 covers survivor bias in more detail) and the fact that industry category 'winners' enjoy most of the spoils — add to this the fact that there are businesses in the modern world that effectively create their own category. A great example is Airbnb, the online accommodation-sharing marketplace. Airbnb was created in 2008 when its founders came up with the idea of offering accommodation in their living room to attendees of a conference being held in San Francisco, for which hotel rooms were proving scarce. Airbnb was eventually floated on the Nasdaq Stock Exchange in December 2020.

Airbnb effectively created a business — homestay accommodation, arranged online — and the brand around it, and tapped beautifully into the network effect. The more hosts that it has on its site renting out rooms, the more likely Airbnb is to attract guests, and then it attracts more hosts, and more rooms . . . The company goes from creating a category to creating a global brand to creating a network effect around that brand — and that can prove very difficult for potential competitors to break down.

An Australian version of this is Afterpay, which essentially created the buy now, pay later (BNPL) model of consumer shopping. Afterpay grew from a $165 million micro-cap stock to a $34 billion member of the S&P/ASX 50 in just over five years, before being taken over. It did this while becoming a verb to its customers, who love using it — more than 90 per cent of its gross merchant volume (GMV) comes from repeat customers. Afterpay's customer base and global underlying sales transactions have been growing hugely, and the shift to online purchases in the wake of COVID-19 has favoured it. Afterpay has shown that its payments business is scalable as it starts to grow in a big way in its new markets of the US, Europe and the UK. As this happens, the operating leverage — when most of a company's costs are fixed, and increased sales volume starts to magnify the profits earned — is potentially massive, particularly in the US.

Afterpay customers tend to transact in greater size, and more frequently, the longer they use the platform. According to Afterpay, its Australian customers who have been using it for more than four years now transact 29 times per year, up from 25 times the year before. Those that have had Afterpay for more than three years use it 20 times a year; more than two years, 16 times; more than one year, 11 times; and first-year users tend to use it four times. The top 10 per cent of users used it 60 times a year at 27 merchants.

Afterpay is also becoming a major referrer of web traffic to retailers, which is why more merchants want to join its platform. Again, that is the network effect in action. As the company expands into new markets, growth managers expect to see these same patterns that happened in Australia and New Zealand repeated in Afterpay's new markets. Of course, the company faces more competition all the time, and it will intensify as it moves into new markets. But a strong business model that's built on rising frequency of use, plus the network effect, is what growth investors are buying with Afterpay — and what attracted its US suitor, Square, Inc. (now known as Block Inc.).

Both growth managers and value managers will have an intrinsic value in mind for a company's share price, and they will have their own measurements on which they focus. Minimum internal rate of return (IRR), return on capital (ROC), free cash flow (FCF)-to-sales (that is, to revenue) ratio, enterprise value-to-sales (EV-to-sales) ratio, research and development (R&D) spending-to-sales ratio, gross margins and current penetration of market versus total addressable market (TAM) in percentage terms can all be important tools for the growth manager. Effectively, growth managers are looking for businesses that can compound. And that potential for compounding is difficult to measure using the standard value investing toolkit.

A growth manager may prefer to look at a sales multiple — for example, enterprise value (see Chapter 14) to sales, because software businesses invest so heavily in research and development (R&D) and marketing their products, which is why there's no profit — so they might consider an EV-to-sales multiple of, say, 10 to 13 times to be cheap. But they will be looking over the horizon at the TAM and adjusting the multiple to that. If a company has sales of $5 billion and it's on an EV-to-sales multiple of 10 times, that implies that it should have a $50 billion market capitalisation; the growth manager may then ask, 'If the company's TAM is $150 billion, and it can take 20 per cent of that market, that's $30 billion worth of sales on 10 times, so the market capitalisation should be $300 billion.' That's the way that growth managers think when they buy stocks that value managers wouldn't touch.

Prior to the COVID-19 crisis, high-growth companies (defined as those showing EPS growth above 20 per cent), were trading at forward P/Es at well over twice the market, and about 60 per cent above their international peers, according to broker Goldman Sachs. The ASX tech stocks, as represented by the S&P/ASX 300 Software and Services sector (the S&P/ASX All Tech had not yet been created) were trading at a forward P/E of 40.7 times earnings — which was 3.6 standard deviations above the market's average forward P/E since 2001, of 19.3 times.

The market can get more comfortable paying a rising P/E: CSL is a great example of a growth stock where the rising P/E, and the expectations that implies, has been borne out by the earnings, and the share price has steadily trended higher (see Figure 5-1). But growth stocks live by the sword, and can die by it, too — when a much-fancied stock growth fails to deliver what the market expects, disappointment can be hefty.

CSL Limited

High: 45.98

Low: 13.42

305.00
45.26

Price — Forward P/E — Average P/E

Source: FactSet Financial Data and Analytics

FIGURE 5-1:
CSL share price
and P/E,
2011–2021.

In the early part of the 2010s, investors pushed Domino's Pizza to a forward P/E of 55 times earnings, as it rattled off several years of 40 per cent–plus profit growth. In the five years to August 2015, Domino's delivered a total return of 732 per cent, compared to a 60 per cent gain in the major index. Even more impressively, any investor who snapped the share up in 2005 was sitting on a total return of 1,762 per cent, compared to a 97 per cent gain from the market. That's what a growth stock can do.

At its core, Domino's is a fast-food company; however, chief executive Don Meij continually told the market that Domino's should be viewed as a technology company. With online ordering, mobile ordering, 'four-click' ordering and customers able to track the progress of their pizza via GPS, Domino's walked the tech talk.

But, in doing so, Domino's raised the bar on what growth investors expected. So, when, after several years of 40 per cent–plus growth, investors were given a forecast of only 20 per cent growth in 2015, they didn't like it. Domino's had been a standout performer, but at 55 times earnings, any bad news does not go down well. Two years later, even a record full-year profit could not save the stock, because it fell short of the company's guidance. (An ugly scandal of Domino's underpaying workers over a four-and-a-half-year period also didn't help.) All of a sudden, Domino's was trading at 20 times expected earnings — with the price following the 'de-rated' P/E lower (see Figure 5-2). In 2019, Domino's was trading at 18 times expected earnings, which was very cheap for its track record. That corresponded to a share price of about $37.50 in mid-2019, a four-year low, and a painful slide from the 2016 peak of $55.83. But investors who trusted Domino's to regain its growth stardom were rewarded in spades, as the company's operations in Australia, New Zealand, Europe and Japan generated increased profits even through the COVID-19 period. The market has lifted the forward P/E back to 47 times earnings, and the share price has surged close to $120 — a growth stock

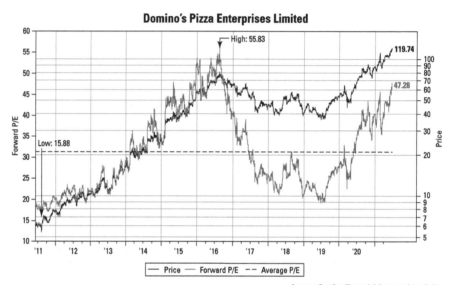

FIGURE 5-2:
Domino's Pizza
share price and
P/E, 2011–2021.

Source: FactSet Financial Data and Analytics

once more.

REMEMBER

The holy grail for a growth manager is to find a stock that is starting out on a journey called the S-curve. The *S-curve* tracks how a company or industry grows over its lifecycle. There comes a point in the lifecycle when growth inflects upward, driven by a structural change. It is the tailwind created by the structural change that allows a company to deliver and create wealth.

Companies like Facebook, Amazon and Apple have ridden the wave of demand for technology products and services that did not exist 15 or 20 years ago, but which are now considered indispensable in our daily lives. All of those companies rode the S-curve.

Apple is a great example, with its iPhone smartphone, which was launched in 2007. Apple didn't invent the smartphone — IBM's Simon 'personal communicator' was well ahead of it, in 1994, and the Blackberry 5810 device hit the market in 2002 — but these handsets didn't have the functionality we've come to associate with smartphones. The iPhone did, and it revolutionised the mobile phone market.

Between 2008 and 2017, while growth in the overall mobile phone market was relatively flat, smartphone penetration zoomed from less than 10 per cent to roughly 70 per cent over the same period. In 2008, investors had ten mobile phone stocks to choose from, but only two really worked out — Apple and Samsung. Household names like Blackberry, Motorola, Eriksson and Nokia failed to seize the structural growth opportunity in smartphones.

There's no better example of the S-curve phenomenon than the trajectory of Apple's domination of the smartphone market, shown in Figure 5-3, for which I'm indebted to global growth fund manager Munro Partners. The two graphs in Figure 5-3 show the growth in smartphone use over the period 2008 to 2018, and the increasing contribution of the iPhone to Apple's revenue over the same period. Apple's share of the overall mobile phone market went from 10 per cent to a 75 per cent share in the space of six years. During this period, Apple's stock increased seven times in value. Ideally, a growth manager likes to invest before the 'inflection point' shown at the bottom left of the chart (before the slope of the S-curve

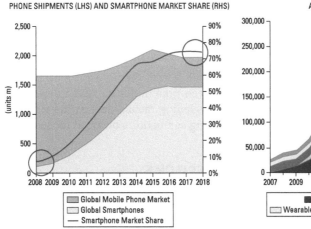

FIGURE 5-3: The smartphone 'S curve' and the composition of Apple's revenue, 2007–2020.

Source: Munro Partners (Munro Asset Management Limited)

steepens) and sell before the second inflection point at the top right of the chart (when the S-curve flattens out).

The smartphone market has now stopped growing; Apple now relies on price rises and its services revenue for growth. The smartphone industry is now at the end of its S-curve — but only Apple really rode it.

Video streaming, however, is a market that's only just starting out on the S-curve; currently, Netflix dominates that market. Netflix started life in 1997 as a DVD-rental-by-mail firm and spent the first five years struggling to get to a sustainable model that was cash flow positive. It spent most of the next five years fighting with Blockbuster in the US. But it began streaming content — that is, showing video in real time over the internet — in the US in 2007, and internationally in 2010.

Initially, Netflix bought content to show to its subscribers, but in 2013 it started producing its own original TV series and movies. Netflix is available virtually everywhere (except in China), and as streaming entertainment disrupts (that is, replaces) free-to-air TV, it remains the biggest player (although there's no shortage of competitors, such as Amazon Prime, HBO Max, Disney+ and Apple, plus Australia's Stan, BINGE and Foxtel Now). According to network services and research company Sandvine, Netflix is the number-one internet application globally, accounting for about 15 per cent of global traffic.

Many growth managers would consider Netflix as being poised for immense growth. It is currently in just 10 per cent of broadband-connected homes around the world, and its monthly pricing is low relative to the value of the content it offers, so its potential for earnings growth is huge. It has reported profits, but it's also reported negative free cash flows — the difference arises from how Netflix accounts for its investment in content. From a growth manager's point of view, that's Netflix doing the right thing — there's only going to be a handful of winners in the streaming market, so Netflix needs to keep spending and attracting subscribers to make sure it's one of them. At present, Netflix accounts for less than 10 per cent of TV screen time in the US, and an even smaller proportion in other regions and when including mobile devices; its runway for growth is still very large, albeit with strong competitors biting at its heels.

Finding value stocks

Value investors want to buy stocks that are trading below what they're worth. To do this, they calculate what they believe is the company's *intrinsic value* (what the company is actually worth, per share: this calculation is subjective, and will depend on quantitative, qualitative and even perceptual factors), and if the market price moves far enough below this, they buy stocks based on the belief that, over time, the share price will revert to the intrinsic value. In this way, they have bought, for example, $1 worth of the company for 80 cents.

Value investing's holy book is *Security Analysis* by US investors Benjamin Graham and David Dodd, which was first published in 1934. Graham believed in viewing a stock as a share of an entire business. His approach to investing was that the investor should try to work out that business's intrinsic value, in the knowledge that the price being offered for the stock by 'Mr Market' could be quite different to that value. But because the calculation of intrinsic value is inherently imprecise, he advised buying only when there was a satisfactory margin between the current market price and the value.

Value stocks are shares considered cheap because they're out of favour with the market and are consequently priced low, relative to the company's earnings or assets. The P/E and the dividend yield are important numbers for a value stock, but so is the ratio of price to net tangible asset (NTA) backing. The NTA backing represents the amount of tangible — that is, real — assets that stand behind each share. To work out NTA, subtract the value of any intangible assets, such as goodwill and brands, from shareholders' equity, and divide by the number of shares on issue. (Under ASX reporting rules, companies must give their NTA in their interim [half-year] and full-year reports to shareholders, and show the equivalent figure for 12 months earlier.)

However, a major problem has emerged in recent years with the price-to-NTA ratio, or what in North America is called 'price-to-book' (as in, the company's 'book value') — the total value at which its assets are 'carried' in the books (financial accounts), minus its total liabilities. Many newer businesses have very little in the way of tangible assets; instead, they may have more 'human capital' (that is, smart employees) or IP (intellectual property) that isn't reflected on the balance sheet. The problem is that traditional accounting practices struggle to measure value for more modern, research and development (R&D)-intensive companies.

Price-to-NTA used to work when companies owned traditional physical assets, such as large factories, manufacturing plants or retail premises. But nowadays, many companies derive their value from more technology-based intangible assets such as patents, algorithms, software and user interfaces — and the massive R&D spending that built these — plus powerful brands. The so-called 'FAANG' stocks in the US — Facebook (which trades under the name of its parent company Meta Platforms, Inc, which is also the parent of Instagram and WhatsApp), Apple, Amazon, Netflix and Google (which trades under the name of its parent company, Alphabet) — have assets that cannot be captured in a traditional NTA figure; however, these 'intangible' assets are extremely valuable and generate colossal cash flow.

As business models evolve, companies are spending more on innovation to drive sustainable growth — but how can an investor accurately value a company's level of innovation? What value might an investor put on the 'network effect' (outlined in the preceding section, 'Buying growth stocks,' and the nearby sidebar 'Anatomy of a Growth Stock')? For a company like Amazon or Xero, it's worth plenty. But traditional measurements of value such as NTAs won't pick up on that value at all.

It's not only price-based valuation metrics that are unsuitable for assessing 'new economy' companies, it's asset-based valuations, too. As an example, the bulk of Microsoft's asset value is determined by its IP, rather than its physical assets.

REMEMBER

A value stock often has a relatively low P/E ratio and a low price-to-NTA ratio, but a high dividend yield (because its price has fallen). Investors look for such value anomalies and buy the stock because they believe that the market will eventually recognise the stock's true value and the stock will be re-evaluated or bid up in price.

The long-term average P/E on the Australian market is about 14 times historical earnings; the average dividend yield is about 3.3 per cent (although full franking, at the large-company tax rate of 30 per cent, turns that into a gross yield of 4.7 per cent).

Value investors are often described as looking for stocks trading at P/Es well below the prevailing market P/E and well above the prevailing market dividend yield; or trading at a markedly lower P/E than those of other companies in the same sector; or trading at a markedly lower P/E compared to its history. But in all of these cases, there is no guarantee that the P/E will catch up and close that perceived gap.

At all times, value investors have to be aware of 'value traps', which are stocks that are trading where they are for very good reason. You can't just pick out the ten lowest P/E ratios or the ten highest dividend yields. The highest dividend yield or the lowest P/E may be a result of a sharp fall in the share price. When aiming to buy stocks that trade at a discount to fair value, it's important to distinguish between those that are cheap, and those which represent good value.

Value investing usually involves buying good stocks at low P/Es — single-digit, if they can be found — that are not value traps, and riding these stocks as the market 're-rates' them to a higher P/E. (Conversely, growth investors like to see their stocks' P/Es come down, as the earnings they were expecting to see finally flow through.) Value investors don't chase high-growth, high-multiple stocks that are highly vulnerable to savage re-rates if earnings disappoint. But investors who lived by that rule would have missed out on stocks like Cochlear and CSL, which have continually traded on high multiples and delivered great returns.

REMEMBER

To be fair, value investment is not as simplistic as just looking for low valuation measures such as the P/E. It's more correct to say that value investing is buying stocks that the investor thinks are priced below the investor's estimate of their value. At its core, value investing is about spotting situations where a company is trading on the market at a price that is significantly lower than what the investor calculates to be its intrinsic value. The larger this difference, the larger is the value investor's 'margin of safety'. (Growth investors also calculate an intrinsic value for their stocks and look to sell when the share price eventually catches up to this estimate.)

A great value stock doesn't have to show a low P/E, but it does have to be trading for less than it's worth. However, value investors are well aware that the 'E' part of the equation is not always accurate. Instead of a P/E ratio, a growth investor may use free cash flow to identify a value stock, which (because earnings can be manipulated) could provide them with a truer picture of the company's economic earnings. Over the last decade, many ASX-listed companies have started reporting an 'underlying' earnings measure in addition to their 'statutory' reporting obligations, because they consider the accounting basis doesn't provide investors with a good understanding of the performance of their core business. The companies want to help investors look beyond things such as revaluations, impairments and one-off transactions so they can really assess what the company is earning (see Chapter 14 for more on evaluating performance). For this reason, the value investor may decide to focus on free cash flow — and to use *enterprise value* (the sum of the company's market capitalisation and its total debt, minus its cash), because it gets around the issue of leverage (a P/E ratio would not necessarily pick-up that a company was potentially over-leveraged, as in, carrying too much debt). The problem for ordinary investors is that free cash flow can be quite a subjective valuation metric, and different fund managers use different methods for calculating it.

Good value investors do a lot of work to avoid value traps. They're aware that a number like the P/E is a snapshot in time, whether they're using a historical or a forward P/E. To get around this, they use a long-term measurement like the cyclically adjusted P/E (or CAPE ratio), sometimes called the Shiller P/E after its inventor Robert Shiller (an American professor of economics at Yale, a Nobel Prize winner and the author of the book *Irrational Exuberance*, published in 2000).

The *CAPE ratio* attempts to measure whether a stock is undervalued or overvalued by comparing its current market price to its inflation-adjusted historical earnings record. The investor takes ten-year average earnings per share (EPS) and adjusts these earnings for inflation, using the consumer price index (CPI), so that they're 'real' earnings. Using ten-year smoothed real earnings is meant to strip out the effect of any big fluctuations, which gives a picture of the company's earnings over a typical business 'cycle' and more accurately represents the ratio between current price and earnings.

The main problem that the CAPE ratio tries to get around is that during an economic downturn (or recession), share prices fall, but company earnings fall sharply as well, which can temporarily boost the P/E ratio. This boost can give the value investor a false signal that the market is too expensive and suggests they shouldn't buy, when it could actually be the best time to buy.

In a similar vein, the value investor may opt to use an enterprise value (EV) ratio — such as the EV to ten-year-average net operating profit after tax — because using EV includes debt and other liabilities like pensions, and thus includes the cost of the capital part of the business. Some value investors would even add a control premium, to arrive at the 'value' that a buyer would have to pay for the company. Whichever ratio they use, value investors usually prefer longer-term cyclically adjusted measures so they understand exactly where the profits are in terms of the business cycle, and they don't get tricked-into buying by *recency bias*, or what the profits have looked like in the most recent years.

Value investors are trying to understand what the future prospects for a company will be, looking a decade or more into the future. They want to see a strong balance sheet, a high level of recurring and predictable earnings, and a healthy conversion of cash flow to profit (as high a cash conversion ratio as possible, but — depending on the situation and the industry — some companies' cash conversion ratios may be affected by capital expenditure and working capital requirements). And, because value investors are not simply numbers nerds, they want to trust the management and believe the company's 'story' and be certain that it has market-leading products and a sustainable competitive advantage.

A lot of the metrics traditionally described as the tools of the value investor — the P/E, the dividend yield, the NTA — are just the initial filtering mechanism they use to try to identify potential cheap stocks. The value investor then forms an opinion on the rate at which the company can grow its earnings, and the return it can generate on future capital invested. Those things in combination help the investor to determine whether the actual P/E multiple makes the company look cheap, or whether it is a bargain worth buying. For the true value investor, the real work comes after they have identified a stock that they want to look at — then, the detailed work that they do to understand the company's future prospects begins.

REMEMBER

Value investing, like growth investing, can take a long time to be borne out by the eventual share price movement.

A major market downturn can turn many stocks into value stocks instantly. That was the case in February–March 2020, when the 38 per cent slump in the Australian market during the COVID-19 crash stripped big chunks out of market valuations, returning many P/E ratios to single-digits. The market's shell-shocked reaction to the pandemic created the market of a value manager's dreams, with shares being sold off without a thought for valuation. As optimism slowly trickled back into the market, many shares began to rise as investors factored in the post-pandemic world, culminating in a market surge on 'vaccine Monday' in November 2020, when news broke that the Pfizer-BioNTech vaccine demonstrated more than 90 per cent efficacy against COVID-19.

Company-specific problems can also cause a stock to suddenly become a value stock — although, when a stock falls precipitately, there is usually understandable reluctance to 'catch the falling knife' (in Wall Street parlance). (Chapter 11 considers some instances where big price slumps opened up value, although that value only became apparent with hindsight.)

An example of a value stock was Qantas Airways, which in October 2017 was trading at a P/E (historical) of 14.5 times earnings. However, a general market slump in the latter half of 2018, weak consumer spending and intense domestic capacity battles saw the share price fall 18 per cent, and the P/E cut to 9 times. Value investors piled back into Qantas at levels around $5.50 to $5.60 a share. That buy was working a treat for them heading into 2020, with the share price above $7 and the P/E back to 13.7 times, but, unfortunately, the airline was pounded by the COVID-19 pandemic — which grounded aviation virtually completely. And like many companies in March 2020, Qantas was suddenly a value stock again, with a P/E of less than 4 times, and a share price of $2.36 — if you believed that travel patterns, both domestically and internationally, would eventually return to pre-COVID levels. Although they are yet to do so (at the time of writing at least), that value investment in Qantas paid off 15 months later, with the share price back to $4.72. Figure 5-4 shows the movement in the Qantas share price to June 2021.

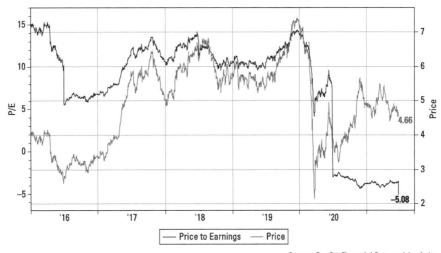

FIGURE 5-4:
Qantas Airways share price and P/E, 2016–2021.

Source: FactSet Financial Data and Analytics

WARNING

As the world emerges from the pandemic, there will likely be fewer people travelling for some time, and the international travel business in particular faces a protracted slowdown. But Qantas will emerge from the pandemic a more streamlined company, cashed-up and with huge untapped value in its Frequent Flyer business. It is a high-quality, very well-run company that should survive and prosper.

REMEMBER

Value stocks and growth stocks don't have a hard border between them — a stock can easily change from value to growth and vice versa. Once a value stock has risen far enough, the value investors sell it to realise their gains. The buyers are often growth investors, who like the way the valuation is expanding. Conversely, if a growth stock's expected earnings fail to come through and the P/E deflates, demoralised growth investors sell it — now the buyers are value investors, who are attracted by the low price and the potential for a return to growth.

Both camps have their adherents, and their respective performances are always on show through the relationship between proxies such as the Russell 3000 Value index — the broadest measure of value stocks in the US — and its stablemate, the Russell 3000 Growth index. Globally, the MSCI World Growth index and the MSCI World Value index are based on the MSCI World index (refer to Chapter 2), and their interplay is closely followed, too. In Australia, the same roles are played by the S&P/ASX 200 Value index and the S&P/ASX 200 Growth index. Investors can back their preference by investing in ETFs based on these respective international indices (although the same isn't true for the Australian indices, yet).

REMEMBER

For investors, the relationship between growth and value stocks plays out in a similar way to the other debates that they hear all the time — shares versus property, active management versus passive. Value versus growth does not have to be a choice between them — investors can have exposure to both as a further layer of diversification.

Knowing How Many Stocks to Buy

Many professional investors believe they can minimise their risk with about 40 stocks in their portfolios. They believe that this number adequately diversifies away the risk. Unfortunately, for most investors, owning 40 stocks isn't an option. For an individual, no matter how much time you devote to monitoring your portfolio, you can't keep track of 40 stocks — unless you're very dedicated! As a single investor taking care of your own portfolio, you probably want no more than 15 shares, with a minimum of ten. Owning around 15 shares allows you to adequately monitor a portfolio and ensure that your investments are well-diversified.

Picking your sectors

The Australian sharemarket hosts companies involved in a huge variety of activities. In March 2002, the ASX adopted the Global Industry Classification Standard (GICS), which was developed by Standard & Poor's (S&P) and Morgan Stanley Capital International (MSCI), and established in 1999. The GICS structure initially consisted of ten sectors and 24 industry groups, into which investors can 'drill down' further to 67 industries and 147 sub-industries. A company is classified into the sector that most closely describes the business activities from which it generates most of its revenue.

In August 2016, a new sector, Real Estate, was created, elevated from its position as an industry group within the Financials Sector. That was the first time a new sector had been created within the GICS structure since its inception in 1999, and the update acknowledged the importance of real estate in the global economy.

TECHNICAL STUFF

The idea behind GICS criteria is that it's a worldwide standard by which companies can be uniformly classified according to their business activities. It doesn't matter where the companies operate or on which stock exchange they're listed: GICS ensures that companies, industries and sectors can be more accurately compared on a global scale. The GICS classification replaced the previous 24 ASX sectors.

When the ASX adopted the global standard, the new classification system had some drawbacks for Australian investors because the resources component of the market was split. The miners were placed in the materials index, which also contains stocks like James Hardie Industries (building materials) and Orica (chemicals and explosives), whereas the oil and gas companies were placed in the energy index. Investors couldn't readily see how the entire resources sector was performing and what proportion of the index resources represented.

To redress this, sector sub-indices have been created, for example the S&P/ASX 200 Resources index, which provides investors with a sector exposure to the resources sector; the S&P/ASX 200 Energy index, which carves-out the energy stocks; the S&P/ASX 300 Metals and Mining index; and the S&P/All Ordinaries Gold index, to provide benchmarks for these important segments of the Australian sharemarket. In addition, separate indices are now calculated for each of the sectors. Table 5-2 gives you the details.

Selecting shares from these sectors can give you a diversified and protected portfolio. However, if you try to cover the entire list of industry groups, your portfolio may become cumbersome and difficult to follow. On the other hand, if you're an income-oriented investor, and the search for a fully franked dividend yield leads you to end up owning shares in National Australia Bank, Commonwealth Bank and Westpac, you have a portfolio that's too dependent on banks.

TABLE 5-2:   **GICS Economic Sectors and Industry Groups**

GICS Economic Sectors	GICS Industry Groups
Energy	Energy
Materials	Materials
Industrials	Capital goods; commercial services and supplies; transportation
Consumer discretionary	Automobiles and components; consumer durables and apparel; consumer services; retailing; media
Consumer staples	Food and staples retailing; food, beverage and tobacco; household and personal products
Healthcare	Healthcare equipment and services; pharmaceuticals, biotechnology and life sciences
Financials	Banks; diversified financial; insurance
Information technology	Software and services; technology, hardware and equipment; semiconductors and semiconductor equipment
Real estate	Real estate investment trusts (REITs); real estate development, management and services
Telecommunications services	Telecommunications services
Utilities	Utilities

Source: Standard & Poor's

Choosing core stocks

The Australian sharemarket is one of the most concentrated in the world. The top ten companies by market capitalisation represent 38 per cent of the sharemarket's total value. The S&P/ASX 20 (the top 20) represents almost 51 per cent of capitalisation, while the S&P/ASX 50 index (the market's largest 50 companies by value) accounts for about 64 per cent of the total value.

That leaves roughly another 2,150 stocks making up the remaining 36 per cent. The 50 largest companies make up the core stocks to invest in and are listed in Table 5-3.

TIP

Most of the core stocks in your portfolio ideally have a record of rising profits and dividend payments. Check that these core stocks pay a fully franked dividend, which gives Australian resident shareholders a tax rebate on taxes already paid by the company on its profits. You can use the rebate, known as the *franking credit* or *imputation credit*, to reduce your tax liability. In some cases, depending on the marginal tax rate, the franking credit can offset the entire tax liability. I discuss dividend imputation in greater detail in Chapter 18.

TABLE 5-3: The Top 50 Companies on the ASX by Value as at July 2021

Stock	Market Value ($billion)
Commonwealth Bank	176.50
BHP	143.02
CSL	129.34
Westpac Banking Corporation	94.06
National Australia Bank	86.52
ANZ Banking Group	80.59
Fortescue Metals Group	72.60
Wesfarmers	66.93
Macquarie Group	57.40
Woolworths	47.65
Rio Tinto	46.67
Telstra	45.07
Transurban	39.13
Goodman Group	38.69
Afterpay	34.25
Aristocrat Leisure	27.18
REA Group	22.45
Coles Group	22.30
Woodside Petroleum	22.11
Newcrest Mining	20.73
Xero	20.37
James Hardie	19.81
Sonic Healthcare	18.19
Brambles	16.47
Fisher & Paykel Healthcare	16.34
Cochlear	16.06

(continued)

TABLE 5-3: *(continued)*

Stock	Market Value ($billion)
QBE Insurance Group	15.72
Sydney Airport	15.68
Reece	15.23
ASX	14.97
Santos	14.85
Ramsay Health Care	14.38
Scentre Group	14.32
Suncorp Group	14.25
South32	13.87
ResMed	13.06
Amcor	12.94
Insurance Australia Group	12.47
SEEK	11.76
Northern Star Resources	11.65
TPG Telecom	11.56
Tabcorp	11.55
Mirvac Group	11.50
BlueScope Steel	11.21
Stockland	11.17
Endeavour Group	11.10
APA Group	10.54
Mineral Resources	10.48
WiseTech Global	10.37
Magellan Financial Group	10.27

Source: Australian Securities Exchange Ltd

TECHNICAL STUFF

Investors love franking credits for the help they provide at tax-return time, but some of the major stocks on the Australian market have cut their franking rates due to the amount of their earnings overseas. Because they don't pay Australian tax on this profit, they can't generate franking credits. Although this isn't necessarily a bad thing — in fact, the profit that these companies generate overseas can act as a hedge against the possibility of their Australian earnings falling — the fact that they don't offer 100 per cent franking must for some investors be considered in the investment decision. Global investment bank and asset manager Macquarie Group generates two-thirds of its operating income overseas; this results in 40 per cent dividend franking. Global insurer QBE Insurance generates 28 per cent of income from overseas, so can only partially frank its dividend — the 2020 dividend was only 10 per cent franked. Global share registry leader Computershare, for example, earns about 90 per cent of its profit overseas so has not been able to generate enough Australian-taxed profit to pay a fully franked dividend — it usually pays a 30 per cent franked dividend.

Since 2019, packaging giant Amcor's parent entity, Amcor plc, has been incorporated in Jersey, with a tax domicile in the UK. Because it is no longer incorporated in Australia, franking is not applicable, and dividends are not franked. Mining heavyweight Rio Tinto, however, is dual-listed, and the London and Australian stocks have equal rights over the company's assets, with the only difference for investors being local tax laws — under this arrangement, holders of the Australian shares receive fully franked dividends.

REMEMBER

The core stocks are the blue chips, considered the most reliable, least volatile issues on the market. However, blue chip status isn't forever (see Chapter 8). AMP was once considered a blue chip — no more. Ditto, Telstra. The old idea that an investor could buy blue chips and hold them forever is outmoded — or, put another way, the kind of stock that constitutes a blue chip is changing. CSL is now a blue chip — it operates in a non-cyclical business model with a constant and growing global demand for its services, particularly with the ageing demographics of the western world. Jobs website operator Seek, real estate sales website operator REA Group and auto sales website operator Carsales.com could also arguably stake a claim to being among the new generation of blue chips, as could Cochlear, ResMed, Macquarie Group and Goodman Group. In time, the 'WAAAX' stocks could feasibly join them as their businesses consolidate and mature.

Each sector has its top 50 representatives. The market has given these blue chip shares a capitalisation (value) that reflects their reliable nature. The S&P/ASX 50 contains the large-caps — the largest 50 companies by market capitalisation, or value. This cuts out at about $9.9 billion. (Market value is not the only criterion for inclusion in the S&P/ASX 50; liquidity, or turnover, is also required.) These are the elite group of stocks from which many of your core portfolio holdings come. Size, however, doesn't necessarily equate to blue chip status.

Evaluating second-liners

Outside the top 50 come the mid-caps, usually considered to be the companies ranked 51 to 100 by value. This group is covered by the S&P/ASX Midcap 50, which starts at about $9.9 billion and ends at about $4.7 billion. Then come the small-caps, generally taken to mean those ranked between 100 and 300 by market capitalisation, as measured by the S&P/ASX Small Ordinaries index. This means that, roughly, any stock between $560 million and $4.7 billion in size is a small-cap.

Institutional investors usually consider only the stocks comprising the S&P/ASX 200 index — with a lower limit of about $1.4 billion — to be *investment-grade* (suitable for investment). Companies with stocks that lie within the 200 to 300 range may make the grade, but haven't yet. But individual investors may have a different view than institutional funds of what constitutes investment-grade.

The institutions typically concentrate their analysis and efforts on the top 100, although an increasing number of small 'boutique' managers look outside the top 300. Individual investors realise that they can use their research skills outside that range to find undervalued companies that the wider market has overlooked.

REMEMBER

The small-caps are more volatile than the large-caps, and they tend to be hit harder when the market falls. The reverse is also true, meaning they can run harder than the large-caps when the market is rising. But the reason many investors find the small-caps attractive is that these stocks are far-less-researched stocks than those in the top 100, meaning that investors who do their homework on an unknown or little-covered stock can 'get set' well ahead of the rest of the market, and make a return of many times what they put in.

Potential leverage is even greater in the 'micro-caps', which are the stocks that lie outside the S&P/ASX All Ordinaries index (consisting of the 500 largest companies by market capitalisation). This cuts out at about $270 million. The companies below that level are even less researched than the small-caps, with many going about their business virtually unnoticed. Not many institutional fund managers go anywhere near the micro-caps because these stocks have low liquidity, meaning that if the manager gets it wrong, the fund may not be able to sell the shares, and so it may make a 100 per cent capital loss. On the other hand, the fund may be one of the only — if not *the* only — institutions on the share register, and may be invited on to the board for that reason.

But the attraction for the retail investor is that you can find value you simply can't find in larger stocks. If you can get a micro-cap investment right, you're looking at a star investment. A compound annual growth rate of 30 to 50 per cent over ten years is possible. As an example, 25 years ago, Sonic Healthcare was a micro-cap; its market cap is now $18.2 billion. Less than 20 years ago, Fortescue Metals Group was a micro-cap — founder Andrew Forrest bought half of its predecessor company Allied Mining & Processing in 2002, at 8 cents a share, and raised its first capital at 13 cents. The Fortescue share price is now more than $25, for a market value of $77.6 billion.

Outside the All Ordinaries index, after you cull resources explorers and research and development stocks, you have almost 600 profitable industrial companies. That's a big universe in which to try to spot the next Fortescue Metals Group or Sonic Healthcare. Although the risk is far greater than investing in S&P/ASX 100 stocks, many investors like this sector of the market.

Gambling on specs

At some point, when delving around the approximately 1,700 stocks that don't make it into the S&P/ASX All Ordinaries index (the top 500 by market value), you'll find yourself dealing with the specialised world of the specs, or speculative stocks.

In Australia, a *spec* once meant a mineral or petroleum explorer. Nowadays, spec refers to any stock that does not have a positive financial track record but may have prospects. Usually these prospects are called *blue sky*, meaning the possibility exists of very large gains in the future. Mineral- and oil-exploring companies are still specs, but a host of biotechnology and telecommunications hopefuls have also joined this category.

REMEMBER

With specs, you pays your money and you takes your chances. Nobody really knows how specs are going to perform in the future because a reliable method of forecasting the potential of these stocks just doesn't exist. If the stock doesn't have a track record, buying a spec share is a gamble.

You can punt on a few speculative shares. If you set a limit on the amount you invest and you have a strategy for buying them, you can even come out ahead.

WARNING

Don't overlook the high risk involved when gambling on a good return. If you have a conservative portfolio, you may enjoy buying a few speculative shares. However, don't risk the children's school fees in a stock that promises a lot but is yet to earn a profit.

Diversifying through Managed Funds

When you analyse a diversified share portfolio, you have to keep in mind that it only contains shares. Full diversification requires another step. To protect your total investment, make sure your portfolio contains (at the very least) shares, property and interest-bearing investments, with a cash component kept in reserve. This kind of balanced portfolio is often most easily assembled using professionally managed funds, whether unlisted or exchange-traded.

REMEMBER

A *managed fund*, or unit trust, is a good example of diversification in action. With a managed fund, small investors pool their money to buy assets that are larger in size and more numerous in spread than they could buy individually. A managed fund has greater buying power and can more easily diversify its assets than an individual investor can. Through managed funds, investors can share in the ownership of assets that they couldn't afford themselves, such as shopping centres, office blocks and airports.

Managed funds also offer the most convenient means of investing overseas. Managed equity (share) funds have the built-in diversification of a large, professionally assembled portfolio. Buying into a managed fund saves you, the investor, the effort of building and researching your own portfolio.

Australian investors are big users of managed funds, with Australia having the fourth-largest managed funds market in the world. According to research firm Rainmaker Information, in 2021 Australians had $3.1 trillion invested through fund managers and super funds (including managed funds, wrap platforms — which allow an investor to hold shares, managed funds and a cash account, all under one umbrella — and all kinds of superannuation). This is up 135 per cent since 2011, and has increased by 9 per cent each year over the past decade. The nation's growing superannuation kitty also accounts for $3.1 trillion (about one-third of super is directly invested by funds, while about one-third of money invested by fund managers comes from non-super).

Managed funds have opened up virtually all of the major asset classes to individual investors. Approximately 5,000 funds (excluding ETFs) are open for retail money. Of the $3.1 trillion investment kitty, more than $2.9 trillion is run through investment managers, with the managed funds pool spread across Australian shares ($659 billion), international shares ($644 billion), Australian bonds ($352 billion), real estate investment trusts ($88 billion), cash ($190 billion), direct property ($222 billion) and international fixed interest ($195 billion). Another $521 billion is invested in infrastructure, private equity, hedge funds and other 'alternative' assets.

Unlisted equity trusts are very popular. The largest of these are two index funds, the Vanguard International Shares Index Fund, with $17.5 billion of investors' money, and its domestic stablemate, the Vanguard Australian Shares Index Fund, with $14.5 billion. Then comes the largest actively managed funds, both international equity funds — the Magellan Global Fund ($13.3 billion) and the Platinum International Fund ($8.2 billion). The currency hedged version of the Vanguard International Shares Index Fund is next, with $6.3 billion, followed by other active funds including the Fidelity Australian Equities Fund ($5.8 billion), the MFS Global Equity Trust ($5.4 billion), the Platinum Asia Fund ($5.4 billion), the Walter Scott Global Equity Fund ($4.2 billion) and the Antipodes Global Fund ($3.3 billion).

Real estate investment trusts (REITs) (see Chapter 8) are now a $155 billion component of the ASX, and property securities funds — these funds offer investors access to a portfolio of REITs, managed by professional fund managers — are a $110 billion sector.

The other basic kinds of managed funds are

» Bond (or fixed-interest) funds, which own portfolios of government, semi-government and corporate bonds

» Cash management trusts (CMTs), which invest in term deposits, cash bank bills or short-term money market securities (instruments that can be quickly converted to actual cash)

» Mortgage funds, which hold a portfolio of mortgages over various kinds of property

» 'Absolute return' funds, which invest for maximum return, without reference to any benchmark index (and carry higher risk as a result)

» Debt securities funds, which invest in sovereign (government) and corporate debt (or bonds)

» 'Hedge' funds, which claim the ability to make money regardless of what the share and bond markets are doing

» Income funds, designed to generate a reliable income for investors

The latest innovations are:

» **Private equity funds:** These funds invest in private companies, which are not listed on the stock market. In 1994, $71.1 million was invested in private equity; Australian investors now have $54 billion invested there.

» **Global property securities and infrastructure securities funds:** In the same way that global equity funds invest in overseas shares, global property securities and infrastructure securities funds invest in the much larger markets in those assets overseas. Global property securities is a $4.6 trillion market (with $2.6 trillion in listed REITs); global infrastructure securities is estimated to be even bigger, at $5 trillion.

» **Socially responsible investing (SRI) funds:** These funds' investments are screened from an ethical or social perspective. They're either directed away from unacceptable investments — for example, arms makers, gambling companies and alcohol/tobacco companies — or actively channelled to acceptable investments, such as companies showing good environmental or social behaviour, or with products that demonstrably serve a good purpose.

SRI is a small but growing market in Australia. According to Rainmaker Information, dedicated ethical/SRI investment funds held $164 billion at March 2021, up from $6.2 billion at June 2010 — but if this is widened to include all of the superannuation funds now managed by fiduciaries that have signed up to environmental, social and governance (ESG) principles, the ESG investment sector in Australia is as large as $1.6 trillion.

DECIDING TO BE AN ACTIVE OR PASSIVE PLAYER

When buying into a managed fund, you buy not only a diversified portfolio, but also the expertise of the managers, which is important if the fund is active in trying to beat the index. This means that the fund manager's goal is to perform better than a particular index, such as the S&P/ASX 200. The fund manager may achieve this by buying under-valued stocks and selling overvalued stocks. Overall, this managed fund is betting that the skills of its stock pickers can earn it a better return than the market. *Active* fund managers may have difficulty in picking the consistent winners and outperforming the market. However, when they succeed, these fund managers can beat the index hand-somely. But investing in managing funds comes with a cost — in fees.

Investors who don't want to invest in aggressive funds that try to beat the index can instead buy into *passive* or *index* funds. An index fund replicates a particular index, reducing the worry about analysing the market.

Depending on the fund, this index could be the S&P/ASX 200 index (for an Australian share fund) or the Morgan Stanley Capital International (MSCI) World index (for an international share fund).

The manager of an index fund or exchange-traded fund (ETF) constructs a portfolio that closely tracks a specific market index by holding all or, in the case of very broad indices, a representative sample of the securities in the index. The index funds buy the poor performers as well as the standout risers, but their investors know that the fund won't underperform the index because their portfolio is the index.

Index funds have lower brokerage costs than active funds because these funds only buy and sell shares when the composition of the index they track changes. If you're paying fees to have your investment actively managed and the manager fails to beat the index, you're losing money.

After several relatively lean years early in the 2000s, and then the GFC-triggered market slump of 2007 to 2009, investors became mutinously conscious that many funds were more concerned with how their performance fared against the relevant benchmark index, instead of how the fund actually performed. In simple terms, to investors it seemed that fund managers didn't mind the fund performing poorly — what fund managers did mind was the fund performing poorly on its own.

A decade or so ago, investors in an older-style, typically growth-oriented equity fund were asked to pay an entry fee as high as 5 per cent (the adviser, or a discount broker, might have rebated this back to the investor in full), and an annual management fee of 2.5 per cent. This meant that they were significantly behind the performance eight-ball from the outset. These days, most modern fund products (and wholesale funds) don't have entry fees, unless the investor goes directly to the fund manager. A retail investor will face ongoing charges, which can be summed up in the management expense ratio (MER) and are typically about 0.5 per cent to 0.8 per cent a year. A platform fee may also be charged, if that is how the investor invested in the product. All up, according to research firm Rainmaker Information, retail investors going into a managed fund should expect to pay 0.8 per cent to 1.5 per cent a year in total fees.

In contrast, the largest Australian equity ETFs are managed for as little as seven to 13 basis points — that's 0.07 per cent to 0.13 per cent — a year. The cheapest international shares ETF — the Vanguard US Total Market Shares Index ETF, which tracks a Total Market index with nearly 4,000 constituent companies across 'mega', large, small and micro-capitalisation levels, and thus represents nearly 100 per cent of the investable US share market — makes that look positively expensive, with an annual management fee of just 0.03 per cent. That is democratisation of access to the sharemarket on steroids, and for that pittance of a management cost, this ETF earned its investors 17.9 per cent a year for the five years to June 2021. For more on ETFs, see Chapter 9.

Another problem that investors may find with managed funds is that through 'process homogenisation' — once known as herd mentality — the larger managers have focused on relative return (that is, relative compared to their peers), crowding together with a tracking error of 2 to 3 per cent, and not wanting to deviate too far from the index. By definition, this makes outperformance difficult to achieve.

Investors who have adopted an index (or passive) strategy — who want a fund that replicates a particular index — don't mind this approach. But those who want active management — they're paying for the skill of the fund manager's stock pickers to beat the performance of the index — do mind paying for what they're not getting, leading to a crisis of confidence in many of the big-brand managers.

(continued)

(continued)

But the perennial problem with active fund investing is that the great majority of them do not beat their benchmark index. Financial data firm Standard & Poor's maintains a scorecard called SPIVA (S&P Indices Versus Active), with the latest SPIVA scorecard, for 31 December 2020, showing that for a one-year period, 86.3 per cent of Australian actively managed share funds did not beat the performance of the S&P/ASX 200 index. Over three years, 73.4 per cent of the active funds failed to match or beat the index. Over five years, 81.7 per cent of the active funds fell short of the index; for ten years, that figure was 79.3 per cent; and for 15 years, 86.3 per cent of active funds underperformed the benchmark. The SPIVA numbers explain why many investors prefer index funds or ETFs for their Australian shares investment — because they know they will receive the index performance (before fees and expenses). They will not beat the performance of the index — the index fund or ETF is not designed to do that — but nor will it under-perform the index, either.

Some active managers do out-perform the index in a given period — but doing it consistently is very, very difficult. And with investors in an active managed fund paying up to 1.5 per cent a year in management fees — and the more actively managed the fund and the more complex the investment strategy, the higher the fee — many investors find it untenable to pay active fees, but get worse returns than a much cheaper index fund or ETF would give them.

Critics of index funds and ETFs say that the inherent problem is that the funds buy stocks purely because they are in the index the fund tracks; in other words, they pay no heed to specific stocks' fundamental valuations. The indexed investment buys the high-quality stocks and the weaker-quality ones, without discrimination. The response of the index fund and ETF issuers is that this results from an implicit trust that the index is doing what it is meant to do — the S&P/ASX 200 has the 200 biggest stocks in Australia, and the investors want that. In effect, investors believe that the index return is the return that they're entitled to in the sharemarket, and that the index fund or ETF will give them that.

One last point to keep in mind is that the index funds and ETFs can affect company valuations. If, say, Fortescue's weight in the index increases due to its share price outperforming, the index fund/ETF manager automatically buys more Fortescue shares. If, say, CSL's fortunes have declined over the past 18 months, index funds and ETFs will have mechanically sold CSL shares in line with its falling index weight — thereby exerting downward pressure on CSL's share price. This can arguably increase the impact of momentum and over-valuation, due to the greater weight of funds automatically buying those companies with share prices that have been rising (and vice versa for share prices that have been falling). The index funds and ETF managers simply say that they react to the changing weightings — it's no concern of theirs what fundamental or performance factors are causing the outperformance or underperformance of individual companies.

Investing outside Australia

One strategy for managing your portfolio is to have some of your investments outside Australia. True diversification involves investment not only across a range of asset categories but also across local and foreign investments. The Australian sharemarket accounts for less than 2 per cent of the total capitalisation (or value) of the world's sharemarkets. Your share portfolio (or asset portfolio in general) isn't truly diversified unless it contains shares outside Australia. For more on international investing, see Chapter 20.

Considering Alternative Investments

Increasingly, savvy investors are considering allocating fairly large (10 per cent to 20 per cent) chunks of their portfolio to 'alternative' investments — that is, those that are not the traditional building blocks of a portfolio, being shares, cash, bonds and property. Alternative assets have different returns streams from mainstream investments, such as bonds and equities, where payments in the form of coupons or dividends can generally be expected every six months. This means alternative assets can help to diversify an investment portfolio.

REMEMBER

Alternative investments also offer diversification because they can have a low — or even negative — correlation to traditional investments. This means, at times when all the traditional markets appear to tear downwards at once, allocations to alternatives may move to a much lesser extent (low correlation) or move in the opposite direction (negative correlation). This ability to absorb shocks can take the risk out of portfolios. But alternatives are not without risk.

The term *alternative investments* is usually taken to include:

» Hedge funds, which are managed funds that can invest across many different markets and strategies, with maximum flexibility, so they can make money regardless of what the share and bond markets are doing. They can lose money, too.

» Managed futures/commodity trading adviser (CTAs) strategies.

» 'Absolute return' equity-based funds, such as long–short funds, which will simultaneously go long (buy) under-valued stocks and short (sell) over-valued securities, and 'market-neutral' funds, which try to deliver above-market returns with lower risk by hedging out market risk. These look to negate the impact and risk of general market movements and isolate the pure returns of individual stocks.

>> Private equity — that is, capital invested in a private company not yet listed on the sharemarket. (A private equity investment made at a very early stage — for example, before the company has earned any revenue — is known as 'venture capital' and is sometimes considered a discrete investment class.)

>> Infrastructure assets, where income streams can be generous but not without risk.

>> High-yield assets — for example, funds that invest in distressed debt, junk (high-yield) bonds and mezzanine debt.

>> Commodities, such as precious and base metals, oil and energy, and soft (agricultural) commodities.

>> Agribusiness, such as investment in forestry, farming or horticultural businesses.

>> Art and other collectible items, such as coins and wine.

More recently, the range of alternative assets available has been widened to include investment in insurance-linked securities (the value of which is driven by insurance events); water entitlements (traded in the Australian water market); 'social impact' investments, where the investment both earns a financial return and generates a targeted positive social outcome; shipping funds; aircraft and other equipment leasing; weather-related derivatives; volatility derivatives; carbon-dioxide emissions trading; other income streams, such as music royalties; and cryptocurrencies, such as Bitcoin. Like gold, Bitcoin is increasingly being seen as a genuine member of the liquid (easily sellable) part of the alternative assets class.

WARNING

The caveat always remains that holding any asset as part of a diversified portfolio as an uncorrelated asset runs the risk, in extreme circumstances such as the GFC Crash and the COVID-19 crash, of the correlation of assets coming together, at least temporarily. Many investors were surprised when this happened in February–March 2020, but the unprecedented external factor — the pandemic and the associated economic hit — made all assets more correlated for some time. This was exacerbated by leveraged investments (that is, investments made with borrowed money) that had fallen in price facing 'margin calls', or the need to rebuild the deposit for borrowing back to the original loan-to-value ratio (LVR). To meet these margin calls or rebuild deposits, the affected investors were selling liquid assets to raise cash — even their liquid alternatives, which temporarily cost those assets their 'uncorrelated' status.

3

Buying, Buying, Sold

Chapter **6**

Buying and Selling Shares

B uying and selling shares can be easy. All you need is an account with a stockbroker, because a broking firm licensed by the Australian Securities Exchange (ASX) must perform all transactions on the securities exchange.

You can buy and sell virtually any quantity of any listed share through your broker, whether you make the transaction over the phone or on the internet. The broker makes the transaction on your behalf and charges you a fee, called *brokerage*.

You can also buy shares before they list on the sharemarket, when a company makes an *initial public offering* (IPO), known as a *float*. Buying shares through an IPO is free of brokerage, but the catch is that you must first obtain a prospectus for the float. Back in the 1990s the general public could easily buy shares in large floats of government-owned entities, such as the Commonwealth Bank and Telstra. However, most floats are a lot smaller and harder to get into than those mammoth floats. (Chapter 13 explores the ins and outs of IPOs.)

In this chapter, I cover how the ASX's trading system works and tracks trade histories and prices, and how to place an order with your stockbroker. I also take you step by step through a trading day on the ASX, and look at floats and electronic registers.

Finding the Market

The actual sharemarket exists on a computer screen that's linked to the ASX's electronic trading system, called ASX Trade, which provides individual share information from the Australian sharemarket, and access to the trading venues, even those not operated by ASX. Launched in 2010 — and overhauled in 2020 — ASX Trade provides for every one of the approximately 2,200 stocks listed on the market, among other data, such vital statistics as the last sale price, the buy quote (*bid*) and the sell quote (*offer*, or *ask*). These statistics tell you the price at which the shares last traded, the price that buyers are presently prepared to pay for the shares and the price that sellers are prepared to accept.

REMEMBER

ASX Trade hosts two trade services, or 'order books':

>> **TradeMatch** is the main market, and handles retail orders. It handles about 60 per cent of all trading. TradeMatch is a 'lit' market, meaning the bids, offers and volumes are displayed, and the market sees each transaction as it is struck.

>> **Centre Point** is a 'dark' market, meaning that buyers and sellers are matched anonymously. Institutional investors strike 'block' trades (trades involving large numbers of shares) in Centre Point, to lessen the impact of such large orders hitting the market. Centre Point pricing exists between two price steps in the ASX market. High-frequency traders, who use complex algorithms to analyse trading patterns and execute orders based on market conditions, also use Centre Point. But depending on the broker you use, so can retail investors.

ASX Trade also gives access to the second Australian stock exchange, Cboe Australia (formerly called Chi-X), which trades company shares and ETFs already quoted on the ASX, but doesn't list or supervise the companies. Cboe Australia also trades a range of ETFs that are only listed on Cboe Australia, as well as Cboe Australia warrants (see Chapter 21) and transferable custody receipts (TraCRs) over US-listed stocks (see Chapter 20).

REMEMBER

Brokers access ASX Trade through a range of interfaces. Brokers and market participants need to have their own proprietary systems or rely on third-party interface providers (such as IRESS Trader, provided by ASX-listed financial software company, IRESS Limited). No end-customer connects directly to an ASX product — any functionality that end-customers see is provided by their broker.

Through whichever interface used, every stockbroker has direct access to the raw sharemarket data from his or her desktop. Investors don't see or interact with ASX Trade — only brokers do. Clients of online brokers see a re-presented version of ASX Trade, based on a feed coming directly from the ASX, when they log in to their broking account. How the market is presented graphically is up to each broker.

Investors can also trade in the daily 'auctions', both the opening auction at the start of the day, and the closing single price auction, which occurs between 4.00pm and 4.12pm (see the section 'Working the Trading Day', later in this chapter, for more). To trade in the auctions, investors instruct their broker accordingly.

Setting the pace — how the ASX trades

Only stockbroking firms that are ASX participants have direct access to ASX Trade. You place an order with your stockbroker by instructing your broker personally or by trading online (which still goes to ASX Trade via a broker), and the order is placed into ASX Trade through your broker's market interface.

ASX Trade provides details on the exact number of buyers and sellers for each stock. Brokers can trade shares at the push of a button (see Chapter 12 for a full explanation of how brokers work). As you place your buy and sell orders, the broking firm's automated system feeds the information into ASX Trade. Bids and offers are lined up, with bids tabulated from the highest down and offers shown with the lowest at the top.

The broker's trading program matches buyers and sellers automatically, giving priority to the highest bid and lowest offer price in the queue. This is called *price time priority*. If prices are equal, the orders that were entered in the system first are filled first, which means that large orders have no priority over small orders. When a bid and an offer match, a transaction occurs.

Price quotes are in cents and fractions of a cent, as shown in Table 6-1. All of this information is updated continuously as the market changes.

The ASX Trade system, as presented through your broker's interface, allows fast, informative communication at a glance.

TABLE 6-1

Price Steps for Equities, Rights Issues and Warrants

Price Range (cents)	Minimum Bid (cents)
Up to 9.9	0.1
10–199.5	0.5
200 and above	1.0

A *ticker* moves across the top of the screen, from right to left, and shows trades as they occur, in groups of stock code, price and number of shares. The ASX doesn't provide the ticker; it is presented by the broker's trading system.

A *Price Information window* is used to view current market prices in a selected stock or a number of stocks. This window displays specific information relating to the performance of a stock, such as the stock identity (ID), a description of the stock (Short Description), the total quantity available at the best bid (BQty), best buy price (Bid), best sell price (Ask), and the total quantity available at the best ask price (AQty). Again, this data is provided by the ASX, but how it is presented is up to your broker's system.

The broker's trading system also shows the difference between the buy price and the sell price — this is the *spread*, which shows you how the shares are priced in current buy and sell situations. These situations include the following:

>> **Open:** The price of the first trade for the current trading day

>> **High:** The highest traded price for the current trading day

>> **Low:** The lowest traded price for the current trading day

>> **Last:** The price of the most recent trade

>> **LQty:** The quantity of the most recent trade

>> **Close:** The price of the last trade at the close of trading on the previous trading day

Again, all this data is provided by the ASX, but it is up to the broker's trading system as to how it is presented.

Users also see:

>> **Volume:** The volume traded during the current trading day

>> **Value:** The value traded during the current trading day in dollars

Getting order depth

Order depth shows the full *market depth* for a particular stock, displayed order by order, as presented by the broker's trading system. The *Order Depth window* is a list of bids (the prices that buyers are prepared to pay) and asks (the prices that sellers are prepared to accept). In the Order Depth window, the buyers will be presented on the left, with the highest bid at the top; the sellers are on the right, with the lowest offer at the top. Market participants can see all the orders at individual prices. The Order Depth window can also be viewed with all orders at the same price aggregated.

The Order Depth window allows brokers to view all of their own orders currently in the market. No other broker can see this information. Brokers enter, amend or cancel their orders via the Order Depth window, which is also where they make any inquiries.

Getting trade history

The *trade history* is used to view information about individual trades, provided by the ASX. For each buy and sell trade, the broker's system's *Trade History window* shows the following information:

>> **ID:** The stock identity.

>> **Qty:** Quantity of shares bought or sold. The shorthand for a thousand is 'T'; for a hundred thousand, it's 'HT'; and for a million, it's 'M'. (For example, 10,000 shares is 10T; 700,000 shares is 7HT; and 2 million shares is 2M.)

>> **Prc:** Traded price.

>> **Time:** The time of the trade.

>> **As of:** The 'as of' date of the trade. If the trade was entered with a date different from the current trading day, it will be displayed in this column.

>> **TType:** The trade type. If the trade is cancelled, the trade is displayed again as a trade reversal; that is, it's displayed as Rev.

Broker numbers are not displayed for trades executed on stocks.

Paying your way

Most stockbroking firms require you to put up a certain amount of money before they accept your first order to buy shares. Not to put too fine a point on it, the stockbroker wants to know that you can pay for the shares, and that the firm won't be left holding the baby.

REMEMBER

After you establish an account, you can then place buy and sell orders through your broker's smartphone app (see Chapter 17) or website, by email, or, if you're old school, over the telephone. As you sell shares, the broker pays the proceeds into your cash account. The account comes in handy later when you settle your trades.

Making a Trade

In order to buy or sell shares, you have to give your stockbroker an *order*, which the broker enters into ASX Trade. If your buy order matches the best sell order, the transaction takes place in full view of everybody viewing a broker interface connected to ASX Trade, and anywhere in the world where someone subscribes to ASX data. You can give your broker an order by telephone, over the internet, in person, or by email, fax or letter. If you have an account with an online stockbroker, you can buy and sell shares with the click of a mouse.

However, you always need a broker to fulfil your order. If the market is moving quickly, success may mean being able to place the right kind of order. Getting, or getting rid of, the shares you want at the price you want may depend on what kind of order you lodge.

Placing an order

The main types of order on the ASX are:

>> Limit orders in the lit market

>> Centre Point orders; that is, orders that are designed only to go to Centre Point

>> 'Sweep' orders, which go to both TradeMatch and Centre Point

TIP

If you want the shares as quickly as possible and won't haggle over the price, you use a *limit order*, which is entered at a defined price. This order can execute at any price that is equal to or better than its limit price, but the order won't execute at a worse price. A limit order ensures that you won't pay more than you specify for the shares you're buying, and, if you're selling, that you won't accept less than you specify.

With a limit order, you set the price at which you want to buy or sell the shares. It doesn't matter what the current market price is — you only trade at a price that's acceptable to you. For a buy order, you set the price below the current market price to try to get the shares at a cheaper price; for a sell order, you enter a price higher than the current market price to try to get a better sale price.

Centre Point orders have the following features:

>> You can enter an optional limit price that ensures the order will not trade at a worse price

>> The limit price can be entered at any full or half tick

>> Orders match anonymously, thereby reducing market impact costs

>> Orders are queued in time priority

Limit orders in the lit market, Centre Point and sweep order types all support a range of order timeliness:

>> **Fill-or-Kill:** Fill or kill orders fill the order entirely when possible, or not at all.

>> **Fill-and-Kill:** Fill and kill means the order is immediately executed to the greatest extent possible, with any remaining unexecuted volume being cancelled.

>> **Good-for-Day (Day/GFD):** These orders expire at the end of the current trading day.

TradeMatch order types also support the following additional variations:

>> **Good-Till-Date (Date/GTD):** The order expires at the end of the specified trading day.

>> **Good-Till-Expiry (Expiry/GTE):** The order expires on the instrument's expiry date.

>> **Good-Till-Cancel (GTC):** The order expires only when cancelled or after the maximum permitted order lifetime for that particular instrument type.

Unlike conditional orders (see the section 'Finetuning your order', later in this chapter), these kinds of orders are managed by the ASX system. This means where conditional orders might fail to be executed, the ASX-managed orders will not.

The second exchange, Cboe Australia, uses Mid-Point orders, which enable you to track the mid-point of what's called the National Best Bid and Offer (NBBO) to provide guaranteed price improvement upon execution. Mid-Point orders can rest in the central limit order book (CLOB), enabling them to interact with all other orders, both lit and dark, maximising the investor's chance of their order being executed.

Other more rarely used types of order are market-to-limit orders and best-limit orders.

A *market-to-limit order* starts out as what used to be called an *at-market order*, which gets filled at the best price available in the market at the time of the order. But if the order isn't completely filled and the price moves away, it converts to a limit order, with the price defined at the price you paid for the filled portion of your order.

For example, suppose you entered an order for 1,000 Telstra shares as a market-to-limit order. The market price is $3.25, but you only get 600 shares 'filled' at this price before the price changes to $3.27. An order is then created for the remainder of the shares you want (in this case, 400 of them) and it is entered as a limit order at $3.25, which is the price you paid for your first 'fill'.

In this case, you can leave the order as it is, or go into your pending orders and amend it. If you are keen to buy and the market price has risen, you may either amend your order back to a market-to-limit order, or change the price on your limit order to a higher price, near or a bit above the current market price. Similarly, if you want to sell and the market price has dropped, you may want to lower the price of your limit order.

If you don't like using market-to-limit orders but still want the current market price, you can use a limit order at a higher price than the current price (if buying) or a slightly lower price (if selling). Your order will still execute at the best price, but it gives you more chance of having your whole order filled straightaway.

A *best-limit* order is an unpriced limit order that is priority-queued at the current best bid price (if selling) or best ask price (if buying). It appears in the market as a limit order with a specified price. Like market-to-limit orders, best-limit orders are only rarely used these days.

Brokers use numbers of shares rather than dollars when discussing trading. If you ask for '10,000 Commonwealth Bank' when you actually mean $10,000 worth of Commonwealth Bank shares, you may (at mid-2021 prices) wind up being billed for $1 million!

Utilising market depth information

Market depth information is now available from online brokers and information services. *Market depth information* allows you to see the various buy and sell orders entered into the trading system at a limit, but yet to happen. Being able to see how many shares are on offer and at what price can help you buy and sell more effectively. Figure 6-1 shows the market depth screen for BHP available through CommSec.

BHP GROUP LIMITED
ASX: BHP Share. Materials. Materials

Last Price (AUD)	Bid / Size	$36.140 / 1,763	Open	$35.910	52 Week High	$42.330
$36.140	Offer / Size	$36.150 / 520	High	$36.180	52 Week Low	$24.050
Today's Change	Volume	4,078.816	Low	$35.610	ASX Status	Open
▼$0.620 (1.69%)	Trades	27.864	Previous Close	$36.760	Chi-X Status	Open
	Value	$146,107,707.525	Last Traded 12:43:47 PM, 12 Jun 20		Primary Market	Open

Buy Sell

As of 12:43:48 PM Sydney Time, 12 Jun 2020. Data sourced from ASX TradeMatch and CHI-X

Summary Announcements Charts Dividends Recommendations About Forecasts & Trends Trade History Financials Derivatives

Prices Orders Course of Sales   Open in new window

Buyers   **Sellers**

NUMBER	VOLUME	PRICE $	PRICE $	VOLUME	NUMBER
12	1,224	36.130	36.140	352	4
16	3,033	36.120	36.150	2,796	13
15	2,937	36.110	36.160	2,297	10
18	5,819	36.100	36.170	2,946	13
13	3,062	36.090	36.180	2,359	12
13	3,034	36.080	36.190	2,388	11
13	2,605	36.070	36.200	9,496	19
16	2,349	36.060	36.210	1,786	7
8	1,630	36.050	36.220	13,730	9
6	2,373	36.040	36.230	1,674	7
6	2,287	36.030	36.240	1,511	5
3,083 buyers for 1,726,404 units			898 sellers for 684,300 units		

Performance Chart

⏱ 1 Year   Daily

■ BHP

BHP appears to be in a Medium-term rally confirmed by multiple indicators. Most importantly, the 5-day moving average is above both the 20 and 50-day moving averages.

View BHP Charting

FIGURE 6-1:
CommSec
Market Depth
Screen for BHP.

Source: CommSec

TIP

If your order is queued up behind a much larger order at the same price, you can tweak your bid (higher for a buy, lower for a sell), effectively starting a new queue, which means your order can get through quicker.

Finetuning your order

Traders take a different view of the order process to investors. Investors usually choose their stocks to hold long term and really aren't interested in quibbling over a few cents here and there on the purchase price. However, for traders, executing the trade as close to perfect as possible — that is, getting the price absolutely right — can make all the difference. Several kinds of conditional order, managed by a broker, are available to both investors and traders.

REMEMBER

These methods are:

>> **Rising sell:** This order helps you take some profit when a stock price rises. You instruct your broker to sell some or all of your shares when the price rises to the 'trigger' level you have set.

- **Trailing sell:** This order can help you take profits when a stock's direction changes from rising to falling. You instruct your broker to sell some or all of your shares when the price rises to a level you've set as your trail start price; you also set a 'trail stop value', and the next time the stock falls by the amount of this trail stop value, it triggers a market sell order.

- **Falling sell:** More often called a 'stop-loss', this order tells the broker to sell the shares if they fall to a certain price. This can help you lock in profits, but can also limit your losses in a falling market. A stop-loss order means if the price falls — that is, if the trade goes wrong — traders can retrieve their capital quickly, take a small loss and live to fight another day. If you're a long-term investor who has carefully chosen the stocks for your portfolio, you're not going to be too worried by the immediate downside. (Unless the stock starts to look terminal, in which case you chose badly!)

- **Falling buy:** This order allows you to tell your broker to buy when the share price falls to or below the price that you have set as a trigger. You can also set a limit price, which means the broker won't buy the shares above this price.

- **Trailing buy:** This order can help you gain when a stock's direction changes from falling to rising. It allows you to tell your broker to buy when the share price falls to or below a level you've set as your trail start price; you also set a 'trail stop value', and the next time the stock rises by the amount of this trail stop value, it triggers a market buy order.

- **Rising buy:** This order helps you take advantage of a stock price starting to rise, and when you want to get in on that recovery. It allows you to tell your broker to buy a stock when the price rises to, or above, a level that you've set as a trigger. You can also set a limit price, above which the broker won't buy.

REMEMBER

Conditional orders are not guaranteed by brokers. They come with a variety of risks, including:

- If the market is moving fast, as it was during the February–March 2020 crash, you risk your limit order not being executed, or your market order being executed at a different (and much less favourable) price point than your trigger conditions.

- Highly volatile securities could trigger a conditional order and then move against you, leaving you out of pocket.

- Conditional orders are taken on a 'best endeavours' basis — in the event of system failure or corporate action (for example, a share going 'ex-dividend', reconstructions and rights issues), your order may be cancelled.

TIP

Cboe Australia has a unique order type called 'Market on Close' (MOC), which allows you to trade eight minutes after normal market hours — up until 4.20pm.

With all of these orders, if you're making trades without a broker's advice, only one person is to blame if things go wrong — you. Most broking firms still believe that their advisers can help you make the most of your investments (but an obvious conflict of interest exists there!). However, they may help you avoid a badly planned order.

Closing an order

After you place a buy or sell order, you want the order filled quickly. If you're a buyer who's prepared to pay the lowest price sellers are asking for the number of shares they have on the market, your purchase can go through while you're still on the telephone.

How long the order hangs around depends on the kind of order. Most orders operate on a *good until cancelled* basis. ASX Trade will cancel or purge any orders overnight that meet the following criteria:

» **Expired:** Orders can be entered with an expiry date. ASX Trade checks the expiry dates of all orders at the close of each trading day, and removes expired orders daily.

» **Price:** If the order price is too far away from the current market, defined as the best buy (or sell) price for the close, the order may be cancelled. How far is too far depends on the market price.

» **Purged:** An order may be purged when the basis of quotation changes; for example, the share becomes ex-dividend (XD).

» **Session State:** Orders for a stock that has been suspended (prohibited from trading) during that trading day may be cancelled.

Working the Trading Day

Equity Automatic Trading takes place on ASX Trade between 10.00am and 4.12pm on weekdays (except public holidays that occur in Victoria and New South Wales on the same day). Not all shares are open for trading at 10.00am. The start of the trading day is staggered to allow orders recently placed into the system to be processed smoothly.

REMEMBER

Orders processed at the start of the trading day may have been entered the previous day, after the close of trading. Between 4.12pm and 6.50pm, the equity market enters an *adjust* phase, where orders cannot be entered. Brokers are able to trade during this period; however, the ASX imposes strict rules in relation to trading after hours. Brokers can conduct *housekeeping* on their trading books, cancelling or amending orders. Orders may also be entered in the morning, during *pre-open*, which begins at 7.00am. During pre-open, broking firms can enter orders, amend or cancel the previous night's orders and generally prepare for the trading day, but are unable to trade. Table 6-2 shows these phases on ASX Trade.

TABLE 6-2   A Day in the Life of ASX Trade

Time	Equity 1–5[1]/ Interest Rates	Warrants (excludes Index, Commodity and Currency Warrants)	Index, Commodity and Currency Warrants
	Trading Sessions		
	Actual Market Times		
5.30am			
6.00am*			
7.00am	Pre-open	Pre-open	Pre-open
9.40am			
9.50am*			Open
10.00am*	Open	Open	
4.00pm	Pre Closing Single Price Auction (CSPA)	Pre CSPA	Pre CSPA
4.10:30pm**	CSPA	CSPA	CSPA
4.12pm	Adjust	Adjust	Adjust
4.20pm			
4.30pm			
4.42pm	Adjust on	Adjust on	Adjust on
5.30pm*			
6.50pm	Purge orders	Purge orders	Purge orders

Time	Equity 1–5[+]/ Interest Rates	Trading Sessions Actual Market Times Warrants (excludes Index, Commodity and Currency Warrants)	Index, Commodity and Currency Warrants
6.59pm	System maintenance	System maintenance	System maintenance
7.00pm	Close	Close	Close
8.00pm			
8.10pm			

[+]*Equity Market 1 A–B: 10.00; Equity Market 2 C–F: 10.02:15; Equity Market 3 G–M: 10.04:30; Equity Market 4 N–R: 10.06:45; Equity Market 5 S–Z: 10.09*

*Random +/– 15 secs

**Random +/– 30 secs

Source: © Australian Securities Exchange Limited

Prior to the ASX opening (*Opening Single Price Auction*, which determines the opening price of a stock), and immediately prior to closing (*Closing Single Price Auction*, which determines the closing price), stocks enter a 'matching phase', during which ordinary price/time priority trading ceases but orders can still be placed on any terms, such that the price on buy orders can exceed the price on sell orders, and an overlap occurs.

In this way, during pre-open, buyers and sellers quote the different prices they are willing to accept (sellers) or pay (buyers) for their shares. At 10.00am (the open), when the market opens for trading, the overlapping bids and offers that exist within the market are matched off against each other.

During 'the match', the ASX uses a sophisticated algorithm to determine a single price at which all overlapping orders will trade. The algorithm determines the volume on the buy side versus the volume on the sell side, as well as the prices at which they have been placed. From this, the algorithm determines an official 'auction' price, which is the price at which the stock opens.

REMEMBER

The algorithm is only applied when an even or overlapping market exists. For example, if all buy orders are lower than all sell orders, the opening price can't be set. That will only occur when a buyer lifts their price to meet a seller, or a seller lowers their price to meet a buyer, at which point a trade is executed and an opening price is generated. With an overlapping market, all buy orders that had been submitted above the auction price will have traded, just as all sell orders that had been submitted below the auction price will have traded. Buy orders below the auction price and sell orders above the auction price will be sitting in the market still, not having yet traded at the prevailing market price.

At 10.00am AEST, the market opens for 'Normal Trading,' but on a staggered basis, with stocks opening alphabetically at set times:

>> Stock codes starting with **A–B** open at 10.00:00am (+/– 15 seconds)

>> Stock codes starting with **C–F** open at 10.02:15am (+/– 15 seconds)

>> Stock codes starting with **G–M** open at 10.04:30am (+/– 15 seconds)

>> Stock codes starting with **N–R** open at 10.06:45am (+/– 15 seconds)

>> Stock codes starting with **S–Z** open at 10.09:00am (+/– 15 seconds)

The times indicated are when that particular group of stocks opens for trading. Any matched orders entered during pre-open will trade at that price. Each group then moves seamlessly into normal 'lit' trading.

For example, if you enter an order for WBC (Westpac Banking Corporation) at 10.05:02am, your order will be placed in the opening algorithm and if it matches, it will cross at 10.09am (plus or minus 15 seconds) — that would be an auction trade. If you place an order for WBC at 10.09:16am and it crosses with an opposing order, then you've traded in the normal 'lit' market.

The market then trades as usual until 4.00pm, when it enters 'Pre Closing Single Price Auction' (Pre CSPA). During this time, between 4.00pm and 4.10pm, orders can be entered into the market and existing orders can be amended.

At 4.10pm, the Closing Single Price Auction (CSPA) takes place, where the algorithm is used again to determine the closing auction price at which any overlapping orders are matched off against each other. After this, the market is effectively in Close phase overnight, and it all starts again at 7.00am with the Pre-Open phase.

The Opening Single Price Auction and CSPA are open for all — you just need to trade in that time window. There's no requirement for a broker to set a flag or trade type in this instance.

Estimating the costs for trading

When you buy or sell shares, you're charged a fee called *brokerage*, which covers the broker's costs and a profit margin. Brokerage is added to the purchase price of a buy transaction and is deducted from the proceeds of a sell transaction.

Stockbrokers earn their income from brokerage on transactions, although some brokerage firms are changing to annual fees for managing a client's portfolio. However, brokerage is still the main game, which means your broker is happiest when you're transacting. Buying or selling really doesn't matter to your broker.

Most brokers apply a tiered scale for charging brokerage, in which the commission rate decreases as the dollar value of the transaction increases. Many charge a flat fee for smaller trades, with brokerage moving to a percentage of the total trade for transactions over a certain amount.

REMEMBER

Brokerage fees differ significantly between stockbroking firms, with the level of service offered usually also determining the fee. If you want research, portfolio management and other services, you can expect to pay more in fees. The charges may be a percentage of the transaction, with discounts on higher value transactions. Some firms charge a flat fee for transactions up to a certain size, and most firms charge a minimum fee for all transactions.

TIP

A broker can provide a range of value-added services, including advice on which shares to buy or sell, recommendations, research, portfolio management, financial planning and access to new floats that the firm is handling. Investors can choose between so-called *full-service* brokers — offering stockbroking with all the trimmings — and *execution-only* (or *discount*) brokers. Chapter 12 gives a detailed explanation of how brokers work.

Stockbroking is a customer- and service-oriented profession; it's also a highly competitive one. Full-service brokers typically charge a minimum amount of as low as $80 (plus GST) for small trades, or a brokerage rate of about 0.9 per cent to 1 per cent. Brokerage rates are usually negotiable and depend on the dollar value of the transactions and the frequency of trades — depending on your volume of business with the firm, you may be able to negotiate a special scale of fees with your stockbroker. Without advice, a full-service broker might be prepared to charge active clients brokerage of 0.1 per cent, because they know they have to try to compete with online brokers. The best online brokerage fees in the market are provided in Table 6-3.

TABLE 6-3

Online Brokerage Fees

Trade Value	Lowest Fee	Average Fee
$1,000	$5.00	$15.57
$5,000	$5.00	$16.62
$10,000	$5.00	$16.94
$25,000	$5.00	$24.30
$50,000	$5.00	$46.33
$100,000	$5.00	$90.59

Source: Canstar (as at 9 June 2021). Based on the online share trading brokerage fees for a single trade per month.

A lot of full-service brokers (and increasingly financial advisers) take on clients through their 'managed account' services, which are generally discretionary — where the broker buys and sells the stocks — or consultative between the broker and the client, and all shades in between. Many self-managed superannuation funds (SMSFs) like the managed account arrangement because it aligns more naturally with their obligations as trustees to develop a strategy for the SMSF and broadly stick to it. In this structure, the client may pay a management fee of up to 1 per cent of the value of the portfolio — up to, say, $500,000 — for portfolio management and administration. Above $500,000, the fee may then drop to 0.75 per cent a year. Such clients may also be paying brokerage at much lower rates than standard, but these arrangements can be highly negotiable.

Making the final settlement

After your broker completes your trade, you receive a contract note setting out the particulars of the transaction. *Settlement* — paying for the shares you bought or handing over the shares you sold — must take place within two business days after the transaction (a system called *T+2*).

TIP

After you place an order and the order is filled, you're required to fulfil your side of the transaction, even if you haven't yet received the contract note. Many brokers can offer you a cash management account to make settlement easier. If your broker has sold shares for you, the broker then deposits the proceeds (minus costs) into your account. If your broker has bought shares for you, the broker debits your account. You don't have to use this arrangement, but many investors find it's convenient.

Transferring off-market

You don't have to use the sharemarket to trade shares. Off-market transfers of shares between parties without using a stockbroking firm as the intermediary are executed through the use of an *Australian Standard Transfer Form*.

TIP

You can also conduct off-market transfers of securities electronically through *CHESS* (Clearing House Electronic Sub-register System), which is an ASX computer system that manages the settlement process (see the next section). You don't need an Australian Standard Transfer Form for transfers through CHESS; for this type of transfer, however, you need to go through your stockbroker.

Off-market transfers are usually private arrangements between family members or transfers from deceased estates. To obtain an Australian Standard Transfer Form, contact the share registry of the company whose shares you wish to transfer.

Playing CHESS Isn't a Game

The ASX has a paperless settlement system, the Clearing House Electronic Sub-register System — or CHESS. Prior to CHESS, shareholders used to receive share certificates for each parcel of shares that were purchased (which usually only clogged up your desk drawers until you sold the shares, and most times you couldn't find the certificates anyway).

CHESS was introduced in 1993 as an electronic transfer and settlement system that improved the bureaucracy of the Australian sharemarket. CHESS operates as a central hub that exchanges money and shares at the same time. The ASX registers all shareholdings electronically on CHESS, and they're known as uncertificated holdings. The cost of using CHESS is included in your brokerage fee. The CHESS Securities Clearing House (SCH), on behalf of companies, issues holding statements to shareholders who are sponsored by brokers or institutions that participate in CHESS. You get a separate statement for each security you have in CHESS. You also get a statement whenever your security holding changes because of a transaction during the month. All of this simply means that when you buy or sell shares, ASX has a record of you owning those shares directly.

REMEMBER

To register your ownership of shares on CHESS, you need a Holder Identification Number (HIN). To get this, you need to be sponsored by a broker who is connected to the CHESS computer system. Your CHESS sponsor registers you on CHESS by opening a CHESS account in your name. The stock exchange then sends you a notice confirming your CHESS registration and gives you your HIN. You can register shareholdings in any number of companies under your HIN. Of course, appointing a broker as your CHESS sponsor restricts your selling to that broker. If you want to sell through any broker, use Issuer Sponsored Registration.

Alternatively, a company that you buy shares in can sponsor you. Here, you register on an Issuer Sponsored Subregister and receive a Shareholder Registration Number (SRN), which records your shareholding in that company. When you buy shares in a company, you automatically get an SRN. If you want to transfer the registration of these shares to CHESS, you can ask your CHESS sponsor. Issuer Sponsored shares can usually be traded through any broker, providing any conditions set out by that broker are met.

TIP

If you hold shares in more than one company and choose to be issuer-sponsored, you have a different SRN for each shareholding. As your portfolio grows, you have to deal with multiple SRNs. Transferring the registration of these shares to CHESS, under one HIN, is much easier on the memory.

Shareholders don't have to manage the paper mountain of printed share certificates. CHESS holding statements accumulate over a financial year (1 July to 30 June). During the financial year, you get a new statement page that reflects transactions from 1 July. The statement tracks share transactions in the same way that bank account statements track cash transactions. The end result is less paper and more accurate records.

Because the ASX handles clearing and settlement, any shares you buy through Cboe Australia will settle on your CHESS HIN or directly with the share registries.

TECHNICAL STUFF

About $2 trillion worth of shares are registered in CHESS: every day, around $5 billion is processed through CHESS, with more than 300 transactions and up to 1,500 messages processed every second. CHESS is undergoing a refresh, with the ASX upgrading CHESS with a new digital ledger technology (DLT) messaging protocol, similar to a private blockchain, which will introduce complete digitisation through to the end investor. Where CHESS currently handles about 7 million trades a day, the ASX expects the replacement system to handle 15 million–20 million trades a day, and ultimately, up to 40 million–50 million.

The ASX has been working on the CHESS replacement project since 2015 and was hoping to go live with the new system in April 2021, but it decided to reassess the design of the DLT system after experiencing a major spike in trading volumes in March 2020, when activity exceeded previous peaks by more than seven times. In June 2020, the ASX announced a new go-live target date of April 2022. But after faulty software took the ASX trading system down for almost a full day in November 2020 when a planned upgrade to ASX Trade went spectacularly awry, the ASIC also expressed 'significant concern' about the outage. That forced the delay of the targeted start date of the DLT system to April 2023.

IN THIS CHAPTER

» Making sure you're ready for the market

» Using fundamental and technical analysis

» Analysing yourself — investor or trader?

» Listening to your broker

» Keeping your ear to the ground

» Assessing the tax implications

Chapter **7**

Knowing When to Buy and Sell Shares

The basic rule for investing in shares is to buy low and sell high. You buy shares when they're cheap and sell them when they're expensive. The trouble is, how do you know what's cheap or expensive? Only hindsight tells you that for sure. You may buy a share and then see its price fall. Conversely, you may sell a share and then watch its price rise. If you sold the share at a profit, remember that you made a profit; and if you bought believing the shares were cheap, don't worry that they're now even cheaper.

In this chapter, I discuss the whys and wherefores of when to buy and when to sell, how to analyse the market, the differences between being a trader and an investor, and ways to keep your tax to a minimum.

Getting Ready for the Action

No perfect method exists by which you can determine the best time to buy or sell shares. Whether you're a long-term investor or a trader focused on short-term opportunities, you have to work this out for yourself. Many people collect and interpret data in order to know when to buy and sell shares, but even the professionals don't always get it right.

WARNING

An experienced investor knows that no perfect method for determining when to buy or sell a share exists, although you can always find a salesperson or a software system that claims to have the key. If only the process were that simple! Whether they use fundamental analysis, technical analysis or even astrology, these systems are far from infallible. Don't be fooled by software programs that promise to make you rich. If the system were foolproof, you can be sure it would be a very tightly held secret.

Before you buy or sell shares, you have to satisfy yourself that the shares are likely to rise or fall. If you're using a software tool to give you trading tips, you have to be able to validate the information it's giving you. Whether you do this through your own research or through consulting a reputable broker or adviser, seeking a second opinion is always wise.

REMEMBER

When you invest in the sharemarket, the only way to have the odds in your favour is to do your homework. You have to study the companies, research their operations, review their history and estimate their potential for profit. This may require reading the company prospectus or annual report, sifting through broker research, trying the company's products or services yourself and even talking to the directors or managers. You may decide to follow the price and the volume of trades and try to understand the many things that they imply. Read, study and ask plenty of questions — and then go back and study some more.

Loving your shares

Emotions play a part in sharemarket investing. Although buying shares means acquiring a financial asset, the main purpose of the investment is to earn money for you. If a share doesn't perform to expectations, sell it and find one that will make you money. That's the objective. However, when you buy a share, you're also starting a relationship. You researched the company or read about it and you're enthusiastic. As with your everyday relationships, the possibilities seem endless, the expectations are all for the best and you're truly optimistic. Perhaps, if this relationship goes well and your stock makes you money, you may come to believe you could never bring yourself to sell. If that happens, you've lost sight of the purpose of investing in shares.

TIP

Sometimes investors are paralysed by the fear that after they sell a share the price goes higher and they could have made more from it if they'd hung on. If this happens, remember that by locking in your capital gain, you protect yourself from the possibility of loss; taking a loss on a share feels a whole lot worse than not making as much profit on a share as you could have.

REMEMBER

A profit is only a profit and a loss is only a loss when it is *crystallised* — when you actually sell the shares. Price fluctuations in the sharemarket continually alter your paper profit or loss, but good or bad, the change in the value of your holdings isn't real until you act on it.

Sometimes you may fulfil your expectations and justify your emotional attachment to the shares. When you're ready to sell, you face two possibilities — either you've made money on the shares, or you haven't. You can bank the money and pay the tax, or learn your lesson, claim the loss and get on with your life in the sharemarket.

If a share purchase goes bad, convincing yourself that the shares can return to your buying price if you just hang in there long enough is easy. However, that's a dangerous assumption to make. Taking the loss and moving on to better investments may be more suitable.

Buying smart

To buy smart, you buy a share when it's undervalued by the market and likely to rise in price and generate a capital gain.

REMEMBER

You can't know what's going to happen to the share price in the future. However, you can make a well-informed guess, based on knowledge, research and help. You're making an educated guess but that's all it can ever be. Sharemarket investors and traders make these assessments every day.

Every sharemarket participant is trying to buy stocks cheaper and sell stocks at a profit. But for every buyer, a seller exists — someone whose view of the stock is the exact opposite of yours. To ensure your side of the transaction is the correct one, do your homework and trust your opinion. That way you can be confident that you're a better-informed investor than the person on the other side. But you won't get every decision right.

Selling smart

Usually, you sell a share when you decide it's more likely to fall than rise. If you bought shares for less than you sold them, that's good, and all you have to worry about is the capital gains tax. If you need cash, selling a profitable shareholding is a quick way to generate free money to spend on things like children's education or overseas travel. I've cashed in shares to spend on travel, and it's an enjoyable feeling, as though the money came out of thin air.

AVERAGING DOWN OR UP

Averaging down means buying more of a share if the price falls. Investors do this to lower the average cost per share of the holding. For example, say you bought 1,000 shares of a company at $5. The price drops to $3, so you buy 1,000 more shares. The average cost of your shareholding is now $4. Instead of the stock having to rise above $5 before you're ahead, your break-even point is now $4. If the share price falls further, you can lower your average buying cost even more. But the risk you're taking is that the stock never recovers, in which case all you've done is throw good money after bad.

For example, anyone who averaged-down into Dick Smith Holdings or Slater and Gordon or RCR Tomlinson (refer to Chapter 4) after they began their terminal slides, and who thought they were lowering their average cost, turned out in the end to hold a one-way ticket to oblivion — unless they eventually claimed the capital loss (see Chapter 18). Averaging down only works if a stock recovers and then moves higher than your average buying cost. When you average down you're taking a big risk, but you can make it work in your favour if you confine it to stocks that you research thoroughly. Then, when the market overreacts to a piece of news and dumps the stock temporarily, averaging down can pay off. Many investors used the February–March 2020 crash, for example, as the opportunity to average down.

As I mention in Chapter 3, even some of the market's biggest long-term success stories, such as CSL, have given investors the occasional opportunity to average down. Fortescue Metals Group is another, over its journey. And that raises one of the drawbacks of the averaging-down strategy — its success really only becomes obvious in hindsight.

Specialist baby goods retailer Baby Bunting is another example. Baby Bunting floated on the ASX in October 2015, and surged from its issue price of $1.40 to $1.99 on its first day, a 42 per cent gain. Let's say, fortunately for you, you received 1,000 shares in the initial public offering (IPO).

The shares more than doubled within a year of listing after the company beat prospectus forecasts. Happy with how the company was performing, say you then bought another 1,000 shares at $2.60 in August 2016 — taking your average buying price to $2.

However, things then started to turn sour for Baby Bunting, as investors started to worry about rising competition in the baby goods sector, intense discounting by rivals and fears about the imminent arrival of Amazon Prime, given that Amazon is a major player in the baby goods category in the US.

The share price ebbed lower and lower, until, at Baby Bunting's annual general meeting in November 2017, the company upset investors with an earnings guidance downgrade, and the shares fell back through their issue price of two years earlier.

In investors' minds, it seemed that Amazon was apparently going to kill off local retailers. In vain, Baby Bunting tried to reassure investors that it expected to be cheaper than Amazon for about half its product range, and that more than half its top 250 selling goods were subject to Australian mandatory safety standards, which Amazon Prime may not have been able to match.

Say you believed the company rather than the market, and bought another 1,000 shares at $1.40, in March 2018. Clearly your initial IPO stake was not making money, but you now owned 3,000 shares with an average buying price of $1.80.

After that, it was time to sit back and watch as Baby Bunting was able to ignore a generally weak retail environment and move to a dominant position in the $2.4 billion baby goods market, gaining a 12 per cent share. The company watched four of its biggest competitors, including Babies 'R' Us and Baby Bounce, go out of business. The company smashed expectations when it reported results for FY19 and, by late 2019, the shares were trading at $3.90 — more than twice your average entry price.

The February–March 2020 COVID-19 crash stripped the Baby Bunting share price back to $1.65. Since I'm setting out this case study with the benefit of hindsight, I'd love to say that you snapped up another 1,000 shares at that price and lowered your average purchase price for Baby Bunting to $1.76 — but that's probably too perfect, because it means you would have been brave enough, and clever enough, to pick that March 2020 bottom. But if you did, you'd have seen Baby Bunting's share price surge, much as spending on baby products has surged (the company's online sales have swelled more than five times between 2016–17 and 2020–21, to $90.8 million, while the proportion of online sales in terms of total sales has tripled, from 6.4 per cent to 19.4 per cent). The company has unveiled plans to push into New Zealand, and at the time of writing, Baby Bunting shares were changing hands at $5.76.

Averaging down worked in this case because Baby Bunting is a high-quality stock that got into an oversold position but was able to see a strong rise in share price as the strength of its business model came to the fore.

'Buying the dips' in a high-quality stock can decrease your average cost and increase your capital gain — assuming that the 'dips' turn out to be temporary.

(continued)

(continued)

'Value' equity fund managers are quite prepared to average down, on the grounds that if they like a stock at $10, they like it even more at $5. Of course, that approach assumes that they have researched the stock thoroughly, and they believe that the market is missing something that they know.

On the face of it, a better strategy is to *average up*; that is, as a company's share price increases, you should buy more of its shares. The theory here is that while you increase your average buying cost, the company is also prospering, the good news is flowing and the stock is steadily rising. In averaging up, you're putting more money into your winners. That's true, but your investments are following the law of diminishing returns. Averaging down — if it works — adds a lot more value.

Another method of averaging is *dollar-cost averaging*, which involves making regular investments of the same amount of money in a stock or managed fund. You're not trying to predict the best time to buy, but dollar-cost averaging makes market fluctuations work for you because you buy more shares when prices are low and fewer shares when prices are high. In short, it takes the emotion out of investing.

This strategy can help to ensure that you're not too exposed to falls in the market when you buy at the top. The strategy can also reward you when the market recovers, through buying when the market was falling. Dollar-cost averaging doesn't need you to have the skill or the advice to help you pick the tops and bottoms; because it doesn't depend on the timing, dollar-cost averaging over time can smooth out the market's ups and downs.

Dollar-cost averaging is most effective in a long-term saving strategy, and it's actually how most people invest in the sharemarket through superannuation (through their employer's regular compulsory super contributions). Superannuation is effectively dollar-cost averaging — your employer must pay your super into your nominated account every quarter, and the super fund buys financial assets on your behalf four times a year. Similarly, most salary-sacrifice contributions are made via regular contributions.

Fintech company Raiz has linked the dollar-cost averaging strategy to micro-investing and exchange-traded funds (ETFs), and automated it to give investors a very low-cost way of starting to invest in the sharemarket. The company's Raiz app allows investors to start investing with as little as $5, and users can invest small amounts regularly into a mix of ETFs that are arranged in seven different portfolios. While investors can also invest lump sums and occasional top-ups, the central focus of the strategy is investing small amounts regularly — and getting started in sharemarket investment early. It's a good way of overcoming people's fears that they need a large amount of money to start investing in the sharemarket, and getting its long-term compounding track record working for them.

Share purchases can go wrong, and you may have to sell shares for less than you paid. In such a case, if you're a disciplined share trader, you may have a concrete rule on how much you're prepared to let the share price fall before you sell. If you're a long-term investor, you may be prepared to ignore the price fall to salvage something from a disaster.

The good news is that the Australian Tax Office (ATO) allows you to use your capital losses to offset against the capital gains that you've (hopefully) made on other shares, in that or future years.

In the absolute worst-case scenario, if you buy the wrong share, you can lose all your investment. This can happen even if you do your homework and satisfy yourself that the shares are a good buy. That's part of the risk.

Going into Analysis

Two tribes seem to dominate the sharemarket according to the pundits — the fundamentalists (fundies) and the technically oriented (techies). Fervent followers of each school exist. Professionals say that fundamental analysis tells you *which* shares to buy or sell and technical analysis tells you *when* to buy or sell. I don't believe these are exact tools, but they're useful and investors can profit from knowing how to apply them.

Fundamental and technical analysis are not for everybody, and peaks and troughs on a share price chart can be seen only with hindsight. However, these tools can be helpful.

Using fundamental analysis

Investors make their decisions based on fundamental analysis. *Fundamental analysis* (see Chapters 14 and 15) concentrates on the financial health of the company, as shown in its regularly published accounts. Among the most important indicators are

>> Profitability

>> Dividend yield

>> Cash flow

>> Assets

>> Owners' equity

>> Liabilities

Fundamental analysis involves relating the company's reported numbers to its price to work out whether the market price is cheap or expensive. It's used to measure risk and to find out whether the company's financial situation is improving or deteriorating. One of the drawbacks of fundamental analysis is that company accounts are furnished only every six months or, in the case of new companies that have listed on the stock exchange without a track record of profitability, every three months. These companies are required to post a statement of cash flows every quarter. Using fundamental analysis, you may spot a trend and try to confirm that trend in the next issue of company statements.

Fundamental analysis is a tool best suited for medium- to long-term investment. Fundamental analysis doesn't suit a trading strategy because it relies on out-of-date data. Four important calculations in fundamental analysis are the price/earnings ratio, the dividend yield, and interest and dividend cover. Other areas that are worth close investigation are gearing, asset backing and cash flow.

Determining the price/earnings ratio

The *price/earnings ratio* (P/E ratio) is a basic tool of fundamental analysis. The P/E ratio is the share price divided by the earnings per share (EPS). The P/E ratio compares the share price to the earnings and determines the value of the earnings bought at that price. Analysts use the P/E ratio to compare companies against their own track record, their industry peers and against the overall market.

TECHNICAL STUFF

To calculate the P/E ratio, you can either use the reported EPS of a company from its most recent financial year annual report or the prospective EPS figure forecast by broking firms. Investors who use a historical P/E ratio feel it shows actual figures based on real earnings, whereas those who use a forecast figure are trying to look into the future. Last year's earnings are cold hard fact, whereas prospective earnings estimates are not. Then again, buying shares means forecasting future growth.

Experts used to argue that investors should look for a company with a low P/E ratio. The general rule was that a value of 10 or lower was cheap and that 20 or above was expensive. However, analysis can be a bit more complicated. For example, a stock may have a P/E ratio of 20 because its growth prospects are better and the market is prepared to pay a premium for it, or a stock may have a P/E ratio of 8 because the market feels the stock won't grow. These days, investors understand that the market goes through phases in which these parameters change. For instance, the market is grappling at present with the question of what are fair P/Es to pay for Australia's technology-oriented 'growth stocks' (refer to Chapter 5).

A P/E ratio on its own doesn't tell you much. You have to use this calculation as a comparison. For example, you can compare a company's P/E ratio to the following:

» The average P/E ratio of its sector group — for example, banks, transport or telecommunications

» The average P/E ratio of the market as a whole

» The history of the company's P/E

By using these comparisons, you can see whether the share is rated at a premium (relatively overvalued) or at a discount (relatively undervalued). Comparing P/E ratios can show you whether the share price of the company is too high or too low.

The American fund manager John Neff built his career on low P/E ratio investing, looking for P/E ratios 40 to 60 per cent below the market average. He says:

> Low P/E stocks can capture the wonders of P/E expansion with less risk than skittish growth stocks. An increase in the P/E, coupled with improved earnings, turbocharges the appreciation potential . . . Unlike high-flying growth stocks poised for a fall at the slightest sign of disappointment, low P/E stocks have little anticipation, no expectation built into them. Indifferent financial performance by low P/E companies seldom exacts a penalty.

Growth-oriented fund managers would beg to differ with that approach in today's market (refer to Chapter 5). I cover P/E expansion in Chapter 11.

According to FactSet, the average historical P/E for the S&P/ASX 200 stocks over the past 20 years is 15.8 times earnings, while the average forward P/E is 14.5 times earnings. At present, the historical P/E for the S&P/ASX 200 stocks is 21.4 times earnings, while the forward P/E is 17.6 times earnings. To many investors, that indicates an overvalued market.

REMEMBER

A low P/E ratio can be that way because the market doesn't rate the stock very highly. Successful investing is about finding opportunities in shares that are undervalued, but not all of them go on to be winners. Sometimes a dog is a dog.

Calculating the dividend yield

To calculate the *dividend yield* — the percentage return of dividend income from a share investment — divide the dividend by the share price and multiply by 100 to convert to a percentage.

You can't compare the dividend yield to the yields on other investments because the dividend is only part of the earnings stream of the company. Some of the earnings are retained or reinvested in the business, and the dividend yield doesn't account for any capital gains (or losses) on the shares.

However, you can compare the dividend yield of the company to the same areas as you did with the P/E ratio; that is, to other companies in its sector, the market as a whole and the company's price history. These comparisons can reveal whether the share is relatively overvalued or undervalued. You want to buy shares with a high yield and sell shares with a low yield. The dividend yield falls as the price rises.

According to FactSet, the average gross historical dividend yield for the S&P/ASX 200 stocks over the past 20 years is just under 4 per cent (equivalent to 5.7 per cent if fully franked, assuming a tax rate of 30 per cent), while the average *gross forward yield* (the expected dividend in the next full financial year) is 4.6 per cent (6.6 per cent with full franking). At the time of writing, the historical dividend yield for the S&P/ASX 200 stocks is 2.4 per cent (3.4 per cent with full franking), while the forward dividend yield is 3.9 per cent (5.6 per cent with full franking). Again, to many investors, the lower-than-average yields point to overvaluation.

WARNING

You need to be careful because a high yield can be a sign of distress (remember risk versus return). The moral here is that you can't use dividend yield or any single determinant on its own as a guide to buy or sell.

Finding interest and dividend cover

Interest cover denotes the number of times that earnings *cover* (can pay for) interest payments. If this ratio is less than 1, it means the company will be unable to pay its current interest obligations. An interest cover of 3 is adequate, while 2 or below is cause for worry. An interest cover level better than 3 means that during periods when earnings are under pressure (such as the post-COVID-19 period for many companies) the company will have a better chance of still being able to meet its interest payments from earnings. An interest cover of 5 or above means that the company is very well managed. Also, many companies have debt covenants (agreements with their bankers) that require them to maintain an interest cover ratio above a certain threshold.

Dividend cover is the ratio of earnings to the dividend. A ratio above 1 shows that the company has earnings left over after paying the dividend. A company with a dividend cover above 2 is considered highly reliable — the dividend comprises less than half of the company's earnings for the year. Dividend cover below 1 means that the company needs something more than earnings to pay its dividend.

Companies can borrow from their reserves of retained earnings from prior years to pay a dividend. As a one-off situation this is fine, but it's not sustainable in the long run and is usually considered a warning sign.

REMEMBER

Mature companies have a lower dividend cover because they don't need to retain cash to finance their growth. The dividend cover is the reciprocal of the dividend payout ratio — with the average dividend payout ratio of the S&P/ASX 200 companies being about 72.3 per cent, according to FactSet, the average dividend cover for the index cohort is about 1.4 times.

This tells you that the S&P/ASX 200 companies feel a lot of pressure to maximise their dividends — which could be because self-managed superannuation funds (SMSFs) own somewhere between 15 per cent and 20 per cent of the sharemarket, and they gravitate to the biggest dividend payers.

Using gearing

Gearing describes the ratio of borrowings to shareholders' equity (or shareholders' funds). A company finances assets from shareholders' equity or through liabilities to external creditors. The gearing (or 'debt-to-equity') ratio shows the relative proportions between these two sources of funding. Gearing is measured by dividing net debt by total equity (assets plus liabilities).

TIP

During good economic times, companies with a high level of gearing generally deliver higher returns to investors. But when the tide turns — as it did in early 2020 — investors find that highly geared companies have a much riskier financial structure. Some (as many did) have to raise equity to pay down some debt. FactSet says the average gearing ratio of the companies in the S&P/ASX 200 index peaked in the last 20 years at 83 per cent, in 2008, but post-GFC the balance-sheet repair saw it slashed to 48 per cent in 2011. Over that 20-year period, the average figure has been 62.4 per cent. At the time of writing, the S&P/ASX 200 index constituents had an average gearing ratio of 68.3 per cent.

Generally, the lower the gearing ratio, the stronger the balance sheet — but relatively high gearing can be okay if a company has a reliable enough underlying cash flow to service (pay off) the debt. Anything over about 80 per cent warrants further investigation.

A negative debt to equity ratio means that the company's debt minus its cash, divided by its equity is negative. That's a good thing! In fact, when it comes to gearing, *net cash* status — where the company has no gearing because its holding of cash and cash equivalents exceeds its liabilities — is as good as it gets. Although occasionally, analysts criticise such companies for having a 'lazy' balance sheet — implying that they should take on some level of gearing to boost their return on equity. However, net cash means that a company is effectively self-funding.

ASX companies boasting net cash status at the time of writing included WiseTech Global, South 32, Cochlear, Fortescue Metals Group, Xero, Breville, Premier Investments, Altium, Lynas Rare Earths, Wesfarmers, Magellan Financial Group, The Reject Shop, Medibank Private, Pro Medicus, JB Hi-Fi, Netwealth Group, Metcash, Beach Energy, Shaver Shop, Codan, Technology One, Super Retail Group, Iluka Resources, Objective Corporation, Appen, Clinuvel Pharmaceuticals, Temple & Webster, NIB Holdings, Jumbo Interactive, Redbubble, Australian Ethical Investment, Data#3, Bravura Solutions, Jupiter Mines, Coles Group, Nick Scali, Gold Road Resources, Nickel Mines, Sims Limited, Integrated Research, Sandfire Resources, Class, Johns Lyng Group, Enero Group, Cyclopharm, SRG Global, Ramelius, Austal, Macmahon Holdings, Michael Hill, EML Payments, Kogan.com, Orocobre, PointsBet, Myer Holdings, G8 Education, NRW Holdings, Regis Resources and Praemium.

Understanding asset backing

Theoretically, each share represents a share of the company's assets, not counting debt. The *net tangible asset* (NTA) backing is a figure based on the assumption that if the company were dissolved and all its debts paid, these assets would be left to be sold. Intangible assets are not counted in this figure, which many argue makes it almost obsolete (refer to Chapter 5).

The market price of a share should be higher than its NTA backing. Ideally, a price premium would exist because the business is flourishing, selling its goods or services, and being well managed. A company that's trading below its NTA backing is cheap, but this may be an indication that it won't survive. Price-to-NTA (called 'price-to-book' in the US, as in, 'book value') is a good indicator of relative value, but don't use it on its own.

According to FactSet, the average price-to-NTA figure for the S&P/ASX 200 index is 2.8 times — which is higher than the average figure over the past decade, which is 2.5 times.

Watching the cash flow

A company's gross *operating cash flow* comes from selling its product or service. From this, you deduct the cost of these sales, such as paying staff, advertising and marketing costs, research and development expenses, leased assets, and other working capital outlays. Other deductions include any dividends or interest paid and income tax paid. What is left over is net operating cash flow. If net operating cash flow is positive, the company is generating cash. When it's not positive, the company is consuming cash.

REMEMBER

A company with negative cash flow can turn this around and bring in cash through its investing activities or by selling businesses, shares, intellectual property or any other assets. The company can receive cash from dividends on its investments, make further issues of equity or options, or borrow from banks or other sources. However, funds garnered from investing or financing are only an adjunct to a company's main activity, which is selling products or services. If a company can't generate positive operating cash flow, investors become wary of purchasing shares.

Working with technical analysis

Technical analysis is the study of the changes in the price and volume of a share that have occurred over a period of time. Using technical analysis, you can chart the share's history and begin to make extrapolations and projections about the share. Ideally, this kind of analysis allows you to make predictions about where the share price will be at a given point in the future. You can also use technical analysis to study an index or a currency, or any commodity that is traded and sold. For more on technical analysis, see Chapter 16.

TIP

On any share price chart, you can draw a trendline using technical analysis. When an upward trendline is breached, the signal says sell. When a downward trendline is breached, the signal says buy.

Charting resistance and support levels

A *resistance level* is a point on a chart that the share price has historically not been able to break through, and from which the share price has fallen away. If the stock is approaching a resistance level, its track record may indicate a sell. But if the stock manages to move through resistance, it's generally headed higher.

A *support level* is a point on a chart at which the share price has historically rebounded. If the stock is approaching a support level, its track record may indicate a buy. But, if a stock falls through a support level, traders sell the stock as soon as they can because it's heading for a lower support level.

Following a moving average

The *moving average* (MA) can appear on a chart in the form of a curving trendline. If you take a specified period of consecutive price data and divide it by that number of time periods, you get the MA. For example, you can take the last 20 days of closing prices, add them together and then divide by 20 to produce a single price. You can plot this price on the chart alongside the market price.

TIP

A moving average identifies a trend after it has already started and is known as a lagging indicator. When the price closes above the MA, it's a buy signal, and when the price moves below the MA, it's a sell signal.

Understanding breakout trading

A *breakout trade* is a form of share buying based on trend theory. When a stock is on an uptrend, it forms a series of waves with higher highs and higher lows. When the share breaches a wave high or a long-term resistance level it means that the share's uptrend is confirmed. Buying at this point is termed a breakout trade.

REMEMBER

Breakout trading sounds strange to novice investors who think that success comes from finding a stock that's languishing near its lows and watching it return to its highs. Breakout trading seems contrary to logic. How can a share be a bargain when it's at its highest price? The answer is that if the uptrend continues, that current price is ultimately a bargain.

Investing or Trading

Investors and traders have different goals when they buy and sell shares. An *investor* wants to identify stocks that provide maximum capital growth over a long period of time. A *trader* buys and sells shares to make a profit without a preconceived idea of how long to hold the shares. This is how they differ:

» **Investors** look for a promising share prospect with low risk and the possibility of increased capital gain. They research the company, understand risk versus return and know that earnings affect share prices. Investors want the right stocks at the right price, and they believe that sooner or later the share price is going to rise. They're patient and prepared to wait for the true value of their shares to be reflected in the share price.

» **Traders** move funds in and out of the sharemarket — whether they're buying or selling doesn't matter. A trader expects to take an amount of money and use it to buy blocks of stocks, which the trader can sell for a profit. Not all the trades are going to be successful, but an experienced trader with a disciplined approach expects to make more on profitable trades than they lose in unprofitable ones.

Buying as an investor

Investors look for particular elements when buying shares. They want a stock that's predictable and shows growing earnings. It doesn't do the investor much good if the company looks 'cheap' on some measures but doesn't have growing earnings. Investors want a share in a successful company to show a profitable trend within five years. They may allow a year of flat or even declining earnings, but in the remaining four years they want earnings growth of at least 15 to 20 per cent a year. The company's business and the sector of the economy in which the company operates must show the potential to create this earnings growth.

Other factors investors are interested in when buying shares include:

» **Capable management:** Investors want to see a settled board of directors and a management team that can demonstrate a track record of success; they also want to know that these people own shares in the company.

» **Reasonable price:** A share with a rising trend in earnings, which trades on a low P/E ratio relative to its peers and the market, is just what a value-oriented investor looks for.

» **Low gearing:** The lower the borrowings, the better, because the less interest a company pays, the higher the proportion of earnings that's ploughed back into the company — and the greater the dividends for shareholders.

» **High cash flow:** A company with a strong cash flow from its business is effectively self-financing and less prone to external shocks, such as interest rate rises.

REMEMBER

Efficient market theory is a point of view that says the market knows all there is to know about every stock at any time and values each of them accordingly. However, investors know that at any time plenty of undervalued gems (and overvalued stocks) are in the market and, with a bit of diligence, you can find them.

Selling as an investor

Investors sell a share when it delivers the return they expect or if the share's story changes and the risk of holding it increases. Investors also sell because of financial need. You may have to finance an emergency or settle a long-planned-for payment. You enter the sharemarket to see your capital grow and build wealth. You can cash in part of this wealth at any time — for the children's school fees, a new car or an overseas holiday. Shares are a financial asset that store buying power today for future use.

KEEPING THE DIVIDEND

A listed company usually fights tooth and nail to keep one major status symbol. It isn't S&P/ASX 200 index status, it isn't a sumptuous glass-and-granite Sydney or Melbourne CBD address, and it isn't an investment-grade credit rating. What's really sacrosanct — once first achieved — is the dividend.

Companies typically pay dividends as a partial distribution of company profits. Whatever they don't pay as dividends goes into retained earnings, which are reflected in the Statement of Financial Position as an increase in shareholders' equity. Companies face the decision on how much to pay out in dividends — the payout ratio — but many are very unwilling to reduce the dividend when profits are lower, worried that it could be construed by the market as a negative signal in relation to the company's recent performance and future prospects.

This has created the expectation that solid companies — certainly companies that think of themselves as blue chips — always lift their dividend. But it isn't as simple as this. The argument is sometimes made that a hefty payout ratio is a sign of a company that can't find suitable options to invest its capital. The investment-versus-dividend dilemma is a constant one for companies.

This dilemma has only increased over the last decade, as interest rates declined and returns from yield-bearing investments like term deposits ground ever-lower. With income-oriented investors in despair at paltry sub-1 per cent term deposit yields, investors are having to look further and wider for income than ever before. (At the time of writing, the Reserve Bank of Australia [RBA] was forecasting that it would not be able to consider lifting the official cash rate until 2024 at the earliest.) As has been the case for the last decade, the income aspect of share dividends has become a major attraction, with investors prepared to take on board the fact that the dividends cannot be considered certain until they are paid. Dividends are paid at the company's discretion and can be cut at any time — even abandoned.

Some of these 'term deposit refugees' who flocked to the sharemarket looking for yield seemed to believe that share dividends were some sort of annuity that they could bank on; however, this belief started to wane in 2017 when Telstra warned the market to expect lower dividends in future. Telstra maintained its FY17 dividend at 31 cents, but surprised the market with a new dividend policy — the company told investors to expect 22 cents, fully franked, in FY18, including both ordinary and special dividends. Prior to the announcement, the analysts' consensus had expected 29.6 cents in FY18. Given how attached Telstra shareholders were to their dividends, this caused a Telstra Tantrum: Telstra shares fell 20 per cent.

Telstra demonstrated the price risk that income-conscious investors run when they are treating shares as dividend cows. When the dust settled, however, Telstra was still offering investors a decent yield, supported by the attributes of the dividend imputation system. At 6 per cent before franking, that yield was effectively worth 7.2 per cent to a SMSF in accumulation phase (that is, paying 15 per cent tax) and worth 8.6 per cent to a SMSF in pension phase (when it is paying pensions to all its members and is thus untaxed).

After 11 straight years of stable or increased dividends, FY18 saw Telstra's dividend fall — and it also came down in FY19. From 31 cents in FY17, Telstra shareholders received just 16 cents per share in FY19.

The big banks, too, showed that dividends were not 100 per cent certain, with a series of cuts — once considered by investors as unthinkable. ANZ Bank cut its interim dividend in 2016, and slashed the level of franking in its final dividend for FY19 from 100 per cent to 70 per cent.

Westpac cut its final dividend for FY19 from 94 cents to 80 cents, its first dividend cut in a decade. National Australia Bank also bowed to the inevitable and lowered its interim dividend from 99 cents to 83 cents in 2019, its first dividend cut in five years.

Then, in the COVID-19 market crash and economic downturn, the banks (as with many companies) reacted to the drastic circumstances with savage cuts to their dividends. ANZ's FY20 dividend was cut by 62 per cent (from 160 cents in FY19 to 60 cents); National Australia Bank's dividend saw a 64 per cent cut (from 166 cents in FY19 to 60 cents); and Westpac's dividend was slashed by 82 per cent (from 174 cents to 31 cents). In these circumstances, Commonwealth Bank only cutting its FY20 dividend by 31 per cent (from 431 cents in FY19 to 298 cents) looked like largesse showered on its grateful shareholders. After these bruising encounters with economic reality, even the most starry-eyed, income-oriented investor had to admit that equity dividends cannot be considered totally reliable as an income stream.

The other main risk of relying on shares for income is that while you are holding the shares for yield, the share price can fall — just ask Telstra's legion of retail shareholders, who watched their yield source fall 58 per cent in value between February 2015 and June 2018. And of course, every dividend-paying company fell in a heap in February–March 2020, with the market crash.

Dividends aren't a bonus for owning shares; over long periods, the dividend return typically delivers just over half of your total return from owning shares.

Investors who adhere to the buy-and-hold strategy don't want to sell. They're trying to replicate the miracle of Westfield Holdings (refer to Chapter 3). If you had invested the equivalent of $1,000 in the float of Westfield in September 1960, and reinvested every dividend and bonus that Westfield had paid to you, by December 2017, when Westfield left the sharemarket (taken over by French-Dutch commercial real estate company Unibail-Rodamco), your investment would have been worth $440 million.

REMEMBER

You can't take the money with you, but shares can play a major part in building inheritable wealth for your family. Even if you're a buy-and-hold investor, you're wise to continually monitor your share portfolio. Ask yourself if you'd buy the stock today. If the answer's no, you should think about selling it and reinvesting the proceeds in a stock you'd like to buy.

The doyen of the buy-and-hold strategy is Warren Buffett of the US investment company Berkshire Hathaway. Buffett is a phenomenally successful money manager, and his company has what it calls 'permanent holdings'. But Buffett does sell when a stock is overvalued or even undervalued. According to Philip Fisher, you hold on to a share until it has done the job, or its circumstances change and you don't think it ever will do its job.

Buying as a trader

If you buy a stock expecting to sell it in a matter of days, even hours, then you're not an investor, you're a trader. Trading in the sharemarket is okay if you know what you're doing and accept the risks. If you try to compress the wealth-creating power of the sharemarket into a short time frame, the sharemarket gods can get very angry.

Traders don't worry too much about the fundamentals of a company, particularly if they're *day traders*. As the name suggests, *day trading* is the buying and selling of shares within the same trading day. Day traders are also not too concerned with the P/E ratio of the stock. The P/E ratio is only a consideration for those who are committing money to the stock for a period of years. Traders are concerned with price movement and volume; that is, the technical indicators and the price momentum of the stock.

WARNING

Day trading is a particularly difficult and stressful form of share investing that's decidedly not for the novice or the long-term average investor. Although knowing how day traders operate may be interesting, I must caution you that this kind of investing is only for professionals.

Selling as a trader

A trader sells when their shareholding drops to a specified point. When a trader buys, they put a *stop-loss* (or 'falling sell') in place that stipulates the amount of loss they're prepared to take before selling the shares. Stops are set in terms of a dollar (or percentage) amount, or they're set using some form of technical parameter, such as when a moving average is crossed. Although the trading mantra says to let profits run, a trader may also decide, after reaching a certain amount of gain, to get out of the trade and look for the next profitable share. Instead of a stop-loss, you can call this a *stop-profit* because that's exactly what it does. To the trader, though, the operative word is 'profit'.

Relying on Your Broker

You can't rely completely on your stockbroker. Although some of their buy recommendations may be good investments, selling is another matter. Stockbrokers talk about underweighting a stock, lightening it, reducing it or even trimming it, but they rarely bring themselves to say 'sell'. Some subscription-based investment websites and newsletters, however, are wholly independent and answer only to their subscribers, and are quite willing to make 'sell' calls.

Sell calls can cause problems for a broking firm. Companies don't like having their shares rated 'sell'. A disgruntled company can blacklist a broking firm from analysts' briefings, conference calls and site visits. If the broking firm has an underwriting arm, a sell recommendation can be even more problematic. The broking firm can forget about any underwriting work from companies it describes as sells. Supporting issues in the after-market (the days after a stock is floated) is an important part of getting underwriting — and if the broker has been unfriendly, the work won't be there.

REMEMBER

Brokers make their money when people buy or sell shares. In fairness, brokers spend more time and effort on buy recommendations because they're directed at an unlimited number of people; that is, anyone who sees the recommendation is a possible buyer. However, only those people who own the shares can sell them — unless they're short-sellers (see the sidebar 'Selling short' for more).

A common complaint of the small investor is that 'my broker never tells me when to sell'. Even if brokers were convinced that a share was about to fall and had the time to call every client on their lists, they probably couldn't get to every client before the share price fell. Brokers naturally wants to take care of their best clients first because they pay their wages.

SELLING SHORT

'He who sells what isn't his'n, Must make it good or go to prison.' This mantra of legendary 19th century Wall Street trader Daniel Drew is no longer true in terms of prison, but anyone who sells shares short and gets it wrong still pays a hefty price.

Short-selling is a reverse of what you're meant to do on the sharemarket. Short-selling is selling a stock first, and buying back the stock later. You don't have the stock when you sell it; you have to borrow it from someone and then sell it. Then you buy it back. Short-selling is rife in the US markets but not so popular in Australia.

Short-sellers profit if the price falls. Then their selling price is more than their buying price. They pay their fees and borrowing costs and pocket the difference.

If the price rises, the short-sellers are in trouble. To cover their short position — because they have to deliver the shares they've sold — they have to buy the shares back on the market. If the price has risen, they've paid more than their selling price. For this reason, short-selling is definitely not for the inexperienced sharemarket participant.

Because you don't own the shares when you sell them short, you must borrow them from someone. Stockbrokers and institutional investors can lend the shares to you, but they charge a borrowing fee and also require collateral for the loan. If your broker permits short-selling, the Australian Securities Exchange (ASX) requires the broker to obtain margin cover of 20 per cent of the value of the trade before placing your short-sold order. If the price of the shares you've short-sold rises by more than 10 per cent, you must provide additional margin cover of 100 per cent to your broker.

Because of the ASX's T+2 settlement period, a short-sold position must be settled within two days; if not, a hefty fail fee will apply. Therefore, to make a profit, the price of the shares must fall within two days. You buy the shares, deliver them, pay your broker's fees and borrowing costs and pocket the difference.

The ASX and the Australian Securities and Investments Commission (ASIC) maintain a list of the approved securities that may be short-sold, and which shares are being short-sold. In early 2020, 519 stocks were on the list, which is updated daily. No more than 15 per cent of the shares on issue may be short-sold. Short-selling is not allowed when:

- The stock is under a takeover offer.
- The order price is lower than the last sale price.

Short-selling is a common strategy employed by managers of hedge funds and absolute return funds, many of whom run long-short funds, which simply aim to capture returns from both rising and falling share prices, within the same fund. In this way, the funds can, in theory, generate a positive return no matter how the sharemarket (or other financial markets) are performing.

Such funds have been termed alternative investments and rose in popularity among retail investors annoyed at the losses posted by their Australian and international equity funds in the early 2000s. But not all of these funds were able to perform well in the GFC, losing too much on the 'long' side.

Short-selling was blamed for some of the excessive volatility at the peak of the GFC market turmoil in late 2008, and for some of the large price falls in stocks targeted by the short-sellers, particularly financial stocks. Some short-selling by hedge funds was deliberately targeted at stocks in which key executives had margin loans to buy their shares; the short-selling triggered margin calls, which pushed the share price even lower and had a disastrous impact on market sentiment.

In response, in September 2008, ASIC and the ASX temporarily banned short-selling. The ban was lifted in May 2009 for 'covered' short-selling, where the sellers had borrowed the stock before selling it; but 'naked' short-selling (where the sellers never even borrowed the stock) remained banned. Following the ban, ASIC and the ASX introduced stricter disclosure rules for covered short-selling.

Because of the clampdown on short-selling, many brokers no longer offer it unless the investors are 'wholesale' investors, meaning that they are either professional investors or are investing a minimum of about $500,000.

In the funds management world, short-selling is a perfectly legitimate strategy. A 'long-short' manager who decides that a stock is overvalued will borrow the stock, sell it, and expect to be able to buy it at a lower price before returning the stock to the lender, thus making a profit on the transaction. This approach simply leverages the manager's analytical work — which leads it to think that the shares are overvalued — to turn a profit.

The company being 'shorted' might not like it — but if the shorting is done ethically, it can both assist the market with appropriate price discovery, and provide the manager with portfolio returns that are not correlated with the market index. For these benefits, short-sellers theoretically run unlimited risk — for example, a surprise takeover bid that sends the share price of the short-sold company spiking can hurt them very badly — and for these reasons, it is a specialised activity that requires a very disciplined approach.

Equity (share) fund managers are always putting prospective stock purchases through painstaking research and analysis to determine whether they will buy them or not. If the manager decides not to buy it, that is usually because they have formed a negative view

(continued)

(continued)

of the stock. The long-short manager that 'shorts' the stock simply takes this negative view a bit further, actively seeking to profit from it. Long-short managers often talk about short-selling requiring a different mindset to 'long-only' (that is, buying stocks and only selling them when they have reached a certain price target) investment.

Of course, the same concept — deciding that a share price is more likely to fall than rise — can also be employed by individuals.

Many traders prefer to short-sell through online share trading platforms. In Australia, two main products are used to do this.

Contracts for difference

Contracts for difference (CFDs) are derivative investment products that allow you to speculate on prices without actually owning the shares. This means that CFD traders can profit whether the prices of stocks, commodities or currencies are going up or down. However, investors must understand that CFDs are complex and risky financial instruments, and many investors lose money this way. Based on a sample of 12 Australian licensed CFD providers, an ASIC report at the height of the COVID-19 crash estimated that retail clients lost just over $428 million gross (or $234 million net) during the week 16–22 March 2020. The 12 CFD providers studied represent about 84 per cent market share of retail CFD trading.

ASIC found that many retail CFD client accounts went into negative balances in the week commencing 16 March 2020. A total of 5,448 retail client accounts of the 12 providers in the sample (or 2 per cent of their retail client accounts that traded during that week) went into a negative balance to the value of over –$4 million in aggregate. That is, they lost their initial investment and owed a further $4 million to the CFD providers.

Options trading

You can buy an exchange-traded option (ETO) on a stock that allows you to sell it at the initial market price within the option's expiry date. If the price goes down, you sell, buy back at the new price and make a profit. If the price goes up, you don't sell at all and only lose the value of the option, thus limiting the risk. With traditional short-selling, you can buy back whenever you want (unless the owner of the stock claims it back), whereas options normally have a fairly short expiry date.

Looking and Listening

Knowing when to buy and sell shares means that you need to be attuned to what is happening in the business community. You need to do your research, and you also need to be aware of events such as takeovers, profit warnings, index changes and more.

Analysing takeovers

A hostile takeover bid is an emotion-packed event for the sharemarket (refer to Chapter 11). If more than one company is involved and a bidding war ensues, the rest of the sharemarket eagerly watches the protagonists slug it out. The shareholders of the sought-after company have the most to gain, mainly because a takeover usually boosts the share price.

When a company's share price is beaten down, or one of its competitors sells its business for a large amount of money, speculators look for possible takeovers. Market rumours swirl around potential takeovers, and some traders buy on rumour, hoping to sell on fact.

REMEMBER

Any company listed on the sharemarket is up for sale, from the biggest blue chip to the smallest minerals explorer. Anybody can come along, any day, and lay money on the table. If the price is right, the board has a duty to recommend that shareholders accept it.

Taking note of profit warnings

A company announcing a profit warning — an imminent downturn in profits — means its investment story has changed for the worse (refer to Chapter 11). The opposite is true for an upgraded profit forecast. Traders often act quickly when they hear a profit warning. However, as an investor, if you don't believe that the long-term outlook for the company has altered and yet the stock is suddenly substantially cheaper, you may want to buy more shares. When a profit warning does alter the long-term prospects of a company, you can then think seriously about selling the shares.

Watching index changes

Thanks to the growth of index funds and exchange-traded funds (ETFs), changes to the composition of the major indices bring both guaranteed buying of the stocks added and guaranteed selling of the stocks discarded, as institutions alter their portfolios to reflect the new make-up of the index. Trading on index changes is short-lived, but generally this trading produces relatively reliable price gains.

Index provider S&P Australia rebalances its indices on a quarterly basis. The quarterly rebalancing is closely watched, as it can directly result in tens of billions of dollars of investment allocation changes in funds that track the indices. The most recent change to the S&P indices was in September 2021. In the larger-cap S&P/ASX 50 index, A2 Milk, AGL Energy and Ampol were dropped, and ResMed and gaming company Tabcorp were added. (There was an additional removal because the index was carrying an extra constituent following the demerger of Endeavour Group from Woolworths in June 2021.) The same factor affected the S&P/ASX 100 index, from which Boral and Beach Energy were removed, with Virgin Money UK plc coming in.

In the benchmark S&P/ASX 200 index, the September 2021 rebalancing saw troubled software firm Nuix depart, along with gold miner Westgold Resources, early childhood education specialist G8 Education and resources contractor NRW Holdings, to be replaced by payments group Tyro Payments, tourism operator SeaLink Travel (now known as Kelsian Group), funds manager stable Pinnacle Investment Management Group and residential community operator Lifestyle Communities.

In May 2020, global index provider MSCI announced changes to its main MSCI Australia 'country' index, under which Alumina, Bendigo & Adelaide Bank, Boral, Challenger, Flight Centre, Harvey Norman, Incitec Pivot and Worley were removed, and Afterpay and gold mining pair Evolution Mining and Northern Star included. That change triggered large share sales, with 10 per cent of some of the affected companies changing hands on the final day before the changes took effect.

Capitalising on turnaround situations

The sharemarket is hard on a poorly performing stock, which usually means the company is in difficult straits. Later, when the company has a new management team, has cleaned up its balance sheet and is back with a plan for business growth, the sharemarket may still be ignoring it. This situation is one in which an astute buyer can make a lucrative investment if they know what they're doing. Investors who follow market fundamentals can benefit from these turnarounds.

Being a contrarian investor

Contrarian investing is buying when buying seems absolutely the wrong thing to do and selling when exuberance reigns. Psychologically, a contrarian investor is going against the herd instinct, which requires considerable self-belief. However, as it turned out, selling all your technology shares in March 2000, or buying back into the battered blue chips in March 2009, or buying back into the market in March 2020, was a very wise thing to do. It just took a lot of guts at the time!

REMEMBER

Contrarian investors can make huge gains if they're brave and patient. Contrarians have great faith in their process of share assessment. However, as the fund manager John Neff says: 'Don't bask in the warmth of just being different. There is a thin line between being a contrarian and being just plain stubborn. At times, the crowd is right. Eventually, you have to be right on fundamentals to be rewarded.'

Watching for insider activity

When individual board members buy or sell shares in their company, investors watch carefully. Naturally, shareholders are happier when board members buy rather than sell shares. In fairness, directors should be allowed to raise cash by selling shares without setting off the market. If directors change their shareholdings, this news has to be announced on the stock exchange but not on the actual day of the transaction; these changes are listed as notices of record. Investors watch the transactions of insiders in the hope of detecting a trend; investors want to know whether a transaction is a one-off or whether a flurry of buying or selling is about to occur.

Taxing Considerations

Letting tax considerations drive investment decisions is always a bad move. Whether you're buying or selling shares, your main objective is to buy future growth. If you concentrate only on gaining a tax advantage, you may lose out in the long term. By all means consult an accountant about your tax liabilities in buying and selling shares, but don't make your decisions based on tax advice solely.

Minimising capital gains tax

Some people decide not to sell profitable shares because they don't want to trigger a capital gains tax (CGT) liability. You can't avoid this tax unless the shares you sell were bought before the law was introduced (19 September 1985). Nothing can protect capital gains from a sudden change in market sentiment, which can turn a gain into a capital loss very quickly.

Selling to take a tax loss

May and June are known as the tax-related selling season. At this time, investors may bite the bullet on shares they're holding at a loss. If they choose, they can take the loss and offset it against capital gains earned in that tax year, or carry the loss forward for future use. Then, if they want to stay with the shares, they can buy them again at the current price.

Offsetting your annual tax with a capital loss is a perfectly legal deduction. However, CGT can be a problem if it overwhelms your investment strategy. Financial advisers always warn against such decisions. (See Chapter 18 for a guide to tax and shares.)

Chapter **8**

Buying What You Know

If you want to buy shares, you're not starved for choice. About 2,200 shares are available on the Australian sharemarket and more are being added every month (of course, companies occasionally get delisted, too). These companies cover virtually every activity that can legitimately be conducted for profit. The ASX presents a dazzling array of opportunities. You can't help but be impressed by the ingenuity and potential on display.

However, you can't own everything, so don't try to stretch a portfolio too far. If you own 20 stocks, you own too many. Diversification is great, but it has its limits. A share portfolio becomes difficult to monitor properly when it grows beyond 15 stocks. That means if you're taking charge of your own sharemarket investments, you have to narrow your sights compared to an institutional investor who may hold 50 or more stocks. In this chapter, I tell you all about the different types of sharemarket sectors and stocks, and show you how to choose what goes in your portfolio. (For more specialised sharemarket products, turn to Chapter 9.)

Acquiring Ordinary Shares

Ordinary shares, those tiny building blocks of a company's equity, can be anything but ordinary in their performance. Most activity on the sharemarket centres on ordinary shares, or what the Americans call *common stock*.

Each ordinary share entitles the owner to:

>> A proportional share of the company's profit after expenses

>> A proportional share of the company's assets after the liabilities have been met in the event of liquidation of the company

>> A vote for the board of directors in the company

REMEMBER

The ordinary share is one of the great inventions of the financial world. It may be ordinary, it may be common, but an ordinary share is a fabulous opening to the wealth created in the economy.

Buying blue chips

Named after the highest-value chip in poker, *blue chips* are the sharemarket's elite stocks. Blue chips have an established track record over many years of consistently rising profits and fully franked dividends.

The blue chips have large market capitalisations, which guarantees plenty of liquidity in the market. They boast well-established businesses, high-quality assets and — usually — good management. Blue chips typically have high dividend yields, in the range of 4 to 7 per cent, with an average of 5 to 6 per cent (except the likes of biotech CSL, which is more of a capital-growth stock than a yield generator). Over time, blue chips usually prove to be reliable wealth generators.

WARNING

Blue chips sometimes fall from grace. At various times, companies considered blue chips, such as Westpac, BHP and AMP, have all turned in billion-dollar losses and lost their blue-chip status. As if a 20-year litany of poor investment performance, strategic blunders, poor acquisitions, write-offs and at least one botched takeover wasn't enough, AMP's diabolical testimony in the Royal Commission into Misconduct in the Banking, Superannuation and Financial Services Industry in 2018 (refer to Chapter 4) left its credibility shattered. AMP was officially an ex-blue chip — finally proving to investors that a household-name brand does not a blue chip make. From a peak of $45 on its first day of trading on the ASX in 1998, AMP has slid all the way to $1.07.

QBE Insurance also cashed-in its blue chip, with its share price spending the 2010s sliding backwards. The big four banks — ANZ Banking Group, Commonwealth Bank, National Australia Bank (NAB) and Westpac — are beloved by investors for their high dividend yields, but in May 2020, they were all showing a negative total return over the last five years. That's not a blue chip stock. A commodity price slump in 2015 took BHP and Rio Tinto down badly, hurting their status.

The 177-year-old newspaper giant Fairfax Media — publisher of The Age, the Sydney Morning Herald and The Australian Financial Review — was once considered an unassailable blue chip because of the reliable earnings from the 'rivers of gold', its newspapers' classified advertising revenue. But the company was not able to react quickly enough when three internet-based start-up businesses stole the lion's share of the rivers of gold out from under its nose — jobs website seek.com.au (ASX code: SEK), real estate sales website realestate.com.au (owned by REA Group, code REA), and auto sales website carsales.com (CAR). As a final humiliation, when Fairfax merged with Nine Entertainment Company in December 2018, its market value, at $1.45 billion, was outweighed more than 12 times by the combined value of the three companies that had disrupted and fatally weakened it.

Telstra has been Australia's largest and most profitable telco and a solid dividend payer but, despite this, Telstra's shares have been disappointing performers since the company was floated on the ASX following an offer of shares from the federal government in 1997 at the $3.30 level (and subsequent sales at $7.40, in 1999, and $3.60 in 2006). A series of disastrous expansions — including a failed move into Asia that lost the company $3 billion — conspired to cut the market value of Telstra in half. Intense competition, new technologies and the government's decision to build the NBN (National Broadband Network) have all affected the sector and Telstra — particularly over the last decade.

Adding to the NBN challenge, the announcement in 2017 of TPG's ambitious plans to become Australia's fourth mobile network provider also weighed heavily on Telstra's share price. Telstra has had to take huge amounts of costs — mainly in the form of employee numbers — out of the business. Telstra has positioned itself as market leader in the rollout of 5G technology, and its rollout of this network will boost its earnings, but Telstra's share price has done very little in recent years — especially for the long-suffering investors who bought into the 'T2' second-tranche float in 1999. In May 2020, it was showing a five-year total return of −7.4 per cent a year; and a three-year total return of −5.7 per cent a year. A better performance since then has put Telstra in the black over one- and three-year periods, but at the time of writing, an investor who'd held TLS for five years had been rewarded with a total return (even with the dividend flow) of −3 per cent a year. Blue chip? I don't think so.

None of the big four banks has performed well over the past five years, at the time of writing: CBA showed a total return of 10.4 per cent a year in that time; ANZ, 7 per cent a year; NAB, 5.6 per cent a year; and Westpac, 1 per cent a year. Investors in the latter two effectively needed their dividends to make any money at all. That's not what a blue chip should do.

In fact, there's been a bit of a rethink in recent years about what constitutes a blue chip. While blue chip status may once have been closely linked to size, some of the giants in the S&P/ASX 20 have given investors quite poor returns in recent years. It doesn't depend on a hefty dividend yield, either: CSL pays a relatively paltry dividend yield — around 1 per cent — but very few long-term holders of the stock would complain about their total returns.

If you look at some of the really strong performers in recent years among the relatively large stocks, you see five-year total return numbers such as 62 per cent a year for diagnostic imaging technology company Pro Medicus; 59.1 per cent a year for Fortescue Metals Group; and 53.4 per cent a year for Kogan.com. Even a 34.3 per cent a year five-year stretch from home appliance manufacturer and marketer Breville Group and 32.8 per cent a year from sleep breathing-aid maker ResMed start to look very consistent.

There may well be a changing of the guard underway in terms of what really are blue chips. Diversified miners BHP and Rio Tinto are holding their own in terms of blue chip status — with five-year returns of 27.7 per cent a year and 28.7 per cent a year respectively — as are logistics property specialist Goodman Group (27.5 per cent a year), Wesfarmers (21.4 per cent a year) and Macquarie Group (21.1 per cent a year). Four-wheel-drive accessories maker ARB Corporation (22.7 per cent a year) and REA Group (21.3 per cent a year) are coming along behind them. Even some of the 'growth' superstars covered in Chapter 5 may in time become blue chips — if they deliver consistent above-average returns.

The other thing that investors must remember about blue chips is that when the market is being routed across the board as it was in 2008, and in early 2020, even the bluest of chips are not immune. The sharemarket is the most volatile of the asset markets — and the blue chips, as the highest profile and most liquid stocks, can be most affected by this volatility. Indeed, because the expectations are higher on blue chips, they can be savagely treated in the short term if they disappoint the market. If you expect a blue chip share only to rise and never to fall in value, you've got another thought coming. Fortescue Metals, for example, at present only mines iron ore. At some point, the record high iron ore prices that currently prevail will weaken as Brazil returns to full production and other mines are brought into production in other parts of the world. Investors have to consider the possibility that Fortescue's future returns may weaken along with iron ore prices.

WARNING

Blue chip stocks are exposed to the same systemic risk as any other stock on the market. The blue chips usually lead the market higher, but when the market suffers a correction, the blue chip stocks plunge too. You can do poorly in blue chips if you buy and sell them at the wrong time, so you need to watch these stocks as closely as your other stocks.

In terms of popularity, the investing public certainly appears to believe that Telstra, AMP and the big banks are still blue chips. According to the most recent company annual reports, Telstra is the most widely held Australian stock, with 1.27 million shareholders (605,000 of them with fewer than 1,000 shares), followed by Commonwealth Bank, with 884,300 shareholders (670,000 with fewer than 1,000 shares), and AMP, with 708,000 shareholders (481,000 with fewer than 1,000 shares). Westpac, NAB and ANZ Bank are next, and after them come BHP, Wesfarmers and Woolworths.

In contrast, the sharemarket's bluest chip, CSL, has a relatively small share register, with 205,290 shareholders, of which 179,000 own fewer than 1,000 shares. Despite its stunning record of capital appreciation, CSL is not a big dividend source, and its dividend is unfranked — which goes a long way to explaining its relative unpopularity.

Looking at industrial and resources companies

Traditionally, the main kinds of companies listed on the stock exchange have been divided into industrials and resources. Resources companies are easy to identify; they include mining and petroleum companies that drill, find, extract, process and sell Australia's mineral commodities. Any company engaged in these activities is a resource company; one that isn't engaged in these activities is an industrial company.

Choosing industrials

The industrial part of the sharemarket is the largest by value and by number of companies. These companies are involved in a vast array of activities — not only manufacturing products but also developing drugs and diagnostic devices, banking, making wine, processing waste, setting up telecommunication networks, farming fish, selling software, collecting financial receivables, building power plants and operating ferries. The more you investigate the Australian stock market — especially the world beneath the top 200 — the more the variety of what listed companies do will amaze you. You want a feel of the different types of companies that make up the sharemarket? It's time to examine the Global Industry Classification Standard (GICS) sectors of the S&P/ASX 200 index.

FINANCIALS: BANKS AND FINANCIAL SERVICES

At the top, the dominant GICS sector is Financials, which accounts for about 30 per cent of the S&P/ASX 200 index, up from 26.4 per cent in 2020, but down from 41 per cent in 2016.

The Financials sector includes 289 companies, coming from three industry groups — banks, insurance companies and 'diversified financials', which covers diversified financial services companies, asset managers and consumer finance companies.

Naturally, the Financials sector heavyweights are the big four banks — Commonwealth Bank, Westpac, NAB and ANZ, in order of size — as well as Australia's home-grown investment bank Macquarie Group. (An investment bank doesn't take deposits and make loans; instead, an investment bank trades on its own account, delivers corporate advice and financial services packages, and manages investment opportunities.) However, Macquarie Group has changed its business model since the GFC, such that the annuity-style businesses (funds management, and banking and wealth products) generate more than two-thirds of its revenue — as opposed to 30 per cent a decade ago.

The sector also contains the operator of the stock exchange, ASX, which is listed on itself; the big insurers Insurance Australia Group, Suncorp Group, QBE Insurance and Steadfast Group; health insurers Medibank Private and NIB; funds management companies Magellan Financial Group, Platinum Asset Management, Pendal Group and Janus Henderson; financial services companies AMP and Challenger; the smaller banks, Bendigo & Adelaide Bank and Bank of Queensland; the buy-now-pay-later (BNPL) cohort, led by Afterpay (which was replaced on the stock market in 2022 after its takeover by US firm Block, Inc. was completed: Afterpay shareholders now hold Block's ASX-listed CHESS Depositary Interests, or CDIs) and Zip Co; and the big listed investment companies (LICs), Australian Foundation Investment Company (AFIC), Argo Investments and Milton Corporation. The 223 exchange-traded funds (ETFs) are in here as well, which bulks up the sector's numbers, and a variety of smaller financial services businesses round out this part of the sector. (Chapter 9 covers ETFs and LICs in more detail.)

REMEMBER

Banks receive and pay the prevailing price of money in the form of interest. A rise in interest rates means added revenue on the asset side of the bank balance sheet and extra cost on the liability side. Banks can lend more than they borrow because they can create credit. Bankers generally don't like high interest rates because they raise the cost of borrowing and lending money. However, depending on the liability costs, a bank can do well in a rising interest rate environment. For example, if a bank has a high proportion of its liabilities in savings and cheque accounts paying a low interest rate, an interest rate rise will increase the bank's profits.

Banks also have non-interest income — revenue generated not from borrowing and lending but from their fees and charges. However, this income has declined markedly as a proportion of total revenue, under intense competition and greater consumer awareness, and the banks have reverted to greater reliance on interest income — non-interest income accounts for about 20 per cent of the major banks' revenue, down from 41 per cent in 2006.

The insurance influence on the sharemarket grew in the 1990s with the demutualisation of several large mutually owned life insurance offices. These companies changed their status from mutually owned societies to companies limited by shares; shares were then offered free to their policyholders pro rata according to the policies held. In this way, AMP, AXA Asia–Pacific (formerly National Mutual) and Insurance Australia Group (formerly NRMA Insurance) migrated to the sharemarket, bringing millions of first-time investors with them. In March 2011, AXA Asia–Pacific merged its Australian businesses with AMP and sold its Asian businesses to its French parent company, AXA.

MATERIALS

The Materials sector accounts for 20.3 per cent of the S&P/ASX 200 index. The Materials sector is a biggie, with 715 companies, but it's something of a grab bag, covering Metals and Mining, the Chemicals industry, Construction Materials suppliers, the Container and Packaging industry, and the Paper and Forest Products industry for forestry plantation, paper and timber companies.

The mining industry provides the largest materials stocks, with the big global miner BHP — producing iron ore, thermal (electricity) and metallurgical (steel-making) coal, copper, nickel, and oil and gas — the largest stock in the sector. (BHP has pledged to exit the thermal coal business by 2023.) BHP is followed by iron ore heavyweight Fortescue Metals Group and global operator Rio Tinto — which produces iron ore, copper, bauxite (aluminium ore) and aluminium, diamonds, and industrial minerals (borates, titanium dioxide and salt). Big gold miners Newcrest Mining and Northern Star (having acquired fellow gold miner Saracen in 2020) are also in the top ten, as is South32, which was spun-off by BHP in 2015 — it produces aluminium/alumina (aluminium oxide), manganese, nickel, silver, lead, coking coal (another term for steelmaking coal) and thermal coal. The fifth-biggest stock in the index is building materials company James Hardie, the world's largest maker of fibre cement products. Rounding out the Materials top ten are global packaging giant Amcor; iron ore and lithium producer Mineral Resources; and global steel products manufacturer BlueScope Steel.

Gold producers Evolution Mining, Regis Resources, St Barbara, Silver Lake Resources, Gold Road Resources, Perseus Mining, Resolute Resources and Alkane Resources are in this sector as well, as is Alumina, which owns 40 per cent of Alcoa World Alumina & Chemicals (AWAC), the world's largest alumina and bauxite business. Also included are copper/gold producer Oz Minerals, nickel/copper/gold miner and lithium producer IGO, nickel producer Western Areas, mineral sands and rare earths producer Iluka Resources and copper/gold miner Sandfire Resources. Lithium producers Allkem and Pilbara Minerals, Zimbabwe-based platinum producer Zimplats, manganese miner Jupiter Mines, manganese miner and processor OM Holdings, lithium/tantalite ore miner Pilbara Minerals, tin miner Metals X, and graphite (in Mozambique) and battery anode material (in the US) producer Syrah Resources are also all in the Materials sector, as are a host of junior gold producers and explorers.

Industrial representatives in the Materials sector also include Orica, the world's biggest supplier of explosives and blasting systems to the resources and construction markets; construction materials companies Boral, CSR, Brickworks, Adbri (the former Adelaide Brighton) and Fletcher Building; agricultural chemicals firms Nufarm and Incitec Pivot; metals recycler Sims; and packaging companies Orora and Pact Group.

TIP

Because the Materials sector is such an eclectic mix, many investors prefer to break out the Resources sector by using the S&P/ASX 200 Resources index, which picks up miners and metal producers, as well as oil and gas companies involved in the oil and gas industry, and the production of other fuels, such as coal and uranium. Several ETFs track this index.

HEALTH CARE

The Health Care sector represents 10.1 per cent of the S&P/ASX 200 index, and contains 182 companies, made up of two industry groups: the Health Care Equipment & Services industry, covering healthcare equipment, supplies, providers, services and technology companies; and the 'biotech' industry, which is Pharmaceuticals, Biotechnology and Life Science. This is the industry that develops drugs and diagnostic compounds and devices.

At the top of the Health Care sector are big industrial companies such as CSL; diagnostics and imaging company Sonic Healthcare; New Zealand-based Fisher & Paykel Healthcare, which makes products used in respiratory care, acute care, surgery and the treatment of obstructive sleep apnoea; global hearing implant maker Cochlear; global hospital operator Ramsay Health Care; ResMed, a leading global maker of devices and software solutions that help treat and manage sleep apnoea, chronic obstructive pulmonary disease and other respiratory conditions; diagnostic imaging technology company Pro Medicus; global gloves and protective personal equipment (PPE) maker Ansell; Kiwi-based marketer, wholesaler and distributor of healthcare, medical and pharmaceutical products EBOS Group; medical centre, pathology lab and diagnostic imaging centre operator Healius; and Kiwi retirement village company Summerset Group Holdings.

Then come the biotechs, which garner a lot of attention from speculative investors trying to emulate some of the Australian biotech industry's success stories, such as Biota, which developed Relenza, an influenza vaccine, becoming the first Australian biotechnology company to take a modern drug to market; and Viralytics, which developed an immunotherapy called Cavatak from a common cold virus and aimed it at cancer. Biota went from a few cents in 1990 to a peak of $7 in 1999 (although when it left the ASX in 2012 to relist in the US, it had retraced to 83 cents). From starting life on the stock exchange in 2006 at 15 cents, Viralytics was taken over by pharma giant Merck in 2018 at $1.75 — Merck's bid was 160 per cent above the share price, and the $500 million deal is an example of the nirvana to which Australian biotechs aspire. Merck still has Cavatak in trials but has shown that when used in combination with immune checkpoint therapies like Merck's Keytruda, Cavatak can almost double the rate at which cancer is destroyed.

Investors love to speculate on what will be Australia's next biotech success story. In 2020, the latest candidate was stem-cell therapy developer Mesoblast, which had reported success in trials of its potential treatment for critically ill COVID-19 patients — a bone marrow product called remestemcel-L, which is intravenously infused in patients suffering from acute respiratory distress syndrome (ARDS), the most common cause of death from COVID-19 infections. Under 'emergency compassionate use' protocols, patients at New York's Mount Sinai hospital with ARDS were given remestemcel-L intravenously, and the results were much better than those seen in ventilator-dependent COVID-19 patients receiving standard-of-care treatment. On the back of these results, Mesoblast began enrolling patients in a Phase II/III clinical trial in more than 20 medical centres across the US to 'rigorously confirm' whether remestemcel-L provided a survival benefit in patients with moderate/severe ARDS due to COVID-19. From $2.10 at the start of the year, Mesoblast shares had pushed to $5.22 by August 2020.

It was all heading in the right direction — but Mesoblast gave shareholders three unpleasant experiences in just a few months. The first was in August 2020, when the US Food and Drug Administration (FDA) released a briefing document that cast doubt over whether the company's remestemcel-L product would pass through a scheduled meeting with the Oncologic Drugs Advisory Committee (ODAC). That stripped 31 per cent from the Mesoblast share price in a day.

The FDA caused more problems for the Mesoblast share price in October 2020 when it announced that Mesoblast would have to conduct an additional randomised control study before it would approve remestemcel-L for use. Mesoblast's shares plummeted 37 per cent on that news.

Finally, in December, Mesoblast told the stock exchange that its trial — to test if remestemcel-L could help reduce mortality in COVID-19 patients — had failed to achieve its objectives. This time the drop was 36 per cent, again in one day. At time of writing, Mesoblast is soldiering on with remestemcel-L, and there is a possibility of a deal with pharmaceutical giant Novartis. But the three canings of the share price in 2020 understandably shook the faith of many investors, and the shares are down 60 per cent on that August 2020 peak. (See the sidebar 'Playing the long game' for more on testing phases and trials.)

PLAYING THE LONG GAME

On the long path to commercialisation of drugs, diagnostics and medical devices, success in biotech investment requires patience. A pharmaceutical company is required to conduct extensive pre-clinical laboratory testing before testing a compound in humans can begin. Pre-clinical trials involve thorough testing of the compound in animals (for example, mice) to prove the compound appears to be safe, and possibly effective in mammals.

Pre-clinical testing usually takes three to four years, and has a success rate of about 1 per cent. If successful, the company provides the relevant information to the US Food and Drug Administration (FDA), requesting approval to commence testing the drug in humans — known as an Investigational New Drug (IND) application.

If the FDA approves the IND, the company is cleared to test the compound in human volunteers in Phase I clinical trials. These trials aim to determine how the drug acts in the human body, and to investigate any side effects that may occur as dosage levels are increased. Phase I usually lasts from several months to one year. According to the Biotechnology Innovation Organization (BIO) in the US — the largest biotechnology industry organisation in the world — the probability of Phase I trials moving to Phase II is 52 per cent.

Because the US is the biggest market for pharmaceuticals, the FDA is considered the gold standard of approval. Australian companies can get approval from the Therapeutic Goods Administration (TGA) in Australia, or gain the CE Mark for approval for sale in the European Economic Area — and there are similar things for other countries too — but if you want to market a drug, a diagnostic or a device in the US, the biggest market for pharmaceuticals, you must have FDA approval.

Once a drug has been shown to be safe in Phase I, Phase II trials aim to evaluate the efficacy — the clinical effect — of the new treatment, in a testing period that may last from several months to two years. Phase II trials determine the dosage and treatment schedules. Phase II is where most experimental drugs fail — only 29 per cent of drug candidates successfully complete both Phase I and Phase II testing, on the BIO's numbers.

Phase III trials then seek to confirm the clinical benefits of the drug in large numbers of patients; this large-scale testing aims to provide a more thorough understanding of the drug's effectiveness, benefits, and the range and severity of possible adverse side effects. Phase III trials usually take one to four years to complete.

Upon successful completion of Phase III — which the BIO says 58 per cent of drug candidates that get that far manage — the pharmaceutical company submits the results of all the studies to the FDA so as to obtain a New Drug Application (NDA)/Biologic License Application (BLA), which means that the drug can be sold to the public. The FDA has initiated a 'fast-track' approval process designed to speed up the development of drugs with the potential to treat serious or life-threatening conditions where there are currently no treatment options.

Going from NDA/BLA status to approval has a 91 per cent likelihood of success, says the BIO. But the sum of all these processes and chances of success is that less than 8 per cent (7.9 per cent) of drug candidates go all the way from Phase I to reach the market. On average, says the BIO, it takes 10.5 years for a Phase I candidate to progress to regulatory approval.

There is also a designation called 'orphan drug', which may be given by the FDA or the European Medicines Agency (EMA) to incentivise companies to develop medicines for rare conditions with only a small population of potential users, which means that the drug would most likely not be profitable to produce without government assistance.

Bringing a medical device to market takes less time than a drug but is still an onerous process, with at best three years, and at worst seven, typically needed to obtain FDA approval. For biotech investors, these time frames need to be well understood — each company needs to ensure that it remains well-funded through the process by tapping investors or taking on a bigger partner.

The biotech constituents of the Health Care sector contain dozens of interesting stories in both drugs and diagnostic devices, such as those shown in Table 8-1. (This is only a small selection of listed biotech companies; there are a number of others listed on the ASX.)

REMEMBER

Not many biotechs have actual earnings, and investors are in many cases relying on the approved drug or the device technology being picked up by larger partners (or even purchasers). Biotech can be a lucrative investment field, but one that is littered with the bleached bones of failed businesses. News flow is crucial to making share price gains, with many companies then finding sustaining and consolidating these share price gains very difficult. Smart investors follow the biotech companies' announcements closely and understand that the further companies move along the approval pathway, the probability of success, the value and the ability to do a deal with a partner all increase.

WARNING

The biotechs can surge on the back of good announcements and plummet on the back of not-so-good ones (refer to Chapter 4). Consider the case of infectious diseases specialist Biotron, which for years has been developing a therapy to treat viral infections, including HIV-1 and hepatitis C. In September–October 2018,

Biotron shares rocketed from 2 cents to as high as 45 cents — a 2,150 per cent surge — in just three weeks. The trigger was Biotron announcing that its flagship drug candidate, BIT225, was 'having a unique effect in patients, over and above viral suppression seen with current anti-retroviral drugs' in patients suffering from HIV, in Phase II trials.

TABLE 8-1 ## Biotech Companies in the Health Care Sector

Biotech Company	Area of Research and Development
Paradigm Biopharmaceuticals	Its Zilosul drug is under evaluation from the US Food and Drug Administration's expanded access program, and has FDA 'orphan drug' status for using Zilosul in treating the rare metabolic disorder MPS-I.
Kazia Therapeutics	Its Cantrixil ovarian cancer drug had success in Phase I trials, and the company is developing its drug candidate paxalisib as a potential treatment for glioblastoma, the most common and most aggressive form of primary brain cancer. Both Cantrixil and paxalisib have 'orphan drug' status from the FDA; paxalisib also has 'fast track' FDA status.
Imugene	It works in immuno-oncology, the anti-cancer field in which the body's immune system is artificially stimulated to boost its natural ability to fight the disease; it's developing four new treatments.
Immutep	Its lead product candidate, eftilagimod alpha (IMP321), has shown success in trials as a chemo-immunotherapy for metastatic breast cancer; it could also be a treatment for autoimmune diseases.
Prescient Therapeutics	A small-molecule drug development company, it works in CAR-T therapy, a type of cancer treatment in which a patient's T-cells (a type of immune system cell) are changed in the laboratory so they will attack cancer cells.
Opthea	Its lead compound, OPT-302, treats several eye diseases, including wet age-related macular degeneration (wet AMD), which results in vision loss and is the leading cause of blindness in people aged over 50 in the developed world. Opthea's shares rose five times on the back of positive trial results in September 2019.
AVITA Medical	A regenerative medicine company that is commercialising the RECELL technology, which was developed by plastic surgeon Professor Fiona Wood at Royal Perth Hospital to treat burns patients.
Neuren Pharmaceuticals	The company is developing two new drugs to treat six distinct, rare and severe neurological disorders, particularly in children; it has FDA 'orphan drug' status for all six of its development programs.
Recce Pharmaceuticals	It's developing a new line of synthetic polymer antibiotics designed to address the urgent global health problem of antibiotic-resistant 'superbugs' and emerging viral pathogens.
Actinogen Medical	It has its Xanamem drug — which blocks cortisol (stress hormones) in the brain — in trials against Fragile X syndrome, a genetic condition that causes intellectual and development disabilities; and against cognitive impairment due to Alzheimer's Disease.

Biotech Company	Area of Research and Development
Dimerix	It's taking its lead compound DMX-200 into Phase III trials against focal segmental glomulosclerosis (FSGS), a nasty kidney disease in children. DMX-200 has 'orphan drug' status in both the US and Europe.
Amplia Therapeutics	It's working on a pipeline of therapies that 'switch off' the particular protein, known as focal adhesion kinase (FAK), that inhibits the penetration and effect of chemotherapy drugs. Amplia has two FDA 'orphan drug' designations.
Nanosonics	Its infection prevention device trophon sterilises ultrasound probes without chemicals. Nanosonics — which has another major product in development — has 25,100 trophon units installed worldwide, in its major market, the US, as well as Asia–Pacific, Europe and the Middle East.
PolyNovo	Its NovoSorb bio-degradable polymer technology works as a wound dressing and burns treatment, and is being used in emergency, trauma and major-surgery applications in a substantial number of countries.
Medical Developments International	Its Penthrox product, also known as the 'green whistle', is a fast-acting non-opioid pain relief product that is used everywhere from the sporting field to ambulances to hospital surgeries. It is used in about 30 countries worldwide, with approval submissions lodged in the US and China.
Exopharm	A regenerative medicine company that has developed a technique to manufacture 'exosomes' (a kind of cellular secretion) derived from human blood platelets, or cultured adult stem cells, for use as therapeutic and diagnostic agents.
SomnoMed	Its SomnoDent device, sold in 28 countries, works against sleep-related breathing disorders such as obstructive sleep apnoea.
4D Medical	A Software-as-a-service (SaaS) company that enables respiratory diagnostic imaging in real-time, generating high-resolution images of the motion and airflow of lung tissue as the patient breathes, to provide sensitive, early diagnosis and to monitor changes over time.
Clinuvel Pharmaceuticals	It's commercialising its Scenesse drug to treat adult patients with the rare genetic and metabolic condition erythropoietic protoporphyria (EPP), which irritates the skin when the patient is exposed to light. Scenesse won FDA approval in October 2019.
LBT Innovations	A medical technology company that has developed the automated plate assessment system (APAS), which speeds-up the process by which microbiologists sift through and interpret hundreds of agar culture plates to diagnose infectious diseases. APAS was the world's first artificial intelligence (AI)-powered diagnostic medical device to receive US FDA clearance, in 2016.
Alterity Therapeutics	Formerly Prana, Alterity develops therapies for neuro-degenerative diseases; its lead candidate, PBT 434, aimed at disorders related to Parkinson's Disease, is in Phase I clinical trials, and has received 'orphan drug' status in the US and Europe.

(continued)

TABLE 8-1 *(continued)*

Biotech Company	Area of Research and Development
HeraMED	It has developed HeraBEAT, a medical-grade foetal heart rate monitor, and a fully integrated smartphone app that monitors foetal heartbeat in the home to hospital standards, to help pregnant women. HeraBeat was approved for use in the US as a clinical medical device in November 2019.
Rhythm Biosciences	This company is developing ColoSTAT, its low-cost blood test for the early detection of colorectal cancer, which could replace the global standard-of-care, the Faecal Immunochemical Test (FIT).
Cyclopharm	A diagnostic imaging company whose flagship medical device is Technegas, a lung ventilation imaging agent contained in a gas. Technegas is an ultra-fine dispersion of radioactive labelled carbon: the patient inhales the gas during a medical imaging procedure, and the labelled carbon helps to produce images that accurately demonstrate lung function.
Bionomics	The company is advancing its lead drug candidate, BNC210, to treat patients suffering from serious central nervous system disorders. BNC210 has FDA 'fast track' designation for the treatment of PTSD and other trauma- and stress-related disorders.
Race Oncology	It has FDA 'orphan drug' designation for its Zantrene (bisantrene) anti-cancer drug, which has shown high potential against acute myeloid leukaemia and melanoma.
Telix Pharmaceuticals	A clinical-stage biopharmaceutical company developing both diagnostic and therapeutic products using molecularly targeted radiation (MTR), aimed at cancer treatment. Telix's lead product, Illuccix, for prostate cancer imaging, has been accepted for assessment by the FDA.

However, Biotron shares slid over 2019 and early 2020 back to levels as low as 5 cents — before BIT225 achieved some more astounding results from a Phase II clinical trial in March 2020. The drug showed that it could 'unmask' hidden HIV cells in the body, allowing the immune system to attack the virus and kill it for good. Ordinarily, HIV-infected cells stay hidden in the body indefinitely, meaning patients need life-long treatment. This time, the share price reaction was far more muted — up just 13 per cent, as investors appeared more worried about the company running out of cash. At the time of writing, Biotron — which is also testing its library of anti-viral compounds against SARS-CoV-2 — had retraced to 5 cents.

INDUSTRIALS

The Industrials sector accounts for 6.6 per cent of the S&P/ASX 200 index. It features 152 companies across three main industry groups: Capital Goods, which covers construction and engineering, machinery, aerospace, building products, electrical engineering and industrial conglomerates; Commercial and Professional Services; and Transportation.

The biggest industrial stock by market value is Transurban Group, one of the world's largest toll road operators. This is followed by Sydney Airport (at the time of writing, under a takeover offer), then Brambles, the global logistics business that operates the world's largest pool of reusable pallets and containers, and plumbing, air-conditioning and refrigeration supplier Reece. Next comes the dual-listed Auckland International Airport, followed by one of its users, Australia's global flag carrier Qantas Airways. Media group Seven Group, Australia's largest rail freight operator, Aurizon, international engineering contractor CIMIC Group (the former Leighton Holdings) and international toll road operator Atlas Arteria round out the top ten.

Global analytical and testing services company ALS is there, as are port logistics company Qube, waste management operators Cleanaway Waste Management and Bingo Industries, plumbing fixture manufacturer Reliance Worldwide Corporation, shipbuilder Austal, infrastructure specialists Downer EDI and Cardno, and intellectual property services firm IPH.

In this sector are also the engineering, equipment and services groups that assist the resources industry, including Monadelphous, Lycopodium, Emeco, Primero, Decmil, MACA, NRW Holdings and Acrow Formwork and Construction Services. You'll also find childcare provider G8 Education, automotive parts and pumps business GUD Holdings, car fleet group SG Fleet and regional airline Regional Express here. It's a very eclectic group.

CONSUMER STAPLES

At 75 companies strong, the Consumer Staples sector makes up 4.2 per cent of the S&P/ASX 200 index. This sector represents the companies that make or sell the things that people need to buy all the time — making it, in theory at least, a highly defensive sector.

The sector is made up of three industry groups: Food, Beverage and Tobacco, which contains packaged foods, agricultural products, brewers, distillers, soft drinks and tobacco companies; the Household and Personal Products industry, which hosts the companies producing products like toiletries, vitamins, supplements and other health and household products; and Food and Drug retailers.

The largest stocks are supermarket archrivals Woolworths and Coles, as well as Woolworths' former liquor and pubs division, Endeavour Group, which was spun-off in June 2021. Then come global wine company Treasury Wine Estates; New-Zealand-based specialised dairy producer The A2 Milk Company; groceries, liquor and hardware wholesaler and distributor Metcash; rural merchandising and essential agricultural services provider Elders; food and dairy products heavyweight Bega Cheese; Australia's biggest vitamin and supplements company,

Blackmores; Australia's largest horticultural company, Costa Group; poultry and fodder supplier and producer Inghams; international malt supplier United Malt Group; the ASX's biggest listed agribusiness, GrainCorp, the country's largest listed grain handler; almond grower and processor Select Harvests; Australia's largest cattle company, the 196-year-old Australian Agricultural Company (it has only been listed since 2001); Kiwi stock Synlait Milk, which is A2's specialist milk supplier; Tasmanian fish farmer Tassal; and rice farmers' co-operative SunRice (listed under the name Ricegrowers). For a tipple, you can also find wine group Australian Vintage, Good Drinks Australia (owner of Gage Road Brewing in Perth and Matso's Brewery in Broome) and Tasmania-based Lark Distilling.

REAL ESTATE

The Real Estate sector represents 6.7 per cent of the S&P/ASX 200 index. Bulked-up by the presence of the 48 A-REITS — the real estate investment trusts — this sector has 82 companies.

REITs are unit trusts that own property and are traded on the sharemarket. REITs give individual investors the chance to share ownership in property assets, such as city office blocks, shopping centres, industrial parks and tourism properties, which they couldn't afford to invest in as individuals. REITs own about two-thirds of the institutional-grade property in Australia.

The REITs offer property investment but with all the advantages of a stock exchange listing. All or part of the property holding can be sold instantly rather than having to sell the actual properties.

REITs are considered a reliable source of high yields because they're required to distribute all of their taxable profit to unit-holders. Most REITs usually pay out about 90 to 95 per cent of their profit as distribution, compared to about 75 to 80 per cent of the major listed industrial companies' profit going out as dividends. (And this figure has come under pressure from the COVID-19-induced slowdown.)

Over the past 20 years, the average yield from the S&P ASX 200 A-REIT index has run at 6.3 per cent, compared to 4.3 per cent for the S&P ASX 200 index. However, REITs do not boast the tax advantages of a fully franked share dividend so this outperformance is not as good as it looks. The REITs' distribution has a *tax-advantaged component*, which comes from the trust's building depreciation allowance — income-tax free — and a *tax-deferred component*, which reflects other taxation deductions available to the trust during the period. However, these components are not as effective in reducing an investor's tax liability as fully franked dividends from shares.

TIP

REITs do offer another advantage. A lease contract usually entitles the property owner to apply annual rent increases, either fixed or linked to CPI — meaning that REITs have inflation protection built-in.

WARNING

While the REITs have usually been seen as a defensive sector in the sharemarket — apart from a dalliance with entrepreneurialism in the 2000s, when many of them geared-up and took on activities such as property development, syndication, management and property services to add earnings streams other than mere rent collection — they are seen as vulnerable in the wake of the COVID-19 pandemic. This is due to their higher exposure to the retail sector than is typical among their global peers.

In 2021, the likelihood of the Australian economy going into recession was seen as high, so A-REIT distributions were pressured because of difficult business conditions and the fact that some of their tenants couldn't carry on normal operations for long periods. The valuations of shopping centres and office towers have come down to reflect changes in consumer behaviour and the re-assessment of space needs on the back of the 'work-from-home' response to COVID-19 of many companies. While the pandemic has altered demand and pricing factors, by what extent remains to be seen.

The REITs were among the worst-hit sectors during the COVID-19 market falls as investors feared for rental returns, distributions and valuations. But in the post-2008 recovery from the GFC, the A-REITs were among the shining stars of the ASX, outperforming in 7 of 12 years, including significant outperformance in 2011, 2012, 2014, 2015 and 2018.

The big fish of the REIT world are the sector's heavyweights. Logistics property giant Goodman Group is by far the largest stock, at $41 billion, with daylight between it and the second-largest, shopping centre heavyweight Scentre Group (which operates the Westfield chain of shopping centres), at $13.3 billion. Then come office, residential, retail and industrial property owner Mirvac Group; Dexus, Australia's largest office property owner; diversified trust Stockland (one of Australia's largest retail property owners); retail, office, and logistics property owning GPT Group; multinational construction, property and infrastructure company LendLease; retail REIT Vicinity Centres (co-owner of Australia's largest shopping centre, Chadstone in Melbourne); and office, retail and industrial owner Charter Hall Group.

Woolworths' property owner SCA Property Group (which was spun-off from Woolworths in 2012) is also here, as is the remnant of Westfield in the form of the merged Unibail-Rodamco-Westfield (in 2018, Westfield Group was taken over by European property group Unibail-Rodamco), which owns and operates 87 shopping centres, including 53 flagships in Europe and the US, all under the Westfield brand.

Specialist REITs are also listed in this sector, such as the BWP Trust, which mostly holds large-format retailing properties — in particular, the Bunnings Warehouses operated by home products and hardware retailer Bunnings Group. The specialists also include self-storage centre portfolio, National Storage REIT; retirement living and budget tourism REIT, Ingenia Communities Group; industrial property trust Centuria Industrial REIT and its office property stablemate Centuria Office REIT; commercial property trust Cromwell Property; Dexus Industria REIT, which mainly owns industrial, warehouse and business park properties, and stablemate Dexus Convenience Retail REIT, which owns service stations and their attached convenience stores; and the similar Waypoint REIT, Australia's largest owner of service stations and convenience stores.

Arena REIT specialises in childcare, healthcare, education and government-tenanted properties. Pubs REIT Hotel Property Investments is also listed. And rural REIT Rural Funds Group is a way to play Australian agriculture as a landowner — its portfolio is based around almond orchards, vineyards, cattle, cotton and macadamia assets.

CONSUMER DISCRETIONARY

The Consumer Discretionary sector accounts for 8.2 per cent of the S&P/ASX 200 index. This sector includes 144 companies, selling people things and experiences that they don't actually need — thus, the sector was hammered by the COVID-19 pandemic and resultant crash, with many stores closing because their likely customers were staying at home and so foot traffic melted away. The sector slumped 45 per cent in the COVID-19 crash, compared to the 36 per cent fall of the market index. However, since then, the Consumer Discretionary sector has surged back impressively, up 118 per cent (compared to the 53 per cent gain of the market index).

Wesfarmers, the Perth-based conglomerate that owns home products and hardware chain Bunnings, department store chain Kmart and office products chain Officeworks — in addition to its chemicals, energy, gas and fertilisers businesses, among others — is top dog in the Consumer Discretionary sector, valued at $69.6 billion. This company is followed by global gaming machine giant Aristocrat Leisure; gambling and entertainment company Tabcorp (created from the December 2017 merger between Australian gambling giants Tabcorp Holdings and Tatts Group); Australia's largest pizza chain, Domino's Pizza (also the world's biggest franchisee for the Domino's Pizza brand, holding the rights for Australia, New Zealand, Belgium, France, The Netherlands, Japan and Germany); international education organisation IDP Education; and the currently troubled casino and hotel operator Crown Resorts, which owns the Crown casinos in Melbourne and Perth (as well as Crown Sydney in Barangaroo on Darling Harbour). In mid-2021, Crown was battling for its Victorian and New South Wales casino licences amid regulatory uncertainty (although Crown Sydney's hotel, restaurant and bar operations have opened). Under a remediation plan worked out with New South Wales regulators, Crown Sydney is targeting a 2022 casino opening.

Next in the sector are retailer Harvey Norman; home entertainment retail chain JB Hi-Fi; global household appliance marketer Breville Group; retail group Premier Investments, owner of the Smiggle stationery chain and the clothing retailers Just Jeans, Jay Jays, Jacqui E, Portmans, Dotti and sleepwear brand Peter Alexander; car dealership group Eagers Automotive; and 4WD accessories maker ARB Corporation. Then comes Star Entertainment — operator of the original Sydney casino, The Star (also on Darling Harbour) as well as The Star Gold Coast (formerly the Jupiters hotels and casinos on Queensland's Gold Coast), and The Treasury hotel and casino in Brisbane. Also here are travel agency chains Flight Centre and Corporate Travel Management; automotive aftermarket parts, service and accessories business Bapcor; corporate bookmaker Pointsbet; and funeral companies InvoCare and Propel Funeral Partners.

REMEMBER

A host of retailers of all kinds are in this sector, such as fallen department store icon Myer, online seller Kogan.com, baby goods specialist Baby Bunting, Super Retail Group (which owns BCF Boating Camping Fishing, Macpac, Rebel Sport and Supercheap Auto), online lottery seller Jumbo Interactive, online homewares and furniture retailer Temple & Webster, women's fashion chain City Chic Collective, manchester and homewares specialist retailer Adairs, footwear chain operator Accent Group, costume jewellery specialist chain Lovisa, lighting store group Beacon Lighting, discount chain The Reject Shop, furniture retailer Nick Scali, motorbike dealerships chain MotorCycle Holdings, Collins Foods (which operates restaurant chains KFC and Sizzler in Australia and parts of Asia) and Restaurant Brands New Zealand (which operates and owns the master franchising rights for the Carl's Jr., KFC, Pizza Hut and Taco Bell brands in New Zealand).

ENERGY

The Energy sector accounts for 3 per cent of the S&P/ASX 200 index. It's made up of two industries: the Oil, Gas and Consumable Fuel producers, and the Energy Equipment and Services industry, which covers oil and gas drilling, equipment and services companies.

The sector hosts 146 companies. Top of the Energy food chain are the petroleum heavyweights Woodside Petroleum and Santos (which merged with the other member of the 'big three', Papua New Guinea-focused Oil Search, in 2021). Fuel supplier Ampol (the former Caltex Australia) is found here, as is Worley, the global engineering and consulting group that specialises in the Resources and Energy sectors. Washington H Soul Pattinson also appears here — despite the fact that it operates the Soul Pattinson chemist chain and has major investments in building materials, finance and telecommunications — because it owns 50 per cent of coal producer New Hope, which is itself a constituent of the sector, along with fellow coal producers Whitehaven Coal, Yancoal Australia and Stanmore Resources.

Electricity and gas supplier Origin Energy is here, as is Australia's largest onshore oil producer, Beach Energy, plus fellow oil producers Cooper Energy, Senex Energy, Karoon Energy and Carnarvon Petroleum, and uranium producers Energy Resources of Australia (ERA) and Paladin Energy. The dual-listed Z Energy, a New Zealand fuel importer, distributor and seller, is a feature, as are hydrocarbons industry service providers MMA Offshore and Matrix Composites & Engineering. Beyond that, a large group of petroleum explorers is also included.

COMMUNICATION SERVICES

The Communication Services sector accounts for 4.2 per cent of the S&P/ASX 200 index. It holds 79 companies, made up of two industry groups: Media & Entertainment, which includes companies involved in advertising, broadcasting, publishing, movies, entertainment, interactive media and services, and Telecommunication Services, covering companies involved in mobile and integrated communications services.

The latter industry group provides the sector heavyweight, Telstra. (Prior to the float of the first portion of Telstra shares in November 1997, the Telecommunications sector didn't exist on the ASX.) Property websites operator REA Group is next in size, followed by telecommunications supplier TPG Telecom (which merged with Vodafone to form Australia's third-biggest telecommunications firm in 2020), employment website operator Seek and auto sales company Carsales. com, separated by the dual-listed Spark New Zealand, which supplies telecommunications and internet services in New Zealand.

Next come media and television group Nine Entertainment, dual-listed New Zealand telecoms infrastructure operator Chorus and property websites operator Domain Holdings.

INFORMATION TECHNOLOGY

The Information Technology (IT) sector comprises just 4.2 per cent of the S&P/ASX 200 index but is the third-largest by population, holding 194 companies. It's where you'll find the heavyweights of the new S&P/ASX All Tech index, and that index's heavyweights are also the leaders of the IT sector. At the time of writing, such heavyweights included buy-now-pay-later (BNPL) fintech Afterpay (now Block, Inc.), worth $30.7 billion; cloud-based accounting software provider Xero; global share registry and financial infrastructure provider Computershare; cloud-based logistics software provider WiseTech Global; data centre operator NEXT DC;

electronic printed circuit board (PCB) design software company Altium; and machine learning and artificial intelligence dataset developer Appen.

As investors would expect, the sector is a hive of serious 'tech' cred, but also a lot of companies that are striving to turn amazing products into revenue, cash flow and profits.

UTILITIES

The smallest sector, Utilities, accounts for just 1.5 per cent of the S&P/ASX 200 index and has 25 constituents. Five industries are present:

>> The Electric utilities industry, which includes electricity generators, retailers and metering providers

>> The Gas utilities industry, which includes gas transmission, storage, processing, compression and gas-powered generation companies

>> The Multi-utilities industry, which includes companies offering a wide range of utility services

>> The Water utilities industry, which includes companies involved in water supply and water and wastewater technology

>> The Independent Power and Renewable Energy Producers industry, which features independent companies that produce energy through renewable and non-renewable sources

The Utilities sector has a strong trans-Tasman flavour, hosting quite a few dual-listed companies from New Zealand. Leading the sector is the $11.4 billion gas pipeline and processing and storage facility operator APA Group. This company is followed by the leader of the Kiwi contingent, New Zealand electricity generator and retailer Mercury NZ; integrated energy business Origin Energy; New Zealand's largest renewable energy power company, Meridian Energy; Kiwi infrastructure, utility, airport and social infrastructure investor Infratil; Australia's AGL Energy, a large generator and retailer of electricity and gas for residential and commercial use; and New Zealand's largest electricity and gas generators and retailers, Genesis Energy and Contact Energy.

Also in the sector are solar power infrastructure business New Energy Solar; renewable energy generator Genex Power; and water investment company Duxton Water (D2O), the only pure water exposure on the ASX.

CLEANTECH

The latest technological wave to grab the attention of investors is *Cleantech*. This term is used to describe companies involved in renewable energy, carbon dioxide emissions control, biofuels, energy efficiency, water purification technology, salinity, carbon sequestration projects, alternative engine technology, electrical switching devices, clean coal technologies and new materials.

TIP

The Australian market has many stocks that qualify as Cleantech candidates. The grouping is similar to Biotech in that many of the stocks involved are yet to commercialise their technologies. But profitable companies such as waste handling and recycling companies Cleanaway and Sims are showing that Cleantech operations are no barrier to strong financial performance.

Exploring resources

The GICS sectors of Energy and Materials contain the Australian stock market's resources stocks. Because of Australia's mineral wealth, the sharemarket is renowned overseas as a resources market. Some international investors still appear to regard Australia as little more than a gigantic mine to be invested in only when commodity prices are rising. These overseas investors hope to get a double benefit if share prices and the Australian dollar are rising.

In the mid-1980s, the Resources sector represented about two-thirds of the Australian sharemarket's capitalisation; now it accounts for about 18 per cent. Although resources activity has grown tremendously, the difference is better explained by the fact that far more of the depth and breadth of the Australian economy has moved on to the sharemarket, and the industrial side of the market has swelled.

REMEMBER

The Australian Resources sector is a huge contributor to the economy. In 2019–20, it accounted for 10.4 per cent of gross domestic product (GDP) and more than half of the nation's exports. Despite the overall economy contracting, mining industry GDP increased 4.9 per cent in 2019–20 and totalled $202 billion.

The sector is also a massive source of export earnings. In 2019–20, Australia exported $103 billion worth of iron ore, up from $4.1 billion 26 years earlier. Indeed, it is the largest producer and exporter of iron ore in the world, with 53 per cent of total exports, more than twice the proportion of its nearest competitor, Brazil. Of Australia's total iron ore, 83 per cent goes to China.

Australia also exported $35 billion worth of coking (steelmaking) coal and $20 billion worth of thermal (electricity) coal in 2019–20, compared to $10.3 billion worth of coal 26 years ago. The country is the world's largest exporter of steelmaking coal, accounting for 54 per cent of total exports, and is the second-largest exporter of thermal coal (behind Indonesia).

Gold exports rose over the period from $7 billion to $25 billion, and Australia has the potential to become the world's largest gold producer by the mid-2020s. Liquefied natural gas (LNG) has risen from a $1.8 billion export market in 1994–95 to $47 billion: Australia is the biggest LNG exporter in the world.

Copper has gone from $1.2 billion worth of exports to $9.6 billion; crude oil from $2.6 billion to $9 billion; lithium from nothing to $1.6 billion, making Australia the biggest producer and exporter; and uranium (where Australia is the third-largest producer, and has almost one-third of the world's proven reserves) went from $281 million to $650 million.

Mining and petroleum drilling companies extract, process and sell Australia's minerals, oil and gas. Australia possesses virtually the full set of mineral commodities, making for one colossal industry.

TIP

The main reason investors invest in resources is to capture the upside of the global economic cycle, and to have commodity price exposure in their portfolio for diversification purposes. Australia's resource companies have enjoyed several years in the sun, powered by the rise in commodity prices, driven mainly by the massive industrial expansion in China. With China looking to power-up its economy to recover from the COVID-19-induced slowdown, commodity prices appear to have strong support.

REMEMBER

Mining companies usually have a fairly stable cost of production and can usually predict their operating costs. These companies measure profits by sales income minus operating costs, so fluctuations in the prices of the commodities they mine — and in the A$/US$ exchange rate — are the key to their profitability, although they can drive costs lower to help their margins, too. After all, their costs are the only one of their profitability parameters that they can realistically control.

The main issue for the investor contemplating the Resources sector is whether to take the lower-risk route — investing in the large-cap diversified miners, such as BHP and Rio Tinto — or to invest in the pure-play companies, such as Fortescue Metals Group, Alumina and Coronado Global Resources, where you're taking a view on their specific commodities (iron ore, aluminium and metallurgical [steelmaking] coal, respectively). The risk is higher with those companies, but you can receive greater earnings leverage at times. Even riskier are the highly speculative junior explorers, where the investor is looking for a strong capital gain related to specific projects that the company has. Alternatively, you can buy a resources-focused ETF and so hold a diversified portfolio of resources stocks.

TIP

The prices of resource shares generally anticipate movements in commodity prices. Resource shares are attractive to buyers when the Australian currency is weak because the supply contracts of the miners are written mostly in US$, while they report their profits in A$. The Resources sector is even more attractive in times of economic expansion, because world economic growth translates to growth in global industrial production, and Australian mineral commodity producers supply a great deal of the global industrial production.

MINING FOR RESOURCES

Since the beginnings of the stock exchange in Australia (refer to Chapter 2) the Resources sector has given the market a lot of its romance, in the tradition of the exploration company hitting paydirt with a drilling hole, resulting in a share price surge. In particular, the names of nickel explorers Poseidon and Tasminex live on as synonyms for instant riches — and the inevitable bust (refer to Chapter 3). It's history that Poseidon — which actually did mine nickel at Windarra — eventually went into receivership in 1976 (although an unconnected company, Poseidon Nickel, owns and operates three high-quality nickel operations in Western Australia), and that Tasminex never mined nickel at Mount Venn. (Mount Venn is now jointly owned by explorers Woomera Mining and Cazaly Resources, but it is a very long way from being mined.)

The excesses of the 1969–70 nickel boom prompted the first serious look at corporate governance in Australia. These days, the veracity of stock exchange announcements — and the qualifications of the geologists who sign them — are strictly enforced. A rigid system is in place — the Joint Ore Reserve Committee (JORC) Code for Reporting Mineral Resources and Reserves, which defines the criteria for publicly reporting resources and reserves.

Under the JORC code, a company proceeds from resource to reserve, where an *ore reserve* is considered to be the economically mineable part of a measured or indicated mineral resource. Ore reserves are subdivided into *probable reserves* and *proved reserves*. Announcements must be signed off by a 'competent person', which means a member of either the Australian Institute of Mining and Metallurgy or the Australian Institute of Geoscientists. Announcements of moves up the chain from resource to proven reserve can be catalysts for big share price jumps.

WARNING

Despite the tighter regulation of announcements and the claims made in them, some tricks of the trade remain. Prime among these are *nearology* and *flexibility*. An outbreak of nearology occurs when one spectacular drilling result sparks a flurry of announcements from any company with ground that shares the same postcode. For example, after Sandfire Resources' breakthrough world-class copper–gold discovery at De Grussa in Western Australia's Bryah Basin in May 2009, the share prices of more than 20 junior companies with exploration projects in the region pricked up. The reasoning of speculators was that if Sandfire had done it — and its shares had rocketed from 7 cents to $2.15 in just a few months — so could its neighbours. Investors poured millions into the ground searching for another company-making DeGrussa-style deposit in the region. But so far, no-one other than Sandfire has succeeded there.

It was the same story for Sirius (see Chapter 11) when it found the world-class Nova nickel deposit in the Fraser Range area of Western Australia in 2012. Sirius was only months away from running out of cash when it hit the bonanza. After the shares went to the stratosphere, from 5 cents to $5.00, more than 40 'nearology' plays flooded the region, sinking millions of investor dollars into exploration to find the next Nova — only to be disappointed. (In fact, the only company to benefit from 'nearology' was Sirius itself, when it found the nearby Bollinger deposit, hitting the jackpot twice. Similarly, the only meaningful discovery near DeGrussa so far has been the small but high-grade Monty deposit, which Sandfire found in 2015 in a joint venture with Talisman Mining.)

In late 2018, BHP reported a big iron oxide–copper–gold find 65 kilometres to the south-east of its Olympic Dam mine in South Australia — in one day, the share prices of the nearest neighbours in that area, Aeris Resources, Argonaut Resources and Cohiba Minerals, spiked 27 per cent, 41 per cent and 100 per cent respectively. All received 'please explain' notices from the ASX, concerned about continuous disclosure requirements — but there was nothing to see; it was nearology again.

REMEMBER

You can see why speculators often try to join the dots quickly — the nearology theory is often based not only on geographic adjacency but also sound geological reasons; for example, one company might have tenements consisting of the iden-tical rock type in which the other company's discovery was made. But, sadly, it rarely works that easily.

Another trap for rookies in the resources area is 'flexibility', which occurs when a particular commodity is running hot and deposits can be re-packaged to take advantage. For example, if nickel is running hot, gold projects can be re-presented as nickel projects. However, this can be genuine. When Kidman Resources paid $3.5 million in cash and shares for the Mt Holland tenement in Western Australia in December 2015, the company — valued at about $10 million on the ASX — hoped the deal would make it a major gold producer. But in April 2016, Kidman's geologists first realised that the ground contained hard-rock lithium. Three-and-a-half years later, as the world was waking up to the scale of lithium demand on the back of electric vehicles and renewable energy, conglom-erate Wesfarmers bought Kidman and its lithium deposit — which had attracted Tesla and the world's biggest lithium producer, SQM of Chile, as partners — for $776 million.

WARNING

Certainly, the potential for excitement in the explorers never goes away. Inves-tors have to beware of the way that announcements are presented because the Australian stock market hosts explorers looking for virtually everything that can be mined.

And the big discoveries keep coming. At Hemi in the West Pilbara region of Western Australia in November 2019, De Grey Mining made one of Australia's best gold discoveries in decades. At Willaura in western Victoria in October 2019, Stavely Minerals found a huge shallow high-grade copper–gold discovery in 2019. Core Lithium encountered high-grade lithium deposits at its Finniss project in the Northern Territory in January 2020. Legend Mining struck a potentially massive nickel orebody in Western Australia's Fraser Range in December 2019. In March 2020, Chalice Mining made Australia's first major palladium discovery — along with the significant presence of nickel, gold, cobalt and silver — with the very first drill-hole it put down at its Julimar prospect in Western Australia (triggering a burst of 'nearology' from neighbouring drillers). In April 2021, St George Mining unearthed a combination of high-grade nickel, copper, cobalt and platinum group metals at Mt Alexander in Western Australia.

REMEMBER

The explorers — whether looking for minerals or hydrocarbons — are highly speculative. In fact, you're not investing when you play in this market, you're punting. The risk is higher because no financial fundamentals exist at all. Rather, you're looking for a strong capital gain related to the company's specific drilling programs or projects. This mode of sharemarket participation is very announcement-driven and fits the day-trader mentality of trading momentum to a tee. But Australian resources investors have shown that they can be very patient; for example, Oil Search began looking for oil and gas in Papua New Guinea in 1931. The first revenues from this venture came in 1991, and the first dividend to shareholders followed a year later.

BUYING GOLD: A SPECIAL CASE

Australia has a long history with gold investing, which was the genesis of the country's informal sharemarket beginnings back in the 1850s. While investors often participate in gold through gold stocks — which at times can give great leverage to gold prices — the ASX has two vehicles that enable retail investors to buy gold in its own right. The first of these products, Gold Bullion Securities (ASX code: GOLD) was launched in March 2003. Each GOLD security gives the investor ownership of one-tenth of an ounce of gold bullion, held in the London vaults of custodian bank HSBC Bank USA. GOLD securities may be sold at any time on the ASX, or (subject to certain conditions and fees applying) holders may redeem them at any time for cash or in exchange for gold bars. The price of a GOLD security is one-tenth of the A$ gold price.

Later in 2003, GOLDs were joined on the ASX by the Perth Mint Gold Quoted Product, or PMG (ASX code: PMGOLD), which is a *security* (technically a warrant) that gives you the right to own one-hundredth of an ounce of gold. That right may be bought and sold on the stock exchange. The gold is held in Perth as bars or coins, and guaranteed by the Western Australian Government.

TIP

Both products enable investors to trade in gold as if the investors owned physical bullion. This type of investing is a very clean and efficient way of 'playing' the gold price; instead of buying the corporate risk attached to a gold miner, an investor buying either GOLDs or PMGs is only 'buying' the gold price. No company-specific factors such as mine life, resource security or hedging activity complicate matters. The stocks simply track the A$ gold price very closely, and may be sold at any time on the ASX. Brokerage is charged on the purchase or sale, and the management expense ratio (MER) of the investment is 0.40 per cent a year for GOLD, and 0.15 per cent a year for PMG.

Gold is also tradeable on the ASX through a range of exchange-traded products (ETPs), which offer exposure, through a listed stock, to the price changes of physical gold. ETPs also offer an investment in physical silver, platinum, palladium and a basket of the three, plus gold.

Deciding What to Buy

With the market divided into specific sectors, you can get a feel for the sectors with which you're most comfortable. Some sectors need a bit more research and effort in order to make successful investments; resources and some of the telecommunications companies operate in a complex environment. As with all share investment, the more you know about the companies that you invest in, the sounder your investment.

Buying what you know

If you use a company's goods or services, you know that company well, and you understand what makes them attractive to consumers. You can see where the revenue is coming from to pay you, as a shareholder, your earnings stream and dividend wage.

REMEMBER

One of the annoying (because it's true) clichés of the sharemarket is that if you can't explain to someone sitting next to you at a dinner party what one of your stocks actually does, you shouldn't own that stock.

Brand power

An extension of the 'buying what you know' policy is *brand power*. The type of companies that have become trusted blue chips of long standing are companies with a trusted brand name that have been around for a long time. Brands don't get to be household names without earning the trust of investors as well as consumers.

Beware a brand that has had huge expenditure put into it and looks established, while the company behind it has not yet made a profit, or has profits that are unreliable. Watching AMP's slow slide from $45 on the day of its float in 1998 to $1.13, or department store 'icon' Myer's similar dismal track from its $4.10 issue price when floated in November 2009 to 36 cents in mid-2021, should also be enough to convince you that the renown of a company's brand has nothing to do with how well it will do on the sharemarket.

However, brand reputation is a major part of how appliance marketer Breville has become a 13-bagger during the period of Myer's slide, from $2.25 to $30.

Companies that dominate

Competition benefits consumers but not investors. If the competition is hot, margins remain down and also earnings — and that's not good. The sharemarket may be the seat of capitalism, but it likes a monopoly best. What the sharemarket wants most is reliable and predictable earnings. A company that dominates its market delivers stability.

The big four Australian banks enjoy enormous size and scale, plus they're considered to have implicit government protection — which is enshrined in the 'four pillars policy' that prevents them from merging, their 'too big to fail' status and the fact that they're allowed by the Australian Prudential Regulation Authority (APRA) to apply lower risk weightings to their home loan assets than the regional banks, because they're 'systemically' more important, and thus considered to be under more intense regulatory supervision. Commonwealth Bank, Westpac, ANZ and NAB thus collectively enjoy competitive advantage.

Research firm Morningstar sums up companies' competitive advantage in its concept of the 'moat' — the combination of attributes such as a strong brand; a cost advantage; a product that is good enough to dissuade customers from changing brands and thereby incur the pain of 'switching costs'; a 'network effect', whereby an increase in the users of a product or service results in a corresponding increase in mutual benefits for both old and new users; and efficient scale, which occurs when a market is effectively served by a small number of producers or sellers.

Morningstar says the best moats on the ASX are:

>> **ASX:** The largest securities exchange in Australia, with a monopoly in listing, trading, clearing and settlement of Australian cash equities, debt securities, investment funds and derivatives.

>> **Cochlear:** A very strong market position as a global hearing implant maker, with 60 per cent of the market, plus the trust of the ear, nose and throat (ENT) surgeons that instal hearing implants.

- **Transurban:** High-quality, well-situated global toll road operator.

- **Wesfarmers:** Strong market position in consumer spending.

- **InvoCare:** The largest funeral, cemetery and crematorium operator in Australia, New Zealand and Singapore.

- **Auckland International Airport:** Monopolistic status as the largest airport in, and international gateway to, New Zealand.

- **Brambles:** The global leader in supply chain equipment solutions for the Consumer Staples sector.

- **Commonwealth Bank, ANZ Banking Group, NAB, Westpac:** Sustainable structural traits that guarantee high returns on equity. Together, the four lenders control more than 80 per cent of the business and consumer lending markets, plus the vast majority of bank deposits.

CSL has been recognised by investors globally for its size and manufacturing scale, giving it a cost advantage over competitors in a market where demand for blood plasma continues to grow.

Other healthcare companies such as ResMed, Ramsay Health Care, Pro Medicus and Ansell have strong competitive advantages. So too does international student placement provider IDP Education, through its one-third ownership of the crucial International English Language Testing System (IELTS). Technology stars Altium and Appen have major competitive advantages — even Afterpay (now Block, Inc.) has a first-mover advantage (particularly in the US market) that gives it an edge despite its core product being easy to emulate. Many companies have surprisingly strong versions of competitive advantage — although for many, the shock of the COVID-19-induced economic downturn may have lessened these advantages, at least temporarily. Seeing whether some advantages considered to be set in stone actually survive is likely to be fascinating.

Top management

Effective management is absolutely vital to the financial health of a company and to your investment. Good management positions your company at the forefront of its market. If the managers fail, so does your investment.

TIP

You can follow the track record of the management teams that run the companies in which you're investing. If you don't have confidence in their abilities, don't wait until the board shares your opinion. Fire them first by selling the shares.

Assessing management is difficult, and made more so by the publicity that some chief executive officers (CEOs) attract. The financial media can fall in love with high-profile CEOs, especially if they're good with a quote, while stock market analysts can be bedazzled by a seeming Midas touch. In the late 1990s, it was Peter Smedley (former CEO of Colonial, then Mayne) who was a market favourite. Then in the early 2000s it was AMP's extrovert American chief executive George Trumbull, who was larger than life while taking AMP on an acquisition binge that later went awry.

Former Telstra CEO Ziggy Switkowski was another whose love affair with the media and market ended acrimoniously when he agreed in 2004 to step down two years early. His departure followed a series of disastrous expansions — including a failed move into Asia that lost the company $3 billion — that cut the market value of Telstra in half. Switkowski was followed by American Sol Trujillo, whose high-profile time in the top seat at Telstra was marked by an adversarial relationship with the federal government, the Australian Competition and Consumer Commission (ACCC), employees and customers — not to mention a 25 per cent slide in the share price.

Then came the boom of the mid-2000s, in which the luminaries of the debt boom such as Eddy Groves of ABC Learning Centres, Phil Green of Babcock & Brown, David Coe of Allco Finance Group, John Kinghorn of RAMS Home Loans and Michael King of MFS were all over the media, not only in the finance pages but in the lifestyle pages too. Their high profiles could not prevent the credit crunch and the GFC exposing their companies as unsound once the debt taps were turned off.

In contrast, not many investors would have heard of the likes of Cameron McIntyre, CEO of Carsales.com; Peter Wilson, CEO of Reece; Paul Perreault, chief executive of CSL; Shemara Wikramanayake, chief executive of Macquarie Group; Dominic Stevens, CEO of ASX; Elizabeth Gaines, CEO of Fortescue Metals Group; Andrew Brown, managing director of ARB Corporation; Mick Farrell, CEO of ResMed; Steve Vamos, CEO of Xero; and Dig Howitt, CEO of Cochlear. Relatively unknown they may be to the wider public, but they all lead management teams doing an excellent job of creating value for shareholders.

Retreating behind defensive stocks

Defensive stocks, considered safe in troubled times, are the most liquid shares in the top 50. A true bear market depresses share prices across the board, and designing a portfolio that performs well in such a market is difficult. In this situation, professional investors sell many of their shares to increase their cash holding.

In the extreme case of a recession, bank shares, high-yielding property trusts and patronage assets (refer to the earlier section 'Choosing industrials') are the best defensive havens because interest and rental income are fairly constant. In the worst cases, you can also move the rest of your portfolio to cash. Defensive stocks are non-cyclical because they experience solid profits regardless of the motions of the broader economy. Even if their prices fall in a bear market, they should not fall by as much as other stocks.

The food retailers are usually viewed as safe havens. For example, the supermarket stocks, Woolworths and Coles, are usually considered premier defensive stocks, as is Telstra — just as people need to eat no matter how bad the economic circumstances are, they also need and want to use their mobile phones and internet for work and pleasure. CSL and Ramsay Health Care are also considered defensive, backed by global cash flows and the growing demand for healthcare as the population ages.

Utilities are sound defensive performers because people still need electricity and gas, and gas pipeline operator APA Group is a good example of a defensive utility stock. Sadly — for the human frailty it speaks of — gambling is also a robust defensive exposure, in the form of stocks such as Tabcorp.

Other defensive stocks are those with dominant market positions. A good example of that in the Australian market is Computershare, the world's largest share registry business, and ASX in Australian financial markets (although this pair depend heavily on the activity of financial markets buzzing along nicely). Australian banks also proved to be sound defensive holdings during the GFC — although their profits suffered as their bad debt provisions mounted, and they were susceptible to movements in credit markets, the fact that they had very little exposure to US housing or to the European debt problem held them in good stead.

Will the banks behave in the same manner in the wake of the COVID-19-inspired hit to the economy? In the midst of the COVID-19 crash, fears of economic recession and a blow-out in bank bad-debt provisions (as business and personal customers struggled to repay their loans) slashed the major banks' share prices, and their FY20 dividends were drastically lowered (the banking regulator, APRA, actually capped their dividend payout ratios at 50 per cent in 2020, concerned at the banks' need to retain capital). The sharemarket was also concerned at what would happen if a slide in commercial property valuations eventuated, as companies faced difficulty in paying their rent. But in mid-2021, those threats to bank earnings and dividends had largely subsided, and the banks' share prices had largely recovered — although breakouts of the Delta variant of COVID-19 were causing concern. Bank losses could occur if areas of the economy are shut down for longer than expected, unemployment rises more than expected and the economic recovery from the COVID-19 downturn takes longer than expected.

REMEMBER

Defensive stocks will not help your portfolio avoid a broad-based fall in the market, and the nature of a defensive stock ultimately boils down to the price you pay.

Cycling your way to recovery

Cyclical stocks are shares with sales and earnings that are affected most by the economic or industry cycle. When the local economy seems to have bottomed or come out of recession, the usual strategy is to sell your defensive stocks, such as the banks, and buy cyclical stocks, such as building materials, media and resources, to ride the recovery.

Cyclical industries include resources, energy, financial services, real estate and discretionary retailers (such as Harvey Norman, Nick Scali and Super Retail Group) that benefit from consumers having more disposable income. The big mining and energy stocks — BHP, Rio Tinto, Fortescue Metals, Woodside and Santos — are typically *high-beta* (that is, they tend to move with the market index) because they are most leveraged to the world growth cycle.

Other cyclical stocks — which tend to move with business and economic cycles — include Qantas, IAG, Ampol, Steadfast, Corporate Travel Management, Webjet, Flight Centre, Qube and Suncorp. The building materials stocks — CSR, James Hardie, Adbri and Boral — tend to be cyclical, as do the discretionary retailers such as Myer, JB Hi-Fi and Harvey Norman.

Other stocks considered cyclicals are jobs websites operator Seek, car sales website operator Carsales.com and real estate websites operator REA Group, plus the stocks that are attached to the automotive industry, such as ARB, AMA Group, Bapcor and Eagers Automotive.

Scooping the small-caps

Small-cap stocks are those with a small capitalisation or market value. However, if you're a large fund manager, small capitalisation may be any share valued at less than $1 billion on the stock exchange, or it could be those outside the top 50 by market capitalisation, or the top 100. As I showed in Chapter 5, small-caps is generally taken to mean the stocks ranked between 100 and 300 by market capitalisation.

Picking successful smaller companies is harder than picking good big companies because, generally, you have to do your own research. Find out as much as possible about the company; reading its announcements to the ASX provides a lot of information on the company's performance, along with its most recent annual report from its website.

Small-cap stocks are difficult to research. However, because most investors are concentrating on the larger stocks, you may be able to find an overlooked company that is already making a profit. When the rest of the market finds your stock, you can sell at a profit. That's the theory, anyway! Many small companies don't ever get picked up. If you have an eye for a good product with growing earnings and dividend streams and a sound balance sheet, buying small can be rewarding.

Punting on speculative stocks

Speculative stocks are those with the most risk but which offer potentially the highest returns. They have no track record and offer only the excitement of a good blue-sky story — the prospect of riches.

Because the Australian sharemarket relied on the Resources sector for such a long time, investors have a history of backing speculative companies. Mineral exploration companies are often in the middle of a boom-and-bust speculative investment. The Poseidon incident in 1969 is one of the most famous speculative debacles. In 1999 through 2000, investors bought speculative stocks (in this case, technology stocks) that were doubling, tripling and quadrupling in a matter of days. The fundamentals of investment such as profit, dividend and interest cover were irrelevant. When the companies didn't produce earnings, technology shares tumbled. In the 2000s, the speculators favoured any stock drilling for copper or uranium, or working in drug development. Technology was back in favour in the second half of the 2010s, and into the 2020s.

The Australian sharemarket is full of speculative situations — the resources explorers can still soar on good drilling results, and they have been joined by many technology and biotechnology stocks that have a similar leverage to good news. Good drug trial results and announcements of tie-ups with big global pharmaceutical companies usually have the same effect on a biotech company's share price that spectacular drilling results have on a resources explorer's.

TIP

While it is risky, investing in speculative shares, if done with a small percentage (5 or 10 per cent) of funds that you're prepared to lose, can be lucrative and fun. Stocks do double, triple and quadruple in value; ten-baggers — even 20-baggers — do come along, but not often.

Chapter **9**

Buying Specialised Shares and Other Listed Products

Some shares are not shares in companies; they are specialised listed securities that perform a particular investment task. For example, shares in listed investment companies (LICs), which are a type of managed fund, widen your investment in the market dramatically. If you feel you don't know enough about the market and lack confidence when picking shares for your portfolio, managed funds may be the way to go. Other types of investment also exist that can offer you specific tax advantages.

One of the biggest revolutions in sharemarket investing in recent years is exchange-traded funds (ETFs) and exchange-traded products (ETPs). ETFs are a subset of ETPs: ETP is the umbrella term for the collection of financial products traded on a stock exchange that include ETFs, as well as exchange-traded managed funds (ETMFs), exchange-traded notes (ETNs) and exchange-traded commodities (ETCs). What these investments have in common is that they are listed securities, they are traded throughout the day (exactly the same as shares) and they are *open-ended*, meaning that the number of units on issue is not fixed but can increase or decrease in response to demand and supply.

In this chapter, I look beyond buying what you know — the more familiar territory I cover in Chapter 8 — and delve into investing in these specialised stocks, including so-called 'hybrid' securities.

Looking at Listed Investment Companies (LICs)

Listed investment companies (LICs) are a kind of unit trust (managed fund). Managed funds are professionally managed vehicles that follow a diversification and asset allocation strategy that's available only to the most sophisticated share-market investors. Two types of trusts exist — trusts that are listed on the share-market and trusts that are not. LICs own a portfolio of other listed shares; in effect, these companies operate as a share that invests in other shares. Like their unlisted cousins, LICs offer built-in diversification and professional management at a cheaper rate for investors.

Non-listed equity trusts are very popular, but the industry often comes under fire for the high fees it charges investors. LICs are more competitive because the brokerage fee on the purchase of a LIC is usually about half the entry fee of an equity trust. The annual management fee for a listed trust is even smaller.

TECHNICAL
STUFF

The share price of a LIC tends to fluctuate around (but mostly under) its asset backing or the value of its net tangible assets (NTA), which is sometimes called net asset value (NAV). The *NTA* is the market value of that company's share portfolio divided by the number of shares on issue. Sometimes the share price of a LIC can fall below NTA, and investors may buy an interest in the portfolio for less than the cost of establishing that portfolio. This means an individual investor's performance could be very different in the same LIC, depending on the discount/premium when they first invest.

For example, over the five years to March 2021, the largest LIC, Australian Foundation Investment Company (AFIC), traded at a discount to NTA of up to 4 per cent and a premium to its worth of as much as 12.6 per cent. The second-largest LIC, Argo Investments, traded at a discount to NTA of up to 4.2 per cent and a premium of as much as 10.8 per cent. The third-largest LIC, Milton Corporation, moved between a discount of 5.9 per cent and a premium of 4.5 per cent. These three LICs combined have a market capitalisation of about $18.2 billion, which accounts for around 31 per cent of the total sector.

An unlisted equity trust is open-ended and the value of the underlying units in an equity trust is determined by its NTA. An investor in an equity trust buys the units by paying the NTA plus fees. LICs are closed-end investment vehicles because, after the initial capital raising, the shares trade at a price set by the market. (No new money comes into the fund unless new shares are issued or through a dividend reinvestment plan.) As with any other stock, supply and demand as well as the health of the sharemarket affects the share price.

Historically, during stronger market phases, the investment companies are at a premium to NTA. Buying at a premium to NTA works against the investor because the trading opportunity lies in riding the move from discount to premium. Longer-term investors can have an investment that tracks the market. Long-term investors who buy investment companies at deep discounts to asset backing are rewarded because their original investment keeps working for them over the years.

REMEMBER

LICs are the tortoises of the sharemarket. They never pick up speed but, over time, generally achieve returns in line with the market average. Selecting a LIC on the basis of discount to NTA may not be the best strategy; the better-performing LICs trade at a premium and the poor performers often trade at a discount — although, in strong markets, even very large LIC portfolios can move into discount temporarily. Medium-cap/small-cap specialist LIC WAM Capital, for example, has never traded at a discount — but over the ten years to March 2021, it has increased its NTA by an average of 8.5 per cent a year, and the share price has appreciated by an average of 11.4 per cent a year. The most important criterion in evaluating a LIC is its track record.

LICs are permitted to report NTA figures before and after provision for unrealised capital gains. Some of the investment companies aim to make a profit and pay a dividend purely from the dividend flow in their portfolio. Others aim to add to profit by trading the portfolio. Most LICs distribute income in the form of fully franked dividends. For LICs with a dividend reinvestment plan, investors can choose to increase their investment exposure rather than receiving cash. The better-performing LICs have outperformed the equity market accumulation indices (which count dividends as reinvested) over quite long periods.

For example, in the 20 years to end-September 2020, Argo Investments earned its shareholders a total return of 8.8 per cent a year (including franking credits), compared to a return of 7.3 per cent a year for the S&P/ASX 200 Accumulation index. Over the ten years to December 2020, fellow LIC heavyweight AFIC reported total return plus franking credits of 9.5 per cent a year, versus 7.9 per cent a year for the S&P/ASX 200 Accumulation index.

TIP

A more recent innovation has been the *listed investment trust* (LIT). The main difference between these two structures is in the tax treatment: as companies, LICs pay tax on their earnings and pay dividends to their investors (which are usually taxable to them but include franking credits). As trusts, LITs are structured to pay no tax directly, but instead must distribute their taxable income to investors, who then pay tax on it at their own tax rates. These distributions usually do not include significant franking or other tax credits.

Since 2018, 17 LITs have floated on the ASX, eight of them in the credit sector, offering investors access to a portfolio of corporate loans, or other private debt instruments, mostly provided by non-bank lenders. These funds offered much higher yields than cash, and found a ready audience: income-oriented investors who had been badly hit by falling yield returns from cash and fixed interest, but were worried about buying stocks for dividends given the potential for capital loss.

This group features the KKR Credit Income Fund, Partners Global Income Fund, Perpetual Credit Income Trust, NB Global Corporate Income Trust, Qualitas Real Estate Income Fund, Gryphon Capital Income Trust, MCP Master Income Trust and the MCP Income Opportunities Trust. However, the COVID-19 crash was not kind to the LIT share prices. As closed-end vehicles, most of the credit LITs fell well below their reported NTA values — to discounts of 20 per cent to 50 per cent — as the market struggled to price accurately their underlying assets. As with the LICs, however, this dislocation opened up the opportunity for new buyers to augment their returns by riding the process (however long it took) of returning to trade closer to NTAs. As well, assuming the distributions remain the same, investors who buy at the lower price stood to benefit from an increased yield based on the lower entry price. As it happened, by mid-2021 there had been strong share-price recovery in the credit LITs. Just as in many other types of stock, the COVID-19 crash showed that LITs — because the 'L' stands for 'listed' — are always susceptible to human behaviour and market fluctuations.

THE LIC MARKET

The LIC market in Australia is relatively small — about $58.3 billion, compared to $595 billion in unlisted Australian equity trusts — and is dominated by longstanding companies like Australian Foundation Investment Company (AFIC) at $9.8 billion and Argo Investments at $6.7 billion in size. AFIC was founded in 1928 and was closely aligned with the JBWere stockbroking group, while Argo Investments was founded in 1946 in Adelaide by a group of stockbrokers that included the world's greatest cricketer, Sir Donald Bradman. Milton Corporation was established in 1938 and listed on the Sydney Stock Exchange in 1958.

Of the 102 LICs listed on the ASX, most invest in Australian shares. Those with a large-capitalisation Australian stocks focus include AFIC, Argo, Australian United Investments (AUI), Milton Corporation, Carlton Investments and AFIC's stablemate Djerriwarrh Investments (which specialises in the buy-and-write options strategy). Those with a small-capitalisation Australian stocks focus include Mirrabooka Investments, WAM Capital, QV Equities and Ophir High Conviction Fund.

Globally focused LICs include MFF Capital Investments ($1.6 billion) and Magellan High Conviction Trust ($990 million), as well as smaller companies like WAM Global, Templeton Global Growth, Platinum Capital, PM Capital Global Opportunities, Pengana International Equities and Tribeca Global Natural Resources.

Other LICs with a specific focus include Argo Global Listed Infrastructure, Platinum Asia Investments, Hearts & Minds Investment (a global high-conviction investor); WAM Microcap, Spheria Emerging Companies, NAOS Emerging Opportunities Company, NAOS Small Cap Opportunities Company and Acorn Capital Investment Fund, which mainly target Australian 'microcap' stocks; and Plato Income Maximiser, an income-focused LIC. 'Long–short' funds are also available, which can short-sell stocks (sell them without owning them by borrowing the stock, hoping to profit from a price fall). A domestic specialist in this group is Absolute Equity Performance Fund, while globally focused long–short LICs include L1 Long Short Fund, VGI Partners Global Investments, Antipodes Global Investment and Regal Investment Fund.

The latest tweak in the LIC market is the exchange-traded managed fund (ETMF), or 'quoted managed fund', in which fund managers no longer have to maintain separate funds, a closed-end LIC and an open-end unlisted fund but, instead, offer a single open-ended fund, with investors choosing the listed or unlisted access point they prefer, priced at NTA, at any time. This structure gets around the discount-to-NTA issue that plagues many LICs. This structure could revolutionise the LIC sector and is likely to prove very popular in the future.

Engaging with Exchange-Traded Funds (ETFs)

Exchange-traded funds (ETFs) are one of the fastest-growing investment products in the world. An ETF is effectively a stock that represents a portfolio. For example, the StreetTracks S&P/ASX 200 Fund (issued by State Street Global Advisors; ASX code: STW) is designed to closely track the performance of the S&P/ASX 200 index, because it comprises all the companies in the index. By buying that ETF, with one transaction, no matter what amount you invest, you will receive a return that matches, before fees and expenses, the return of the S&P/ASX 200 index.

REMEMBER

Part of the explanation for the huge growth in ETFs in recent years is the fact that they offer investors cost-effective, simple, instant and liquid exposure to different markets, different asset classes and different strategies by buying one product, which is itself a listed stock. Equity ETFs have grown to challenge LICs as convenient listed investment vehicles that provide relatively low-cost access to diversification through buying a portfolio.

ETFs emerged out of the 'index fund' movement that started in the US in the early 1970s, with the first index fund having an investment objective of approximating the performance of the Dow Jones Industrial Stock Average. The first actual ETF was listed in March 1990 on the Toronto Stock Exchange: it was known as the Toronto 35 Index Participation Fund, or 'TIPs'. That ETF, now owned by BlackRock, still exists today and is now known as the iShares S&P/TSX 60 index ETF, with assets of C$10.4 billon (AU$11.3 billion).

The market really got going with the launch in January 1993 of the Standard & Poor's Depositary Receipt — the SPDR, or 'Spider' — which trades on the New York Stock Exchange Arca market under the ticker 'SPY'. It remains the largest ETF in the world, with a market capitalisation of US$397.1 billion (AU$540 billion), and is the most liquid ETF, with an average daily volume of US$65.8 billion (AU$90.1 billion).

From US$1 billion in market size in 1995, ETFs have grown to a US$8.5 trillion (AU$11.7 trillion) market around the world (US$5.4 trillion of that in the US), with just over 7,000 ETFs trading worldwide. In total, ETFs account for about 37 per cent of US trading value.

Like their counterparts abroad, Australian investors have embraced the ETF revolution. From a humble beginning in August 2001, when State Street Global Advisors launched two ETFs on the ASX, worth $48 million in total, ETFs have grown to the point where the ASX Monthly Funds Report for June 2021 listed 223 ETFs/ETPs on the ASX market, with a total market capitalisation of $113.5 billion, from a total of 30 issuers. There are also 18 ETFs that trade only on the Cboe Australia market.

The largest 'pure' ETF on the ASX is the Vanguard Australian Shares Index ETF, which is capitalised at $8.8 billion, followed by the SPDR S&P/ASX 200 Fund (one of the first two listed in 2001), which is valued at $4.7 billion. The largest international equity ETF is the iShares S&P 500 ETF, with a capitalisation of $4.5 billion. (The largest ETF is the Magellan Global Fund [MGOC], which was converted from an unlisted managed fund to an ASX-listed active ETF in November 2020: MGOC now manages $14.6 billion.)

Australia's ETF listings cover Australian shares, global shares, infrastructure, property securities, bonds (government to corporate), cash, mixed assets, currency and commodities (precious metals, industrial metals, crude oil and agricultural commodities).

REMEMBER

ETFs offer an individual investor a simple means of gaining exposure to a broader portfolio. They are structured to provide, in one stock, exposure to the 'beta' (market performance) of the stock portfolio. The approach is similar to that considered in the active-versus-passive debate described in Chapter 5 — in deciding to use an ETF, you accept that you're giving up the chance to benefit from any 'alpha' (that is, performance above the relevant benchmark index) that an active manager (refer to Chapter 5 for more on 'active' and 'passive funds) may be able to achieve; instead, you simply want to gain the performance of that relevant index. (Although active ETFs do exist — see the section 'Active ETFs', later in this chapter, for more.)

An equity ETF holds the shares on behalf of its investors, so all dividends from the underlying companies are paid directly to the ETF. The ETF then collates any income the assets generate — including dividends, interest, capital returns, capital gains — and pays this to investors through regular distributions, rather than immediately as the dividends are received. This timing could range from monthly to annually. Many investors find one payment with one statement attractive, compared to receiving multiple dividends from multiple holdings. As with shares, ETFs are traded on the ASX and settled through the CHESS clearing system (the Cboe Australia exchange also trades a range of ETFs).

TIP

The appeal of ETFs is the instant diversification and versatility that they offer to investors. They can provide core exposure to various asset classes within an investment portfolio — investors can gain access to a variety of asset classes at a relatively low cost, and ETFs can be used as the building blocks of multi-asset portfolios. For example, you could buy a broad Australian-market ETF to serve as your 'core' holding of Australian shares in your portfolio, around which other selected diversifier holdings can be established, such as US shares or a broad global shares ETF. Buying a global share ETF is an instant, cost-effective way to add international exposure to a portfolio, and hold it long term, to reduce the concentration risk of Australian stocks.

The ETF menu also offers funds tracking sector-specific indices, such as resources, or ones that carve out different sharemarket 'factors' to focus on, such as high dividend yield or 'quality' (including companies that have strong balance sheets, encouraging growth prospects, relatively high return on equity and which show consistent improvements in their earnings).

TECHNICAL STUFF

Factor investing, which some ETFs are structured to implement, is an investment approach that involves targeting quantifiable stock characteristics (or 'factors') that can explain differences in stock returns. This approach is simply another way of slicing and dicing the sharemarket to choose the stocks in which the investor wants to invest. 'Value', or where the stock is selling at a market price below the true intrinsic value, is a factor; 'momentum', where the investor focuses on stocks that have performed well over the last, say, 12 months, is another factor, based on the likelihood that such stocks will continue to outperform the market for at least a short period in the future. 'Low volatility' is another factor — stocks that display a lower level of volatility than the market index often outperform when the overall market is falling, but frequently lag when the market is rising. 'Size' — that is, market capitalisation — is a factor based on the belief that smaller companies are often more capable of outperforming the market than larger companies. 'Quality' is another factor that prioritises the companies showing financial strength, efficient management and a relatively predictable earnings profile. Applying the factor investing approach is often described as *smart beta investing*, which seeks to enhance risk-adjusted returns above the performance of the market index (the 'beta' return), which is usually a capitalisation-weighted index.

ETFs share three main characteristics:

>> They are open-end rather than closed-end funds. This means that the number of units on issue and available to be traded on the stock exchange will fluctuate according to demand.

>> They are involved in a simultaneous primary market (for ongoing unit creation and redemption) and secondary market, which is traded on the exchange.

>> They are designed to ensure that the unit price on the secondary market does not diverge too far from the net asset value (NAV) of the units.

REMEMBER

ETFs are the cheapest way that an individual investor can 'buy' the overall market in a particular asset class. Because ETFs can be used to establish instant invest-ment in a range of asset classes — Australian shares, overseas shares, Australian bonds, overseas bonds, property, infrastructure, commodities, foreign currency — they can make it easy to do the job of asset allocation. *Asset allocation* is the big-gest long-term determinant of portfolio performance but can often be a difficult task. However, virtually your entire asset allocation process can be completed using ASX-listed ETFs or ETPs. The ETFs that invest in international shares will either be currency-hedged or unhedged, with investor decided whether they wish to take currency risk (refer to Chapter 5).

In Australia, ETFs usually account for just under 6 per cent of total ASX trades, after surging in activity during the COVID-19 Crash in 2020. The number of transactions and volume and value figures reached all-time highs. In March 2020, the ASX ETF sector transacted on average about $770 million worth of trades a day, nearly four times higher than the previous peak. The 748,000 transactions for March was about two-and-a-half times higher than the previous month. A lot more people seemed to be more active in the market, because the versatility of ETF uses allowed them to do what they wanted to do. However, by mid-2021, that had settled back to 387,000 trades a month, worth about $339 million a day.

Active ETFs

Not all ETFs are structured solely to follow an index. Some ETFs are actively managed (refer to Chapter 5), where the fund manager chooses its own portfolio and constantly researches it, deciding what to buy, hold and sell, and in what proportions. The manager will actively manage weightings of the stocks depending on stock valuations, industry trends and views on likely macroeconomic and geopolitical developments. They can also hold cash to manage the overall risk of the portfolio and to take advantage of opportunities when markets move. The manager of an actively managed ETF will try to beat the performance of the relevant benchmark index, while also trying to avoid (or lessen) a fall in the benchmark index.

REMEMBER

If that sounds similar to what an unlisted managed fund does, that's because an active ETF is really more accurately described as a listed managed fund — and in the Australian market, they are called exchange-traded managed funds (ETMFs) or quoted managed funds (QMFs), which is the term under which they trade on the Cboe Australia exchange. They function like managed funds but are traded like shares that can be bought and sold during the trading day on the stock exchange. This means, although ETMFs operate in a similar way to traditional managed funds, they have the added benefit of transparent, live intra-day pricing on the ASX, and market-making ability that ensures liquidity for investors.

Active ETFs were only introduced into Australia in March 2015, when funds management group Magellan listed its Magellan Global Equities (MGE), which closely resembled the firm's unlisted Magellan Global fund (the two were united in an ASX-listed vehicle, MGOC, in November 2020). In 2021, 52 active ETFs were trading on the ASX, with a total capitalisation of $20.8 billion (18.3 per cent of the value of the entire ETF cohort). MGOC is by far the largest, at $14.6 billion.

Active ETFs usually cost more than passive ETFs because of the involvement of portfolio managers and researchers; you are paying for the team's skill. In the Australian marketplace, the management fees (the cost to the investor) of active ETFs range between 0.35 per cent and 2.05 per cent a year — but, in general, active ETFs' annual fees are between 0.5 per cent and 1.0 per cent.

REMEMBER

Active managers give you the possibility of outperforming the index — which of course the traditional ETF cannot do — but the flipside is much higher return variability, and much higher management costs.

ETFs can also be used tactically to take a short-term trading view. They suit the 'core/satellite' strategy, where investors use ETFs as core asset-allocation holdings to pick up market 'beta', and then choose active managers and/or direct shareholdings to add 'alpha'.

For example, an investor may hold a broad Australian equity ETF in the core portion of their portfolio, and add active managed funds to the satellite portion of the portfolio to seek to enhance performance. Using ETFs will help to keep the overall portfolio costs low, allowing the investor to choose unconstrained, high-conviction or absolute-return managers that represent the best chance for alpha. It's important to ensure that the satellite funds generate a return that differs as much as possible from the market return. This 'blending' of a passive, low-cost indexed core and higher-cost active management can deliver market outperformance for less than a fully active portfolio would cost.

TIP

When using active managers as satellite holdings, make sure you don't get panicked out of the investment by short-term underperformance — which is the bane of active management. Hold the managers long enough — at least through a full economic cycle — to give each enough time to potentially generate positive active returns through their skills and insight.

The satellite investments to an Australian equity core ETF can also be direct shares. This is a popular strategy in low-interest environments, where franked dividends are a crucial source of income for yield-oriented investors. This is especially the case for self-managed superannuation funds (SMSFs) that are able to use the partial or full rebate of the unused franking credits (depending on whether the fund is in 'accumulation' or 'pension' phase, where the applicable tax rate is 15 per cent and nil, respectively; Chapter 18 explains this process in more detail).

Themed ETFs

ETF issuers have put a lot of effort into developing 'thematic' ETFs that aim to capitalise on emerging trends. Examples include biotech, environmental change, demographic shifts and technology EFTs — and within technology, 'hot' areas, such as artificial intelligence and robotics, and cybersecurity, are also covered. Thematic ETFs usually track custom-made indices, and thus cost more than those that follow broad-based indices, such as the S&P 500 index or the MSCI World index, but plenty of investors want these kinds of specifically targeted exposures.

A good example of a thematic ETF is the iShares S&P Global Healthcare ETF, which taps into the increased spending on healthcare as populations in many countries — developed and developing — age. Adding this global healthcare exposure — which is difficult to achieve on the ASX — can provide a targeted investment while also improving the portfolio's international diversification.

ETFs COME THROUGH THE CRASH

The spectacular market slump and price dislocation experienced over February–March 2020 put all of the sharemarket under stress; however, the ETF sector was perhaps more closely watched than others. Of course, broad index-based ETFs gave their investors the fall — and the rebound — of their underlying indices, because that is what those ETFs are designed to do, and what their investors expect those ETFs to do.

ETFs did exhibit volatility in pricing during the COVID-19 crash — but only in line with the volatility or the structural set-up of the underlying assets and indices. This volatility was more pronounced in some asset classes. In the heightened volatility of the global market crash, the spreads on many ETFs were wider than usual, which reflected the extreme market movements in underlying exposures.

ETFs have *market makers*, which are firms paid to provide buying and selling quotes (bids and offers) on the ETFs throughout the trading day. The market makers play an important role in ensuring that buyers and sellers of the ETF can transact at prices close to the net asset value (NAV). They provide liquidity through the trading day and frequently update their quotes to reflect changes in the NAV of the ETF.

During the COVID-19 crash, buy–sell (bid–offer) spreads were quite volatile. For any stock, the buy–sell spread is the difference between what a seller is asking for the stock and what a buyer is willing to pay, generally calculated off the highest bid offer. As for any managed fund, the buy–sell spread is the invisible cost of investing, paid each time an investor enters or exits the fund, and covering the costs incurred by the market maker or fund provider.

As the ETF market has grown over the past decade, the average bid–offer spread has fallen from 75 basis points (0.75 per cent) to 29 basis points. For many of the largest and most liquid ETFs, average bid–offer spreads are typically 5 basis points to 11 basis points (0.05 per cent to 0.11 per cent). And the 'tighter' the spread, the easier it is for the market makers to trade in the market.

But in March 2020, a month of significant volatility on global financial markets, the average bid–offer spread for Australian ETFs blew out to 85 basis points (0.85 per cent). Even in April 2020, as markets calmed down slightly, the average only returned to 51 basis points (0.51 per cent). Even the $4.5 billion iShares S&P 500 ETF, the largest global shares ETF in the Australian market, saw its average bid–offer spread move from 4 basis points in February 2020 to 15 basis points in March.

This reflected the fact that during the Australian trading day, market makers are pricing the global shares ETFs on the basis of the US stock index futures contracts, which are trading outside US sharemarket trading hours. (Stock index futures trade

(continued)

(continued)

virtually 24 hours a day, with a rise or fall in index futures outside normal market hours often used as an indication of whether the sharemarket will open higher or lower the next day.)

But several times in March during the Australian trading day, US stock index futures stopped trading because the futures went 'limit-down', meaning they fell by more than 5 per cent, and thus trading was temporarily suspended. This gave rise to 'gapping risk', in which nobody is quite sure what price to quote until trading resumes. However, the market makers maintained pricing on the ETFs, using their modelling techniques and other methods to try to reflect the prices accurately. By taking that risk on to their balance sheet, they were able to give investors the ability to buy or sell on the ASX.

This situation was repeated in many ETF sectors and asset classes during the COVID-19 crash, when price discovery was made suddenly very difficult. In some of the fixed-income sectors — corporate bonds and high-yield bonds, for example — market makers also had to take balance-sheet risk to maintain a buy–sell spread as prices gapped, and this pushed spreads wider.

Whenever spreads widen, it's because of the difficulty of price discovery in the underlying assets. During the COVID-19 crash, in some of the fixed-income ETFs, such as those investing in corporate bonds and high-yield bonds, problems arose from the fact that bonds do not trade on public exchanges (such as the ASX) like shares do; instead, they are traded directly between institutions and rely on a core group of banks to do most of the trading. Amid the dislocation of the COVID-19 crash, no-one quite knew what the current prices of the underlying bonds were. The market makers — firms that are some of the biggest buyers and sellers of bonds in the world, and probably better placed than anyone to understand what the prices are of some of these fixed-interest products — took risk on their balance sheets to maintain a market as prices gapped and spreads widened.

In those cases, the ETFs actually provided a more accurate reflection of the pricing than the underlying market was providing at the time. However, some bond ETFs on the ASX did trade at prices well below their NAVs — discounts of up to 10 per cent were common — catching some investors who use bond ETFs by surprise.

Australian ETF spreads have largely returned to the kind of average spreads that prevailed before the COVID-19 crash, with the largest and most liquid equity ETFs showing *slippage* (how much you lose by crossing the spread when buying or selling) of 0.05 per cent to 0.06 per cent.

Protection ETFs

Several of the active ETFs issued by ETF provider BetaShares are 'inverse' ETFs, designed to generate a return that is negatively correlated to the return of either the Australian or the US sharemarket; in other words, they are structured to rise when a sharemarket index falls. Because of this, these ETFs can be used for short-term trading, to 'short-sell' the index — that is, to profit from a fall — but they can also be used to protect a share portfolio to some extent.

TECHNICAL STUFF

Two of the BetaShares inverse ETFs (known as 'bear funds') are *geared* (leveraged) so as to potentially magnify the profit from the 'short' strategy. The simplest of the bear funds, being ungeared, is the BEAR fund (that is the ASX code), which simply targets a return that is negatively correlated with the return of the Australian sharemarket, in a roughly one-to-one relationship. In effect, if the fund's benchmark index — the S&P/ASX 200 Accumulation index, which includes dividends — falls by 1 per cent, the fund should rise by somewhere in the range of 0.9 per cent to 1.1 per cent. (The reverse is also true — if the S&P/ASX 200 Accumulation Index rises by 1 per cent, the BEAR fund should fall by 0.9 per cent to 1.1 per cent.)

The other Australian bear fund, the BBOZ (ASX code) fund, is also designed to be negatively correlated with the return of the S&P/ASX 200 Accumulation index, but in a magnified way: it uses internal leverage (that is, BetaShares borrows money to put on a larger position) to try to achieve a return of 2 per cent to 2.75 per cent for every 1 per cent fall in the S&P/ASX 200 Accumulation index. And, of course, the opposite reaction in the event of a 1 per cent rise in the index.

The third product, the US Equities Strong Bear Hedge Fund — Currency Hedged (ASX code: BBUS) is designed to generate magnified positive returns when the US market (as represented by the S&P 500 Total Return index, which includes dividends) goes down, and vice versa. BBUS is structured to deliver a 2 per cent to 2.75 per cent increase in the value of the fund's units for every 1 per cent fall in the benchmark index (and vice versa).

In the COVID-19 crash, all three funds did what investors expected them to do. The BEAR fund gained 16.9 per cent in March 2020, compared to a fall of 20.7 per cent in the S&P/ASX 200. For the March 2020 quarter, BEAR was up by 20.1 per cent, compared to a 23.1 per cent slump in the index.

As investors would also expect, BBOZ, the geared Australian short fund, did even better. It appreciated by 33 per cent in March 2020, compared to the 20.7 per cent fall in the S&P/ASX 200 and, for the March 2020 quarter, BBOZ rose by 40.6 per cent, against the 23.1 per cent fall in the index.

BBUS, the leveraged US fund, surged by 22.6 per cent in March 2020, compared to a 12.4 per cent fall in its benchmark index, the S&P 500 Total Return index. For the March 2020 quarter, BBUS gained 47.8 per cent, versus a fall of 19.7 per cent for the index.

Visiting the Hybrid Part of the ASX Zoo

The ASX also hosts a $46.9 billion sector of 'hybrid' securities, so named because they combine features of debt and equity securities — the debt features being that investors are paid an interest 'coupon', and the equity features being that the securities have no maturity date, or very long maturities.

Hybrid securities have been popular with retail investors in recent years because they are issued by banks, mainly, and offer high yields; however, they also involve higher risk than traditional fixed-income investments. Hybrid securities typically promise to pay regular interest, at a defined margin above the bank-bill rate (that is, a floating rate). However, unlike a bond, the amount (and timing) of interest payments are not as certain. Because hybrids can be exchanged for shares of the underlying company's shares (they have a fixed date for optional repayment or conversion to shares), they are much more like equity and do not provide the same level of protection as bonds in a market downturn.

REMEMBER

In the corporate capital structure, hybrids generally sit between equity and debt, and as with debt, they are ranked ahead of equity in the event of the company being wound up. Most hybrids are issued by banks and insurers, and have historically had around one-quarter to one-half the risk of shares, but higher volatility than investment-grade floating-rate notes. If the hybrids don't have a set date when they're called in (or repaid), most modern (or so-called Basel 3) hybrids automatically convert to equity at around ten years. Alternatively, the prudential regulator of banks and insurance companies, the Australian Prudential Regulation Authority (APRA) can demand that they be converted into ordinary shares if the issuer is in distress. If the hybrid issuer suspends distributions, penalties normally apply — if they don't pay the income or interest on their hybrids, the issuer is not allowed to pay dividends on their equity, either.

Hybrids are broadly split into three varieties:

>> Convertible/converting debt securities (that convert into ordinary equity securities at some stage)

>> Preference shares (equity securities with debt-like features)

>> Capital notes (debt securities with equity features), which may be perpetual (no maturity), subordinated bonds and securities where the issuer can redeem the securities under certain conditions

REMEMBER

Investors choose to invest in hybrid securities for a number of reasons, including the income, the diversification, and the better liquidity and price transparency than provided by corporate bonds. Coupons are both optional and variable, and the timing of the maturity payment is the choice of the issuer — or the issuer can convert the security into equity. Since the cash flows in a hybrid are relatively unknown, investors look at the 'running yield' — the ratio of the expected yearly distribution relative to the current market price of the hybrid.

Considering exchange-traded bonds

The ASX also hosts exchange-traded bonds (XTBs), with the range of XTBs including underlying bonds from Australia's largest companies. Currently, about 29 XTBs are available on the ASX, issued by 20 companies, all of which are major names from the S&P/ASX 200 index — for example, AGL Energy, APA Group, Bank of Queensland, Dexus, Vicinity Centres, Stockland Group, Mirvac, National Australia Bank, Ampol, Qantas, Macquarie Group, Transurban, Telstra and Westpac.

Each XTB represents a fraction of a corporate bond, which is traded on the ASX. Investors buy and sell XTB units on the ASX with minimum amounts starting from $500. All XTBs have a face value of $100, meaning investors receive $100 per unit at maturity. The performance of the XTB should reflect the underlying performance of the corporate bond.

REMEMBER

The XTBs have the same coupon rate and maturity date as their underlying bond. They effectively mirror the cash flows of individual corporate bonds issued in the wholesale market. They combine the predictable income and capital stability of corporate bonds, with the transparency and liquidity of the ASX market. Investors can choose fixed or floating-rate coupons (interest payments) across a range of sectors.

TIP

The XTBs have made it easier than ever before to incorporate the diversification benefits and the regular, predictable cash flows of corporate bonds into a portfolio. In the wholesale bond market, institutional investors are typically required to buy bonds in large amounts ($500,000 or more), but XTBs over corporate bonds offer participation for as little as $500.

Since XTBs began trading on the ASX in May 2015, 33 XTBs have matured, with $130 million returned to XTB investors in face value payments at maturity, and $46.2 million paid in coupon (income) payments to XTB investors.

In a similar manner, Australian Government Treasury Bonds are also traded on the ASX, in the form of exchange-traded Treasury Bonds, or eTBs. This is also done through fractional ownership, where a one-unit holding of an eTB provides beneficial ownership of $100 of face value of the Treasury Bond over which it has been issued.

An eTB holder has beneficial ownership of the bonds in the form of CHESS Depositary Instruments (CDIs), which means that the eTB holder has all of the economic benefits (including coupon and principal payments) attached to legal ownership of the Treasury Bonds over which the eTBs have been issued.

Exchange-traded treasury indexed bonds (ETIBs) are also available, and these work the same way as eTBs, except the value of ETIBs is adjusted with the consumer price index (CPI) — that is, inflation — meaning the interest received can fluctuate.

Moving with the mFunds market

In 2014 the ASX introduced the mFund platform, allowing investors to buy and sell unlisted managed funds through their broker in the same way that they trade shares. This eliminates the traditional paper-based processes for investing in managed funds and uses the same CHESS electronic system used for settling ASX stock transactions.

When you buy units in an mFund, your holdings may be electronically linked to your Holder Identification Number (HIN) through the ASX, which means they can be tracked along with other investments such as shares and ETFs in the one spot, such as via an online broker.

Several costs are associated with investing in mFunds, including brokerage fees, management fees, the minimum investment and price per unit. For example:

>> **Brokerage fees:** These are charged by the broker or online share trading platform for any settled trades. Each time you want to buy additional units in the fund, you need to pay this fee, which tends to range from $30 to $40.

>> **Management expense ratio (MER):** These are the annual fees charged by the fund issuer, which range from around 0.2 per cent to 1.9 per cent.

The ASX lists 240 mFunds — all actively managed funds — from 73 fund managers. Most mFunds offer much lower minimum investment amounts than required when investing directly in the equivalent funds through the fund manager or an investment adviser.

TECHNICAL
STUFF

Unlike ETFs, mFunds are not actually listed on the ASX (they are listed on the ASX's mFunds platform), which means investors aren't buying or selling mFund units from or to other investors. However, mFunds are settled by the ASX's mFund service, so the ASX is responsible for transferring ownership of units to buyers after payments have been processed.

Chapter **10**

Choosing Shares Wisely

Whan you buy a stock, you're hoping to increase your capital. You invest in the sharemarket to accumulate long-term personal wealth and to accomplish this, you want to choose stocks that beat inflation and make money for you. Remember also that trading in shares attracts fees, and capital gains tax can add up over time.

In this chapter, I discuss different types of investment strategies, including pure speculating, and how to choose a method that suits you.

Selecting a Strategy That Works

Drawing up a share selection strategy is important (I discuss this in detail in Chapter 3). Think of the process of choosing shares as though you were conducting a job interview. Look at each share's résumé, its record and what other owners say about it. When you select a share, you're employing this stock to work for you. In this instance, you're trusting these shares with part of your life's savings. If you don't want to do the research that stock selection entails, you're better off in a managed fund that chooses stocks for you.

Sticking with your strategy

You buy stocks that you believe are one day going to be worth a lot more than you paid for them. You choose your stocks by comparing what the market believes a stock is worth to what you think the same stock is worth.

You can make this decision by using *fundamental analysis* — choosing stocks for the medium to long term — or by using *technical analysis* — spotting a short-term trading proposition. With either method, you should be following a defined strategy; otherwise, you're just throwing darts at the newspaper. (I introduce analysis in Chapter 7, and get deeper into fundamental and technical analysis in chapters 15 and 16, respectively.)

Your strategy can be complicated or simple. A strategy can be as simple as looking for a price/earnings (P/E) ratio under 10 or looking for industrial stocks with fully franked (grossed-up) dividend yields over 5 per cent. At this point, you're not just relying on tips or dinner party hearsay.

You could develop your strategy a bit more by looking for stocks with the following elements:

>> Stocks capitalised at between $500 million and $2 billion

>> Sales growth running 10 per cent higher than GDP growth

>> P/E growth factor of less than 0.5

>> Debt/equity ratio of less than 50 per cent

>> Dividend yield forecast of at least 2 per cent higher than the cash rate

TIP

Some of the points in this chapter rely on calculations and methods that I explain further in Chapter 14.

Throwing darts as a strategy

If you think throwing a dart at the stock list is a strategy, remember that 2,200 companies are listed on the ASX (this number has stayed the same for several years as companies arrive and leave the market). These companies cover a bewildering variety of industries. You need more than a dart to zero in on the companies that will be successful.

Professional investors screen companies first by *capitalisation*, or sharemarket value. The value of a company dictates where it will be in the hierarchy of indices, such as the S&P/ASX 20, S&P/ASX 50, S&P/ASX 100, S&P/ASX 200, S&P/ASX 300 and S&P/ASX All Ordinaries (refer to Chapter 2). The smallest stock in the S&P/ASX 20 is valued at $21.3 billion; the smallest stock in the S&P/ASX 50, at $11.6 billion; the smallest stock in the S&P/ASX 100, at $5.8 billion; the smallest stock in the S&P/ASX 200, at $2.6 billion; the smallest stock in the S&P/ASX 300, at $1.5 billion; and the smallest stock in the S&P/ASX All Ordinaries index, at $705 million.

Managers of index funds and exchange-traded funds (ETFs) (refer to Chapter 9) replicate these indices by buying shares according to the composition of the indices. Shares listed in the major indices are well researched by the market.

This means that although the 100 share leaders — perhaps even the S&P/ASX 200 — are researched in detail by broking firms, investment banks and fund managers, shares outside this list get less scrutiny. Outside the All Ordinaries, market research is almost non-existent, although some small broking firms research the lower reaches of capitalisation if they have a focus on specific sectors, such as small resources explorers. The small-cap companies are generally considered to be those ranked between 100 and 300 by market capitalisation; this could be anywhere between $1.5 billion and $5.8 billion. In practice, these days companies below $1 billion are the micro-caps. With the $1 billion market cap level finishing at about number 390 on the capitalisation ladder, this means about 1,800 stocks are smaller than small-caps; however, many specialist micro-cap investors prefer to fossick around at the sub-$500 million capitalisation level. At this level of capitalisation, you're often on your own when it comes to research, although some smaller brokers (and newsletters — for some useful examples, see Chapter 17) like to spend a lot of time at these depths looking for undiscovered gems.

Giving your strategy time

When you decide on a strategy for choosing stocks, you also have to allow time for your strategy to work. Your overall investment goal is to earn a return better than inflation and allow that return to compound over time. A strategy that includes chopping and changing stocks works against this goal.

One strategy, which I discuss in detail in Chapter 3, is to buy and hold. With a buy-and-hold strategy, you choose the very best stocks you can and hold them for a long time — at least five years, and probably ten for the best benefits. This strategy works well, but it's not called 'buy, hold and forget'. You still have to monitor your portfolio and replace poor-performing shares with good ones.

REMEMBER

Assess your portfolio at least every six months. Put your shares through the job interview process again. If you have shares you wouldn't buy today, think about replacing them with ones you would buy.

Playing it smart and safe

Investors know they must diversify their portfolios to be safe. However, this strategy usually means doing what most of the market is doing — buying stocks in the S&P/ASX 50. An index fund or ETF can do this better and cheaper than the rest of us.

REMEMBER

A strategy that allows you to buy shares that grow in value and are reliable means you have to do the research. You have to work to get information about companies that the market doesn't know much about. If your strategy is to find unknown but potentially valuable shares before the rest of the market becomes aware of them, then you may be a successful investor.

Choosing small over big

The smaller the company, the less liquid — meaning that, with a large spread between the buyers and the sellers, trade doesn't happen as frequently as with larger stocks. Buying and selling shares in small companies can be difficult and stocks of smaller companies are more volatile.

These companies rely on a relatively small number of customers for their cash flow. They also suffer from high levels of debt and are more vulnerable to cash flow crises that can increase debt problems.

However, small companies can offer unique qualities that aren't available with other companies — you may be buying a future blue chip. The market may price smaller companies at a discount to the industrial market because they're not as liquid, their earnings are more volatile or because the market doesn't know enough about them.

Developing Your Strategy

When you're deciding what shares to buy, information is the most important aid. (I discuss the research materials readily available online in Chapter 17.) With the ubiquity of the internet, people are able to research, analyse and corroborate their information about listed companies far more easily than ever before. Twenty years ago, the only information available for investors came from newspapers or company annual reports; even getting an annual report was difficult. Investors were limited to using historical data and had little access to market forecasts.

Today, doing your own research on a listed company is easy. The result can be as good as the advice the professionals offer. (I cover all of these elements in detail in Part 4.) However, bear in mind that, even when you have done your research, no magic formula pops up to tell you when to buy. The criteria against which you evaluate stocks are based on financial calculations, and you use them to compare and contrast the stocks.

You can establish your own rules in each case. For example, you can set up parameters beyond which you're not prepared to commit your funds. For revenue and earnings, you can set targets based on growth in *gross domestic product* (GDP), which is the value of all goods and services produced in the economy. For the dividend yield, you may say that the official cash rate is your benchmark and you're only interested in stocks showing a yield representing a certain margin over this benchmark. Using this approach, you may set a target of GDP plus more than 10 per cent as the growth rate for revenue and earnings. If the country's GDP is growing at 3.5 per cent a year, you won't invest in a stock unless its revenue and earnings per share are growing at more than 13.5 per cent a year. You might also set a particular target for grossed-up dividend yield — this strategy has been particularly compelling for income-oriented investors over the past decade, as interest rates and spreads (margins above bond rates) have ground lower. Any time you're using numerical limits on particular criteria, you have the makings of a strategy.

You can add some other criteria to your parameters, such as:

>> Price must be 75 per cent of net tangible assets (NTAs) or less

>> Debt/equity ratio must be less than 50 per cent

>> Forecast P/E ratio must be less than 12 times earnings

>> Profit margin on sales must be higher than 8 per cent

>> Price/earnings growth factor must be less than 0.5

You're no longer choosing stocks haphazardly. You have a strategy. Of course, numbers are only part of your research. You can also assess listed companies for their competitive position, and the quality of their products and management. If you can, try to use the products or services yourself and talk to customers, employees and suppliers. Discover as much as you can about the company's public demeanour.

Taking a mechanical approach

You can use a straightforward mechanical strategy to make choosing shares relatively easy. You select a valuation criterion (or criteria), plug in the stock list and look for those stocks that seem to be good buys.

The following valuation criteria are applicable:

>> Highest-yielding stocks

>> Lowest P/E ratios

>> Lowest price-to-NTA ratios

This relatively simple approach reveals the cheapest stocks available. (You can find out how to do these calculations in Chapter 14.)

A well-known mechanical strategy is the Dow Dividend approach in the US (sometimes called the 'Dogs of the Dow'). With this strategy, which is meant to identify undervalued blue chips, you study the 30 stocks in the Dow Jones Industrial Average (DJIA) and at the end of each year, buy the ten that show the highest dividend yield (using the most recent dividend). After a year, when the top ten yielding list is updated, you keep the ones that are still on the list and sell those that have fallen off. Follow this and you should — theoretically, anyway — out-perform the Dow Jones that year.

This strategy is based on *mean reversion* — it works on the assumption that things eventually return to the mean, so in this case high-dividend-yielding stocks will lower their relative payouts by improving their prices.

At first sight, it appears to work. The website dogsofthedow.com ran the numbers to find that the Dogs of the Dow's average annual return for the ten-year period between 2009 and 2019 was 15.9 per cent — versus an average annual gain of 13.9 per cent for the Dow overall. However, if you only considered the five-year span between 2015 and 2019, the average Dogs of the Dow yearly gain of 13.4 per cent is pretty much the same as the Dow's 13.3 per cent average annual gain.

Worse, in 2020, the DJIA gained 7.2 per cent in 2020, while the Dogs lost 12.7 per cent all-up. This one bad year would have negated years' worth of any outperformance an investor might have enjoyed by using the Dogs of the Dow strategy.

Mechanical strategies take the subjectivity out of choosing stocks. Selection isn't based on compiling information. You assess your purchases on the basis of the shares' rankings according to various statistical criteria.

Investing in a style to suit you

The two main investment strategies are based on value and growth. The former means buying stocks that appear to be good value and the latter dictates buying stocks that show huge potential for growth in sales and earnings. Everybody hopes, when they buy a share, that someday that share is going to be worth more than they paid; in other words, that they've bought good value. And, everyone hopes that company earnings are going to rise when they buy shares. The difference is which strategy — value or growth — you emphasise.

You can follow other strategies that are variations on the two main ones. You may be looking for a steady income, you may decide the market has misread a stock, or you may engage in top-down and bottom-up investing. I explain value and growth investing further in Chapter 5, but here I share a quick summary of these styles and these associated variations.

Value investing

Pioneered by Benjamin Graham, *value investing* involves finding those shares that are undervalued in the market. The value investor has to have something to compare the share price against, and this something is *intrinsic value* — what the business would be worth if it were sold tomorrow.

Value investors usually look to smaller companies for their long-term holdings, because analysts quickly pick up any underpriced value in the Top 100 stocks. In contrast, small companies sometimes go unnoticed and an undervalued small stock could take months to be discovered by the market.

Growth investing

Growth investing means trying to locate above-average growth in earnings of particular shares, ideally, when this trend is just beginning. A growth investor is looking for evidence that shows a company's prospects for producing earnings and dividends are growing faster than the market average. This could mean increasing market demand for the company's products, a technological or scientific edge, or outstanding management. Whatever the factors, the company is producing earnings growth and growth investors believe that if the earnings keep growing so will the share price.

Growth stocks deliver very large percentage rises in revenue and earnings per share. Growth investors aren't put off by lack of dividends because a growth stock is, after all, growing, and needs the retained earnings. Growth investors don't mind paying a price premium for their stocks. They're mainly interested in P/E growth ratios and the return on equity (ROE), which is a major determinant of growth in earnings.

Growth stocks like CSL generally reward investors for paying high P/E ratios over time. Along the journey from an effective IPO price of 77 cents to $290 in share price (with a peak of $336), CSL has consistently rewarded investors — who buy it and watch it go higher. The P/E 'asked' by the market to buy CSL has risen from 13.4 times in 2011 to 45 times, but investors have been happy to pay this.

But because nothing happens in a linear fashion on the sharemarket, that is not to say that CSL's share price growth has proceeded smoothly. Like the market itself, CSL has occasionally suffered a pull-back in price — which has given many a professional investor a bargain entry to the stock, albeit not in response to the traditional value-investing indications of a bargain.

Most recently, CSL slid 29 per cent in the 'COVID crash' of February–March 2020; and before that, the stock lost nearly one-quarter of its value in late 2018, when the market saw a flight from growth stocks that was linked to rising US interest rates. And it has often been the subject of arguments over its high P/E ratio investment, as high P/Es can often indicate 'expensive'. Over time, CSL has traded at an average historical P/E of about 27 times earnings, meaning that it is hardly ever considered 'cheap' — and it certainly doesn't look cheap at the moment, trading on a historical (FY20) P/E of 44 times earnings and a prospective FY22 P/E, on analysts' consensus estimates, of 42 times earnings.

That doesn't happen by accident — CSL almost routinely under-promises and over-delivers in terms of earnings. The quality of the franchise — its balance sheet strength, outstanding track record of management and confidence in future earnings growth — has justified a high P/E multiple throughout its listed life.

WARNING

The risk with growth stocks is that if the company's earnings falter, the price can fall dramatically. If the company falls behind expected profit forecasts or has to write down a recent acquisition, the lofty share price premium can deteriorate. What's worse is that a high P/E stock that shows an earnings fall will be hammered by P/E contraction (see Chapter 11), so a high P/E can be a double-edged sword.

Income investing

Some investors are mainly interested in *income investing*. These people are usually self-funded retirees who have made their money and now want to draw down income from their share portfolio to live on. Although most retirees are income-oriented investors, it's not a bad idea for any long-term portfolio to contain some income-generating stocks.

The sharemarket can be a very lucrative source of high yields. Don't forget, over the long term, dividends generate just over half (51 per cent) of the market's total return. But there is a catch — dividends are not guaranteed. When it comes to individual stocks, dividend yield expectations can be very rudely disappointed (refer to Chapter 7). Moreover, while you wait for the dividends you expect, the share price can fall — defeating the purpose of hanging around for the dividend.

That said, many shares can be very consistent dividend payers. Investment conglomerate Washington H. Soul Pattinson has paid a dividend every year since it listed in 1903 — the last year in which the company did not increase its dividend was 2000. Infrastructure heavyweight APA Group has lifted its dividend every year since 2004, on the back of the reliable annual cashflow it generates from its huge national gas pipeline network.

Various industries wax and wane when it comes to being yield favourites. In Chapter 7, I explained how Telstra and the big four banks lost their dividend shine from about 2016. Strangely, one of the industries that replaced them in the affections of income investors was mining — in particular, iron ore, as the price of that commodity began to rise strongly in the 2000s, and then again in the latter half of the 2010s (refer to Chapter 4), on the back of Chinese demand. This flowed into improved dividends from the iron ore behemoths, helped by a change of policy.

Between 2000 and 2010, global mining giants BHP and Rio Tinto operated a 'progressive dividend' policy, which guaranteed that dividends never fell. When slumping commodity prices pitched both into losses in 2016, they both bit the bullet. In February 2016, BHP slashed its interim dividend by 75 per cent — the first cut since 1988 — to 16 US cents, about half of what the market expected, after reporting its first loss in more than 16 years. The mining giant abandoned the progressive dividend policy, committing to a payout ratio of 50 per cent of underlying earnings over the longer term, with the possibility of extra amounts depending on circumstances at the time. Similarly, Rio Tinto told shareholders at the release of its interim 2016 results that a progressive dividend policy was 'not appropriate' for a cyclical industry such as mining, and so from 2017, returns to shareholders would be based on profit.

Almost immediately, in 2017, the benefits of this flexibility were on show. BHP more than tripled its final dividend, while Rio Tinto showered its shareholders with the biggest interim dividend in the company's history, more than double the previous year. Fast-forward to 2020, and the big miners were dishing out rivers of cash. While it paid a full-year dividend of 83 US cents (106 Australian cents) in 2017, in 2020 BHP paid 120 US cents (174 Australian cents). The dividend amount in Australian shareholders' hands does depend on the A$/US$ exchange rate, but the iron ore price strength has boosted the dividend significantly. Special dividends have helped along the way, too.

It's a similar story at Rio Tinto, which has also been a regular special-dividend dispenser. In 2017, Rio Tinto paid a full-year dividend of 290 US cents (366.25 Australian cents); for only the first half of the 2021 financial year, Rio dropped an interim dividend of 561 US cents (760.06 Australian cents) into its shareholders' accounts. The same occurred at Fortescue Metals Group — from a full-year dividend of 45 (Australian) cents in 2017, by the halfway stage of the 2021 financial year, it had already paid an interim dividend of $1.47.

Temporarily, at least, the big miners have become to income-oriented investors what Telstra and the big four banks were for much of the 2000s.

But there is another stunning little secret to dividend yields that can truly start to make income-oriented investors salivate. Even though dividend yield figures are quoted everywhere, they are usually based on the current share price — which means that the quoted yields do not represent the yield in the hands of a shareholder. That yield is individual, and depends on the average price the shareholder paid for their holding.

This is where yield gets really interesting. Imagine you happened to buy Commonwealth Bank (CBA) shares 20 years ago, in June 2001, at $32 a share. In 2020–21, CBA paid you a dividend of $3.50 a share. On what you paid for the shares, the yield on that dividend was 10.9 per cent. With full franking, that is a grossed-up yield of 15.6 per cent.

Now imagine that you bought your CBA shares in the initial float, back in 1991, for $5. On CBA's 2020–21 dividend of $3.50 a share, the yield on the investment is 70 per cent. Grossed-up, that is 100 per cent. For a year, as a shareholder. It's almost ridiculous.

Or, imagine you bought Fortescue Metals Group when things looked really bad for iron ore, back in January 2016, at $1.50 a share. In 2020–21, Fortescue paid you a dividend of $3.58 a share, fully franked, that is more than twice what you paid for the stock. The yield is 238.7 per cent; grossed-up, it comes to 341 per cent. When you bought it, the stock paid a dividend of 5 cents.

And when you consider that Andrew Forrest raised the first capital for Fortescue, when he was getting it off the ground in 2003 — parcelling-up iron ore tenements that Rio Tinto did not want, because it thought the iron ore was of a low quality — at 13 cents, it truly doesn't bear thinking about what the yield is on those original shares. There's a good reason why Andrew Forrest and his wife Nicola — who own 36.2 per cent of Fortescue Metals Group through their family company Tattarang — direct almost all of the $2 billion or so they receive in dividends a year to their philanthropic group, the Minderoo Foundation.

Looking for the highest yields when using the sharemarket to generate yield can be a trap because yields rise as share prices fall. The share price could have fallen for very good reasons, indicating that the company is in trouble, or the yield might be calculated using a very optimistic dividend assumption.

Putting together a high-yield portfolio is all about using the dividends that you believe are maintainable. If they come in better than that, that's a bonus. This means looking at a company's track record of paying dividends and its dividend cover, and discarding any rogue yield figures you see. You've got to be confident that the companies can pay the dividends when they're supposed to. A growing dividend stream can deliver some truly spectacular yields on shares that have been held for a long time — without any smoke or mirrors. (See Chapter 19 for how this effect can deliver astoundingly good income for self-managed super funds.)

Sick shares investing

A certain kind of investor likes to invest in *sick shares* or companies whose share price has fallen spectacularly. This investor tries to diagnose the symptoms of the company's illness and determine why the share price fell. If their diagnosis shows that the problems can be fixed, the investor is prepared to buy shares. Their reasoning is that once the market realises it has overreacted in selling off the stock, the share price will return to its former rating. This is known as *contrarian investing* because not only is the investor going against what everyone else is doing, what they're doing seems to be contrary to common sense. This type of investing is dangerous, even though the rewards can be high. Contrarian investing is value investing taken to extremes. It's gutsy investing because contrarians back their hunches when other investors are saying that the stock is on the slide — even worthless.

In the preceding section on income investing, I described a scenario where you bought Fortescue Metals Group in 2016 (when the iron ore price was slumping at $1.50 a share). If you had done this, you would be a contrarian — not only would you have picked up an almost unbelievable yield, but the stock would have proved to be a 16-bagger. The same applies to anyone who bought rare earths producer Lynas Corporation (now Lynas Rare Earths) in mid-2015, when Malaysians who live near its processing plant in that country looked increasingly likely to win their fight to have the plant shut down. The electric vehicle and clean energy revolutions weren't yet on the horizon, and the problems in Malaysia, as well as high debt and tumbling prices for rare earths, had driven the company to the brink of collapse — at a share price of 3.3 cents.

But a brave contrarian, who also had the foresight to see those revolutions coming — and that the developed world would be desperate for a non-Chinese source of rare earths — now sits on a stock worth $7 a share, which, after a one-for-ten share consolidation in December 2017, has delivered them 21.2 times their purchase.

These are extreme kinds of contrarian gains; professional contrarians are happy with far humbler gains. In November 2017, baby goods retailer Baby Bunting got caught up in an aggressive discounting war, which caused the company to slash its profit guidance. With the market worried about the imminent arrival of Amazon in the Australian market — given that Amazon is a major player in the baby goods category in the US — the confluence of concerns stripped 60 per cent from Baby Bunting's value, to lows of around $1.34. A contrarian who believed the company when it said that it could hold its market share in the face of competition, and who invested then, has made more than four times their money.

Similarly, in 2014, no-one wanted to invest in job website operator Seek because American giant LinkedIn was coming to Australia and was expected to dominate the online job ad market. But Seek possessed the network effect (refer to Chapter 5) and it wasn't going to be so easy to knock it from prominence — employers and recruiters knew that SEEK was where active jobseekers were most likely to look, so if they wanted to place a job ad as efficiently as possible, Seek was the platform they needed to use. A savvy contrarian would have tripled their money investing in Seek.

Sometimes, contrarian investing doesn't require company-specific situations like these; at other times, it's a market-wide slump that opens up opportunities for contrarians. During the global financial crisis (GFC) market slump in 2007 to 2008, and during the COVID crash of February–March 2020, cheap situations were appearing everywhere an investor looked.

However, when contrarian investing is unsuccessful, in the words of the old Wall Street saying, 'It's like catching a falling knife.' Investors who bought stocks such as Myer and AMP during their years-long respective slides would have been very disappointed contrarians.

During the 54 per cent market fall that accompanied the GFC, it was raining knives. That slump was different to the COVID crash, because the reckoning that hit over-debted companies was terminal for many of them. During the GFC, plenty of contrarians were prepared to punt that the likes of ABC Learning Centres, Centro Properties, MFS, Allco Finance Group and Babcock & Brown (refer to Chapter 4) would recover. They didn't, and people lost the money they put into them. Of course, during the GFC, contrarians also made some wonderful purchases if they had the courage and the faith in the companies to buy the stock. And in the throes of the COVID crash, they obtained huge bargains — although it was scary for a while as investors struggled to come to terms with a disaster-movie scenario like a pandemic.

Top-down investing

Top-down investing focuses on economics. Analysts look at the global economic environment and how this may affect the Australian economy. They decide which sectors of the economy will benefit or suffer and choose stocks accordingly.

The drawback of top-down investing is that this type of investing is usually only useful in assessing the Top 100 stocks. Many of the smaller companies operate in special niches of the economy that don't rise or fall with the level of economic activity in Australia or overseas.

Bottom-up investing

Bottom-up investing focuses on individual stocks rather than the larger economic picture. Here, an investor researches the company's business activity and potential. The bottom-up approach is difficult because you have to know a lot about the companies concerned to be successful. Though modern technology has made available more information than ever before, it requires sophisticated interpretation to be useful in company research.

MONKEYS, CAMELS AND DARTBOARDS

A few years ago, in Germany, a camel won a stock-picking competition with a porn actress and a sharemarket analyst. The analyst came third. The camel picked its shares with nose nudges. I don't know how the actress picked hers.

This kind of exercise has been popular since Princeton economist Burton Malkiel published *A Random Walk Down Wall Street* in 1973, debunking the efficient market theory. Malkiel argued that if the sharemarket was truly efficient, meaning share prices accurately reflected all information known about companies, then a blindfolded monkey throwing darts at the listing of stocks in the financial pages of a newspaper should do as well as professional investors in selecting a good portfolio.

The *Wall Street Journal* began testing the theory in 1988, except that it used its own reporters, blindfolded, to throw the darts instead of a blindfolded monkey. The exercise lasted more than six months and these primates won about 40 per cent of the time.

In Britain in 2012, *The Observer* newspaper ran a stock-picking competition between a house cat named Orlando, three professional fund managers and a team of students. Each team invested a notional £5,000 in five companies from the FTSE All-Share index at the start of the year. While the professionals used their decades of investment knowledge and traditional stock-picking methods, Orlando chose stocks by throwing his favourite toy mouse on a grid of numbers allocated to different companies.

After every three months, the competitors could exchange any stocks, replacing them with others from the index. By the end of September, the professionals had generated £497 of profit compared with £292 managed by Orlando. But a strong final quarter saw

(continued)

(continued)

the cat's portfolio ending the year at £5,542.60, compared with the professionals' £5,176.60.

A similar exercise in Russia in 2010 pitted Lusha, a performing chimpanzee from a circus, against a panel of bankers. Each participant was given one million roubles to invest — choosing from a list of 30 stocks, from which they could choose eight. Lusha — whose day job was riding a scooter — tripled the value of her portfolio in a year, outperforming 94 per cent of her competitors.

In January 1999, during the tech boom, Raven Thorogood III, a six-year-old female chimpanzee, picked the MoneyDex, the internet's first index of internet stocks, by throwing ten darts at a dartboard containing the names of 133 internet-related stocks. By the end of June 1999, Raven's picks were up by 55 per cent and by the end of the year, her portfolio was up by 200 per cent.

Unfortunately, the MoneyDex came and went. Like many luminaries of the tech boom, Raven got cleaned out when the market went bust. This experience could be the lot of all super-star short-term stock-pickers. Getting every stock-pick right is impossible.

Buying profits or buying blue sky

When you buy a share, you're buying a flow of future profits and dividends. You can value these potential earnings using the P/E ratio, which converts profits and share prices to a comparable base.

On the other hand, 'blue sky' refers to the potential of a stock; the multi-billion-dollar markets that it could one day crack. When you buy blue sky, there's nothing tangible on which to base the valuation.

REMEMBER

The correct term for buying blue sky is *speculating*. If your portfolio has a well-diversified spread of core holdings, nothing is wrong with having 5 to 10 per cent of it in speculative stocks. However, if your portfolio has only speculative stocks, you're not investing — you're gambling.

Knowing When to Buy Resources

The first thing to remember is that resources stocks are different (refer to Chapter 8). Earnings and dividend flows are far less predictable than with industrial stocks. You have to use different methods of choosing stocks and timing your moves with resources. This is necessary to weather the fluctuations in the commodity price cycles and exploration or production issues.

Resources companies produce commodities that are inputs in industry, so they perform best when global industrial production is rising. Australian mineral commodity producers supply much of this production to the Asian, US and European markets. When those economies falter, Australia's resource companies are the losers.

The proportion of capitalisation of the Australian sharemarket represented by resources stocks has fallen from about two-thirds to about 25 per cent in the past 30 years, as the representation of other industries has increased. Resources stocks have a place in a portfolio as long as investors understand their cyclical nature.

The resources sector is usually attractive when the Australian dollar is weak because the supply contracts of mining companies are written mostly in US dollars. With a weak currency and the prospect of a global economic upswing, the resources sector benefits. The price of the commodity (or commodities) your company produces and the exchange rate between the A$ and the US$ are the big drivers of share prices. It's usually not worth trying to predict these variables because even the professionals can't do it successfully.

However, resources investors were handed a free kick in the early 2000s as the Chinese economy expanded; this economic phenomenon sent commodity prices surging and created hugely profitable conditions for miners and petroleum producers. Resources investment became a no-brainer for much of that period, on the back of the *super-cycle theory* — which holds that, mainly because of Chinese demand, commodity prices are going to stay higher for much longer than a normal commodity cycle.

However, Chinese growth was slowing even before the COVID-19 pandemic hit. China did hit the stimulus button to power its economy through the pandemic slump, and both the global economic recovery and ongoing strength in Chinese steel production have continued to support the prices of Australia's main commodity exports — in particular, iron ore. But while China has experienced one of the strongest post-pandemic economic recoveries globally, the diplomatic and trade tensions between Australia and China (see Chapters 4 and 11) have tempered the benefit for Australia in some areas — particularly coal, where non-market forces (that is, government policy) have crimped demand for Australian coal.

That said, other growing markets for Australia — such as India, South Korea and Vietnam — are helping to pick up some of the slack. But although iron ore demand is still strong (mainly because of the quality of the Australian product), China doesn't have the same insatiable interest in Australian commodities that it had in the early 2000s.

Like all companies, mining companies are now on watch for being good corporate citizens under environmental, social and governance (ESG) requirements. The industry's heavyweights were all stung by the backlash following two major mining tailings dam failures in Brazil: firstly in 2015, at a project jointly owned by Australia's BHP and Brazilian miner Vale; and then in 2019, at a wholly Vale-owned project. Both companies were pilloried for the incidents, particularly Vale, which had pledged 'Never again!' after the 2015 dam collapse.

The 2019 disaster brought ESG issues in the mining industry to centre stage, and into a very bright spotlight.

While investors had looked askance at BHP's tailing dams issue, its multinational diversified mining rival, Rio Tinto, basked in ESG approbation. Under its then chief executive Jean-Sébastien Jacques, who had succeeded Sam Walsh in July 2016, Rio Tinto made a deliberate play for ESG cachet. Between 2016 and 2018, it sold completely out of the coal business, touting itself as the only major diversified miner that didn't produce fossil fuels.

In 2018, it sold its 40 per cent stake in the Grasberg gold-copper mine in Indonesia for $3.5 billion, drawing a line under Rio's exposure to the mine's constant labour disputes, its poor safety record and its waste disposal method, which involved the mine's tailings being poured into nearby rivers. This disposal arrangement had prompted what was probably the world's most influential arbiter of ESG issues (before they became mainstream) — the Norwegian Sovereign Wealth Fund — to blacklist Rio.

But Rio worked hard to remove ESG problem areas from its operations — and business portfolio — and to embrace indigenous land rights. For these efforts, it was rated the top mining company in the World Benchmarking Alliance's Corporate Human Rights Benchmark for two years running in 2018 and 2019. In 2019, when ratings agency S&P Global Ratings published its first ever series of ESG report cards for the mining and oil and gas sectors, Rio won an 'A' rating. In October 2019, the Norwegian Sovereign Wealth Fund bought the shares again after a decade of shunning Rio.

And then, in May 2020, Rio Tinto blew up (legally) the 46,000-year-old cultural site at Juukan Gorge in Western Australia's Pilbara, despite knowing (it was told in 2014) that the site was of 'the highest archaeological significance in Australia', containing evidence of Aboriginal existence since the last Ice Age, and several 'staggering' artefacts, including a 28,000-year-old kangaroo-bone tool.

Rio Tinto blasted the site, by its own admission, to get at \$135 million worth of high-grade iron ore, which it needed for its premium 'Pilbara blend' product. Its act was fully legal, as the Western Australian government had granted Rio Tinto permission for the blast in 2013. The blast was permitted due to a state law from 1972, which apparently didn't allow for renegotiations even when new information had come to light — as was the case with Juukan Gorge.

To say there was outrage is an understatement. Rio Tinto conceded that it had failed to grasp the significance of the site and had communicated poorly with the owners about its plans. The Australian Parliament convened an enquiry into the destruction of the Juukan Gorge caves, hauling Rio Tinto executives before it. An unedifying spectacle of mealy-mouthed apologies and attempted blame-shifting from the company's leadership to previous management only added to the disgust. As Queensland MP George Christensen put it to Jacques: 'I'm trying to understand what "sorry" means . . . what is the sorrow? That it actually happened, or is the sorrow that this is now in the news?'

THE CLEAN ENERGY CONUNDRUM

Over the last decade or so, the resources industry has increasingly encountered the world of environmental, social and governance (ESG) considerations, which has big potential ramifications for companies in all areas. The link between fossil fuels and climate change makes it tougher by the day for fossil-fuel producers — countries are under pressure to reach 'net-zero-emissions' of carbon dioxide by a certain date, while various groups are trying to thrash out the framework by which companies will account for their carbon dioxide emissions (not only those they cause in their own business, but those that their customers and suppliers cause). The transition to carbon-dioxide-emission-free 'clean energy' — which is taken to mean 'renewable' energy sources such as wind power and solar power, and definitely not nuclear energy — continues apace, a process that, theoretically at least, will eventually put fossil-fuel producers out of business at its logical extension.

The paradox is that 'clean energy' will actually require staggering increases in the use of mined commodities such as copper, lithium, nickel and the 'rare earth' basket of metals, and so it therefore is likely to underpin a major expansion of mining activity. This is because 'clean energy' applications (such as solar cells, battery cells, wind turbines and permanent magnets) require metal inputs. If electric vehicle (EV) use replaces the internal combustion engine, as some believe must (and will) happen, the commodities that enable this shift need to be found, mined, processed, transported and smelted — and as a result the world will move from a fuel-intensive economic setting to a materials-intensive setting.

Juukan Gorge was a full-blown ESG watershed, and in September 2019, Rio Tinto announced that — after it had 'engaged extensively with shareholders, traditional owners, Indigenous leaders and other stakeholders' – Jacques would step down as CEO. Chris Salisbury, chief executive of iron ore, and Simone Niven, head of corporate relations, also stepped down at that time. This was a turning point for the resources industry (and indeed, the wider corporate world), when ESG considerations were revealed as having teeth.

Chapter **11**

Why Share Prices Change

From the moment the Australian Securities Exchange (ASX) opens for business at 10.00am, until the trading day closes at 4.12pm, shares in most of the 2,200 listed stocks are being priced continuously, upwards or downwards. Some stocks remain dormant, waiting to be traded.

A company's value on the sharemarket reflects the sum of investors' perception of its earnings (profit) flow. Theoretically, if the sharemarket detects something about a company that may harm its earnings flow, the company's share price falls. If the sharemarket hears news that makes it more optimistic than before about the company's earnings, its share price rises.

The process of setting a company's value on the sharemarket is subject to the reality that the sharemarket is, on a day-to-day basis, hugely influenced by the prevailing collective investor sentiment regarding the health of the global economy, and geo-political happenings. Anything that is perceived to be negative for economic growth, world trade or a company's ability to conduct its business profitably can potentially affect that sentiment — in both directions — and cause a widespread general rise or fall in share prices. Investors are always looking to market information for guidance, including economic news (particularly changes to interest rates) and political events, which can cause share prices to rise or fall.

For each individual stock, the sharemarket's objective at any time is to place a value on the company's future earnings flow. If the market can't place that value because the company doesn't yet have earnings, the market tries to estimate the potential value of the company. This methodology is not an exact science; looking into the future is never certain. Experienced investors, however, try to use all the tools available to them to predict the direction of the share price. In the short term, investors have to grapple with the reality that the share price can also be affected by intangible factors such as sentiment, hype and word-of-mouth.

In this chapter, I discuss all the different types of things that can make share prices rise and fall.

Influences on the Price of a Share

Share prices change because sellers and buyers are constantly reviewing companies' earnings prospects. Over the long term, two factors determine the direction of share prices — future expectations of earnings and the price-to-earnings (P/E) multiples (see the sections 'Earnings, earnings, earnings' and 'The pull of the P/E', later in this chapter). Both of these factors depend on an evaluation from buyers and sellers as they learn more about the listed companies.

REMEMBER

Put simply, share prices react to supply and demand. The sellers are in charge of the supply and the buyers provide the demand. Both camps are driven by their expectations of future value. You can see the buyers and sellers in the market depth screen (refer to Chapter 6).

If more buyers move into the market, the demand grows and share prices go up — especially if there is limited supply. If supply and demand are just about equal, the share price is likely to move around in a narrow range for a while, until one of the factors outweighs the other. Share prices come down when supply is greater than demand, and when more investors start to sell.

An increase in demand for a company's shares means an increase in price, unless supply increases to match it. If an increase in demand is accompanied by a decrease in supply, the rate of the price rise increases. To coax sellers into parting with their shares, buyers raise their bid prices.

From the sellers' position, if their shares can't find buyers, the asking price drops until the shares sell. The keener sellers are to sell, the lower the price at which they offer their shares.

Share prices don't always change — the share prices of successful companies that are growing their revenue and earnings do go up, but even the best can't be expected to rise continually. Sometimes a kind of equilibrium happens when buyers are happy to pay and sellers to accept at the prevailing price. Investors who chart prices call this a *trading range* or *sideways trading* — so termed because on a price chart, a price that isn't rising is moving sideways — just like the sharemarket index.

While sharemarkets have historically generated positive returns of more than 60 per cent on a monthly basis, and more than 70 per cent on a calendar-year basis, on a day-to-day basis it's closer to 50/50 as to whether the share market will go up or down (see Figure 11-1).

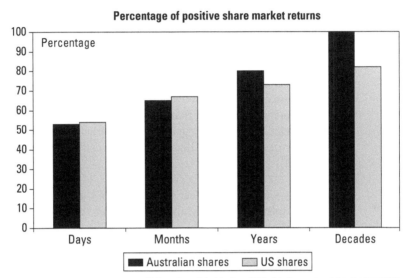

Percentage of positive share market returns

Daily and monthly data from 1995; data for years and decades from 1900.

Source: AMP Capital

FIGURE 11-1:
Percentage of positive sharemarket returns over time periods.

REMEMBER

The Australian sharemarket, like all sharemarkets, is greatly influenced by the US sharemarket. If the major US indices — the S&P 500 index, the Dow Jones or the Nasdaq Composite index — fall substantially, Australian share prices are likely to be under pressure for no other reason than because US prices fell. Not fair, maybe, but it happens, and should be factored in to any short-term assessment of the local market.

Between 2016 and 2020, investors had to consider another unpredictable influence on the US sharemarket — the US's then-President Trump's penchant for tweeting his thoughts. His tweets could cause market conniptions. Often this happened while Australian investors were asleep, and they would wake to find that the US markets, or their futures versions, were down. It's not just ex-President Trump, though. Tweets from Tesla founder Elon Musk have also been adjudged to have the potential to move the market in Tesla stock, and the US Securities and Exchange Commission (SEC) has warned him about this several times.

The following sections explore some of the key company-specific factors that can impact supply and demand and therefore influence the price of a company's shares.

Pricing and liquidity

Liquidity — the ease of buying or selling a share — can be a major influence on a share price. If a company's shares are rarely traded, even just one active buyer or seller can decisively influence the share price in the short term.

If a share is not liquid, sudden trading can deplete the possible sellers without satisfying demand. Now, the buyers have to tempt other sellers by bidding up the stock and paying more for it than they intended. Similarly, a large selling order can overwhelm the possible buyers in the market. Now, the share price will go down to attract buyers. Non-liquid stocks are usually more volatile in price than liquid shares.

While supply and demand affect share prices in the market, it's just as important to ask what influences supply and demand (see the nearby sidebar 'Buying back the farm').

BUYING BACK THE FARM

Increased demand for a company's shares could be coming from the company itself. Companies often buy back chunks of their equity as part of their continuing focus on capital management — if companies realise that if they have excess capital, for which they cannot find an effective use, they have a duty to return the capital to the company's owners, the shareholders. A company can do this through a capital return, a special dividend or increased dividend, or by buying back its own shares.

Many Australian companies have bought back their own shares in recent years, including Rio Tinto, ANZ Banking Group, Qantas, AGL Energy, CSR, Woolworths, Aurizon and Amcor.

Share buybacks have been a popular tool for companies because they tend to increase share prices by boosting earnings per share. Another, more cynical, view is that they can also benefit company executives with remuneration linked to company share prices.

Buybacks certainly appeared to get out of hand in the US over the period 2016 to 2019 when, spurred on by President Trump's tax cuts, companies in the S&P 500 index spent US$2 trillion on buybacks, 30 per cent more than what they spent over the previous three years, according to S&P Global Market Intelligence. Investment bank Goldman Sachs said in May 2020 that buybacks had been 'the only source of net demand for shares in the past decade'.

Buyback programs certainly appeared to sustain the ten-year bull market in the US after the global financial crisis (GFC), especially in its latter phase. Morgan Stanley analysts found that, on average, a company's shares were 13 per cent higher a year after its management had announced cash return measures. Arguably, that benefited share-holders; however, critics argued that it was simply a lazy use of cash. The COVID-19 crash of February–March 2020 stopped buybacks in their tracks — suddenly, companies needed to retain the cash. And US companies that received government stimulus money to stay in business during the COVID-19 shutdown were banned from using it for share buybacks.

Share buybacks come in two types: on-market and off-market. *On-market* share buy-backs involve a company buying its own shares on the market; *off-market* share buy-backs are where the company sets a price at which it will buy shares, and invites acceptances. In both cases the bought-back shares are cancelled, increasing the earn-ings and dividend per share on those that are left (assuming the company's profit remains the same).

Being able to get excess franking credits out into the hands of shareholders, who can make use of them — whereas the company cannot — has made off-market buybacks more popular with Australian companies. Shareholders like them, and the company can buy the shares at a relative discount to the market price — generally, it's a win-win.

Each buyback proposal must be assessed differently, on its merits. When you consider a buyback, you have to consider what is different about the buyback offer compared to selling on the market or, alternatively, whether you're happy to hold the stock after the buyback opportunity closes.

Since 2008, Australian companies have bought back about $112 billion worth of their own shares, at an average of about $8 billion a year — with a peak year of $41 billion in 2018–19, powered by a swathe of multi-billion-dollar buybacks from the likes of BHP ($14.5 billion) and Rio Tinto ($8.3 billion). Another bumper year may be pending in 2021 — analysts say the banks alone are sitting on at least $30 billion in surplus capital available for capital returns.

Earnings, earnings, earnings

The three most important words when you're dealing with the sharemarket are earnings, earnings and earnings. Over the long term — which you should be thinking about when investing in shares — rising share prices follow rising earnings.

TIP

If a secret to sharemarket investing exists, this is it — the sharemarket creates wealth when well-managed companies with a competitive advantage make money, and their shares grow in value. From their revenue, according to their margins, these companies earn a profit. Every year, they pay some of this profit (usually about two-thirds) out to their shareholders in the form of dividends, and they retain the rest for reinvestment.

Over the long term, just over half of the total return of the Australian sharemarket comes from dividends (51 per cent, according to AMP Capital). The rest comes from the increase in the value of companies, which rises as the retained earnings compound inside the company and the P/Es expand. Given good management, the earnings — and thus the dividend — grow over time.

Table 11-1 shows a simplified version of how a company — and thus its shares — grows in value. In the example shown, a business is started with $100 in assets. The business makes a profit of $10 in its first year: a return of 10 per cent. Of that profit, the business decides to pay half out as a dividend to shareholders, and retain the other half for reinvestment. Table 11-1 shows what happens to business assets if these returns and payout rates continue for six years.

TABLE 11-1 **The Earnings Matrix**

Year	Business Assets ($)	Profit (Return on Equity) ($)	Dividend ($)	Retained Earnings ($)
1	100.00	10.00	5.00	5.00
2	105.00	10.50	5.25	5.25
3	110.25	11.00	5.50	5.50
4	115.75	11.60	5.80	5.80
5	121.25	12.20	6.10	6.10
6	127.65	12.80	6.40	6.40
7	134.05			

Source: Investors Mutual Limited

As Table 11-1 shows, in its second year, the company also makes a return of 10 per cent. But this figure now applies to a larger asset base, by virtue of the $5 of retained earnings from year one. The dividend payout ratio remains at half of the profit, so it increases — as does the amount of retained earnings. In this example, the return is a consistent 10 per cent; because this applies to an ever-increasing asset base, if the payout ratio remains the same, the dividend and the amount of retained earnings increase every year.

If dividends are a poorly understood feature of sharemarket investment, retained earnings are even less visible. But as retained earnings compound over time, the part they play in building wealth is very important.

Successful companies grow their revenue and profits. When CSL was privatised by the Australian government in 1994, it had revenue of $193 million and profit of less than $20 million. In the 2020 financial year, the company (which these days reports its results in US dollars) earned revenue of US$8.5 billion (A$11.4 billion) and a net profit of US$2.1 billion (A$2.8 billion).

While the sharemarket is extremely prone to short-term sentiment swings, over the long term, a company's profits (or earnings) are the major influence on its share price. That's not only the profits earned today, but the profits that you and other investors expect the company to earn in the future. The link between the price and the earnings is the price/earnings (P/E) ratio.

The pull of the P/E

The *price/earnings (P/E) ratio* simply relates a share's price to its earnings. However, it is also a strong driver of a company's share price because it reflects the going rate for the company's earnings, in that the market pays a premium for companies with earnings that are growing faster.

If investors are excited about the prospects for a given company, they may be willing to accept a higher P/E ratio in order to buy its shares. At the other end of the spectrum, if investors believe that future earnings will be underwhelming, the company's P/E ratio may languish at a relatively low level.

TECHNICAL STUFF

The P/E can be historical, where the 'E' refers to the most recently reported earnings, or forward-looking or 'prospective', where the 'E' figure is the consensus of analysts' expectations. According to financial data firm FactSet, over the last 20 years the Australian sharemarket has traded at an average historical P/E of 15.7 times earnings and an average forward P/E of 14.5 times earnings (for a chart of the fluctuations around these averages, see Figure 11-2).

REMEMBER

The P/E is not an exact method of assessing value. While a high P/E ratio can certainly indicate that a stock is expensive, it can also tell you that professional investors are prepared to value the company more highly because they respect the earnings growth rates the company has been able to achieve. Conversely, a low P/E ratio could be an indicator of poor performance by the company — and that the stock could be a 'value trap', where the low P/E looks attractive, but the price keeps falling. In other words, the stock was cheap for a reason.

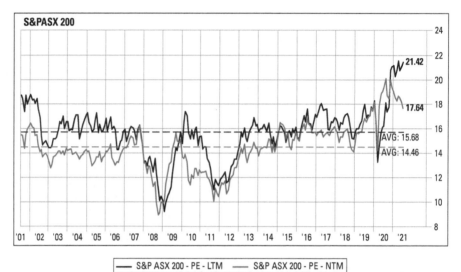

FIGURE 11-2:
S&P/ASX 200
P/E changes,
historical and
forward, 2001–21.

Source: FactSet Financial Data and Analytics

I provide more detail on the P/E ratio in chapters 5 and 7, including how to use it when assessing what is a 'value' stock and what is a 'growth' stock.

P/E expansion and contraction

Share prices rise for two reasons — fundamental reality and the perceptions of that reality — which in a perfect world should work in concert but, in reality, are often at odds. Perception, as in investor sentiment, can push the P/E higher than the fundamental facts can justify.

Enthusiasm on the part of investors can lead to P/E expansion, while disappointment on the part of investors can result in P/E contraction.

P/E expansion refers to a period when investors become convinced that the outlook for a stock is improving, and as a result, they become more willing to pay more for a dollar's worth of earnings. The stronger the earnings growth, the higher the prospective P/E is pushed — the P/E expands. *P/E contraction* refers to the opposite situation — investors detect a worsening outlook for the stocks, and they accept paying less for a dollar's worth of earnings. (Sometimes P/E expansion is called 'P/E re-rating', while P/E contraction may be called 'P/E de-rating'.)

P/E expansion is one of the three components of return from the stock market, along with earnings growth and dividend yield. When it works well, P/E expansion is a turbo-charger for share prices. When it reverses — and becomes P/E contraction — it can wipe out several years of capital growth.

P/E expansion and P/E contraction can be seen in individual share prices, and in the overall market, in terms of a share's average P/E.

For example, CSL has consistently grown its revenue and profit over time, with only three years of declining revenue in the 20 years to 2020, and four years in which net profit fell. The upshot of that record is an average revenue gain of 20 per cent and an average net profit increase of 37.2 per cent. The company's P/E has expanded to reflect the high degree of certainty that investors have that revenue and profit will continue to grow.

Refer back to Figure 5-1 in Chapter 5, which shows how the forward P/E that investors have been prepared to pay for CSL has grown since 2011 — a period that has seen CSL increase revenue in nine years out of ten, and lift its net profit in eight years. Because of this track record, paying an increasingly high P/E for CSL's earnings stream has not concerned investors at all.

Look back at the overall market's P/E, as shown in Figure 11-2. The big market slumps of the GFC (2007 to 2009) and the COVID crash of February–March 2020 are readily apparent, as is the return to optimism that followed both downturns. In 2019, the forward P/E of the S&P/ASX 200 moved from 15 times earnings in January to 19 times earnings a year later. The market slump in the COVID crash stripped that P/E back to 14 times earnings, before the rapid recovery in optimism from 'Vaccine Monday' (9 November 2020, in the US) pushed it to 20 times. Despite the expected rebound in corporate earnings, the market's forward P/E has been pruned to 17.6 times earnings.

In terms of the overall market, the 'market return' really comprises only three things: *P/E change* (whether the market values companies more or less, for a given level of earnings — in other words, P/E expansion or contraction); earnings growth; and dividends reinvested. Where income and earnings are part of companies' 'fundamental' measurements, P/E change is the 'speculative' component of return, because it is ultimately driven by investor expectations, which are unpredictable, being prone to sentiment. Figure 11-3 shows how these components have contributed to the Australian market's total return over the past five decades.

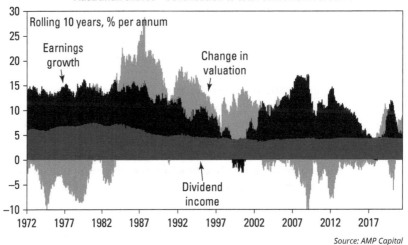

Australian shares - contribution to total sharemarket return

Rolling 10 years, % per annum

Earnings growth

Change in valuation

Dividend income

FIGURE 11-3:
Components of Australian shares total returns (per cent a year) 1972–2021.

Source: AMP Capital

When a share's valuation expands it can have a dramatic positive impact on total return. But share valuation's contribution is highly erratic — sometimes positive, sometimes negative. When the P/E ratio expands, the stock market generally produces double-digit returns. And when the ratio contracts, returns fall into the single digits.

Earning growth and dividends have had a consistently positive effect on total return over the last 50 years (especially dividends). In fact, for much of the last 20 years, earnings and dividends have continued to boost total return; unlike the highly volatile P/E ratio, which has hindered market performance.

In the second half of the 1980s and the second half of the 1990s, for example, the P/E ratio was a strong driver of the era's spectacular market returns. But P/E change actually detracted from market performance through the years 2000 to 2015 when valuations subsided from the start of the high-tech bubble.

The tyranny of expectations

Because company earnings are a major factor in determining share prices, any change in the direction of earnings or earnings forecasts causes a market reaction. This reaction immediately affects the supply and demand for a share. For example, a surprise in reported profit, or an upgrade or downgrade to a profit forecast, generally results in a reaction from buyers and sellers. The rule here is that the market hates to be surprised with bad news. However, the market likes a surprise of good news, especially a rise in profits and earnings.

Because of the 'continuous disclosure rules' of the ASX, all listed companies must immediately inform the market of any news likely to influence their share price. If the information directly affects earnings prospects, the share price can change instantly. Of course, company management tries to put the best possible spin on any new information, good or bad, in order to placate the professional analysts covering the market.

The companies' investor relations departments, and their management, work with analysts to keep them as informed as possible — without breaching commercial confidence, of course, or giving them priority over the market.

Watching out for announcements

The continuous disclosure regime means that a constant stream of announcements comes out from the 2,200 listed companies, all day, every trading day. Many of the announcements are mundane corporate housekeeping, but occasionally a genuine bombshell is flagged with a red dollar sign — meaning 'must read, could affect the share price'. If a disclosure is virtually certain to affect the share price, the stock will usually be placed in a trading halt before the announcement and stay temporarily suspended to allow the market to digest the new information.

Things are happening to companies all the time that they have to report to the market. If the news is good — for example, a mineral discovery, successful drug trial or a takeover bid — it's a good feeling for the shareholders, who know the stock is likely to jump on its return to trading. But if the news is bad, they get the opposite feeling.

An example of good news came in October 2019 for shareholders of biotech company Actinogen Medical, which announced excellent results for its drug candidate Xanamem in a trial against Alzheimer's disease. The Phase I clinical trial (for more information on clinical trials, refer to Chapter 8) demonstrated a 'significant improvement in cognition' in the trial volunteers — and Actinogen shares surged five-fold in less than a week. At the time of writing, the company has announced that Xanamem will enter a Phase II clinical trial to test whether it can improve cognitive ability in patients with mild cognitive impairment, the first clinical stage of Alzheimer's disease.

In May 2019, fellow biotech Orthocell announced the results of the first patients completing a trial of its CelGro tissue repair technology in regenerating damaged nerves. Results from the first four patients showed they transitioned from having zero muscle usage to significant return in their muscle performance after operations using CelGro. The share price skyrocketed by 700 per cent in a day and a half.

Less-liquid companies, with wide bid-ask spreads (the difference between the buy quote, or bid, and the sell quote, or ask), can go ballistic under the right circumstances. The most eye-watering take-off in stock price in recent years was that of Stemcell United, which extracts plant stem cells for use in traditional Chinese medicine. In March 2017, Stemcell United told investors it had appointed a medical cannabis expert to look at opportunities to use its plant genetics and stem-cell technology in the medical cannabis sector — which was 'hot' at the time. The stock surged almost 3,000 per cent in one day, from 1.2 cents to 37 cents. The stock has since retreated to 2 cents.

The same kind of thing is a feature of the junior resources stocks — a share surge on the back of a promising drilling result, or a new discovery, has been one of the great traditions of the Australian sharemarket since its earliest days. In particular, the names of nickel explorers Poseidon and Tasminex live on as synonyms for instant riches — and the inevitable bust. On one day in January 1970, Tasminex shares surged from $3 to $96 on the basis of a false report that the company had struck nickel at Mount Venn in Western Australia. Fellow nickel explorer Poseidon made that jump look paltry, rocketing from 50 cents to $280 in a few months, on news that it had struck nickel nearby at Windarra.

In more recent time, in July 2012, nickel explorer Sirius Resources was trading at 5 cents until news of two huge nickel discoveries, first Nova and then Bollinger, in Western Australia's Fraser Range area, sent the stock soaring to $5 by March 2013 — a 100-bagger. The second discovery sent Sirius rocketing from $2 to $5 in only a few days. Sirius was taken over by Independence Group (now IGO Limited) in 2015.

REMEMBER

On any given day, somewhere on the market, you can be sure something is soaring skyward — however temporarily. Price movements are usually more staid in the industrial sector of the market, although good news is still good news, and quick-fire, double-figure gains in share price are often seen in this sector. But generally speaking, it's hard for a stock to hold on to a stratospheric share price rise if there is nothing of substance to underpin it. CSL has moved from (the equivalent of) 77 cents to $305, but it has taken the stock 27 years to do so — and there is plenty of substance to justify the rise.

Profits, expectations and 'confession season'

Companies report their financial results to the stock exchange at least twice a year — an interim (half-yearly) and a preliminary final result. During the reporting seasons, January–February and July–August, the market is inundated with profit announcements. The two main reporting dates are 31 December and 30 June.

Most Australian companies use the 30 June ending date for the financial year, but some follow the American model and use the calendar year as the financial year. Companies with a financial year that ends on 30 June report their final results for the year in July–August. At this time, companies that use the calendar year as their financial year report their interim (half-yearly) result to 30 June. The reverse occurs in January–February.

TECHNICAL STUFF

Not all companies use these dates. Many banks, such as National Australia Bank, Westpac and ANZ, use 30 September as their end-of-year balance date, although a few use 31 August. Macquarie Group balances on 31 March, along with CSR. Agricultural chemicals group Nufarm's year ends on 31 July, while Sigma Healthcare, the drug wholesaler and manufacturer, uses 31 January.

For most of the year, expectation of profit is what influences the share price. However, on the two trading days when the interim and preliminary reports are released, a company's actual profit results affect the share price.

TIP

Sometimes, investors are confused when a result seems to bring a contrary reaction. For example, a company's share price may fall after a large profit rise is recorded. This happens because the sharemarket buys and sells on the expectation of results. What's most important about the actual profit result is whether it meets, beats or falls short of the consensus expectation, and to what extent (in the case of the latter two cases).

REMEMBER

Company profits wax and wane along with economic performance and company-specific factors. The ASX's full-year reporting season for 2019–20 came after the appearance of COVID-19 in the second half of the financial year had caused a market crash and plunged economies — Australia's included — into turmoil. According to AMP Capital, of major ASX companies (the bulk of the S&P/ASX 200 index) with a 30 June balance date, 64 per cent reported a worse result than the previous corresponding period — the highest such rate since 2009. But by the 2020–21 full-year reporting season, with the economy recovering, that proportion fell to just 25 per cent. Figure 11-4 shows the score.

The weaker profits inevitably flowed through to dividends. AMP Capital reported that only 27 per cent of companies increased their dividends in 2019–20, well below the longer-term norm of 62 per cent. And 55 per cent of companies actually cut their dividends, almost twice the previous worst figure of 28 per cent (in 2018–19). But in the reporting season a year later, in 2020–21, 67 per cent of companies lifted their dividends, and only 12 per cent saw a cut. Figure 11-5 shows the tale of this dividend taper and recovery.

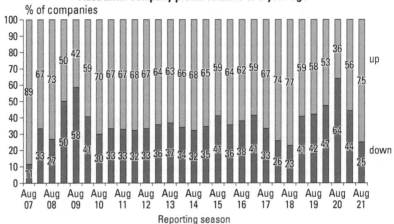

Australian company profits relative to a year ago

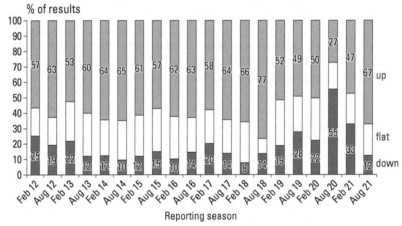

Australian dividends relative to a year ago

The sharemarket loves being surprised with good news, but a profit report that doesn't meet expectations usually results in a fall in the share price. Very severe (20 per cent to 40 per cent) price falls can easily happen if the market feels let down by a company reporting a profit that falls well short of what previous information had led the market to believe. If the expected profit turns out to be a loss, the reaction could be even worse.

It is often a surprise to new investors that a company can report an increase in profit and yet still get pummelled by the sharemarket — but that can happen if the market is expecting an even higher revenue or profit. On the day of the profit announcement, what the market had been led to expect — either by the company's guidance, or analysts' consensus estimates that the company had not talked-down if it felt they had become overstretched — is what the result is actually assessed against. Figure 11-6 shows how the major ASX companies' profit results have performed in recent years relative to these all-important market expectations.

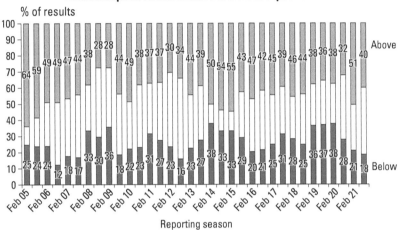

Australian profit results relative to market expectations

FIGURE 11-6:
Australian company profit results relative to market expectations 2005–21.

Source: AMP Capital

TECHNICAL STUFF

In the weeks leading up to their reporting season, companies usually try to prepare the market for a profit rise or fall. This process is called *guidance*, meaning the practice by which companies seek to manage the market's expectations of their profit, either by giving specific forecasts themselves or by commenting publicly on the forecasts posted by research analysts. The move to guidance arose from a crackdown in 1999 by the Australian Securities and Investments Commission (ASIC) and the ASX on selective briefings given to analysts. Traditionally, companies told analysts in these briefings whether their forecasts were accurate; if not, the analysts changed their forecasts and the altered expectation filtered out to the market. But ASIC and the ASX were rightly concerned that this practice breached the continuous disclosure requirements, and suggested instead an informal system of guidance. Providing guidance is neither a stock exchange listing rule nor a Corporations Law requirement — it is voluntary, but it has effectively become expected by the market.

When guidance alerts the market that the company is poised to announce a big profit increase — called a *profit upgrade* — the reaction is equally quick, with a price rise in the shares. But with the opposite, a *profit warning*, the reaction is also equally quick — and savage. Share price falls of up to 40 per cent are common when highly favoured companies shock the market with a profit warning. This movement is P/E contraction in a very short period of time, and unfortunately — if you're holding the shares — the 'P' (price) contracts with the P/E.

In early 2020, as the economic impact of the Covid-19 pandemic spread, the ASX told its listed companies that they did not have to provide forward-looking statements, and could — in light of how the economic situation had changed so drastically, so quickly — 'withdraw' previously lodged guidance. A flurry of retracted guidance statements ensued, and any company maintaining its existing guidance was treated as if it had upgraded its expectations.

The move to guidance means that the market effectively has a 'confession' season before each reporting season. The main confession season happens in April and May after companies see their results for the March quarter. If companies realise that they're not going to meet the market's profit expectations for the full year, they tell the market about it.

The reaction of the market to a profit downgrade can be horrendous — especially if it happens more than once. From levels above $8 in 2018, horticulture operator Costa Group had its value cut by 70 per cent by late 2019 as it downgraded its profit guidance four times in a little over a year due to a series of issues, including drought, in its Australian and Moroccan growing areas. The market brought the stock price down from a clearly too-optimistic level. Costa Group worked its way back with a 100 per cent gain by May 2021, but another disastrous downgrade — this one largely driven by labour shortages among fruit and vegetable pickers due to COVID-19, but with pest outbreaks and hailstorms thrown in — stripped 31 per cent from its value.

Shareholders of building materials group Boral endured six profit downgrades over two years in 2019–20, that cumulatively slashed its market value by 70 per cent. That lower price attracted Kerry Stokes' Seven Group on to the share register — at the time of writing, Seven had just taken control of Boral, having bought more than half the shares.

Well before its China troubles, which slammed its share price in November 2020 — and were not really its fault (turn to Chapter 4 for more) — Treasury Wine Estates had dismayed its shareholders with a surprise profit downgrade in January 2020, mainly on the back of problems in its commercial wine business in the US, where it was hit by a glut of cheap wine. Over two days alone, its share price took a 30 per cent dive, stripping $3.9 billion from its market capitalisation.

Manchester and homewares specialist retailer Adairs has rebuilt its credibility after a disastrous profit downgrade in late 2016, when it admitted that it had got its inventory wrong in the crucial bed linen category, which at the time accounted for about 40 per cent of total sales. Failing to get bed linen fashion trends right was an embarrassing look for a specialist — the shares fell 42 per cent in a day, to $1.48. Almost five years later, Adairs was trading at $4.21 and had been forgiven by shareholders.

Judging quality of earnings

Sometimes a financial report shows a healthy jump in profit but doesn't produce a share price rise. The reason can be the poor quality of the earnings. The term 'quality of earnings' refers to how much of the reported earnings are derived from actual operating cash flow.

The cash earnings from the business can be boosted, or reduced, by one-off items that don't recur. A company may sell a business or a property, and book the profit. If you look at the underlying profitability of the company, you need to discount such abnormal profits, which aren't expected to happen again.

A large abnormal loss in profit, on the other hand, may not be a disaster if the actual underlying earnings of the company have risen. Depreciation, provisions for bad and doubtful debts, adjustments to meet the new reporting standards and tax rates may detract from the quality of earnings.

The Economy as a Predictor

Because economic conditions directly affect companies' earnings prospects, economic news is an important influence on the sharemarket. A bewildering array of economic statistics is published each year and not all of those statistics are easily understood. The following are some of the economic conditions and statistics that affect the sharemarket (all of them affect investors' and traders' perception of the health of the sharemarket, what local and global economic data means in that context, the constant interplay between risk and return, and the relative attractiveness of shares versus bonds):

>> **Australia's official interest rate:** Set by the Reserve Bank of Australia, the official interest rate is the overnight (or *cash*) rate used in the money market, where banks and financial institutions store money overnight. The official interest rate has been held at a record low of 0.1 per cent since November 2020.

As a rule, stock markets don't like rising interest rates. When interest rates rise, two major effects take place on the stock market: borrowing costs for companies go up, effectively lowering profits; and money moves from shares to bonds, which become more attractive compared to shares.

>> **Exchange rate:** This rate, which is constantly changing over the 24/7, five-days-a-week (New York time) foreign exchange market, shows how the Australian dollar fares against other currencies. A company that exports or imports products or services, or has receipts or payments in other currencies, is affected by the exchange rate between the Australian dollar and foreign currencies.

REMEMBER

The most important of these currency crosses is the rate of the A$ to the US$. A lower A$ is actually good for the Australian economy, making both exports and local import–replacement industries more competitive. On the other hand, a rising A$ is often a function of improving global economic conditions. For this reason, investors are advised not to use the exchange rate in isolation to decide whether to buy or sell stocks. A lower A$ is particularly good for the miners who sell their commodities in US$ but take their profits and report their earnings in A$. Since it was 'floated' in December 1983 — meaning the foreign-exchange market was allowed to set its value, not government or Reserve Bank of Australia (RBA) policy — the Australian dollar has fluctuated from a low of 47.75 US cents in April 2001 to a high of US$1.10 in July 2011. At the time of writing, an Australian dollar bought you 75 US cents.

>> **Inflation rate:** This rate reflects the rate of increase in consumer prices. Interest rates are the primary weapon against inflation, which is the tendency of goods and services to rise in price over time. The sharemarket dislikes inflation because inflation pushes up costs for companies faster than the companies can pass them on to customers, adversely affecting their earnings.

Australia's inflation rate has averaged 4.87 per cent from 1951 until 2021, reaching a record high of 23.90 per cent in the fourth quarter of 1951 and a record low of –1.30 per cent in the second quarter of 1962.

>> **Rate of growth of Australia's gross domestic product (GDP):** The value of all goods and services produced in the economy is recorded in the GDP.

According to research firm Trading Economics, Australia's annual GDP growth rate has run at 3.33 per cent from 1960 until 2021, reaching a record high of 9 per cent in the first quarter of 1967 and a record low of –6.30 per cent in the COVID-19-slammed second quarter of 2020. The quarterly GDP growth rate averaged 0.84 per cent from 1959 until 2021, reaching an all-time high of 4.40 per cent in the first quarter of 1976 and a record low of –7 per cent in the second quarter of 2020.

>> **The US economic growth and interest rates:** The United States is the world's largest economy, and its health is vital to the sentiment of the sharemarket.

According to research firm Trading Economics, the US GDP's annual growth rate averaged 3.12 per cent from 1948 until 2021, reaching an all-time high of 13.40 per cent in the fourth quarter of 1950 and a record low of –9.10 per cent in the second quarter of 2020 — with this 'outlier' reading reflecting the shock-and-awe of the COVID-19 slump (which was followed by a significant snap-back).

>> Trading Economics also reveals that the US's official interest rate (the 'Fed Funds Rate') averaged 5.50 per cent from 1971 until 2021, reaching an all-time high of 20 per cent in March 1980 and a record low of 0.25 per cent in December 2008. Since March 2020 the rate, which is used as a benchmark both for short-term lending for financial institutions and as a peg for many consumer rates, has been targeted at 0–0.25 per cent, down from a previous target range of 1–1.25 per cent.

>> **US non-farm payrolls (NFP):** The monthly NFP shows the total number of jobs that were created in the US economy in the previous month. The number is known as 'non-farm' because it excludes people working at the basic level of the agricultural sector.

Investors watch the NFP closely. It is often called the most important piece of economic data of them all because it provides an update about the overall health of the US economy — more jobs tend to be created when the economy is doing well. Like company profits, market reaction to the NFP usually revolves around how the announced figure relates to market expectations.

>> **China's economic growth rate:** The Chinese boom since the late 1980s has had a huge influence on commodity prices worldwide, as China's unprecedented industrialisation and economic expansion has required raw materials. Both the Australian economy and sharemarket have been big beneficiaries of this effect, with China hoovering up Australian commodities as soon as they can be mined or pumped — and directly contributing to the massive profit growth of Australia's big miners and petroleum companies. That's why the Australian sharemarket watches Chinese economic statistics very closely — although the numbers come out so quickly after the end of each quarter that many Western watchers take them with a grain of salt.

According to Trading Economics, China's annual economic growth rate has averaged 9.27 per cent from 1989 until 2021, reaching an all-time high of 18.30 per cent in the first quarter of 2021 and a record low of –6.80 per cent in the COVID-19-hit first quarter of 2020. For the quarter ending June 2021, the Chinese economy advanced 7.9 per cent year-on-year. This figure fell short of market consensus, which expected 8.1 per cent.

>> **Purchasing managers indices (PMIs):** The PMI is an economic indicator that consists of monthly reports and surveys from private sector manufacturing firms. The PMI surveys product managers, who are the individuals that buy the materials needed for a company to manufacture its products; for this reason, PMI data is used to assess industry conditions and provide an insight into the possible future growth — or lack thereof — in the sector. PMIs are created for all the major economies, and different PMIs exist for the manufacturing and services sectors.

In China, 'official' PMIs are published by the country's National Bureau of Statistics (NBS), and 'unofficial' Caixin/Markit PMIs are published by Chinese financial news site caixin.com and UK-based research firm IHS Markit. The official PMI survey typically polls a large proportion of big businesses and state-owned enterprises, while the Caixin indicator is considered a more accurate gauge of China's privately run medium- and small-sized manufacturers and exporters. A PMI reading above 50 suggests growth, while a number below 50 indicates contraction. Market reaction to PMIs depends on how the announced figure relates to market expectations.

>> **Commodity prices:** Gold, oil, iron ore, nickel and so on trade continuously, and price changes have potentially large ramifications for producers of such commodities. Some commodity prices — certainly oil, and arguably iron ore, in the context of Chinese demand — have implications for broader economic health, and can also have geo-political effects, so investors follow them closely for their potential to affect the sharemarket.

Usually, what drives commodity prices higher is world industrial production, which depends on economic growth. In the short term, prices are affected by sudden alterations to the supply–demand situation; depending on the level of world inventories, an alteration to supply or demand can cause a quick price spike up or down.

AUSTRALIAN COMPANIES AND THE EXCHANGE RATE

Some Australian companies with big global operations report their results in US$, including biotech giant CSL; mining companies BHP, Rio Tinto, South32, Newcrest and Fortescue Metals Group; oil and gas heavyweights Woodside Petroleum and Santos; global securities registry leader Computershare; insurer QBE; medical device heavyweight ResMed; investment firm Janus Henderson; logistics giant Brambles; packaging group Amcor; healthcare companies Ramsay Health Care and Sonic Healthcare; building materials producer James Hardie; protective equipment maker Ansell; and electronics design software company Altium.

Generally speaking, a stronger A$ is bad news for shareholders in these companies — while they report their results on a 'constant currency' basis, which eliminates foreign exchange movements from one year to the next, the Australian dollar dividends will be reduced if the A$ appreciates against the US$, depending on the exchange rate at the time the dividend hits their bank account (Fortescue Metals Group pays dividends in A$). These stocks may also show a weaker share price when the A$ is strong.

A strong A$ can also be a problem when Australian companies earn revenue overseas — the stronger the Australian currency is against an overseas currency, the less revenue companies can earn in A$ terms (in other words, the stronger the A$ against an overseas currency, the less A$ each 'unit' of overseas revenue buys when it's converted to A$ in the reported financial results).

Companies with significant percentages of their revenue coming from offshore include Appen, Boral, Treasury Wine Estates, Macquarie Group, Worley, CSR, BlueScope Steel, Zip Co, Austal, Cochlear, Flight Centre, SDI, Carsales.com, Aristocrat Leisure, Ainsworth Game Technology, Hansen Technologies, Reliance Worldwide Corporation, Seek, Sims, Orora, GrainCorp, Breville, Adbri, GWA, Bega Cheese, Incitec Pivot, Transurban, WiseTech Global, Nufarm and Orica.

Most of these companies use hedging contracts to reduce the volatility, but the higher the A$ rises (for example, against the US$), the more *translated earnings* (earnings converted to A$ at the half-year and full-year balance date) will suffer. Conversely, translated earnings increase as the A$ goes lower.

The biggest losers from a higher Australian dollar are exporters — the lower the A$ the better for them, as their offshore earnings increase when converted. Conversely, a higher domestic currency benefits companies importing products into Australia to sell — it takes less Australian dollars to buy goods or services denominated in a foreign currency.

Of course, in the long run, the health of a company's business, and the investor appetite for the shares, is more important than currency impacts on earnings in the short term. If the valuation is attractive and the profit outlook good enough, investors will buy the stock notwithstanding any headwind from the currency — above-market earnings growth is more important than the currency effect. (It is a similar story with buying an overseas-listed stock — get the stock selection right, and the currency risk will not matter in the long run.)

Reacting to News

The sharemarket is ravenous for information, and the continuous disclosure requirement ensures a constant flow of news about all aspects of company operations. Investors are also able to access economic, political and scientific news.

Any news that affects company earnings also influences the share price — industrial companies win new contracts; biotechnology companies release the test results for their drugs; explorers announce spectacular drilling results. All this news has to be weighed and evaluated as to how it will affect the earnings of your stocks.

In the following sections, I look at some of the kinds of news that moves share prices.

Boosting power of takeover bids

Any company listed on the sharemarket is up for sale. Another company or group of investors can make an offer to its shareholders at any time. A takeover bid is the kind of news that has little to do with earnings but can quickly affect a share price. Takeover activity can happen anywhere on the market at any time — from the depths of the resources exploration tiddlers to the very heights of the market, as with BHP's unsuccessful $165 billion bid for rival Rio Tinto in 2008.

REMEMBER

A takeover bid can be *on-market* — mounted through a broker buying shares on the ASX — or *off-market*, where an offer document is sent to the shareholders of the target company. Most takeover bids are made off-market because this allows conditions to be included in the offer. When a bid is made, shareholders of the target company receive a written offer to buy their shares.

Another option is a *scheme of arrangement*, which requires court and shareholder approval. A scheme of arrangement is usually the case with an agreed merger, but takeovers can also be hostile — and very bitterly fought.

TECHNICAL STUFF

Once an investor owns 5 per cent of a listed company, the investor must notify that company and ASIC of the shareholding, and any subsequent changes of 1 per cent or more. Once the shareholding exceeds 20 per cent — or where the shareholding is increased between 20 per cent and 90 per cent — the acquiring company must make an unconditional offer to all shareholders for their shares. The only exception is the *creep* provisions, under which an unconditional offer is not required providing that the holding of a shareholder with more than 19 per cent increases by less than 3 per cent every six months. If the market notices creep happening, you can bet that the shares will start to rise in anticipation of a takeover bid.

Usually, the shareholders of a company undergoing a takeover bid are happy with the instant boost this gives the share price. If the bidding company offers a substantial premium to the market price, shareholders may be coaxed into selling their shares. When another company gets involved, the takeover becomes a bidding war. This situation can bring an increase in share price worth several years of capital growth — or which reinstates some of the market value lost in market slumps such as the GFC and the COVID-19 crash.

A company considered a takeover target is said to have *corporate appeal*. When rumours of a takeover occur, speculators buy the company's shares hoping to turn a quick profit when a bid is announced. The kind of bids speculators are looking for include:

>> A bid that doesn't prise open the target company's share register, meaning the predator company has to lift its offer

>> A bid that flushes out another potential predator and the two of them (or even more!) slug it out

REMEMBER

Hostile takeover offers generally result in big rises for the target's shares because the prospective acquirer has to offer the company's shareholders a 'control premium' (typically in the range of 20–40 per cent, depending on the stake the prospective acquirer already has) to take their company, and the share price rises to match the bid. Once a takeover bid is announced, the bidder must make an offer to buy your shares within two months. The target company will also make a written response to the bid to its shareholders.

A takeover bid can be an instant spark for the target company's share price. In September 2019, milk and infant formula producer Bellamy's Australia soared 55 per cent to $12.89 after receiving a $1.5 billion takeover offer from China Mengniu Dairy Company. Remote-site energy provider Zenith Energy jumped 45 per cent on receiving a takeover bid from private equity group Pacific Equity Partners in March 2020. And junior resources company Capricorn Metals rocketed more than 59 per cent after gold miner Regis Resources lobbed a takeover bid (which was ultimately unsuccessful) at it in September 2018.

The paradox for investors is that companies can be takeover targets for different reasons. A company may be attractive because the company is underperforming and is being valued by the sharemarket lower than it could be, or because the company is performing well. Investing for takeover potential is a difficult game. Specialist investors — such as hedge funds — try to pick potential takeover targets, or special situations, but for most retail investors, sticking to high-quality companies, in case a takeover doesn't happen, is probably safer. That way, you're at least protected by buying a good investment.

Shareholders of the predator company may not fare as well. Sometimes, if the two companies are really a perfect fit, the share price of the buyer also rises. More often, a negative reaction occurs because the purchasing company has to spend a large amount of money on the takeover, which could incur debt. Also, the two companies might prove difficult to integrate smoothly or the purchase may be seen as an error of management — a bad move. Corporate appeal can add a significant premium to the share price, but the appeal can vanish quickly if the situation changes.

Accepting a takeover bid means selling your shares. Depending on the price you originally paid for the shares, accepting a cash takeover bid will give rise to a capital gain or loss. If you've made a capital gain, you may be liable for capital gains tax (CGT) if your total capital gains exceed capital losses in the tax year. If you've made a capital loss (capital losses exceed capital gains in the tax year), you can use your capital loss to offset capital gains in the current year, or carry it forward to offset against future capital gains (see Chapter 18).

A takeover bid can get complicated if the bidding company uses its own *scrip* (shares) as currency in making the bid. The problem with doing this is that the currency is being revalued on a daily basis by the sharemarket — since the share price is changing all the time, so is the value of the bid. (If the company is a foreign company, you have the 'double-whammy' of the exchange rate as well.) You may not want to own shares in the company that is offering its scrip for yours.

One advantage of a scrip bid is that if you accept, you're not deemed to have sold your shares, and thus are not slugged for CGT — CGT will not occur until you sell the new shares.

If a takeover battle ever gets too confusing, remember that another bid is always close by — the bid for your shares on the market. You can always take that bid in the marketplace and let somebody else make the decision.

TIP

The rule for retail investors is don't rush to react to a bid made for a company. You can afford to sit tight because you have the downside protection of that bid being there. If the company is in an area where it's possible for multiple bidders to arise, you're prudent to sit and wait. Potential bidders take time to work through what price they're prepared to pay and what tactics they're likely to adopt.

The first bid can only be the start of proceedings. When you learn that one of the shares in your portfolio is the subject of a takeover bid, you don't have to do anything at first. The bidder is required to contact you and set out its case for buying the shares, in the Bidder's Statement. Your company's board is required to examine the bid and make a recommendation to you as to what it believes you should do.

The bidder must offer a price above the prevailing market price, to induce the company's shareholders to part with their shares. If the target company's board believes the bid price is fair and reasonable, and that no higher bid from another party is likely, the board recommends that shareholders accept the bid.

If the board decides to recommend against acceptance of the bid, the board is required to present its case, in the Target's Statement. This document may include an independent expert's assessment of the likely future worth of the shares, and the company's future prospects should it continue under its current management. The bidding company may respond to this with a letter to the target's shareholders, but it is not required to do so. From this point, the success of the bid depends on the conditions of the bid and the price being offered. The price may be raised.

The bid has an expiry date, which may be extended. If the bidding company reaches 90 per cent of the shares, the bidder may proceed to compulsorily acquire the rest.

What investors most want to see is a bidding war in which their company is sought by more than one party (see the nearby sidebar 'Warrnambool Cheese & Butter takeover tussle'). Of course, takeover action can go the other way.

As if it had not given shareholders enough grief over its painful 23 years as a listed company (refer to Chapter 8), AMP was approached in October 2020 by US investment firm Ares Management Corporation with an offer to buy 100 per cent of the company at $1.85 a share. In a sudden reversal of the long-term trend, AMP shares jumped 31 per cent in two days, to $1.68.

Despite long negotiations, the takeover did not eventuate. A new joint venture between the companies was proposed in its place, in February 2021, in which Ares would take over 60 per cent of AMP's private markets business, for $2.3 billion. That deal fell through one month later, sinking AMP shares back to $1.07 — or 21 per cent lower than they were when shareholders first learned of the Ares bid. At the time of writing the shares were trading at $1.10, and AMP shareholders could only dream of someone offering $1.85 for their shares.

WARRNAMBOOL CHEESE & BUTTER TAKEOVER TUSSLE

In 2013 the sharemarket was riveted to what would hitherto have been considered a highly unlikely event — a frenzied international takeover tussle in the world of cheese, which sent the price of listed dairy producer Warrnambool Cheese & Butter (WCB) soaring.

The western Victoria-based WCB, Australia's oldest dairy processor, was listed as a farmer's co-operative in May 2004. The highly profitable company had developed strong export networks, particularly into Asia, for its cheese, skim milk and milk powder. By September 2013, that had attracted the close attention of other dairy players.

WCB was trading on the ASX at $4.51 when fellow listed dairy company Bega Cheese lobbed a cash-and-scrip (that is, Bega offered some of its shares as part payment) bid that valued WCB shares at $5.78 — a 28 per cent premium. WCB described the bid as 'inadequate', saying it did not reflect fair value.

(continued)

(continued)

The next month, Canadian dairy giant Saputo countered Bega with a bid for WCB, at $7 cash. That bid was recommended by the board of Warrnambool Cheese & Butter. Already there was 'competitive tension' — which is good for the shareholders of the target company. But this got even better a few days later, when a third bidder, Australian dairy co-operative Murray Goulburn, entered the fray with a cash bid of $7.50.

The fourth bid came from Saputo, also in October 2013, when it lifted its bid to $8. Things settled down for a few weeks, but in November, Murray Goulburn returned with a $9 offer. The next day, Bega threw in bid six, lifting the shares part of its offer such that it matched Murray Goulburn.

Saputo fired back with bid seven, also at $9, but saying that its bid was 'unconditional', whereas the other two had to get approval from the Australian Competition and Consumer Commission (ACCC). Saputo then increased its offer to $9.20, if it were to reach greater than 50 per cent of WCB's shares during the offer period. In late November, Murray Goulburn lifted its bid to $9.50.

In December, bid ten came when Saputo boosted its bid to $9.40, if it were to garner greater than 75 per cent of WCB's shares during the offer period, and to $9.60 if it were accepted by more than 90 per cent. Bega Cheese said its offer would close at the appointed time, 20 December, meaning it would not be increasing its offer.

By late January 2014, Murray Goulburn had admitted defeat, accepting Saputo's offer for the shares it had accumulated. Murray Goulburn's acceptance meant that Saputo's tenth bid would prevail, at $9.40. In February 2014, Saputo's takeover of WCB closed, with 87.92 per cent acceptance.

Ten bids and counter-bids had been thrown into the ring, while WCB shareholders delightedly watched the auction more than double the value of their shares over a four-month period.

Relying on rumours and tips

The Australian sharemarket began as a predominantly gold-based sharemarket, where a strike meant instant wealth. The late 1960s nickel boom (refer to Chapter 8) confirmed that drilling results — even if unreliable — could bring spectacular share price rises. Because of this, Australians have always been fond of a hot tip, and still are.

The cliché of the share tip picked up at a dinner party or around a barbecue is real. According to the ASX's 2020 Investor Study, for most categories of investors (male, female, next-generation, wealth accumulator, retiree, high-value investor and non-high-value investor), getting investment advice from friends and family members is just as likely as getting it from their financial adviser. Next-generation investors are more likely to take advice from family and friends than advisers (34 per cent to 29 per cent), as are wealth accumulators (33 per cent to 28 per cent). Of the ASX's categories, only retirees and high-value investors clearly favour professional advice over that from friends and family.

Given such strong reliance on family and friends, social gatherings are a perfect environment for rumours to spread. In an online world, rumours are propagated far more quickly. The various online chat forums are conduits for a vast linkage of information sharing, and it happens in an instant — but much is rumour and speculation.

Investors need to be on their guard in sorting out rumour from hard information. Under the continuous disclosure requirements of the ASX, Australian-listed companies must inform the market as soon as practicable of any news likely to have a material effect on their share price, to ensure a fully informed market.

By the time you notice a potentially undervalued stock, speculators who are quicker off the mark are already in it. The saying is, 'Buy on the rumour, sell on the fact.' You don't have to be plugged into an online chat forum to pick up a spicy bit of goss. Rumours can spread anywhere — at a bar, sitting on a train, anywhere you're on your phone. If the rumour is hot enough and you buy the shares and then sell them at a profit, technically you've broken the law. If the rumour hasn't been divulged to the wider market, what you've just done is insider trading.

Insider trading

Insider trading is referred to in Section 1002G of the Corporations Law, which says that insider trading occurs when a person possesses information not generally available to the market and they know, or ought reasonably to know, that the information is not generally available to the market. A person who transacts shares on the basis of that information, knowing that if the information were generally available it might have a material effect on the price or value of the securities, is guilty of insider trading.

The law does not specify that the person in possession of the information must be a director or an employee of the company. Insider trading can be practised by anyone who 'knows something not generally available to the market and who acts on that knowledge'. In other words, if you act on a rumour, however you came by the rumour, this description could apply to you.

Every day, about $5.8 billion worth of shares are traded on the ASX, and another $1.4 billion worth are traded on Cboe Australia. Usually, this translates to about

1.5 million individual share transactions, just on the ASX. Of that number, between 5 and 10 per cent are tainted by one of the parties having insider information. That's the conclusion of studies conducted by the University of Technology, Sydney, and the University of Western Australia. This figure matches the findings of similar studies from other countries.

The paradox is that the ASX knows that insider trading occurs occasionally — most notably, when company share prices move markedly prior to an important announcement. The exchange's surveillance of market activity (SOMA) system is onto any such irregularities in trading as fast as a seagull is onto a sick prawn. But picking up instances of possible insider trading is one thing; to secure a conviction — to prove beyond reasonable doubt that a criminal act was committed — is quite another.

Both the ASX and the market's regulator, ASIC, are very willing to prosecute insider trading. In March 2021, ASIC said that since 2011, 35 people had been criminally prosecuted for insider trading as a result of ASIC investigations, with a conviction rate of over 85 per cent. There have been charges laid since — insider trading is a crime that doesn't seem to go away. It isn't confined to the sharemarket, either; in 2021, ASIC brought charges against Westpac Banking Corporation, alleging insider trading and unconscionable conduct towards its clients over a multi-billion-dollar transaction linked to the 2016 privatisation of NSW energy assets. Westpac denies the allegations and at the time of writing, the case hadn't made it to court.

In 2015, two individuals — one a former employee of the Australian Bureau of Statistics (ABS) — were gaoled over an insider trading scam that saw the ABS employee forewarn his accomplice over a mobile phone about soon-to-be-published economic data; the accomplice, knowing the data would affect the A$/US$ exchange rate, used the sensitive information to trade in foreign exchange derivatives through two trading accounts. Supreme Court Justice Elizabeth Hollingworth described the case as 'the worst instance of insider trading to come before the courts in this country'. The scam netted the pair $7 million — but also landed them in gaol.

Rejecting Murky Offers

Human nature being what it is, some people don't want to wait patiently for the market to push their share price higher over the long term. They want to help the process along with a bit of manipulation, which by definition interferes with the free and fair operation of the market.

Trying such manipulation methods is not advisable because the ASX passes on any irregularities that its SOMA system detects to ASIC, which investigates the relevant trading, and if necessary, briefs the Director of Public Prosecutions, who may lay charges.

Investors have to be aware of the schemes and manipulations that can lure them into bad investments. Being aware and doing your research are the keys to avoiding these pitfalls.

Manipulating the price

One way to manipulate the price is to place large buy or sell orders (or both) into the trading system in order to change or maintain the price of a stock. Manipulators want to create a price rise and thus subsequent demand into which they can sell. This specialised form of manipulation is called *pump and dump*, or pushing the share price higher then suddenly lower.

Marking the close

Another method of manipulation involves buying a share just before the close of the day's trading in order to push the closing price higher. This is called *marking the close*. If a flurry of small parcels of the shares is traded just before the market closes, the exchange people take notice. Marking the close might be done to artificially lift the value of a portfolio (called window dressing) or to avoid a margin call (see Chapter 22 for more detail).

Wash trading

A *wash trade* is a trade in which the buyer and the seller are one and the same, but are transacting through different entities. A wash trade can create the impression of heavy volume where there isn't any — but it serves its purpose of grabbing the attention of speculators, pushing up the price.

Ramping

Companies can sometimes gild the lily in their announcements, making them sound better than the facts justify. During every boom, company announcements are packed with over-exuberant, wildly optimistic projections full of questionable assumptions. In that kind of environment, a fine line exists between enthusiastic announcements and deliberately deceptive information. Pumping up a company's shares using false or misleading information is called *ramping*. Today, the various online chat forums are fertile ground for share ramping. Investors have to beware of this 'hype and dump' strategy.

TECHNICAL STUFF

The ASX cracked down on ramping in June 2021, issuing an update to Guidance Note 8. Particular examples of 'ramping announcements' identified by ASX included:

>> Announcing a contract with a major customer to leverage off the customer's reputation, without properly quantifying the benefit to the entity. In one instance, this included disclosure of a 'material commercial agreement with a leading financial entity', under which the company making the announcement was to receive less than $1,000.

>> Announcing a 'contract' when in fact it is only a non-binding 'heads of agreement' or 'framework agreement' that merely establishes contractual arrangements that will apply to future orders (if any are made); the ASX does not consider these types of agreements between companies, while promising, as equivalent to an actual contract.

>> Projecting substantial revenues without reasonable grounds.

>> Describing a contract as 'material' when clearly it is not.

The ASX told companies it had observed instances of ramping announcements being made just prior to or after a capital raising, presumably with the intent of boosting the raising price or the post-raise trading price — or following the appointment of advisers who are remunerated in securities.

If the ASX suspects a ramping announcement has been made, it can suspend trading and issue a query letter to the company seeking further information about the announcement, and asking it to explain the purpose of the announcement and — if the announcement includes any projections or forward-looking statements — the reasonable grounds on which those statements are based. The ASX may also require a corrective disclosure to be made where information in a ramping announcement was not material or was incomplete or misleading; in these cases, the offending company must disclose that it has been asked to amend the announcement, and state that investors should not make investment decisions based on the original announcement.

Clocking Emotions and Biorhythms

Share prices can change because of perceptions, greed, hype, momentum and fear. Sometimes, the sharemarket can be seen as the sum of the emotions of its human entrepreneurs, subject to arbitrary whims and flights of fancy. In fact, there is a new field of study called behavioural finance that looks at the emotional aspects of investing.

According to a Wall Street saying, only two influences are at work on the sharemarket — fear and greed. Most of the time fear and greed are in equilibrium, with greed staying dominant only long enough to produce the long-term trend depicted on a sharemarket graph. Occasionally the equilibrium snaps and the pendulum swings sharply. The 1999 to 2000 technology boom was a stark example of greed taking over. So was the 2003 to 2007 China story, when greed set in and became complacency. Then the GFC hit, and fear marauded through the market for a couple of years, until a fresh boom kicked-off in 2009 — lasting, notwithstanding the odd correction, until a strange disease reared its head in early 2020.

Booms have always been a feature of the Australian sharemarket, but traditionally they were in the resources exploration stocks. In the 21st century, that propensity has extended into areas such as technology, biotech, buy-now-pay-later (BNPL) and even selling infant formula to China. Hype and momentum (which refers to the rate of change in share prices) are clearly at work during these periods, while in downturns, it's doom-and-gloom ('reverse hype') and downward momentum holding sway. In periods like the GFC crash and the COVID crash, the headlines can be uniformly gloomy — at one point in late 2008, the survival of the global financial system seemed actually to be in doubt, while in early 2020 it seemed that a real-life Hollywood disaster movie was coming real. However, it was only in hindsight that people realised that the worst of these crises had actually been a great time to buy good-quality shares.

CHARTING THE PLANETS

Don't laugh. Some technical analysts (even non-chartists who happen to be superstitious) swear by the effect of planetary alignment on the financial markets. Sometimes this study is called *planetary harmonics* or *astro-vibrations* to make it all sound more respectable. There are financial astrologers (Bill Meridian is a famous one) who believe that astrological cycles and the transit of planets can help investors pick sharemarket winners. Who knows, it might be the answer to the whole hill of beans!

Pacing the Seasons

'To every thing there is a season, and a time to every purpose under heaven,' wrote the anonymous author of the Book of Ecclesiastes in The Bible. He (or she) could have been talking about the sharemarket.

Seasonal patterns have long been observed in sharemarkets. Yet, despite the potential they provide for astute investors to profit from them — and in so doing arbitrage them away — they seem to persist. The 'January effect' has perhaps been the most famous, where January typically provides the best gains for US stocks, but anticipation of it in recent years has seen it morph into December, such that it has become the strongest month of the year for US shares. However, it is part of a broader seasonal pattern, which is positive for shares from around October/November to around May and then weaker from May. Figure 11-7 shows the seasonal pattern of average monthly changes in US share prices (using the S&P 500 index).

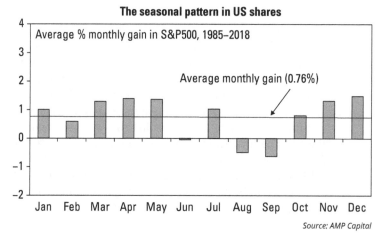

FIGURE 11-7: The seasonal pattern for US share trading, showing the average monthly gain in the S&P 500 index (per cent), 1985–2018.

Source: AMP Capital

According to Shane Oliver, head of investment strategy and chief economist at AMP Capital, the key factor behind the US seasonal pattern is the regular ebb and flow of investor demand for shares relative to their supply through the course of the year. In the case of US shares, the main drivers of the seasonal pattern are:

» Investors and mutual funds selling losing stocks to realise tax losses (to offset against capital gains) towards the end of the US tax year in September, which tends to happen at a time when capital raisings are solid

>> Investors buying back in November and December, at a time when capital raisings wind down into year-end, which then combines with both the tendency for investors to invest bonuses early in the new year, and new-year optimism as investors refocus on the future, put any disappointments of the past year behind them and downplay bad news — all at a time when capital raisings are relatively low. The illiquid nature of investment markets around late December and January (due to holidays) make these effects all the more marked.

The net effect has been that the US share market is relatively weak around the September quarter and then it strengthens into the new year, with January often being the strongest month. The year then remains solid until around May, by which point new-year optimism has started to fade a bit — and as noted previously, anticipation of the 'January effect' has started to pull buying forward into December.

Calendar-year-end window dressing by fund managers may have also added to this tendency. Since 1985, US share prices for December have shown an average monthly gain of 1.5 per cent monthly gain. This compares to an average monthly gain across all months of 0.76 per cent. By contrast, August and September are the weakest months, with falls on average.

A similar seasonal effect can be seen in Australia, although it is a little different. Figure 11-8 shows the seasonal pattern for the Australian sharemarket.

FIGURE 11-8: The seasonal pattern for Australian share trading, showing the average monthly gain in the S&P/All Ordinaries index (per cent), 1985–2018.

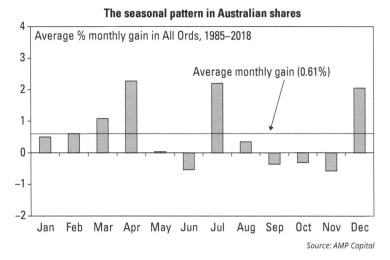

The seasonal pattern in Australian shares

Source: AMP Capital

Shane Oliver says the seasonal effect means that from the end of November to the end of May, the Australian market usually earns just over 10 per cent, while from the end of May to the end of November period usually gives a 3 per cent rise. While the strongest months of the year in the Australian market are April and July, December also tends to provide above-average gains.

Since 1985, Australian share price gains in December have averaged 2.1 per cent, with April averaging 2.3 per cent and July 2.2 per cent. This compares to an average monthly gain for all months of 0.6 per cent. The lower average monthly gain for all months in Australia compared to the US partly reflects the fact that a greater proportion of the return from Australian shares comes from a higher dividend yield compared to the US.

Chapter **12**

Working with Brokers

B rokers seem always to get pretty bad press. Their huge salaries and flashy Porsches, combined with the latest float fiasco and discredited recommendations, have lowered their standing in the investor community. Following the 2000 tech stock crash, and again following the global financial crisis of 2008 to 2009, a facetious definition of broker was 'poorer than you were last year'.

But no matter how much you may complain about stockbrokers, as an investor, you can't do without them. Stockbrokers are an essential part of the investment process because in most cases you can't buy or sell shares without using a broker. Only a qualified broker can place your order to buy or sell shares via the Australian Securities Exchange (ASX) system. However, this 'broker' could just be an online broker's interface to the ASX, on your computer screen.

In this chapter, I show you how to deal with brokers effectively. Finding a broker isn't difficult, but you need to know what brokers do and how they do it before you make your choice.

What a Broker Does

A *stockbroker* is licensed by the Australian Securities and Investments Commission (ASIC) to offer investment advice; a stockbroker also works for a firm that's licensed by the ASX to trade in the sharemarket. The sharemarket is a public marketplace, but only stockbrokers can place orders.

Shares can be transferred outside the market without involving a stockbroker, but the shareholder has to find the other party to the transaction and settle on a price. Shares can also be transferred privately without any payment; for example, you can transfer shares between family members. In all off-market transfers, a standard transfer form must be used to advise the company's share registry. The transferor and the transferee must sign this form. Off-market transfers don't require a broker because technically the shares aren't going through the physical market.

REMEMBER

A broker acts as your agent, buying or selling shares on your instructions. Stockbrokers charge a fee for this — called brokerage — and they may also offer other services, such as advice on which shares to buy or sell, portfolio management and financial planning.

In Australia, about 58 broking firms (called ASX or Cboe Australia *market participants*) are active, including Australian branches of global investment companies, such as UBS, JP Morgan, Goldman Sachs and Morgan Stanley, as well as full-service local retail firms, such as Macquarie Equities, Morgans, EL & C Baillieu, Bell Potter, Shaw and Partners, Taylor Collison, State One Stockbroking, Phillip Capital, Euroz Hartleys, Wilsons and Canaccord Genuity.

The vast majority of transactions in the Australian sharemarket are undertaken by institutional brokers, both in terms of number and value; these brokers are responsible for about 80 per cent of all trading. They are usually big international banks, but Macquarie Equities (owned by Macquarie Group) also operates in this market (it also offers full-service broking to retail clients). The institutional brokerages deal solely with the institutional investors (managed funds), superannuation funds and insurance companies that own most of the sharemarket. You probably won't deal with this kind of heavy-duty broker; fortunately, the kind of broker that you deal with probably needs you more than you need them.

The retail brokers — there's about 25 of them active across the ASX and Cboe Australia — represent, on average, about 20 per cent of value traded on the Australian market. Broadly, these are the full-service local firms (the upcoming section 'Stockbroking for Everyone' explains what I mean by 'full-service').

Then there are the nine online brokerages that are also market participants — but there are actually 31 online brokers offering services in the Australian market, on about 52 platforms.

The difference between the nine and the 31 here is that many of the online trading platforms are 'white-label' products that are operated by market participant brokers. The online retail broker market participants are CommSec, nabtrade, Bell Direct, CMC Markets, Amscot and Interactive Brokers; there are also three wholesale online brokerages that are participants: Openmarkets, FinClear and AUSIEX. Between them, these firms provide white-label broking platforms for IG Share Trading, ANZ Share Investing, Macquarie Online Trading, Saxo Capital Markets, Bendigo Invest Direct, SelfWealth Trading, St. George Bank Directshares, ThinkMarkets, Westpac Online Investing, First Prudential Markets, HSBC Online Share Trading, Sequoia Direct, Netwealth Investments, Suncorp Share Trade, Bank of Queensland Online Share Trading and Superhero. For example, both Macquarie Online Trading and HSBC Online Share Trading transact through a white-label service provided by Bell Direct.

Stockbroking for Everyone

Stockbroking was once a sellers' market. Stockbrokers held the monopoly on transactions in securities listed on the stock exchange and brokerage rates were fixed. If you wanted to buy shares, you had to use a broker. They knew you needed them and if they didn't like you as a potential customer, you were locked out of the sharemarket. You could go to smaller firms, but if your investment was too small the broker would tell you to use a managed fund. Indirect share ownership was the best you could hope for.

In the past, stockbroking firms charged high prices to cover their transactions as well as their other costs, including opulent offices, well-paid research analysts and client advisers, client newsletters, and a labour-intensive back-office shuffling of the firm's paper. A brokerage rate of 2–3 per cent of the value of a transaction was considered justifiable.

That scenario is no longer true. Although stockbrokers still hold the monopoly on transactions, the difference is that, since 1984, they've been free to price their charges according to the service offered. Today, you can choose among *full-service* and *execution-only* (or *discount*) brokers, which these days operate almost exclusively online.

Buying full-service

Full-service brokers offer their clients the whole traditional kit and caboodle — advice on shares to buy and (much rarer) sell, research reports, client newsletters, access to floats, portfolio management and financial planning. Full-service brokers also know how to charge for their services. (Refer to Chapter 6 for a rundown of typical costs for full-service brokers.)

REMEMBER

Under the attack of online broking, full-service broking has evolved away from transactional, commission-driven sales to remuneration based on a percentage of assets held in portfolios that are managed for the long term. Essentially, which type of broking suits best depends on the client. The benefits of a full-service broker may be worth the cost. Such brokers offer you research and advice on stocks and other investments, and, potentially, access to upcoming floats. Brokerage fees are usually negotiable with advisory brokers; if you're trading frequently enough, you can probably negotiate a better rate.

Many full-service brokers have diversified to become wealth managers, bringing in expertise in superannuation, insurance, taxation, retirement planning and estate (wills and inheritance) planning. They may offer discretionary services, where they manage portfolios and make investment decisions for their clients. The full-service menu may include access to international shares, alternative investments, credit products, 24-hour futures and foreign exchange. The fee will reflect the meal of services the client chooses from the menu.

Increasingly, many full-service brokers are trying to move upscale to specialise in 'sophisticated' and 'wholesale' investors, who are eligible for investment opportunities at an institutional level.

The *Corporations Act 2001* permits offers of securities to be made to persons defined as 'sophisticated investors' without a disclosure document, meaning that these people get access to investment opportunities that run-of-the-mill retail investors do not get.

The 'sophisticated investor' criteria are either:

>> Net assets of at least $2.5 million (including the net assets of a company or trust controlled by the person)

>> A gross income (including the income from a company or trust controlled by the person) of at least $250,000 a year, for each of the two previous financial years

The category of 'wholesale' investor is also used, defined as someone able to invest more than $500,000 in any security or product.

The rise of online broking has not killed off full-service broking; far from it. If you have a client adviser who's helpful, courteous, interested in you and how your financial knowledge develops, and who becomes a trusted confidant, you're in good shape. If you're happy with the firm's research, recommendations, newsletters and other services, excellent. Any investor in this position would consider the increased cost of the service cheap. Many investors have the same adviser for years and stick with them as the adviser moves on to different firms.

Going online — or on the phone

Online broking certainly democratised access to the market, and smartphones took this to a whole new level. All the online brokers have apps that allow trades to be completed on a smartphone or tablet — and portfolios, charts, research and lots else to be viewed. You can buy a parcel of shares while you're sitting on the bus and sell them while jogging at lunchtime. It's great that people have this ready access to the sharemarket.

The smartphone has changed online broking in recent years. People hold in their hands the trading capability that only an institution would have had 20 years earlier. They can look at the buy and sell orders in a stock, place an order and instantly see what's happening with their portfolio. CommSec, the leading online broker, conducts around 55 per cent of its trades through its CommSec smartphone app.

Online broking certainly suits self-reliant investors, but not everyone can be that. Plenty of investors welcome the help of their stockbroker. Not all investors want to follow the market closely or trade frequently. Some are more interested in a very strategic approach to long-term investment.

Most online brokers offer *straight-through* processing, which means that trades are fully automated — you're trading directly into the market yourself. But the brokers also have filters, and if an order looks like an error (for example, it's too far away from the last trade of the stock) or possible market manipulation, it won't be lodged and you'll be asked to check it.

The 44 trading platforms offered by the 24 online brokers give investors open, cheap access to the market, for as little as $6 a trade (for amounts up to $1,000). As of 2021, online brokers accounted for about 13 per cent of all ASX trades. Effectively, that represents more than 70 per cent of retail trading. The average trade size on the online market was $19,000 in 2020, and this is increasing all the time.

CommSec controls about 40 per cent of the online share-trading market in Australia, while CMC Markets (and its ANZ Share Investing white-label customer) hold about 12 per cent, Bell Direct has about 7 per cent and nabtrade has about 5 per cent of the market. Wholesaler Openmarkets holds about 10 per cent — it clears more than $50 billion worth of trades annually, across 200,000 accounts (it also has Opentrader, which is a self-directed platform for active investors).

The extent to which Australians flocked online to trade shares during the COVID-19 pandemic is shown by the growth in the average weekly value traded through CommSec, which ballooned almost four-fold, from $1.7 billion before the pandemic to $4.2 billion during the COVID-19 period. Between 20 February and 7 August 2020, according to data from corporate advisory and research firm Vesparum Capital, retail investors were net buyers of $9 billion in stocks on CommSec, Bell Direct, CMC Markets, nabtrade, Westpac Share Trading and ANZ Share Investing.

In 2020, *retail participation* in the market — that is, regular individual investors as opposed to fund managers and investment professionals — reached almost twice what had previously been considered 'normal' levels, with $2.8 billion in daily turnover, up from $1.6 billion before the pandemic.

Research firm Investment Trends found that in 2020, the total number of active online investors (defined as those buying or selling shares at least once in 12 months) in Australia hit a record high of 1.25 million, after 435,000 people placed their first trade on the sharemarket that year. The number of online traders was up 66 per cent over 2020 and almost doubled in two years. Of the new-to-market traders in 2020, 18 per cent were younger than 25, and 49 per cent were between 25 and 39, indicating an unprecedented spike in activity by Millennial (those aged 26 to 40) and Generation Z (aged 18 to 25) Australians.

Another study by financial comparison website Canstar estimated that two-fifths of young Australians invested in the sharemarket in 2020. It found that 44 per cent of Millennial respondents and 42 per cent of Gen Zers participated in the market for the first time. Of those, the majority (58 per cent) directly invested in shares, 30 per cent invested via a managed fund, 20 per cent invested via a micro-investing app and 17 per cent invested through an exchange-traded fund (ETF). (The results do not include investments within superannuation.)

Many of these new investors were fans of Robinhood, the US-based, brokerage-free trading app on which their American counterparts were trading stocks for free. But what its Australian fans didn't know was that Robinhood was earning more than 80 per cent of its revenue from being paid by exchanges for its order flow — in other words, the exchanges take Robinhood's retail volume and sell it to institutional market-makers and traders on the other side, who use it in their own execution. Because it makes money in a different part of the trading process, Robinhood doesn't have to charge brokerage (instead, it charges a Spotify-style subscription fee). Because neither the ASX nor Cboe Australia pays for order flow, free brokerage cannot be offered in Australia.

The major online brokers are not the cheapest: CommSec charges (for clients whose cash account is with Commonwealth Bank) $10 a trade for up to and including $1,000; $19.95 for between $1,000 and $10,000; $29.95 for between $10,000 and $25,000; and 0.12 per cent of the transaction if over $25,000. Nabtrade charges $14.95 on transactions up to $5,000, then $19.95 for up to $20,000, and 0.11 per cent of the trade if it is more than $20,000. Bell Direct charges a minimum of $15 for a trade up to a transaction value of $10,000, but it gets down to $10 if you trade more often.

A new generation of low-cost trading platforms is looking to undercut the established online brokers. The lowest brokerage cost online is charged by Superhero at about $5 for a transaction worth up to $15,000 on the ASX or Cboe Australia; the same trade will cost you $7.50 at IG Share Trading, $8 at ThinkMarkets and $9.50 at SelfWealth Trading.

Another angle is offered by online trading platform Trade For Good. After investors make a trade, and after the ASX and settlement fee are deducted from the brokerage, Trade For Good divides what is left of the brokerage fee in half and donates one half to the investor's charity of choice, keeping the other half to invest in running the Trade for Good business.

In 2019, CommSec launched CommSec Pocket, an app that allows investors to invest in ETFs from a minimum investment of $50, and pay $2 each time they invest (or sell) up to $1,000. The app offers seven themes of ETFs, including Aussie Top 200, Emerging Markets, Tech Savvy and Sustainability Leaders. Pocket was designed to allow investors to get into the market with very small amounts of money — it can accommodate investments of as little as $50, with brokerage of $2 a trade up to $1,000, and 0.20 per cent of the trade value above $1,000.

CommSec was reacting to the rise of the 'micro-investment apps', which are investment platforms that don't actually go through online broking, but are designed to make sharemarket investing more accessible than ever for small investors. The first mover in this space was the ASX-listed Raiz (refer to Chapter 7), founded in February 2016, which has built seven diversified 'instant portfolios' featuring 16 ASX-listed ETFs, representing seven different asset classes. The Raiz portfolios range in risk from 'conservative' to 'aggressive', and include a socially responsible portfolio — also, the Sapphire portfolio contains Bitcoin.

The Raiz platform allows customers — mostly Millennials — to round-up purchases and automatically invest the 'spare change' in their chosen ETFs, so any dividends or distributions are automatically reinvested. The technology allocates fractional interests in ETF units, allowing users to open an account with as little as $5. There is no brokerage; investors pay a flat fee per month, based on account size. Raiz has also launched a superannuation account.

Investment app Spaceship, launched in 2017, offers both investment and super-annuation products, specifically aimed at younger Australians under the age of 45. Spaceship Voyager is a fractionalised managed fund, allowing users to invest as little or as much as they want. You can choose from three funds — the Universe Portfolio, Origin Portfolio and Earth Portfolio. Each fund is made up of shares from various different companies from around the world (users can't customise their own investment portfolios). Investors are charged a percentage of their balance for amounts greater than $5,000 (there are no fees for balances under that amount). Spaceship has hit $1 billion in funds under management and has almost 200,000 customers.

Platforms like Superhero, SelfWealth Trading, Pearler and Sharesies have all hit the Australian market in the last 18 months, joining existing 'challengers' in offering cheap brokerage and lower entry thresholds, which seem to be making a mark with younger and first-time investors. Sharesies, which trades in Australian, New Zealand and US shares, offers rates of 0.5 per cent of the transaction if below $3,000, and 0.1 per cent of the transaction if above $3,000. Sharesies is the first broker to let customers buy fractions of Australian shares rather than whole shares — with no minimum investment. Instead of paying $100 for one Common-wealth Bank share, Sharesies allows investors to buy one-tenth of a share, or any fraction.

Fractional investing is also possible with US shares on specialised app-based plat-forms such eToro, Stake and Interactive Brokers. It means that you can invest dollar amounts into a stock so you can buy a portion of it. For example, instead of buying one Alphabet (Google's parent) share for US$2,500, you could buy one-tenth of a share for US$250 — or one-hundredth of a share for US$25.

Some of the newer platforms operate under a 'custody model'. Normally, when you buy shares listed on the ASX, you need to invest a minimum of $500 per com-pany. In return, you get a holder identification number (HIN) from the ASX and your ownership of that stock is recorded by the exchange on the CHESS registry. Part of having your own HIN means that you must abide by a few rules — such as investing at least $500 when buying shares in any ASX-listed company.

To get around the minimum $500 investment, Sharesies and Superhero use one HIN for all investors. Your investments and your share ownership details are held and recorded by these platforms (not by the ASX) in a trust — this is the *custody model*. You are the 'beneficial' share owner, which means you get all the monetary benefits, including dividend payments, but you may not get voting rights. For some investors, this may not represent enough protection — there are potential trade-offs for the very cheap transaction costs.

While smartphones (and, of course, the internet) have certainly democratised access to the sharemarket, one of the criticisms of any form of execution-only broking has always been that what is not democratised is investment knowledge, experience and insight. Instant access to the sharemarket can mean the instant ability to make big mistakes. But while they do not offer advice as full-service brokers do, many of the online broking services do their best, as standard, to equip their customers with extensive research, recommendations, information, software, charting and analytical tools.

Given the surge of new investors into the market since the COVID-19 pandemic hit, some online brokers are endeavouring to help them start their investing journey with care by supplying them with research and data, helping them to educate themselves. In 2021, for example, CommSec launched CommSec Learn, an investor education website that was designed for that purpose. It also launched CommSec Check-In, a tool it uses to survey 500,000 customers every six months; its purpose is to make sure that clients are checking their portfolio health, looking at using some of the different tools that are available, and thinking about where they've invested and how they've diversified their portfolio.

For its beginner and novice traders, Bell Direct has an education series that guides clients through the investing process. It is designed to help investors create and generate wealth, with a long-term investing mindset. For more advanced traders, Bell Direct's Technical Insight Tool can help investors time the entry or exit out of a stock. Clients can check for strength and weaknesses by applying over 30 types of chart patterns, candlesticks, indicators and oscillators (see Chapter 16 for more on these types of technical analysis chart).

Bell Direct also has a tool called Strategy Builder that helps investors identify new opportunities and strategies, choose from a list of pre-built expert strategies, or create their own strategy to identify opportunities based on fundamental and technical analysis. Clients can also test their chosen strategy and see how it would have performed over the last six months.

TIP

Online brokers offer different product features to different sectors of the market. For example, customers new to online broking are provided with fundamental and economic research, educational material and portfolio management tools, while active traders — those who meet a minimum level of activity — are offered features such as dynamically updated data, price alerts, upgraded charting packages and the ability to make conditional (or 'stop-loss') orders for free. Customers also have access to tax reporting tools.

Different customers may also have different data requirements. Your data needs largely depend on how frequently you intend to buy and sell. You can access three types of data delivery:

>> **Delayed:** The data you see is 20 minutes old

>> **Live:** You click to refresh your browser for market updates

>> **Dynamic:** The data is streamed live from the market

It may not be necessary for an active investor to pay for dynamic data. Whether you choose to depends on whether you need to react to changes within minutes, over the course of a day, or over a week.

So much functionality is offered in terms of education, information, research and charting that the online brokers have moved well beyond their 'execution-only' beginnings. They may not give direct advice, but they certainly give self-reliant investors the tools and the knowledge base that they need to make more informed decisions.

While online brokers don't give advice, they do try to give their customers access to as much information and insight as possible. They help their clients make better investment decisions by offering educational content that's relevant to first-time investors, such as economic and company research, news feeds, relevant and timely market information, and scanning and number-crunching tools. Online traders want fundamental and technical research available at the click of a mouse; they want to be able to put in the parameters, filters and indicators that they feel are important to their trading decisions. They want to set 'stop-loss' or 'stop-profit' orders — either on price or percentage moves — so that they can control their entry and exit strategy. These days, online brokers offer these options, seeing themselves as one-stop-shops for investment, wealth creation and trading — providing everything short of actual advice.

Some online brokers have expanded beyond simply offering cheaper transactions, increasing their offering to include extensive research, recommendations, information, software, charting and analytical tools. Some offer 'model portfolios' provided by third-party research houses. These model portfolios are selected to complement a client's individual requirements, investment time horizon and appetite for risk.

TIP

Online brokers are well represented on social media, with some hosting online 'communities', where clients can exchange ideas, post real-time news, speak to the firm's analysts, or talk to the firm's trading services team if they have any issues with the trading platform or their account. Some (for example, eToro) offer *copy trading*, a form of trading that allows would-be traders to follow and copy automatically the positions opened and managed by selected expert investors, usually through a 'social trading' network. However, this service is not offered for Australian-listed stocks; it is limited to the experts' trading in foreign shares, currencies, commodities and crypto-currencies.

Investors need to work out what kind of investor they are before they decide which medium — online or full-service — to use.

Chapter 17 explores your online and app-based trading options in more detail, including where to find information about share investing online and which investing podcasts might be worth a listen.

Choosing the Best Broker for You

To choose the kind of broking service that best meets your needs, you need to answer the following questions:

>> How much are you prepared to pay?

>> How many trades are you likely to make?

>> What services do you need?

If you're new to the sharemarket, you're investing a relatively large amount of money and you want to establish a well-diversified portfolio designed for patient capital appreciation, you can benefit from a consultation with a full-service broker. If you know the sharemarket well and want to use your knowledge to trade your portfolio, you can opt for an online broker.

TIP

You don't have to confine your trading activity to one or even two brokers. By all means spread your activity around. If you want to participate in floats, opening and maintaining an account at one of the larger retail brokers makes sense. Large retail brokers have access to the big company floats. The more transactions you put through this firm, the better your chances of getting in on the float action.

REMEMBER

Cheaper brokerage means less service, which can lead to poor purchases. If you save 1per cent in brokerage fees but pay an exorbitant price for the shares, you haven't achieved a saving. You need to know what you want from a broker before making your choice.

Fighting for full-service

After several years of copping the online assault, full-service brokers made a comeback through one of their trump cards — access to floats. The stockbroking industry earns 90 per cent of its revenue from 10 per cent of its clients — that's why full-service brokers get first crack at the floats. A stockbroking firm handling a sought-after float is under no obligation to offer the shares to the wider public, unless the floated company so requests. Most floats are small enough to be handled comfortably by the large full-service brokers.

TIP

However, online brokers have built up the distribution ability to challenge for the large floats; after all, CommSec's 1.1 million customers is a pool of potential investors that is very hard to ignore!

REMEMBER

Usually, brokers fill float issues from their own client base first. If the brokers know they can achieve this without help from another firm, only their clients receive an offer of shares. That's why many online clients also work with a full-service broker, although larger floats increasingly use the online brokers as a distribution tool.

Doing the research

Research analysts from stockbroking firms produce a huge amount of information. Their newsletters contain a good deal of research for private clients, but this is only a fraction of the pixel (and paper!) mountain of analysis sent to institutions. Since the Australian market is one of the most concentrated in the world, the top 50 companies are the most scrutinised and researched. Stocks that aren't large enough for the S&P/ASX 200 index are less likely to be researched.

The bulk of the research produced is aimed at the institutional buyer. This information can be a problem for the investor who's receiving recycled institutional research, laden with jargon, diagrams and acronyms. What your full-service broker should be doing is advising you when to buy and sell shares.

REMEMBER

Unfortunately, brokers rarely tell you when to sell — unless you're one of their best clients, brokers prefer to offer buy recommendations. Only people who already own shares can act on sell recommendations.

Companies don't like to see their shares rated as a 'sell' since they never think they deserve it. In the best broker–client relationship, for example, your broker may recommend selling a particular stock at $5 and buying back in at $4, not because they hate the company, but because their research has shown that at $5, the stock has gone past fair value.

WHERE ARE THE CUSTOMERS' YACHTS?

A well-known story relates that a visitor to New York was being shown the wonders of the city. Down on the river, at the New York Yacht Club, his guide said: 'And there are the brokers' and the bankers' yachts.'

Came the reply, 'Where are the customers' yachts?'

This reply also became the title of one of the best available books on investment, written by Fred Schwed Jr, called *Where Are the Customers' Yachts? A Good Hard Look at Wall Street*, first published in 1940. The story also explains something about the paradox of the sharemarket and sheds light on who benefits most from the broker–client relationship.

Paying for service

Let's face it, the reason full-service brokers aren't cheap is because they don't want small clients who generate only a small amount of brokerage. They'd rather let small clients go to online brokers.

If you buy $1,000 worth of shares through a full-service broker who charges a minimum brokerage of $80, the brokerage on your purchase is 8 per cent of the total. The share has to rise by more than 8 per cent before you're ahead. The same investment can be made through an online broker for as little as $6. According to research house Canstar, in 2021 the average brokerage on a $1,000 share purchase through an online broker was $15.57, while for a $10,000 share buy, the average brokerage was $16.94.

REMEMBER

If you're a longstanding or highly active client, you're probably able to negotiate a discount, but if price is your only criterion, clearly you'd be mad to go through a full-service broker. But the story is different if your relationship with the full-service broker is a good one — if you get sound personalised service and good long-term strategic advice, this relationship can pay for itself many times over.

Interviewing for a Broker

Always remember — stockbrokers need you more than you need them. The market today is a buyers' market for stockbroking services, particularly if your stockbroker thinks you may defect to an online broker.

A full-service firm assigns an adviser, who asks you how much you have to invest. For a full-service broker, an investment less than $10,000 wouldn't be considered worthwhile. For that amount of money, the broker may argue that achieving proper diversification is difficult and that you're better off with the in-built diversification of an ETF or managed fund. (Refer to Chapter 5 for an explanation of how ETFs and managed funds diversify.)

Although the ASX's trading system could accommodate the purchase of one share in any company, the brokerage fee would be likely more than the cost of the share. If you pester a broker enough, they'll buy or sell your small parcel — but expect to pay a hefty fee if it's a troublesome transaction.

Your adviser establishes

>> How comfortable you are with risk

>> How well you understand the sharemarket

>> Whether you want capital growth or income

>> Whether you intend to invest in capital for the long term, or whether you want to trade shares

A good broker may tell you that your $10,000 would probably be better off in an ETF or managed fund rather than buying several shares; if one of the stocks purchased doesn't work, the portfolio is in trouble. For the money invested, a managed fund makes more sense.

You don't have to accept that advice, but you then have to do your own research and analysis to make your small portfolio work (refer to chapters 7–11 and 17 for details on how to research companies).

TIP

If you decide to work with a full-service broker, be ready to ask the broker some questions, such as:

>> Where do they invest?

>> What sort of shares do they prefer?

>> How many floats have they participated in? (Check this against a list of floats that have taken place over the same period.)

>> Are they willing to have a two-way relationship? (Ideally, your adviser will be prepared to listen as well as talk.)

TIP

THE RETAIL CLIENT'S GLOSSARY OF BROKERS' RESEARCH TERMS

If you're going to work with a broker, you're going to have to talk the broker's talk. Here are some important terms — some simple, some more technical — to get your head around:

Accumulate: A nothing call. The broker can't manage to say 'buy'.

Avoid: This share is a dog. The broker has been wavering between fear of upsetting the company and fear of embarrassment at being caught out as the only firm supporting a dog. The latter fear has won.

Buy and sell: These terms explain themselves. You'll hardly ever hear the latter. Some cynics claim that these mean, respectively, 'We've got a load of these we want to get rid of' and 'We're desperate to pick up as many of these as we can for a large client.'

Get on this, it's headed to the stratosphere: As an ordinary retail client, you're never going to hear this. All up, that's not a bad thing.

Hold: After exhaustive study, the broker wants to sit on the fence, because no-one else has made a buy or sell order.

Indexweight: A jargon word for 'hold'. (The institutions prefer this word to 'hold'.)

Marketweight: See previous entry.

Overweight: You can think of this as, 'We mean buy, but we want to sound more impressive.'

Reduce and lighten: The broker wants to say sell, but doesn't want to upset the company. Let's face it, to reduce or lighten a holding without selling some shares is difficult.

Speculative buy: In other words, 'Some huge gains could be made, but, hey, don't blame me if it goes belly-up.'

Switch: Your broker is saying, 'Sell, and buy the one we want you to buy.'

Take profits: Another less harsh term for 'sell'.

Underweight: An impressive-sounding technical term that doesn't hurt the company's feelings as much as the word 'sell'.

It's not okay if your adviser patronises you or obviously fails to prepare for your consultations. Nor should you accept being badgered to buy or sell stocks. A broker's income comes from commission on transactions. To make money, the broker must be raking in commissions. Repeat this mantra: 'My broker needs transactions to make money. Ergo, they want transactions to occur. Ergo, they are happiest when I am transacting.' A broker's business is a sales business. The best clients, who generate the most sales, receive the best service.

If your broker says a company looks good, ask why. Ask the broker for the price/earnings (P/E) ratio, the net asset value, the revenue and earnings track record over the past three years, the consensus forecasts for the next two years, and the proportion of its sales that go to export markets. Put pressure on your broker to provide factual substance to the recommendation, otherwise all you're getting is a tip, and you can get enough of them at dinner parties.

Making the most of full-service

If you decide to take the full-service route, make sure that the broker earns their commission. When your broker commits to maintaining a properly structured investment portfolio, some essential steps must be taken. These steps should

>> Determine your risk profile and the level of risk that you're comfortable with that will meet your investment objectives

>> Locate the investments that fit your risk profile and meet your investment objectives

>> Monitor your investment portfolio and your financial situation

>> Structure your financial affairs in the most tax-efficient manner to maximise your potential to create wealth and minimise tax

In a full-service broker–client relationship, you pay for extra services that help to maximise your ability and opportunity to create wealth.

Forging a new relationship

Some brokers, notably the Australian arms of major US investment banks, have embraced a deliberate strategy of moving away from transaction-based commission revenue to an annual fee levied on assets under management. Under this model, called *relationship management*, the brokers manage the portfolios of their customers in return for annual fees. In this situation, the broker brings in the services of experts to take care of the client's overall financial needs — in fields such as taxation, banking, property investment, derivatives and futures.

This approach is based on the 80:20 rule, which dictates that 20 per cent of the firm's clients generate 80 per cent of its revenue. This rule is more like a 90:10 rule at the high end of stockbroking, and some firms allocate their resources to the most lucrative area — those with the most to invest. In other words, the firms cull their client list and encourage their advisers to build assets under management rather than generate trades.

REMEMBER

Stockbroking is a buyers' market and willing investors can easily find a firm happy to carry their business, although some clients may find it a wrench to leave an adviser they trust. Investors who prefer to conduct high-volume, low-cost business are not suited to relationship management; these investors find that an online, execution-only broker is the best fit for their needs.

Using broker sponsorship

Shareholders can arrange to be sponsored by a broker in their dealings with the CHESS clearing house (refer to Chapter 6 for a full explanation of CHESS). It doesn't cost anything, but a formal agreement is required. The shareholder is allocated a holder identification number (HIN) that covers the client's shareholdings and acts as an identifying password into CHESS. Your HIN must be quoted when placing orders.

Alternatively, listed companies can sponsor their own shares. Shareholders electing to use this system are allocated a security holder reference number (SRN), which covers only the holding in that particular company. Issuer sponsorship is popular with shareholders who don't want a formal relationship with a broking firm. With broker *sponsorship*, if you want to sell through another broker, you must first transfer your shares into the sponsorship of the other broker, which is unnecessary paperwork. Discount brokers also offer CHESS sponsorship facilities. Your account and paperwork are the same but you're paying a lot less to trade.

Locating the ideal broker

You can try several effective ways to find a good full-service stockbroker. Word-of-mouth is a good starting point. If your friends are happy with their brokers, these brokers may be worth contacting; it helps if you can contact a broker armed with a referral from an existing client. The ASX also offers a referral service, and its website (www.asx.com.au) lists all brokers' contact details. Visit these brokers' websites and assess their offering.

For online brokers, Canstar at www.canstar.com.au, Finder at www.finder.com.au and Mozo at www.mozo.com.au provide a summary of all online brokers' fees and charges, and which services they offer.

Chapter **13**

Initial Public Offerings

A company *floats* when it tries to raise capital by offering its shares to the public for the first time. The process is known as the *initial public offering*, or IPO, but it is more commonly described as a float. With its connotation of a ship being launched, this word is perfect — a float is like a ship sliding down the slipway, with an excited crowd watching its first voyage. However, sometimes, a company does not float at all: it sinks.

Floats are a big part of the excitement of investing in the sharemarket — especially for the stags. *Stags* are investors who buy the shares through the prospectus, hoping to sell for a quick gain when the shares list. The stags are often in conflict with *institutional investors* (that is, super funds, fund managers and insurance companies) that may have invested in the pre-IPO stage and want to sell their positions on listing.

A float can flop on its first day on the stock exchange and still survive. In his first Test match, cricketer Sir Donald Bradman scored a grand total of just 19 runs. He retired two decades later with an average of 99.94, which will probably always stand as a record. In the same way, the future potential of some shares can't be guessed on their first trading day.

In this chapter, I discuss how to read and understand a company's prospectus before it issues you shares, how to pick a winner and what to do if your ship sinks.

The Float Slipway

The stock exchange's 'float slipway' is usually a conveyor belt that is quite full. IPOs have been a major part of Australia becoming a nation of 6.6 million share investors. Many people bought shares for the first time through the privatisations of Telstra Corporation, Commonwealth Bank and Qantas in the 1990s. According to the Australian Securities Exchange (ASX), more than 2,500 companies have listed on the exchange through an IPO since October 1998, raising about $170 billion from large and small investors. The full picture of Australia's vibrant IPO market is shown in Figure 13-1.

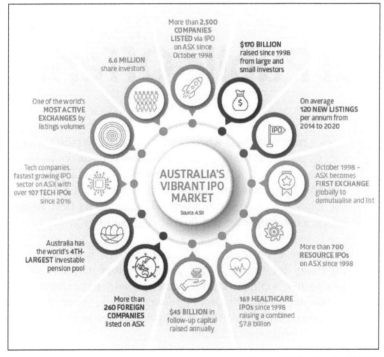

More than 2,500 COMPANIES LISTED via IPO on ASX since October 1998

$170 BILLION raised since 1998 from large and small investors

6.6 MILLION share investors

One of the world's MOST ACTIVE EXCHANGES by listings volumes

On average 120 NEW LISTINGS per annum from 2014 to 2020

Tech companies, fastest growing IPO sector on ASX with over 107 TECH IPOs since 2016

October 1998 – ASX becomes FIRST EXCHANGE globally to demutualise and list

AUSTRALIA'S VIBRANT IPO MARKET
Source: ASX

Australia has the world's 4TH-LARGEST investable pension pool

More than 700 RESOURCE IPOs on ASX since 1998

More than 260 FOREIGN COMPANIES listed on ASX

$45 BILLION in follow-up capital raised annually

169 HEALTHCARE IPOs since 1998 raising a combined $7.8 billion

FIGURE 13-1: Australia's IPO Market.

Source: Australian Securities Exchange

The float pipeline has been relatively consistent in recent years, but with capital-raising amounts occasionally skewed by the bigger IPOs. In 2014, there were 73 listings, raising $16.1 billion, including the $5.7 billion Medibank Private float conducted by the Australian government, which was the second largest government privatisation behind the $10 billion Telstra first tranche in November 1997. Cleaning and services group Spotless returned to the share market (after private equity group Pacific Equity Partners had removed it in 2012) in a $955 million float (the company was taken over by Downer in 2019).

In 2015, the market saw 97 IPOs, raising $8.6 billion, including the $950 million float of superannuation fund administration company Link Group, accounting software company MYOB's $833 million IPO, fleet management and vehicle leasing group Eclipx's $250 million float, PSC Insurance Group's $225 million issue, and specialist baby goods retailer Baby Bunting Group Limited's $175.8 million float.

In 2016, 96 IPOs raised $8.3 billion, with the Charter Hall Long WALE REIT ('REIT' stands for real estate investment trust) the biggest listing, with an offer size of $1.12 billion, while international plumbing fixtures supplier Reliance Worldwide Corp raised $918.8 million, service station owner Viva Energy REIT (now known as Waypoint REIT) brought in $911 million, and Australia's largest chicken producer, Inghams Group, raised $440 million.

In 2017, the market racked up 113 floats — almost ten a month — raising $6 billion. The largest three were all listed investment companies (LICs) — the largest listing, Magellan Global Trust, raised $1.5 billion. Fellow LICs VGI Partners Global Investment and MCP Master Income Trust raised $550 million and $516 million, respectively. Waste management company Bingo Industries mounted a $439.6 million float.

In 2018, 95 floats raised $7.8 billion, with the three biggest IPOs — oil refiner and marketer Viva Energy ($2.4 billion), LIC L1 Long Short Fund ($1.3 billion) and US-Australian steelmaking coal producer Coronado Global Resources ($1.2 billion) — accounting for nearly two-thirds of the total capital raised. Manganese producer Jupiter Mines raised $240 million, while Indonesia-based nickel producer Nickel Mines brought in $200 million.

In 2019, 63 companies joined the ASX, raising a total of $5.4 billion, led by listed investment vehicles KKR Credit Income Fund ($925 million) and Magellan High Conviction Trust ($862 million), while fintech business Tyro Payments raised $287 million.

The COVID-19 crash of February–March 2020 slammed the IPO market but it roared back to life in the second half of the year, with three-quarters of the 113 floats in total arriving after June, raising $5.3 billion. Infrastructure facility Dalrymple Bay Infrastructure, which raised $1.29 billion, and analytics software company Nuix, which raised $953 million, were the two largest offerings of the year, while financial services group Liberty raised $321 million, the HomeCo Daily Needs REIT raised $301 million, online beauty and personal care products retailer Adore Beauty raised $269 million, and speciality retailer Universal Store garnered $148 million.

In the first half of 2021, 85 companies joined the ASX screens, raising $3.5 billion of capital and listing with a combined market capitalisation of $22.8 billion. The IPOs were led by non-bank lender Pepper Money, which raised $500 million, pathology services provider Australian Clinical Labs, which raised $411 million, and Kiwi-based online food delivery business My Food Bag, which raised $314 million. In early July 2021, digital property settlements platform PEXA was floated by its owner Link Administration Holdings (which kept 42.8 per cent of the shares) in a $1.2 billion float.

Today, the average float raises about $88 million (at the time of writing), though nearly one in two IPOs raises less than $10 million. Floats that raise $1 billion-plus are still rare; there have been only eight such floats in the last ten years.

Floats generally do quite well. Table 13-1, from capital-raising platform OnMarket, shows the performance of IPO companies for the six years up to 2020, covering performance on the first day of the IPO, the first month after the IPO and at the end of the calendar year in which the IPO took place.

TABLE 13-1   **IPO Performance 2015 to 2020 (Simple Average Returns)**

Year	No. of IPOs	Average raising ($ million)	Total capital raised ($ billion)	One-day return (%)	One-month return (%)	Return at 31 December (%)
2020	79	70.9	5.6	32.4	27.9	46.9
2019	63	85.7	5.4	24.1	27.5	35.2
2018	95	82.1	7.8	11.0	8.0	–14.9
2017	113	53.1	6.0	17.1	16.0	61.6
2016	96	86.4	8.3	16.6	20.0	25.4
2015	85	101.2	8.6	11.5	15.2	21.7

Source: OnMarket

Staying afloat

Investing in successful floats can prove highly lucrative. Afterpay listed at $1 a share in May 2016 and was later taken off the sharemarket in 2021 by US payments group Square, Inc. for $126.21; CSL turned a float price of 77 cents (the original $2.30 shares were split three-for-one in 2007) into a market price of $306 a share (refer to Chapter 3 for more on this impressive story); and even CSL's journey is put in the shade by the long-term wealth creation efforts of Westfield (also explored further in Chapter 3). Another great performance was Cochlear's

100-fold rise (refer to Chapter 4). But investors also have to keep in mind that floated companies can go the other way.

That sinking feeling

One of the most spectacular examples of a float sinking like a stone was BrisConnections, an infrastructure trust that floated in July 2008. BrisConnections raised $1.2 billion after winning a $3.5 billion contract to build an airport toll road in Brisbane. Shares were issued at $3, with a first instalment of $1 paid in the IPO and two subsequent amounts of $1 each to be paid.

BrisConnections got off to a bad start, falling 59 per cent to 41 cents on the first day of trading. With the credit crunch biting hard, institutional investors bailed out quickly from an infrastructure stock with high debt levels; by October 2008, the shares had fallen to 0.1 cents, the lowest tradeable price on the ASX. And unitholders still owed another $2 on each unit! In the end the stock's underwriters, Macquarie Group and Deutsche Bank, took the IPO units off retail investors' hands in 2009, waived the payments, coughed up the $2 to make each unit fully paid and put them back on the ASX. But BrisConnections finally went into voluntary administration in February 2013, when the value of the company slid below its amount of debt. The last price at which an investor could have got out was 40 cents.

The BrisConnections debacle followed another disastrous Brisbane motorway stock, RiverCity Motorway, which floated in August 2006 after raising $690 million through its IPO. The shares cost 50 cents in the IPO, with another 50 cents due in August 2007. The shares fell 8 per cent on the first day. After the second instalment was paid, the shares briefly climbed to 90 cents, but the company was soon in trouble again. By the time the road opened in March 2010, its shares were trading at 24 cents; when the traffic fell well short of what had been forecast in the prospectus, the shares fell further. RiverCity Motorway took a $1.5 billion write-down on the value of the road tunnel and institutional investors were talking about suing the company over the traffic forecasts made by the engineering consultant to the IPO. RiverCity Motorway slid into administration in February 2011 — the shares last traded at 7 cents. However, because the road only carried one-quarter of the forecast traffic — which caused the financial difficulties — hundreds of RiverCity Motorway shareholders won a class action settlement in the Federal Court of Australia in August 2016 of $121 million. The court found that the investors had suffered loss as a result of the misleading traffic forecasts.

US drilling contractor Boart Longyear listed on the ASX in April 2007 at $1.85 a share, in a $2.3 billion IPO; the shares quickly cruised to $2.70 by October 2007. However, after that, Boart Longyear turned into a disaster. The company had to raise $770 million in 2009 to repay a $650 million term loan; it also mounted recapitalisations in 2014 and 2017, during which the equity holders lost control of the company to the debt holders. In November 2019, the company consolidated its shares so that every 300 shares became one share and the 0.7 cents share price became $2.10. Boart Longyear still lingers on the ASX, at 30 cents — each original share has lost 99.99 per cent of its value.

More recently, shares in forensic intelligence software company Nuix disappointed investors severely, despite having appeared to be a highly successful IPO. Offered in the IPO at $5.31, the shares listed on the ASX in December 2020 at $8.50 for a 60 per cent stag premium, and quickly moved to $11.16 in January 2021. The float was backed by Macquarie Group, which owned 76 per cent of the company pre-float and retained a 30 per cent holding (after pocketing $586.7 million of the $953 million raised). But things went south very rapidly.

The December 2020 half-year result, released in February 2021, disappointed investors, with the company plagued by COVID-19 and US election-related sales challenges, which affected US government contracts, as well as unexpected currency headwinds. The share price was slashed by 34 per cent, but chief executive Rod Vawdrey said its sales pipeline remained strong and US government deals would bounce back in the June 2021 quarter. The company stuck to its prospectus forecasts.

In March 2021, it was reported in the *Australian Financial Review* that the company's revenue recognition policy was under scrutiny because the December 2020 first-half result included the company's recognition of up to 80 per cent of the revenue from multi-year contracts in one lump sum. The newspaper said questions had been raised with the securities regulator ASIC (the Australian Securities and Investments Commission) by a third party about Nuix's prospectus, but ASIC declined to act.

In April, Nuix confirmed that it would not meet its prospectus revenue forecasts, while also noting that its earnings would be higher than predicted. That took another 15 per cent from the share price.

However, this was only the start of the bad news for Nuix shareholders, the Macquarie Group and its joint lead manager Morgan Stanley (*the lead manager* arranges the share issue, and may also underwrite it), as well as Nuix's auditor PwC (which wrote the investigating accountant's report in the prospectus). Nuix's then-chief financial officer was accused of insider trading, and ASIC also began to investigate how the Nuix prospectus and its company accounts from 2018 to 2020 had been put together.

In June 2021, Nuix fired its chief financial officer Stephen Doyle and announced that chief executive officer Rod Vawdrey would leave by the end of the year. At that stage, the company was still facing an ASIC probe, potential investor class action suits, an ongoing Australian Federal Police investigation into former chair Tony Castagna over potential breaches of the Corporations Act, and legal action in the Federal Court from former chief executive Eddie Sheehy.

With the company plagued by corporate governance scandals, two earnings down-grades, three profit warnings and extreme share price volatility, the share price had plunged by 80 per cent in less than five months in the first half of 2021, immolating more than $2 billion in shareholder wealth.

A much higher profile dud has been Telstra, particularly for the investors who bought the second tranche of Telstra shares, known as Telstra 2, in 1999. Telstra 2 retail subscribers paid a total price of $7.40 (paid in two instalments) for shares that by mid-2021 were worth $3.76 — a capital loss of 49 per cent. To lessen the pain a little, they have received $5.79 in dividends, comfortably putting them in the black by 29 per cent. But that's not a great return for tying up cash for 22 years — in fact, it is about 1.2 per cent a year. That's not great when the share-market (as shown by the S&P/ASX 200 index) has earned a total return of 8.3 per cent a year over the last 20 years.

Telstra retail shareholders who entered the stock through the Telstra 3 issue, in November 2006, paid $3.60 in two instalments. With the shares trading at $3.76 nearly 15 years later, they're sitting on a capital gain of 4.4 per cent, but the $3.80 in dividends they have received puts them 110 per cent ahead. Again, at 5.2 per cent a year, that's not exactly princely.

The original retail shareholders, who paid $3.30 in two instalments starting with $1.95 in November 1997, have made a capital gain of 13.9 per cent, but the $5.93 in dividends along the way means they have earned 2.9 times their investment — which sounds okay, but at 4.7 per cent a year, investors could have done a lot better.

Department store giant Myer has also been a dismal performer on the market since its November 2009 listing. Myer is a textbook case study on how the sumptuous-ness of the prospectus has no correlation with the quality of the company. The company's prospectus bore on the cover a lovely photograph of its star model, former Miss Universe Jennifer Hawkins — who had also been prominent in pre-float advertising — but the photo was not delightful enough to compensate shareholders for the fact that in more than a decade on the sharemarket, Myer shares have never traded above the issue price.

Sold through the prospectus at $4.10, Myer shares opened on the market at $3.88 and have slowly subsided until, at the depths of the COVID-19 crash in March 2020, the shares changed hands at 10 cents. For the statistically minded, that is a compound loss of more than 30 per cent a year. (At 32 cents in mid-2021, the shares are down 92.2 per cent, having slid in value by 18.5 per cent a year.)

The Myer experience put many investors off floats for a long time — particularly ones that, like Myer (and Dick Smith Holdings, refer to Chapter 4), were sold on to the sharemarket by the private-equity firms that owned them. To be fair, the likes of electronics retailer JB Hi-Fi, funerals business InvoCare and employment websites operator Seek were all private-equity-backed floats that have been very successful investments for subsequent shareholders.

Figure 13-2 shows what can happen to the share price when a float goes well (in the case of CSL), and Figure 13-3 illustrates what happens when it doesn't (in the case of Myer).

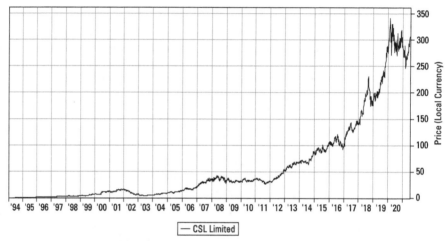

FIGURE 13-2:
CSL share price
1994–2021.

Source: FactSet Financial Data and Analytics

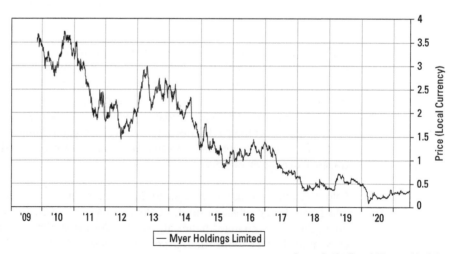

FIGURE 13-3:
Myer Holdings
share price
2009–2021.

Source: FactSet Financial Data and Analytics

THE 'BIG DADDY' IPOs

All around the world, IPOs are happening virtually every day as companies seek to raise capital and move on to publicly traded exchanges. They come in all shapes and sizes — and occasionally, a whale of a company hits the stock exchange.

The biggest of them all was Nippon Telegraph and Telephone (NTT), way back in November 1987, when the Japanese giant raised US$40.3 billion as the government privatised it on to the Tokyo Stock Exchange. NTT was back at the top of the IPO pyramid in October 1998, when it threw off its mobile subsidiary, NTT DoCoMo, this time for US$18.4 billion.

In May 2006, the first big Chinese IPO came to market, with the first of the country's 'Big Four' banks to float on the stock market via the US$11.2 billion share issue of the Bank of China. This was followed in October 2006 by the $21.9 billion issue of shares in the Industrial and Commercial Bank of China (ICBC), China's largest lender by assets, in a dual listing in Hong Kong and Shanghai. Next up was the China Construction Bank, which mounted a US$7.7 billion IPO in September 2007, and China's Big Four bank listings became complete in July 2010 when the Agricultural Bank of China (AgBank) raised US$22.1 billion. AgBank was originally founded as a bank for the country's peasants in 1951 by Mao Zedong, who probably did not envisage his creation eventually finding a home on the Hong Kong and Shanghai stock exchanges, bought by capitalist running-dog investors.

The daddy of all Chinese floats was ecommerce and internet giant Alibaba Group, founded by Jack Ma, which floated 9.2 per cent of its shares on the New York Stock Exchange (NYSE) in September 2014, garnering US$25 billion. Ma was poised to follow up that success by listing 11 per cent of Alibaba's financial arm, Ant Group — which operates the group's Alipay mobile payment service — in a US$37 billion IPO in November 2020, but Chinese regulators stopped the IPO shortly before share trading was due to start in Hong Kong and Shanghai. The official reason given was that the regulators wanted Ant Group to overhaul its business practices; however, it was widely reported that the Chinese leadership — that is, President Xi Jinping himself — had canned the float after Ma had made comments critical of Chinese financial regulators and banks in a conference speech in Shanghai in October 2020. (At the time of writing, Alibaba, Ma and Ant Group were trying to resurrect the IPO.)

Other mega-floats include the US$29.4 billion IPO (at 1.5 per cent of its equity) of Saudi Arabian national oil company Aramco in December 2019; the US$17.9 billion Hong Kong float of AIA, the Asian life insurance arm of American International Group (AIG), in October 2010; the US$19 billion NYSE IPO of Visa Inc. in March 2008; the US$17.4 billion float of 35 per cent of the shares in Italian electricity giant Enel by the Italian government, on the NYSE and the Italian stock exchange in Milan, in November 1999;

(continued)

(continued)

and Facebook's US$18.4 billion IPO (selling 17.7 per cent of the shares) on Nasdaq in May 2012.

General Motors was re-floated by the US government in November 2010, after its Chapter 11 bankruptcy in 2009, whereupon the US Treasury took shares in return for a capital injection to save the company. The 2010 IPO (technically, the re-IPO) raised US$20.1 billion for the Treasury (which also sold Ally Financial, the former GMAC — GM's finance arm — in an IPO in April 2014, raising US$12 billion).

Australia's largest-ever IPO, Telstra 1, in November 1997, was not in the same league as these big daddy IPOs, raising US$8.8 billion. But all up, by the time the sale of the three tranches of Telstra shares on the ASX had been completed in June 1998, the Australian government had raised US$31 billion.

Understanding the Prospectus

When a company intends to float on the stock exchange, it first submits a prospectus to ASIC. A *prospectus* details a company's business and the proposed share issue; a prospectus is also lodged with the ASX.

A prospectus contains enough information about the company's business, financial details, prospects and risk factors to allow an investor to make an informed choice about subscribing for the shares. The disclosure requirements of the Corporations Law dictate the contents of a prospectus. Here, the Australian Government has tried to strike a balance between the need to protect investors and the costly nature of a modern prospectus, which can run to 350 pages long. Unfortunately, the details that have to be crammed into a prospectus in order to avoid liability make the document almost unreadable.

The legal requirement is that a prospectus must contain all the information that investors (and their professional advisers) would reasonably require, and reasonably expect to find in the prospectus, to make an informed assessment of material matters relating to the company, including:

>> The assets and liabilities, financial position, profits and losses, and prospects of the company

>> The rights attached to the securities being offered

The ASX requires that a prospectus must be presented in a 'clear, concise and effective' manner so that investors (especially *retail investors*; that is, individuals investing for themselves) can understand the potential opportunities and risks associated with an investment in the company. However, these documents can't be said to be perfectly presented in plain English — companies don't want to disclose commercially sensitive information or trade secrets, and legal drafting notoriously tends towards the long-winded.

TIP

No connection exists between either the size or the sumptuousness of the prospectus and the quality of the company — unless you can buy shares in the printing company that did the job. Every year, the financial community is bombarded with magnificently presented prospectuses for companies that don't cut the mustard on the market — such as Myer (refer to the earlier section 'That sinking feeling').

REMEMBER

Issuing a prospectus and getting ASIC approval isn't enough to list shares for trading on the sharemarket. The company must be approved by the ASX, which means it must be large enough for there to be a market in its shares. To qualify, the company must agree to abide by the ASX Listing Rules, and meet the following requirements:

>> **Number of shareholders:** Attract a minimum of 300 non-affiliated shareholders investing $2,000 each

>> **Float:** Offer a free float (the number of shares that can be freely traded) of at least 20 per cent

>> **Company size:** Pass a profit or asset test:

• Profit test: Have at least $1 million aggregated profit from continuing operations over the past three years, and at least $500,000 consolidated profit from continuing operations over the last 12 months

OR

• Assets test: Have at least $4 million in net tangible assets, or at least $15 million in market capitalisation.

Foreign companies can seek either a primary or dual listing on the ASX in order to access the Australian capital market and create a new market for the company's shares. The ASX can admit non-New Zealand overseas companies under a *foreign exempt* listing, where the company's home exchange is acceptable to the ASX, and the Australian exchange is satisfied that the company complies with the listing rules (or their equivalent) of its home exchange. Foreign exempt listings must meet one of the following two criteria:

>> Operating profit before tax for each of the last three financial years of at least A$200 million

>> Net tangible assets of at least A$2 billion or a market captalisation of at least A$2 billion.

THE ASX: A GLOBAL EXCHANGE

The ASX is increasingly active in seeking foreign listings, and companies are voting with their feet, attracted by the $3 trillion superannuation pool — the fourth-largest pension pool in the world — as well as globally recognised indices and, in many cases, a broader population of specialist investors.

New Zealand is the most obvious source of listings, and in recent years, this migration to a deeper and more liquid capital market has seen more than 60 Kiwi companies — around one-quarter of the 260 foreign listings, most of which also remain listed on the New Zealand Exchange (NZX) — come across the Tasman, to tap into a pool of investable funds that is more than four times larger than the pool available in New Zealand. In September 2015, the ASX introduced a new category of dual listings, *NZ Foreign Exempt*, which made it easier and cheaper for NZ companies listed on NZX's main board to dual-list in Australia. Many New Zealand companies have made the move and instantly been bought by Australian fund managers whose investment mandates specify that they can only invest in ASX-listed stocks. (Only two of the NZX top ten, Ryman Healthcare and Mainfreight, are not also ASX-listed, and well over half of the NZX Top 50 have put one foot across the Tasman.)

The benefits can flow both ways. Privatisation of NZ energy assets in recent years has augmented the ASX's exposure to renewable energy assets. The IPO of Mighty River Power (now Mercury Energy) in 2013 was followed that year by Meridian Energy. Contact Energy listed on the ASX in 2015.

Kiwi companies listed on the ASX include national airline Air New Zealand and Auckland International Airport; dairy products companies A2 Milk, Synlait Milk, Keytone Dairy (now Halo Food Company), Fonterra (listed in Australia as a shareholder fund, which gives economic exposure to Fonterra but not a vote) and Happy Valley Nutrition; global medical devices group Fisher & Paykel Healthcare; adventure clothing company Kathmandu; infrastructure operator Spark New Zealand; buy-now-pay-later (BNPL) provider Laybuy; church donation software platform Pushpay; soft-tissue regeneration company Aroa Biosurgery; homeware retailer Briscoe Group; customer engagement software company Plexure; glass supplier Metro Performance Glass; media company NZME; healthcare and veterinary products distributor EBOS Group; peer-to-peer lending platform Harmoney; medical analytics software company Volpara Health; vehicle fleet management technology provider EROAD; cervical cancer screening company Truscreen; billing and customer management software company Gentrack; GPS data software company ikeGPS; travel and expense management technology company Serko; cinema management software company Vista Group International; IT service management company SmartPay; chemicals manufacturing and storage company DGL Group; cloud-based translation services provider Straker Translations; and meal-kit home delivery service My Food Bag.

Global small-business accounting software leader Xero was one of these companies, listing on the ASX in November 2012, but in February 2018 Xero moved to a sole listing — its ASX one.

The next biggest foreign contingent is US stocks, which might surprise many given that the US is home to the world's largest stock market. US companies list on the ASX through securities called *CHESS Depositary Interests* (CDIs), which are ownership interests that are traded in the same way as shares, and the holders are entitled to vote at general meetings and receive dividends. (CDIs are not required for companies incorporated in New Zealand, Israel, Bermuda or Papua New Guinea.)

Among the Yankee contingent on the ASX are media heavyweight News Corporation, global sleep-breathing device leader ResMed (established in Australia, but which moved its domicile to the US in 1990), metal and plastics recycler Sims, family communications app developer Life 360, online lending marketplace Credible Labs, US-Australian coal producer Coronado Global Resources, regenerative medicine company AVITA Medical (which moved its domicile from Australia to the US in June 2020) and drug development company Nyrada.

Israel has also emerged more recently as a source for ASX listings, starting with the listing of digital audio speaker company Audio Pixel Holdings in December 2004. The ASX has attracted about 25 dual-listed Israeli companies, mainly small and early-stage technology- and biotech-oriented companies, which feel that an ASX listing can put them on the radar of Asian investors on a well-known exchange that is much smaller than Nasdaq. The ASX recognises the listing rules of the Tel Aviv Stock Exchange (TASE), which reduces the compliance requirements of a dual listing. (The ASX has similar arrangements with the NYSE, Nasdaq, NZX, Tokyo Stock Exchange, Hong Kong Stock Exchange, TSX in Canada and the Deutsche Boerse in Germany.)

In September 2020, Israeli BNPL company Splitit — which listed on the ASX in January 2019 — was added to the ASX's S&P/ASX All Technology index, becoming the first Israeli company to be a constituent of an Australian stock index, and thus benefit from investment from local institutions.

Foreign companies that hold a 'foreign exempt' listing on the ASX are exempt from many of the ongoing disclosure requirements imposed on companies that hold a 'primary' listing.

The ASX retains the discretion to decide whether to list companies according to their individual circumstances.

Companies — whether foreign or domestic — can also come to the ASX through a *compliance listing*, which is when a privately owned unlisted business lists and quotes its existing securities without making a public offer. A compliance listing is made only to create a trading facility for a company's shares; that is, the company does not raise additional capital. For example, South Pacific lender BSP Financial Group (formerly Bank of South Pacific Limited) listed on the ASX in May 2021 through a dual listing (it remains listed on the PNGX, Papua New Guinea's national stock exchange) because it was seeking new sources of liquidity and growth.

Similarly, Victoria-based olive oil producer Cobram Estate conducted a compliance listing in August 2021, moving its unlisted shares to the ASX but not raising capital.

Anatomy of a (Successful) Prospectus

The Baby Bunting Group Limited float of October 2015 is a good prospectus to examine, given that the company has now been on the stock market for almost six years. Baby Bunting raised $52 million through the issue of 37.2 million shares (29.6 per cent of its capital) at $1.40 each. The float was one of a group of specialist retailers that arrived on the sharemarket within a few years of each other, and Baby Bunting was well received by the sharemarket. The shares hit the ASX screens at $1.965, for a 'stag' premium of 40 per cent, which widened to 44 per cent on its debut day.

Baby Bunting has gone on to enjoy a profitable life on the stock market, although, as I pointed out in chapters 7 and 10, it has given shareholders occasional conniptions. In mid-2021 the shares sold for $5.80 and the company was valued at $750 million. The company is now very well-known as the only national baby goods retailer and has about a 15 per cent market share. Its main competitors are Kmart, Big W and Target.

In its prospectus, Baby Bunting said it was Australia's largest speciality retailer of baby goods, operating 33 stores across Australia as well as its website, baby bunting.com.au. Its major product categories include prams, cots and nursery furniture, car safety, toys and clothing. The company stated its aim was to have more than 70 stores in Australia, and that it believed it had a substantial growth opportunity ahead in Australia's $2.3 billion baby goods market.

Baby Bunting was founded by Arnold and Gail Nadelman in 1979, with the opening of their first store in the Melbourne suburb of Camberwell. Their vision was to be 'the one-stop baby shop', supporting new and expectant parents with the widest range of products and expert advice. Sydney-based private investment company TDM Asset Management invested in the company in 2012, taking a 42 per cent interest.

TDM sold a 12.7 per cent shareholding into the IPO, taking its stake down to 29.4 per cent. It entered voluntary escrow until August 2016 (three days after the 2015–16 full-year result was released — this result was released on 12 August 2016). Escrowed shareholders held 36.8 per cent of the shares as at the IPO. TDM subsequently sold 22 million shares at $2.90, through a block trade to institutional investors that cut its stake to 10.4 per cent. TDM fully exited its investment in August 2018 — its final total return (including dividends) on the Baby Bunting investment was approximately nine times its initial investment.

TDM said that when it invested in Baby Bunting, the company was looking for growth capital to enable its vision of becoming a national 'category killer' in the baby goods market. While TDM was on the board, Baby Bunting fulfilled this vision, becoming 20 times larger than its nearest competitor, growing from 6 stores to 50, and boosting its annual revenue from $40 million to more than $360 million.

TECHNICAL STUFF

Escrow, from the old French *escroe*, meaning a bond or roll of writings, is used to describe a rule by which some shareholdings in a company about to list are frozen voluntarily for a specified period of time, generally one or two years. Usually, the company's vendors own the shares placed in escrow. Escrow is designed to prevent early shareholders from selling their shares before the market has had the opportunity to fully value, through trading, the company's securities.

The founding Nadelman family sold half its stake into the IPO, going from 12.2 per cent to 6.1 per cent. New shareholders entering through the IPO owned about 30 per cent of the company. Table 13-2 shows Baby Bunting's growth on the ASX, using some of the most important sales and profitability figures that investors follow.

The following sections explore the key elements of a prospectus, using Baby Bunting's 2015 prospectus as an example.

Getting an overview of the company

A prospectus opens with a statement about the company's mission, vision or strategy, or some combination of the three, a summary of the company's financial status, an address by the chairperson, and an introduction to the company's activities — past and future. It gives the key dates in the timetable of the IPO, and the main investment numbers relating to the shares.

TABLE 13-2   **Baby Bunting Group Limited as a Listed Company**

	Prospectus forecast for FY16	Actual for June 2016	June 2017	June 2018	June 2019	June 2020	June 2021 (forecast)	June 2022 (forecast)*
Revenue ($ million)	218.6	236.8	278.0	303.1	368.0	405.2	468.4	515.8
Earnings before interest and tax ($ million)	13.2	15.5	18.9	14.3	18.9	33.3	42.3	n/a
Net profit after tax ($ million)	9.1	10.6	13.0	9.6	12.4	19.3	26.0	29.6
Earnings per share (cents)	7.2	8.9	10.3	7.6	11.4	15.2	20.2	22.3
Dividends per share (cents)	5.4	6.3	7.2	5.3	8.4	10.5	14.1	16.0
Share price at end of financial year (cents)	–	233	192	136	216	330	542	–
Store numbers	36	36	42	48	53	56	60	–

Source: Baby Bunting Group Limited prospectus and annual reports
*Forecasts: Stock Doctor/Thomson Reuters

Figure 13-4 and Figure 13-5 show the key dates and the offer statistics for Baby Bunting from the initial overview of its prospectus.

Reading the chair's letter

The chair's letter is a necessary part of the prospectus and usually spells out the company's key characteristics, what it does and the size of the market opportunity it sees, including the investment highlights.

Baby Bunting's chair's letter from its 2015 prospectus spelled out how the company was Australia's largest speciality retailer of baby goods, operating 33 stores across Australia and a website. It outlined Baby Bunting's mission — to provide customers with the widest range of products, high levels of service and low prices every day — and its main product categories.

key dates

Retail Offer opens	1 October 2015
Retail Offer closes	9 October 2015
Settlement	13 October 2015
Issue and transfer of Shares (completion of the Offer)	14 October 2015
Expected commencement of trading on ASX (on a deferred settlement basis)	14 October 2015
Expected completion of dispatch of holding statements	15 October 2015
Expected commencement of trading on ASX (on a normal settlement basis)	16 October 2015

Source: Baby Bunting Group Limited

key Offer statistics

Offer Price[a]	$1.40
Total number of New Shares issued under the Offer	18.1 million
Total number of Existing Shares offered under the Offer	19.0 million
Total number of Shares to be offered under the Offer	37.2 million
Total number of Shares on issue at Completion of the Offer	125.6 million
Market capitalisation at the Offer Price	$175.8 million
Enterprise value at the Offer Price[b]	$171.2 million
Pro Forma Net Cash (as at 28 June 2015)	$4.6 million
Enterprise value to pro forma forecast FY2016 EBITDA multiple[c]	10.5x
Offer Price to pro forma forecast FY2016 NPAT per Share multiple[d]	19.4x
Forecast FY2016 dividend yield	3.9%
Forecast FY2016 dividend yield, annualised	5.5%

Notes
(a) Shares may trade below the Offer Price upon Listing.
(b) Enterprise value is calculated as the market capitalisation at the Offer Price minus pro forma net cash as at 28 June 2015 as set out in Section 4.7.
(c) This ratio is commonly referred to as an EV/EBITDA ratio. The EV/EBITDA ratio is calculated as the enterprise value divided by pro forma forecast EBITDA (refer to Section 4.11 for more details).
(d) This ratio is commonly referred to as a price earnings or PE ratio. The PE ratio is calculated as the Offer Price divided by pro forma forecast NPAT divided by total Shares on issue immediately after Completion of the Offer (refer to Sections 4.11 and 7 for more details).

Source: Baby Bunting Group Limited

It talked about the size of the Australian baby goods market, estimating that its addressable market at that time, based on the company's product focus, was approximately $2.3 billion a year. It described how market demand for baby goods was underpinned by resilient long-term drivers, such as the number of births and population growth. It described the state of the industry as being highly fragmented across small independent speciality retailers, a number of online-only retailers and a few larger retailers (where baby goods are part of their overall offering — for example, department stores).

The chair's letter described how Baby Bunting's senior management team, led by CEO and Managing Director Matt Spencer, had a track record of delivering strong financial performance and growth. It said the company had achieved three-year compound annual growth in sales and EBITDA (earnings before interest, tax, depreciation and amortisation) of 19.8 per cent and 81.5 per cent respectively to FY2015.

It went on to describe the size of the offer, the stakes that new and existing shareholders would have in the company, and the market capitalisation Baby Bunting would have upon listing. It described the escrow restrictions to which the board, senior management and the major shareholder TDM Asset Management would be subject. It described how the money raised in the IPO would be used — in this case, to strengthen Baby Bunting's financial position by repaying all its outstanding bank debt of $8 million and increasing the company's cash balance by $1 million (to $4.6 million), which would contribute towards the funding of the company's roll-out strategy in the immediate term. Further, the capital raising would be used to pay a special dividend to existing shareholders and pay for the costs of the offer, as well as to pay out any shareholders who sold existing shares under the offer.

Getting the investment highlights

One of the most interesting parts of any prospectus is the investment overview, perhaps presented in bullet points, of the company's activities and the key selling points for the float. The summary is the first indication of financial prospects and it summarises the earnings outlook of the company — if there is one.

At this point in its prospectus, Baby Bunting presented an industry overview — the size of the market; the drivers of the market in terms of birth numbers in Australia and economic performance; the structure of the baby goods retail industry and its competitive dynamics; and the safety standards that applied to the products sold by the industry. Baby Bunting then set out the size of the Australian baby goods market for the interests of prospective investors, including baby apparel, food and consumables — it estimated this market to have annual sales of approximately $5 billion a year, with Baby Bunting's addressable market at that time — assuming a 45 per cent market share — being about $2.3 billion a year.

Then the prospectus gave a business overview, which talked further about Baby Bunting's history, product range and stores (and where they were situated). The business overview also covered how Baby Bunting generated its income, what its strategy was and how it funded its operations, as well as setting out the recent financial performance of the company and sharing some forecasts. It also laid out Baby Bunting's key strengths and the factors that drove its competitive advantage; described its business model, as well as the major risks it faced; and delineated what the dividend policy would be.

The business overview described how Baby Bunting designed and presented its stores, what plans it had for its online business, its procurement operation and its suppliers, how it conducted its sales and marketing, its logistics and supply chain, its IT systems, and its organisational structure. It went through the company's growth strategy, its plans for increasing store numbers, and the financial parameters and profile of a typical store. It talked about the company's margins and how it planned to improve them.

REMEMBER

The investment overview section is the starting point where you can get an idea of whether you want to buy into the float or not — you know the price of the shares, and you've been given the earnings and dividend outlook. You have to price the expected flow of earnings and dividends against those of other similar investments.

Digesting the financial information

The next part of Baby Bunting's 2015 prospectus was the financial information section. This section goes beyond the investment overview to set out in more detail the main financial figures and data — historical and forecast — that investors need to make an informed choice as to whether or not to invest in a float.

The financial information section reveals the nuts and bolts of a company's financial statistics. It describes the business in terms of the source of funding, gives an historical view of the company's financial performance and offers forecasts based on selected financial data. Sometimes, the information that is presented reflects what the company will look like post-floating, not as it existed before; in this case, the information is set out as *pro forma* information (which translates as 'a matter of form', but is used to indicate that the information is presented using certain projections or assumptions). Examples of situations in which pro forma information may be provided are if the company being floated is an amalgamation of existing companies, or if the purpose of the float is to acquire a business.

The Baby Bunting prospectus set out pro forma financial information and forecasts because its *statutory* (reported) financial information needed to be adjusted to reflect the company's intended operating and capital structure following the IPO, and to exclude certain non-recurring items.

Baby Bunting's financial information section defined the financial terms the prospectus used and contained previous-year key operating and financial figures, plus forecasts. It set out the historical and forecast consolidated statements of profit or loss, the historical consolidated statement of financial position and the historical and forecast consolidated statements of cash flow, all on a pro forma basis. It took prospective investors through the company's debt position, its banking facilities and its lease commitments; Baby Bunting also provided prospective investors with a management discussion and analysis of the financial information and the forecasts that were being presented, including the general factors affecting the company's results over the years leading up to the float. To this end, the prospectus applied a sensitivity analysis to the forecast financial information, to give investors an idea of the business, economic and competitive uncertainties to which investors could expect Baby Bunting to be subject, many of which were beyond the control of the company, the directors and management. Lastly, the financial information section reiterated what the company's dividend policy would be.

Dealing with risk factors

This section takes investors through all the different risks for the company as it runs its business. These risks could be specific to the company's industry or more general business risks.

Risks highlighted as being specific to Baby Bunting in its 2015 prospectus included:

>> Increased competition in the baby goods market

>> Loss of exclusivity regarding the sale of crucial products (where Baby Bunting may once have been an exclusive seller)

More general business risks included:

>> The unforeseen potential for worsening retail environment and general economic conditions

>> Disruptions to the company's supply chain

>> Products failing to comply with mandatory Australian safety standards, creating potential liability for the company

>> Failing to achieve its growth objectives or meet its financial forecasts

>> The departure of crucial management personnel

>> Operational and business risks, such as failure of IT systems

>> Foreign exchange rate changes could affect the prices and viability of imported products

Other risks you may encounter in a prospectus are some of the more general risks of investing in shares of any kind — for example, the share price on the ASX post-listing could fluctuate because of fluctuations in the domestic and international sharemarkets, and general economic conditions, including:

- » Interest rates

- » Inflation rates

- » Consumer sentiment

- » Changes to government fiscal, monetary or regulatory policies and settings

- » Changes in legislation or regulation

- » Inclusion in or removal from market indices

- » Changes in the nature of the markets or industries in which a company operates

Baby Bunting's 2015 prospectus stated that there could be no guarantee that an active market for the shares would develop — in other words, there may be relatively few potential buyers or sellers of the shares on the ASX at any given time. This consideration may increase the volatility of the market price of the shares, and it may also impact the prevailing market price at which shareholders are able to sell their shares.

TECHNICAL STUFF

The prospectus also covered risks around the escrow arrangements under which certain shareholders' holdings would fall, and for what period. It told shareholders that the company may decide to issue shares or other securities in future, and that there was consequently a risk of *dilution* (where relative shareholdings may be diminished by new shares being added to the number already on issue). Other risks were that there could be changes in tax laws; the company may find itself unable to frank its dividends (either partially or at all); Australian accounting standards may change and the implementation of the new standards may adversely affect Baby Bunting; that the company may not be able to refinance its existing or future bank facilities as and when they fall due, or face not as favourable terms to do so.

This section concluded with the standard description of *force majeure* events that may occur within or outside the markets in which Baby Bunting operates and which could impact upon global or regional economies, the operations of Baby Bunting, and/or the price of its shares. These events include (but are not limited to) acts of terrorism; an outbreak of international hostilities; natural disasters, including fires, floods and earthquakes; labour strikes; civil wars; outbreaks of disease; or other natural or man-made events or occurrences that may have an adverse impact on the demand for Baby Bunting's products and its ability to conduct its business. Although 'outbreaks of disease' is commonly stated in the standard description of force majeure events, COVID-19 did not cause any such problems for Baby Bunting; in fact, despite the pandemic, new and imminent parents still needed cots, clothes, car seats and other baby supplies, and Baby Bunting's sales (especially online) actually grew in 2019–20 and 2020–21.

Checking out the key people

The next section of a prospectus outlines the backgrounds and experience of the directors and senior management staff, as well as their pay, shareholdings in the company, interests and benefits. In Baby Bunting's case, the section was headed 'Key people, interests and benefits'.

TIP

It's always good to see that the directors and management have 'skin in the game', with material shareholdings!

In Baby Bunting's case, this section also outlined any related-party agreements that applied, the corporate governance principles and actions that would be in place, and how the various board committees would be established and would operate. This section also set out how Baby Bunting would be subject to continuous disclosure requirements in the ASX Listing Rules and the Corporations Act, and how its formal Code of Conduct would outline how Baby Bunting expected its employees to behave and conduct business in the workplace, as well as how the company's securities trading policy would govern how its employees could transact in its shares. In addition, this section discussed the company's diversity and inclusion policy with respect to the composition of its workforce, as well as its policy for communicating with shareholders.

The nuts and bolts of the offer

This section, which may be called the 'Details of the Offer' section (as in Baby Bunting's case), gets down to the nuts and bolts of the IPO on offer.

In Baby Bunting's 2015 prospectus, it started by dealing with who could obtain the shares. The offer comprised:

» The Retail Offer, which consisted of the Broker Firm Offer, open to Australian resident retail clients of brokers who had received an invitation to participate from their broker

» The Employee Gift Offer, which was open to eligible Baby Bunting employees

» The Priority Offer, which was open to selected investors in Australia who had received a priority invitation

» The Institutional Offer, which was an invitation to institutional investors in Australia and certain other eligible jurisdictions to bid for shares

This section also covered the purpose of the share offer, and how Baby Bunting would use the proceeds of the offer. The purpose of the offer was to:

>> Provide Existing Shareholders with an opportunity to realise all or part of their investment in Baby Bunting

>> Provide Baby Bunting with access to capital markets to improve its financial flexibility for growth

>> Provide a liquid market for its shares.

The proceeds of the offer were to be used to:

>> Repayment the debt drawn on the company's debt facilities ($8 million in aggregate)

>> Pay existing shareholders who were selling existing shares into the offer

>> Fund the pre-IPO dividend to existing shareholders

>> Increase its cash and cash equivalents

>> Pay the costs associated with the offer

The offer section also carried information about the major shareholders existing in the company prior to the IPO, and how their shareholdings would look once the offer had been completed and the Baby Bunting shares had been listed.

The offer section concluded with a summary of the actual terms and conditions of the offer, including:

>> The offer price

>> When the offer would open and close

>> How much money would be raised

>> Whether the offer was underwritten (Baby Bunting's offer was fully underwritten by the joint lead manager, Morgan Stanley)

>> Minimum and maximum application amounts

>> The allocation policy that would govern who received the shares, and how and when share allocation would occur

>> Any restrictions on distribution of the shares

>> When the shares would be listed on the ASX

Similar details were provided for the Broker Firm Offer, the Employee Gift Offer, the Priority Offer and the Institutional Offer.

The offer summary also included:

>> Details of what each applicant would be legally deemed to have acknowl-edged, accepted, understood, declared, agreed and authorised

>> The company's discretion with respect to the offer (the circumstances under which Baby Bunting could have withdrawn the offer)

>> Details of how the company's shares would be listed, traded, settled, trans-ferred and registered in CHESS, and under what ASX code they could be traded (in this case, BBN)

>> A legal description of the rights attached to each share

>> Reiterations of important company governance policies

>> The contact details of the company

Reviewing the independent experts' reports

At this point in a prospectus, it's time for some analysis. At the very least, an independent 'investigating accountant's report' is required, and there may also be legal assessments, and a word from the directors.

The company floating usually commissions a report on assets, intellectual prop-erty, industry-relevant aspects (such as geology, if it is a resources company) and other elements of the prospectus that may require verification. A biotech company will have an independent report on its patents and intellectual property in its pro-spectus. An independent expert who has expertise in the relevant fields and is demonstrably independent from the company can provide this information. While an independent expert's report can contain a lot of technical detail (depending on the company/industry), it's useful for checking against the company's projections.

Deloitte Corporate Finance Pty Limited acted as investigating accountant for the Baby Bunting prospectus. It was engaged by the directors to review the historical financial statements and the forecasts presented in the prospectus. While Deloitte was careful to stress that its review was not an audit, it stated that nothing had come to its attention that caused it to believe historical financial statements and the forecasts had not been 'presented fairly in all material respects'.

Searching for additional information

At the end of the prospectus is a catch-all section containing anything else that an investor might want to know but couldn't find elsewhere. This section may cover outstanding litigation, interests in the company held by directors, float expenses and any consents that need to be given. The section may also have a glossary (a handy dictionary of useful financial terms) and, last of all, the disclaimers — the watertight fine print that means 'Buyer beware!'

Baby Bunting's 2015 prospectus included two appendices: Appendix A, which outlined the significant accounting policies the company adopted in preparing the prospectus; and Appendix B, a glossary of terms and acronyms used throughout the prospectus (this can be a handy reference tool for investment terms in general).

Getting to the application form

In their haste to sign on the dotted line, the application form is often the only part of the prospectus that people read — and their only reason for requesting it. Filling out an application form, and sending off a cheque, used to be the only way to get hold of the shares offered in a float. These days, however, the prospectus may direct investors to an online link at which they may apply for the shares, typically using a unique customer reference number, and pay the application price. Prospective investors also have the option of using the application forms in a printed copy of the prospectus (if one is available) or of printing the application form attached to the electronic version of the prospectus and sending the form, with a cheque for the number of shares applied for, to the address given in the prospectus.

REMEMBER

An original completed and lodged application form (or a paper copy of the application form from the online prospectus), together with a cheque or online payment for the application amount, constitutes a binding and irrevocable offer to subscribe for the number of shares specified in the application form.

Pricing a Float

A company seeking to float approaches a stockbroking firm (or an investment bank) to act as its underwriter, the corporate midwife that will bring it to market. The *underwriter* will effectively buy the shares that the company wishes to sell and then resell these shares to its clients. The underwriter's reputation may also provide some assistance to a newly listed company seeking to establish its credibility in the market. But the underwriter doesn't have to be a stockbroking firm. The underwriter may be another kind of financial services firm, in which case the shares need a sponsoring broker to guide them through the listing rules and requirements. Underwritten capital raisings are a good sign of the confidence the broker or investment bank has in the strong demand from investors for buying shares in a company.

The underwriter agrees to market the shares to prospective subscribers, and to buy any shares that are not bought by investors during the IPO — known as the *shortfall* — giving the company certainty that it will achieve its targeted capital raising. The main purpose of having underwriters is firstly, to ensure the raising takes place, and secondly, to give confidence to the investors that the underwriter has studied the company and knows its value so investors can buy with some confidence.

While most medium-sized to large IPOs tend to be underwritten, there is no requirement for underwriting. Typically, one or more of the *lead managers* (which is usually an investment bank or stockbroking firm, or corporate advisory firm) will also underwrite the offer; however, unless the lead manager agrees also to act as underwriter, it is not obliged to take the shortfall.

The underwriter won't sign the underwriting agreement until after successful investor roadshows have been completed and the underwriter is virtually certain that the offer will be fully subscribed. This is normally immediately before the prospectus is lodged with ASIC. Typically, the underwriter will require certain shareholders and key management personnel to enter into voluntary *escrow* (or lock-up) agreements in relation to their shareholdings to assist in marketing the IPO to investors, who do not want to see the major existing shareholders bail-out straight away.

Voluntary escrow is different to ASX mandatory escrow, which applies to major existing shareholders in a company that is admitted to listing through the assets test — in such cases, the ASX will impose an escrow period on certain sharehold-ers which prevents that shareholder from selling the escrowed shares for a pre-scribed period. Voluntary escrow arrangements are typically shorter than mandatory escrow periods, and are a matter of negotiation between the company and the underwriters to achieve a balance between ensuring an orderly market after listing, while also achieving adequate levels of liquidity.

For earlier-stage companies, the escrow rules require various types of recipients, related parties, promoters or associates who held shares in the company before its IPO to retain those shares for a minimum period (usually 24 months) after quota-tion on the ASX. These rules help ensure the interests of seed and early-stage investors in a company are better aligned with those of new shareholders who invest through an IPO.

REMEMBER

Escrow is a good rule because it prevents owners of floated companies from making instant riches on floating, leaving them with no subsequent incentive to work to build shareholder wealth.

A number of factors go into (or may influence) the price of a float — here are just a few points to consider.

Running the numbers

After the underwriter has accepted the job of taking a company through to flotation, it conducts months of *due diligence* — a study of every aspect of the business and its prospects. The underwriter tests the marketability of the company by discreetly querying its major clients on how much they would pay for the stock. The underwriter then prepares a prospectus, setting out every conceivable piece of information a potential investor needs to know about the company. Based on comparative valuations of the company's peers and the underwriter's observations of what the market will bear, the underwriter sets the price of the shares in the prospectus.

The underwriter is trying to strike a balance between conflicting interests. The company being floated wants to raise as much money as possible, while the underwriter has to think in terms of satisfying the market. The underwriter wants to get the best possible price for its client (the floating company) while also satisfying its other clients (the investors in the after-market, or the secondary market). The underwriter also receives a fee based on the market capitalisation, so it has a vested interest in pricing the shares as high as the market will bear.

The final prospectus must be lodged with ASIC before the offer can open. ASIC does not pre-vet a prospectus before lodgement — it has a seven-day 'exposure period', which it can extend to 14 days to review the prospectus. ASIC undertakes a detailed review of the prospectus, both in terms of content and presentation. It is common even for the most carefully prepared prospectus to receive comments from ASIC requiring amendment. These can usually be addressed quite quickly by the company and its advisers, and they often require only minor amendments, which are implemented through a *supplementary* or *replacement* prospectus.

For prospectuses where it has serious concerns, ASIC can issue a stop order preventing the IPO from proceeding. In recent years, examples of companies whose prospective IPOs have been stopped by ASIC include foreign exchange brokerage FXprimus and streaming music service Guvera, which were planning IPOs worth $200 million and $1 billion, respectively.

If new information comes to light after lodgement of the prospectus with ASIC that may result in the information provided in the prospectus becoming misleading, or a new circumstance arises which would have been required to be disclosed if it had been in existence at the date of the prospectus, a supplementary or replacement prospectus will need to be prepared if ASIC considers the new information to be materially adverse from an investor's point of view.

Building the book

Sometimes the underwriters call for tenders for shares from institutional investors, who may make offers for a certain number of shares at a certain price. Using this knowledge, the underwriters can delay setting the final price of the shares until they know what the demand is, so in theory the underwriters get it close to what the market can actually bear. This process is called *building the book* (or a *bookbuild*). The downside of this approach is that it limits the flexibility for a large premium on the day of the float because much of the demand based on institutional interest is already built into the final price.

The importance of timing

The timing of the float can also affect its price. The listing date assigned by the sharemarket is like a lottery. If the Nasdaq Composite Index or the Dow Jones Industrial Average in the USA loses 5 per cent overnight, any Australian stock listing the next morning local time is staring at an immediate discount to its issue price. If the overnight fall is bad enough, the work done by the underwriter in pricing the shares is probably irrelevant.

If an IPO had been scheduled to hit the ASX lists on 12 March 2020, for example, when the S&P/ASX 200 index fell by 7.4 per cent; or on 16 March 2020, when it fell by 9.7 per cent, the stock was going down, along with everything else.

That's why it was a splendid effort for rapid blood test company Atomo Diagnostics to list on 16 April 2020, at more than double its IPO price of 30 cents. Aged care health-tech start-up InteliCare also pulled off a successful listing on the ASX, this time on 25 May 2020, with its shares rising by more than 50 per cent on day one. Such heroics aside, both companies have sadly retreated below their respective issue prices.

A much bigger example was Chinese smartphone maker Xiaomi, whose July 2018 IPO in Hong Kong ran headlong into headlines of a trade war between China and the US, with the countries imposing tit-for-tat tariffs on US$34 billion ($45.8 billion) worth of goods just three days before it was due to list. The US$3 billion ($4 billion) float came on to the market 6 per cent below its HK$17 issue price. Xiaomi plumbed depths of HK$8.39 — less than half its issue price — by November 2019, and it didn't trade above its issue price until August 2020. However, at the time of writing, it was trading above HK$25 and has (hopefully) put such bad experiences behind it.

Getting into the Action

Large, mass-participation IPOs are rare. Retail investors don't usually get a chance to buy shares unless they are clients of the full-service stockbroking firms involved as underwriters or lead managers. The reason for this is that the companies and brokers need the certainty of filling the book-build and raising the target amount, and it is easier to do this through a smaller number of larger participations rather than dealing with many smaller investors. The book-build process is integral to the success of the IPO, so obtaining commitments from institutional investors and clients with large amounts of funds under management with the participating brokers lessens the risk of under-subscription. Often, institutional investors are given an 'early look' at the book-build process, and if the book can be covered from that, the underwriters and lead managers are happy; once the book-build has been completed, the offer may open up to the underwriters' and lead managers' retail networks.

In the following sections, I talk about different ways you can participate in an IPO.

The undemocratic world of allocations

The shares are a penny and ever so many

are taken by Rothschild and Baring

and just as a few are allotted to you

you wake with a shudder, despairing.

That's how W S Gilbert put it, and it's still mostly true. The underwriters have the say about who gets shares in a float, and the public is usually allotted what's left over.

When a broking firm or investment bank acts as an underwriter for an IPO, its duty is to get the company listed with an acceptable spread of shareholders. Unfortunately, fairness is not part of that agreement; the underwriter offers shares to its own client base, starting at the top.

The underwriter is taking the risk that it won't be able to sell all the shares and will end up holding them itself, which it may not want to do. If the shares are a flop and nobody wants them, the underwriter is obligated to take the shares, which may not be saleable for some time. That's the risk for underwriters, and they try to offset this by making sure the shares are bought up as quickly as possible. For this reason, the underwriter will look for the quickest, least risky way to sell the shares — it will offer the shares to its VIP clients first, which will largely include institutional investors and wealthy, high-net-worth customers.

Shares are distributed according to the following hierarchy:

>> Seed investors, who helped get the company started

>> Staff, family and friends of the company

>> Institutional investors

>> Underwriting broker's best clients

>> Underwriting broker's best mates

Only then — if any are left — are the shares released to the retail market.

This access has been made even more difficult for retail investors in recent years with the consolidation in the numbers of full-service brokers. Opportunities for retail investors to participate in IPOs have narrowed even further.

However, in recent years, the IPO market has opened up and there are now more channels for retail investors to participate, with the growth of online book-builders that aggregate retail bids and allow individuals to invest directly in upcoming IPOs. Investment platforms such as OnMarket, launched in 2013, offer retail investors access to IPOs with or without a broker account. OnMarket works with lead managers to help with shareholder spread, broad investor distribution and capital; it has provided retail investors access to almost 200 IPOs, most of which have been raisings of between $5 million and $50 million — but it has worked with the likes of Macquarie Bank on larger offerings.

The OnMarket platform allows retail investors (who will have signed a one-off agreement with their broker) to bid on shares of selected IPOs at the offer price, in an auction format. Retail investors bid on the number of shares they wish to buy, not the price. Investors don't need a broker account to bid, although they will need a broker account to sell the shares. Although retail investors may not get as many shares as they would like, they will pay the same price as institutional investors — every bidder pays the same final price for the new shares. Investors can bid through a smartphone app, tablet or desktop computer. OnMarket has worked with more than 70 lead managers and brokers and typically provides access to about one-third of all ASX IPOs.

TECHNICAL STUFF

Similar aggregator platforms, for example 180 Markets and Fresh Equities, operate in the area of *sophisticated* and *wholesale* investors, categories of investors who, under the Corporations Act 2001, are permitted access to offers of securities without a disclosure document, meaning that these people get access to investment opportunities that run-of-the-mill investors do not get, but they give up many of the documentation protections that ASIC ensures investors receive. The definitions of these categories are:

- » Sophisticated (having one of the following):
  - Having or controlling net assets of at least $2.5 million, either in your own name or through an entity
  - Earning a gross income of $250,000 or more per year in each of the previous two years
- » Wholesale (or *professional*) and having one of the following:
  - Having or controlling more than $10 million in gross assets, either in your own name or through an entity
  - Holding an Australian Financial Service Licence (AFSL)
  - Controlling a company that employs more than 20 people (or if the business includes or is directly involved in the manufacturing of goods, 100 people)
  - Controlling a foreign entity that, if established or incorporated in Australia, would be covered by one of the preceding options

Investors in these categories, if they obtain a verified Section 708 (Section 708, that is, of the Corporations Act) certificate from their accountant, can participate in pre-IPO raisings and other *excluded offers*, which are unpublicised capital raisings not open to the retail public.

TECHNICAL STUFF

The Corporations Law doesn't allow a public share offer without a prospectus. However, a company can offer shares to so-called professional investors through an excluded offer, by invitation, in $500,000 lots. These offers are accompanied by an information memorandum, or IM, which includes only summarised information, compared to a prospectus, and doesn't have to be lodged with ASIC. It's assumed that professional investors understand the risks involved in an excluded offer better than retail investors and require less information. In other words, they're big enough and ugly enough to look after themselves.

Using subbies and firms

A firm underwriting a float may try to reduce its exposure to risk by using sub-underwriting agreements and firm allocations. An underwriter who thinks it may need help to lock away a share issue may sign sub-underwriting agreements with other broking firms, offsetting some of the underwriter's risk, or the underwriter may give firm allocations to broking firms. A firm allocation is not as binding as a sub-underwriting agreement, but a firm wants to do its best to find homes for the shares to ensure it's asked to participate in other floats.

GETTING IN (VERY) EARLY

Shares don't have to be listed on the ASX to be a worthwhile investment. A great many companies have a great business idea with the possibility it will take off, but it is often very difficult for them to raise capital, fund expansion and grow their businesses. The finance-raising possibilities usually start with the FFF (friends, family and fools) model; next comes bank lending, which will probably involve pledging your house; and then possibly government grants. Private equity — capital invested in a private company not yet listed on the sharemarket — and venture capital (a private equity investment made at a very early stage) are both potential sources of investment, but they're usually the domain of specialist investors. However, in 2017, the Australian government legalised an avenue for proprietary limited companies to raise funds from investors through equity crowdfunding laws — if they became unlisted public companies and produced audited accounts each year. If they did this, they could raise up to $5 million from investors each year.

While it sounds good at first, this was widely criticised as being too onerous for these early-stage companies. In September 2018 the public company requirement was removed, allowing proprietary limited (private) companies to raise funds through equity crowdfunding without changing their legal status. The new rules also got rid of the requirement that Australian private companies were limited to a maximum of 50 non-employee shareholders (previously, if they'd had any more, they would have had to change their status to becoming an unlisted public company). Under the September 2018 amendment, investors acquiring shares through a crowdfunding offer were excluded from this cap, allowing private companies to raise funds from potentially hundreds or thousands of investors through a licensed equity crowdfunding intermediary platform.

At the time of writing, unlisted public companies and private companies with less than $25 million in consolidated assets and revenue can now raise up to $5 million a year. Companies seeking to use equity crowdfunding are subject to a range of obligations to ensure that investors are appropriately protected. These include related-party transaction rules and enhanced reporting and disclosure obligations. Every crowdfunding offer — regardless of its size — must produce an offer document, including prescribed information about the company, its directors and senior management; the offer itself; financial information; and major risks and warnings. (Companies targeting only 'sophisticated' or wholesale investors need only to produce an IM)

Intermediary platforms hosting crowd-sourced funding offers must conduct background checks on companies and key people, and review the offer document to ensure it meets the minimum statutory requirements and is not misleading. You also cannot trade the shares easily — they are typically restricted from sale or transfer within the first 12 months of issue.

Depending on the platform, the minimum investment can be quite low — as low as $50. Retail investors are capped at an investment of $10,000 per company, per year. Sophisticated and wholesale investors have no limit on how much they can invest.

According to licensed platform Birchal in mid-2021, since equity crowdfunding became legal more than 144 Australian small-to-medium-sized companies have used this route to raise more than $100 million, backed by 68,000 investors.

More than a dozen licensed equity crowdfunding platforms operate in the Australian market, with the three largest being Birchal (birchal.com), Equitise (equitise.com) and OnMarket (onmarket.com.au). The largest trading platform for trading shares in unlisted companies is PrimaryMarkets, at primarymarkets.com.

How the process of investment works depends on the platform you choose; typically, once you have researched the company, you can invest through the platform website, and you may be given a five-day cooling-off period in case you change your mind. If you decide to go ahead with the investment, you will receive shares in the company. It may take a while, but you may also receive dividends once the company starts making a profit. Your exit could come if the company is sold or decides to conduct an IPO on the stock exchange.

The result is that retail investors may find it impossible to obtain shares in a float unless they have a relationship with the underwriter, sub-underwriter or a firm with an allocation. Companies generally like to have a spread across retail and institutional investors if possible.

Stagging a float

Stagging a float, or selling out the day the shares hit the market, is one of the great traditions of the Australian sharemarket. Before the advent of day trading in 1999, stagging was the most popular way of trying to turn a quick profit, albeit one not without risk.

To stag a float, you subscribe to the issue through the prospectus, then sell your shares the moment they begin trading (or as soon after that as you can manage). You pocket the stag premium and away you go. Subscribing through the prospectus issue doesn't cost you anything in terms of brokerage. The only disadvantage is the capital gains tax.

WARNING

Underwriters and companies would much rather see a stock priced at a premium of 10 to 20 per cent, and rise steadily. The danger with a spectacular premium is the share can go only one way in the short term — down. Usually, these monster premiums quickly erode and the shares settle down to a more reasonable valuation.

Online stockbroking makes it easy for punters to stag share issues. Online traders watch the market depth very closely, which allows them to be in and out quickly on float day. Selling out of a popular float at a nice premium can deliver you the kind of instant capital growth that usually takes the rest of your portfolio months to achieve.

Stagging is great when it works. For example, when Nuix Limited finished 50.9 per cent higher on its first day on the ASX, in December 2020, that was good, quick, easy money. Stags might have felt aggrieved as the shares pushed to $11.86 in January 2021; however, they felt a lot better seeing the shares at $2.21 just five months later.

A 50.9 per cent premium is a stellar result for such a large ($953 million) IPO — especially as the shares were soon to crater.

The presence of a large population of potential stags is a crucial part of the liquidity needed to get floats underway. That's why underwriters, during the pricing process, want to leave something on the table for the stags. Stags are an important support mechanism for the capital-raising process, and it's not good for the market if they're discouraged during a float. But, securing an allotment of shares in a major float is not a guarantee of a substantial instant capital gain.

Even Nuix pales against the all-time top performer on record (in the modern era of the ASX, that is). On 3 March 2000, at the height of the 1999 to 2000 technology boom, Axon Instruments Limited set an Australian sharemarket record when it hit the ASX screens at $1.65. Axon had been issued in its prospectus at 20 cents. That day, Axon traded as high as $1.92, before settling back to trade at $1.54. On its third trading day, Axon peaked at $2.29 — 11.5 times its issue price. Axon's performance of striking a first trade more than eight times its issue price matched up with the best that the US tech stocks managed in the tech boom.

Axon was a designer, maker and marketer of software, hardware and instrumentation for cellular neuroscience. The company's share offer was only open to clients of the underwriting brokers and shareholders of its parent company, Circadian Technologies Limited. Sixty million shares were issued at 20 cents to raise $12 million. Australia's then richest man, the late Kerry Packer, emerged with 5 per cent of the company. The rumour of Packer involvement on the share register was one of the ingredients that stoked the fire of market desire for Axon.

Those investors who managed to stag the float did very well because Axon suffered badly from the collapse of the tech boom, making a string of losses and slipping as low as 13.5 cents a share in November 2002. Sadly, Axon is no longer on the stockmarket — the company was taken over by US firm Molecular Devices Corporation in July 2004 at 39 cents a share. But Axon lives on in the memory of sharemarket watchers because there has not been a stag premium to match it.

THE URGE TO DEMERGE

Companies can come to the sharemarket through a *demerger* — sometimes known as a *spin-off* — in which a business unit owned by one company is holus-bolus moved on to the sharemarket by means of the parent company carving it out, transferring a proportional number of shares in the demerged entity to its shareholders and listing it separately. The parent company tends to retain a substantial stake in the spun-off company.

Usually, the shareholders in the parent company don't have to do anything — they automatically acquire shares in the new company. The moment the new shares list, the parent company's market capitalisation falls by the amount of the new entity's now-independent market value. A separate tax cost base is calculated for capital gains tax (CGT) purposes, and the new entity sails off into its own listed existence.

Analysts usually find this a win-win over the long term. Often demergers fare better on their own because they have struggled for attention in a bigger company, and as a result are not valued appropriately.

That is why BHP Billiton (as it was then known) demerged South32 in May 2015. The new company was created to hold BHP's non-core aluminium, manganese, nickel and zinc mines, as well as some metallurgical (steel-making) and thermal (electricity) coal mines, spread across Australia, South Africa, Brazil and Colombia. These were mostly Tier 2 assets (in the production cost curve) and were starved for capital because BHP had higher-quality Tier 1 operations elsewhere, in other commodities.

It was a disparate group of assets, and initially the market wasn't enthusiastic. After the stock debuted in May 2015 at $2.13 a share, giving it a market capitalisation of $11.3 billion (which made it Australia's third-largest miner), South32 shares sank to 94 cents by January 2016, for a market value of just $5 billion, as Chinese economic growth slowed, dragging commodity prices lower. But as recovering steel prices helped to lift nickel, manganese and metallurgical coal prices, and aluminium prices surged, the market pushed the stock to $4.23 by October 2018, at which point it was valued at $22.4 billion. South32 is now back at $2.84, for a market valuation of $13.2 billion.

Demergers have a largely positive track record in Australia. Macquarie Group spun-off its remaining shares in Sydney Airport (a 17 per cent stake) in January 2014, in a $1.3 billion demerger; in mid-2021, that stake in the ASX-listed Sydney Airport, having rejected a $22 billion takeover bid from IFM Investors, QSuper and Global Infrastructure Partners, was worth $20.8 billion, and was regarded as one of Australia's premier infrastructure stocks (assuming that airline travel recovers after COVID-19).

(continued)

(continued)

Other major demergers include the following:

- Beverages business Foster's Group spun off its wine business as Treasury Wine Estates Limited in May 2011, only four months before Foster's itself disappeared from the Australian sharemarket, taken over by Anglo-South African brewer SABMiller (which became AB InBev in 2016).

- Chemicals and explosives company Orica demerged its paint business DuluxGroup in July 2010 with a market capitalisation of $850 million; nine years later, a successful $3.8 billion takeover bid by Japanese company Nippon Paints gave shareholders a total return of 483 per cent.

- National Australia Bank demerged its UK banks, Clydesdale Bank and Yorkshire Bank, through the listing of Clydesdale and Yorkshire Bank (CYBG) Plc in London and on the ASX in February 2016. In October 2019. CYBG PLC merged with Virgin Money UK PLC, under a single UK banking licence, and the combined entity still trades on the ASX under the name Virgin Money UK PLC as a CDI, where it is valued at $5.7 billion.

- In 2012 Woolworths spun-off 69 Australian and New Zealand shopping centres into a $1.4 billion listed REIT called Shopping Centres Australasia (SCA) Property Group, now a $2.9 billion REIT.

- Packaging heavyweight Amcor spun-off its Australasian metal canning, glass bottling and fibreboard packaging business, together with its Australasian and North American packaging distribution assets, into Orora Limited, in a $3 billion demerger in December 2014.

- The $16.95 billion spin-off of supermarket giant Coles by Wesfarmers in November 2018 would have ranked as the biggest market float on the ASX in 2018. Coles is now valued at $24.1 billion.

- Retail drinks and hotels business Endeavour Group landed on the ASX in June 2021 following its $12 billion demerger from Woolworths.

Fund managers often prefer demergers to IPOs as a way of bringing fresh stock into their portfolios because demerged assets are already well-known in the market, even if their subsequent experience proves that they were not appropriately valued. Remember the Cochlear situation from Chapter 4? Hardly anyone would even remember that it was once owned by Pacific Dunlop — or that there even once was a major listed company called Pacific Dunlop.

Demergers usually work because:

- They allow good businesses previously obscured inside a larger group to be valued more accurately by investors

- Management can have shares as part of their remuneration and be rewarded through the growth in the stock market value of the company, thereby driving positive outcomes

- Demerged companies can be taken over — or, if not, a control premium can at least start to be factored into the share price

The Australian experience indicates that there are more successful demergers than failures, but they do not always go smoothly.

Despite a successful carving-off of Orora, Amcor has delivered investors one of the worst experiences, too. In April 2000, the company spun-off its $1.5 billion printing paper and industrial packaging division to create a new company, PaperlinX. Amcor shareholders got the shares at $3.17. By 2003, Amcor was being criticised in the press after PaperlinX's share price had risen to $5.40. At the same time, PaperlinX was expanding globally, after paying $1 billion to buy Europe's largest fine paper merchant, and becoming the world's largest paper merchant.

But PaperlinX was hit hard by the GFC, and at the end of 2008 the company breached one of its financial covenants set by its senior lenders. The company had to start selling its best assets to improve its financial position; subsequently, it was hit by a combination of an economic downturn, a substitution of digital channels for print marketing and the impact of new press technology. The UK paper merchanting business went bust in April 2015, causing the company to exit Europe.

To avoid further reputational damage, shareholders of PaperlinX voted to change the company's name to Spicers Paper in October 2015, with their shares trading at 4 cents, and the company having just reported a $392 million loss. The whole sorry saga ended when Spicers Paper was bought by Japanese paper group Kokusai Pulp & Paper in July 2019, for 7.3 cents a share.

Placements and Rights Issues

Companies have other options to raise additional equity funding. A *placement* is a way for listed companies to raise equity capital quickly, through an offer of new shares to investors. Placements have fewer disclosure and reporting requirements than other forms of equity capital raises. This means companies can complete a placement quickly — usually within days — to make an acquisition or pay down debt.

A placement involves creating new shares and issuing them to selected investors, usually institutions, or wholesale investors. The shares are typically issued without a full disclosure document, so they can only be aimed at these investors. Placements are the preferred method of raising capital by companies, and typically are not announced to the public until they're complete (although usually before such shares are listed on the ASX). Placements are often sold at a discount to the current share price to make it worth the capital suppliers' while, and can cause the share price to fall accordingly. Placements are often underwritten, providing certainty to the company that it will get its funds.

Placements are good for companies because they can raise the funds they need quickly, and they're good for institutional investors too because they get a cheap entry to the stock. But they're not so good for retail investors, who are diluted by the issue of new shares (their holding is reduced, in proportion, by the larger number of shares now on issue). Companies often attempt to redress this by also offering a share purchase plan (SPP) alongside the placement, to allow existing retail investors to increase their holding and allow the company to raise further funds. This component of the capital raising sees retail shareholders also offered newly issued shares, usually at the lower of the institutional price or the five-day volume-weighted average price at the end of the offer. The SPP is typically capped; for example, a maximum of $30,000 in new shares per investor. And unfortunately, high demand means they're often scaled back heavily, somewhat defeating the purpose.

Companies were previously allowed to raise up to 15 per cent of their capital, in any 12-month period, without having to seek approval from all shareholders. But the ASX and ASIC extended that limit to 25 per cent in April 2020 in response to the COVID-19 pandemic, and removed entirely the cap on non-renounceable rights issues, in order to help listed companies raise large dollops of capital quickly.

Rights issues are capital raisings in which the company makes an offer to existing shareholders to invest new capital in the company by buying additional shares. The *rights* (the right to buy the additional shares) are issued via a predetermined ratio based on the shareholder's current holding of shares. The new shares are usually available at a discount to the current market price.

Imagine an investor already owns 100 shares of company XYZ, and the shares are currently trading at $20 each. In order to raise more money, company XYZ announces a rights issue for current investors at a price of $15 a share, which will last for 30 days. The company also sets a conversion rate of five for ten, meaning that a current investor can buy five discounted shares for every ten that they currently own. As a result, the investor could buy 50 more shares for $750 — a discount of $250. The company raises funds while the shareholders increase their stake in a company for a reduced cost.

The rights issue will be either renounceable or non-renounceable. In a *renounceable* rights issue, shareholders are allocated 'rights' that are tradeable on the market while valid. Owners of renounceable rights have the following options:

>> Exercise the rights before the expiry date (buy the new shares)

>> Sell them on the market (while the rights are valid), and let the buyer, whether an existing shareholder or not, exercise them

>> Choose to do nothing (the rights will expire on a specified date)

A *non-renounceable* rights offer does not allow investors to sell their rights — they must either be taken up or lapse. Most listed company rights issues are non-renounceable because of the additional complexity and cost of having the rights quoted on the ASX so they can be traded.

The fairness (or not) of rights issues, particularly where retail investors are diluted by capital raises in which they didn't participate, has been a subject of fierce debate for many years. Placements are automatically diluting, but even rights issues can be if not everyone can partake — and sometimes the raising simply happens too quickly.

TIP

A renounceable rights issue is fairer than a non-renounceable one as not all investors have the money or desire to participate in all the rights issues from the companies that they own. It can be challenging for investors, particularly where the rights issue is at a significant discount to the company price, to not be able to participate. Using a renounceable rights issue allows those investors who don't want to participate in the capital raising to sell their rights, which trade separately to the shares and extract some value.

In response, investment banks developed the *accelerated renounceable entitlement offer* (AREO) and *simultaneous accelerated renounceable entitlement offer* (SAREO), which largely replaced the traditional rights issue. But those structures typically only achieved a maximum of 50 per cent retail investor participation. In 2011, investment bank Merrill Lynch pioneered a structure called the *pro-rata accelerated institutional, tradeable retail entitlement offer* (PAITREO), a capital-raising structure that allows renouncing retail holders to trade their entitlements on the ASX for 14 days from the close of the institutional book-build.

The beauty of the PAITREO is that retail investors are automatically compensated for dilutions arising from any capital raises they didn't participate in. The PAITREO is good for small investors, because it is pro rata, and all non-participants are compensated in a book-build, but retail investors get the additional advantage of being able to sell their rights on the market.

The PAITREO structure is designed to provide fairness for all shareholders, in particular retail shareholders, as it allows retail shareholders to potentially receive value for their entitlement throughout the offer period. However, companies have been slow to adopt the PAITREO structure as standard, and it has only been used 36 times in the past decade. The most important point in a PAITREO is whether non-participating institutional or retail shareholders receive the bigger compensation payment from separate book-builds for the respective shortfall components. The newsletter The Mayne Report (maynereport.com) tracks the outcome of PAITREOs (and other capital raisings), and declares each one a 'win for retail' (retail investors) or a 'win for the instos' (institutional investors).

PUTTING ON THE GREENSHOE

Some IPOs use a greenshoe arrangement, which allows the vendor (or its underwriting panel) to buy in the secondary (post-listing) market more shares than were offered through the prospectus. In effect, the *greenshoe* (so named because it was first used in the IPO of US company Green Shoe Manufacturing Company, in 1960) establishes a floor that is below the market price.

When Telstra 2 arrived on the sharemarket in October 1999, the greenshoe was called into action within 90 minutes of the listing of the instalment receipts. The greenshoe enabled the government's broking panel to buy on the secondary market up to 144 million instalment receipts above the number offered through the prospectus — 6.75 per cent more than were issued — if the price fell below the $4.50 paid by retail subscribers. Within 48 hours, normal buying took over and the greenshoe's job was done.

To some investors, the greenshoe is market manipulation — it's certainly not normal buying practice. Greenshoe buying is designed to support a sagging market price; it's a practice that guarantees buying in the after-market. A greenshoe facility is not meant to be a long-term arrangement, and usually lapses after 14 days. Telstra 3 in late 2006 also had a potential greenshoe situation, as did Myer in November 2009 and QR National (now Aurizon) in November 2010. QR National's underwriters had the option to buy back 6 per cent of the shares in its first 30 days as a public company in order to stabilise a volatile share price.

The greenshoe, while common in the US and Europe, is little used in Australia. Plumbing supplies company Reliance World Corporation was the last IPO on the ASX to use a greenshoe, in April 2016.

4

Doing Your Homework

Get comfortable with numbers.

Make sense of fundamental analysis.

Chart your way to technical analysis success.

Discover a host of useful online share investing resources.

Tackle tax with confidence.

IN THIS CHAPTER

» **Keeping an eye on liquidity ratios**

» **Calculating company debt**

» **Finding out where the profit's coming from**

» **Understanding how performance affects earnings**

» **Making your calculator work overtime**

Chapter **14**

Crunching the Numbers

To invest in the sharemarket, you need to become comfortable with numbers. If you don't understand the calculations that link prices to earnings, for example, you're flying blind at night in a snowstorm.

The good news is that you don't have to go back to university to master the techniques. All you need is a grasp of the basic financial ratios and calculations. When you're comfortable with these concepts, you may want to move on to the more esoteric areas of professional share valuation.

In this chapter, I concentrate on the fundamentals.

Getting the Price Right

The first thing you need to know about a share is its price. That's as easy as punching its ASX code into a search engine on your smartphone to see the price virtually, in real time; or, if you're old school, looking up yesterday's close in the newspaper.

Given the price and the number of shares on issue, you can work out the company's market *capitalisation*, which is the value the sharemarket places on it at that point in time.

Market capitalisation is calculated as follows:

Market capitalisation = current market share price × number of shares on issue

The price of an individual share, however, is not what professional sharemarket participants really mean when they speak of a company's worth. The share price doesn't tell you whether the share is cheap or expensive. The market price tells you only what buyers are willing to pay, and sellers to sell for, at a particular moment. By the time you come out of a meeting and check your smartphone — certainly, if you wait to read the price in a newspaper — the situation will have changed.

In deciding whether a share is likely to rise or fall in price, you need to consider more than price — you need to work out what you think is the stock's *fair value* — what you think it is inherently worth right now.

If you work out a fair value that is higher than the current share price, you may be looking at a bargain. But if you work out a fair value that is lower than the current share price, it might be worth selling while the going is good.

The problem is that your fair value for a stock might be different to someone else's. Fair value is ultimately only someone's opinion. To start working out fair value, you can relate the price of the share to the company's *fundamental* data — revenue, cash flow, earnings and dividends. You can also compare some of these data to the company's *assets* (what it owns) and *liabilities* (what it owes others). You can find this information in the company's financial statements, such as the profit and loss (P&L) statement (these days, known as the *income statement*), the balance sheet (these days, known as the *statement of financial position*), the statement of cash flows and the statement of changes in equity (or alternatively, the statement of recognised income and expenses).

You want to construct a set of *ratios* (or calculations) that boils down these data to a more manageable set of numbers. This allows you to make comparisons between the financial performance and status of a company in terms of:

>> The track record of past performance

>> Competitors

>> International peers

>> The Australian sharemarket in general

These calculations can be expressed in a variety of ways — percentages, dollars and cents, and even years.

Working Out Liquidity Ratios

Liquidity ratios show how well a company can fund its needs and obligations from its ready cash. I mention liquidity in Chapter 1, as a major attraction of shares as an asset class. If there's good *liquidity* in the shares, it means they are easily bought and sold. In the accounting sense, a company's *liquidity* refers to how readily it can convert its assets into cash.

You can calculate liquidity ratios by using information from the balance sheet. The *current assets* in the balance sheet are those that will be used — that is, converted to cash — within one year; the *current liabilities* are the debts that fall due within one year.

Usually, current liabilities are met from current assets. Current assets minus current liabilities gives the company's *working capital*, which tells you how much the company has in liquid assets in excess of its obligations. From this information, you can create two commonly used ratios that evaluate the company's ability to pay its short-term debts.

Current ratio

The *current ratio*, also known as the working capital ratio, is calculated by dividing the amount of current assets by the amount of current liabilities.

$$\text{Current ratio} = \frac{\text{current assets}}{\text{current liabilities}}$$

In this equation, 'current assets' is the *numerator* (the number to be divided) and 'current liabilities' is the *denominator* (the number by which the numerator is to be divided). The result is the number of times current liabilities are covered by current assets. The current ratio shows the ability of the company to meet its short-term debts — if that ability needs to be demonstrated.

TIP

Investment analysts look for a current ratio of 2 or above, depending on the type of business. A business with a long lead-time between manufacturing a product and selling that product needs more working capital to fund its activities, so you'd expect to see a higher current ratio.

Quick ratio

The *quick ratio* is a modified version of the current ratio, which envisages the need to meet current liabilities quickly. The quick ratio ignores the effect of inventories (which might not be able to be sold quickly), and the bank overdraft (which could probably be converted to a non-current liability depending on the company's relationship with its bank).

$$\text{Quick ratio} = \frac{\text{current assets} - \text{inventories}}{\text{current liabilities} - \text{bank overdraft}}$$

The quick ratio is also known as the *acid test ratio*, because it cuts to the short-term chase.

Analysts look for a quick ratio above 2, but the larger the inventory a company carries, the lower its quick ratio.

TIP

Understanding Debt Ratios

Most companies are financed by a mixture of *equity* (funds that investors invest) and *debt* (funds the company borrows). Debt ratios show you the extent to which your company is *geared*, or funded by debt, and how well the interest payments on that debt are covered by earnings.

Debt-to-equity ratio

The *debt-to-equity ratio* shows the extent to which a company is financed by debt; it's also called the *gearing ratio*. A highly geared company has a high proportion of debt.

In this case, debt means financial debt, which is any liability on which interest is being paid, including lease charges. Equity means shareholders' equity (sometimes called shareholders' funds), which is assets minus liabilities (see the following formula). Cash in the bank and short-term deposits are ignored.

The ratio is calculated as follows:

$$\text{Debt / equity ratio} = \frac{\text{total financial debt} - \text{cash}}{\text{shareholders' funds}} \times 100\%$$

The general rule here is that a debt/equity ratio of less than 100 per cent is sound.

You may come across a debt/equity ratio that is negative. This isn't necessarily bad and can happen when cash holdings exceed borrowings. In this case, the negative value means nothing. In fact, if cash holdings exceed borrowings, the company's debt could easily be paid in full.

REMEMBER

A negative debt/equity ratio is definitely bad if a company's shareholders' funds figure is negative, meaning its liabilities are more than its assets, and it is technically bust.

Shareholders' equity

Shareholders' equity (or shareholders' funds) is what the company's shareholders own. In the balance sheet, shareholders' equity is the difference between assets and liabilities. The equation is calculated thus:

$$\text{Shareholders' equity} = \text{assets} - \text{liabilities}$$

Shareholders' equity consists of share capital, reserves and retained profits (that part of the company's profit not paid out in dividends) and is the same as a company's net assets.

The share capital is the amount received by the company when it issued shares. The reserves come from things like realised capital gains, asset revaluations (every time certain types of asset are revalued, an amount the same as the increase in value is added to the asset revaluation reserve) and profits on foreign currency translations.

Interest cover

Interest cover reveals the ability of the company to service its debt. The calculation gives the number of times the company's earnings can pay its net interest payments (interest paid minus interest received). Interest cover shows whether the company earns enough to pay its interest bill, and how much of a safety margin it has.

$$\text{Interest cover} = \frac{\text{EBIT}}{\text{net interest payments}} = \text{times covered}$$

Earnings before interest and tax (EBIT) is the figure used to calculate earnings, but some analysts also take finance leasing charges into account, because they're also liabilities on which interest is being paid.

In this case, the finance leasing charges are taken out of the numerator, which becomes earnings before leasing charges, interest and tax (EBLIT) and are added back to the denominator as follows:

$$\text{Interest cover} = \frac{\text{EBLIT}}{\text{net interest} + \text{finance lease charges}} = \text{times covered}$$

TIP

Generally, an interest cover of three times covered or above is considered acceptable. If interest rates go up, interest cover is one of the first calculations you should check. The lower the interest cover, the greater the risk that higher interest rates may cause the company problems.

Debt to cash flow ratio

Another indicator that a company is adequately servicing its debt is the *debt to cash flow ratio*. This measures the number of years it would take for the company's cash flow to pay off its outstanding debt.

You can use the figure for 'operating cash flow' given in the cash flow statement. The calculation is as follows:

$$\text{Debt to cash flow ratio} = \frac{\text{total financial debt}}{\text{operating cash flow}}$$

Some people prefer the more traditional method of using *gross cash flow*, which means net profit after tax (NPAT), with depreciation and amortisation added back in, but this is a messy figure compared to 'operating cash flow'.

More recently, some analysts have started to invert the ratio to 'cash flow to debt', by dividing operating cash flow by debt. This gives a ratio or 'times covered' figure rather than a figure in years.

Ideally, the calculation would show that the company's cash flow was at least 20 per cent of its debt. In other words, cash flow covers debt by 0.20 times. Here, the higher the number, the better. Cash flow can't be expected to cover all debt, some of which is very long term, so you're not going to get a coverage of one. Around levels of 0.3–0.4 times coverage, the balance sheet would be starting to look 'lazy'; analysts would be asking whether the company is going to pay the cash flow out in dividends, or do something with it like an acquisition or a share buyback.

Other investors prefer to use *free cash flow*, which is the operating earnings plus non-cash charges (depreciation and amortisation) minus capital expenditure on plant, property and equipment. Alternatively, you could look at the cash flow statement, start with the figure for 'cash flows from operating activities', and take away the capital expenditure figure to get a good proxy for free cash flow.

REMEMBER

While cash flow refers to the cash left over after paying the bills, free cash flow measures the cash that remains after the company has paid the bills and then reinvested into the business. It's the cash left over after paying the costs of doing business, interest and taxes, and making long-term investments — which means it's the cash that can be used to pay dividends, make a takeover bid or buy back stock. Free cash flow is the lifeblood of the company.

Positive free cash flow tells you that the company is generating more cash than it needs to run the business, so it has money available to invest in growth opportunities. Such a company is less reliant on external finance, such as making a *share placement* (issuing new shares, which dilutes existing shareholders).

You might come across the *free cash flow to operating cash flow ratio*, which measures the amount of free cash flow for each dollar of operating cash flow.

$$\text{Free cash flow to operating cash flow ratio} = \frac{\text{free cash flow}}{\text{operating cash flow}}$$

A high free cash flow to operating cash flow ratio suggests that the firm generates enough cash flow to be able to distribute money to capital providers without negatively impacting its growth or acquisition plans.

Using Profitability Ratios

Profitability ratios aren't concerned so much with the amount of profit the company makes, but focus on how the amount of profit relates to the investment the company made to generate that profit. They are also an effective means of assessing management's ability to optimise profits. Two important calculations can give you this information.

Return on equity

Shareholders own equity in the company. The *return on equity (ROE)* measures the return the company's management generates on that equity. ROE is the ratio of net profit after tax or NPAT, to shareholders' equity. The higher the ROE, the more profit is being made on that equity.

If NPAT has any outside equity interest — that is, any equity holders other than the parent company entitled to a share of the NPAT — that figure is taken out of the NPAT for the ROE calculation, as follows:

$$ROE = \frac{NPAT - profit\ attributable\ to\ outside\ equity\ interest}{shareholders'\ equity - outside\ equity\ interest} \times 100\%$$

The amount shown in the balance sheet as 'outside equity interest' is not the amount that is deducted from NPAT in calculating the ROE. The amount that should be deducted is the portion of the NPAT that is attributable to the outside equity interest.

REMEMBER

The ROE isn't the same as the return that shareholders receive because not all profits are paid out as dividends; some profits are retained for investment. The ROE is the return that's generated on all the funds invested by the shareholders.

Return on assets

As well as equity invested in a company, a company has assets that it puts to work to generate a profit. (These activities could be funded by equity or debt, or a mixture of both.) The *return on assets* (ROA) shows how well a company's assets are being used. At the very least the ROA should exceed the current cash benchmark rate; otherwise, the company would be better off liquidating its assets into cash and investing those funds into a high-yielding bank account. As counterproductive as that might sound at first, the company would get a better return for much less risk.

The ROA factors in net profit after tax, or NPAT. Some analysts prefer to use EBIT, in order to remove the effect of financing the company's operations through borrowings or tax benefits. Cash and any interest-bearing investments are deducted from total assets.

The calculation is as follows:

$$ROA = \frac{NPAT\ (or\ EBIT)}{total\ assets} \times 100\%$$

TIP

The higher the ROA, the better. The ROA assesses how much the company made for shareholders from both the equity invested and the assets on hand. You can compare the ROA against companies in the same industry, as well as the company's overall track record — you want to find a rising ROA trend.

Linking the Margins

The term *bottom line* is used to mean profit, because the net profit is found at the bottom line of a company's profit in its P&L statement (formally known as the *income statement*). A company's sales (its *revenue*) is often described as *top line* because the revenue figure appears in the top line of the income statement. The margin is the calculation that links the top and bottom lines.

A company's *margin* represents the percentage of each dollar of sales revenue (as distinct from the company's 'income', which could be augmented by the sale of non-current assets) that's turned into net profit. The net profit margin is calculated by dividing net profit by revenue:

$$\text{Net profit margin} = \frac{\text{NPAT}}{\text{revenue}} \times 100\%$$

Dividends are paid from the net profit. The higher the margin, the better. The nature of the company's business, to some extent, determines its margins. A high-volume retailer, such as a supermarket, makes a small margin on each sale, while a medical device manufacturer generates a much higher margin.

The *gross margin* is the percentage of revenue the company can keep for each dollar of sales, after taking away the *cost of goods sold*, which represents all the costs of making the sales. It is calculated as follows:

$$\text{Gross margin} = \frac{\text{Revenue} - \text{cost of goods sold}}{\text{Revenue}} \times 100\%$$

Some or all of the gross margin may still need to be spent on paying shareholders or other business expenses — gross margin only flows into gross profit. While gross margin is also a measurement of profitability, the net margin, which is the residual earnings left after all the company's total expenses have been deducted from revenue, is considered a more definitive profitability measure.

REMEMBER

A growing trend in margins means increased profits, but even stable margins can deliver profits if the company can bring costs down. Falling margins means a company either has no pricing power, or its costs are out of control.

Drawing on Performance Ratios

Performance ratios are used to value earnings and dividends from listed shares. These calculations are simple, but you have to be careful to compare like with like. Performance ratios are not absolute figures that fit into a range of acceptable values, but they're meaningful as a comparison with similar calculations, made on the same basis, for other companies. This method of comparison, known as 'peer analysis', is ideally performed on companies in the same industry with similar operations.

Price/earnings (P/E) ratio

One of the most common terms in the investment lexicon is the *price/earnings ratio*, known as the P/E ratio or PER, or earnings multiple (if it's being calculated using forecast earnings). The P/E ratio can be a confusing statistic.

When you buy a share, you're buying a share of an earnings stream. The *P/E ratio* relates a company's share price to this earnings stream. For any share price, the P/E ratio tells you how many times the price is a multiple of the earnings or how many times the price covers the earnings. The P/E ratio also indicates how many years the earnings stream needs to pay off the purchase price, assuming the company's profit remains the same.

The P/E ratio is calculated by dividing the current share price in cents by the company's earnings per share, or EPS. The P/E ratio may be *historic*, that is, using the most recent EPS, or *forward* (or *prospective*), using an estimated EPS figure for a future period.

$$P/E \text{ ratio} = \frac{\text{market price in cents}}{\text{earnings per share in cents}}$$

If the historic P/E ratio is 7, you're paying $7 a share for every $1 of current earnings. If the P/E ratio is 12, that same dollar of earnings costs you $12.

Assume that you have two stocks. The first is trading at $3.50 and earning 50 cents a share; the second is selling for $1.20, earning 10 cents a share. The first stock, trading on a P/E ratio of 7, seems better value than the second stock, which is on a P/E ratio of 12, because the earnings pay off the purchase price sooner — all things being equal. However, on the sharemarket, all things are not equal. The P/E ratio also indicates what the market is prepared to pay for a stock, so it becomes a subjective measurement.

A P/E ratio rises with a rising share price. A stock with a high P/E ratio might be a bargain compared to a stock with a low P/E ratio, if its earnings are expected to grow at a higher rate. In such a case, the market knowingly pays a premium for the company whose earnings are growing faster. The company with a low P/E ratio may have a low share price for a good reason, such as major sales problems.

As I covered in Chapter 11, there are often periods on the sharemarket where investors are benefiting from *P/E expansion* — a beautiful combination of rising earnings and rising P/Es. P/E expansion is a 'double whammy' of growth. But if the earnings growth expectations implied by a high P/E ratio are not met, the consequent downward re-rating of the P/E ratio, and thus the share price, can be both sudden and harsh. P/E 'contraction' caused by the share price coming down is bad enough, but what investors really don't want to see is when earnings start falling as well — and they get the reverse 'double whammy'.

You can't find a correct range of P/E ratios to signify that a stock should be bought or sold. The P/E ratio doesn't tell you much on its own since the P/E ratio is useful only when you compare it to other P/E ratios and measure the relative attractions of different shares. Armed with a stock's historic and prospective P/E ratio figures at any given time, you can compare the stock to its historic performance, its peers or the market as a whole. The P/E ratio changes every time the numerator (the share price) changes. The denominator (the earnings per share figure) doesn't change until next year's earnings are reported, or (if you're using a prospective earnings figure) the forecast is altered.

The recent track record of the Australian sharemarket indicates that when the average P/E ratio falls under 10, the market is undervalued and poised to rebound. Conversely, when the P/E ratio approaches 20, the market is overvalued and ripe for a fall. This track record has given rise to the simple investment approach of looking for stocks with single-digit P/E ratios to buy, and selling out of stocks whose P/E ratios rise above 20. This value investment approach won't always work. Growth investors, for example, are happy to buy shares at P/E ratios that horrify value investors because they believe the high P/E ratio indicates a stock with huge potential for growth in earnings (refer to Chapter 10 for an explanation of the two investment strategies, value and growth).

The example of Commonwealth Bank (CBA) shows how the P/E ratio can be used. Assume CBA trades at a share price of $100. In its most recent financial year (to 30 June 2021), CBA earned a net profit of $8.7 billion, which came to $4.89 a share. The historic P/E ratio for NAB quoted in the financial media is calculated as follows:

$$\text{CBA P/E ratio} = \frac{10,000}{489} = 20.44 \text{ times earnings}$$

The consensus estimate of the analysts who follow CBA is that the bank will lift its earnings per share to $5.22 in the year to 30 June 2022. The prospective P/E for CBA becomes:

$$\text{CBA P/E ratio} = \frac{10,000}{522} = 19.16 \text{ times earnings}$$

Again, these calculations are of use only when compared to other bank stocks (at home and abroad), CBA's historic P/E ratio range and the P/E ratio of the Australian market as a whole.

Earnings per share

Earnings per share, or EPS, measures the portion of profit earned for every ordinary share on issue. Think of it as each share representing a piece of the company. EPS measures how much each piece of the pie is generating in terms of profit. Over the long term, if the company keeps growing the EPS, then other investors will pay more to own the increased earnings, and therefore the PPS — the price per share — goes up.

Another way that investors like to think of EPS is as the maximum amount that can be paid out to shareholders as dividends in a given year without dipping into reserves. This is important as dividends are usually paid to investors from after-tax profits.

To calculate earnings per share:

$$\text{Earnings per share} = \frac{\text{NPAT attributable to ordinary shareholders}}{\text{average weighted number of ordinary shares}} \times 100$$

The average weighted number of shares is used because during the year a company may experience changes to its capital base as a result of events such as the issue of new shares through either capital raisings or director remuneration; or even shares being removed from the market through the company buying back shares to improve the returns for existing investors. The average weighted number of shares on issue is given in a numbered note in the company's annual report.

NPAT is expressed in millions of dollars and the number of shares is expressed in millions of shares, so multiplying by 100 is necessary to bring the figure to cents. The earnings per share is the net profit (minus dividends on preference shares) divided by number of shares on issue.

EBITDA multiple

Instead of the P/E ratio, many professional investors prefer to use a calculation called the *EBITDA multiple.* EBITDA stands for earnings before interest, tax, depreciation and amortisation. EBITDA is a measure of the earnings from the business, before working capital and capital spending requirements.

Instead of price, the EBITDA multiple uses as a numerator the company's *enterprise value* or EV (the sum of the market value of its equity — that is, its market capitalisation — and its net debt plus any minority interests or preference shares, which have to be added back in). This figure is divided by the company's EBITDA. EBITDA is used because it gives a company's underlying cash flow, and strips out factors such as tax rates and depreciation policies.

EV is used because it represents the total intrinsic value of the company. The reason for using EV is that anyone buying a business buys its debt as well as its assets. EV is what you would have to pay to own the business outright, after paying off all the debts. For this reason, EV is often called the 'takeover multiple'.

To find the EV and then the EBITDA multiple:

$$\text{Enterprise value} = \text{market value of equity} + \text{market value of debt} - \text{cash}$$

$$\text{EBITDA multiple} = \frac{\text{enterprise value}}{\text{EBITDA}} = \text{times}$$

The EBITDA multiple is used like a P/E, with one difference. Where the prospective P/E presents a picture of future expectations of earnings growth and what that earnings growth costs in terms of the price, the EBITDA multiple gives a picture of cash flows relative to the total value of the company. In both cases, a higher multiple represents greater growth prospects, and/or lower risk, because the market is prepared to pay more.

Many professional investors prefer the EBITDA multiple over the P/E on the grounds that it includes the company's debt, while using the EBITDA figure as the denominator provides a better indicator of the company's profitability because it removes the impact of non-cash expenses (such as depreciation and amortisation) that reduce net profits. The EBITDA multiple is often used to value companies that operate in global sectors, such as telecommunications and airlines.

The free cash flow figure can also be used to calculate a multiple, substituting for EPS or EBITDA, whether as a denominator to capitalisation (share price) or with EV as the numerator. In either case you're comparing the company's current market value to its amount of free cash flow, on a per-share basis, but you're valuing the company on the basis of the cash it is generating to fund its growth in order to be able to compare it to its competitors, the market as a whole or its own track record.

Pricing growth by PEG

The *price/earnings growth factor*, or PEG, relates the price/earnings (P/E) ratio to the earnings growth rate. The PEG assumes that a company with earnings growing at a rate of 15 per cent a year should be rated on a P/E ratio of 15. If the P/E ratio is divided by the growth rate, the result is the price/earnings growth (PEG) factor. If a stock is trading at fair (or full) value, its PEG is 1. A PEG of less than 1 is cheap.

The PEG was created to value companies with high rates of earnings growth and high P/E values, which made the P/E multiple difficult to use. Like the P/E, the PEG can be *historical* (using the previous year's earnings) or *forward/prospective* (using forecast earnings). The rate of earnings growth is the key to the PEG. Like the P/E ratio, the PEG has its limitations; it works only with companies valued primarily on their flow of operating earnings. Although most stocks are valued in this way, stocks that rely on assets in their valuation lessen the PEG's effectiveness. A company that records a loss has no PEG and you have to rely on forecast earnings to calculate one. The result can only be a guess.

TIP

As a general rule, the ideal range for the PEG ratio is 0.5 to 0.75. You can buy stocks in this PEG range with a reasonable expectation that you can make money. However, when it goes above 1, the PEG ratio indicates a sell.

Earnings yield

If you invert the P/E ratio, you get the *earnings yield*, which is earnings divided by price. You calculate the percentage as follows:

$$\text{Earnings yield} = \frac{\text{earnings per share in cents}}{\text{market price in cents}} \times 100\%$$

As a measure of company performance, earnings yield is more useful than the dividend yield. The earnings yield measures the yield on the earnings before they are split, with one portion going into retained earnings, and one going out to shareholders as dividends, according to the company's payout ratio.

REMEMBER

Because the earnings yield measures the performance of the company to the investor, it gives a better comparison to interest rates on other investments than the dividend yield.

Dividend yield

Dividend yield (dividend divided by price) can also be calculated using the historic dividend or the prospective (forecast) dividend:

$$\text{Dividend yield} = \frac{\text{dividend per share in cents}}{\text{market price in cents}} \times 100\%$$

Using the example of CBA, for the year ended 30 June 2021, CBA paid a dividend of $3.50 a share. The historic dividend yield is calculated as follows:

$$\text{CBA dividend yield} = \frac{350}{10{,}000} \times 100 = 3.50\%$$

Broking analysts who follow CBA estimated that the bank would increase its dividend for the year ended 30 June 2022, to $3.93 a share. Based on that estimate, the prospective dividend yield for CBA becomes:

$$\text{CBA dividend yield} = \frac{393}{10{,}000} \times 100 = 3.93\%$$

REMEMBER

Investors looking at the prospective dividend yield must remember that until the dividend is actually declared and paid, the forecast is really no more than an opinion. But the historic dividend yield is cold hard fact.

WARNING

Because the share price is the denominator, the dividend yield falls as the share price rises. The lower the dividend yield, the more expensive the shares. An increasing yield may look attractive, but it is a cause for concern because the share price is falling. When a company has a high yield, look at its dividend cover. When the dividend yield is unsustainable, the dividend cover will be low. When the yield is rising, investors have to ask why the price is falling.

A rising dividend yield could mean the market is adjusting the share price down because it believes the company can't maintain its dividend.

Shares, unlike bonds, don't have a guaranteed interest return. The dividend earned on shares depends on the profits earned by the company. In any given year (or half-year), the directors may decide to increase or lower the dividend. They may even decide not to pay a dividend — but they had better have a very good excuse, otherwise the shares will be dumped!

Talking a certain kind of investor out of the conviction that a higher-yielding stock should be bought is difficult. Some investors don't realise that, in share investment, a falling dividend yield is a good thing because the price of the shares is going up.

Dividend cover

Dividend cover is the number of times the amount of recent earnings could pay the dividend. The earnings per share is divided by the dividend per share to give the dividend cover. The best rule is that a dividend cover over 1.3 is comfortable. This figure wouldn't be acceptable in other countries, but Australian investors are accustomed to a healthy dividend payout due to the dividend imputation system (see Chapter 18). A dividend cover of less than 1 tells you the company has paid out more than it earned by dipping into its reserves.

The ratio is calculated as follows:

$$\text{Dividend cover} = \frac{\text{earnings per share}}{\text{dividend per share}} = \text{times covered}$$

The 'earnings' being used here is earnings per share, which comes out of NPAT.

Payout ratio

The *payout ratio* is the percentage of NPAT that is paid out as dividends:

$$\text{Dividend payout ratio} = \frac{\text{dividend per share}}{\text{earnings per share}} \times 100\%$$

The payout ratio varies according to the stage of life of a company. When a company is young, earnings are retained and ploughed back into the business, so the payout ratio is small (if there's a dividend at all). Resources companies, too, unless they are well established as commodity producers, are not famous for their payout ratio.

REMEMBER

The payout ratio is the reciprocal of the dividend cover. A suitable payout ratio depends on a company's cash needs and investor expectations. About 60–70 per cent is standard for industrial companies — over the last 20 years, according to FactSet, the average payout ratio of the S&P/ASX 200 stocks has been 67.4 per cent.

Free cash flow yield

Free cash flow yield is a figure that represents the income (free cash flow) created by an investment. It compares free cash flow and market capitalisation (or EV if you want a more accurate measure of the value of a company as it includes the debt):

$$\text{Free cash flow yield} = \frac{\text{free cash flow}}{\text{enterprise value}} \times 100 = \%$$

TIP

The inverse of the free cash flow yield is the enterprise value-to-free cash flow ratio.

Revenue multiples

Sometimes, when companies are not yet profitable, investors link the share price to the revenue to get a feel for the company's valuation. The *price-to-revenue (sales) ratio* shows how much the market values every dollar of the company's sales, for comparative purposes with its peer companies — in the same way that the P/E or EV multiple is used.

TIP

A revenue multiple is most useful for comparing companies within a sector or industry because 'normal' values for this ratio vary from industry to industry. In general, low price-to-revenue ratios are more appealing because they suggest that a company is undervalued.

The basic price-to-revenue ratio is calculated the same way as the P/E:

$$\text{Price-to-revenue ratio} = \frac{\text{share price in cents}}{\text{revenue per share in cents}} = \text{times}$$

TECHNICAL STUFF

In some situations, particularly with fast-growing software-as-a-service (SaaS) companies, analysts and investors prefer to plug in the annual recurring revenue (ARR) figure to hone their valuation basis further. Again, the purpose of this is to provide a basis for comparison with peers.

Whether it is revenue or ARR, the investor can use a reported (*historic*) or forecast (*prospective*) revenue number — the important point is to be consistent with the one you're using for comparison. Many tech companies are valued based on a forward multiple of ARR, with the multiples higher or lower based on how fast the company is growing. Enterprise value-to-revenue multiples are also increasingly common.

Net tangible asset value

Each share in a company would have a value if the company were broken up and sold tomorrow. That value is the *net tangible asset (NTA)* backing (in North America, this is called the 'book value' because it is taken from the company's accounts, or its 'books'). To calculate the NTA, you divide shareholders' funds by the number of shares on issue. Some adjustments are made to shareholders' funds, such as subtracting intangible items and discounting any outside equity interest.

The calculation is as follows:

$$\text{NTA} / \text{share} = \frac{\text{shareholders' equity} - \text{intangibles \& outside equity interest}}{\text{no. of ordinary shares}} = \$$$

The NTA per share figure tells you what each share would be worth if all tangible assets were sold, all debts paid and whatever was left was distributed to the shareholders.

Because the NTA calculation doesn't use intangible assets, companies with a large proportion of intangible assets have a poor NTA. Intangibles, however, do have value. *Intangible assets* are defined as identifiable non-monetary assets that cannot be seen, touched or physically measured; examples include patents, intellectual property, software, product designs, copyrights, trade secrets, confidential information, trademarks, domain names, customer lists and licensing agreements.

Consider the value of an ecommerce business like jobs website seek.com.au; arguably, almost all of its value comes from software development, its brand, its internet presence, its copyrights and its user base. Or take media companies — their mastheads (newspaper and magazine titles) or broadcasting licences are valuable assets.

Innovations in technology in recent decades have allowed some of the world's biggest companies to develop business models based on intangible assets — for example, data and software platforms such as Facebook (which trades under its parent company's name, Meta Platforms). Intangible assets are now the main source of economic value for many businesses, accounting for 75 per cent of business value globally, according to multinational insurance group Beazley. In 2020, according to the Ocean Tomo Intangible Asset Market Value Study, intangible assets accounted for 90 per cent of the total value of the S&P 500 companies' assets, at more than US$2 trillion. Apple's intangible assets alone were worth US$2.1 trillion in 2020, according to brand valuation consultancy Brand Finance.

If a company buys assets at prices above the book value, it may carry goodwill on its balance sheet. *Goodwill* reflects the difference between the price the company paid and the book value it places on the assets.

In some cases, it might be fairer to use net assets in order to acknowledge that some intangible assets have value, even in the potential break-up of a company. Note that most asset values are only as accurate as the company's valuation of these assets; for example, real estate investment trusts (REITs) need care on this score.

Price to NTA

The NTA figure is most useful when compared to the current share price. If the price is less than the NTA, the share appears to be undervalued. The calculation is thus:

$$\text{Price} / \text{NTA} = \frac{\text{share price (cents)}}{\text{NTA (cents)}} = \text{times}$$

In North America, this is called the *price-to-book (P/B) ratio*. A price-to-NTA ratio of 1 indicates that the company's market valuation is the same as that of its tangible assets.

WARNING

The obvious problem is that using net tangible assets does not take into account intangible assets — for technology-oriented stocks, it will be of little use.

Crunching More Numbers

The range and depth of calculations used by analysts in the world of share investment are limited only by time and imagination. Professional analysts aren't referred to jokingly as rocket scientists for nothing. In this section, I discuss some of the more common calculations that don't fit into any of the well-known categories.

EBIT and EBITDA

You need *EBIT* (earnings before interest and tax) and *EBITDA* (earnings before interest, tax, depreciation and amortisation) for several calculations, but not every company provides them in their income statement. You may have to work them out yourself.

If EBITDA is given, subtract the figures given for depreciation and amortisation expense from EBITDA to arrive at EBIT.

If EBITDA isn't given, work up the P&L from the pre-tax profit figure. Add net interest (interest paid minus interest received) to pre-tax profit and you have EBIT (subtract any outside equity interest you find). To arrive at EBITDA, add the figures given for depreciation and amortisation expense to EBIT. The income statement given in Table 14-1 shows how the bottom line is reached.

TABLE 14-1

Income Statement Showing the Hierarchy of Money

Total revenue	529.9
Cost of sales	(428)
EBITDA (Earnings before interest, tax, depreciation and amortisation)	101.9
Depreciation	(25.7)
Amortisation	(1.2)
EBIT (Earnings before interest and tax)	75
Net interest	(13.1)
Pre-tax profit	61.9
Income tax	(18.6)
Net profit after tax attributable to members	43.3

Effective tax rate

When a company refers in its income statement to *income tax*, the company is talking about its current and deferred tax, which represents all tax consequences facing the company, not just those relating to the current year's profit. A company has *deferred tax liabilities*, *deferred tax assets* and *current tax payables*. Here's how the effective tax rate in a given year is calculated:

$$\text{Effective tax rate} = \frac{\text{current tax payable}}{\text{pre-tax profit}} \times 100\%$$

The company could be using past losses to lower its tax bill, or have expenses that aren't deductible. A numbered note to the accounts explains why the company is paying a different rate of tax to the statutory rate.

Dilution

In theory, the number of shares used in the calculation of a company's earnings per share, cash flow per share and NTA/share should take into account not only the actual number of shares on issue, but also the number of potential shares — in other words, all the securities the company has issued that could be converted to shares, such as options and convertible notes. If all of these become shares, the holdings of the current shareholders will be *diluted*.

Basic earnings per share (EPS) is calculated by dividing earnings available to shareholders by the weighted-average number of shares on issue during the year. A *fully diluted* EPS figure is calculated on the assumption that all of those possible conversions into ordinary shares will take place.

The number of shares on issue can cloud the figures. Earnings per share is directly comparable between years only if the number of shares on issue is static. However, if the number of shares on issue changes during a financial year, the EPS needs to be adjusted.

Capital adjustments

A company's capital doesn't necessarily remain static. At any time, a company could issue shares or other securities. It could also buy shares back on the market, consolidate its shares (make the total number on issue smaller) or split each share (make the total number on issue larger). You must take these capital adjustments into account when you calculate the company's performance per share.

When you look at a company's profitability or cash flow per share, you need to know the effect of changes to the capital structure. Here, a time-weighted average of the number of shares is used to reflect the capital changes. For example, a company has 100 million shares on issue for nine months of the financial year and an extra 25 million shares on issue for the last three months, after a one-for-four bonus issue. In this case, there were:

» 100 million shares for 274 days

» 125 million shares for 91 days

The dilution factor (DF) is calculated as follows:

$$DF = \frac{\text{no. of new shares held}}{\text{no. of old shares held}}$$
$$DF = \frac{100}{125}$$
$$DF = \frac{4}{5} = 0.8$$

If the company paid a dividend of 10 cents a share last year and 8 cents a share this year, the two dividends are not directly comparable, because of the altered capital base. To compare like with like, last year's dividend is multiplied by the dilution factor, and works out to: $10 \times 0.8 = 8$ cents. What appeared to be a 2-cent (20 per cent) fall in the dividend per share is actually an unchanged dividend.

Here's how to calculate a time-weighted average of the number of shares on issue:

$$1 \text{ July} - 31 \text{ March}: 100{,}000{,}000 \times 274 \div 365 \quad = \quad 75{,}068{,}493$$
$$1 \text{ April} - 30 \text{ June}: 125{,}000{,}000 \times 91 \div 365 \quad = \quad 31{,}164{,}384$$
$$\text{Time-weighted average number of shares on issue} \quad = \quad 106{,}232{,}877$$

The figure is used in the calculation of earnings per share, cash flow per share and NTA/share for the year. If you don't keep track of capital changes and make the necessary adjustments to your figures, your calculations will go awry — and so will your investing.

REMEMBER

You should be able to find the average weighted number of shares on issue in a numbered note in the company's annual report.

IN THIS CHAPTER

» Tracking a company's figures

» Checking an income statement

» Understanding a balance sheet

» Watching the company cash flow

» Getting practical lessons in fundamental analysis

Chapter **15**

Following the Money Trail: Fundamental Analysis

T o choose successful shares, you need to be familiar with all aspects of a company's fundamental data, which are set out in its financial reports. Company reports are reasonably reliable because their contents are specified in the stock exchange listing rules and the Corporations Law. However, sometimes companies stretch the facts in order to give a more positive slant to the information presented.

In this chapter, I show you how to get familiar with financial statements so that you can read the figures for yourself.

The Fundamentals of Fundamental Analysis

Fundamental analysis is an important tool that allows an investor to evaluate a company's performance and estimate how well the company is managed. The records analysed are mainly numerical and statistical records, including revenue, earnings, expenses, dividends, assets and liabilities.

Fundamental analysis can also include the examination of a company's products, management and markets. Every six months, listed companies report their financial and operating performance to their shareholders; these annual and interim (half-year) company reports provide fundamental analysts with the data they need to start digging and follow the money trail.

The financial statements in these reports track the flow of money through the company. The major parts of the financial statements are the income statement (formerly known as the profit and loss statement, or 'P&L'), the statement of financial position (formerly known as the balance sheet), the statement of cash flows and notes to the accounts. These financial reports provide the nitty-gritty of a company's financial performance — not the chairman's or chief executive's reports at the front.

TECHNICAL STUFF

There is a fourth statement, the *statement of changes in equity* (also known as the *statement of recognised income and expenses*), which is the reconciliation between the opening balance and closing balance of shareholders' equity (for more on this, see the later section 'Shareholders' equity'), but it is best left to those obsessed with company accounts — the really important stuff is in the other three statements, which I explore in more detail in this chapter.

Reading the Income Statement

The *income statement* is a summary of the company's revenue and expenses over a period of time. The income statement shows whether or not the company's operations for the year generated a profit.

REMEMBER

A net profit occurs when income exceeds expenses. A net loss happens if costs outweigh income. Shareholders' equity is increased by a net profit and decreased by a loss. The income statement has several key elements, which fall into one or other of the following two categories.

Revenue

Revenue is sometimes called *turnover* and is the money that comes into the company. The first item given is *sales revenue*, generated through selling the company's products or services, and other revenue, which could be in the form of dividends, rent or interest received. Income excluded from revenue, such as the proceeds of sales of non-current assets or government grants, appears below revenue as *other income*. Thanks to the Americans, sales revenue is known as the *top line* because it stands at the very top of the income statement. A company's profit is often referred to as its *bottom line*, because it appears as the last line in the income statement — as the saying goes, 'That's the bottom line.'

Profit (or loss)

The key figure in the income statement is the *operating profit* after tax. This is the amount left over after all wages, operating costs, overheads, interest, taxes and allowances for the depreciation and amortisation of assets have been subtracted from income.

The income statement also gives the company's gross operating profit, or *EBITDA* (which means its *earnings before interest, tax, depreciation and amortisation*). Subtract the figures given for depreciation and amortisation expense to arrive at *EBIT* (a company's *earnings before interest and tax*), another common measure of profit. Another way to work out EBIT is to add *net interest* (interest paid minus interest received) to the pre-tax profit.

Sometimes you hear companies talking of their *statutory profits* — the statutory figures are those presented by the company in its formal company report. Strict accounting standards apply, and the figures are independently audited. They include all items and costs that impact profit (income statement), financial position (statement of financial position) and cash flow (statement of cash flows).

Companies also usually present *underlying* figures — the underlying figures (sometimes also described as *normalised*, or *cash* figures) are adjusted to remove the impact of items that are considered 'one-off' (or *non-recurring*). What's included and not included in underlying measures is crucial to getting an accurate picture of performance.

TECHNICAL STUFF

Unusual one-off profits or losses that have a significant impact on a company's business can happen in any year as a result of the company's operations. An example is a one-off profit on the sale of a business or some other asset, or the *write-down* in the value of an asset. Any non-recurring items that affect the reported profit for the year (or half-year) can be carved out of the income statement — that is, clearly identified and given their own line in the income statement — so that investors can see the underlying net profit before the non-recurring items are taken into account.

There's nothing wrong with companies using underlying profit figures so that investors can better compare operating performance across trading periods. But the underlying profit measure is not the legal definition of profit in Australia; it is presented at the company's discretion, and investors must understand that it gives companies the flexibility to paint a more flattering picture.

The best approach is to take the audited statutory net profit figure, which legally must be presented, and then compare it critically to the underlying net profit figure also cited. Companies sometimes report a loss but argue that the 'underlying' business was profitable; and in some cases, they may be right.

The Chanticleer column in the *Australian Financial Review* analysed the 172 members of the S&P/ASX 200 that reported full-year results in the 2019–20 financial reporting season and found that their combined statutory net profits were 76.5 per cent (or $28.6 billion) lower than the underlying profits they trumpeted — which starkly shows the grounds for concern. A company that's being completely transparent will provide a clear reconciliation of their statutory and underlying profit figures, showing logically what has been excluded or included, and why, so investors can make up their minds as to whether there is any 'massaging' going on.

WARNING

Underlying profit can exclude items for which management should be accountable. Above all, be careful as underlying profit could be used as the basis for executive remuneration or incentives; if this is happening, it should be disclosed — and explained — in the remuneration report.

Finding Balance Sheet Bliss

The *statement of financial position* (the old 'balance sheet') is a one-page summary that is a snapshot of the net worth of the company at balance date. The *balance date* of the company is the day on which it balances accounts for the year (a statement of financial position is also included in the half-yearly report).

Working capital is the capital that the company can use to fund daily business. You can calculate this figure by looking at the balance sheet and deducting current liabilities from current assets. Working capital tells you how much the company has in liquid assets, so the more working capital you see in the company's reports, the better.

Working capital can be negative if current liabilities are larger than current assets. This isn't a good situation because the company has to concentrate too hard on paying short-term debts rather than building its business.

TECHNICAL STUFF

The statement of financial position records the company's assets and liabilities at a point in time that relates to, and is part of, a period that has gone before. The process is repeated at set periods to enable comparisons to be made. The statement of financial position shows what assets are owned by the company at that date, what amounts are owed to lenders (liabilities), the surplus of assets over liabilities and the amounts contributed by the company's owners (shareholders' equity).

Assets

Assets are what the company owns or controls, such as cash, investments, property, plant and equipment, which can be either *current* or *non-current* assets. Assets can be amounts that the company is owed by others and items paid for in advance, where the benefits will be received in future years. Assets can include intangible items, also.

Intangible assets

Intangible assets are those that can't be touched — for example, goodwill, media titles, brand names, trademarks, broadcasting licences, manufacturing licences, management, and even market share and distribution networks. Although these assets aren't 'real', they can contribute to a company's value.

Current assets

Current assets are those that the directors believe could be turned into ready cash within 12 months, or taken through the income statement as an expense, within that time. Current assets show how much money the company can call on relatively quickly to pay bills — expected or otherwise — or use to take advantage of investment opportunities.

Current assets could be:

>> **Cash:** Specifically, ready cash held in the bank to meet day-to-day expenses and bills.

>> **Inventories:** The value of stocks held by the company at balance date.

>> **Receivables:** These consist of money held in short-term investments to pay expenses and bills expected in the next few months, money owed to the company by customers (mostly for goods or services sold but not yet paid for), and any other money owed to the company.

Non-current assets

Non-current assets are assets the directors don't expect to turn into cash within 12 months. The largest item in non-current assets is usually 'property, plant and equipment'. This group includes the major capital items owned by the company, which it uses to produce income. The value given for these items in the statement of financial position is usually calculated by subtracting from the original cost of each capital item a specific deduction representing the value of each item diminished by wear and tear. If the asset is building, plant or machinery, this deduction is called *depreciation*; if the asset is an intangible asset, the equivalent deduction is called *amortisation*.

DEPRECIATION

You can use two methods to determine depreciation. The first is *straight-line depreciation*, which spreads the cost evenly over a chosen time period. In this method, the asset depreciates by the same amount each year, which is treated as an expense through the income statement, and the value of the asset in the balance sheet falls accordingly.

The second method is called *diminishing value*, in which a fixed percentage of the value of the asset is expensed each year; the amount of depreciation charged decreases each year. This process results in a depreciation rate of about 1.5 times the rate obtained using the straight-line method.

Some non-current assets — for example investment property, or shares or bonds held for trading — are not depreciated, but *fair-valued* each year. To get a fair value, the company looks at market price, or looks at prices of similar assets to infer a value, or uses some other form of valuation technique. This valuation must be done every balance date. Fair value of these assets can go up or down — any changes go straight to the income statement.

AMORTISATION

Amortisation of intangible assets is usually done by the straight-line method, over a period in which the intangible asset might generate a benefit for the company. Intangible assets have no maximum amortisation period.

Goodwill

Goodwill arises when a company buys the business or assets of another entity and pays more than the total value of those assets or the business, net of liabilities. The buyer is prepared to pay more as consideration for the *goodwill* — effectively, its clientele, brands and commercial reputation — that the business has built up over the years.

Intangible assets that have an indefinite useful life and goodwill are not amortised but are, instead, tested for impairment each year, based on the expected future cash flow that the asset is expected to generate. In effect, the company must make an assessment at each balance date of the amount it would have paid had it bought the asset again that year; based on that assessment, it can evaluate whether the goodwill is still sustainable.

REMEMBER

Goodwill can only be written down in value, not up — once written down, that amount cannot be reinstated.

Write-downs

Asset *write-downs*, where the value of the asset is reduced in the statement of financial position, are often excluded from underlying earnings. But a write-down should not be dismissed as unimportant: it should cause shareholders concern. By writing-down an asset's valuation, the company is effectively telling shareholders that it is not going to earn as much money from that asset (or investment) as it expected when it acquired it (or entered into it). The bigger the write-down, the lower the expected future earnings compared to the original expectations (and effectively, the more the company overpaid for the asset when it acquired it).

Liabilities

Liabilities are the amounts that the company owes to others. As with assets, liabilities are divided into *current* and *non-current*, depending on how soon they could be called on to be repaid.

Usually, the major item in liabilities is the company's borrowings from banks and other lenders. Convertible notes can also be listed as liabilities; these notes could become future shares in the company and then become equity. Liabilities also include accounts payable for goods and services that have been supplied to the company, but not yet paid for.

Net assets

Net assets are the difference between the company's total assets and total liabilities. The figure represents the net worth of the company to shareholders, and is the same as the shareholders' equity.

Shareholders' equity

Shareholders' equity is the money that has been raised from shareholders. In the statement of financial position, shareholders' equity must balance with net assets (they're the same amount) because the latter shows where shareholders' equity has been spent. Shareholders' equity consists of share capital, reserves and retained profits. Shareholders' equity is sometimes called *shareholders' funds* because the equity is what the shareholders own.

Share capital and reserves

The *share capital* is the amount received by the company when it issues shares. The company's *reserves* are capital built up by transfers from profit. Reserves can also be built up when certain types of assets are revalued and the increase in value is added to the asset revaluation reserve (it may also be taken away if the revaluation is downward), or when foreign currency used in the company's business is trans-lated at a profit and the amount is added to the foreign currency translation reserve (this reserve can also diminish).

Retained profits

Once the profit for the year has been calculated, the directors decide how much the company pays out to the shareholders as dividend, how much (if any) is to be spent on buying back the company's shares, and how much is to be retained to fund the business. The retained portion is shown in the statement of financial position as *retained profits*. The entry is really only an accounting entry — the amount of retained profits is recorded in the company's accounts — and is useful for paying shareholders a dividend when the company hasn't earned enough to pay one.

Examining the Statement of Cash Flows

The *statement of cash flows* summarises the company's cash receipts and payments for a period — *cash flow* refers to the money 'flowing' in and out of a business. A company's cash is held in ordinary bank accounts, and short-term deposits and bank overdrafts are also treated as cash.

TIP

A company statement of cash flows refers to 'cash and cash equivalents' — where *cash equivalents* usually refers to short-term deposits and securities, with an original maturity of three months or less, that are readily convertible to known amounts of cash.

Generating company cash

The company's cash is provided from, and employed in, three areas: operations, investing and financing. A company doesn't have to rely on operations to generate an overall positive cash flow; it can bring in cash at any time through investing or borrowing.

REMEMBER

Eventually, a company must make a living from selling products or services. If operating cash flow doesn't provide enough cash, the two other wells will run dry.

Operating cash flow

A company's *operating cash flow* comes from sales to customers. The company brings in money by selling products or services. A positive operating cash flow figure shows that the core business activities of the company are strong and that the company is generating cash from existing operations.

All cash received from customers is paid into the company's bank account. The cash needed to pay for wages, goods, services, interest and taxes is taken out of that account. Overall operations should contribute a net cash flow to the company.

After you have the total receipts from customers, you can calculate net cash flow from operating activities (operating cash flow) by subtracting the cost of sales, such as paying staff, advertising and marketing costs, research and development expenses, leased assets and other working capital outlays. You then subtract the interest, bank charges and tax paid by the company. What is left over is *net operating cash flow*. If the company has a cash surplus, it's generating cash. If it has a loss, the company's activities are consuming cash.

WARNING

Customer receipts may not be the same figure as sales revenue in the income statement. Receipts from customers represent the actual cash paid into the company's bank accounts over the period. Sales revenue could contain amounts that have been invoiced and booked as sales but not yet received.

Investing cash flow

Any time the company buys or sells a business, shares, intellectual property or any other asset, the movement of cash is part of the *investing cash flow*. Cash is taken from the bank to pay for these items and paid in when the assets are sold. Receiving interest or dividends on its own investments is also part of a company's investing cash flow.

TIP

'Growth' companies often show negative investing cash flows, as cash is invested into assets to support long-term growth.

Financing cash flow

Financing cash flow is affected when the company pays shareholders a dividend, makes lease payments, makes issues of shares or options, borrows from banks or other sources, or repays these loans. This section of the statement of financial position tells you how much external funding the company has used, and is a sign of its dependence on outside capital.

Calculating net cash flow

Once you know the net operating cash flow, the net investing cash flow and the net financing cash flow, you can add them together to arrive at the net increase (or decrease) in cash held for the period. If you add to this the cash at the beginning of the period, your final figure will be the cash at the end of the period. The difference is the net cash flow for the period.

The net change in cash can be a decrease, which may or may not be a problem depending on the company's activities. A company may have a good reason for a negative net cash flow — but it had better be a very good one. Usually the only time it is acceptable is if the company is growing. Examples on the ASX are rare, but in the US, Netflix had negative cash flow for years because it was investing in original content and marketing to entice subscribers, especially in international markets. Netflix took a calculated gamble to spend to dominate the global streaming-TV market, using external debt funding, and investors loved the stock for it.

The statement of cash flows may not include some assets that could improve the company's financial position. Assets such as commercial bills, government bonds or listed shares may be a source of readily accessible cash, but they cannot be considered as cash for the purposes of an ASX *entity commitments test*, which is the quarterly reporting regime required of companies that listed on the ASX under the *assets test* (refer to Chapter 13). These companies are called *commitments test entities* (CTEs). Investors must remember that assets are not cash until they are sold.

Free cash flow is the cash flow available to the company after all capital expenditure and maintenance requirements have been met and the dividend paid. Free cash flow is the cash flow remaining after all the items required to keep the company in business as it stands have been deducted. This cash is available for use in growing the business. A company generating a substantial free cash flow is able to pay dividends and fund growth without raising more funds, and is on the way to a healthy future; a company with negative free cash flow will need to issue shares, borrow money or cut costs to survive.

Factoring in quarterly cash flow reports

The statement of cash flows has always been required in the preliminary final and interim reports, but the ASX also requires certain companies — for example, mining, oil and gas exploration companies, and companies that were not yet profitable when they listed (and so they listed under the assets test instead of the profits test) — that is, they are CTEs — to produce an *Appendix 4C statement*, which is a quarterly statement of cash flows.

For example, many technology companies have floated on the sharemarket with a business plan to commercialise a particular product or service, and yet at the point of entry they had generated little in the way of revenue, profit or dividend. These companies were capitalised because investors had faith in their business plans. With no receipts from customers, these companies recorded negative operating cash flow. If the net decrease in cash over a period is larger than the cash held at the end of the period, the company has problems. If the spending continues at the same rate and isn't replaced by cash coming in, the company eventually runs out of money. In this case, the company can alter operations to preserve available cash — for example, they could sell something, issue shares or look to attract a cashed-up rescuer.

Biotechnology companies are similar. While biotech companies may not generate immediate receipts from customers, they count on long-term commercial profits from human therapeutics. Investors can treat biotech companies as though they are resources explorers who have raised money to drill wells and (hopefully) bring them to production.

Biotech companies may see cash flow into the company in different ways. They can expect to receive an R&D (research and development) tax incentive rebate payment; they may have equity draw-down facilities or loans, or may be about to have a capital raising; some may even be in a position to expect a milestone payment from a partner for achieving a specific stage of a clinical development program.

WARNING

However, investors must keep an eye on the cash position of any company that is not making a profit. If it is using up its *cash reserves* (cash balance), it's said to be in 'cash burn'; in other words, it has *negative free cash flow*. Such a company has a *cash runway*, defined as the length of time it would take to run out of money if it kept spending at its current rate of cash burn.

TIP

The Appendix 4C statement (known as a 5B if the company is a mining or oil and gas explorer) shows you (in Section 8) the *estimated quarters of funding* available to the company (consisting of cash on hand plus undrawn debt plus outflows). If this is less than two quarters, then you need to consider whether the company is going to be able to continue to fund itself or if it may need to raise further cash. In such a situation, you would want to see an outline of the steps it proposes to take to raise this cash.

The Appendix 4C statement needs to include details of the company's business activities for the quarter, including any material developments or material changes in those activities, and a summary of the expenditure incurred on those activities. If no substantial business activities have taken place during the quarter, that fact must be stated.

REMEMBER

An Appendix 4C (or 5B) statement details how a company manages its cash flow, while also allowing investors to form a judgement as to the growth prospects of that stock. This makes it one of the most important announcements to monitor if you intend to buy or sell small-cap stocks that tend to be risky and more volatile than established businesses that generate consistent profits or self-funding activities through positive operating cash flow.

Looking at a Case Study: XYZ Limited

To help you understand how fundamental analysis works, I've created a case study of a fictional company, XYZ Limited.

XYZ's fundamental details

Gizmo manufacturer XYZ Limited has had a tough year in the face of a weak gizmo market. XYZ has cut costs and brought in revenue of $529.9 million (down 19 per cent) and made a net profit after tax of $43.3 million (a drop of 13.4 per cent). On a per share basis, XYZ's earnings have fallen by 13.4 per cent, from 15.70 cents a share to 13.59 cents. The company has lifted its dividend from 11 cents a share last year to 11.5 cents, a rise of 4.5 per cent.

XYZ, however, is pretty well positioned in the gizmo market, where its intellectual property is considered second to none. Last year, XYZ signed a deal with gizmo giant Opple to make Opple's new iGizmo product, when it is eventually launched. The iGizmo will be the most powerful gizmo ever and this licence is a highly valuable property in the gizmo-making world.

XYZ has 318.5 million shares on issue. The share price fell from $1.80 last year to a current price of $1.50. Table 15-1 shows XYZ's income statement; Table 15-2 shows its statement of financial position; and Table 15-3 shows its statement of cash flows.

TABLE 15-1　　XYZ's Income Statement ($ million)

	This year	Last year
Sale of goods	529.9	653
Cost of sales	(428.0)	(540.2)
EBITDA (Earnings before interest, tax, depreciation and amortisation)	101.9	112.8
Depreciation	(25.7)	(25.0)
Amortisation	(1.2)	(1.2)
EBIT (Earnings before interest and tax)	75	86.6
Net interest	(13.1)	(15.2)
Pre-tax profit	61.9	71.4
Income tax	(18.6)	(21.4)
Net profit after tax (NPAT) attributable to members	43.3	50.0

TABLE 15-2　　XYZ's Statement of Financial Position ($ million)

	This year	Last year
Current assets		
Cash and equivalents	60.8	74.8
Receivables	77.0	85.0
Inventories	118.4	93.6
Other current assets	2.4	2.4
Total current assets	258.6	255.8
Non-current assets		
Receivables	54.6	55.3
Property, plant and equipment	259.3	255.1
Investments	90.1	106.5
Intangible assets and goodwill	174.1	166.5
Total non-current assets	578.1	583.4
Total assets	836.7	839.2

(continued)

TABLE 15-2 *(continued)*

	This year	Last year
Current liabilities		
Accounts payable	57.3	59.3
Borrowings	0.0	0.0
Provisions	50.7	67.9
Total current liabilities	108.0	127.2
Non-current liabilities		
Borrowings	298.5	276.4
Provisions	14.1	16.6
Total non-current liabilities	312.6	293.0
Total liabilities	420.6	420.2
Net assets	416.1	419.0
Equity		
Capital	344.3	344.3
Reserves	30.0	30.0
Retained profits (accumulated losses)	41.8	44.7
Equity attributable to members	416.1	419.0
Total equity	416.1	419.0
Shareholders' funds	416.1	419.0

TABLE 15-3   XYZ's Statement of Cash Flows ($ million)

	This year	Last year
Cash flows from operating activities		
Receipts from customers	529.9	641.5
Payments to suppliers and employees	(446.2)	(542.9)
Interest paid	(16.5)	(18.0)
Income tax paid	(21.5)	(21.1)
Net cash flow from operating activities	45.7	59.5

	This year	Last year
Cash flows from investing activities		
Proceeds from sale of property, plant and equipment	6.5	8.0
Interest received	3.4	2.8
Dividends received	1.5	3.0
Purchase of property, plant and equipment	(56.6)	(30.1)
Net cash from/(used in) investing activities	(45.2)	(16.3)
Cash flows from financing activities		
Proceeds from borrowings	23.7	6.7
Repayment of borrowings	(1.6)	(1.4)
Dividends paid	(36.6)	(35.0)
Net cash from/(used in) financing activities	(14.5)	(29.7)
Net increase/(decrease) in cash	(14.0)	13.5
Cash at beginning of period	74.8	61.3
Cash, at end of period	60.8	74.8

XYZ's ratios

For a detailed explanation of how the following ratios are calculated, refer to Chapter 14.

Looking at the current ratio, XYZ should be comfortable with a ratio above the value of 2 since the company has improved markedly from last year.

$$\text{Current ratio} = \frac{\text{current assets}}{\text{current liabilities}}$$
$$\text{This year} = \frac{258.6}{108} = 2.39 \text{ times}$$
$$\text{Last year} = \frac{255.8}{127.2} = 2.01 \text{ times}$$

XYZ is comfortable with a quick ratio well above the level of 1, which is considered healthy. As a manufacturer with large inventory holdings (46 per cent of current assets), the company could operate with a quick ratio of less than 1 without too many problems. (Note that XYZ does not have a bank overdraft.)

$$\text{Quick ratio} = \frac{\text{current assets} - \text{inventories}}{\text{current liabilities} - \text{bank overdraft}}$$

$$\text{This year} = \frac{258.6 - 118.4}{108} = 1.3 \text{ times}$$

$$\text{Last year} = \frac{255.8 - 93.6}{127.2} = 1.28 \text{ times}$$

For an industrial company, XYZ has a high level of intangible assets. The company's goodwill, brand names and intellectual property account for 42 per cent of net assets. A heavy reliance on intangibles could raise the risk of *write-downs* (devaluation of the assets on the company books). While such write-downs will not affect the company's ability to generate free cash flow, they may reduce investor interest.

The net debt-to-equity figure represents something of a blow-out in *gearing* (proportion of debt to equity) for the year, as XYZ increased its borrowings to buy a state-of-the-art robotic gizmo assembly line from Switzerland, but the company still shows prudent gearing, with a debt well covered by equity. Financial risk appears to be moderate.

$$\text{Net debt-to-equity} = \frac{\text{total financial debt} - \text{cash}}{\text{shareholders' funds}} \times 100 = \%$$

$$\text{This year} = \frac{298.5 - 60.8}{416.1} \times 100 = 57.12\%$$

$$\text{Last year} = \frac{276.4 - 74.8}{419} \times 100 = 48.11\%$$

With a net interest cover of 3 considered to be healthy, XYZ receives a big tick on the score of interest cover.

$$\text{Net interest cover} = \frac{\text{EBIT}}{\text{net interest}} = \text{times covered}$$

$$\text{This year} = \frac{75}{13.1} = 5.73 \text{ times covered}$$

$$\text{Last year} = \frac{86.6}{15.2} = 5.7 \text{ times covered}$$

The time that it would take for XYZ to pay its *outstanding debt* (debt to gross cash flow) increased over the last year, following the higher gearing level, but this figure doesn't present a major problem.

$$\text{Debt to gross cash flow} = \frac{\text{total financial debt}}{\text{NPAT} + \text{depreciation} + \text{amortisation}} = \text{years}$$

$$\text{This year} = \frac{298.5}{43.3 + 26.9} = 4.25 \text{ years}$$

$$\text{Last year} = \frac{276.4}{50.0 + 26.2} = 3.62 \text{ years}$$

With a return on equity of more than 10 per cent on the funds invested by share-holders, XYZ is doing a fine job — just not quite as fine as it was doing last year.

$$\text{Return on equity} = \frac{\text{NPAT}}{\text{shareholders' funds}} \times 100 = \%$$

$$\text{This year} = \frac{43.3}{416.1} \times 100 = 10.40\%$$

$$\text{Last year} = \frac{50.0}{419} \times 100 = 11.93\%$$

Shareholders have little reason to complain about the job of XYZ's operating management. The company is using assets to generate profit. Management has acknowledged it had a tough year in the gizmo market but shareholders can be happy with a return on assets of almost 10 per cent.

$$\text{Return on assets} = \frac{\text{EBIT}}{\text{total assets} - \text{cash}} \times 100 = \%$$

$$\text{This year} = \frac{75}{836.7 - 60.8} \times 100 = 9.67\%$$

$$\text{Last year} = \frac{86.6}{839.2 - 74.8} \times 100 = 11.33\%$$

As a gizmo maker, XYZ is not going to make the margins of a luxury goods business, but neither is it a high-turnover business with wafer-thin margins. The company is making a solid living with 14.2 cents in the dollar remaining in the company after pre-tax expenses — its EBIT margin.

$$\text{EBIT margin} = \frac{\text{EBIT}}{\text{sales}} \times 100 = \%$$

$$\text{This year} = \frac{75}{529.9} \times 100 = 14.15\%$$

$$\text{Last year} = \frac{86.6}{653} \times 100 = 13.26\%$$

The net profit after tax (NPAT) margin figure is a solid margin on the net profit, with plenty of room for a dividend, which comes out of this margin.

$$\text{NPAT margin} = \frac{\text{NPAT}}{\text{sales}} \times 100 = \%$$

$$\text{This year} = \frac{43.3}{529.9} \times 100 = 8.17\%$$

$$\text{Last year} = \frac{50.0}{653} \times 100 = 7.66\%$$

XYZ's earnings per share is still healthy and the result is a relatively low P/E ratio for an industrial stock.

$$\text{Earnings per share} = \frac{\text{NPAT}}{\text{number of ordinary shares}} \times 100 = \text{cents}$$

$$\text{This year} = \frac{43.3}{318.5} \times 100 = 13.59 \text{ cents}$$

$$\text{Last year} = \frac{50.0}{318.5} \times 100 = 15.70 \text{ cents}$$

$$\text{P/E ratio} = \frac{\text{market price in cents}}{\text{earnings per share in cents}} = \text{times earnings}$$

$$\text{This year} = \frac{150}{13.59} = 11.04 \text{ times earnings}$$

$$\text{Last year} = \frac{180}{15.70} = 11.46 \text{ times earnings}$$

XYZ's dividend yield has increased (which could make it attractive to new buyers), but with a relatively low dividend cover, the company may find it difficult to sustain its attractive dividend policy.

$$\text{Dividend yield} = \frac{\text{dividend per share in cents}}{\text{current market price in cents}} \times 100 = \%$$

$$\text{This year} = \frac{11.5}{150} \times 100 = 7.67\%$$

$$\text{Last year} = \frac{11}{180} \times 100 = 6.11\%$$

$$\text{Dividend cover} = \frac{\text{earnings per share}}{\text{dividend per share}} = \text{times covered}$$

$$\text{This year} = \frac{13.59}{11.5} = 1.18 \text{ times covered}$$

$$\text{Last year} = \frac{15.70}{11} = 1.43 \text{ times covered}$$

The dividend payout ratio is large for an industrial company and is high enough to worry about whether the dividend can be maintained. The company must strike a balance between rewarding shareholders and retaining a prudent amount of profit. This year it has leant too far to the former.

$$\text{Dividend payout ratio} = \frac{\text{dividend per share}}{\text{earnings per share}} \times 100 = \%$$

$$\text{This year} = \frac{11.5}{13.59} \times 100 = 84.62\%$$

$$\text{Last year} = \frac{11}{15.70} \times 100 = 70.66\%$$

XYZ is still trading well above its net tangible asset (NTA) backing; in fact, investors are buying the assets at a 100 per cent premium, which is acceptable to professional investors for a couple of reasons. One, they understand the value of XYZ's intellectual property and manufacturing licence from Opple, which doesn't show up in XYZ's NTA figure; and two, they like XYZ's relatively high dividend payout. Also, XYZ is a fairly efficient profit generator and the market likes this aspect as well.

Net tangible asset

$$(\text{NTA}) \text{ backing per share} = \frac{\text{shareholders' funds} - \text{intangible assets}}{\text{number of ordinary shares}}$$

$$\text{This year} = \frac{416.1 - 174.1}{318.5} = \$0.76$$

$$\text{Last year} = \frac{419 - 166.5}{318.5} = \$0.79$$

Cash flow per share is above earnings per share, which generally means that cash is being generated that can go to debt repayment, although the margin of cash flow per share above earnings per share probably needs to be higher before this can be accomplished. This shows, however, that XYZ's earnings are good quality and the cash flow is definitely there to pay the earnings that are reported.

$$\text{Cash flow per share} = \frac{\text{net operating cash flow}}{\text{number of ordinary shares}} \times 100$$

$$\text{This year} = \frac{45.7}{318.5} \times 100\% = 14.35 \text{ cents}$$

$$\text{Last year} = \frac{59.5}{318.5} \times 100\% = 18.68 \text{ cents}$$

IN THIS CHAPTER

» **Drawing and interpreting charts**

» **Turning up the volume**

» **Trending in the right direction**

» **Sorting the bulls from the bears**

» **Navigating the market without charts**

Chapter **16**

Charting the Intricacies of Technical Analysis

The saying that a picture is worth a thousand words could be used to describe what *technical analysts*, or *chartists*, believe. They think that clues to the future behaviour of a share price can be recognised on a chart, or graph of its history. Technical analysis is sometimes seen as the opposite of fundamental analysis. While each approach has partisans, the two theories complement each other — fundamental analysis tells you what to buy, while technical analysis tells you when to buy.

Most experienced investors concede that fundamental analysis may not tell the whole share price story. A stock can have attractive fundamentals, yet be out of favour with the market. At the same time, a technical analyst might produce an appealing chart, but of a stock that is too speculative. If you use a combination of fundamental and technical analysis, where the fundamentals are strong and the chart also looks good, you can invest (or trade) with more confidence and be less prone to speculation.

In this chapter, I show you how to create and read the different kinds of charts, patterns and trends used to measure activity on the sharemarket — in short, how to be your own technical analyst.

Understanding Technical Analysis

Technical analysis studies the movement of prices through the use of charts for the purpose of assessing the probable direction of future market action. Technical analysts create price charts and look for recurring patterns, which allow them to infer the likely direction of the share price. The theory is that a share price chart reveals not only the historical record of movement, but also the patterns of behaviour that might take place in the future. In other words, the chart is a visual representation of the past and present performance of a market, and allows the trader to use this information to anticipate future trends before entering a trade.

What technical analysts are looking for are patterns of buying or selling pressure on the chart. Once they have identified the pattern, they believe they know where the share price is headed — that the chart gives them, in effect, clear signals of when to buy and sell. Technical analysis differs from fundamental analysis because it doesn't rely on information about the company whose shares are being considered (or the index, or the commodity). Technical analysis doesn't really consider the intrinsic value of a stock; rather, it concentrates on identifying actual buying or selling pressure on the chart. The reasons behind this pressure don't matter, but once analysts identify the pattern, they believe they know where the share price is headed. At this point, they can join the action, preferably before the market as a whole has found the share.

REMEMBER

Technical analysis appeals to short-term traders who are interested in quick turnaround based on recognising trends. It is also applied to understand long-term trend behaviour. Fundamental analysis suits the long-term investor, who tries to identify undervalued shares to buy, and overvalued shares to sell.

Many traders use technical analysis to help with risk management — with proper position-sizing strategies, they believe they will be profitable over a large number of investments. Other investors use technical analysis to provide a 'second opinion' after analysis of the fundamentals.

Technical analysis can be a complicated topic with hundreds of technical indicators of varying complexity that traders can use to give buy and sell signals. Many experienced traders have their own indicators, developed over years of study. Chartists think of a chart as a road map for the sharemarket. Charts record the price of shares (or commodities, interest rates, currencies and indices) and give a picture of which routes the prices have travelled in the past, where prices are now and where they could lead to in the future.

Charting is useful because of the tendency of price charts to repeat the same formations, which come to be known as either positive or negative depending on the direction. Technical analysts look for patterns, both bullish and bearish, that can be shown on charts and give clues to future trend directions. The patterns could either signal a continuation of the trend or a change in the trend.

However, it is best to think about technical analysis not as predicting where the market's going to go, but as identifying a change in the balance of probabilities — a change that suggests, based on past behaviour, that the market is likely to move towards a certain level.

As you delve into the literature of technical analysis, you'll read about head and shoulders, double tops, double bottoms, triangles, flags and pennants. To the chartist, these are important phases where a change of direction could occur.

Creating the Chart

The basis for technical analysis is a *chart* — a graph of the price of a share, or the value of an index, currency or commodity. Charts can help an investor by showing the levels at which a share becomes cheap in relation to its past performance and also at which points the share should be sold.

Many varieties of charts have been developed, but the basic format remains the same. The typical chart represents price and time, with price on the vertical (y) axis and time on the horizontal (x) axis. The four common kinds of chart are the line chart, the bar chart, the point-and-figure chart and the candlestick chart. The vertical (y) axis may also use one of two different scales: arithmetic or logarithmic.

Drawing a line chart

With the *line chart*, you connect dots drawn on a graph to represent the closing price over any period — daily, weekly, or for longer or shorter periods. This type of share price chart is often used on television, in newspapers and on many online investing articles because it is simple and easy to digest — it typically displays closing prices and nothing else, plotting the closing price as a solid line. Each closing price is linked to the previous closing price to make a continuous line that is easy to follow.

A line chart tracks the performance of a share price over a long period and is good for observing historic highs and lows. It tends to smooth out daily fluctuations in price, sometimes giving a better picture of the overall trend. However, it is only giving a simplistic market view — because it doesn't capture the highs and the lows (it only captures the close), the information that's available from a line chart is the least amount of information, and the least useful, for trading purposes. At the same time, beginning with a line chart allows you to at least start to visualise and track the direction of prices. The line chart in Figure 16-1 shows the daily closing price of ANZ Banking Corporation (ANZ), over the period December 2020 to June 2021.

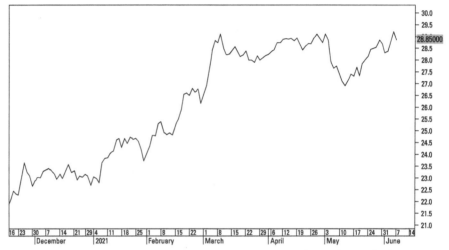

Source: Guppytraders.com/chart from MetaStock

FIGURE 16-1:
A line chart showing ANZ Banking Corporation's daily close over seven months.

Stepping up to a bar chart

The more sophisticated *bar chart* consists of dots drawn to represent the highest and lowest price reached over a given period, with a vertical line drawn between them. The vertical line represents the trading range over that period — it is created by the high and low price for the bar. To the left of this bar, a small dash represents the opening price for the period and to the right is another small dash that shows the closing price.

TIP

Bar charts are sometimes called OHLC charts, because they show the opening, high, low and closing price. Being able to identify whether a bar closes up (usually shown as green) or down (usually shown as red) indicates to the trader the market sentiment (bullish/bearish) for that period.

TIP

An OHLC chart — whether it's a bar chart or a candlestick chart (see the later section 'Lighting the candlestick chart') — immediately gives you more information about a stock. The trader can evaluate volatility by the height of the bars and the conviction of the buyers and sellers by the price range between the open and close marks. In other words, you can see how *volatile* the stock is, and how far it's likely to move.

Figure 16-2 shows a daily OHLC chart for ANZ, over the period December 2020 to June 2021. If you look at the rise for ANZ in March 2021, for instance, where you have six bars going up very strongly, and compare that to what you're seeing in the same period on the line chart, you can see the difference in the information that's available when you compare the two charts.

In March 2021, on the first high bar, it closes at the high; then it closes at the high the next day, and the day after that. However, the day after that it closes near the low. That tells you immediately that the impetus is going out of that particular rally because it couldn't sustain the highs. You can't get that information from a line chart.

If you look at the beginning of May 2021 in Figure 16-2, you can see a strong downtrend day where it opened and then closed on the low. That gives you a good warning that the downtrend is likely to continue. Again, you can't derive such information from the line chart.

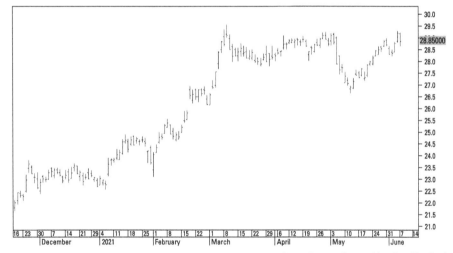

FIGURE 16-2:
A bar (or OHLC) chart showing ANZ Banking Corporation's daily prices over seven months.

Source: Guppytraders.com/chart from MetaStock

Getting the point-and-figure chart

The *point-and-figure chart* differs from line and bar charts in that it ignores time, concentrating only on share price movements, trade by trade. Share traders use point-and-figure charts to track only the significant changes in the price of a share.

To draw a point-and-figure chart, the chartist first chooses a certain price movement, called the *box size*, to be the minimum price movement required to generate a new entry on the chart. The box size chosen depends on the price of the stock being charted (if the stock is trading at 20 cents, the box size may be half a cent; a $3 share price may be 10 cents; trading at $30, the box size may be 50 cents).

Once the box size is chosen, if the price rises by that amount, an X is drawn; if the price falls by the amount of the box size, an O is drawn. If the price moves by two box sizes, two Xs or Os are drawn. In the paper days, point-and-figure charts were drawn on arithmetically scaled graph paper. Successive Xs are added above each other in a column. As soon as an O occurs, it's drawn in a new column to the right of the preceding column.

REMEMBER

An X represents demand. An O represents supply. If Xs are being added to the column, buyers are taking on the stock; if Os are being drawn, sellers are dominant.

Horizontal movement happens only when the trend changes. Time is irrelevant — each column could represent days, weeks or even months; it doesn't matter until the price changes enough to register an entry on the chart. Advocates of point-and-figure charts believe that by filtering out less-significant price movements, they can focus only on important trends. Trends show up more clearly than on other types of chart.

Figure 16-3 shows a point-and-figure chart for ANZ, over the period September 2016 to June 2021, with a box size of 25 cents.

In this case, every one of those Xs or Os represents 25 cents and the reversal is three boxes; in other words, it has to retreat by 75 cents before you move to a new column. It's a way of weeding out the noise of the market — the daily fluctuations that you consider unimportant — and extracting what you believe is the significant price movement that takes place, which, in turn, is the important underlying trend behaviour. The changes in the price of a share that you regard as significant are determined by the parameters you have set, which is the box size, and then the *reversal* — the amount that is required to change before you add a new X or move to a new column.

REMEMBER

When you're using a point-and-figure chart, you are ignoring time — that's the key factor. If you look at the timescale underneath these charts, it's all over the place. If you go back to Figure 16-2, quite clearly, it's a calendar display.

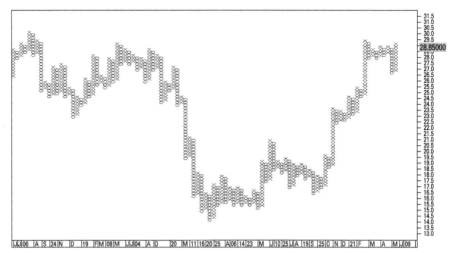

Source: Guppytraders.com/chart from MetaStock

FIGURE 16-3: A point-and-figure chart for ANZ Banking Corporation's share price, September 2016 to June 2021.

Lighting the candlestick chart

The *candlestick chart* was developed in the Japanese rice exchanges of the 18th century and has been widely adopted in the West only in the past 40 years. The candlestick chart gives the same information as a bar chart, but it is presented differently.

A candlestick chart is drawn from the same information as a bar chart, using the opening, high, low and closing price for the period. In a candlestick chart, a rectangular box is drawn between the opening and closing price. The box is known as the *real body*. The thin lines that extend from the body represent the high and low price of the period and are known as the *shadows*. Different types of candle combinations have different names and represent different market situations.

TIP

Because the candlestick chart appears very effectively on computer screens, it has become the dominant type of chart. The candlesticks are easy to see, and easy to identify.

If the closing price is higher than the opening price, the box is green (or white/clear in a black-and-white candlestick chart) and the candle is bullish. If the closing price is lower than the opening price, the candle is red (or black [or *filled*] in a black-and-white chart) and is bearish. Figure 16-4 shows a weekly candlestick chart for ANZ, over the period December 2020 to June 2021.

Strangely enough, the green-and-red colour scheme is reversed in Chinese candlestick charting systems! So, if you see on TV, or in a picture, a 'disappointed' Chinese investor in front of a screen full of red stocks, they would in fact be very happy because that means their stocks are all going up.

Source: Guppytraders.com/chart from MetaStock

FIGURE 16-4:
A candlestick chart for ANZ Banking Corporation showing bearish and bullish candles, and shadows.

Charting with arithmetic and logarithms

You'll encounter charts with two different kinds of scale on the vertical (y) axis. They are the *arithmetic* chart, which measures the actual (or absolute) price rise, and the *logarithmic* chart, which measures price growth in per cent.

A rise from $5 to $10 covers the same vertical distance on both kinds of chart. On the arithmetic chart, the share price has gained $5 and on the logarithmic chart, it has doubled. After that, on the arithmetic chart, the share price must move to $15 to cover the same vertical distance, but on the logarithmic chart, the share price must move to $20 (it must double again).

REMEMBER

No hard-and-fast rule is found for which kind of chart to use. Some of the tools of technical analysis — such as trendlines and indicators — work just as well on arithmetic or logarithmic charts. If you want to study long-term charts (more than two years in duration), logarithmic scale is one way to fit your data into the chart. Most charting packages automatically re-scale charts to fit the screen display.

INTERPRETING VOLUME TRADING

Although price and time represent the y and x axes of the chart, some chartists consider *volume* — the number of shares traded during a given period — as the third major element in technical analysis. Volume indicators may be added to a chart along the horizontal (x) axis.

In many technical analysis books, volume is described as a leading indicator of price, which tells the technical analyst that a change in trend may be imminent. On this theory, volume is low when a stock *bottoms out* — traders lose interest — but picks up as the new uptrend gains interest or momentum.

Diminishing volume is usually considered a sign that the prevailing trend is petering out. However, a more modern view is that volume is not a particularly useful indicator. When the precepts of technical analysis were first being quantified in the 1930s, the sharemarket was much smaller than today in terms of participation and thus volume — the general feeling was that volume preceded price. The big players would have come into the market and they'd buy shares, and if you'd followed the volume, you would have been able to track the price rises. But markets have changed in the last 90 years. Most of the volume theory of the past is based on the idea that information was restricted, and only the large players really had access to it. However, today the flow of information has increased exponentially, both in terms of speed and reach, to a vastly larger pool of market participants. People are using trading software (which is infinitely more powerful than the tools available a century ago) that gives them information on a stock direct to their computer screens almost instantaneously, and they're looking for price increases, not volume increases. These days, price often leads volume, not the other way around.

To the modern share trader, volume becomes important only in terms of the liquidity in the stock — whether it is possible to enter and exit the stock relatively quickly, in a share parcel size that suits the trader.

The following figure shows a bar chart depicting price and volume history for ANZ over the period November 2020 to June 2021. The chart shows the ANZ share price rising steadily until March 2021, then moving sideways during the March to May period, showing a small drop in May and then a resumption of the uptrend. But the volume information at the bottom of the chart doesn't really provide any clue to what's going on with the price.

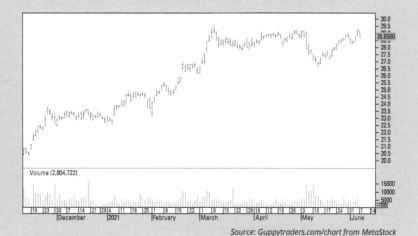

Source: Guppytraders.com/chart from MetaStock

Watching Market Trends

Trend is the direction of the market. The aim of technical analysis is to identify and join the share price trend. On a chart, a *trend* represents a consistent change in prices as well as a change in investor expectations.

A rising trend means the stock is recording successively higher highs and higher lows. Buyers are in control and are pushing the price higher. This situation is what investors want to see. Conversely, a falling trend means the stock is recording successively lower highs and lower lows. Here, sellers are forcing the price lower.

A *trendline* is drawn on a chart to represent both an uptrend and a downtrend, connecting the ascending troughs for an uptrend or descending peaks for a downtrend. It is drawn above peaks for a downtrend and under troughs for an uptrend, on a line of best fit. Figures 16-5, 16-6 and 16-7 show a variety of trendlines.

REMEMBER

A trendline is not considered valid until it has been tested at least three times and the price has moved away each time. The more the trendline is tested and the longer it remains intact, the more important the trendline becomes as a *support* or *resistance* feature.

Support and resistance are crucial concepts that analysts use to determine a change in share price direction. A *support* area on a chart is where a price fall has stabilised repeatedly at a consistent level and then turned upward again. A *resistance* area shows a price level that has historically retreated repeatedly from a consistent level, acting as a barrier. Support and resistance areas develop when market participants have a strong memory of previous price levels.

A trendline on a chart requires an *anchor point*, which is often the low point of a previous trend — a rally (or a retreat) of relatively major significance that comes back and then rallies (or retreats) again. You then have a total of three points — an anchor point and two subsequent points that the trendline connects between, and which is then projected forward into the future. The trendline acts as a support level — what the trader is looking for in the future if a price falls is for it to come back to that line and find support at that level before rebounding.

REMEMBER

Trends differ from support/resistance levels; trends represent change, while support/resistance levels represent barriers to change.

A sloping uptrend is very dynamic. It shows activity with a 'crowd' of people very interested in buying the stock, and this keeps pushing the price upwards because they believe the stock will have a higher future value. But prices tend to feel the impact of gravity, falling much faster than they rise. Downtrends tend to be much faster and swifter than uptrends.

Figure 16-5 shows an uptrend in a weekly chart of the S&P 500 index, over the period February 2020 to July 2021. An uptrend line simply tells you that prices are still moving in a rising trend and that the crowd emotion has not changed. When prices drop below this line, this tells you there is a strong probability that the uptrend is over because there has been a change in crowd behaviour.

Figure 16-6 shows a downtrend in the AGL Energy share price, over the period September 2020 to June 2021. This is the reverse situation to that of the S&P 500; it is a simple downtrend, with the crowd predominantly bearish. The trendline shows that prices are still moving in a falling trend and that the crowd emotion has not changed. When prices move above this line, this tells you there is a strong probability that the downtrend is over because there has been a change in crowd behaviour.

REMEMBER

When traders believe that a trend is about to change, they trade against it — what is known as a *breakout trade*.

Another kind of trend is a *sideways* trend, where the price is neither rising nor falling, just moving sideways left to right along the horizontal time (x) axis. This means the value of the stock has stalled and the market is waiting for either the bulls to push it into an uptrend or the bears to push it into a downtrend. Figure 16-7 shows a sideways trend in the share price of software company Dubber Corporation Limited, over the period October 2020 to May 2021. While a stock in a sideways trend isn't actually falling (so it is not creating a loss for a trader), sideways trends do numb investment success; ultimately, a sideways trend isn't great. The breakout trading above the sideways trendline in April 2021 would have been a welcome sight for investors in Dubber.

REMEMBER

A trendline is *breached* (or *penetrated*) if the price records a close outside the trendline, in the direction of the trend (that is, below an uptrend line, and above a downtrend line).

The following sections look deeper at two types of market trend: the moving average and support/resistance levels.

Moving average

The *moving average* (MA) is a calculation that smooths out price action to show the underlying trend. The MA is drawn on the same chart as the price, and curves under and over the price line (or bars, or candlesticks). Moving averages plot the average price over a set number of periods, and they're a very popular tool used by traders to see what direction a market is heading.

FIGURE 16-5:
An uptrend on the weekly chart for the S&P 500 index, February 2020 to July 2021.

Source: Guppytraders.com/chart from MetaStock

FIGURE 16-6:
A downtrend on the daily chart for AGL Energy, September 2020 to June 2021.

Source: Guppytraders.com/chart from MetaStock

The MA is the average price of the share, on a rolling basis, at any given time. You calculate the MA by taking a set number of days' closing prices and dividing by the number of days to produce a single average price figure that is plotted on the same chart as the share price.

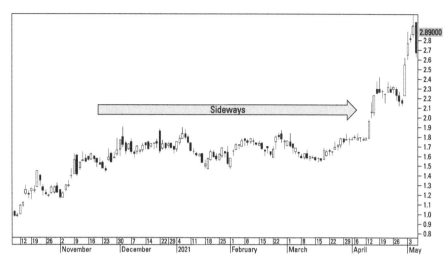

FIGURE 16-7:
Dubber
Corporation, daily
chart, October
2020 to
May 2021.

Source: Guppytraders.com/chart from MetaStock

Because the MA follows the trend, it also identifies the start of a trend. Traders use the MA as a signal. When the price closes above the MA, that's a buying signal; when the price moves below the MA, that's a red-light signal. The fewer the number of days in the period of your MA, the more frequently the share price will cross the MA. A longer period of days will generate fewer trading signals, but the catch is that you won't see a new trend as quickly as with a shorter MA.

Moving averages are most commonly used as a combination of two moving averages — a shorter-term MA and a longer-term MA. Crossover signals represent trend reversals and give positive and negative indications: when the shorter-term line moves above the longer-term line, that's a bullish (buy) signal, while the shorter-term line falling below the longer-term line is taken as a bearish (sell) signal. The combination of two averages also helps to reduce false signals.

A moving average can be a *simple moving average* (SMA), which applies an equal weight to all observations over the period, or an *exponential moving average* (EMA), which puts a greater weight and significance on the most recent data points. An exponentially weighted moving average reacts more significantly to recent price changes than a SMA.

Figure 16-8 shows a combination of a ten-day EMA and a 30-day EMA in the price of energy infrastructure company AusNet Services, over the period October 2020 to August 2021. It shows that between November and February, on average, AusNet's price was trading below its 30-day value; and from March through to May, it was, on average, trading above its 30-day value.

TIP

The MA provides you with a useful understanding of trending behaviour: if the price is consistently below the MA, then the stock is in a downtrend; when the price is consistently above the MA, the stock is in an uptrend.

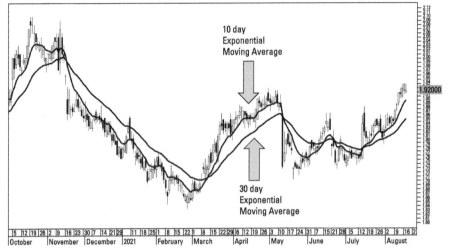

FIGURE 16-8:
A daily ten-day exponential moving average and a 30-day exponential moving average for AusNet Services, October 2020 to August 2021.

Source: Guppytraders.com/chart from MetaStock

One moving average tells you this, but a combination of two MAs tells you a little bit more. When the shorter-term MA and the longer-term MA cross-over, it indicates that there may be a change in price direction taking place. When the shorter-term MA moves above the longer-term, it is potentially a bullish signal; conversely, if the shorter-term MA moves below the longer-term, it's potentially a bearish sign.

Support and resistance

Technical analysts use support and resistance levels to identify price points on a chart where the probabilities favour a pause or reversal of a prevailing price movement. This happens because of demand and supply. *Support* occurs where a downtrend is expected to pause because of a concentration of demand. *Resistance* is in play when an uptrend is expected to pause temporarily, due to a concentration of supply.

TIP

Effectively, support and resistance levels show market psychology at work; they show when buyers and sellers gain control over the direction of the share price.

On charts, support and resistance are indicated as lines, but in the real world, support and resistance indicators aren't usually that precise. It's more helpful to think of support and resistance as narrow *areas*, or *ranges*, on a price chart where activity and price direction are more likely to change.

If a share price trades for a long period between a support and a resistance level and is unable to breakout either way, the share is said to be in a *trading range* or *rangebound*. Support and resistance become interchangeable. Once this impasse is breached, a resistance level has the potential to act as a support if the price later retreats. Similarly, when a support level fails to hold, that level becomes a resistance level if the price later rises. (This is described as the resistance or support level *changing its polarity*.)

When the price breaks through a resistance level and is headed upward, the trader will look for the next resistance level at which the price can reasonably be expected to stabilise again (the reverse is true for support levels).

Figure 16-9 shows the Blackstone Minerals share price declining in November and December of 2020, and rebounding from the same level. That same price level was tested again in May and June of 2021 — that's the support level. The late-2020 resistance level (at around 40 cents) became a support level in January 2021. The resistance that appears in November and December 2020 influences the market in May and June 2021. The support level in November and December 2020 again influences the market in May and June 2021. These levels show a consistent value over time, acting as a support or resistance level.

FIGURE 16-9:
A daily chart showing support and resistance levels for Blackstone Minerals, September 2020 to June 2021.

Source: Guppytraders.com/chart from MetaStock

If the share price pushes through the resistance level or falls below the support level, a breakout has occurred. When resistance is breached, the share price is headed higher, which happened with Blackstone Minerals in January 2021. But when a support level is breached, the price is headed lower, which happened with Blackstone Minerals over March–April 2021. The chart may show the next support level and give you a reasonably good idea of how far the price has to fall before it pauses and rebounds.

When strong resistance is broken, it means that long-term selling pressure has finally been overcome. The more powerful the resistance level, the more powerful the breakout. The stronger the resistance level — the more prolonged the period over which it can resist — the stronger it is as a support level when the level changes its polarity from resistance to support.

Interpreting the Chart

No matter what style of chart you use, your aim is to interpret the chart by identifying a trend, or a pattern, which you believe can indicate the balance of the probability of where the market in that share is headed. If the trend is rising, you try to identify it as soon as possible and buy shares. Then, you monitor the trend to identify when it changes to a sideways or falling trend in order to sell the shares.

Finding channels

A *channel* is similar to a trading range, in which a share price moves sideways for a long period between a support and a resistance level; the difference is that in an upwards-sloping channel, the price is appreciating, because both the highs and lows are being struck at progressively higher levels.

A channel occurs when a trendline is drawn under successive lows, then a parallel line known as the *return line* (or *channel line*) is drawn above the peaks and above the successive highs. The direction of the trendlines, up or down, defines the trend direction.

The combination of a trendline and a return line in a price channel is shown in Figure 16-10, showing the price action in the daily chart of listed investment company Australian Foundation Investment Company (AFIC) over the period January to August 2021. The lower trendline is the support level changing value over time; the upper trendline is the resistance level changing value over time. The channel breakout occurs in July, when the price pushes through the return line.

A channel is said to have failed when the price is unable to reach the return line and breaks through the trendline. Figure 16-11 shows a channel failure in the share price of wagering company BetMakers Technology Group in May–June 2021. Once the share price closes below the lower trendline, it signals a change in the trend for BetMakers — in this case, a fairly dramatic change in the trend.

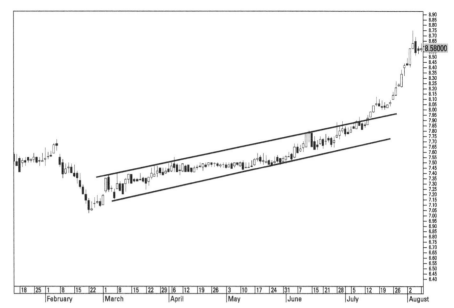

FIGURE 16-10:
A daily chart showing channel breakout for the Australian Foundation Investment Company, January 2021 to August 2021.

Source: Guppytraders.com/chart from MetaStock

FIGURE 16-11:
A daily chart showing channel failure for the BetMakers Technology Group, January 2021 to June 2021.

Source: Guppytraders.com/chart from MetaStock

Locating gaps

Gaps are places on the chart where no trading takes place at certain prices. In an uptrend, a gap occurs when a stock opens higher than it closed the day before and the high of the preceding day is lower than the low of the following day. The opposite occurs in a gap in a downtrend.

Figure 16-12 shows the price action for Woodside Petroleum (now known as Woodside Energy) over April–June 2021.

FIGURE 16-12: A daily chart showing gaps in trading for Woodside Petroleum, April 2021 to June 2021.

Source: Guppytraders.com/chart from MetaStock

Gaps are a feature of OHLC (bar) charts and candlestick charts, which track the opening, closing, high and low prices. A line chart will not show gaps because it tracks only the closing prices; a point-and-figure chart also ignores gaps because for these charts, time is irrelevant. A gap up means a runaway share price, while a gap down is very bad news. Some technical analysts believe that the price always returns to fill a gap, but this is by no means 100 per cent accepted — and you could be waiting a long time to see these results.

Gaps appear when the 'crowd' — as in, the market — changes its opinion on the value of the stock overnight, usually related to a news event. Australian traders are very familiar with gaps; quite often, news from overseas breaks overnight and is immediately reflected in markets that are open and trading, but this news has to be incorporated into prices at the next open of the Australian market, which often results in a gap. Alternatively, a gap may appear if an Australian company releases news after the local market has closed for the day — for example, an earnings downgrade — and the news is important enough to ensure that tomorrow's open will be at prices well away from that day's close.

REMEMBER

Gapping-up doesn't always indicate a runaway share price, and gapping-down isn't necessarily bad news every time. Gaps can bring trading opportunities — in cases when the market over-reacts to the gap, for example, low selling positions may appear shortly after the open, before the local market stabilises at a new level.

Identifying consolidation patterns

When a trend takes a breather, it consolidates, and trades sideways. If the price continues in that direction, the sideways pattern is known as a *consolidation* pattern. The main consolidation patterns are the *triangle* (sometimes called a *pennant*) and a *rectangle*.

Triangles and pennants

A *triangle* is a medium-term sideways trading pattern that narrows into the form of a small triangle. A triangle occurs when two trendlines converge to form an equilateral (or symmetrical) triangle. Other triangle types are created by a trend-line and a support/resistance level. Of the three triangle patterns — up-sloping, down-sloping and equilateral — the equilateral triangle is the least useful because it has a 50 per cent probability of breaking up or down.

Triangles are useful precisely because they allow the measurement of price targets. The triangle direction is decided by the slope of the trendline: up- and down-sloping triangles identify a higher probability direction for the breakout. The triangle pattern also has a well-defined vertical base.

Figure 16-13 shows a triangle in the chart of financial services company Prae-mium Limited, over the period July to November 2020. The anchor point is the base of the vertical base. This is an up-sloping triangle, so it has a resistance level. This level is tested on several occasions — there is a brief hint of a breakout that takes place, but the closes are all on that resistance level. The trendline comes off the anchor point; it has three rebound points. The crucial factor is the base of the triangle, which is usually three to five days of continuous price action — in other words, most of the candles are green or most of the candles are red.

GETTING INTO ADVANCED TECHNICAL ANALYSIS

Once you delve into technical analysis, there seems to be no end to the complexity of theories. You can find devotees of stochastic oscillators, Moving Average Convergence Divergence (MACD), Relative Strength Indicators (RSIs), Bollinger Bands, Guppy Multiple Moving Averages, the Chaikin Oscillator, the Williams per cent R momentum indicator (momentum usually refers to the speed or strength of price movement) and the Gann indicators developed by WD Gann in the mid-20th century.

Some of these have fascinating histories, seemingly unrelated at first glance to the financial markets. Much of Gann's work, for example, was based on geometry, astronomy, astrology and ancient mathematics. The Coppock Indicator was invented in the 1960s by Edwin Coppock, an investment adviser who was asked by the trustees of the American Episcopalian Church pension fund to spot points in the investment cycle when the odds of profitable investment were at their highest. Instead of analysing figures, Coppock turned to psychology and how people might react to changes in market conditions. He studied grief, and the time it took for people to recover from traumatic events such as bereavement and divorce, and related all this to the sharemarket.

Many analysts base their charting on one of a number of strategies that have been developed and refined over time. One popular theory is the Elliott Wave Principle, named after Ralph Nelson Elliott, who is famous for accurately predicting the low point reached by the Dow Jones Industrial Average following the crash of October 1929. Building on the wave theory of physics, Elliott observed that the stock market tended to move in waves. Elliott discovered patterns that recur in a liquid market, and his theories have been developed into a complex system of technical analysis that has many devotees.

Other chartists swear by the Fibonacci sequence of numbers: 0, 1, 1, 2, 3, 5, 8, 13, 21, 34, 55, 89 and so on ad infinitum, named after the 13th century Italian mathematician (you add the previous two numbers to get the next in the sequence.) After 21, the Fibonacci sequence grows at the rate of 1.618, a rate of growth that is found commonly in nature and science (it was known by the Ancient Greeks as the golden ratio). The sequence is used by many chartists to predict price movement.

Without a technical analysis software program, most people would have no hope of calculating the values used for these indicators; computers and smartphones have revolutionised the field. Some people can get a little obsessed with technical analysis, but so can the advocates of fundamental analysis with their P/Es and NTAs.

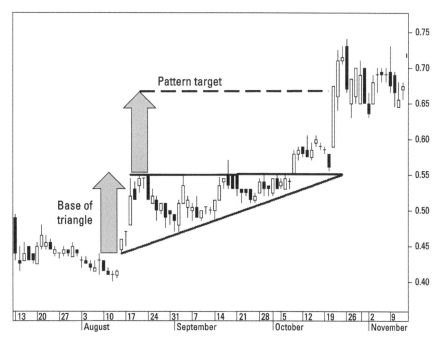

Source: Guppytraders.com/chart from MetaStock

FIGURE 16-13:
A daily chart showing a triangle for Praemium Limited in the period July to November 2020.

Consolidation patterns are a measured move — you measure the base of the triangle, and project that upwards, and that projection becomes a high-probability target. When the breakout develops in Figure 16-13, where the triangle pattern appears in a bull market, there's about a 90 per cent probability that the projected target will be hit. The vertical base on the Praemium Limited chart is 12 cents, so the projection target is 12 cents above the resistance level on the triangle. Having used the three points on the trendline to identify this as an upward-sloping triangle, the trader has a reasonable expectation of a run from about 55 cents to about 67 cents.

For a down-sloping triangle, this would work in reverse — you measure the vertical base of the triangle and project downwards to give the price-fall target.

A short-lived equilateral triangle with an upward or downward slope is called a *pennant*, and appears after a very fast rise (or fall) in price. Figure 16-14 shows a pennant in the chart of investment company Absolute Equity Performance Fund. Again, the pennant has to have a valid uptrend and downtrend line. The base of the pennant is measured. That value is then projected upwards from the point at which the price breaks out above the pennant (or below it, as the case may be).

A pennant pattern demonstrates almost equal upward buying pressure, followed by almost equal downward selling pressure. A price breaking out of a pennant is not considered to have as high a probability as in a triangle, but when the breakout takes place, the trader knows that there has been a change in the market's understanding of the price and value for this stock.

Source: Guppytraders.com/chart from MetaStock

FIGURE 16-14: A daily chart showing a pennant for the Absolute Equity Performance Fund in the period April 2020 to September 2020.

Rectangles and flags

A *rectangle* is a sideways trading pattern that forms over one to three months, in either an uptrend or a downtrend. It forms when the share price leaves the main trendline and trades between two new horizontal lines, a support level and a resistance level. A rectangle is a variation of a *trading band* (the range of prices at which the stock, or whatever else is being charted, has previously traded over a certain period of time; a trading band forms a floor and ceiling over the current trend). A rectangle is traded the same way — it is a pattern projection target, with the width of the trading band projected upward to define the target for the breakout.

Figure 16-15 shows rectangle trading bands in the weekly chart of the SPDR S&P/ASX 200 exchange-traded fund over the period May 2020 to July 2021.

While many stocks show a *secular* (that is, long-term, so not seasonal or cyclical) uptrend, the price movement takes place along trading bands. In these cases, every time there is a breakout, as part of the uptrend, the trader can tell where the target will be. In the SDPR chart in Figure 16-15, a trader would have been a buyer in September, out in November, a buyer again in January and out again in April, because they were trading between the bands.

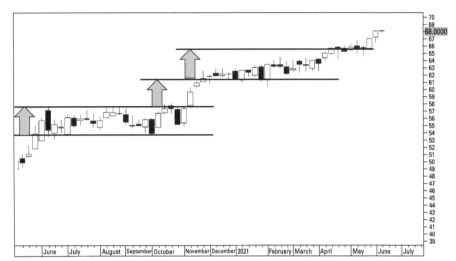

Source: Guppytraders.com/chart from MetaStock

FIGURE 16-15:
A weekly chart showing rectangle trading bands for the SPDR S&P/ASX 200 exchange-traded fund, May 2020 to July 2021.

A *flag* is a slanting parallelogram that appears when the price movement is not horizontal but a series of progressively lower highs and lows for an uptrend. A *flagpole* is what you get when a sharp near-vertical advance or decline precedes a flag. A valid flag pattern is quite famous in technical analysis and only appears at the end of a flagpole created by a few days of very rapid price rises. The height of the flagpole is used to calculate the breakout target.

REMEMBER

The essential feature of a flag pattern is the flagpole, which is created by between one and five days of really strong price action. Then, the price pulls back; the pull-back is defined by two parallel down-sloping trendlines. Not a pennant, not lines that are converging, not lines that are expanding — the lines are parallel, just like a flag. The crucial feature of a flag pattern is that you measure the height of that flagpole from the point of the breakout, which sets the upside target — it's a high probability that the price will reach that upside target as the flag is considered a reliable trading pattern.

Figure 16-16 shows the daily chart for expenses management software company Bill Identity Limited over the period August–September 2020. It shows a clear flag pattern.

Identifying reversal patterns

Reversal patterns point to an imminent change of direction in the trend, so are important trading points if they can be identified correctly. The patterns sometimes resemble their names, such as the head and shoulder and double tops and bottoms patterns.

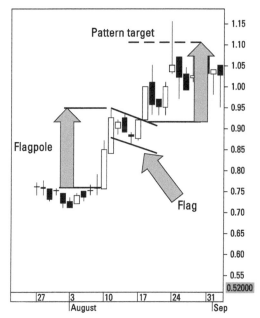

FIGURE 16-16:
Bill Identity
Limited, daily
chart, August
2020 to Septem-
ber 2020.

Source: Guppytraders.com/chart from MetaStock

Head and shoulders patterns

A *head and shoulders* pattern in a share chart signals problems — it is always a reversal pattern. Figure 16-17 shows a head and shoulders pattern for the S&P/ ASX All Ordinaries index over 2007–08, with each candle representing a week.

A head and shoulders reversal pattern forms after an uptrend, and its completion marks a trend reversal. The pattern contains three successive peaks, with the middle peak (the head) being the highest and the two outside peaks (the shoulders) being low and roughly equal. The reaction lows of each peak can be connected to form the neckline, which is a support level. A share price that has made a head and shoulders pattern on the chart has topped out and has a high probability of falling.

The shoulder-head-shoulder pattern is clear in Figure 16-17, with the lows connected with the neckline. Again, the value of the head and shoulders pattern is that it is a measured move. You measure the distance from the head to the neckline, project that downwards, and that gives you your downside target. In 2008, once traders saw the retreat coming off the shoulder in Figure 16-17, starting in May, they were able to recognise a confirmational head-and-shoulders pattern, and project their downside target at 3,700 points.

An inverted head and shoulders pattern, however, is just what the doctor ordered for a prospective buyer. The inverse head and shoulder signals a market bottom.

It is similar to the standard head and shoulders pattern but forms after a down-trend, and its completion marks a trend reversal — in this case, a market turning bullish. The first and third trough are considered shoulders, and the second trough forms the head. Traders typically buy-in when the price rises above the resistance of the neckline.

Source: Guppytraders.com/chart from MetaStock

FIGURE 16-17:
A head and shoulders pattern by week for the S&P/ASX All Ordinaries index, 2007 to 2008.

Figure 16-18 shows an inverted head and shoulders pattern in the daily share price chart of Equity Trustees Limited from January to October 2020. Here, a successful trader would have identified the inverted head and shoulders pattern, and bought-in as the market began to recover in June, selling-out at the target level in October. Being a *recovery trade* — which needs new money coming into the market — inverted head and shoulders patterns usually take longer to complete than head and shoulders reversals, which are brought about by people selling.

REMEMBER

Like flags and triangles, the head and shoulders pattern is considered to be highly reliable.

Double tops and bottoms

A *double top* occurs when a share price tests a resistance level twice and fails to break through. With a *double bottom*, the support level is tested twice but holds. A double top is negative and a double bottom is positive for the share price. For obvious reasons, a double top is sometimes known as an M pattern, and a double bottom as a W pattern. If either of them tries the resistance level again and fails, they become a triple top or triple bottom, and they are, respectively, even more bearish than a double top or a double bottom, with an even higher probability of retreat away from the resistance level or rebound off the support level.

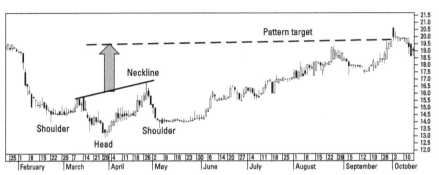

Source: Guppytraders.com/chart from MetaStock

Figure 16-19A shows a double top in the share price chart of Australian iron ore miner Mount Gibson Iron Limited, while Figure 16-19B shows a double bottom in the price chart of the main Japanese share market index, the Nikkei 225. The most important feature of the double bottom is that the height of the pattern from the bottom to the peak of that middle rise is a measured move — take that value, project it upwards, and it gives you your upside target. That upside target is usually reached within three to six months.

Source: Guppytraders.com/chart from MetaStock

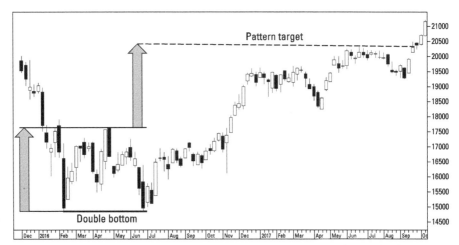

Source: Guppytraders.com/chart from MetaStock

FIGURE 16-19B:
A weekly chart showing a double bottom for the Nikkei 225 index, December 2015 to September 2017.

Leaving the Charts Behind

Keep an open mind about technical analysis. These theories aren't a guaranteed way to wealth, nor are they as enigmatic as reading tea leaves or a horoscope. I've spoken to chartists who say that they can look at a price chart without knowing what it represents, and they can tell you whether to buy or sell; and it must be said that some have strong track records of success. Technical analysis is a tool, not a dogma, although watching a share price move exactly as Fibonacci analysis projected can be unnerving!

REMEMBER

Keep in mind that technical analysis takes no account of a stock's intrinsic worth — for the long-haul investor, this information is still crucial.

IN THIS CHAPTER

» **Scrutinising company websites**

» **Trading shares**

» **Checking out investment websites**

» **Finding share apps at your fingertips**

» **Tracking down a good podcast**

Chapter **17**

Using Online Tools to Research Your Investments

Eleven years ago, when I was writing the third edition of this book, I wrote, in this spot: 'The internet makes investing easier by opening up access to information. Armed with an internet connection, you can now research, analyse and buy shares with virtually the same speed and performance as a stock-broker. While access to information is now available to everyone, the ability to correctly interpret that information is still an acquired skill. In this chapter, I show you how the web can work for you when it comes to getting information on stocks and shares.'

Today, it seems totally redundant to write such a thing. You can now access information of all kinds instantly over the internet, on any device you choose — computer, laptop, tablet or smartphone. You can look up anything you want and buy any stock, anywhere and at any time; you can sit in a café or on a train while researching your investment portfolio wirelessly, using a variety of sites. Now, you have much more than access to information — you have the tools at your fingertips to research your investments, sell and purchase shares, and develop your understanding of the sharemarket through apps, podcasts and expert-driven newsletters.

Which is why this chapter is now about so much more than getting information. In this chapter, I consider the many ways that the internet and modern technology can make it easier than ever to understand the sharemarket and trade in shares.

Making the Most of the Web

You can type any topic in this book that piques your interest into a search engine and within seconds, a cornucopia of information cascades onto your monitor. Some of this information won't be of any use, but a staggering amount of it is helpful. Free sites and subscription sites with free trials abound. Online, you can teach yourself fundamental and technical analysis, and visit a company and view its operations. You can look inside the financial innards of almost any company, run a ruler over its price chart, buy the company's stock and chat to other investors, not all of whom have the same view of the company's merit.

Back in 1994, I started doing a 6.30am radio broadcast on the overnight figures and moves in the finance markets. When I started my broadcasts, I had to rely on the market figures given by the television and radio morning news bulletins. I would catch a bulletin and hastily scribble down the figures. Eventually, I cultivated a relationship with one of the broking houses, which had people working the early shift. I would ring my contact just prior to going on air for the very latest figures for gold, oil, the Dow Jones Industrial Average and the Nasdaq Composite Index in the US, the FTSE100 in the UK, and the A$/US$ exchange rate. Sometimes I would find (to my horror, as air time was looming) that the brokers were too busy to talk to me.

By the time I gave up the early mornings, I had simply bookmarked the key websites I relied on for a full account of trading that had taken place in the northern hemisphere markets while I slept. It took me just a few minutes to collect all the information I needed. Quite a bit of that time was taken up with the sounds of a dial-up connection. . . another thing of the past.

REMEMBER

Today, connecting to the latest investing updates is instantaneous. Anyone reading this book can go online to get instant access to almost as much information as the professionals.

The point about using the internet as an investment tool is not only related to the ease and convenience of making transactions there, but lies in the potential of the internet as a conduit of information. The variety of information you can find on a company in just a few seconds is staggering. You can sit at your computer and research a stock, read through its financial statements, check what its charts look like and buy it with just a few clicks, and with all that information on your computer screen at the same time. The internet is unparalleled at getting information to your fingertips and democratising access to the sharemarket. The internet can't make you a better investor — but it can certainly bring to you a lot of the information you need. You have to supply the experience, knowledge and insight.

Virtually every publicly quoted company realises that having a website is an ideal way to communicate up-to-the-minute news and financial information. A company website also keeps private investors informed and ensures they get the same timely information as professional investors. Most companies use their websites (and their social media) as the centrepiece of their communications strategy — they can keep their investors informed of the latest company news in real time.

Using the internet, you can put together a dossier on a company and its competitors. If the company belongs to an industry association, its website may also be helpful for commentary and outlook.

TIP

The company website should be your first port of call before you buy a stock, and subsequently, while you own it. As a first step, plug the name of the company you're interested in into a search engine such as Google to go directly to its information, so you can find out what people are saying about the company.

WARNING

The standard of information and presentation on company websites varies, as does the frequency of their update. But if a company you're interested in doesn't have a website to tell the world about itself, that should be a concern.

A company puts every profit result and stock exchange announcement it makes on its website, as well as any presentations and briefings its executives give. The news section of the website is good to follow — it may feature information that has not been in a market announcement, although everything that could affect the price will have been reported to the market. You can also find descriptions of the company's business and operations, complete with photographs and maybe even video footage, as well as stories from other media sources.

The current trend is for more interactivity on websites. Most companies want to be as open and informative as possible in order to maintain and enhance their relationships with the investment community. Many companies broadcast their meetings over their website; some even allow shareholders to vote online.

WARNING

Although a website can be useful, you can't rely completely on the positive broker reports it features. A company is hardly likely to post critical or negative media and broker research reports on its website!

Finding Investment Websites

Investment websites abound, from free sites to subscription-only sites where only members have access to the recommendations, to forum sites where like-minded enthusiasts gather to talk shares, to broker websites where clients are given a password for access to online research and recommendations. Every stockbroker has a website that features a rich seam of research, recommendations, tools and education but they are usually client-only, so registering with several stockbrokers is worth doing just to get a password to visit their websites. Check out the stockbroker listings page on the Australian Securities Exchange (ASX) website (asx.com.au).

The ASX site is a great place to start learning about sharemarket investment, and a great site to explore as your understanding grows. Novice investors will find an outstanding array of information online. The ASX website is a gold mine, packed with up-to-the-minute data, such as the prices of listed securities, dividend dates, index values and company announcements, trading volumes and market statistics, and it is brimful of educational material, information on floats, stockbroker contact details, company reporting and even a meeting calendar.

TIP

Most *fund managers* (refer to Chapter 5 for more on managed funds) issue an investment report every month — these can be a great source of investment thinking, strategy updates, research articles, or explanations of which stocks the manager bought and sold that month. Google is all you need to get started here — simply type in search terms such as 'Australian equities' and 'fund manager'.

Many sources of great share investing tips offer free advice; some provide paid-for, subscription-based content if you're willing to invest in building your knowledge base; and your broker may have a useful website full of resources.

Getting information for free

Here are some of the really helpful free websites:

>> **Australian Securities Exchange** (ASX; asx.com.au): Aside from up-to-date prices and announcements that ASX-listed companies make (and have made, back to 1998, if they're old enough), the ASX website is packed full of

information and resources for share investors, as well as the housekeeping information to be expected of the nation's main stock exchange.

TIP

The ASX's Investment Products Monthly Update, published on its website, can be a bountiful place to start looking for fund managers and evaluating their thinking. Go to the listed investment companies/listed investment trusts (LICs/LITs) section on the ASX website, find the announcements for the LIC you're interested in (using its ASX code if you know it), and find its monthly reports to identify the fund manager. For unlisted fund managers, the Investment Products Monthly Update also shows you the managers involved in the ASX mFunds program; armed with all those names, you can start searching the managers' websites — many of which are great sources of market insights and discussions regarding the stocks that the manager is interested in.

>> **BetaShares** (betashares.com.au): Exchange-traded fund (ETF) issuer BetaShares has a good website that features not only information about ETFs and its own products, but readable and accessible investment education material and insights. The site also features investment, market-sector and economic updates, and a blog from chief economist David Bassanese.

>> **ETF Securities** (etfsecurities.com.au): ETF issuer ETF Securities has a site packed with information, including a weekly summary of the global and Australian sharemarket. The site hosts articles about the themes and industries behind the issuer's ETFs, and includes a range of resources for both professional and individual investors.

>> **Firstlinks** (firstlinks.com.au): Owned and operated by research firm Morningstar Australia, Firstlinks is a publisher providing content — in both article, and longer research 'white paper' form — written by financial market professionals with experience in wealth management, superannuation, banking, academia and financial advice. The website focuses on investing, economics, strategy, taxation and retirement planning.

>> **iShares** (blackrock.com/au/ishares-etfs): ETF issuer iShares, part of global funds management giant BlackRock, has a site that is replete with ETF market updates, investor education and insights, plus a range of market and economic commentary, both Australian and global.

>> **Listcorp** (listcorp.com): Listcorp is a personalised information service for investors. Providing instant access to information from companies and research analysts, along with data-driven insights, Listcorp is a digital publishing, distribution and data analytics platform designed to bring together listed companies and investors, giving investors an easy-to-use, intuitive, one-stop resource for relevant listed company information, sharemarket research and industry insights.

>> **Livewire** (livewiremarkets.com): Livewire is a free social media platform (though you have to sign up) for investors and market professionals. It brings

together leading financial companies, fund managers and commentators on a single platform to share insights and discuss what's happening in the markets. It aims to give self-directed investors access to the ideas, research, and investment insights and strategies from some of Australia's best professional investors, financial advisers, analysts, stockbrokers and independent research providers.

>> **Nestegg** (nestegg.com.au): Personal finance website nestegg that is not solely focused on share investing — it also covers saving, the economy, investing, borrowing, wealth creation, superannuation and retirement. It is aimed at a wide spectrum of readers, from the beginner saver to the novice asset owner or the expert investor, as well as anyone in between.

>> **Proactive Investors** (proactiveinvestors.com.au): Proactive Investors is an international company with offices in the US, UK and Canada. It offers breaking financial news, sharemarket commentary, company articles, research and analysis. Listed companies and companies about to mount an IPO pay for news and video coverage.

>> **ShareCafe** (sharecafe.com.au): ShareCafe aims to create informed investors by producing engaging digital and educational investment content to help all types of investors with their financial decisions. ShareCafe's long-term goal is to be Australian investors' primary source of financial information on topics such as advice, wealth, ASX-listed companies, property and equity research. (**Note:** I have written for ShareCafe.)

>> **Share Prices** (shareprices.com.au): This website provides its subscribed members (who must register) with a large and comprehensive array of sharemarket data, investment products and trading tools in one place. Share Prices features educational content and videos on investment, trading, and fundamental and technical analysis. While it is free, occasionally the site offers members access to investment products that may contain management, brokerage or service fees.

>> **SmallCaps** (smallcaps.com.au): A website for market news and information on ASX-listed small-cap companies. All sectors of the market are covered, from mining, resources, biotech and pharmaceutical to technology, oil and gas explorers and new producers (often called *juniors*), and companies looking to list on the stock exchange. Listed companies pay for coverage, which is provided via articles, videos, podcasts and detailed sector reports.

>> **Stockhead** (stockhead.com.au): Stockhead covers the stories of little-known listed companies, those hailing from what Stockhead calls the 'ASX 2,000' — that is, the companies outside the S&P/ASX 200 index. Emerging ASX-listed companies pay Stockhead for journalistic coverage; Stockhead says it focuses on the companies driving the next wave of innovation, economic growth, societal progress and shareholder wealth.

>> **StocksDigital/Next Investors Group:** StocksDigital/Next Investors is an investment firm that takes long-term positions in portfolios of carefully selected ASX-listed companies, and shares in-depth articles, research, commentary and updates on the companies it owns with readers for free. The featured companies pay Next Investors a fee (usually in shares) in return for sharing updates, commentary and opinions about them with their readers. (***Note:*** I have written for StocksDigital.)

The group's websites each cover a discrete portfolio of stocks:

- **Next Tech Stock** (nexttechstock.com) focuses on tech stocks.

- **Next Biotech** (nextbiotech.com.au) focuses on biotech stocks.

- **Next Oil Rush** (nextoilrush.com) focuses on oil stocks.

- **Next Mining Boom** (nextminingboom.com) focuses on oil stocks.

- **Finfeed** (finfeed.com) focuses on early-stage biotech and life science stocks.

- **Catalyst Hunter** (catalysthunter.com) targets fast-moving stocks, providing alerts when a stock is close to a *share price catalyst* (an expected event or a piece of news that triggers a significant price rise — a *negative catalyst* would trigger a fall) that may potentially initiate a share price movement.

- **Wise-Owl** (wise-owl.com) is the website for an investment fund seeking long-term returns through investing in a small, carefully chosen portfolio of high-quality ASX listed micro-cap stocks.

>> **The Bull** (thebull.com.au): This independent sharemarket news website has articles, data and stock tips. The advertising-funded site conducts in-depth online broker reviews, so readers can find the best brokerage or adviser for their investing needs. Each year, The Bull's team of traders test and assess broking firms on more than 290 variables to formulate their star ratings for various categories, as well as the scoring for the Annual Review. Every fortnight, The Bull gives buy, hold and sell recommendations from an ever-changing cast of brokers and analysts. (***Note:*** I have written for The Bull.)

>> **The Inside Network** (theinside.network): Full disclaimer — I am contributing editor at The Inside Network, which is a global community of investment professionals, academics, researchers and thought leaders, spanning three pools of global capital: institutional, adviser, and individual. The Inside Network hosts investment events and publishes three digital newsletters (*The Inside Investor, Investor Strategy News* and *The Inside Adviser*), and it also has a YouTube channel packed with informative video content on investment.

- **The Market Herald** (themarketherald.com.au): Itself an ASX-listed company, The Market Herald website features editorial articles and video covering the sharemarket and business news. Listed companies pay for a package of coverage and services. The Market Herald also operates HotCopper (at hotcopper.com.au), which is Australia's largest free and independent stock market trading forum for ASX investors to discuss share prices, the sharemarket and other asset classes.

- **VanEck** (vaneck.com.au): ETF issuer VanEck makes a considerable effort to educate ETF investors through its Learning Hub, Investor Centre, Research and Insights sections, as well as its videos and blog.

- **Vanguard Education Centre** (vanguard.com.au): Global funds management giant Vanguard has a really handy Client Education Centre on its site.

- **Wallmine** (wallmine.com): Wallmine is a US-based website built to provide investors with reams of sharemarket and cryptocurrency news, data and information in a single place, but also to allow them, once registered, to monitor their investments and use tools to gain insights to understand that information. Investors can create personalised filters, portfolios and watchlists. For an Australian investor, one of the handiest things about Wallmine is the presence of consensus analysts' price targets.

- **Yahoo Finance** (au.finance.yahoo.com): Yahoo provides Australian finance and investment news and articles, stock quotes, currency information and a blog. Investors can use tools such as watchlists and portfolio monitoring to track the performance of their shareholdings, using real-time data and customised views, and can look up any stock.

Paying for content

You can also access a broad range of investment websites that are subscription-based, although each may offer some content for free as a loss-leader. Among the leaders in this field are:

- **AtlasTrend** (atlastrend.com): The AtlasTrend blog features regular articles on investing, with a particular focus on the themes around which the company's portfolios have been built.

- **Australian Investors Association** (investors.asn.au): The Australian Investment Association (AIA) is a not-for-profit organisation dedicated to providing high-quality, independent investment information that helps Australians decide their financial future. It isn't aligned to any institution, which allows it to filter and choose the best possible information for its members. The AIA doesn't offer advice, but it can help investors understand their share investing and risk management process; keep abreast of local and global news and developments that may impact their investing activities; establish and manage a self-managed super fund (SMSF); invest in managed funds or other instruments, such as ETFs; and build portfolios and strategies across asset classes.

>> **Australian Shareholders' Association** (ASA; australianshareholders. com.au): Australia's largest, independent, not-for-profit shareholder association, the ASA's mission is to be the voice of retail shareholders through educating investors and standing up for shareholder rights. The ASA offers members access to a resource centre full of investor information and educational material, as well as its magazine, Equity, recorded webinars, articles, presentations and podcasts. The organisation wants all shareholders to be treated equitably and will advocate for change in company governance and behaviour where fairness is lacking. The ASA also runs a broad program of member events.

>> **Australian Stock Report** (australianstockreport.com.au): This website offers affordable market research and Australian and global stock market news to everyday Australian investors through curated research reports, a daily newsletter containing recommendations of stocks to buy now on the ASX, and live events to its subscribers and members, as well as general advice advisory, managed funds, investment software and more.

>> **Barefoot Investor** (barefootinvestor.com): The Barefoot Investor (former stockbroker Scott Pape) is an independent finance expert and author of the books under that title. The Barefoot Investor broadcasts and publishes financial education through newsletters, emails, websites, television, radio, audio recordings, seminars and written reports. The focus of the overall service is personal finance.

>> **Fat Prophets** (fatprophets.com.au): Established by Sydney stockbroker Angus Geddes in 2000, Fat Prophets' mission is to combine fundamental and technical analysis to recommend to members the best-value shares at the best possible price. It is an analysis firm, a wealth manager offering portfolios and separately managed accounts (SMAs), and a fund manager, running two LICs on the ASX (Fat Prophets Global Contrarian Fund, or FPC, and Fat Prophets Global Property Fund, or FPP). Fat Prophets has grown to cover the New Zealand, UK and European sharemarkets.

TIP

The Fat Prophets philosophy is macro/thematic — it looks to identify sectors that are set to prosper from underlying economic conditions — as well as contrarian; in other words, it looks to where the crowd is not investing. It is a fundamental 'value' manager and stock-picker, using technical analysis to sharpen its timing.

» **Fat Tail Investment Research** (`fattail.com.au`): Fat Tail Investment Research publishes a range of investment research newsletters and advisory services that aim to help investors meet their financial goals for capital growth and wealth protection. Its iconoclastic newsletters are definitely not bland — they are highly outspoken, and often feature different newsletter editors each arguing a bull and bear case. The newsletters and advisory services cover everything from small-caps, mining stocks and technology trends to market cycles, precious metals, global macro-economic and geo-political analysis, and asset allocation.

The two flagship newsletters have their own sites:

- **Money Morning** (`moneymorning.com.au`)
- **The Daily Reckoning** (`dailyreckoning.com.au`)

Check out the Fat Tail website for more on its other newsletters and subscription options.

» **FN Arena** (`fnarena.com`): FN Arena is a subscription service that combines financial news, sharemarket articles, reports, commentary and insights, videos, and fundamental and technical analysis tools (some of them unique to FN Arena) with a search engine containing a mine of information on specific topics, sectors or ASX-listed companies. Like Stock Doctor (also in this list), FN Arena is useful for obtaining consensus estimates of company earnings, dividends and analysts' price targets, as well as regularly updated commentary from the broking firm analysts that cover each stock.

» **Intelligent Investor** (`intelligentinvestor.com.au`; see also `eurekareport.com.au` and `investsmart.com.au`): Operated by the ASX-listed company InvestSMART, an online financial advisory, portfolio management, investment education and funds management company, Intelligent Investor is a high-quality newsletter and research website that provides sharemarket editorial content, stock research and recommendations, special alerts, sector summaries, and investment updates and ideas. The company also publishes the *Eureka Report* investment newsletter, helmed by renowned financial journalism veteran, Alan Kohler. (***Note:*** I have written for Intelligent Investor.)

» **MakCorp** (`makcorp.net.au`): MakCorp provides a wide range of services and information sources related to the mining and oil and gas industries. While some of its services are for actual mining companies and suppliers to the industries, investors can use its research and analytics tools to find out more about the resources companies listed on the ASX. A variety of subscription plans are offered.

» **Marcus Today** (`marcustoday.com.au`): Founded in 1998 by stockbroker Marcus Padley (confession — an old mate), the Marcus Today is an insightful, independent daily source of sharemarket research and ideas, as well as articles on various investment-related topics. It also publishes podcasts and videos, and has an education section offering short courses and ebooks. Marcus Today is also a fund manager, offering two separately managed accounts (SMAs) — a Growth portfolio and an Income portfolio. (**Note:** I have written for Marcus Today.)

» **Market Matters** (`marketmatters.com.au`): Market Matters is owned and operated by a group of professional money managers that have decades of experience navigating domestic and international stock markets. Market Matters runs a real portfolio and invest its own money in the recommendations it makes. The subscription-based service offers advice from investors, with the ability to tailor content to your interests and investments.

» **MineLife** (`minelife.com.au`): MineLife specialises in covering the Australian junior resources sector. Headed by highly regarded resources analyst Gavin Wendt, the MineLife team sifts through the hundreds of junior resource companies listed on the ASX — a population that continues to grow significantly through new listings — to find, research and watch the most promising stocks across the resources spectrum. MineLife maintains a list of the stocks it follows in its in-house portfolio. The firm's research encompasses companies in the precious metals, energy, battery materials, base metals and bulk commodities sectors.

» **Morningstar** (`morningstar.com.au`): Morningstar is a global research house that investors can join, with packages divided into Morningstar Basic and Morningstar Premium. Some of the information can be accessed for free, including the fund screener tool, which enables you to search for funds that suit your criteria. The site offers qualitative research on more than 1,600 companies, 350 managed funds and 70 ETFs, plus data on over 48,000 global securities. Members gain access to Morningstar's top equity picks, including sustainable dividend-generating stocks, as well as Morningstar's analysts' fund and ETF ratings, which are based on their ability to outperform the index on a risk-adjusted basis over time.

TIP

Morningstar Premium includes complimentary access to Sharesight's Investor Plan, one of Australia's leading portfolio trackers.

» **Motley Fool** (`fool.com.au`): The Australian arm of the US-based Motley Fool (one of the most well-known stock-picking services in the world) provides a mix of free content and subscription-only investment guidance. The Motley Fool's name comes from William Shakespeare's play *As You Like It*. The court jester, known as the Fool, could speak the truth to the king and queen without having his head lopped off. (It's also worth checking out the US parent site at `fool.com`, especially for its education section; you can also try the UK version at `fool.co.uk`.)

» **Rask Australia** (rask.com.au): Confession: I know Owen Raszkiewicz and the Rask team well, and I think Rask is a great product. The directors of The Inside Network, at which I am contributing editor, are also investors in Rask. Rask is a finance and investment website that provides news, research articles on listed companies (which give a view on whether they should be bought or sold), and investment ideas for subscribers on growth shares and dividend shares, as well as a core/satellite strategy with ETFs as the core. Investors can join Rask for free, but they can also access premium subscriptions for the package of content that suits them. The Rask Core membership service is the company's premium research service, which seeks to identify and recommend compelling investment ideas from both the ASX and global markets. Rask has a comprehensive education section offering short courses on investing.

» **Rivkin** (rivkin.com.au): Coming out of stockbroking firm Rivkin Securities, Rivkin offers research, analysis, education and strategies on local and global sharemarkets. It also specialises in asset management for wholesale investors, stockbroking and contracts for difference (CFD) dealing, as well as SMSF administration and general accounting services. Its subsidiary Rivkin Asset Management offers two wholesale managed funds (the Australian Equity Fund, AEF, and Global Equity Fund, GEF).

» **Sharesight** (sharesight.com): A portfolio management, monitoring and tax reporting website, Sharesight allows members to track shares and ETFs from over 40 exchanges worldwide, plus Australian LICs and managed funds. Members can also track cash and over 75 currencies, as well as unlisted investments such as fixed interest and investment properties, and the site features an easy-to-use online portfolio tracker. Members can get started for free, and then move to pricing packages depending on the features, resources and tools they use.

» **Spotee** (spotee.com.au): Spotee's main aim is to make what it calls 'DIY investing' accessible to everyone by empowering investors to make more informed decisions with objective and independent perspectives. The site offers three main services: Spotee Connect, a community-directed service where members can ask questions about any ASX stock (all members see the questions and Spotee's answers); Spotee Consulting, a specialised support and education offering comprising portfolio diagnostics, investment strategy development, individual stock analysis, targeted share investing education, and ongoing mentorship and support; and Spotee Education (SpoteeED), a range of courses covering all aspects of share investing.

» **Stock Doctor** (stockdoctor.com.au): Stock Doctor is run by Lincoln Indicators, which has developed a methodology for indicating the health of any business with a high degree of accuracy by analysing its financial statements to arrive at an assessment of its financial health. The Stock Doctor website has adapted this methodology into a proprietary sharemarket research platform that generates what the company describes as some of the most reliable investment insights in Australia, providing early warnings of companies whose financial position is weakening or strengthening. Stock Doctor carries a wealth of historical financial data on any ASX-listed stock, interpreted through its filters, and a wide array of tools enabling investors to organise this information to suit their needs. The website is particularly useful for obtaining consensus estimates of company earnings, dividends and analysts' price targets.

>> **Stock Specialist** (stockspecialist.com.au): An online sharemarket research company that provides stock market analysis reports to investors, Stock Specialist aims to provide investors with easy-to-understand analysis so that they can be confident about choosing the right companies to invest in. The firm's fundamental and technical analysis is presented in clear and succinct research reports, with actionable recommendations.

>> **Stockradar** (stockradar.com.au): An independent investment education and advisory service, Stockradar provides guidance on stock trading, teaching an investment philosophy that is disciplined, consistent and methodical. Stockradar has developed a focused trend following strategy that it says gives readers a market edge by combining trend, volume, moving averages and momentum price indicators to identify stocks with compelling trending qualities that offer the best prospects of sustained price movement.

>> **Stocks Down Under** (stocksdownunder.com): This site offers investors company research and insights, detailed information on investing, weekly investor webinars, and regular publications on all market sectors (with in-depth analysis of S&P/ASX 200 stocks, emerging companies, small-cap companies and resources companies).

>> **Stockspot** (stockspot.com.au): Stockspot offers customers a diversified portfolio of ETFs that track a broad range of global assets, including global shares, Australian shares, and government bonds. Stockspot asks a series of questions to establish a customer's risk profile and investment timeframe, and then recommends a portfolio that matches the customer's individual circumstances. Stockspot reviews and rebalances the portfolio regularly, and manages the reporting; the customer can then send the portfolio straight to their accountant at tax time.

>> **Switzer Group** (switzer.com.au): The Switzer Group, run by Australian business and financial commentator, radio and television presenter, lecturer, and author Peter Switzer, operates the Switzer Daily website, which provides insights and information on current financial, economic and business matters, as well as the daily news update '5 things you need to know today'. The group also operates Switzer TV, The Peter Switzer Show podcast, and the *Switzer Report*, a subscription-based financial newsletter that provides succinct analysis of current financial trends, along with share analysis, tips and recommendations. (***Note:*** I write for the *Switzer Report*.)

» **Under the Radar Report** (undertheradarreport.com.au): Under the Radar, edited by Richard Hemming, is managed by an investment committee whose principal responsibility is to act as a sounding board both for the small-cap stock and small-cap share tip ideas the report generates, as well as for its Australian small-cap model portfolio.

» **Value Investing for a Living** (valueinvestingforaliving.com): An affiliate of Sharesight, this blog is focused on event-driven, activist and deep-value investing.

» **VEye** (veye.com.au): VEye is an independent shares research subscription site profiling ASX-listed companies and giving recommendations. The site combines the disciplines of fundamental and technical analysis. Subscribers receive a daily analysis report, plus their choice of regular subscriber reports.

Turning to your broker

Anyone who wants to do their own research, and is willing to forgo the advice and support of a full-service stockbroker can make their investment in the market very cheaply, not just trade in the market very cheaply. As an online broker customer, you don't have to be armed with trading software and glued to your internet chat forums, waiting for the smell of blood in the water to attract you to a stock on the rise. With the amount of research and educational assistance available on some online broking sites, buying stocks cost-effectively can be only one of the reasons why online broking makes sense. Online broking can also provide a great deal of valuable help and knowledge, often for free. (I talk about using online brokers in chapters 6 and 12.)

You can find a comprehensive list of the online brokers operating in the Australian market, with all their fees, charges and services, at the main comparison sites: Canstar at canstar.com.au, Finder at finder.com.au and Mozo at mozo.com.au.

If you want to trade with an online broker, visit these websites first for a feel of what the brokerage rates are around the marketplace. Then, follow the links to the various online brokers and check out their service offerings — not just fees and charges, but also news, charts, research, portfolio management, and so on. Online broking is a very competitive market and you can find a service that meets your needs.

Don't overlook the full-service brokers. Most of them have comprehensive websites as well. Check out the list of broker websites at the ASX site and take a tour of what they have to offer: just remember that full-service brokers are trying to keep their clients, so they show their best goodies only to clients who have a log-in password. They don't show the research and recommendations to people who are just dropping in — because they know that visitors could take that recommendation to an online broker and buy it. Chapter 12 clarifies the differences between online and full-service brokers.

The App Revolution

The rise of easy-to-use *apps*, the software applications you can add to your computer, smartphone or tablet, has been a huge feature of the sharemarket in recent years. In 2021, consumer advocacy magazine/website *Choice* estimated that there were approximately 145 investment-related apps on the Australian market at the time. Some of these specialise in particular areas of investing, such as property, commodities or crowdfunding, but many give users greater access to understanding the sharemarkets — just as any traditional trading and investment management firm would — at any time, on any device.

WARNING

While the democratisation of access to the sharemarket is on balance a good thing, be aware of the flipside. Financial services regulator the Australian Securities and Investments Commission (ASIC) has warned several times in recent years that many of these apps may be dangerous for novice traders. ASIC says apps may induce new traders and investors to transact more than they should due to the fact that they are so easy to use, often with zero *brokerage* (the cost of execution of the actual trade) and because the number of clicks a user needs to actually buy assets — whether they are shares, futures contracts or contracts for difference (CFDs, see Chapter 22), foreign exchange, or cryptocurrencies such as Bitcoin — has been minimised by design.

ASIC has also warned that some apps have copied features from the gambling industry to get their (usually younger) users addicted to the app, with tactics including celebrity endorsements, offers of free shares and benefits if you refer someone to the platform. Some apps also regularly 'nudge' users with pings, suggestions and messages in an effort to keep them trading, which people should only do when they've done their homework and found reliable advice that can improve the chances of successful trading for the app's users.

REMEMBER

Online share trading is an investment tool, not a computer game.

Another big concern for the regulator is that many first-time traders get their advice from social media forums such as Reddit, Facebook and LinkedIn; ASIC has warned that information and advice found on such forums may be conflicted because some companies and product issuers pay promoters to post favourable comments and encourage first-time traders to invest. *Copy trading* — where an app allows users to copy the trades of an ostensibly more experienced investor — is also a worry for ASIC.

However, it is the age-old dilemma; should a tool be banned because some people misuse it? In the hands of a person who knows what they're doing, many investment and trading apps are simply another conduit for access to the sharemarket, making it easier for people to use their online connectivity and smart devices to trade and invest on their terms, using their skills and knowledge to try to build wealth. As long as investors do their homework and make informed decisions, considering who is offering the app and the benefits of using it (as well as the trading decisions they use the app to enact), apps themselves are not the problem.

In any case, many of the apps are not trading services; many are investment portfolio monitoring and market information apps, which give you additional opportunities to understand the sharemarket.

TECHNICAL STUFF

Apps and websites are different. Although both are used on the same devices (computers, smartphones and tablets), an app is a program that is downloaded and installed onto a user's device, whereas a mobile website is simply a website adapted to tablet and smartphone formats. For example, the Stock Doctor website doesn't have an app (at the time of writing, at least), but it does have a mobile site that has been designed to adapt to a smartphone's smaller screen to provide a more user-friendly experience, with small variations in content and layout compared to the full site. Many of the websites mentioned in this chapter will have an optimised mobile site, even if they don't have an actual app.

In the following list, I share a selection of some of the most widely used investment and portfolio monitoring apps available that you may like to check out:

>> ANZ Share Investing

>> ASX

>> AvaTradeGO

>> Bell Direct

>> Bendigo Invest Direct

>> Capital.com

>> CommSec

>> CMC Markets Invest

>> Computershare Investor Centre

>> Eightcap

>> eToro

>> Finder

- IBKR mobile
- IG Trading
- InvestSMART
- nabtrade Mobile
- Netwealth
- Opentrader
- Plus500
- Raiz
- Saxo Trader GO
- SelfWealth
- Sharesies
- Sharesight
- Simply Wall Street
- Spaceship Voyager
- St. George directshares
- Stake
- StockLight
- Stockspot
- Superhero
- ThinkTrader
- Tiger Brokers
- Westpac Share Trading

Perusing the Podcast Pack

If you're interested in learning more about investing, then one helpful thing you can do is subscribe to a good finance podcast (a *podcast* is an audio form of digital content made available for download over the internet). You can find a wealth of options in the podcast world — with more springing up all the time — and it should be easy to find one to suit your interests and needs.

TIP

Many of the investment websites I mention in this chapter (refer to the earlier section 'Finding Investment Websites') have their own podcasts: Nestegg, MakCorp, Morningstar (Investing Compass), Motley Fool, Rivkin, Spotee, Stockhead (The Stock Doc and Stockhead Radio) and the Switzer Group (The Peter Switzer Show) are notable examples, and more may follow.

While Google is your friend here, the following podcasts are also good places to start if you want to listen to the experts talk money (thanks to the team at Canstar for their help with this!):

>> **Aussie Firebug:** Run by the anonymous 'Firebug', this podcast focuses on helping listeners attain financial independence — making enough from your investments so that you don't need to work.

>> **Buy, Hold, Sell:** From the above-mentioned Livewire Markets, the highly informative Buy, Hold, Sell forum features fund managers discussing stocks and whether they are buyers, holders or sellers of those stocks. It features some interesting disagreements!

>> **Chris Judd's Talk Ya Book:** Former AFL star Chris Judd, a dedicated sharemarket investor, investigates the investment processes used by Australia's best investors as they talk through their highest-conviction investment ideas.

>> **Equity Mates:** Equity Mates is hosted by Bryce and Alec, two young Australians with a strong interest in finance. They provide an accessible and entertaining introduction to investing.

>> **Inside the Rope:** Experienced financial services professional David Clark, a partner and adviser at Koda Capital, one of Australia's leading wealth management firms, interviews some of the leading minds in the investment and wealth management fields.

>> **Magellan: In the Know:** A monthly investment podcast from one of Australia's leading global equities investors. Magellan investment staff bring listeners timely, unique and thought-provoking insights to help them make sense of today's investment landscape.

>> **Market Pulse:** This podcast offers weekly information, insight and commentary on Australian and International markets, economic and business, news and all things investing.

>> **Money and Investing with Andrew Baxter:** Successful trader and investor Andrew Baxter discusses investment and wealth creation strategies for everyday Australians.

>> **My Millennial Money:** This podcast is hosted by Glen James (the founder of sortyourmoneyout.com) and John Pidgeon (from online property investment guide, Solvere Wealth). In each episode, the hosts discuss a different topic

related to personal finance, talk about your money mindset, or share interviews with industry leaders and everyday Australians.

>> **Oz Investing:** Oz Investing is a finance and investing podcast for the 'everyday investor', based on the experiences and research of two mates, Sam and Jude. The focus is on investing in Australia and stocks on the ASX.

>> **QAV:** Standing for 'Quality at Value', QAV is a value-investing podcast in which successful private investor, Tony Kynaston, teaches co-host Cameron Reilly about investing. QAV discusses ASX-listed stocks, applying a checklist to find companies that are performing well (that is, represent quality) but which can also be bought at a discount (that is, at value).

>> **Seneca Financial Solutions:** Luke Laretive, investment adviser and CEO of Seneca Financial Solutions, educates listeners on best investment principles and practice for making their money grow. Listeners discover how to examine the markets, identify value in a stock approach investing. (**Note:** I know Luke very well and have worked closely with him. He has even filled in on my basketball team!)

>> **Shares for Beginners:** Hosted by Phil Muscatello, Shares for Beginners mainly includes interviews with finance experts. As the name suggests, Shares for Beginners breaks down complicated investment topics and questions and presents them in a way even those very new to investing can understand.

>> **She's On The Money:** Hosted by millennial money expert Victoria Devine, She's On The Money has become Australia's number-one money podcast. While the podcast definitely discusses investing, it also tackles other finance-related topics, such as budgeting and health insurance. Presented by a woman and predominantly for women, this podcast is helping a whole generation of women become more financially savvy.

>> **Talking Wealth:** Dale Gillham and Janine Cox from share investment education business Wealth Within host this podcast, talking about effective stock trading and investing, wealth creation, and expert stock market analysis.

>> **The Acquirers:** Hosted by founder Tobias Carlisle, a former hedge fund analyst, The Acquirers is a podcast about finding under-valued stocks, deep value investing, hedge funds, shareholder activism, buyouts and special situations. It uncovers the tactics and strategies for finding good investments, managing risk, dealing with bad luck and maximising success.

>> **The Australian Investors Podcast:** Hosted by Owen Raszkiewicz, the founder of Rask (refer to the earlier section 'Paying for content' for more on Rask), Owen interviews a different finance or investment guru each episode, who shares their investment insights and tips. Rask also offers The Australian Finance Podcast, aimed at helping investors get on top of their entire financial strategy.

>> **The Ideas Exchange:** Presented by the ASX, The Ideas Exchange gives listeners a view of investing opportunities and strategies, hearing from ASX insiders and industry experts.

>> **The Investment Interlude:** Hosted by Thomas Patterson, an economics and finance student at the University of Wollongong, this podcast aims to inspire and inform people to learn about money, finances, the stock market and the economy.

>> **The KOSEC Show:** Each week, the team at Sydney-based stockbroking and wealth management firm Kodari Securities (KOSEC) discuss macro-economic events, S&P/ASX 300 top performers, currencies, commodities and the panel's stock picks for the week.

>> **The Money Café:** Alan Kohler and James Kirby, two of Australia's most renowned financial journalists, join in this weekly podcast to discuss the week's financial news and investment insights.

>> **The Richards Report:** Ted Richards, former AFL player and director of business development at investment services firm Six Park, hosts this podcast, covering the basics of investing and interviewing a broad range of investment industry and business figures.

>> **The Rules of Investing:** Another podcast from the Livewire Markets stable, The Rules of Investing showcases ideas, analyses and strategies from hundreds of Australia's most respected fund managers and investment professionals.

>> **The Yarra Exchange:** One of Australia's most experienced business journalists, Malcolm Maiden, interviews senior business leaders to get their take on the big topics dominating the markets and the business world. The podcast is sponsored by independent Australian fund manager Yarra Capital Management, but Maiden ranges well outside the firm for his interviewees.

>> **The Young Investors Podcast:** Two young Australian investors, Hamish Hodder and Brandon van der Kolk, who both run their own investing-related YouTube channels, explore the ideas and concepts behind value investing.

>> **Wattle Partners Market Thinkers:** Investment advisers Jamie Nemtsas and Drew Meredith of Wattle Partners bring the insights of global thought leaders directly to listeners through two-way conversations on this podcast. These sessions cover everything from the basics of investment markets and stock ideas to the outlook for asset classes. (***Note:*** I work with Jamie and Drew, as contributing editor at The Inside Network.)

>> **Your Wealth:** Gemma Dale, director of SMSF and Investor Behaviour at nabtrade, hosts this podcast, discussing strategies and tips to build your wealth, with a strong emphasis on investing. Each week, Gemma examines a different topic, from different tools and investment instruments through to the influence of technology, and investing abroad.

Chapter **18**

Taxing Matters

S hares generate income for their owners through the flow of dividends paid out of the company's profits. Before you get too excited about this, remember that the Australian Taxation Office (ATO) takes its cut of this income, too. Not only are your dividend payments part of your assessable income, but the tax office also claims a cut of any money you make when you sell your shares. Because of this, shares play an important part in managing your tax affairs.

In this chapter, I explain the system of dividend imputation, which gives Australian investors a tax credit for tax paid by the company on its profit. I describe how you can use fully franked dividends for tax-effective investing, particularly in a self-managed superannuation fund (SMSF). I also cover how your capital gains on shares are taxed, and how you can manage capital gains tax (CGT) and try to offset losses against gains.

Benefiting from Dividend Imputation

Dividend imputation allows investors who've been paid a dividend to take a personal tax credit on the tax already paid by the company. The rebate, known as the *franking credit* or *imputation credit*, can be used by a shareholder to reduce their tax liability. In some cases — depending on the marginal tax rate — the franking credit can offset the individual's total tax liability. In certain circumstances, excess franking credits (after the total tax liability has been extinguished) can be claimed as a refund.

For Australian resident investors, franking credits are the third element of total shareholder returns, after capital gains and dividends. Over the long term, franking credits add about 1.4 per cent to 1.5 per cent to the total return (capital gain plus dividends) from Australian shares.

TIP

For an investor with an SMSF that is in the 'accumulation' phase — that is, all members still contributing — dividend imputation is particularly important. First, because it can snuff out the tax liability on the fund, levied at 15 per cent. Properly balanced, a flow of imputation credits can offset the tax on contributions to the fund, which is a practical and legitimate form of tax planning. Second, once the fund moves into 'pension phase' — that is, begins paying a pension to all members — no tax is paid on the income or capital gains from the assets and any unused franking credits can be refunded fully in cash.

Franking credits made easy

The 3,000 largest Australian companies by employment (which effectively covers the stock market's dividend-paying companies) pay corporate tax at the full rate of 30 per cent. When one of these companies pays tax, it builds up credits in its *franking account*. The company's ability to frank its dividend depends on the credit balance in this account. With a surplus available in the franking account, the company may declare a fully franked dividend; if the credit balance isn't large enough, a partly franked dividend may be paid.

TECHNICAL STUFF

Unfranked dividends are paid out of company profits that have not been subject to the full Australian corporate tax rate. Such dividends don't have any franking credits associated with them and are taxable at the shareholders' marginal tax rate. When the company makes a loss, it pays no tax that year, and doesn't receive any franking credits. The only way the company can pay a franked dividend the following year is if it has sufficient franking credits in its franking account from prior periods.

Legally, companies can pay franking credits only by attaching them to cash dividends, whether ordinary, special or the deemed dividend components in off-market share buybacks. Franking credits are of no value to companies — they are only valuable in the hands of shareholders. On average, about 90 per cent of credits are distributed. The Australia Institute notes that about $25 billion to $30 billion in franking credits is distributed each year, split equally three ways between households; superannuation funds, charities and trusts; and other companies.

Australian companies are among the most generous in the world in terms of dividends. In 2019, Australia's top 200 companies paid out a record $88 billion in dividends, not including the benefits of franking credits. According to funds manager Janus Henderson, 40 per cent of that payout came from the banks, which were paying out more than 80 per cent of their profits in dividends in the five years to 2019. But on the back of the COVID-19 pandemic's economic impact, dividends fell sharply as profits slumped, and the banks were told by their regulator, the Australian Prudential Regulation Authority (APRA) to 'materially reduce' their dividends. (APRA's European equivalents actually ordered banks to stop paying dividends altogether during the crisis.)

In 2020, bank dividends were cut by 60 per cent on average, and total Australian dividends fell to $63.3 billion in 2020. The miners and banks made up the bulk of the top ten dividend payers in Australia, contributing almost 78 per cent of Australia's total dividend haul.

But with a swag of upgraded payouts for the 2020–21 financial year, the Australian market's dividend flow was expected to return to about $73 billion in 2021.

For example, with the strength of the iron ore price delivering record profits for producers BHP, Rio Tinto and Fortescue Metals Group, the mining behemoths took over from the banks in 2020–21 as major dividend sources, with $37 billion flowing out to shareholders between the trio — and that's with Rio Tinto's financial year only half completed.

In 2019, franking credits became a federal election issue, with the Australian Labor Party running on a policy to disallow tax refunds on franking credits for those on zero tax rates. Companies responded by significantly ramping up off-market share buybacks and special dividends to try to get their franking credits into their shareholders' hands, given the uncertainty around tax policy. Due to the strong opposition to Labor's proposal, and the party's subsequent defeat in the 2019 election, tax refunds on franking credits look set to remain — into the near future, at least. At the time of writing, Labor had officially abandoned its franking credits policy.

In 2021, according to a study by *The Australian* newspaper, Australian companies held a stockpile of franking credits estimated at about $66.4 billion, which would be worth about $31.9 billion in shareholders' hands. That war chest of franking credits had swelled by more than two-thirds since the beginning of the pandemic in early 2020. The four big iron ore miners (adding Mineral Resources Limited to BHP, Rio Tinto and Fortescue Metals Group) saw their combined franking credit balance lift by a combined $19.2 billion between 2019 and 2021, representing more than 70 per cent of the net gain made by the entire S&P/ASX 100 group of companies.

The stockpile arises because Australian companies generally pay out about two-thirds of profit as dividends, and the excess franking credits go into franking accounts. One way to distribute excess franking credits is to mount an off-market share buyback where part of the buyback price is identified as a *deemed* dividend (see the section 'Biting on a buyback', later in this chapter).

Fully franked dividends

Shareholders who receive fully franked dividends must add the imputation credit on the dividend to the amount of dividend in order to arrive at the taxable income represented by the dividend. This procedure is called *grossing up* the dividend.

REMEMBER

With the company tax rate at 30 per cent, dividends are grossed up by $30 for each $70 of dividends received. This means that Australian companies that pay tax at the 30 per cent company tax rate have $428.57 of attached franking credits for every $1,000 of fully franked dividends they pay out.

As a shareholder, you have to include the grossed-up dividend amount in your assessable income. You receive a tax credit of $30 for each $100 of grossed-up franked dividend included in your assessable income.

After the tax liability on the grossed-up amount is worked out, the imputation credit is subtracted from the tax liability to give the actual tax payable. Table 18-1 shows the situation where an investor on the current top marginal tax rate of 45 per cent (plus the 2 per cent Medicare levy) invests $10,000 in shares and receives fully franked dividends of $700.

TABLE 18-1

Tax Liability ($700 Dividend Fully Franked)

Investment	$10,000
Fully franked dividend income	$700
Gross yield	7%
Imputation credit $700 × 30/70	$300
Included in taxable income	$1,000
Tax payable at 47%	$470
Less imputation credit	$300
Tax payable	$170
After-tax income	$530
After-tax equivalent yield	5.30%

The franking credit reduces the investor's tax liability on the cash amount of dividend received from 47 per cent to 24.28 per cent ($170 of the $700 received). At the same time, the 7 per cent dividend yield becomes the equivalent of an after-tax yield of 5.30 per cent. If the income came from fixed interest or rent, the 7 per cent yield after tax would reduce to 3.71 per cent.

Partially franked dividends

Depending on its franking account, a company may declare a partially franked dividend or an unfranked dividend. An unfranked dividend carries no tax credit and is simply added to the investor's assessable income. A *partially franked dividend* carries a partial imputation credit. To calculate the tax payable, the franked portion is grossed up by the proportion of tax paid. In the example shown in Table 18-2, it's again assumed that the marginal tax rate is 45 per cent, plus the Medicare levy (2 per cent), and the dividend received is $700. This time, however, it's 80 per cent franked.

As shown in Table 18-2, the franking credit reduces the investor's tax liability on the cash amount of dividend received from 47 per cent to 28.8 per cent ($201.80 of the $700 received). At the same time, the 7 per cent dividend yield becomes the equivalent of an after-tax yield of 4.98 per cent.

TABLE 18-2

Tax Liability ($700 Dividend Partially Franked)

Investment	$10,000
Dividend income	$700
Franked income = 80% of $700	$560
Gross yield	7%
Imputation credit $560 × 30/70	$240
Included in taxable income	$940
Tax payable at 47%	$441.80
Less imputation credit of	$240
Tax payable	$201.80
After-tax income	$498.20
After-tax equivalent yield	4.98%

Franking credit refunds

Taxpayers (including superannuation funds) can claim cash rebates on any excess franking credits. Excess franking credits arise when the shareholder's marginal tax rate is lower than the corporate tax rate of 30 per cent.

For investors on a marginal tax rate higher than 30 per cent, imputation credits reduce the tax liability on the dividend. For those on a marginal tax rate of less than 30 per cent, excess imputation credits may be offset against tax payable on other income in the year of receipt, or be claimed as a cash rebate if no other tax is payable.

Investors on the 15 per cent tax rate (for example, an SMSF in the 'accumulation' phase) actually get a tax refund of $215 for every $1,000 of fully franked dividends they receive, because this amount is not needed to offset tax on the dividends. For such investors, a dollar of fully franked dividend income is effectively worth more than a dollar.

Even better is when an SMSF moves to the 'pension' phase; that is, you can choose to have your fund pay you a pension. In this case, the assets are held in the fund's 'pension account', which means they're being used solely for the purpose of paying out a pension. In this case, no tax is payable on the income or capital gains from the assets, and the franked dividends can actually be refunded fully by the ATO.

Table 18-3 shows the effect of the franking credit rebate on the tax status of individuals on the four individual marginal tax rates above the tax-free threshold. (Not included in the table is the 15 per cent rate paid by an SMSF in the 'accumulation' phase; once the fund moves to the 'pension phase', its tax rate is zero.) The workings ignore the Medicare levy of 2 per cent.

TABLE 18-3 ## The Benefits of Dividend Imputation*

	Nil taxpayer	19% taxpayer	32.5% taxpayer	37% taxpayer	45% taxpayer
Dividend	$1,000	$1,000	$1,000	$1,000	$1,000
Grossed-up dividend	$1,429	$1,429	$1,429	$1,429	$1,429
Gross tax payable	Nil	$271	$464	$529	$643
Franking credit rebate	$429	$429	$429	$429	$429
Tax payable	$429 refund	$158 refund	$35	$100	$214

*Amounts rounded

Obeying the 45-day rule

Shareholders who receive more than $5,000 worth of franking credits in a tax year must own each stock in their portfolio for more than 45 days (not counting the day of purchase or sale) before being entitled to a franking tax offset from dividends paid or credited on the shares. For preference shares, the holding period is 90 days. The rule was introduced to prevent tax-driven investors from trading shares merely to gain the imputation credits on fully franked dividends, and so lower their tax liability. (In fact, because the days of purchase and sale aren't counted, the rule could more accurately be called the 47-day rule.)

Watching Your Capital Gains

As part of the tax system, Australia has a *capital gains tax* (CGT), which taxes the gains made on the sale (or disposal) of shares (and other assets), at the individual's marginal tax rate — although you may get a tax discount depending on how long you've held the shares. CGT isn't payable on shares bought before 20 September 1985, but if you've bought any shares since then and sold them for a gain, that gain will be taxed.

Calculating your liability

You're liable for CGT if your capital gains exceed your capital losses in any income year. When filling out your annual tax return, you add up your capital gains and capital losses. Your net capital gains (capital gains minus capital losses) figure is added to your taxable income, and taxed at your marginal tax rate.

REMEMBER

If you have a net capital loss figure, you can carry the amount forward to help offset future capital gains, but your loss can't be used to offset any other income received for that year. Capital losses can be offset only against capital gains, but they can be carried forward indefinitely until fully used up by being offset against future capital gains. Nobody likes to sell a share for a loss, but reducing the tax office's take of your capital gains helps to lessen the pain of buying dud shares.

Reducing the tax office's take

If you hold shares for at least 12 months, you pay CGT on only half of the profit made, which makes receiving a capital gain much more attractive than receiving income. For shares bought and sold within a year, CGT is levied on the entire capital gain at the individual's marginal tax rate.

Say you're on the top marginal tax rate of 45 per cent, plus the Medicare levy of 2 per cent; for the 2020–21 tax year, this rate cuts in at $180,001 of income plus taxable gains. Say you also achieve a capital gain of $50,000 on an asset you've owned for a year and a day. This means you're eligible for the CGT discount. Your gain is halved to $25,000 and the tax rate of 47 per cent is applied, meaning that CGT payable on the gain is $11,750. On the $50,000 capital gain, the tax incurred is 23.5 per cent of the gain.

TECHNICAL STUFF

Although the Medicare levy itself isn't halved, in effect the maximum CGT rate for assets held for at least a year is 23.5 per cent, which is half of the top marginal rate plus Medicare levy. But the discount doesn't technically apply to the individual's tax rate; it's a discount on the gain taxed.

If you own shares that you bought between 20 September 1985 and 21 September 1999, you have a choice of methods to calculate your CGT liability. You can use *inflation indexation* (using the consumer price index or CPI) with indexation frozen at 30 September 1999. This way, you're taxed only on the real, or after-inflation, capital gain that you made. No corresponding inflation adjustment is available for losses. With the other method, you can elect to have half of your net capital gain taxed. You don't get this concession, however, if you choose the indexation method.

REMEMBER

You're within your rights to use the method that gives the tax office the least. Given that asset price inflation was far more dominant in the 2000s than inflation, most people will find that they get a better result using the 50 per cent discount method.

An SMSF that is in its 'accumulation' phase, in which its tax rate is 15 per cent, earns a one-third CGT discount if it holds an asset for more than 365 days. This means the gain made on the subsequent sale of the asset incurs CGT at 10 per cent — unless the asset has been transferred into the pension account of the fund, at which point the tax rate on income and capital gains from the asset becomes zero.

REMEMBER

If you have different parcels of a shareholding that have been acquired at different times and for different prices, it's necessary to keep track of these 'tax lots', since the capital gain or loss may be different for each. The shareholder can choose to their advantage; for example, selling a parcel with a capital loss to realise the loss immediately, or keeping particular parcels until they've been held for one year to qualify for the discounted CGT rate. Some portfolio management software systems can help with this task. Most online brokers offer clients a tax monitoring tool that keeps track of 'tax lots'.

REMEMBER

As always, investors should think investment first, and tax considerations second. Shares can change in value very quickly — and with some shares, waiting until your shareholding is a year old just to qualify for the CGT discount is pointless because the 'CG' part may have disappeared by then! Having to pay CGT should be viewed as a good thing because it means you've made a capital gain. That's what sharemarket investing is all about.

TIP

Although you don't have to be an accountant to benefit from the tax treatment of shares, talking to an accountant at least once a year helps. Chances are your accountant can help you keep more of your investment gain from the tax office — perfectly legally, of course.

Taxing Tactics

You can use your share portfolio to make strategic tax decisions. You can sell shares before the end of the tax year to crystallise a capital loss and take a tax liability on a capital gain made in the same year. But while tax can play a big part in your buying and selling decisions, it should never be the sole reason for buying or selling a share.

Tax-loss selling

Nobody likes making a capital loss on a share, but using it to soak up a capital gain that you've (hopefully) earned elsewhere in your portfolio is a perfect way to ease some of the pain. Rather than moaning about shares that have fallen in value, investors should look to use this situation to reduce the tax office's take of their capital gains.

If you have a $10,000 loss on a stock that has gone down and a $10,000 profit on a stock that has risen, and you sell both, you're square with the ATO. Tax-loss selling is common in June, towards the end of the tax year, when people are looking to crystallise capital losses to offset against gains. You can make good use of the fact that your shares have fallen in value.

TIP

When using a capital loss to offset a capital gain, a good idea is to use it to offset a capital gain on a stock that you've held for less than 12 months — where you pay CGT at the full rate — rather than the discounted CGT. That way, you get the full value of the loss offset.

You can always buy a stock back if you really want to hold it for the long term. Selling the stock gives rise to a handy tax loss that can be offset against a capital gain on another share. If you buy it back at a lower price, you've lowered the average buying price of your long-term holding.

WARNING

You can't buy back a stock you've sold too quickly. People used to sell on a Monday and buy back on the Tuesday; as long as two separate trades were registered, they had crystallised a tax loss. But this was red-carded by the ATO in 2008. It said that if it considered this kind of *wash sale* (sale and purchase within a short period of time) as being done to obtain a tax benefit, it would deny the loss.

You're allowed to change your mind and buy back into a stock, but to avoid an ATO rejection of your capital loss you may need to show that the sale has another purpose, such as restructuring your portfolio, or that the repurchase has been made because the market has changed, or on the basis of new research. If in doubt, consult your accountant.

Another possible strategy is to sell capital loss-making shares to an SMSF or a discretionary master trust that handles direct shareholdings. This is an *in specie* transfer where you as an individual are deemed to have disposed of the shares for a capital loss, which you can use in your tax return for the year. The shares then become the property of the super fund or master trust, at the price on the day. Shares can also be transferred in this way to a company, or into a spouse's name.

Using a delisted dog

Generally speaking, shares make a remarkably successful investment asset, but occasionally companies go bust, as shareholders in the likes of high-profile collapses such as ABC Learning Centres, Dick Smith Holdings, RCR Tomlinson and Virgin Australia know only too well. It happens occasionally. Nobody wants to see a share they buy end up in the company graveyard with these stocks, but some benefit can be extracted from the disaster if the capital loss is claimed.

WARNING

The firm handling the burial of your unbeloved 'dog' — its administrator, receiver or liquidator — has to ascertain how much the company's secured and unsecured creditors are claiming before it declares the shares worthless, allowing you to claim the capital loss. Unfortunately, this can take years.

The problem is that if the company has collapsed, its shares will be suspended and you have no way to sell them in order to gain the capital loss. Normally a capital loss (or a capital gain) for tax purposes only occurs after a CGT event. Common CGT events include the sale of shares or units, distribution of a capital gain by a managed fund, declaration by an administrator or liquidator that they have reasonable grounds to believe shareholders are not going to receive any further distribution, or the creation of a trust over a CGT asset and deregistration of a company.

The creation of a trust has been used extensively (since an ATO Determination in 2004) to facilitate the crystallisation of losses in companies suspended from ASX quotation and in administration. As shares can no longer be sold on the market, shareholders may enter into an agreement to dispose of their shares and create a trust over those shares until transfer of ownership can be registered. This is the only way to achieve effective change of ownership pending the subsequent registration of an accompanying transfer when and if the company emerges from administration. These transactions have to be at 'arm's length' and should be executed professionally to satisfy taxation and other requirements.

The creation of a trust doesn't help with companies in liquidation but it does with those suspended from quotation and in administration, which covers most of them.

TIP

A helpful service is provided by the website delisted.com.au, which tracks what's going on with the hundreds of companies trapped in the limbo of administration, receivership or liquidation. Many of these companies eventually return to the stock exchange lists as 'shell' companies, through a 'backdoor' listing. The website keeps in touch with the administrators and posts any news on delisted stocks so that shareholders know whether a recovery is possible — or, at least, the latest developments during an administration.

This website also operates a service whereby it buys worthless shares — in companies that have collapsed, entered administration, have been suspended for many years — through a mechanism whereby shareholders essentially transfer their stocks into a trust, meaning that it acquires the stocks pending the registration of the transfer, which satisfies the ATO that the shareholders can claim a loss. This service comes at a cost, which works out to be about $151 per parcel of shares that delisted.com.au acquires, but in return you may have a potential capital loss worth thousands to put to work in your tax return.

Biting on a buyback

Although they were prohibited until 1989 — and then heavily regulated until 1995 — share buybacks have become a common feature of the Australian sharemarket. In 2020, ASX-listed companies bought back more than $50 billion of their own shares, with a further $35 billion bought back over 2020 and 2021.

Companies undertake share buybacks as part of their capital management strategy. They may want to improve earnings per share (EPS), return on equity (ROE) for shareholders or return on assets (ROA), or they may want to return surplus capital or franking credits to shareholders.

The company can either buy back its own shares on-market, or conduct an off-market buyback, inviting eligible shareholders to offer to sell their shares within a certain time frame, and usually at a discount to the current market price. The shares bought back are cancelled, reducing the number of shares the company has on issue.

REMEMBER

When you sell shares into a buyback, you must work out the capital gain or capital loss on the sale of your shares to include in your tax return. You may also have to include in your tax return a dividend as part of the buyback — in an off-market buyback, part of the buyback price including a fully franked dividend is common. This is not an actual dividend, but a *deemed dividend* that is the difference between the *capital component* of the buyback price and the actual price. The ability to deem part of the price to be a dividend enables companies to distribute their excess franking credits to shareholders. In an on-market buyback, the proceeds are treated as a return of capital only.

The tax consequences of a share buyback depend on what kind of buyback it is. If you're looking at an off-market buyback where part of the price is treated as a franked dividend at below the prevailing market price, the buyback may be unattractive to a retail shareholder on the highest marginal tax rate, but very attractive to lower taxpaying shareholders (for example, a superannuation fund) receiving a large distribution of franking credits, as well as a capital loss to use in offsetting capital gains.

The company may make special arrangements with the ATO to reduce the amount of tax that shareholders accepting its buyback offer will pay. The ATO often provides fact sheets on its website (ato.gov.au) that spell out the consequences for different taxpayers of buyback proposals in the market.

Borrowing a tax deduction

If you borrow to invest in shares or use an instalment warrant, the interest costs are tax deductible because the borrowing is used to produce assessable income. If you *negatively gear* a share portfolio, meaning that you pay more in interest than you get back in dividends, you can also claim this difference against your other income. The loan product may also allow you to pre-pay interest before the end of the current tax (financial) year, no more than 12 months in advance, and claim the full amount as a tax deduction in the current financial year.

Keeping tax breaks in perspective

Your decision to buy or sell an investment should never be driven by tax considerations. Always use investment factors when you decide to trade shares and let any tax benefits come as a bonus. If you have some poorly performing stocks in your portfolio, and you're convinced that they're not going to recover in the near future, sell them to realise some capital losses to offset your capital gains. However, when you try to create losses by selling shares you don't want to sell, you can encounter problems.

WARNING

Buying and selling for tax advantages can be complicated. You can sell your shares at a loss and then buy them back afterwards. However, because you're buying the shares again, at a lower price, you now have a lower cost-base for CGT purposes. You have deferred CGT, but any recovery in the share price is taxable when you eventually sell the shares. When you buy the shares again, you have to keep them for at least 12 months to be eligible for the CGT discount of only half your capital gain being taxed (which effectively halves your CGT rate).

Similarly, you don't want to take a share loan or buy a structured product, such as an instalment warrant, just to get a tax deduction. The share portfolio you buy with the loan, or the shares your instalment warrant is based on, may fall in value. In these situations, you can lose money — perhaps more than you saved with the tax deduction the loan gave you.

Trading as a business

The ATO treats individuals who conduct a business of buying and selling shares differently from ordinary investors. If you meet certain criteria set by the tax law and the ATO's guidance, you may be classified as a professional trader and the profit you make from share trading will be treated as ordinary income, not capital gain. With this classification, you may be able to claim expenses, such as brokerage, as a tax deduction. You cannot declare yourself a trader — your level of activity dictates whether the ATO treats you as such.

To be a share trader means that you're in the business of trading shares for gain. As such, you're allowed to use all the provisions that relate to business, one of which is that your shares are treated as trading stock.

Traders are taxed on the income derived in the course of carrying out their business of trading in shares (dividends or profitable sales) and are allowed to offset any losses incurred in their share-trading business against any gains made in that business, any capital gains from other sources and indeed, any other income.

For traders, gains are not actually 'capital' gains because the trader isn't assessed under the CGT regime. Any change booked in the value of a trader's stock is either assessable as income or deductible as a loss. This means that unrealised losses may be claimed in a tax year, but gains don't have to be brought to account until they're realised.

For all other shareholders, capital gains incur CGT and the only losses that can be claimed are realised capital losses, which can be offset only against realised capital gains, in the same year or future years. Net sale value is minus brokerage paid. The cost of buying shares isn't an allowable deduction, and profit from sales isn't assessable income.

Traders are allowed to value their closing stock at the lower of cost — what the shares cost to buy — or net realisable value, which is the market price on the last day of the tax year (the financial year). Say that you own shares that cost you $100 when you bought them on the first day of the year, and the market value of the shares at year-end was $75. If you're classified as a trader, you can write down the value of the holding to $75, and claim a loss of $25.

Assume that at the end of year two you still hold the shares, but their market value is $150. You make no stock adjustment at all, and the holding remains valued in your books at $75. The stock has doubled to $150, but you have no assessable gain. You don't have to mark up the value because you hold it at the lower of cost or net realisable value.

At the end of year three, you sell the shares for $125. You then have an assessable gain of $50, but on income, not capital. You incur tax on this income at your full marginal tax rate.

The introduction in 1999 of the 50 per cent CGT discount applying to assets held for more than 12 months took away much of the perceived advantage of professional trader status. When a trader sells shares, the profit is liable for income tax at up to 47 per cent, whereas for an ordinary investor on the top marginal tax rate, if the shares have been held for longer than 12 months, only half of the capital gain incurs CGT, meaning that the investor pays CGT effectively at a maximum rate of 23.5 per cent.

TIP

Potentially, investors using the CGT regime may fund share purchases through debt, gaining an interest deduction of 47 per cent, yet pay CGT at only 23.5 per cent on any gains — an extremely profitable arrangement! Whether being treated as a share trader is best for you depends on your marginal tax rate and your level of trading activity.

If you want to be classified as a trader, you have to meet various criteria set by tax law and interpreted by the ATO. No specific law on share traders exists, but the ATO publishes a fact sheet with guidelines based on previous court rulings. The ATO website says that the following factors have been considered in previous court cases:

» Amount of capital employed

» Nature of the activities, particularly whether they have the purpose of making a profit

» Organisation in a businesslike manner, the keeping of books or records, and the use of a system

» Repetition and regularity of the activities

» Volume of the operations

The ATO needs to satisfy itself that you're running a business dealing in shares. You have to show regular activity employing substantial capital. You should possess or have undertaken the following:

» A business plan (your trading strategy written down), with profit targets, budgets and records, and details of any software systems used

» A detailed trading history of profits and losses, dividend income, bonus issues and changes to capital structure (for example, splits, consolidations, share buybacks and capital returns)

» A financial year statement with opening and closing inventory

» Relevant educational courses and/or qualifications gained

A possible alternative to seeking trader status is to conduct your share trading activities through an SMSF. Your share profit within the fund is taxed at a maximum of 15 per cent, regardless of whether the profits are treated by the tax office as income or capital. The drawback in this case is that losses are quarantined within a superannuation fund and can't be used to offset tax on your other income or capital gains.

Keeping a record

For CGT purposes, you need to maintain a share register. Often shares in the same company are purchased at different times. You must maintain separate records in order to correctly calculate the total CGT liability when the shares are eventually sold.

TIP

Sufficient records for tax purposes include:

>> Brokerage charged on each transaction

>> Company name

>> Date of transaction

>> Incidental expenses

>> Number of shares or units bought or sold

>> Price per share on buy or sell transactions

>> Type of transaction (buy or sell)

You usually include as incidental expenses any expenditure the ATO allows as furthering your investment knowledge, such as the cost of financial books, and subscriptions to magazines and financial websites. Other items may include money spent travelling to annual general meetings of companies in which you own shares, or even visiting your companies' factories and mines, although this will depend on the facts of each case. Always check with your accountant or tax adviser about what to include in your record keeping. At worst, a taxpayer can use the system of private rulings to get an ATO determination on their particular circumstances — or circumstances they're contemplating.

5

Shares Are for Everyone

IN THIS CHAPTER

» **Using the sharemarkets to invest for the future**

» **Making the best of tax incentives**

» **Facing up to super fees**

» **Choosing your own super fund**

» **Self-managing your super**

Chapter **19**

Bankrolling Your Superannuation

The Australian sharemarket is the cornerstone of the *superannuation* system, which is the basis (along with the age pension) of retirement funding in this country. Since superannuation comes out of people's wages and savings, and the age pension comes out of the public purse, the government is anxious for the superannuation system to provide the funds for retirement of the majority of Australians. This means a shot in the arm for the sharemarket.

In this chapter, you find out exactly what superannuation is, the different types of super, how super assets are invested in the sharemarket system, and what it all means to you as an investor.

Dissecting Superannuation

Superannuation (affectionately known as *super*) has become the major pillar of retirement funding in Australia. Super is a specially designed long-term invest-ment vehicle, whose purpose is to provide retirement savings.

Officially, Australia operates a 'three-pillar' retirement-funding system: the government-funded age pension; compulsory superannuation under the Superannuation Guarantee (SG), which requires employers to pay 10 per cent of their employees' wages (set to rise to 12 per cent by July 2025) into their nominated super accounts; and voluntary contributions by individuals to their super accounts. An additional, unofficial fourth pillar is made up of a person's non-superannuation investments. Despite being taxed at a higher rate, these investments are easily accessible.

Back when the SG kicked off in 1992, superannuation assets totalled $148 billion. But from 1 July 1992, employers were required to make superannuation contributions on behalf of their employees equal to 3 per cent of their pay. This has progressively increased, and was lifted from 9.5 per cent to 10 per cent in July 2021. Along the way, the nation's superannuation pool has grown to approximately $3,300 billion — invested on behalf of the 16.1 million Australians who hold at least one superannuation account.

At present, about 26 per cent of this amount is invested in the Australian sharemarket, counting real estate investment trusts (REITs) — just short of the 27 per cent invested in international shares, the largest investment portion. A large part of the sharemarket's growth in the future will come from further growth in savings invested to fund retirement income. Shares are particularly well suited to this task because they show a better long-term record of capital growth, which is important for superannuation funds.

But although shares are integral to what super funds are trying to achieve, super funds are also very conservative investors and follow the principle of diversification. Super fund managers consider a portfolio invested wholly in Australian shares as too risky.

Super funds are managed with the emphasis on long-term capital growth. Superannuation works because of its long-term nature, which allows the principle of compounding to get to work on the invested funds. The basis of compounding is that as an investment earns a return, that return keeps being added to the original capital, swelling the pile. For example, an investment compounding at a constant rate of 7 per cent will double every ten years. A professionally managed super fund seeks to achieve the best balance between diversification of investments — for safety — and long-term capital appreciation.

The superannuation kitty is estimated to grow to more than $8 trillion by 2036. If the proportion held in the sharemarket stays the same, Australian shares would then have $2.1 trillion of super money. The government's fifth intergenerational report (IGR), released in June 2021, said that super assets were 157 per cent of the nation's GDP in March 2021; the IGR projected that super assets would be about

244 per cent of GDP by 2061, making it worth $34 trillion (in 2061 dollars). Again, if the proportion held in the sharemarket remains the same, there would be $8.8 trillion of super money invested in the sharemarket. The entire market was worth $2.5 trillion in 2021.

At present, about $145 billion a year flows into the superannuation pool in contributions, according to superannuation and managed fund research house Rainmaker Information; that is equivalent to about 15 per cent of total wages and salaries, meaning that voluntary contributions effectively match SG contributions. About $130 billion a year is paid out in benefits. That means that each week, $2.7 billion is paid into super in contributions, and $2.5 billion is paid back to members in benefits. The super system grows by more than that net $200 million (about $15 billion a year), because what is already invested is growing by about 7 per cent a year on average, going on the performance of the median balanced growth fund (which has about 70 per cent of its assets in growth-style investments and 30 per cent in defensive assets). Balanced growth funds hold more than 80 per cent of Australian super.

The median-performing balanced growth fund has returned 6.9 per cent a year over the 20 years to June 2021, and 8.3 per cent a year over the decade to June 2021. It surged by 17.6 per cent in the 2020–21 financial year. The balanced options of most super funds have an objective to produce returns that beat the annual inflation rate by at least 3.5 percentage points — so, at present, they're aiming for 5.5 per cent to 6.5 per cent. If you go back to the start of compulsory superannuation, in July 1992, the growth fund return is 8.2 per cent and the annual inflation (CPI) increase is 2.4 per cent, giving a real return of 5.8 per cent a year — well above that 3.5 per cent target. By any standards, super has done a great job.

Even when severely tested by the COVID crash of February–March 2020, super came through. According to research firm Chant West, despite the battering that sharemarkets took during that period, the diversification built into growth funds enabled them to limit the damage to a small loss of 0.6 per cent for the 2019–20 financial year, which was a much better result than expected. Then, the median growth fund returned a stunning 18 per cent for the 2020–21 financial year FY21 — the second highest return since the introduction of compulsory superannuation in 1992, only bettered by the 19.4 per cent recorded back in 1996/97.

Such a return would have been inconceivable at the start of the 2020–21 financial year. Fund members who held their nerve and remained patient through the depths of the COVID-induced market crisis, and did not panic and switch to their fund's cash option, were well rewarded. With more than half of the growth fund portfolios allocated to listed shares, these funds were able to capture a meaningful proportion of the upside as markets staged a strong and sustained rally. As Chant West put it, the experience over these two financial years highlighted the resilience and robustness of super funds' portfolios.

Funding your future

REMEMBER

Super is the government's preferred source of retirement funding. Successive Australian governments have encouraged the growth of superannuation because it provides for the funding of retirement in a manner that the age pension never can. The age pension is meant to be a safety net that supplements superannuation, not to be an alternative to it. Different rates of age pension payments exist for single and partnered people, and Services Australia uses income and assets tests to work out how much pensioners receive. The maximum age pension income level at the time of writing was, for a single retiree, $484 a week, or $25,170 a year — not far above the poverty line.

Most people would say that they require a larger income than that to live comfortably — especially with Australians living longer. This is where superannuation comes in.

A super concept

How super works is that over a person's working life, their employers make contributions to their super accounts on their behalf (through the SG) and the individuals can also contribute themselves. These contributions are invested over many years in a range of asset classes: Australian and international shares, property (listed property trusts and direct property), infrastructure and other 'alternative' assets, bonds and cash.

When a super fund member retires, resigns or dies, the fund pays out the member's share of the fund: the member gets back their total contributions plus the investment earnings (and dividend income) on their money. On retirement, the money payable to a super fund member may be paid as a lump sum (that is, a large cheque), a pension (that is, a regular income stream) or a combination of the two. On a member's death, the fund usually pays out contributions to the nominated beneficiary or into the estate.

The super system now holds about $3,300 billion in funds. About 16 million Australians now have money in the super system and, for many of them, these funds are their largest asset after the family home. The government's 2021 IGR said people were retiring with an average nest egg of $125,000; that figure is forecast to be more than $450,000 in 2060, in today's dollars.

TECHNICAL STUFF

Superannuation has two broad phases — the *accumulation* and *retirement* (what used to be called the *pension* phase) phases, but they are not distinct phases with a hard border. A person can have some of their super in accumulation and some in retirement. The accumulation phase is the first stage of everyone's superannuation life — when you are contributing to your superannuation account, or when your super balance is accumulating (combining your contributions with the capital growth on the investments your super fund makes). This combination of the total contributions you make during the accumulation phase and what is earned by investing these is 'locked away' (*preserved*) until your retirement.

REMEMBER

Australians have access to their super money as early as age 55; you can access your super at your *preservation age*, which is between the ages of 55 and 60, depending on your date of birth. Once you've reached your preservation age and you retire from the workforce, you can access your super.

TECHNICAL STUFF

If you've reached your preservation age but aren't ready to retire permanently, you can gain access to a portion of your super through a *transition-to-retirement* pension, if you take it as an income stream, in regular payments, even if you're receiving an income from an employer or business. This is designed for people making the transition to retirement, who might move from full-time to part-time work in preparation for retirement. Under these rules you can't actually cash out the super benefit because you're still working, but you can supplement your employment income with super income — although under current rules, you will generally only be able to obtain between 4 per cent and 10 per cent of your super each financial year.

The simplest condition of release is to turn 65 — once you turn 65, you can access your super even if you haven't retired. But you can access your super if you're aged between 60 and 64 and you stop working, even if you subsequently get another job with another employer. If you're aged 60 to 64 and stop working (for any amount of time), you're considered retired for the purposes of accessing your super. This is the case even if you have no intention of retiring completely.

TIP

You may be able to access your super early on compassionate grounds provided you meet strict eligibility conditions (medical, or financial hardship) and your super fund allows it. If you're approved, the amount is paid and taxed as a lump sum.

Super payments are generally tax free once you turn 60. When you die, your dependants or nominated beneficiaries will be entitled to receive what's left of your super.

Super funds are transferred into the retirement phase when a member begins receiving a super income stream (or pension). Under current rules, a maximum of $1.6 million can be transferred into the retirement phase; amounts above this cap need to remain in the accumulation phase.

WARNING

Contributions (up to the concessional contributions cap) and fund earnings in the accumulation phase are taxed at the rate of 15 per cent. Fund earnings on assets transferred into the retirement phase to support the pension income stream are generally tax free (and are known as *exempt current pension income*). But the earnings on assets supporting transition-to-retirement pensions are subject to tax.

TIP

You may convert your superannuation to a pension stream if you have reached your preservation age and met a condition of release. Standard conditions of release for super pension withdrawals are:

» Retiring

» Beginning a transition-to-retirement income stream

» Ceasing an employment arrangement after the age of 60, even if you get a job with a new employer

» Turning 65 years of age

» Becoming permanently incapacitated

» Being diagnosed with a terminal medical condition

Your dependants can also gain access to your super as a pension when you die if you have arranged for this to occur, although there are likely to be tax implications.

REMEMBER

At age 60, a person can get their super out tax free — but they can take it as a lump sum only if retired. At age 65, whether a person is working or not, super can be taken out tax free, whether as a lump sum or an income stream. But for many, gaining access to their superannuation still may not be enough to fund retirement.

The adequacy dilemma

According to the Association of Superannuation Funds of Australia (ASFA), Australians need to retire with a super balance of at least $545,000, which is what ASFA says is a 'comfortable retirement standard' that allows retirees to maintain a good standard of living in their post-work years. It accounts for daily essentials, such as groceries, transport and home repairs, as well as private health insurance, a range of exercise and leisure activities and the occasional restaurant meal.

Importantly, it enables retirees to remain connected to family and friends virtually — through technology, and in person with an annual domestic trip and an international trip once every seven years. The minimum annual cost of this 'comfortable' retirement was, at June 2021, estimated at $44,818 for a single retiree, and $63,352 for a couple. Both budgets assume that the retirees own their own home outright and are relatively healthy.

But ASFA also says that, at present, Australians aged between 60–64 are retiring with a median balance of $154,453 for males and $122,848 for females. Although this median figure is improving, clearly the amount is a long way short of ASFA's 'comfortable retirement standard' — even when considered as a couple — and such amounts cannot be spread over 20–30 years of retirement.

WHEN THE RAINY DAY CAME . . . EARLY

The purpose of superannuation is to save for retirement, but when the COVID-19 pandemic hit Australia in 2020, the government responded to the fact that millions of workers were suffering hardship through no fault of their own. In March 2020, it announced (surprising the superannuation industry) that eligible people could withdraw up to $20,000 from their super balances — $10,000 before 30 June 2020, and up to another $10,000 in the next financial year.

The official guidance from the Australian Taxation Office (ATO), which administered the scheme, was that to be eligible to withdraw an amount under the COVID-19 early release of super, the money must have been used to help the person deal with the adverse economic effects of COVID-19. The eligibility grounds of hardship were broad, and included at least a 20 per cent fall in a person's usual income.

By the time the scheme wrapped-up, in December 2020, the Australian Prudential Regulation Authority (APRA) reported that 3.5 million fund members had collectively withdrawn $36.4 billion, according to research firm Rainmaker Information. Forty per cent of these applications were from people who made two withdrawals. While people under 35 make up just one-third of all super fund members, they accounted for more than half of all the people who applied for emergency COVID-19 superannuation withdrawals. Many of these people withdrew almost all their superannuation savings. The average withdrawal for each tranche was $7,645; 1.4 million repeat applications were approved.

The upshot of this was that in the June quarter of 2020, Australians pulled more money out of the superannuation system than they put in — the first quarterly drop in net contributions since the compulsory super regime began in 1992. APRA says benefit payments surged by 77 per cent to a record $37.4 billion in the quarter, driven by the spike in lump sum payments as people took advantage of the emergency COVID-19 measures.

There was plenty of consternation at this; that younger people, while getting access to some of their money to tide them over in an emergency, not only missed out on the big recovery in super funds' investments after the COVID crash, but were also missing out on the compounding benefits of that money over the longer term, with potentially dire long-term impacts on their retirement outcomes.

But it seemed that those super fund members who withdrew money recognised the risks, and made up for their emergency withdrawals where they could by replenishing their super accounts. In the June 2021 quarter, total contributions to super jumped almost 40 per cent on the previous quarter, to $40.8 billion. Despite this late surge, for the 2020–21 financial year, total contributions rose by just 5 per cent. Rainmaker described this as super fund members trying to 'renormalise' their contributions.

Australians' life expectancy is increasing. In 1980, the life expectancy at birth in Australia was 71 years for a male and 78.1 years for a female, a gap of 7 years. In 2000, the life expectancy at birth in the year 2000 was 77.1 for a male and 82.2 for a female, a gap of 5.1 years. By 2019, the average life expectancy for a male at birth was 81.5 years, and for a female, 85.4 years. The average life expectancy at birth in Australia in 2019, for both sexes combined, was 83.4 years. Living longer is great, if your health remains good — and you have the money to fund that longer life. People usually find that they overestimate their spending needs in retirement, but even so, increased life expectancy will put many people in a financial bind. To be on track to have enough for a comfortable retirement, ASFA recommends that an Australians have $112,000 in super by age 35, $164,000 by 40, $219,000 by 45, $285,000 by age 50, $360,000 by 55 and $449,000 by 60.

The ASFA 'comfortable standard' was initially designed as, and continues to reflect, a standard for the top 20 per cent of income earners. Further, it constitutes a standard of living higher than that experienced by most Australians during their working lives. It does not account for the trade-off between working life and retirement living standards.

The gaps in super

There are quite alarming gaps in the super system, arising from many things, including people having been out of the workforce for long periods, people having been self-employed, or people participating in the 'gig economy' or 'task-related economy' as sole traders or freelancers. Despite more than 16 million Australians having at least one superannuation account, one in three women and one in four men — across all ages — have no superannuation account. Approximately 25 per cent of women and 13 per cent of men are retiring with no superannuation, says ASFA.

A large and persistent gender gap also exists, as women retire with 36 per cent less super than men, and women tend to have less super at every stage. Gender pay differentials mean that men receive $12 billion more in employer superannuation contributions each year than women. Factors such as work patterns, wages, risk aversion, financial literacy, interest in investment, general education and lower voluntary contributions all play a part in the gender super gap.

The government's Retirement Income Review (RIR), which reported in July 2020, said that most Australians would need 65–75 per cent of their pre-retirement income to fund their current lifestyle in retirement. If your household income is $100,000 before retirement, you need an income from your retirement investments of at least $65,000 a year if you want to maintain your standard of living.

Two carrots but no stick

To make super more attractive, taxation is concessional. The earnings of a super fund are taxed at 15 per cent. The lower rate of tax means your money can grow faster than investments held outside the super system, which are taxed at a higher rate.

Capital gains made by a super fund are also taxed at 15 per cent, unless the fund owns the asset for at least 12 months, in which case it can discount capital gains by one-third. In other words, only two-thirds of the capital gain is taxed, meaning that the effective capital gains tax rate for super funds can be as low as 10 per cent.

Although the lower super tax rate helps, super is actually taxed twice: 15 per cent on contributions and 15 per cent on earnings within the fund.

If concessional tax is one carrot to encourage people to save for their retirement, then another carrot, in the form of compulsory super, is also beckoning. Realising that not enough people were covered by some form of superannuation savings plan, the Australian Government moved, in 1986, to include super in industrial award agreements; then, in 1992, the Superannuation Guarantee (SG) was introduced, requiring employers to pay 3 per cent of their employees' wages into the employees' designated super accounts. This was lifted to 9 per cent in 2002, to 9.5 per cent in 2014, and to 10 per cent in July 2021. Four annual increases of 0.5 per cent are now due until the SG reaches 12 per cent from 1 July 2025.

TECHNICAL
STUFF

Currently, employers are required to make contributions equivalent to 10 per cent of an employee's annual earnings. Unfortunately, after tax of 15 per cent is levied on the contributions, only about 8.5 per cent of the amount contributed by the employer is actually invested. But this system is better than nothing: compulsory super is a form of savings that many Australians, if left to their own devices, probably would not make!

If you're worried about retirement funding, you should consider 'salary sacrifice', where you simply ask your employer to make additional contributions to your super account from your pre-tax salary.

TIP

One of the benefits of this is that the extra contributions are taxed (like your employer's contributions) at only 15 per cent, meaning that you can earn more by investing in your own super than by investing in other assets. But the major benefit of 'topping up' your super with extra contributions is that it can make a huge difference to the amount that you accumulate during your working lifetime.

Apportioning the super pool

The process by which super funds apportion their investments is called *asset allocation*. Super funds have the choice of a variety of investments, including shares; property (direct or through listed property securities); hybrid securities (products that are a mix of debt and equity); fixed interest investments, in Australia and overseas; credit investments, or bonds issued by companies; cash; and 'alternative' assets, a class of assets that doesn't fall into traditional groups, and shows little or no correlation to them, such as hedge funds, private equity and infrastructure assets.

REMEMBER

Most super funds offer members a choice of investment options. These range from the totally safe cash or capital-guaranteed investments offering relatively low (but virtually certain) yields to higher-risk 'growth' options.

The typical fund offers at least five investment risk options, including cash or capital-guaranteed options, capital-stable, balanced, growth and high-growth asset mixes. The main choices are balanced, growth and capital-stable.

WARNING

Growth super funds invest most of their money (61 per cent to 80 per cent) in shares and property, looking for higher returns over the long term. But if the sharemarket has a bad year, the fund may suffer a loss that reduces the accumulated savings. Although shares are the best investment for long-term capital growth, shares also run the highest risk of a short-term capital loss. Investors must keep this in mind when considering where to invest their super.

Balanced

A balanced investment option usually has 70 per cent or more of the portfolio's assets invested in assets such as shares, property or alternative investments

Growth

A growth investment option is for investors with 25 to 30 years to go before retirement, and who are still focused on wealth creation. This option usually has up to 80 per cent of the portfolio's assets invested in growth assets, such as shares, property and alternative assets, with the remainder invested in fixed interest and cash.

Capital-stable

A capital-stable investment option is for investors approaching retirement as the emphasis is on low-risk investments. This option usually has 70–80 per cent of the portfolio's assets invested in safer asset classes, such as fixed interest and cash, with the remainder invested in shares, listed property and alternative assets.

A capital-stable fund is less risky than a growth fund because more of the money is invested in fixed interest and cash — the trade-off for investors is a lower return over the long term.

REMEMBER

The default option — where your money will be placed if you don't know which of the categories to choose and do nothing — is usually a balanced or growth option. According to research house Rainmaker Information, more than 80 per cent of Australians in major super funds are investing in their fund's default investment option (see Table 19-1).

The Australian government introduced a simple, cost-effective super product called 'MySuper', in July 2013. MySuper products are not allowed to charge entry fees, hidden fees, or commissions to financial advisers. MySuper replaced existing default funds — only those funds whose default product meets the MySuper standards were able to operate as a default fund.

Most retail funds have adopted a lifecycle design for their MySuper defaults where members are allocated to an age-based option that's progressively de-risked as that cohort gets older. For example, the proportion of growth assets held in the lifecycle MySuper default funds, for the decade of members' births, are as follows:

>> 1940s: 45 per cent

>> 1950s: 50 per cent

>> 1960s: 70 per cent

>> 1970s: 87 per cent

>> 1980s: 89 per cent

>> 1990s: 90 per cent

There was $903 billion — 27 per cent of the total super pool — held in MySuper funds products at June 2021. About two-thirds of super owned by people younger than 65 years of age is in MySuper, says Rainmaker Information.

Accumulating funds

The first super funds were *defined benefit funds*, which paid out a specific or 'defined' amount of money regardless of how much had been contributed or how well the fund had performed. What you were paid on retirement was calculated based on your annual salary and the number of years you'd worked with the employer.

TABLE 19-1

Asset Allocation — Typical MySuper Fund

Asset Class	Percentage
Australian shares	20
International shares	30
Australian fixed interest	9
International fixed interest	7
Unlisted property	6
Listed property securities	2
Infrastructure	8
Private equity	5
Other alternative assets	7
Cash	6

Source: Association of Superannuation Funds of Australia

These days, it's considered fairer if the contributions — not the benefit — are defined, and the final benefit is determined by the return on the assets in the fund and the length of time the individual has been a member in the fund. Thus, most super funds are *accumulation* funds: employees save money by regular contributions over many years to the super fund, which invests across a diversified range of asset classes.

Managing the nation's super

Australia's $3,300 billion of super is managed by more than 600,000 funds, with more than 24 million accounts. These include corporate funds, large industry schemes run jointly by unions and employers, public sector (government) funds, and retail funds offered by the big fund managers, as well as small family-run and personal self-managed super funds (SMSFs).

Of the 600,000 funds, the vast majority — 599,934, or 99.97 per cent — are SMSFs. These funds hold just under 25 per cent of Australians' super — second only to the 'industry' fund sector — at $824 billion, despite only representing just over 4.5 per cent of super accounts. The industry funds have the most accounts, about 11.3 million, and they hold $927 billion, or 28.1 per cent of super. The largest industry fund, AustralianSuper, holds about $225 billion on its own — and openly talks about its planning for when it manages $500 billion.

Superannuation funds come in seven main types:

>> **Retail 'public offer' funds:** These are super funds offered by professional fund managers, banks and insurance companies; membership is open to anyone. These funds are operated to make a profit, and use financial planners to sell their products.

>> **Corporate superannuation funds:** These are operated for the benefit of their members, who are employees in a particular company. These funds are not-for-profit funds and don't pay sales commissions. A fund's trustees, who are appointed by the company and employees, are not paid. A well-run corporate superannuation fund is able to provide its employee members with a customised retirement savings vehicle. In effect, the various superannuation services — for example, investment management, insurance and administration — are out-sourced, and the best providers of each chosen. The corporate-fund sector is shrinking, but large employers still offer such funds, for example, the Telstra Super Fund and Qantas Super.

>> **Industry funds:** These 'not-for-profit' funds (meaning that any profits are returned to members) began life as superannuation vehicles for workers in defined industries, for example, the Retail Employees Superannuation Trust, now REST Industry Super. Most of these industry funds have evolved into public-offer funds and are open to anybody. In other words, they're just like the retail super funds offered by large investment institutions, with one important difference — they're much cheaper. Trustees are drawn from employers and employees in the particular industry.

>> **Public-sector (or government) funds:** These funds are established by governments for their employees in the public service and government agencies.

>> **Self-managed super funds (SMSFs):** These super funds have up to six members and are often set up for families or individuals. If you're prepared to take the responsibility of managing your super nest egg yourself, you can control the investment of the fund's assets, and can invest in just about any asset you choose. When you retire, your SMSF pays you a pension.

>> **Master trusts:** These are 'platforms' or systems for administering an investment portfolio, run by financial institutions. These funds are used by employers and individuals who want access to a range of different investment managers and styles within one overall account. Super master trusts may be wholesale (offered to groups of employers) or retail (open to individual investors). A 'wrap' account is similar to a master trust but it is for an investor's non-super monies, or for small super funds. The platform provider determines the choice of managed investments available under the platform, but you can usually include direct shares (or other assets) you own.

>> **Retirement savings account (RSAs):** These accounts are offered by banks, building societies, credit unions, life insurance companies and prescribed financial institutions (RSA providers). These accounts are used for retirement savings and are similar to a superannuation fund. RSAs are capital guaranteed, which means that contributions and interest on the account can be reduced only by fees and charges. RSAs are fully portable, so the balance of the account can be transferred to another RSA or superannuation provider at your request.

Boards of trustees run the corporate, industry and public-sector super funds. The board has the legal responsibility for managing the members' money. In most cases, they hire specialist investment managers and give them a mandate to invest a certain amount of the fund's assets. Some of these managers also manage retail money; some are specialist wholesale managers. The investment consultants try to spread the fund's assets to different managers for different asset classes.

Tantalising Tax Breaks

Because the government wants people to provide for their own retirement, super receives generous tax incentives. Investment income and the capital gains of a super fund are taxed at only 15 per cent. The low annual tax rate means that imputation credits from fully franked dividends can lessen or even eliminate the fund's tax liability (refer to Chapter 18 for information on how to calculate imputation credits). Imputation credits can deliver substantial tax refunds.

A super fund lodges an annual tax return the same as the individual investor does by adding the imputation credits on the fully franked dividends the fund has received to the amount of the dividend received. This is called grossing up the dividend (refer to Chapter 18 for more information on grossing up a dividend). After the tax liability on the grossed-up amount is worked out, the imputation credit is subtracted from the tax liability to give the actual tax payable. Table 19-2 shows you how imputation credits can affect the tax liability of a super fund that has received a fully franked dividend of $1,000.

Here, the super fund gets a tax refund of $215 for every $1,000 of fully franked dividends. If the super fund holds assets other than shares that pay fully franked dividends (true for most self-managed super funds), these tax credits can soak up the tax liability produced on this income.

TABLE 19-2

Tax Liability on a Super Fund's Dividend

Dividends received	$1,000
Imputed tax (30/70 x $1,000)	$429
Included in taxable income	$1,429
Gross tax liability (at 15%)	$214
Franking credit	($429)
Tax refund	$215

TIP

Franking credits are particularly useful to investors with self-managed super funds (SMSFs) because the excess franking credits can be used to offset the 15 per cent tax on super contributions as well as tax on other investment income. In broad terms, the difference between the company tax rate and the super fund tax rate means that a dollar of fully franked dividend income in a super fund shelters a further dollar of the super fund's income. Once you move to receiving a superannuation pension (that is, your fund has moved into retirement phase), the benefits are even greater as pension funds pay no tax on their earnings, so all franking credits are refunded.

TECHNICAL STUFF

In this case franked dividends become extremely tax-efficient; any franked dividends from the fund's assets can actually be refunded fully by the Australian Taxation Office (ATO). Say the SMSF owns CBA shares and all of its members are in retirement phase, drawing pensions from the SMSF. CBA is forecast to pay a dividend of $3.90 in 2021/22. Imagine that the fund bought its CBA shares at $40, in 2009. At $3.90, the yield on that dividend for the fund, based on its purchase price, is 9.75 per cent. But the refund in full of all franking credits — because the fund is a zero taxpayer, and does not need them — increases that yield to the after-tax equivalent of 13.9 per cent.

That's pretty good — in fact, in the low-interest-rate environment of the early 2020s, it is staggeringly good. But imagine that the fund bought its CBA shares for $10, back in 1995. A $3.90 dividend gives the fund a yield of 39 per cent. The full tax refund of the franking credits swells this to 55.7 per cent! Have you heard the saying that if a return promised on a dividend looks too good to be true, then something's dodgy about it? Well, the only time that's not true is when you're talking about how a growing stream of fully franked dividends, and time, work together to give stunning results. And remember, now that the fund is in retirement phase, it won't pay capital gains tax (CGT) if it sells its CBA shares either.

The Not-So-Super Part of Super: Fees

For such a hugely important feature of people's lives — funding the way they will live in retirement — superannuation is a notoriously poorly understood issue. Behind tax, the fees aspect of super is one of the most confusing of all.

According to Rainmaker Information, Australian investors pay almost $30 billion in fees a year on their superannuation. The problem is that:

>> Many types of superannuation fees are charged.

>> The fees are charged in many different ways.

A super fund can charge approximately 20 types of fees, but the funds don't have a consistent framework to describe their fees and costs, making it very confusing for investors.

However, super funds are working hard to become more efficient and lower their costs; the industry's fee impost dropped by 3 per cent during the 2020–21 financial year. Overall fees average 1 per cent across super. Fees for the flagship default MySuper sector averaged 1.08 per cent in 2020–21, after falling from 1.13 per cent in 2019–20. Of the 1.1 per cent that members pay in fees, 0.7 per cent is paid for investment fees and 0.4 per cent for administration and product-related fees, on average.

Sixty per cent of default MySuper products reduced their fees in 2020–21, with these funds representing three-quarters of all the members of these funds. The fee range for MySuper products is 0.58 per cent a year to 1.45 per cent a year. If not in a MySuper product, fees for the most expensive personal super products can be as high as 3 per cent a year.

Rainmaker says superannuation fees overall have fallen by a quarter over the last decade, with almost half of the decline happening during the three years to 2020–21, as the traditionally higher-fee retail superannuation sector responded to market pressure (and political pressure in the wake of the government's 'Your Future, Your Super' reforms, announced in the 2020–21 Budget, to take effect in November 2021) to cut their fees by innovating and catching up with the generally lower-fee not-for-profit sector. The fee gap between not-for-profit funds and retail funds is closing fast, with the average total expense ratio for not-for-profit and retail funds now being almost identical, at 1.07 per cent and 1.08 per cent respectively. As at 30 June 2021, the average Australian was paying about $2,200 annually in fees — pretty good, suggested Rainmaker, given the overall investment returns the super system is delivering for members.

If this pressure on super fund fees were to stay on its current track, it could mean that by 2026, average Australian super fund fees could be as low as 0.85 per cent, says Rainmaker, with Australia's 'sharpest priced funds' by then charging total fees below 0.5 per cent. If this were to happen, says the research firm, Australia could be on track to have one of the best-value superannuation fund systems in the world.

REMEMBER

The level of fees that you pay on your super can have a big impact on your final amount. But over time, a super fund's asset allocation strategy is far more important in determining your final balance.

In assessing the many fees that can be charged by super funds, the simplest approach by far is to think in terms of:

>> **Staying-in fees:** Charged on the account balance — ongoing fees for services, such as asset administration, custody, trustee services, and so on

>> **Member fees:** Charged as flat-dollar amounts — variously known as administration charges, policy fees, member fees and plan fees

>> **Investment fees:** Paid by the fund to its investment managers

Australian workers are able to choose the super fund that works best for them. It's your money, says the government, and you should have a say in where your money goes. Each individual worker can choose the super fund into which their employer pays their SG contributions.

The government has tried to simplify the disclosure of fees and charges by superannuation funds. It requires the Australian Securities and Investments Commission's (ASIC) fee template to be included in product disclosure statements (PDSs) and periodic statements to investors. For each fund, the ASIC template distinguishes between:

>> **Ongoing fees:** The total of all administration, investment management (the fees paid by the fund to its investment managers), expense recovery and any other fees charged by the fund

>> **Switching fees:** The fee charged when you switch between investment options offered by the fund

>> **Adviser service fees:** The fee charged by your adviser for advice about your investments in the fund

The ASIC template gives you a separate breakdown of the ongoing fees. The package also mandates a 'health warning', which sets out the effect of different total fee levels on a $50,000 balance. The information provided under this template tells you the total of the investment fees charged each year, plus the total of the administrative fees, which equal the 'cost of the product', which must be shown to you in the form (so if your balance is $50,000, the template will show you how much you have been charged that year for that particular superannuation option and amount). You can use this figure to compare the product you're looking at with other super products.

TIP

The earlier you can start saving for your retirement, the better. According to Rainmaker, if the average super fund continues to earn 8 per cent as it has over the past decade, every dollar contributed to superannuation at age 20 will be worth about $32 at retirement at age 65.

The exact amount of savings people need to accumulate for their retirement depends on when they start putting money aside, how long they have left in the workforce and how much money they feel they need to retire.

TIP

Most fund managers — and many super funds — offer handy, free calculators on their websites to enable visitors to check whether their current superannuation contributions will give them the retirement income they require and, if not, how they could alter their contributions to bring about a better outcome. The calculators are interactive and enable a variety of contribution/outcome situations to be simulated.

The Selecting Super calculator (at www.selectingsuper.com.au) is particularly handy because it helps you work out what super pension you may be on track to receive and whether you have enough money saved. You simply key in your age, existing super, estimated retirement age, current salary and estimated future increases, your super contributions as a percentage of salary, contribution fees and an estimate for investment performance (net of fees).

Taking Control: Self-Managed Super

Don't forget — you can run your own super fund and have total control over the investment process. Any super fund with four members or fewer is considered to be a *self-managed super fund* (SMSF).

A SMSF is officially known as an excluded fund because it doesn't have to comply with many of the requirements of larger funds that accept money from the public (known as public offer funds). Excluded funds have to comply with the Superannuation Industry (Supervision) Act 1993, known as SIS. SIS sets out the rules for trustees running a super fund.

In 1994, about 80,000 SMSFs were operating, holding about $11 billion in assets. There are now almost 600,000 SMSFs, controlling about $824 billion in assets, second only to the $927 billion held in super industry funds. Many Australian investors have voted with their feet for control of their investment destiny.

According to the ATO, at 30 June 2021 the membership of SMSFs was 53 per cent men and 47 per cent women, with men having an average balance of $844,474 and women having an average balance of $706,258. Women are gradually closing this gap.

Data from the ATO shows SMSF member numbers grew in 2020–21 at their fastest rate in five years, with 43,000 more people signing up in 2020–21 to take the total past 1.11 million. The ATO statistics also reveal that both men and women aged between 35 and 54 have been the most active in terms of recently establishing new SMSFs. Women are starting their own SMSFs at a faster rate than men in all age groups between 25 and 44. Overall, 56 per cent of new members are men and 44 per cent are women.

The investment income and capital gains of your fund are taxed at only 15 per cent, and you can reduce this rate even further by using the imputation credits on franked dividends to lessen (even eliminate) the fund's tax liability on its earnings and the tax on contributions, and also by using the discounted rate of capital gains tax (CGT) for assets held for more than 12 months. Then, when your fund moves to paying you a pension, it pays no tax on earnings or capital gains.

For this reason, dividend-paying Australian shares are the cornerstone investments of SMSFs. In a public-offer fund, franking credits are applied against all the tax liabilities of the fund, meaning that members may not receive the full advantage of the franking credits. But in an SMSF, the franking credits can be applied to the full advantage. Also, franking credits are particularly valuable once the fund has begun pension payments: the fund will receive 100 per cent rebate on the franked dividends because income from assets used to fund pension liabilities is exempt from tax.

Diversifying SMSF assets

Many SMSFs make the mistake of having too much cash and too little money invested overseas. As of June 2021, SMSFs held $151.3 billion in cash and term deposits, or 19 per cent of their assets (compared to a 10 per cent cash allocation for super funds in general, and a 6 per cent cash allocation in the MySuper options). Conversely, SMSFs are starkly under-invested in international shares, which are a major generator of capital growth. ATO figures show that as of June 2021, SMSFs had 29 per cent of their assets in shares, and 1.5 per cent in overseas shares. The latter figure is alarming in terms of poor diversification (although SMSFs are probably getting overseas diversification through a significant chunk of the 25 per cent of their assets that are held in managed investments).

WARNING

It is critically important for an SMSF to be well-diversified. Holding too much cash — through nervousness of market moves — means the fund can miss out on market gains. As people get older, it is understandable that they get more nervous because it's harder to replace the money, so many SMSF investors tend to hold more in cash than they perhaps should. Growing life expectancy means that even in the retirement phase, you're going to need growth assets like shares to replenish your nest egg. According to Rainmaker Information, people earn two-thirds of the superannuation investment income they will ever earn after they retire. It has never been easier for an SMSF to build highly diversified portfolios, with ETFs, managed funds and listed investment companies (LICs) offering virtually the full menu of investment exposures that a professional fund would use.

The role of property in SMSFs is a major area of debate, particularly with the use in recent years of *limited recourse borrowing arrangements* (LRBAs), which have enabled many SMSFs to borrow money in order to acquire a variety of property investments. While property can be an excellent investment in an SMSF, as long as it conforms to super regulations, issues definitely exist with property within super that cannot be ignored.

WARNING

If you hold property within an SMSF, it tends to be quite a large asset, and you may find it's a large percentage of your overall fund. There is also, with such a large single asset, the issue of concentration in a particular location and particular state and territory.

WARNING

SMSFs investing in property need to fully understand, and allow for, the rules once the fund enters retirement phase. In retirement phase, a certain minimum percentage of the fund has to be drawn down as pension income each year, and meeting that requirement can be a problem if the main asset in the fund is a large property. The trustees of an SMSF that owns property and is paying out on pensions need to be very aware of these rules — you can't sell one bedroom of a property to meet pension requirement costs.

Following the asset allocation policies of professional super funds helps. Note how the asset choices of these funds change over time — you can check these figures in the media. If the proportions of your SMSF's holdings differ widely from professional funds, ask your financial adviser whether you may need to make changes.

Complying with the law

An SMSF gives you a greater ability to tailor your portfolio to suit your needs and invest directly. An SMSF also gives you more control over how you design your benefits; you can optimise the tax and estate planning benefits that you get from superannuation. However, for all of the flexibility and control — and the ability to make individualised decisions on investment, retirement income and estate planning — there are many responsibilities and requirements that SMSF proprietors must fulfil, and potentially onerous penalties for SMSFs that do the wrong thing.

The regulations governing SMSFs are strictly enforced. An SMSF must have a trust deed and trustees. A lawyer will supply a deed, and then what is needed are two people who meet the trustee qualification — usually your spouse and yourself — but it can be yourself and anyone else who doesn't work for you, as long as neither of you has a criminal record or an event of bankruptcy.

An SMSF must choose to be regulated under SIS to be eligible for the concessional tax treatment of super funds. The ATO requires that every member of the fund must be a trustee (there are special rules for single-member funds) and with that comes trustee responsibilities.

Under the sole purpose test set out in SIS, the trustees must ensure that the fund is maintained for the sole purpose of providing retirement benefits to members. The trustees must 'formulate and implement' an investment strategy for the fund, 'having regard to liabilities, risk and return, diversification and liquidity'. If the fund maintains reserves, it must have a defined strategy for managing those reserves, in line with its investment strategy and its ability to meet liabilities. Since 2013, SMSF trustees have also been required to consider in their strategy the life insurance needs of the fund's members.

A portfolio in a super fund must meet four conditions: liquidity; the matching of cash flows to liabilities in the pension phase; risk; and diversification. Diversification, of course, means that you can't have all your assets in one investment. In considering risk, the fund has to look at the age of the members, when they plan to retire, and match its portfolio to those factors. If you fail to administer your super fund properly and the fund loses its status as a 'complying' fund, the penalties are severe, including penalty rates on the fund's earnings.

The penalties start from a financial penalty, increasing to the maximum punishment, which is the ATO making your fund *non-complying* if it determines that you're really misusing your funds — such as by drawing the money out and using it for personal purposes before you are allowed to do so. If your SMSF is found to be non-complying, it means you are going to get taxed at the highest marginal rate on the whole balance amount.

Because the investment strategy requirement is listed under SIS as an operating standard, if the fund suffers a loss, the trustees can be fined if they're found to have breached those conditions. This means that everything you buy for your SMSF has to have been 'envisaged' in the fund's investment strategy. Many people fall into the trap of thinking that they can buy a beach house for their SMSF, or a nice piece of art to hang on their wall. Buying either of these assets is perfectly legal, but if you do buy them, very strict conditions on their use will apply — they must be used only by people at 'arm's length' to you — which excludes you, relatives and friends.

Because of this, choosing the investments for an SMSF is a very important decision. You shouldn't treat the share component of your personal super fund in the same way as the share portion of your investment portfolio. Your personal super fund isn't the place for stock-picking or speculative stocks. A super fund is a long-term plan, and you need to invest in large companies with demonstrable track records for growth in earnings per share and dividends.

The existence of the obligations on a SMSF and the possible penalties mean that 'self-managed' is somewhat of a misnomer, because most SMSF trustees will be taking advice from a variety of specialist service providers. SMSF Association research shows that an SMSF proprietor actually needs to work with up to nine different specialist service providers, including a tax adviser, lawyer, financial adviser, investment adviser, accountant and auditor. The SMSF Association firmly recommends that people contemplating establishing an SMSF go to the lengths of understanding exactly what they want in their personal, financial, business or family situation, and their future, and how an SMSF fits into that.

The average age of people establishing SMSFs is showing a gradual trend lower over time. SMSFs are becoming cheaper to operate, reflecting the fact that cheaper vehicles such as exchange-traded funds (ETFs) make the asset allocation task a lot easier; and digital providers are bringing technology-based SMSF support services to market. Younger people are coming into the SMSF world too, and while it was often cited in the past as a truism that an SMSF needed at least $500,000 to be viable — otherwise the annual costs were too expensive as a percentage of the balance — this figure has come down, given the general cost compression that technology has brought to financial services. SMSF balances of $100,000–150,000 are now considered competitive with APRA-regulated funds, provided a cheaper service provider is used or trustees do some of the administration.

REMEMBER

You can elect to have your do-it-yourself super fund regulated by either APRA or the ATO. If you choose APRA, the fund is referred to as a small APRA fund (or SAF). If regulated by the ATO, it's an SMSF.

Whichever type of self-managed fund you choose, running your own super is all about taking control of your retirement savings and managing them directly rather than leaving it to someone else. Although you have far greater flexibility than an investor in an ordinary pooled super fund, you have only yourself to blame for poor or negative returns — and there are plenty of strict rules with which you have to comply. But if you use the support structures that are available to you, and you're prepared to do your homework, managing your retirement funding can be very rewarding. However, if you don't think you can give it the time, and you don't really feel you understand the investment markets and the requirements of running an SMSF well enough, professional super fund management does a pretty good job and saves you the risk.

Chapter **20**

Investing in Overseas Shares

The more you know about investment, the more you understand that diver-sification is an investor's best weapon against the threat of loss. *Diversification* means investing across a range of asset categories, including geographical locations. Since the Australian sharemarket accounts for about 2.3 per cent of the total *capitalisation* (or value) of the world's sharemarkets, a properly diversified share portfolio should include overseas investments. Even though diversification is the main reason for investing overseas, the returns are more than worthwhile.

In this chapter, I cover the different ways you can access the international market, and how to cope with currency fluctuation. Time to spread your wings and enter the big wide world of overseas investing.

Going Offshore

Like all investors, Australian investors are prone to 'home bias'. Only 15 per cent of Australian shareholders own international shares, according to the ASX Australian Investor Study 2020.

There have always been good arguments for why Australian investors (like any group of investors) feel more comfortable investing at home. They understand the companies better; overseas companies can be difficult to research; potential currency movements often feel like too much of a risk; and, lastly, investing in overseas stocks is difficult and costly. But there have always been equally good arguments as to why investors should invest outside Australia.

The major reason is the relatively small size of the Australian market. Australia represents only about 2.1 per cent of the MSCI World index, although it is the eighth-largest stock market represented — the index is heavily weighted to the US, which represents more than two-thirds of it (67.2 per cent). In the broader MSCI All Country World index (which covers 50 markets — 23 developed and 27 emerging markets), Australia's weighting (at 30 July 2021) is 1.9 per cent (this index is also dominated by the US, at 58.6 per cent).

The diversification argument is only strengthened by the fact that the Australian stock market is one of the most concentrated in the world, with the top ten stocks making up about 44 per cent of the main benchmark index, the S&P/ASX 200.

Many industries aren't represented or are under-represented in Australia. For example, the MSCI World index has an allocation of just under 35 per cent to the fast-growing Information Technology and Health Care sectors. By comparison, Australia has less than 15 per cent in these sectors.

REMEMBER

The problem is not just that the Australian market is small. The Aussie market is also highly concentrated, dominated by a small number of companies (and sectors) that account for the lion's share of market capitalisation. For example, if you buy an exchange-traded fund (ETF) that tracks the S&P/ASX 200 index, you will be heavily exposed to the two big resources companies, BHP and Rio Tinto (9.2 per cent of your investment), and the Big Four banks (20.9 per cent of your investment).

That is more than 30 per cent of your holding straight off. Financials (30 per cent) and Materials (19.9 per cent; this sector holds the miners) make up just under half of the S&P/ASX 200 index. That can be a big problem if an issue crops up in one of those industries — which has actually been the case at different times in the past two decades, for both mining and banking. BHP, for example, did very little in share price growth terms between 2008 and 2016. Having such large exposures to financials and materials means that a large chunk of many investors' sharemarket returns are affected by the credit (interest rate) cycle and commodity price cycles.

Of course, the Australian market isn't as concentrated as it once was — having biotech giant CSL as your third-biggest investment in an S&P/ASX 200 index ETF (6.1 per cent of it) does help (and in recent times, CSL has been the largest index constituent, with a weighting above 9 per cent). In 2000, the Health Care sector accounted for just 1 per cent of the S&P/ASX 200, but it has grown to become the third-largest sector, at 10.3 per cent of the index, powered by CSL's rise to the top echelon of market capitalisation (CSL represents about 70 per cent of the S&P/ASX 200 Health Care sector by market capitalisation). The Health Care sector's weighting has grown at a compound annual rate of about 18.5 per cent over 20 years. Since March 2011, the combined weight of Financials and Materials — Australia's largest sectors — has decreased from 59.4 per cent to 48.3 per cent, while Health Care has more than tripled in weighting, from 3.2 per cent.

REMEMBER

Investing internationally increases your diversification and gives you access to industries and companies that are not available in Australia.

Around the world, technological trends such as ecommerce, automation, miniaturisation, artificial intelligence (AI), machine learning, the Internet of Things, driverless vehicles and drone technology are becoming increasingly powerful economic forces — and Australian investors arguably have never needed the much wider range of global investment exposures more.

Australian superannuation funds have recognised this, increasing their overseas investments from about 14 per cent in 1996 to about 30 per cent in mid-2021 (a larger allocation than to Australian shares, at 20 per cent), according to financial intelligence firm Rainmaker Information.

TECHNICAL
STUFF

Australia's largest super fund, and arguably one of the best and most consistent performers, is AustralianSuper, which holds $225 billion. Its 'balanced' fund, which targets 70–75 per cent in 'growth assets' (such as shares and property) and 25–30 per cent in defensive assets, is used by roughly 90 per cent of its members. For international shares, it targets an allocation in the range of 10–45 per cent, the same size range as that for Australian shares. In 2021, it had 33.5 per cent of its assets invested in international shares, well ahead of its 22.7 per cent exposure in Australian shares. Most of the other major industry super funds (such as Rest, Cbus or Aware Super) also have significant holdings in overseas shares. Professional investors understand the benefits of sending money out into the world to make their fortune.

Financial planners advise clients to allocate their investable funds across the asset classes. They typically employ an allocation model based on historical performance correlations between the different asset categories such that, given a desired level of risk, the highest expected return is achieved. Depending on the risk profile, the allocation to overseas shares for a 'balanced' or 'growth' investor is about 20–30 per cent, and can be as high as 40 per cent.

WARNING

However, there is a problem with Australia's army of 600,000 self-managed super funds (SMSFs), with their 1.1 million members, who hold $824 billion in assets. The latest data from the Australian Taxation Office (ATO) shows that SMSFs are starkly under-invested in overseas shares, with a weighting of about 2 per cent on average, compared to 29 per cent for Australian shares. The ATO data isn't perfect (it doesn't show how much SMSFs have invested overseas in the 'managed funds and trusts' categories), but even if it is out by a factor of five times, SMSFs have a massive home bias. Even with the tax-advantaged nature of income from the fully franked dividend flow from their Aussie shareholdings (see Chapter 18), this imbalance in SMSF share allocations is not serving SMSFs well.

Investing in the mega-stocks

Australian investors don't have access on their home market to some of the more advanced investment exposures. For example, the Australian Securities Exchange (ASX) has no major telecommunications suppliers, integrated energy companies, large utilities or aerospace companies. Australians can't invest at home on a large scale in the technology industry; although it does have some emerging tech leaders, it has nothing of the scale of businesses such as Apple, Microsoft, Samsung, Amazon, Alphabet (Google's parent company), Twitter, Meta Platforms (the owner of Facebook, Instagram and WhatsApp), Netflix, Tencent, Alibaba, Tesla and Taiwan Semiconductor Manufacturing. Australians also have no home-based large-cap drug companies, such as Pfizer and AstraZeneca (although they are now household names to us, thanks to COVID-19), or Johnson & Johnson, Roche, Novartis and Merck, or consumer champions of the likes of Nestlé, Unilever, AB InBev and Procter & Gamble. Investors who want to be well-diversified have to look outside the Australian market more than ever before to tap into long-term growth opportunities in a range of industries and sectors that are not accessible in a purely domestic share portfolio.

REMEMBER

Most of the products Australians eat, drink, work with, wash with and drive are made by global companies offshore and/or by their Australian subsidiaries. More than 70 per cent of the world sharemarket is made up of companies that operate their business across a multinational framework.

The Australian sharemarket doesn't have the kind of global household name stocks that other, bigger markets have. Most investors who buy foreign stocks deal mainly in the US because they want to invest in the world's largest capital market in the world's strongest currency. Investors want access to the great household name stocks that they can't get in Australia, such as Apple, Microsoft, Coca-Cola, McDonald's, Procter & Gamble, Gillette, Colgate-Palmolive, Exxon-Mobil, Intel, Microsoft, Boeing and 3M. Investors are more comfortable with these companies because they know the products well. There's no reason why shares in US companies can't be part of an Australian investor's portfolio.

REMEMBER

Australian investors aren't limited to US stocks. Investors can also buy into world-class companies such as Honda, Siemens, Sony, Samsung, Louis Vuitton Moët Hennessy (LVMH), Philips, Carlsberg and Unilever. If a company is listed, investors can own it.

TIP

Many world-class companies now list in New York through *American Depositary Receipts* (ADRs), through which non-US companies list on the New York Stock Exchange (NYSE), the Nasdaq Stock Market and the NYSE-owned American Stock Exchange (NYSE Amex, the third-largest US stock exchange).

The New York ADR market is a popular way for individual investors to buy shares in world markets. There are more than 2,000 ADRs available representing shares of companies hailing from more than 70 countries. ADRs trade in US dollars and clear through US settlement systems, allowing ADR holders to avoid having to transact in a foreign currency. Each ADR represents a particular number of the foreign shares. For example, each Nestlé ADR, by which the Swiss-based food giant (the world's biggest food company) is listed in New York, represents ownership of one of the Nestlé shares listed on the Swiss Exchange, while each Toyota ADR covers two of the Tokyo-listed shares. But an investor would need to buy five L'Oréal ADRs to own the equivalent of one of the cosmetics luminary's Euronext Paris-listed shares, and eight Alibaba shares to own the equivalent of the Chinese tech heavyweight's Hong Kong-listed shares.

Getting a bite of the FAANGs

In 2013, Jim Cramer, the television host of CNBC's *Mad Money* program, coined the term 'the FANGs' to denote the tech mega-stocks that were "totally dominant in their markets", in his words: Facebook (now known as Meta Platforms), Amazon, Netflix and Google. After Google was restructured in 2015, and Alphabet became the parent company and took over the Nasdaq listing, the G remained; Cramer added Apple to the acronym in 2017, making it 'FAANG'. Since then, the term has been widely understood to be 'FAANG+M' (as in, plus Microsoft); some investors even discard Netflix for Microsoft, making it 'FAAMG'.

As of August 2021, the FAANGs (plus Microsoft) make up almost 24 per cent of the S&P 500 — a staggering figure, considering that the S&P 500 is generally viewed as a proxy for the entire US economy. The group also makes up almost 38 per cent of the Nasdaq Composite index.

The FAANG stocks have historically outperformed the S&P 500 index. As of July 2021, the worst-performing FAANG stock, Alphabet, has returned more than double the index average since the market bottom in March 2009. Meanwhile, Netflix stock is up more than 100-fold, and Amazon and Apple shares are up more than 50 times.

In the Australian market, the acronym 'WAAAX' has been coined to encompass the local market's tech stars — WiseTech Global, Afterpay, Appen, Altium and Xero. But anyone can come up with an acronym. I enjoyed it when Rupal Bhansali, chief stock picker for the US$19 billion fund Ariel Investments, was in Australia in early 2020 and came up with her own acronym. She told the *Australian Financial Review* that her portfolio emphasised MANG (French tyre-maker Michelin, US-listed Israeli telecom billing software company Amdocs, Finnish tech company Nokia and US biotech Gilead) over FAANG.

In 2020, investment bank Goldman Sachs — which has acronym form, having introduced the world to the BRIC (Brazil, Russia, India, China) group of emerging-market powerhouses in 2001 — introduced the world to the GRANOLAS, a group of 11 heavyweight global stocks from Europe: British pharma giant GSK (GlaxoSmithKline); Swiss pharma heavyweight Roche; ASML, the Dutch supplier to the world's semi-conductor industry; Swiss-based Nestlé, the world's biggest food company; Swiss-based global healthcare company Novartis; Novo Nordisk, the big Danish pharmaceutical firm; French cosmetics and personal care giant L'Oréal; French luxury goods conglomerate LVMH; British-Swedish pharma company AstraZeneca; French pharmaceutical heavyweight Sanofi; and German enterprise resource planning software giant SAP.

TIP

While the GRANOLAS have not quite captured investor attention to the extent that the FAANGs-plus-Microsoft have, the common thread in the group is that they are among the largest stocks in Europe; they have global reach in the healthcare, consumer basics and technology sectors; they have huge businesses and strong balance sheets that enable them to generate earnings growth and sustainable, steady dividend flows; and they generally trade with low volatility. As such, they should be able to remain attractive to investors. As with the FAANGs-plus-Microsoft, investing in such companies means potentially benefiting from their business success — not just being a user of their products.

The passport to performance

Over the long term, international shares generate returns reasonably similar to those you would expect from Australian shares. For example, according to research house Andex Charts, over the 30 years to December 2020, international shares (MSCI World ex-Australia Gross Total Return index) returned 8.5 per cent a year, compared to the 10.1 per cent a year return for Australian shares (S&P/ASX All Ordinaries Accumulation index), as shown in Table 20-1 (both indices count dividend income as well as share price rises). Over 20 years, Australian shares also comfortably outperformed the international holding, with 8.3 per cent a year against 4.8 per cent a year.

But over one, three, five and ten-year timeframes, global shares generated better returns than local shares. Investors benefit from this disparate performance. But the true value of having international shares in your portfolio is not just the return aspect. The true value is the added diversification these international shares give you, in the 97.7 per cent of the 'investable' stock market universe that is not in Australia.

TABLE 20-1   ## Australian Shares versus International Shares (Percentage Returns as at 31 December 2020)

	1 year	3 years	5 years	10 years	20 years	30 years
S&P/ASX All Ordinaries Accumulation Index	3.6	7.4	9.3	7.9	8.3	10.1
MSCI World ex-Australia Gross Total Return Index	6.3	11.8	11.6	13.8	4.8	8.5

Source: Andex Charts Pty Ltd

International shares show similar risk/return characteristics to Australian shares (refer to Chapter 3). Andex Charts has calculated the risk and return from international shares (as measured by the MSCI World ex-Australia Gross Total Return Index) over the period, 1 January 1970 to 31 December 2020, measured over one, three, five, ten and 20 years, with investments made at month ends. Andex measured 601 one-year periods, 577 three-year periods, 553 five-year periods, 493 ten-year periods and 373 20-year periods (see Figure 20-1).

The one-year investments showed great volatility, with a best return of 94.4 per cent and a worst performance of minus 33.1 per cent. The average gain was 12.6 per cent, but nearly one in four (23 per cent) of the short-term investments showed a loss.

Over three-year periods, the probability of success rose to 81 per cent. The best return was 54.3 per cent a year, while the worst performance was minus 18.2 per cent a year. The average gain was 11.6 per cent a year.

The average return over five years was 11.5 per cent a year, with a best return of 44.7 per cent a year and the worst performance being a loss of 7.8 per cent a year. The risk of loss in the five-year periods was still present, however, with 17 per cent of the periods failing to make a positive return.

Whereas with Australian shares, all ten-year investment periods showed a positive return, 9.5 per cent of the ten-year investments in international shares ended in the red. The best result was 26.9 per cent a year, the worst was minus 4.7 per cent a year and the average gain was 11.4 per cent a year.

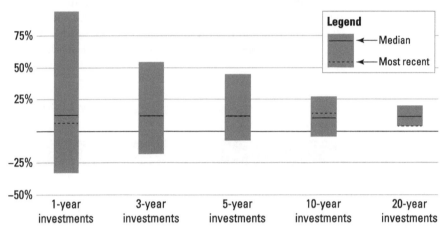

This chart graphs the range of returns observed for international shares between 1 January 1970 and 31 December 2020.

Legend
— Median
— Most recent

75%
50%
25%
−25%
−50%

| 1-year investments | 3-year investments | 5-year investments | 10-year investments | 20-year investments |

MSCI World ex-Australia Gross Total Return Index in AUD terms.
Chart: Andex Charts Pty Ltd

Source: Andex Charts Pty Ltd

FIGURE 20-1: How time tempers the risk and return on international shares.

For a span of 20 years, the average investment in international shares showed a gain of 11.3 per cent a year. The best two-decade period returned 19.8 per cent a year, while the worst came in at 3.7 per cent a year. But no 20-year period showed a loss.

REMEMBER

Both portfolio theory and funds management practice accept that the addition of foreign shares to a domestic share portfolio lowers the portfolio's level of risk without jeopardising the return; or, conversely, it increases the return for the same level of risk.

ETFs: Revolutionising offshore investing

If the ETF (*exchange-traded-fund*) vehicle hadn't been invented, Australian investors looking to invest overseas would have had to invent it. A listed stock that represents a share market (or other asset class) index or portfolio, the ETF is perfect for the purpose of solving the need to diversify an investment portfolio outside Australia. Australian investors have looked to ETFs to gain access to international shares — US and non-US — in a broadly diversified way. They like the broad, diversified international coverage that buying one ETF gives them, particularly when it comes in a cost-effective and transparent form compared to unlisted international share funds.

The investment management cost is often lower than wholesale managed-fund rates, and investors get diversified global exposure without paying relatively high fees for active management. The attraction of global ETFs for Australian investors is that they can be extremely cost-effective, with no entry and exit fees, and an annual management fee that can be as low as seven basis points (0.07 per cent) a year. Investors will also only pay normal brokerage when buying and selling ETFs.

The easiest way to establish international diversification is to buy an ETF over one of the large global indices. For example, iShares' iShares S&P 500 ETF (ASX code: IVV) simply tracks the return (before fees) of the S&P 500 index; Vanguard's MSCI index International Shares ETF (VGS) does the same for the MSCI World ex-Australia index; and SPDR's S&P World Ex-Australia ETF (WXOZ) similarly tracks the S&P Developed ex-Australia LargeMidCap index.

From *first-generation global equity ETFs*, which give access to the recognised mainstream market-cap indices (such as the MSCI World, the S&P 500, and so on), product development has moved through *second-generation ETFs*, which cover single countries in both the developed world and emerging markets, as well as sectors (such as healthcare and consumer staples), and into third-generation ETFs. These *third-generation ETFs* encapsulate exposure to fundamental 'factor-based' (*factors* are fundamental underlying drivers of share returns — for example, low-volatility or high yield) or 'style-based' strategies (for example value, growth or ethical investments), catering for investors who want international exposure but would like that exposure to be designed so as to either maximise, or avoid, a particular factor.

ETF design is becoming very specific — refer to Chapter 9 for some of the more targeted global exposures, built around particular themes, that have come to the ASX. In this way, ETF issuers have been able to move well beyond the major global indices.

TIP

Global ETFs may be the best alternative for inexperienced investors with only small amounts of money to invest, as there is often no minimum investment; however, some brokers will insist on at least a $500 initial purchase. Some of the global ETFs that track the major indices have an annual cost to the investor that is amazingly low — as low as three or four basis points (0.03 per cent or 0.04 per cent). Investors who started investing overseas 20 years ago would be staggered by how cheap that is!

A large number of actively managed global funds are available to investors, offering unlisted share funds, many of which are on the ASX's mFund platform (Chapter 5 covers active fund management in more detail). Australian-based investment firms such as Magellan Financial Group, Platinum Asset Management, WAM, Cooper Investors, Hyperion Asset Management, Alphinity, Pengana, Antipodes Partners, First Sentier Investors, PM Capital, Orbis, Fairlight, Insync, Munro Partners, Nanuk, Ausbil, Plato, Lakehouse, Australian Ethical, Bell Asset Management, Orca and Aoris Investment Management all run global share funds.

Some of these managers have created *exchange-traded managed funds* (ETMFs), which are actively managed funds that are traded on the ASX — examples include the Magellan Global Fund and the Fidelity Global Emerging Markets Fund, which are available in listed and unlisted forms, giving investors more choice and flexibility. Some investors prefer the liquidity, lack of a minimum investment amount, and lack of paperwork and bureaucracy that the exchange-traded version offers. ETMFs are built like managed funds but trade like shares, meaning that their pricing is transparent and they can be bought and sold during any trading day — just like ordinary shares. The listed investment company (LIC) sector of the ASX (refer to Chapter 9) is also worth checking-out for global investment funds with good long-term track records.

TIP

Using professional management relieves you from having to choose from the bewildering array of international stocks. Managers of international equity funds do the research on which sectors and which countries are likely to perform best, and they follow predictions of a slowdown or rise in global economic growth. Getting all the information that's needed to make sound decisions in this area of investment is difficult for individual investors.

Where to Invest?

For the vast majority of Australian investors, *international equities* means shares from one of the major sharemarkets, most of which are in countries that are members of the Organisation for Economic Co-operation and Development (OECD). Table 20-2 charts Australia's peer group of developed sharemarkets (these are the countries used in the MSCI World index).

TABLE 20-2

Developed Sharemarkets

Australia	Hong Kong	Portugal
Austria	Ireland	Singapore
Belgium	Israel	Spain
Canada	Italy	Sweden
Denmark	Japan	Switzerland
Finland	Netherlands	United Kingdom
France	New Zealand	United States of America
Germany	Norway	

Source: MSCI

Standard & Poor's adds South Korea, Luxembourg and Poland to the list shown in Table 20-2.

Outside the first tier are the emerging markets, as shown in Table 20-3. These are the countries from the MSCI Emerging Markets index. Shares from the emerging markets are a separate and riskier asset class than the shares from the major world markets.

TABLE 20-3

Emerging Sharemarkets

Brazil	India	Russia
Chile	Indonesia	Saudi Arabia
China	Malaysia	South Africa
Colombia	Mexico	South Korea
Czech Republic	Peru	Taiwan
Egypt	Philippines	Thailand
Greece	Poland	Turkey
Hungary	Qatar	United Arab Emirates

Source: MSCI

TIP

South Korea sits uncomfortably outside the 'developed markets', despite being the tenth largest economy and 11th largest individual sharemarket in the world. MSCI classifies it as an emerging market because of problems with the convertibility of currency and restrictions on foreign stock transfers imposed by the government.

Trailing the emerging markets are the 'frontier' markets — the stock exchanges in places like Vietnam (which MSCI considers the largest frontier market), Iceland, Kazakhstan, Bahrain, Bangladesh, Kenya, Croatia, Estonia, Jordan, Sri Lanka, Oman, Lithuania, Romania, Nigeria, Tanzania, Morocco and Tunisia.

A separate category of 'secondary emerging' markets sits between the emerging and frontier markets — the 'secondary' signifies that a market has clearly left the frontier world and is heading higher. For example, Argentina and Romania were promoted from frontier to secondary emerging in 2019; Kuwait followed them in 2020; and it is widely expected that Vietnam will be next to be similarly upgraded.

REMEMBER

About three decades ago, emerging markets accounted for about 18 per cent of global GDP. By 2022, that figure is expected to grow to 62 per cent. Emerging markets are where most of the world's population lives, and as these countries move up the wealth ladder and become more middle class in their spending patterns, huge growth trends are likely to emerge. A growing middle class can play a crucial role in a country's development by spurring (consumption-led) economic growth.

The emergence of a global middle class has been one of the most economically significant trends of the past few decades, and this cohort of consumers was expected to continue to grow relentlessly as rising incomes in developing countries lifted millions out of poverty each year. However, the unforeseen COVID-19 pandemic has crimped this growth, as countries have grappled with the virus at different paces, with varying levels of success, amid uneven global vaccine rollouts.

TIP

Adding shares from emerging markets to a portfolio can enhance a portfolio's return and, surprisingly, lower overall risk over time, because returns from these markets don't always move in lockstep with those from developed markets, so they could be rising when the latter is struggling. The key to success in diversification is having a wide enough range of investments to protect your overall portfolio.

Deciding the Best Way to Invest

While there are good reasons to explain Australians' 'home bias' — for example, the benefits of dividend imputation (refer to Chapter 18) and their familiarity with Australian companies — Australian investors have responded to the need for wider diversification. The three ways to invest in overseas shares are called direct, indirect and direct indirect, summarised as follows:

>> **Direct investment** involves buying foreign-listed shares, ETFs or ADRs on your own account for your personal portfolio. You can pick and choose the international stocks that you want to buy directly from the exchange where they're traded.

>> **Indirect investment** is when you buy shares through international equity trusts, which are unit trusts (managed funds) actively managed by professional investors (refer to Chapter 5). Australians have $644 billion invested in international share funds (up from $142 billion in June 2003). This kind of exposure means you have professional managers picking the stocks and monitoring the portfolio on your behalf.

>> **Direct indirect investment** is done through managed funds that are themselves Australian-listed ETFs (refer to Chapter 9). Of the ASX's $122.8 billion cohort of ETFs, $62.9 billion — just over 51 per cent — is invested in global share ETFs.

Going directly to the source

Direct investment in foreign shares is almost as easy as buying local shares. You simply put in an order with your broker, whether over the phone or online, and the broker's platform fills the order as soon as the foreign market in question opens.

This way, an Australian investor can trade on virtually the same basis as a New York investor, while using the same approach as in their securities trading in Australia. The mechanics of buying are the same: investors can set at-limit orders or at-market orders.

When you broaden your horizons to international markets, a larger variety of companies will appear on your radar — along with a staggering range of specialist investments you can tap into through overseas-listed ETFs. More than 2,000 ETFs are available on the US market — some that are very vanilla, and just give exposure to a major index, but others with a highly specific focus. For example, ETFs are available that target Millennial interests such as AI, videogaming and space industries. Virtually anything you can think of in which you would like to invest, someone has created an ETF for it.

Access to international stock markets has benefited from the general price war in financial services that has swept through stockbroking. Many trading platforms do not charge commission at all to buy or sell foreign shares for you; these platforms make their money by taking a cut of the foreign exchange transactions that you need to make when buying and selling your overseas shares.

The 'zero commission' international stockbroking platforms include:

>> CMC Markets

>> Dabble

>> eToro

>> Monex

>> Stake

>> Superhero

International stockbroking platforms that charge minimal costs per overseas transaction include (with costs specified in Australian dollars, except where noted otherwise):

>> **St. George Bank:** $59.00

>> **ANZ Share Investing:** $59.00

- **Westpac:** US$19.95

- **CommSec:** US$19.95

- **nabtrade:** $14.95

- **Philip Capital:** US$10.00

- **IG Markets:** US$10.00

- **SelfWealth:** US$9.50

- **Saxo Markets:** US$4.00

- **Interactive Brokers:** US$1.00

Price is what you pay, value is what you get. Make sure you check all the conditions, and the entire offering, for each of these service providers to see what suits you (and your level of activity) best.

The price war — and the 'functionality' and 'features' wars — in which the broking service providers are engaged is working in the customers' favour. Some stockbroking service providers (Stake is a good example) have used technology to digitise the whole investment process, including the infamous W-8 BEN forms for the US tax office, which usually take several days for clients to work through (global ETFs handle the W-8 BEN situation for their investors, too). The newer platforms are designed to make it as easy to buy foreign shares as it is to buy a pair of sneakers from the US online from a mobile phone, because that's what their Millennial customers expect. The incumbent platforms have to try to match that offering.

Micro-investing app Raiz (refer to Chapter 7) deserves a special mention here. Raiz allows anybody with a few dollars spare to invest automatically in a range of seven pre-designed portfolios, without the hassle of going through a broker, paying brokerage or trying to save a big lump sum to kick off their investment journey. Raiz customers can invest a lump sum; set a recurring daily, weekly or monthly investment amount to invest in their portfolio; or 'round-up' the change from their daily purchases to plug into their portfolio. Among the seven options available, Raiz customers can choose to use a US large-cap share ETF (the iShares S&P 500 ETF), a European large-cap share ETF (the iShares Europe ETF) or a global socially responsible large-cap share ETF (the BetaShares Global Sustainability Leaders ETF). When a young barista proudly shows you their Raiz portfolio on their phone, and how it is performing — as happened to me recently — it's wonderful to see that the global sharemarket is working for them already.

FRACTION MEANS LESS FRICTION

Innovation in financial services is always working to bring better opportunities to investors. Online stockbroking app Stake operates a share trading platform that gives Australians, and other users outside the US, access to US sharemarkets without the need for a US trading account. Stake allows investors to trade *fractional* shares, which are portions of whole shares of a stock or exchange-traded fund (ETF). This means that Australian investors can trade a dollar amount of a stock irrespective of the share price — they have the flexibility to invest as much or as little as they want.

Why is this option so attractive? Consider Berkshire Hathaway, the publicly listed investment vehicle of Warren Buffett and Charlie Munger, which trades at a share price of US$419,820 on the New York Stock Exchange for one of its 'A' shares — it's the most expensive publicly traded share ever. At $559,760 for an Australian investor, it's out of most people's league — unless you can buy it in smaller portions.

On Stake, an investor could stump up US$1,000 ($1,333) to buy 0.0024 of one share of Berkshire Hathaway and have full beneficial interest, with the same rights as full-stock owners — and receive dividends and any other corporate actions on a pro-rata basis. The fractional shares are held in the investor's name with Stake's broker and custodian. Amazon is another US share in which fractional investment makes sense for many people; however, at US$3,677 ($4,902) a share, it's a lot cheaper than Berkshire Hathaway.

TIP

Australia's second stock exchange, Cboe Australia, trades a product called Transferable Custody Receipts (TraCRs), which are securities that give Australian investors access to the benefits of owning US shares in some of the world's biggest brands. TraCR holders own a beneficial interest in the underlying US shares (and the right, subject to the terms of issue, to convert their TraCR holdings into that share). They also hold an Australian security that is traded, cleared and settled in Australian dollars under Australian regulation, during Australian trading hours. Dividends are also paid in Australian dollars, making them easy to manage within an investment portfolio. Investors buy and sell TraCRs the same way they buy and sell other Australian securities.

At the time of writing, Cboe Australia traded TraCRs of the following US shares: AT&T, Alphabet, Amazon, Apple, Bank of America, Berkshire Hathaway, BlackRock, Boeing, Caterpillar, Cisco Systems, Coca-Cola, Costco, Disney, ExxonMobil, Facebook, General Electric, Gilead Sciences, IBM, Intel, JP Morgan Chase & Co., Johnson & Johnson, Lockheed Martin, Mastercard, McDonald's, Merck, Microsoft, NVIDIA, Netflix, Nike, Oracle, PayPal, PepsiCo, Pfizer, Procter & Gamble, Starbucks, Stryker, Tesla, Visa, Walmart and Zoom.

Another product that gives access to global shares is fund manager AtlasTrend's diversified portfolios, of ten to 15 major international shares each, with capitalisations of US$1 billion or more, built around three major 'trends', which are long-term structural investment themes that the manager believes have global impact and strong growth characteristics. At the time of writing, AtlasTrend offered the following such portfolios:

>> **Big Data Big:** This portfolio invests in areas such as technology, software, cloud computing, data centres, cybersecurity and networking. Examples of stocks held in this trend were Alphabet and Apple.

>> **Clean Disruption:** This invests in areas such as renewable energy, battery technology, electric vehicles, recycling and energy-efficient materials. Examples of stocks held in this trend were BYD Company and Vestas Wind Systems.

>> **Online Shopping Spree:** This invests in areas such as ecommerce retailers, logistics and online marketplaces. Examples of stocks held in this trend were Amazon and FedEx.

AtlasTrend makes global investment very easy, with minimum investment amounts of $1,000 (in one dollop) or $100 a month. Investment costs are 0.99 per cent a year, plus a 15 per cent performance fee if the investment makes a return above the MSCI World Net Total Return ex-Australia Index, in Australian dollars.

Dealing with currency risk

When you buy shares in another country, you need to consider the price of the shares and the exchange rate between your home currency and the currency of the country where you bought the shares.

REMEMBER

Currency volatility can substantially alter profits and losses on international shares. If you make a capital gain on foreign shares, what matters is what happens when you convert your profit to Australian dollars.

The currency risk posed by the A$ must always be factored into the decision to invest money overseas. But while the volatile A$ can potentially slash any gains made, it can also increase them, in the right circumstances.

WARNING

In essence, the currency effect on overseas investments can go one of four ways, doubling the risk of simply buying an overseas asset.

Say you have made a capital gain on some foreign shares. Here's what can happen because of currency movements:

>> If the currency in which the shares are quoted strengthens against the A$, your capital gain increases.

>> If it loses ground against the A$, your capital gain is less.

>> If your foreign shares fall in price, you hope that the foreign currency in which the shares are quoted rises against the A$, to offset some of your capital loss.

>> If the share price falls and the foreign currency weakens against the A$, you have copped a 'double-whammy' loss — the rise of the A$ has worsened your loss on the investment.

Currency has been a very important factor in overseas investing because of its remarkable volatility. After being floated on the foreign exchange markets in December 1983 — that is, the value of the A$ was set by the market, not a fixed daily value set by the Reserve Bank of Australia — the A$ has fluctuated from US$1.08 to a low of 47.75 US cents in April 2001, back to parity with the US$ again in October 2010, to a peak of US$1.10 in July 2011, retracting to 58 cents in March 2020, and back to 71 cents at the time of writing. Over that time the average exchange rate has been about 73 to 75 US cents.

For example, imagine you bought 100 Cisco Systems shares in August 2016, with the share price at US$30.87. The purchase cost US$3,087, which, with the A$ buying 76 US cents, cost you A$4,062.

Five years on, your Cisco shares are trading at $56.20, and you sell them, for a nice gain of 82 per cent. The Australian dollar has weakened to 71 cents, which nets you A$7,915 — boosting your gain in A$ to 95 per cent.

If the A$ had gone the other way, and strengthened by 5 US cents to 81 cents, your gain would have been cut to 70 per cent.

WARNING

Unless a foreign investment is *currency-hedged* — that is, its foreign-currency exposure is hedged back to Australian dollars, at a locked-in price — investors run the risk of the US$/A$ exchange rate affecting returns (this is known as *currency risk* — refer to Chapter 4 for more on currency risk). However, because most Australian investors hold at least 70 to 80 per cent of their assets in Australian dollars, many actually want exposure to currency fluctuation, seeing it as an extra layer of portfolio diversification. These investors want to include the relative performance of the foreign currency to the Australian currency as part of their investment strategy.

Without question, the fluctuations of the Australian currency can have a big effect on the returns earned on overseas shares. But over the long term, if you buy the right share, the capital gain on it should outweigh any currency detriment.

Although there are fluctuations, as Table 20-4 shows, over the longer term, the returns were reasonably similar. In periods when the Australian dollar is rising — for example, the rise from 68.85 US cents to 75.07 US cents over the year from 30 June 2020 to 30 June 2021 — investors would have been happy to pay the fee to hedge against the rise of the Australian dollar.

TABLE 20-4 **Effect of Currency Risk on International Share Investments (Percentage Returns as at 30 June 2021)**

	1 year	3 years	5 years	10 years	20 years	30 years
International shares (hedged)	37.7	15.4	15.4	12.4	7.2	8.4
International shares (unhedged)	28.1	15.1	15.3	15.5	5.7	8.8

Source: Andex Charts Pty Ltd

But to many investors these days, there is no distinction between Australian shares and international shares in their portfolios — the combination is, simply, their 'shares' allocation.

Chapter **21**

The Exotic World of Derivatives

ecause shares are financial assets, they lend themselves to the creation of financial entities called derivatives. *Derivatives* are financial instruments that derive their value from the price of something else. Different kinds of derivatives can be created based on the value of indices, currencies or commodity prices, or anything that has a numerical value — even, in the futures markets, the weather.

Share derivatives make a thriving market because they can be used for leveraged investment, outright speculation and even for insuring a share portfolio.

A leveraged, or *geared*, investment is one in which you control an asset of larger value than the amount you have actually invested. This may be done by borrowing money to make a larger investment rather than relying on your own funds, or by buying an asset by making a deposit. Both these leveraged situations increase your profit if the investment makes a gain, but they also magnify any loss.

In this chapter, I talk about the most common form of share derivatives, which are options and warrants, each of which gives you the right to buy or sell a certain amount of shares at a specified price at a future date.

Understanding Options and Warrants

With options, the underlying assets are shares, but derivatives can also be spun off indices, currencies or commodity prices; the warrants on the Australian Securities Exchange (ASX) cover all of these.

Holders of options and warrants don't have to buy the shares they're entitled to buy. The main reason for buying warrants is that they normally increase in value as the underlying share price rises (or falls). As the buyer spends only a fraction of the underlying share price, their leverage to the share price movement is far greater than if they owned the shares outright. By using a warrant, the investor can earn a much higher return than by buying the underlying shares.

WARNING

Whether you leverage an investment using share derivatives such as exchange-traded options (ETOs) and warrants, or the more sophisticated investment warrants, or you borrow to establish (or augment) a share portfolio, always remember that gearing is a two-edged strategy. If you get the share price movement wrong, you'll most likely lose money.

Exercising your options

An *option* gives you the right to buy or sell shares at a later date. Most options contracts are bought by investors who want to speculate in the options themselves rather than deal in the shares. Nothing's wrong with that, but options contracts require a level of understanding that's a step up from general sharemarket savvy. ETOs need to be distinguished from their less-exciting cousins, company options.

Trading in company options

REMEMBER

Companies often issue options that trade along with their shares on the stock exchange and carry the right, but not the obligation, to be converted into shares at a later date, on the payment of a certain price. If the options aren't converted, they lapse. Option holders don't receive a dividend and don't have a vote; they have only the option of becoming a shareholder in the future.

The price the option holder pays to convert the options to shares is known as the *exercise*, or *strike* price. Whether the options are worth converting depends on the share price. If the share price is above the exercise price when the options are due for conversion, option holders can buy the shares cheaply by exercising the options. If the share price is below the exercise price, the options are not worth converting because you're paying more money for the shares than you'd pay for them on the market.

Options can be issued at any time and a company may have multiple options issues outstanding. Often, when a company floats, it offers free options attached to the shares being sold through the prospectus as an added inducement to take up the shares.

TIP

Company-issued options are tradeable in the same way that ordinary shares are, and they're denoted by the letter O after the company's ASX code, or *ticker*. Subsequent issues of a new series of options then carry an additional letter starting with A, moving one letter forward for each additional issue (for example, OA, OB, OC, and so on). The expiry and strike price of each series will usually be different.

Companies issue options for a range of reasons. They may issue them for free, or at a nominal price to existing holders, so as to raise capital at some future time. They may issue them for free as part of a 'sweetener' during a capital raising, on a stated ratio to the shares held; they may also issue them as part of a bonus issue, or at the time of listing, to reward investors for holding the shares for a particular period.

Company options are a feature of many *employee share-ownership plans* (ESOPs) and are used by companies to attract, pay and retain executive staff. Options are issued over shares in the company, giving the employee the right to buy the shares in the future at a predetermined price (when the options are exercised).

Dealing in exchange-traded options

Exchange-traded options (ETOs) are contracts over parcels of underlying shares. ETOs aren't issued by the companies but are made available for trading by the stock exchange. In this case, the companies over whose shares the options are issued have no connection to the options trading.

TECHNICAL STUFF

Two kinds of ETO exist — a *call* and a *put*. A *call option* gives the buyer (or *taker*) the right to buy a specified number of shares on or before a specified date, at a predetermined price. A *put option* confers a similar right to sell (or *write*) the underlying shares under the same conditions. You can buy options, or sell them.

A call option is a punt that the underlying share will rise in value. Buyers of call options bet that the shares will rise; sellers bet that the shares will fall. A put option is a bet on a falling share — buyers gamble that the shares will fall; sellers gamble that the shares will rise. But even if you bet correctly on the share price direction, you can still lose if the price doesn't move far enough for your option to make money.

WARNING

Buyers of options contracts are not obliged to take up the right conferred on them, but the seller's (or writer's) side of the contract must be fulfilled if the option is exercised. This makes writing options far riskier than buying them.

On the ASX, each options contract controls 1,000 of the underlying shares. The contract sells for a fraction of the price of the shares, making options a *leveraged* investment, meaning the buyer has control over a large number of shares for a much smaller outlay than buying the shares directly. If you get the movement in the share price right, you get all the benefits of leverage — because your option controls a larger number of shares and the option price moves more dramatically than the price of the shares.

The purchase price of an options contract is known as the *premium*. The premium is expressed in terms of what it costs to secure the right to trade a single share, but the quoted price must be multiplied by 1,000 to arrive at the price of the actual contract. An option premium is made up of two parts. An option has *intrinsic value* when the share price is above the strike price (for a call), or below the strike price (for a put). If you have a call option with an exercise price of $6 and the shares are worth $7.50, the intrinsic value of the option is $1.50. The other part is the *time value*, which represents the chance that the option will be profitable before it expires. At expiry, the time premium is zero.

If you have an option that could be exercised now at a profit, it's said to be *in the money*. For a call option to be in the money, its strike price is below the share price; for a put option, its strike price is above the share price. In options, time is money because time has a value. In-the-money options are those that could be exercised now at a profit and have intrinsic (real) value. *Out-of-the-money* options have time value, whereby you are buying time to be right.

Only those options that are in the money are exercised because doing so is profitable. Exercising an in-the-money call means you buy a share for less than its market price and can sell it for a profit straight away. Exercising an in-the-money put option means that you are selling the shares for more than they're worth on the market. All other options lapse worthless. If an option expires worthless, its owner loses, but the writer of the option pockets the premium for which they sold it.

Timing your trade in options

To buy and sell options, you need some experience and knowledge of share prices. For example, if you think a share price is about to rise, you could buy a call option, hoping to obtain the stock for less than you believe it will be worth by the exercise time of the option. You could also write a put option, giving another investor the right to sell the stock to you at a cheaper price than what you think the share price will be by exercise time. If you think the share price is about to fall, you would do the reverse. You could buy a put option, establishing a selling price higher than you believe you could get by exercise time, or as a 'floor' should you decide to sell later. You could also write a call option, giving the taker of the option the right to buy the shares from you now, for more than you believe they will be worth at expiry.

REMEMBER

You can also use options to insure shares that you own against a fall in price. If you're worried at the prospect of your shares falling in price, you can buy a put option, which locks in a selling price. As the shares fall, your put option becomes more valuable. Alternatively, you can write call options over shares that you own, receiving a premium for doing so.

Recognising the highs and lows of options

If you're careful, you can keep buying and selling options and set up a nice cash flow that effectively makes your share portfolio work harder.

WARNING

If you get this strategy wrong, you could lose your shares.

The benefits

Options offer four main benefits to the private investor:

>> **Hedging:** You can protect a share portfolio against a price movement.

>> **Leverage:** You can buy control over a large number of shares with a comparatively small outlay.

>> **Speculation:** The price volatility of options, and the leverage involved, makes them ideal for short-term speculation. Traders can decide where a company's share price is heading and make quick money if they're right.

>> **Tax considerations:** If you think that a share price is going to fall but don't want to sell the shares because of capital gains tax (CGT), you can use options to benefit from the expected fall in the share price.

WARNING

Against these attractions is the fact that the options market is a dangerous place for the inexperienced and the unwary. You can make money quickly — but you can lose money just as easily.

The drawbacks

WARNING

The major risk in buying options is that the option can expire and be worthless, in which case you lose your entire investment. The risks are even greater if you write an options contract because your potential loss is unlimited. If you sell a call option, you could find yourself having to sell shares to the option buyer for much less than the market price. If you sell a put option, and it's exercised, you could theoretically have the shares put on you — meaning you have to buy them — at much more than the market price.

For each option contract, three outcomes are possible at expiry — the price of the underlying shares can rise, stay the same or fall. Option buyers lose on two of these possibilities and options writers win on two possibilities.

When you buy a call option, you lose if the underlying share price stays the same or falls. You also lose if you buy a put option and the underlying share price stays the same or rises. You can win when writing a call option if the share price falls or stays the same. With writing a put option, you win if the share price rises or stays the same.

WARNING

Clearly, then, writing options is better than buying them, right? Wrong. Repeat that word: Wrong! Writing options is much riskier than buying options because you must fulfil your obligation. When writing a call option, you risk being exercised against; that is, the buyer of the option calls away their shares and you have to sell at a lower price than you can sell on the market.

Writing a put option is definitely not for the faint-hearted, because you agree to buy a stock on a specific date for a price determined at the time of writing the option. If you're exercised against, you must buy the stock at that predetermined price. If the stock price falls in the meantime, bad luck! What's happened is that you sold someone the right to sell shares to you at a price higher than the market price. Unless you bought back your option, you must take the shares at the higher price.

Working through options transactions

You can get a better view of options transactions by following the market in options over the shares of an imaginary company, XYZ Limited. The month is September and the underlying security (that is, XYZ shares) is trading on the market at $5.

As shown in Table 21-1, XYZ has ten call options series on issue. You can identify options by type (put or call), stock, expiry dates of the options and strike price. All these options expire on the Thursday before the last business Friday in the quoted month, except occasionally when a public holiday intervenes. As one series expires, a new one is added, and so on, indefinitely.

Open interest shows how many contracts are alive in the market in this series. A healthy open interest means exactly the same as large volume in a particular share in the physical market. If you need to get out of your options position, the higher the open interest, the more likely it is that you can do so.

The Status column in Table 21-1 shows that some of these call options are in the money, because they offer the right to buy shares below the market price. In-the-money options have intrinsic (real) value. Some are out of the money, because the market price of the underlying shares is below the exercise price of the option (or above the exercise price, in the case of a put option).

REMEMBER

Out-of-the-money options have time value — you're buying time to be right. These options can't be exercised at a profit now, but the situation could change, depending on the share price, the closer they move to expiry. Some of the call options are at-the-money, meaning they could go either way. If they stay at-the-money, they expire worthless.

TABLE 21-1

XYZ Call Options

Month	Strike price ($)	Last sale ($)	Open Interest	Status
October	4.80	0.25	160	In
October	5.00	0.17	640	At
October	5.20	0.06	3,250	Out
October	5.40	0.03	2,350	Out
November	4.80	0.33	270	In
November	5.20	0.12	290	Out
November	5.40	0.08	120	Out
January	5.00	0.30	1,600	At
January	5.20	0.23	1,550	Out
January	5.60	0.10	440	Out

The most expensive call option at the moment is the November $4.80 calls, in which investors are buying the right to buy XYZ shares for $4.80 in November.

Table 21-2 shows the market in XYZ put options. Here, the options that are in the money offer the right to sell shares above the market price and the out-of-the-money options are those where the market price of the underlying shares is above the exercise price of the option.

Of the puts, the most expensive is the one that grants the right to sell XYZ shares at $5.60 in January. As long as XYZ stays below $5.60, this option is in the money. The further that XYZ drops below $5.60, the more valuable this option becomes.

TABLE 21-2

XYZ Put Options

Month	Strike price ($)	Last sale ($)	Open Interest	Status
October	4.80	0.08	1,020	Out
October	5.00	0.14	1,600	At
October	5.20	0.30	1,060	In
November	5.00	0.21	240	At
January	5.00	0.27	610	At
January	5.60	0.68	130	In
April	4.60	0.22	80	Out

Buying calls

The last sale price in Table 21-1 for the November $4.80 call options is 33 cents. This means that an investor who believes that XYZ will rise in price, and who wants the right to buy 1,000 XYZ shares for $4.80 apiece in November, is up for a premium of $330 a contract, plus brokerage and a small registration fee.

As long as XYZ stays above $4.80, this option is in the money. If XYZ rises in price, this option rises in price too, because buyers want an in-the-money option. The break-even price for the $4.80 call is $5.13 (the strike price plus the premium). Above this price, this option earns its holder $10 for every cent above $5.13.

At expiry, XYZ is trading at $6 and the options are trading for $1.20, having risen in price as the underlying stock appreciated. As the investor, you may exercise your options contract, and buy 1,000 XYZ shares at $4.80. With your initial $330 premium, your total cost is $5,130. You might then decide to sell these shares on the market at $6,000, making a profit of $870 on the transaction before costs.

That's if you want the shares. Alternatively, you could have traded the option at any time as it rose from 33 cents to $1.20. All you have done here is buy a certain form of security on the market at 33 cents and sell it later for a capital gain. Buying call options in this way, looking for leverage to a rise in the price of the underlying share, is the most basic options strategy.

Buy and write

Keep in mind that the *buy and write* strategy is often used by shareholders who want to generate extra income from their shares, but who don't want to part with their shares. For example, they may not want to incur capital gains tax by selling. In this case, you always have the risk of being exercised, or having to buy the option back if things look like going wrong.

You can lodge the shares with a broker and write call options over them. Because you own the shares, these are known as *covered calls*. The buyer of the call options has the right — but not the obligation — to buy the shares at an agreed price by a specified date. Lodging the shares means that no cash margin has to be put up. The shareholder takes the premium (the cost of the put option) but has agreed to sell the shares at a certain price to the option buyer. The consolation in this situation is that you've written an option with a strike price high enough to lock in a capital gain on the shares.

You're giving up the right to some of the upside, but you're being paid for that today. If you expect the share price to trade sideways, or rise slightly, over the life of the option, you can gain extra income on your shareholding.

The strike price you select will be based on where you think the share price will finish. Because you don't want to be exercised against — you want to keep the shares — you will choose an exercise price higher than where you think the share price will finish. The trade-off is that the further away the exercise price is from the share price, the less option premium you will receive.

Assume you own 5,000 XYZ shares and you write (sell) five $5.50 calls over your shares, and receive 5,000 × $0.10, or $500. Your break-even point is $5.60, which is your effective sale price. If XYZ doesn't reach $5.50, the option expires worthless — you've pocketed the $500, kept the shares and can do it again. But if XYZ rises through your strike price, the buyer of the call option you sold will want the shares. To keep the shares, you have to buy the option back (not literally, but a similar option) in the market. You may lose money doing this, but you're making money on the stock rising.

When the share price goes above the exercise price — if this happens — and you don't want to sell the shares, you have to buy back the option. If you don't want to sell the stock, you simply roll the option up and out — that is, a higher strike, and longer-dated. The higher the strike price of the call options you write above the current market price, the less likely that your shares will be called away. You can roll out this strategy indefinitely by writing new options. But if you're exercised early, and you don't want to lose the shares, you have to buy other shares to deliver to the call holder.

The covered-call strategy forfeits uncertain potential upside in exchange for assured current income. This strategy can therefore improve returns and reduce volatility relative to an equivalent share portfolio in falling, flat or slowly rising markets, in which strike prices are not being exercised.

In effect, the covered-call strategy is expected to perform in the following manner:

>> **Bull market:** An investor will likely underperform an equivalent share portfolio, as they will keep the option premium but forfeit some of the upside.

>> **Flat market:** The investor will likely outperform an equivalent share portfolio as they will benefit from the added option premium, while there is little portfolio upside to sacrifice.

>> **Bear market:** The investor will likely outperform an equivalent share portfolio as the option premium will offset some of the loss of value in the share portfolio.

For more income-focused portfolios, the added income from the option premium can be useful, particularly when traditional income-generating investments such as bonds are falling short of investors' needs in a low-interest-rate environment.

TIP

The covered-call strategy doesn't really suit a small retail shareholding; if you're not able to do at least five contracts at a time (that is, you own at least 5,000 shares), the amount of premium income is arguably not worth the trouble. But it can suit a self-managed superannuation fund very well.

The strategy works just as well with index options, which are offered over the S&P/ASX 200 index (ASX code: XJO), the sharemarket's main benchmark index. A similar strategy can be applied using ETOs over the SPDR S&P/ASX 200 ETF (exchange-traded fund), which has an ASX code of STW. Instead of a strike price, index options have a *strike level*, which is a certain index level, expressed in points. Investors who own a portfolio of stocks benchmarked to an index can sell a call option over that index to bring in income, as well as cushion the portfolio from some downside risk.

The ASX says buying-and-writing is the most common trade that retail investors use in the options market. It's also commonly used by institutions to add value to their shareholdings. The ASX has also introduced an index to track this strategy — see the nearby sidebar 'The Buy Write index' for more.

THE BUY WRITE INDEX

In May 2004, the ASX introduced the S&P/ASX 200 Buy Write index, designed to track the buy and write strategy and give share fund managers who use it to augment their portfolio returns a benchmark against which to measure their performance. The underlying index is the S&P/ASX 200 Accumulation index (which counts all dividends as reinvested); over this, each quarter, an S&P/ASX 200 index call option is sold. The strategy writes (sells) at-the-money index call options each quarter, on the day of expiry.

Writing calls over stock held has been a better strategy than buying-and-holding shares alone. Since inception, the S&P/ASX 200 Buy Write index has generated a return of 8.2 per cent a year, versus 8 per cent a year for the S&P/ASX 200 Accumulation index (which counts dividends) and 3.5 per cent a year for the S&P/ASX 200 Index (which counts only share price gain).

Just as importantly, the total risk (annualised volatility) of the Buy Write portfolio has been significantly lower than that of the Accumulation index portfolio, at 12.4 per cent a year compared to 17 per cent a year. In simple terms, the index shows that investors could have *increased* their overall returns and *lowered* the volatility of those returns by using the Buy Write strategy.

The Buy Write approach best suits a market that is trading sideways to slightly higher, because essentially what you are doing by selling the call option is giving up some of the upside potential for payment now. But using the strategy in a rising market is difficult because of the increased possibility of the shares being called away. Buy Write is not a 'set and forget' strategy.

In November 2012, ETF issuer BetaShares issued its BetaShares Australian Top 20 Equity Yield Maximiser Fund exchange-traded managed fund (ASX code: YMAX), which runs a covered-call strategy to enhance the dividend income from a portfolio of the top 20 ASX shares by market capitalisation. In September 2104, BetaShares then issued a similar product over the S&P 500 index, the S&P 500 Yield Maximiser Fund (ASX code: UMAX). Both of these stocks represent a way for investors to participate in options strategies through a listed vehicle.

REMEMBER

A LOSER FOR EVERY WINNER

If you write an options contract, for the life of that contract you have a potential obligation to the market because the taker of the option may exercise their side. At the end of each trading day, the Options Clearing House (a part of the ASX) calculates a *margin*, an amount necessary to ensure that you can meet that obligation. You may have to pay a margin call to keep your option position open. In effect, you put up collateral in order to cover a potential loss.

Options is a *zero-sum game*, meaning that if you make a profit on a contract, someone else makes the equivalent loss. This means that every option that is traded on the market is covered by a margin. Truly, in options trading, you have no gain without pain — but at least it's somebody else's.

Writing naked calls

WARNING

When you write call options against shares you don't own, you're said to be writing *naked calls*. If you're exercised against, you may have to buy the shares on the market to deliver them at the strike price. You have your premium income, but you'll incur a loss if the share price rises above the strike price. When this happens, you make the same loss if you deliver shares or buy back the option.

Because you may have to buy the shares in the market to make delivery if you're exercised early, this strategy is a risky one — as the share price rises, your potential loss escalates and, in theory, this potential loss is unlimited! In fact, you'll have a hard time convincing a broker to let you write naked calls — because if you blow-up, it's the broker that needs to stump up the losses to the exchange.

Buying puts for protection

You can get insurance for your share portfolio by buying put options over shares. These options give you the right to sell shares for a higher price than you think the market price will be at exercise time. If the shares go above the strike price, you've effectively bought insurance. With call options, you don't know the intention of the buyer, who can take the shares. Buying put options gives you the right to decide on the disposal of the shares and you won't lose your shareholding if things go wrong.

For example, assume you bought 1,000 shares of XYZ at $3 a share and you've watched it rise to $5. You're worried about a fall. Working from the figures given in Table 21-2, buying an XYZ $4.60 put for $220 gives you the right to sell the shares for $4.60, which gives you a substantial capital gain. If the share price falls, and you want to keep the shares, you can sell the put at a profit. If the share price rises, you may lose your put premium, but this means your capital gain on the shares is increasing. You can keep up this strategy indefinitely by buying new puts.

Writing puts

If you don't believe that XYZ will fall in price, again, looking at Table 21-2, you could write a put option for April at $4.60. For 5,000 of these, the premium you'll receive is 5,000 × $0.22, or $1,100. You're now exposed to possibly having to buy $23,000 worth of XYZ shares (5,000 × $4.60).

Your gamble will pay off if XYZ stays serenely above $4.60 for the life of your option. But if the market suffers a correction during the life of your option and XYZ falls to $3, you have sold someone the right to dump $23,000 worth of shares on you, which you would only be able to sell for $15,000. In this case, your $1,100 worth of premium would be of little comfort. To get out of this bind, you would have to buy the option back, at a loss because it would have been increasing in value as XYZ shares fell. With writing puts, you can lose more than the premium you receive if the shares fall significantly.

Trading in the World of Warrants

Warrants share many of the same characteristics of options. Warrants are issued by third parties, financial institutions approved by the ASX. As in the options market, the companies over whose shares the warrants are issued have no connection to the warrant trading.

Like options, warrants are bought and sold through a broker, in the same way that shares are. However, if you want to transact in warrants or options, you will have to sign a one-time extra agreement form with your broker to show that you understand the risks of these leveraged products.

Investing in trading warrants

Trading warrants is the name given to the basic warrants over listed shares that trade on the ASX. These warrants represent the right to buy or sell a share at some future time, at a certain price. The main difference between trading warrants and ETOs is that trading warrants are issued by financial institutions, whereas ETOs are created by (and quoted on) the ASX.

Unlike options, some warrants can remain open for years. Trading warrants can be exercised at any time up to and including the expiry date, and the exercise is always at the choice of the warrant holder, not the issuer.

Like option holders, warrant holders don't receive dividends. Depending on the structure, you can use a call warrant or a put warrant, and go *long* (benefit from a rising price in the underlying asset) or *short* (benefit from a falling price in the underlying asset). Call warrants benefit from an upward price movement in the underlying instrument, whereas put warrants benefit from a downward trend. But unlike ETOs, you cannot write (sell) a warrant.

On the ASX, you have trading warrants and investment warrants. *Trading-style warrants* are frequently traded and are generally short-dated. Typically, they are also more highly leveraged — up to about 95 per cent (that is, the investor funds 5 per cent of the purchase). *Investment-style warrants* tend to be longer-dated, have lower leverage (in the range of 30–80 per cent) and are less frequently traded. They have a lower risk/return profile and often have a higher initial outlay compared to trading-style warrants. Both styles of warrant combine gearing/leverage with the potential to only lose the initial premium you paid. The later section 'Graduating to Investment Warrants' covers these types of warrants in more detail.

REMEMBER

Call warrants give you the right — but not the obligation — to buy shares at some time in the future, for a predetermined exercise (or strike) price. In the future, when you want to take up the right to buy the shares, you can exercise the warrant. *Put warrants* carry the right (but not the obligation) to sell shares at a certain price in the future. When you buy the put warrant, you lock in the price at which you can sell the shares. You buy put warrants when you think that the share price will fall. The initial cost of the warrant depends on the current price of the underlying share, its volatility, the exercise price and the time to expiry.

Because warrants are leveraged, they take on some risk. Just as the warrant price will outperform the underlying share if the share price rises, the loss is magnified when the share price falls. In this case, the buyer of the warrant can lose their investment. Unlike options, warrants are not standardised; the *conversion ratio* (the number of warrant contracts per share) differs between warrants. The issuer of the warrant is a bank (Citi is by far the biggest issuer on the ASX), not the companies whose shares are involved. The institution stands behind its warrants, but if it goes under, warrant holders can lose their investment.

Warrants attract two kinds of investor:

>> The investor who has a longer-term view on the stock than can be satisfied in the options market; by buying longer-dated warrants, such as *instalment* warrants, they want to make a geared investment while limiting the downside to the amount they invest.

>> The short-term speculator, who wants to make a quick profit using leverage and volatility.

Tracking the index

Index warrants are the same as trading warrants, except that they give you the right to buy or sell the notional basket of shares that makes up the ASX's S&P/ASX 200 index. This is as close as you can come to buying the entire market, because the index closely tracks the performance of the vast bulk of the market.

TECHNICAL STUFF

Since an index doesn't have a price, index warrants set an exercise level (at a point value of the index) rather than an exercise price. For example, instead of a warrant to buy one share of National Australia Bank at, say, $28, an index warrant may have an exercise level of, say, 7,000 points on the S&P/ASX 200. With a call warrant, it is in the money if the index rises above this level; with a put warrant, it is in the money if the index falls below 7,000 points.

Index call warrants allow investors to profit if the level of the index rises, while put warrants allow investors to profit if the index falls. You can buy a call warrant (the right to buy) if you think that the market is set to rise. When you're pessimistic about where the market is heading, you can buy a put warrant (the right to sell).

Index warrants can also be used as a means of hedging the risk being run in owning a share portfolio. Buying a put index warrant gives you an asset that rises in value when the market falls, compensating for the drop in the value of your portfolio. If the market rises sharply, you can lose the amount you paid for the warrant; however, that's the insurance cost, and your share portfolio benefits from the rise.

You settle index warrants by cash, since you can't buy an index. On exercise, the holder of an index call warrant will receive an amount of cash for the amount, if any, by which the index exceeds the exercise level. If the index is below the exercise level on exercise, no cash settlement is paid. On exercise, the holder of an index put warrant will receive an amount of cash for the amount by which the index is below the exercise level. If the index is above the exercise level, no cash is paid.

Put warrants can act as an insurance policy as they guarantee a minimum value for the underlying security — in this case, the index. Should the market fall, the value of the portfolio will fall with it, but this loss can be either partially or fully offset by the appreciation of the put warrants. On the ASX, index warrants are traded over the S&P/ASX 200 index.

The mighty MINI

By far the major warrant product is the MINI. *MINIs* are open-ended warrants with no expiry date, offering leveraged exposure to either rising or falling markets. They are issued by Citi, and trade on both the ASX and Cboe Australia. MINIs are available over a wide range of shares, indices, currencies (for example, A$/US$, A$/Euro) and commodities (such as oil and gold), and are used for leveraged trading on rising or falling markets.

MINI warrants are classified as either 'long' (buying) or 'short' (selling), enabling the investor to benefit either from the rising or falling price of an underlying instrument.

MINI longs (similar to calls) offer exposure to rising markets, while *MINI shorts* (similar to puts) give traders the opportunity to profit from falling markets, and can also be used to hedge existing positions. MINIs allow investors to track the value of an underlying asset on a *one-for-one basis* — that is, the MINI moves cent-for-cent with the underlying asset — for a small up-front outlay. For any share over which MINIs are traded, there will be a range of MINIs offered on the market, all with different levels of leverage.

MINIs have an in-built *stop-loss* that limits any losses to the MINI price you pay on the ASX/Cboe Australia to open a trading position. The stop-loss is set above the strike price for MINI longs and below the strike price for MINI shorts. This feature ensures that investors cannot lose more than the original amount they put in. With no set expiry dates, MINIs can give the investor exposure to a trading position for a time that suits them, without the need to 'roll' maturities (enter a new position when one expires) like other derivatives. Investors have the flexibility to trade *intra-day* (within a single day) or hold for as long as they wish to maintain their exposure.

REMEMBER

MINIs can be exercised at any time; they are settled by cash. Since MINIs have no fixed expiry date and are open-ended, they are a low-maintenance leveraged instrument that minimises the hassle of expiries and rollovers.

The value of a MINI long or MINI short varies depending on the underlying investment to which you are gaining exposure, but generally it will be equal to the difference between the share price and the strike price. For example, if you have a single-stock MINI long, its value is the share price minus the strike price; however, if you're holding a single-stock MINI short, its value is the strike price minus the share price.

For example, say BHP is trading at $40 and an investor believes it will rise in price. Instead of buying BHP shares, the investor buys a BHP MINI long with a strike price of $37. The MINI price is $3 — the investor buys 1,000 units, outlaying $3,000.

BHP subsequently rises to $41. The MINI long still has a strike price of $37, so it is now worth $4. The investor sells the 1,000 units of their MINI long, fetching $4,000.

If the investor had bought the shares, the profit on the move to $41 would be $1, or 2.5 per cent. But having bought the MINI long, the investor's profit is $1,000, or 33.33 per cent. The potential loss on the BHP share is $40; the potential loss on the MINI long is $3.

Because holding a MINI short gives you exposure to the share price falling, it can help you hedge your underlying shares without having to sell them. You have an asset that rises in price as the shares fall, protecting you, to some extent, against a fall in the market.

To buy a MINI, you need to pay a fraction of the share price up-front. The strike price of a MINI is set daily. You also need to consider the funding costs of MINIs, which cover the cost of holding the stock position overnight; this funding cost is added to the strike price before trading opens the following morning, meaning that the strike price will change each day. If the investor buys and sells the MINI on the same trading day (intra-day), the funding cost won't come into the equation.

You don't have to pay for funding costs up-front — interest costs are added to the strike price daily for MINI longs, or a credit is received for MINI shorts (although as interest rates fell to record lows in recent years, the funding cost aspect became much less important).

Holders of MINI longs don't physically receive the dividends paid by the underlying shares, but they 'earn' the amount of the dividend, in their MINI prices. In contrast, holders of MINI shorts effectively 'pay' the amount of the dividend. On the day that the underlying shares trade ex-dividend, the issuer will adjust the MINI price for the dividend, to offset the theoretical fall in the share price that takes place on the ex-dividend date. Say the Commonwealth Bank (CBA) pays a $2 dividend. When CBA goes 'ex'-dividend (the dividend amount comes out of the share price), if you are holding a MINI long, the issuer will adjust your MINI price by $2. If you are holding a MINI short, the opposite happens; the adjustment makes your MINI value less by the amount of the dividend.

With index MINIs, an index multiplier figure is used to convert the underlying index level to a dollar amount; if you're trading an international index, currency or commodities MINI, the foreign exchange rate will also affect the value at any time.

Index MINIs are also traded over the Dow Jones Industrial Average, the S&P 500 index and the Nasdaq 100 indices of the US sharemarket, the Nikkei 225 index of the Japanese sharemarket, and the Hang Seng Index of the Hong Kong sharemarket.

Citi, the dominant (virtually only) MINI issuer, says the turnover in MINIs is about $20 million a day; because its MINI 'book' is on average about 80 per cent leveraged, that equates to about $100 million worth of notional underlying turnover a day. For example, if CBA is trading at $100 and you buy the stock through a warrant with an 80 per cent loan, your warrant costs you $20 and your final payment is $80; when you trade the warrant, you have traded $20 in the warrants market (as turnover), but the notional exposure traded is $100.

Graduating to Investment Warrants

Investment warrants are designed to allow investors to trade on their estimation of where share prices, indices, currencies and commodities are heading, but using less leverage than trading warrants.

Investment warrants typically go for five years, but some of them go for longer than ten years, with the longest term being 15 years. They offer long-term leveraged exposure to the underlying shares, but as well as being longer-dated than trading warrants, they are also less frequently traded, with a lower risk/return profile.

Instalment warrants

The dominant product in the investment warrant marketplace is the *instalment warrant*, which is very similar to the instalment receipts used in all the portions of the sharemarket float of Telstra in 1997, 1999 and 2006 (refer to Chapter 13), and the third (of three) tranches (portions) of the CBA float in 1996. As in the Telstra and CBA third-tranche floats, a portion of the stock's value is paid up-front and the rest later. In an instalment warrant, the split is usually about 50 per cent of the share's (or ETF's) current value paid on purchase and the rest later, although some instalment warrants represent 30 per cent of the overall purchase price.

An instalment warrant incorporates a limited recourse loan, which is used to buy the stock together with the initial capital amount paid up-front. Even though you pay only a portion of the share's value, you receive all the benefits of stock ownership, including franking credits and entitlements to dividends. This means that for lower capital outlay, investors are able to magnify their capital gains as well as income.

Hundreds of instalment warrants are traded on the ASX, issued by the bank issuers (mainly Citi) over shares and ETFs. Although there are no index instalment warrants, investors can use instalment warrants over index ETFs — for example, the SPDR S&P/ASX 200 ETF or the iShares S&P 500 ETF A$ — to achieve the same effect.

The instalment warrant is a limited recourse loan because if the warrant holder defaults on the final payment, the issuer's only recourse is to sell the shares held on trust to meet the loan obligations.

The first instalment is paid up-front and is composed of a capital component, pre-paid interest and a borrowing fee. The first payment depends on the underlying share price, volatility of the market, time to maturity and prevailing interest rates.

You can sell the warrant at any time on the ASX. At the end of the warrant's term, there is a second, fixed payment that you can choose to make, after which you own the shares. If the shares have risen in price, you have a capital gain that approximately reflects the change in the share's value from when you first bought the instalment warrant.

The risk is that in the meantime, the share price has fallen; however, you're under no obligation to make the second payment or take delivery of the shares on the final instalment date, and in this scenario, you would not do so. You would simply walk away from the loan, and you can buy the shares on the market at a lower price if you wish to do so.

TIP

Because an instalment warrant is technically a loan for the purpose of producing assessable income (share dividends or real estate investment trust distributions), the interest cost (included in the first payment) can be claimed as a tax deduction in the year that it is incurred.

The warrant issuer may find itself saddled with shares that have fallen in value. When the issuer sells instalment warrants in the market, the investor buys the shares, which sit in trust for them; the investor receives a limited recourse loan from the issuer and also buys from the issuer a put option over the underlying shares, which gives the investor the right to sell the shares back to the issuer. The limited recourse nature of the loan and the put option enable the investor to walk away from the loan should they wish to do so. The issuer simply packages this structure together and sells it.

Instalment warrants are popular with the nation's self-managed super funds (SMSFs), as they represent one of the few ways that leverage can be used in an SMSF. This is allowed because it is a limited recourse loan. Instalment warrants are often used to build a portfolio of blue-chip shares and ETFs.

Instalment MINIs are also offered, providing investors with straightforward and transparent leveraged exposure to Australia's leading companies and ETFs. Designed for individuals and SMSFs seeking medium- to long-term exposure, investors gain the economic benefits of share ownership, including dividends and available franking credits, for a small portion of the cost of buying the shares outright. No margin calls or credit checks are required with MINIs and, importantly, investors are unable to lose more than their original investment amount.

An instalment MINI will typically involve two separate payments — the first instalment (which gives the holder the benefits of share ownership) and the second instalment, which is the loan amount plus interest on the loan. Instalment MINIs have an embedded stop-loss feature that ensures that the final instalment, or loan amount, is non-recourse in nature, which means that the investor cannot lose more than their initial investment amount.

Depending on individual circumstances, the interest expenses and borrowing fees incurred when buying an instalment MINI may be eligible for tax deductions.

Gearing into the dividend

Because an instalment warrant carries full entitlement to the dividend and any franking credits attached to the underlying share — which is a unique feature in the warrant world — investors like the opportunity of gearing into the dividends of high-yielding stocks to enhance the yield they receive.

TECHNICAL STUFF

Effectively, instalment warrant investors wanting to gear into dividends must buy the instalment warrants before the ex-dividend date, and then are limited only by the '45-day rule', which states that investors who receive more than $5,000 worth of franking credits in a tax year must hold the shares (or the instalment warrant) for 45 days (plus the day of purchase and of sale) to receive the associated franking credits.

Within this requirement, the most popular use of instalment warrants is to *gear into* a dividend. Investors buy instalment warrants over a dividend-paying share holding them long enough to 'harvest' the dividend, which boosts the effective yield of that dividend significantly as the investor outlays only part of the purchase price of the shares — and the yield is already augmented by the franking credits. Dividend harvesting is popular because while most of the big dividend-paying stocks — for example, CBA, Telstra and, more recently, the big miners BHP, Rio Tinto and Fortescue Metals — pay dividends in March and September after declaring them in their results for the December 31 and June 30 half-year periods, Westpac, ANZ Banking Group and National Australia Bank pay dividends on a different schedule. These three companies have a financial year that ends on 30 September, and they pay interim dividends (for the period ending 31 March) in June/July and final dividends (for the period ending 30 September) in December/January.

Instead of owning CBA shares for the full 12 months (collecting two dividends in March and September) and owning Westpac for the full 12 months (collecting two dividends in June and December), instalment warrants allow investors to harvest a dividend by holding the warrant for two to three months — and to 'switch' that instalment warrant four times a year, enabling them to pick up payments from both the June 30 balance-date stocks and the September 30 balance-date stocks.

Self-funding instalments

In self-funding instalment warrants (SFIs), the dividends are used to reduce the loan amount, and annual interest is capitalised (added to the loan amount). They suit investors wanting low-maintenance leveraged exposure to shares and ETFs.

The investor makes a first payment, which is about half the price of the underlying share. They are then entitled to all dividends and franking credits. The dividends are used to reduce the second payment. Once a year, interest is added to the loan balance. With conservative gearing —say, 50 per cent — most SFIs are positively geared, meaning that the annual interest cost is less than the annual cash dividends.

At maturity, investors have the flexibility to pay the final instalment and receive the underlying shares or ETF units, or walk away from their investment, receiving the residual value remaining in the investment. The second payment is optional — losses are limited to the first payment.

SFIs allow an investor to 'lock in' a conservatively geared investment in shares and ETFs for up to five years. Once they have bought the SFI, investors don't have to outlay any more cash until maturity. SFIs have no margin calls, so fluctuations in the share price during the term of the investment won't result in an obligation to inject more cash.

SFIs are typically geared at about 50 per cent, and may be a positively geared investment, where the forecast dividends are expected to be greater than the interest charged on an annual basis. You can still pre-pay the interest up to 12 months in advance, but you won't receive any tax benefits for doing so.

The benefit you're getting is that you're locking in five to ten years of geared exposure to a good-quality stock, with no requirement for ongoing payments. The interest and future pre-paid interest components are added to the loan on an annual basis. Dividends are retained by the issuer and reinvested back into the instalment structure to repay the loan outstanding.

TIP

Most SFIs on the market offer five- to ten-year terms. Self-funding instalments suit long-term investors — they allow you to take the dividends that you receive to pay off your loan component, over a long period of time. As long as your dividends are more than your loan costs, you can own the shares without having to make the second payment. Sometimes, better-than-expected dividends, special dividends and corporate actions (such as capital returns) can pay off the second payment early, and the investors receive the shares unencumbered.

Some instalment MINIs are also structured to be self-funding. The MINI holder won't receive any dividends or special dividends payable in relation to the underlying shares — they will be applied to reduce the final instalment payment.

Chapter **22**

Leverage and Speculation

s well as patient long-term wealth appreciation, the sharemarket offers leverage and speculation opportunities aplenty. *Leveraging* means using borrowed money to invest in the sharemarket, a tactic that can magnify your gains — but also your losses. Leverage can be very risky and bring a matching level of return, but it can also be put to work in a far more sober and reliable fashion, with a handy tax benefit as well.

In this chapter, I discuss how a lot of the risk has been taken out of leveraging into shares with the introduction of capital-protected lending, but the interest rate has increased to reflect this protection. Alternatively, investors can utilise the speculative vehicle of contracts for difference (CFDs). Both are simple in concept and potentially profitable if you know what you're doing. But remember — just because something is easy to do, it doesn't mean it's easy to get it right!

Leveraging through Margin Lending

Margin lending is another way of leveraging a sharemarket investment, by borrowing money to buy more shares — Australian or global — exchange-traded funds (ETFs) or managed fund units than you can afford. To many, this might sound terrifying, but the concept should be very familiar to most Australian investors since it's how most people buy their first house. Taking out a loan to buy shares is similar to taking out a home mortgage, the only difference being that the house doesn't have a sign out the front showing its value fluctuating every minute, and you don't have the daily prospect of a visit from your nervous banker. Oh, and perhaps one more difference — you can't live in a share portfolio.

Borrowing to buy shares

When you take out a home mortgage, you're making a geared investment in property — you're using a bank loan to make a larger investment than would be possible using your own funds alone. You make a deposit, the bank lends you the rest of the money to buy the house, and over the years you pay off the principal and the interest until you own the house outright.

Gearing a share portfolio is exactly the same. You borrow money to buy a larger portfolio of shares than you could otherwise buy; also, with a larger amount of money to invest, you can use the extra funds to diversify your investment portfolio more broadly than before. Investors may contribute cash or an existing portfolio in order to borrow the funds. You gain access to a tax-effective source of funding to buy assets that will hopefully increase in capital value. Because your investment is geared, both profits and losses are magnified. Lenders won't lend on every share; they keep a list of approved securities, which will generally be from the non-speculative end of the sharemarket. The shares (or ETFs or managed fund units) are used as *collateral*, or security for the loan.

Assume that you have $30,000 in cash and you borrow $70,000 from a margin lender to buy a share portfolio worth $100,000. This portfolio is said to be geared to 70 per cent. In other words, you have $30,000 worth of equity in the portfolio, and the loan-to-value ratio (LVR) is 70 per cent. The margin is $30,000.

If the value of the portfolio increases by 20 per cent to $120,000, your equity in the portfolio rises from $30,000 to $50,000, an increase of two-thirds, without any effort on your part. That's the good side of leveraged investment. On the other hand, a decrease in the value of the portfolio ratchets up the fall in your equity. If the sharemarket goes down and the value of the portfolio falls by 10 per cent, to $90,000, your equity falls to $20,000 (the difference between what you borrowed, $70,000, and what the portfolio is now worth), which is a decline of one-third.

As the borrower, you own the shares and are fully entitled to all dividends and bonuses. Because a margin loan is for the purpose of earning assessable (taxable) income, the interest payments on that loan are fully tax deductible. You can claim the whole of the annual pre-paid interest bill, for up to 12 months ahead, as a tax deduction in the current year. Interest can also be paid in arrears. Your interest costs may be covered by the share dividends.

Most margin loans are interest-only, meaning you only have to service the interest and don't have to make regular loan repayments, and they can have variable or fixed interest rates. At the time of writing, a margin loan will cost you between 4.82 per cent and 6.04 per cent, depending on the terms you choose. If you pay the bank in advance (so you can claim a tax deduction early), you will pay less in interest than if you paid in arrears (which is how you make your mortgage repayments).

REMEMBER

The magnifying effect that leverage has on capital gain increases with the amount of leverage used. However, leverage also magnifies capital losses.

WARNING

If the shares fall in value, you may be asked to sell some shares or deposit more cash to bring the margin back to an acceptable level. This is known as a *margin call* and protects the lender if your investment drops in value (see the nearby sidebar 'Meeting a margin call'). Generally, you will only have 24 hours to correct the situation.

Most lenders will provide a *buffer* — if the value of the security falls and the loan value exceeds the limit by only a few percentage points, the account is 'in the buffer' and no action is required. The buffer will be 5 per cent (10 per cent for some lenders). This allows you to absorb small market fluctuations without triggering a margin call. However, when the loan balance exceeds the limit by more than the buffer, action is required. These days, a margin call should not come as a surprise. The margin lenders provide real-time calculators and simulation tools of position and gearing ratios, and other risk management tools.

When a margin call is made, the borrower must do one of three things:

>> Provide additional cash so that the LVR is restored

>> Lodge additional shares to increase the loan limit

>> Sell part of their portfolio and use the proceeds to repay part of the loan

Typically, borrowers will settle margin calls by putting in extra cash. A margin call can be alarming, but another way to look at it is that it forces you to address the situation while you still have equity left. A margin call focuses your attention on deciding whether or not the securities are worth holding on to — which can be a good thing. You receive a margin call if the shares are falling, which is a big test of your investment case for holding those shares.

WARNING

If you don't have the cash to meet a margin call, you may be forced into selling your shares at possibly the lowest point of the downturn, just when the shares are poised to rebound.

The possibility of a margin call tells you that the leverage you're using can go wrong. Like all leverage, a margin loan can be dangerous if the user doesn't understand it. There's a lovely quote from one of my favourite investment books, Fred Schwed Jr's *Where Are the Customers' Yachts?* (see Chapter 24), from 1940, in which the author uses the analogy of a short rail journey in New York City to describe the feeling of holding a margin loan in a falling market: 'They got on the Twentieth Century Limited at Grand Central Station. They only intended to ride as far as 125th Street, where they would get off and visit Grandma. But the first thing they knew they were making seventy miles an hour through Fort Wayne, Indiana.'

My own analogy is that leverage is like a chainsaw — it's dangerous if you don't know how to use it. But if you do know how to use (and control) the chainsaw, it can be very handy. I'm happy for leverage to be available to those who do know how to use it.

Most lenders have no minimum loan amount. This means that even small investors can use margin loans in the hope of leveraging their gains. The amount that you can borrow depends on the securities in your portfolio, their LVR and a credit limit based on an assessment of your financial position. The LVR on which your lender will lend depends on the combination of investments you want to buy, as the lender will assess some stocks differently (depending on whether you want to buy them alone or in combination with others).

Generally, individuals are not charged establishment fees on a margin loan. Some lenders also charge a fee for each transaction through the margin loan, or for transactions over a set limit. If you happen to cancel your loan within the first three, six or 12 months of taking out the loan, additional fees may apply.

Most of the online brokers offer a margin loan linked to an online broking account, and some margin lenders offer a specific limited recourse borrowing arrangement (LRBA) margin loan for self-managed super funds (SMSFs). The only way that SMSFs can borrow to invest is through an LRBA, which ensures that the lender only has recourse to the shares bought with the loan — the lender cannot have any claim over any other assets owned by the SMSF. National Australia Bank's Super Lever product is an example of a lending product that allows SMSFs to borrow money to invest in shares, ETFs and managed funds, albeit with a smaller approved securities list on which it will lend compared to a normal margin loan.

MEETING A MARGIN CALL

Gearing magnifies the investment returns on the portfolio. Say you have $30,000 to invest, and you borrow $70,000 from a margin lender to buy a share portfolio worth $100,000. Borrowing 70 per cent of the portfolio value will effectively produce percentage gains or losses that are 3.3 times the level of an ungeared portfolio. Now imagine that the value of the portfolio falls to $90,000. With $70,000 borrowed and the portfolio worth $90,000, the loan-to-value ratio (LVR) has climbed to 78 per cent. The lender will ask for the LVR ratio to be restored to 70 per cent (in other words, the margin to be restored to 30 per cent), which means the equity must rise to $27,000. You receive a margin call to pay this $7,000. If you can't meet a margin call, the lender will sell the shares and you'll still owe the lender money. Other ways of meeting a margin call are to buy more shares to raise the portfolio's value, or to sell some shares to raise cash to lower the loan amount.

With a conservatively geared portfolio, however, the likelihood of a margin call lessens considerably. A portfolio geared to 70 per cent will enter margin call territory if the sharemarket falls by just 6.7 per cent. Gearing a portfolio to 60 per cent means the portfolio will need to fall by one-fifth in value to incur a margin call. Gearing to 50 per cent means a 33 per cent buffer; if the portfolio is geared to 40 per cent, the market would need to fall by 45 per cent before a margin call would be made.

Of course, the market has fallen by as much as 54 per cent before — as the Australian market did between November 2007 and February 2009. More recently, of course, the Australian market plunged by 36.5 per cent in early 2020, in just 22 trading days. But even in these extreme market falls, leveraged investors who had been conservative with their gearing weren't burned. According to the Reserve Bank of Australia, when the credit crunch hit in late 2007, investors had, on average, borrowed half of their credit limit — which tempered the pain of a market slump substantially. For example, an investor whose portfolio had a maximum LVR of 70 per cent but who had actually borrowed to an LVR of 30 per cent could have coped with a 60 per cent fall in sharemarket prices before incurring a margin call. The most recent RBA statistics available (to the end of June 2021) show that investors, on average, are borrowing about 58 per cent of their credit limit, and that the aggregate LVR of the margin lending 'book' was 21.5 per cent.

Margin lending has had an interesting couple of decades. According to Reserve Bank of Australia (RBA) data, in 2000, just 84,000 investors had borrowed $7 billion; activity ballooned over the 2000s, to a peak of $41.6 billion worth of loans, in December 2007, held by 248,000 investors. But the dire market fall associated with the global financial crisis (GFC), and a resultant rise in margin calls — the number of margin calls reached a record high of 8.6 a day per 1,000 borrowers in December 2008 — brought activity down substantially. By December 2016, just

$10.7 billion had been borrowed by 130,000 client accounts. The low point of participation was reached in June 2019, when just 98,000 borrowers were active, with loans worth $11.1 billion in total.

By June 2021, borrower numbers were still only 98,000, but the value of borrowings had climbed back to $20.7 billion, for an average loan balance of $211,200. Strong sharemarket rises had lifted the value of the borrowed shares to $95.9 billion — which is finally back above the previous high of $93.2 billion, recorded in March 2008, just before the full onset of the GFC. In terms of the LVR, Australian margin borrowers were sitting on a very conservative aggregate of 21.5 per cent, down from 26.8 per cent in December 2019 (before the COVID crash) — and less than half the aggregate LVR of 44.6 per cent with which borrowers entered the GFC slump. From the outset, margin loan LVRs are usually between 60 to 70 per cent of the shares' value.

Margin calls fell to an average of seven a day in the quarter ending June 2021, across the 98,000 loan accounts — for every 1,000 loans, there were 0.07 margin calls. In the quarter ending March 2020, which contained the COVID crash, there were 7,434 margin calls (116 a day) — for every 1,000 loans in that quarter, there were 0.9 margin calls.

The possibility of a margin call, however, means that some investors who want to borrow to make bigger investments prefer to use the equity in their homes to buy shares. This strategy uses your home equity as security for the loan, rather than the shares themselves. Using the equity in your home to buy shares could help you manage the volatility of the sharemarket, and save you money, because the interest rate on a loan secured by your home will be lower than that charged on a margin loan — the average variable interest rate for owner-occupiers paying both principal and interest at the time of writing was 3.1 per cent, compared to the 4.8–6.0 per cent range for margin loans. With the cheaper cost of investment, your return on your investment should be higher. And having no margin calls removes the risk of being forced to sell your shares if the value drops.

Homeowners looking to use the equity in their home to buy shares would typically set up a line of credit — this keeps the loan completely separate from the main home loan, which is convenient for taxation purposes. As you are using the line of credit for investment purposes, the interest is tax-deductible, which is not the case with the interest you pay on your owner-occupier home loan. The line of credit could have interest-only payments, or principal-and-interest repayments, depending on your investment strategy and goals.

TIP

If your strategy is more aggressive, you would probably choose to make interest-only payments and try to build up additional funds as quickly as possible to buy more shares. Principal-and-interest repayments might be the best option for someone who is taking a long-term view and looking to pay-down the debt as the shares potentially increase in value.

Another option would be to arrange a 'cash-out', where you take out a fully drawn loan against the equity you hold in the property in order to buy shares. Such a strategy may use interest-only or principal-and-interest repayments, and the loan would be separate from the main home loan.

Alternatively, investors can use internally geared ETFs and managed funds, where the borrowing and security are managed within the fund itself, with no recourse to the investor (other than loss of the original capital) should the market value of the secured assets fall. The fund manager uses the fund's assets to support the borrowing. The investor's liability and loss is limited to the amount they invest, so there are no margin calls for investors to meet. As such, in the worst case, your total investment may suffer but, unlike a margin loan, there is no requirement for you to service or repay any residual loan.

Borrowing against your shares

You can use an existing portfolio as collateral to buy more shares. If you use this strategy and incur a margin call, the lender will request additional shares to the value required to top up the LVR. You have to deposit the shares with the lender. The advantage of taking out a margin loan secured by your shares is that you get capital for investment without having to sell the shares and incur capital gains tax (CGT). But if the LVR drops below the allowed level, you will get a margin call.

Using the tax tactic

Another attraction of gearing into the sharemarket is the ability to claim the interest costs of the loan as a tax deduction, provided that the borrowed funds are used to invest in income-producing securities. Negative gearing is when your income from the investment (the dividends on the shares) is less than the interest cost of the investment. The difference between the two amounts is usually a deduction against your taxable income.

TIP

The Australian Taxation Office (ATO) considers a *margin loan* — a loan to buy shares — to be an investment made to generate assessable income, so the cost of the investment (the interest on the loan) qualifies for a deduction. For income derived from fully franked shares, you can use the imputation credits to reduce the actual rate of tax payable.

Margin loans are popular towards the end of the tax year because borrowers can pay 12 months' interest expense in advance and claim that amount as a tax deduction in the current tax year.

REMEMBER

Imagine that you've borrowed $100,000 at an interest rate of 6 per cent, and you've bought a share portfolio. You can choose to pay — assuming interest rates don't move — $500 a month for the next 12 months, or you can pay $6,000 up front. If you pre-pay, that $6,000 is able to be offset against tax payable in the current tax year, and may be used elsewhere. But if you have a negatively geared portfolio but you don't have any other income, you can't use the deduction.

Of course, that's not the only catch. Because a margin loan is a leveraged investment, while any profits on the share portfolio are magnified, so are any losses.

Sleep-friendly leverage: Protected loans

Investors who are nervous about the sharemarket, and want the certainty of capital protection, can also use tax-effective leverage through a protected equity loan. These are typically fixed-term investment loans (interest only with principal repaid in one lump sum at maturity) that allow you to borrow up to 100 per cent of the value of an investment portfolio.

These are *limited recourse loans* — the investor is protected from a fall in the price of the shares as the loan facility includes a capital protection feature that gives the investor the right to transfer the shares back to the lender as repayment of the loan. The lender in turn covers this risk by buying a put option, the cost of which is passed on to the borrower. The obvious attraction is that in a falling market you don't lose your capital, yet you retain the benefits of any increase in the value of the shares and any dividends received during the term of the loan. These products are also SMSF-friendly.

The ATO places restrictions on the deductibility of interest expense associated with protected equity loans. The portion of interest expense related to the cost of capital protection is not deductible; it is treated as a capital expense rather than an income expense. While not deductible, this portion is included in the cost base of the investment for CGT purposes. A benchmark is used to determine the portion of a capital-protected borrowing's interest expense that is tax deductible, with the remainder treated as a capital expense. The current benchmark is the Reserve Bank's standard housing rate plus 100 basis points.

Speculating with Contracts for Difference

From a standing start in the United Kingdom in 1999, *contracts for difference* (CFDs) have emerged as one of the fastest-growing financial products in the world. A CFD emulates the underlying price of the share, index, exchange rate or commodity to which the CFD applies. When you trade a CFD you are speculating on the market price without taking ownership of the underlying asset.

An investor buying a 'long' CFD benefits from a rise in the share price, while a 'short' CFD gives the benefit of a fall in the share price. The investor's profit or loss is determined by the difference between the opening and closing price, with the difference paid at the close of the contract — hence the term 'contracts for difference'.

Each CFD represents an agreement between the client and the CFD provider to settle, in cash, the difference between the price at which the client 'opens' the CFD and the price at which the position is 'closed'.

Introduced to Australia in March 2002, CFDs grew rapidly here, becoming a $2 billion market before regulatory intervention by the Australian Securities and Investments Commission (ASIC) in 2021 curtailed the market significantly.

How CFDs work

Say an investor has a positive view on Telstra (TLS), which is quoted on the ASX at $3.84–3.85. The CFD provider should offer the CFD at the same spread as the live ASX market (but may not do so). The maximum leverage allowed for an individual share CFD for a retail client is five-to-one, or a 20 per cent margin that the investor lodges to *control the position* (that is, the investor can act as if they own the much larger shareholding). The investor 'buys' 1,000 Telstra CFDs at the offer price of $3.85.

> Buy 1,000 TLS CFDs at $3.85
>
> Initial margin required in account: $3.85 × 1,000 × 20% = $770
>
> Total CFD outlay = $770

One week later, Telstra has risen in price and the spread quoted on the ASX (it should be the same for the CFD provider, but may not be) is $4.15–4.16. The investor decides to take the profit, closing the transaction by 'selling' 1,000 CFDs at the bid price.

> Sell 1,000 TLS CFDs at $4.15
>
> Gross profit = $4.15 – $3.85 = 30 cents
>
> 30 cents × 1,000 = $300

That $300 profit, on a $770 outlay, represents a profit of 39 per cent. If you had bought the Telstra shares at $3.85 and sold them at $4.15, your profit would have been 7.8 per cent.

Now assume the investor had instead a negative view on Telstra, and decided to 'go short' on the stock using CFDs. At the quoted spread of $3.84–3.85, the investor 'sells' 1,000 Telstra CFDs at the bid price.

Sell 1,000 TLS CFDs at $3.84

Initial margin $3.84 × 1,000 × 20% = $768

Total receipt = $768

A week later, Telstra has fallen in price and the spread quoted on the ASX (and the CFD provider) is $3.44–3.45. The investor decides to take their profit, closing the transaction by 'buying-back-to-close' 1,000 Telstra CFDs at the offer price.

Buy 1,000 Telstra CFDs at $3.45

Outlay = $3.45 × 1,000 × 20% = $690

Gross profit = Receipt − outlay to close trade = $78

These examples don't include trading commissions, or the funding charges that it costs to keep a position open, which are paid on the full face value of the CFD position. Ordinarily, 'short' (or selling) CFD positions in Australia earn interest. However, with benchmark interest rates (on which these debits/credits are based) at record low levels at the time of writing, these amounts are negligible. As interest rates rise, they will become factors to consider once more.

REMEMBER

CFDs are also offered over overseas shares, indices (local and overseas), commodities, currencies and cryptocurrencies.

Equity CFDs have no time delay and can be used one-for-one to hedge or protect underlying share portfolio positions. If you have 1,420 BHP shares, you can sell 1,420 BHP CFDs against that position, to hedge it; if BHP falls in price, you have an offsetting gain on the CFDs.

REMEMBER

The CFDs available in Australia are *over-the-counter* or *OTC* CFDs, which are traded directly between the CFD provider and the client. Around ten provider firms operate in this market — commission rates in the Australian CFD market, for local shares, are about $5–8. Above $10,000, the charge may be as low as 0.09–0.1 per cent, either side of the transaction, which makes CFDs just about the cheapest leverage available on the stock market. The maximum leverage available is 20 to one (a 5 per cent margin) for a CFD over a major share index. CFDs allow speculators to 'short-sell' stocks much more easily than on the stock exchange.

ASIC's CFD crackdown

Over the 2010s, Australia's corporate and investment regulator, ASIC, was watching the CFD industry closely, and becoming increasingly concerned at what it was seeing.

ASIC was particularly troubled by the amounts of leverage available in the market. Although the amount of leverage providers could offer was essentially up to them, Australian share CFDs commonly offered leverage of 20 to one (where a $5,000 deposit could control a $100,000 share position); index CFD leverage was 200 to one (where a $5,000 deposit could give $1 million worth of exposure). Currency-paired CFDs had leverage of up to 500 to one (so putting down $5,000 could control a position worth $2.5 million!).

ASIC reviews in 2017, 2019 and 2020 found that most retail clients lose money trading CFDs. According to ASIC, 72 per cent of clients who traded CFDs lost money in 2018 alone.

Its 2020 review looked into the effect on the CFD market of the COVID crash — during a volatile five-week period in March and April 2020, the retail clients of a sample of 13 CFD issuers made a net loss of more than $774 million. During this period:

» More than 1.1 million CFD positions were terminated under margin close-out arrangements (compared with 9.3 million over the full year of 2018).

» More than 15,000 retail client CFD trading accounts fell into a negative balance, owing a total of $10.9 million (compared with 41,000 accounts owing $33 million over the full year of 2018). Some debts were forgiven.

In 2019, ASIC estimated that CFDs in Australia had one million clients, with 675 million transactions a year and a gross annual turnover of $22 trillion worth of underlying positions. But that estimate would have encompassed foreign exchange CFDs — which is by far the largest portion of the CFD market — as well as commodity, index and share CFDs, which are the smallest part of the market. Clients based in Australia accounted for just 17 per cent of the market: Asian clients transacting in Australia were 62 per cent of the market, with 21 percentage points of that figure being from China.

WARNING

In November 2020, ASIC announced that it would impose conditions on the issue and distribution of CFDs to retail clients, to take effect in March 2021 and be assessed in September 2022, after which time the conditions may be extended or made permanent. ASIC also required CFD providers to close-out more loss-making trades more quickly. ASIC banned *binary CFDs* — instruments by which investors could speculate on whether a sharemarket index would close up or down (by any amount) at the end of the trading day — and *spread betting*, which enabled clients to bet that the price of a share (or index, commodity or exchange rate) would go up or down. The regulator also banned 'free gift' account-opening and trading inducements for CFDs.

Since 2021, ASIC restricts CFD leverage offered to retail clients to a maximum ratio of:

>> 30:1 for CFDs over an exchange rate for a major currency pair

>> 20:1 for CFDs over an exchange rate for a minor currency pair, gold or a major stock market index

>> 10:1 for CFDs over a commodity (other than gold) or a minor stock market index

>> 2:1 for CFDs over crypto-assets

>> 5:1 for CFDs over shares or other assets

This means that the margin for share CFDs is 20 per cent, so a $1,000 deposit controls a position worth $5,000.

Immediately following ASIC's tightening of the regulations in 2021, CFD volumes traded in Australia fell by up to 80 per cent, depending on the provider, as clients who wanted to retain the ability to use higher leverage redirected their business to accounts based in other jurisdictions not subject to ASIC regulation. Traders using technical analysis (refer to Chapter 16), for example, who may have identified a pattern with a reasonable expectation of generating a 10 per cent rise in the share price, would chafe at having the leverage available to them cut from 20 to one to five to one on a share CFD, and to 20 to one on an index CFD.

As with margin lending, I accept that CFDs are a product where you need to know what you are doing; however, in its zeal to protect those who don't have the necessary understanding of the market, ASIC has penalised those who do. After the rules changed, anecdotal evidence from CFD providers suggested that leverage-hungry traders had already found a legal way around the rules by becoming a 'wholesale investor'. Instead of using the existing test used to classify a wholesale investor in Australia (that they have assets exceeding $2.5 million or an income of more than $250,000 a year), CFD providers have suggested that retail clients need to pass a 'short' knowledge quiz on CFDs, and prove they have used CFDs regularly, to be classified as a 'sophisticated' investor who is able to access higher leverage levels.

Some CFD providers also add an additional income test, requiring customers to show they have an income of more than $100,000 a year or assets exceeding $500,000. The 'knowledge' and 'usage' approaches were originally intended to allow professional traders, working in the industry, to have access to wholesale products without them needing to pass the assets or income test.

At time of writing, ASIC was monitoring the offering of professional accounts to retail investors, and the knowledge quizzes, looking for any misclassification of retail clients as wholesale clients, which it feels would risk denying them important rights and protections. For its part, while broadly accepting much of ASIC's actions, the CFD industry has been arguing for the use of CFDs, and their higher leverage, by clients who understand the risks, understand the products and have the financial capacity to trade the products. Watch this space.

6

The Part of Tens

Get to know the strategies of great investors.

Add extra investing finesse to your bookshelf.

Recall the sharemarket's calamitous crashes.

Discover some Australian share success stories.

Save yourself from some tricky investing missteps.

Chapter **23**

Ten Great Investors and Their Strategies

nvestors come in all shapes and sizes. Here I select nine of the best-known and most successful investors of the past 85 years — and one (Charles Viertel) perhaps not so well known, but no less effective. Each has followed a fairly stringent set of principles to achieve their success — Benjamin Graham was the 'father' of value investing, while Philip Fisher took a different point of view with his strategies for growth investing. These investors had these features in common — each took his task seriously and each has added to our understanding of the investment process.

Warren Buffett and Charles Munger

Much has been written about the investment philosophies of Warren Buffett, who's known as the 'Oracle of Omaha'. He built a US$104 billion fortune from a $50 start in 1956. Warren Buffett is part of a two-man team that has long managed the legendary investment firm Berkshire Hathaway, and is certainly more famous than his partner, Charlie Munger, vice president of Berkshire Hathaway, who acts as the Dr Watson to Buffett's Sherlock Holmes (although these days, portfolio managers Ted Weschler and Todd Combs are more likely to be helping Buffett make the calls).

The stated aim of the company is to

... increase Berkshire's per-share value at a rate that, over time, will modestly exceed the gain from owning the S&P 500. A small annual advantage in our favour can, if sustained, produce an anything-but-small long-term advantage. To reach our goal we will need to add a few good businesses to Berkshire's stable each year, have the businesses we own generally gain in value, and avoid any material increase in our outstanding shares.

Warren Buffett doesn't dwell on Berkshire Hathaway's share price or its earnings; instead, he examines the company's net tangible asset (NTA) value, or what Americans call 'book value'. Since 1965, Berkshire Hathaway's annual percentage change in book value has beaten the S&P 500 (with dividends reinvested) in 37 of 56 completed years. Over that time, Berkshire Hathaway's value has grown at a compound annual growth rate of 20 per cent, versus 10.2 per cent a year for the S&P 500 index. In only 19 years has the index beaten Berkshire Hathaway, with the most recent occasion being in 2020 at the time of writing, when Berkshire's book value grew by 2.4 per cent, while the S&P 500 gained 18.4 per cent in total return.

Berkshire Hathaway has had 11 losing years, versus 12 for the S&P 500. Buffett's fund has twice doubled in one year; 129.3 per cent in 1976 and 102.5 per cent in 1979. The index's best year was 37.6 per cent in 1995, a year in which Berkshire gained 57.4 per cent.

Berkshire Hathaway's success means that an investor who put US$1,000 into the company in 1964 now has a stake in the company worth US$28.1 million. Another investor who put US$1,000 in the S&P 500 index in 1964 has earned US$230,234. That is the power of compounding — which Buffett describes as a 'simple concept capable of doing extraordinary things'. He describes Berkshire Hathaway as simply a 'compounding machine'. A 56-year record of a compound annual growth rate of almost twice that of the market index is successful investing, in anyone's language. Yet Buffett earns a modest annual salary of US$100,000 — and hasn't had a pay rise in 40 years. Of course, owning US$104 billion of stock helps ease the pain of a modest salary.

How do Buffett and Munger do it? They look for companies with a track record of financial success. This means the companies have competitive advantage, excellent management and superior products or services with a respected brand name. Buffett and Munger also try to buy these companies at a reasonable price. That's the simple secret of buying a stream of earnings reliable enough to fuel Berkshire

Hathaway's growth. The key statistics these fund managers look for in companies are

>> Growth in sales and earnings

>> High return on equity

>> Low gearing (33 per cent or less)

>> Rising book value

>> Strong and growing profit margins

Buffett and Munger also look for growth in *owner earnings*, which is earnings (per share) minus depreciation (per share) plus capital expenditure (per share). Owner earnings represent the cash that the business has left after its required maintenance spending — cash that it can spend however it wants. This pair also prefers a company with a relatively high price/earnings (P/E) ratio — they're long-term investors and figure that a stock trades on a high P/E ratio because the market is prepared to pay a premium for it.

For a long time, Buffett and Munger were known for having 'permanent' stock holdings: Buffett says his ideal investment horizon is 'forever'. Berkshire Hathaway is the biggest shareholder of Coca-Cola Co. and American Express Co., and Buffett has held those stocks for 33 years (Coca-Cola) and 58 years (AmEx); indeed, Berkshire has never sold a Coke share, and hasn't touched the AmEx holding since 1998. However, this status is not set in stone — retailer Walmart and banking group Wells Fargo were also once thought to be permanent holdings, but Berkshire sold out of Walmart in 2016 and ditched almost all of its Wells Fargo stake in 2021.

A rare dud for Berkshire Hathaway is Kraft Heinz. Since the merger of the venerable Kraft and Heinz brands in July 2015, the shares of the combined company have lost 47 per cent in value. Berkshire Hathaway, previously an investor in HJ Heinz, owns 26.6 per cent of the company and is estimated to have lost nearly US$5 billion on its investment so far. Buffett admitted in February 2019 that Berkshire had paid too much for Kraft Heinz stock.

Many Australian fund managers say that they follow similar principles to those of Berkshire in terms of valuation precepts. But even managers considered to be Buffett-oriented, such as Magellan, Clime and Caledonia, will tell you that using the basic premises that Buffett and Munger espouse is one thing, but putting them into practice on a Berkshire scale is difficult in the Australian market. Our market is both much more limited in terms of high-quality businesses than the US market and has a higher component of resources investment, and so many of those principles do not work.

Buffett and Munger have been able to pick the fundamental eyes out of an industrial-based economy like the US through 'information arbitrage' — learning more about a company than anyone else. Not only is this harder to do these days in the US, but it's also very difficult to do in Australia, where the market's resources orientation means many of the major Australian companies experience tremendous swings in earnings.

Moreover, no Australian manager can invest in exactly the way that Berkshire does, because Australian fund managers have to service their investors' capital. Since its inception, Berkshire has paid only one dividend.

The compounding effect of retaining earnings and retaining dividend flows gives the company its dramatic earnings power. Buffett also has the ability, as he did at the height of the global financial crisis (GFC), to invest in companies through instruments other than shares; he has occasionally loaned money to companies and converted it to shares later. In fact, this was Buffett's preferred method of investing after the GFC hit in 2007.

Quotable Buffettisms abound, such as: 'When a management with a reputation for brilliance tackles a business with a reputation for bad economics, it is the reputation of the business that remains intact'; 'When you combine ignorance and leverage, you get some pretty interesting results'; and 'I don't care if the stock exchange closes down for five years. I've got my stocks and I like them.'

Buffett's annual letter to Berkshire Hathaway shareholders has become over the years a compendium of investment insight. For example, in the 2019 letter, he told shareholders that he and Munger did not view the constituents of their US$248 billion ($353 billion) share portfolio as:

[A] collection of stock market wagers — dalliances to be terminated because of downgrades by 'the Street,' an earnings 'miss,' expected Federal Reserve actions, possible political developments, forecasts by economists or whatever else might be the subject du jour. What we see in our holdings, rather, is an assembly of companies that we partly own and that, on a weighted basis, are earning more than 20% on the net tangible equity capital required to run their businesses. These companies, also, earn their profits without employing excessive levels of debt.

John Neff

John Neff managed Vanguard's Windsor fund for 31 years, from 1964 to his retirement in 1995. The Windsor fund was closed to new investment in 1985 and was, at that time, the largest mutual fund in the USA. Neff beat the market 22 out of 31 years, turning each dollar invested in Windsor in the first year to $56 by 1985. The total return of the Windsor fund was 5,546 per cent, more than twice as good as that of the S&P 500 index over the same period. The average return of the Windsor fund was 13.7 per cent a year, versus 10.6 per cent for the S&P 500.

REMEMBER

Neff's strategy was to look for stocks trading at a low P/E ratio. Often described as a value investor, the label that Neff thought best described his style was *low P/E investor*. He bought companies that were in line for a re-rating in the medium term, reasoning that a re-rating was more likely to happen to a company with a P/E about half the market average than to a high P/E growth stock.

He looked for companies with an earnings growth of 7 per cent or better. Above 20 per cent, Neff thought the stock too risky. Neff considered yield a return that investors could pocket. He said that share prices 'nearly always sell on the basis of expected earnings growth rates and shareholders collect the dividend income for free'.

The total return that Windsor was looking for was annual earnings growth plus dividend yield. Because the P/E ratio showed what it paid to achieve that annual return, Windsor divided total return by P/E ratio to give a total return ratio. Neff bought stocks with a total return ratio at 2 or above. He was happy to buy cyclical stocks — but at low P/E ratios based on the earnings that he thought were achievable at better points in the cycle. He looked for solid companies in growing fields.

He also looked for companies with what he called a *strong fundamental case*, which meant that the trends in cash flow, sales and margins combined to drive earnings growth. Neff would sell when he felt that the fundamental case was deteriorating, or if the price approached his expectations. Typically, he held stocks for about three years.

My favourite Neffism is: 'Falling in love with stocks in a portfolio is very easy to do and, I might add, very perilous. Every stock Windsor owned was for sale. When you feel like bragging about a stock, it's probably time to sell.'

Benjamin Graham

Benjamin Graham, who died in 1976, was one of the most influential investors the stock markets have known. He developed his ideas about value investing during the Great Depression, and co-wrote, with David Dodd, the 1931 classic text *Security Analysis*. He followed this up 18 years later with *The Intelligent Investor*. These two books set out the concept of value investing, which is based on the fact that a company's share price is different from its intrinsic value.

REMEMBER

Value investing involves buying stocks that are trading at a low price relative to the company's net worth per share, which is its value as though it were to be sold off tomorrow, or its NTA backing. According to Graham, this is a stock's intrinsic value. He compared this intrinsic value to the current market price to determine a share's true value. The further the share's market price was below what Graham had worked out as its intrinsic value, the bigger he considered his margin of safety.

Benjamin Graham's ten rules for choosing stocks were

>> Current ratio greater than two.

>> Dividend yield of at least two-thirds that of the AAA bond.

>> Earnings growth of at least 7 per cent a year, over the preceding ten years.

>> Earnings-to-price yield of at least twice the yield offered by the best AAA bond. (The earnings-to-price yield is the reciprocal of the P/E ratio. For Australian investors, this yield is twice the yield of ten-year bonds.)

>> P/E ratio less than 40 per cent of the highest P/E ratio the stock had traded at over the past five years.

>> Share price of less than two-thirds of book value (NTA) per share.

>> Share price of less than two-thirds of net current asset value, which Graham defined as the current assets of a company minus all of its liabilities.

>> Stability of growth of earnings. (No more than two annual falls of 5 per cent or more in profit in the preceding ten years.)

>> Total debt less than book value (NTA).

>> Total debt less than twice net current asset value.

Over four decades, Benjamin Graham honed this set of ten criteria to what he described as a 'practically foolproof way of getting good results out of common stock investments with a minimum of work'.

Philip Fisher

What Benjamin Graham is to value investors, Philip Fisher is to growth investors. His strategy was to identify growth companies early, buy them and hold them for a long time. Fisher was averse to bargain hunting. He wanted to identify the business characteristics of superbly managed growth companies. He felt that great growth stocks show gains in the hundreds of per cent each decade, while a value-oriented investor rarely finds a stock that is more than 50 per cent below its real value.

Fisher did not use economic data to help him decide when to buy stocks because he thought economists were not accountable. He preferred to use what he called 'scuttlebutt', which involved talking to suppliers, customers, company employees, people knowledgeable in the industry and, eventually, company management. Not all investors can do this, although the internet era makes it a bit easier.

Fisher developed a series of questions you can ask before buying a stock:

» Are there aspects of the business, somewhat peculiar to the industry involved, which will give the investor important clues as to how outstanding the company may be in relation to its competition?

» Does the company have a management of unquestionable integrity?

» Does the company have an above-average sales organisation?

» Does the company have depth to its management?

» Does the company have a short-range or a long-range outlook in regard to profits?

» Does the company have a worthwhile profit margin?

» Does the company have outstanding executive relations?

» Does the company have outstanding labour and personnel relations?

» Does the company have products or services with sufficient market potential to make possible a sizeable increase in sales for at least several years?

» Does the management have a determination to continue to develop products or processes that will still further increase total sales potentials when the growth potentials of currently attractive product lines have largely been exploited?

» Does the management talk freely to investors about its affairs when things are going well, but 'clam up' when troubles and disappointments occur?

» How good are the company's cost analysis and accounting controls?

>> How effective are the company's research and development efforts in relation to its size?

>> What is the company doing to maintain or improve profit margins?

>> Will, in the foreseeable future, the growth of the company require sufficient equity financing so that the larger number of shares then outstanding will largely cancel the existing stockholders' benefit from this anticipated growth?

Fisher is famous for the comment that 'if the job has been correctly done when a common stock is purchased, the time to sell it is — almost never'. However, he would sell in three situations:

>> When he decided he'd made a serious mistake in assessing the company

>> If the company no longer passed his tests as clearly as it did before

>> If he simply decided to take a profit and reinvest the money in another, far more attractive company

Jim Slater

British investor Jim Slater's theories of share investment centred on the price earnings growth factor, or PEG. The *PEG* is a measure of the relationship between a P/E ratio and the expected rate of earnings per share growth. To calculate the PEG, you divide the P/E ratio by the forecast growth in earnings per share (EPS).

Any company trading on a PEG of 1 or less is generally considered appealing, while those on PEGs of 0.6 are cheap as chips. To qualify for a positive calculation, a company must have displayed solid normalised EPS growth going back at least three years, with no setbacks.

Slater found that PEGs tend to work best for what he called small, dynamic companies. He formulated ten critical points against which a candidate for investment must be assessed:

>> Competitive advantage linked to reliability of earnings growth based on well-known brand names, patents, copyrights, market dominance or a strong position in a niche business.

>> Dividend yield — it doesn't matter how low, as long as dividends paid are growing in line with earnings.

- » High relative strength of the shares compared to the market — when the market's strong, the shares are strong; if it's not, you're on red alert.

- » Low P/E ratio relative to the growth rate (in other words, the PEG).

- » Optimistic chairman's statement (in the annual report).

- » Positive rate of growth in earnings per share in at least four of the past five years. Cyclical stocks not allowed!

- » Reasonable asset position. Very few growth shares in a dynamic phase, said Slater, were priced near to or below asset value. A share price as low as 33 per cent of asset value is 'passable for a growth share'.

- » Shares must have a 'story', that offers potential reasons for growth in earnings.

- » Small market capitalisation — elephants don't gallop! Slater preferred companies valued at £10–50 million, and would not invest above £100 million. (Bear in mind, though, that the UK is a larger and deeper sharemarket than Australia.)

- » Strong liquidity, low borrowings and high cash flow. Liquidity here means ability to convert assets to cash. Avoid capital-intensive companies; look instead for those generating cash.

Slater also looked for management with significant shareholding in the company because investors wanted to see shareholder-oriented management that would look after their interests with an owner's eye. Slater believed these criteria allow investors to identify smaller growth stocks, which give investors substantial capital and earnings growth.

Charles Viertel

Charles Viertel was one of the great unsung heroes of the Australian Securities Exchange. From a fairly humble start in life, Viertel left a $60 million charitable foundation when he died in 1992, which has since appreciated to about $215 million — from which about $8.6 million a year flows to charities. He advocated the principle of buying and holding quality shares and picking up more of them after a correction. Viertel was one of the great exponents of the buy-and-hold investment strategy.

Viertel started buying shares and property during the Great Depression, but later sold all his property to concentrate on the sharemarket. Reportedly, he was so shamed by the notice written on the blackboard at primary school, 'Viertel owes threepence' (for schoolbooks), that he never again borrowed a cent. Nor did he smoke, drink or own a car. Until he died, he lived in the same modest home in Brisbane that he bought in the mid-1950s.

Trained as a cost accountant, Viertel based his sharemarket investment strategy on the forensic study of financial statements. He looked for value, whether it was a company that showed potential to grow its business or be taken over. He liked to buy Queensland companies. Once he decided to concentrate on shares as his investment vehicle, Viertel looked for companies with strong dividend yields that gave him the cash flow to expand his portfolio.

According to an interview that long-time friend George Curphy gave to *Personal Investor* magazine in 2001, the three fundamentals on which Viertel placed most emphasis were:

>> NTA backing

>> P/E ratio

>> Track history

Viertel was a voracious and methodical reader of company financial statements. He was always alert for takeover appeal and was reportedly a large buyer of shares when the market crashed in October 1987. He stuck to his principle of solid long-term investing.

REMEMBER

Any person living today has an almost unbelievable advantage over Viertel in terms of accessibility, and ease of accessibility, to information. That makes his success — and the gift, which keeps on giving, that he and his wife left the nation — even more admirable.

Peter Lynch

Peter Lynch became a household name in investment through his work at the Boston-based international fund Fidelity Magellan. Lynch retired in 1990, handing over to his successor a fund worth $14 billion. In his 13 years at the helm, Lynch managed the fund to an average compound return of 29 per cent a year, a record for funds of that size. This translates to a total return of 2,510 per cent, more than five times the appreciation in the S&P 500 over the same period. Lynch believes that individual investors who know what they're looking for can spot good stocks before professional investors. He says that products or services you deal with in your workplace, buy in the shops, or use in your spare time and on holidays are a great source of ideas for investment in the companies that make or offer them.

He divides companies into these main types:

>> **Asset plays:** Companies trading at a discount to their NTA backing.

>> **Cyclicals:** Those companies with earnings that closely follow the economic cycle.

>> **Fast growers:** Small, aggressive companies growing at more than 20 per cent.

>> **Slow growers:** Companies with earnings growth that matches the rate of growth in gross domestic product (GDP).

>> **Stalwarts:** Companies with solid growth in earnings of about 10–12 per cent a year.

>> **Turnarounds:** Poor performers that have cleaned up their act and are poised for recovery.

Of these types of companies, Lynch is interested only in fast growers, turnarounds and asset plays. Lynch likes companies that have a low PEG ratio (their P/E ratio is below their forecast rate of growth in EPS), a strong cash position, low gearing and a high profit margin.

John Bogle

John Bogle, who died in 2019, deserves to be considered one of the great investors — for inventing the index fund. An *index fund* owns a portfolio of stocks that is constructed to match the investment returns of a specified market index. The manager of the fund buys and holds that index, and doesn't try to actively manage the portfolio.

Bogle was an economics student at Princeton University in 1949, researching his thesis on mutual funds managers, when he first hit on the idea. He founded the Vanguard Group in 1974 to practise his theories. His approach was that funds managers couldn't consistently beat the market. A bond fund manager can't out-guess interest rates; nor can a share fund manager outperform the market, on a cost-adjusted basis. As Bogle put it: 'What's the point of looking for the needle in the haystack? Why not own the haystack?'

This philosophy flowed on to the exchange-traded fund (ETF), although Bogle (who did not invent the ETF) was not a fan of all ETFs, worrying that some were being manipulated by speculators. In his final book, he urged investors only to use ETFs as long-term investments. But broad-based index ETFs do allow any investor to 'own the haystack'.

John Templeton

John Templeton rose from poor beginnings in Tennessee to found the huge Templeton Mutual Fund group, and was one of the first US fund managers to invest in foreign shares. The Templeton group paved the way for US investment in the Japanese stock market in the 1960s but, by the 1980s, the company felt that the Japanese market was overpriced and sold its holdings. The company looked silly for a few years, but with the Nikkei losing 80 per cent of its value over the period 1989 to 2003, you'd have to say that Templeton was right. Before selling out, his funds management company had made five times its investment in Japan.

Templeton's value-based investment credo has been set out in ten points:

>> **Avoid the popular:** Too many investors can spoil any share selection method or any market timing formula.

>> **Buy when the market is most pessimistic:** Conversely, sell when the market is most optimistic.

>> **Hunt for value and bargains:** In the sharemarket, the only way to get a bargain is to buy what most investors are selling.

>> **Invest for real returns:** The true objective for any long-term investor is to get maximum total real return after taxes and inflation.

>> **Learn from your mistakes:** 'This time is different' are among the four most costly words in investing history.

>> **Never adopt any type of asset or selection method permanently:** Stay open-minded and sceptical.

>> **Never follow the crowd:** If you buy the same shares as everybody else, you'll get the same results as everybody else. To be a true contrarian, buying when others are selling and vice versa requires the greatest courage, but pays the greatest reward.

>> **Recognise no-one knows everything:** An investor who has all the answers doesn't even understand the questions.

>> **Search worldwide:** If you do, you'll find more and better bargains than if you confine your investing to only one country.

>> **Understand everything changes:** Bull or bear markets, they've always been temporary.

Because he was a pioneer in overseas investing, Templeton also had a set of rules to cover his decisions. He avoided countries plagued by socialist policies and/or inflation and favoured those with high long-term growth rates. Templeton especially favoured countries that showed a trend towards economic liberalisation or privatisation, anti-union legislation and greater openness and transparency in sharemarket dealings. Although the anti-union bit might fall foul of today's ESG focus, Templeton felt that an unethical enterprise would fail, 'if not at first, then eventually'.

Templeton certainly lived his investment principles. When the Second World War broke out when he was aged 27, he borrowed money from his boss to buy 100 shares each in 104 New York Stock Exchange companies whose share price was $1 or less (37 were in bankruptcy, but he bought them anyway). Only four turned out to be worthless and he made large profits on the others, holding them for an average of four years.

IN THIS CHAPTER

» Getting it from the horse's mouth

» Investing with humour

» Learning from the experts

» Digging for knowledge on mining

» Keeping cool in a crash

Chapter **24**

Ten Great Books to Read Next

Yes, I know that most of these books are by US investors — but books on successful Australian investors are emerging. You can get a good grounding in investment strategy from the former, and filter that information through an Australian context in the latter.

In choosing the books in this chapter, I hoped to get away from stock-picking texts, although I have more than a few of those on my bookshelves! I want to point you in the direction of the burgeoning field of financial history and also show you that humour is plentiful when discussing investment. Let's face it, anyone who spends a lot of time around the sharemarket needs the occasional laugh.

The Warren Buffett Way

Of the top 100 individuals or families worth more than US$1 billion, only Warren Buffett made his fortune through investing. That striking fact tells you that Buffett must be on to something. So why would he allow author Robert Hagstrom Jr to reveal the secrets behind his success? Because (a) it's pretty simple; and (b) he's not averse to doing so himself.

In *The Warren Buffett Way* (Third Edition), by Robert G Hagstrom, Jr (John Wiley & Sons, 2013), Buffett says the two people who influenced him were Benjamin Graham, author of *The Intelligent Investor* and the doyen of value investing, and Philip Fisher, the author of *Common Stocks and Uncommon Profits*, the standard-bearer for the growth investment camp. According to Hagstrom, the genius of Buffett's approach is that he thinks about stocks as businesses and not as a set of statistics. Buffett tries to buy exceptional businesses rather than chunks of stock, and the Buffett approach to picking stocks has changed very little over the past 50 years.

Buffett thinks about the company, the management, the financials and the asking price — in that order. Once he has bought, he ignores the price on the sharemarket, trusting that the economic progress of the business he has chosen will determine the long-term value of his shareholding.

In 1999, Hagstrom published a sequel, *The Warren Buffett Portfolio: Mastering the Power of the Focus Investment Strategy* (also published by John Wiley & Sons). This book covers the Buffett approach to managing those businesses (shares) after you've bought them. Hagstrom's books are well worth reading because they're very good summaries of the huge field of Buffettology.

I think people can go a bit overboard about Buffett. You'll find it very difficult to invest exactly as he does because he can afford to take a very long-term view, and during times of market crisis he has effectively been able to buy at very deep discounts — but his principles of what to look for in a stock are pretty handy.

TIP

Make sure you pick up the third edition; it brings in behavioural finance to explain how investors can overcome the common obstacles that prevent them from investing like Buffett.

One Up on Wall Street

Another famous investment guru from the US is Peter Lynch, who wrote *One Up on Wall Street* (latest edition published by Simon & Schuster in 2000) after a successful career at the helm of the Fidelity Magellan Fund. Lynch's approach is very engaging, especially when he urges his readers not to listen to stock market professionals. Of course, as a fund manager who invests other people's money, he's one of the good-guy professionals. It seems that the stockbroking analysts are the bad-guy professionals you have to beware of.

Lynch firmly believes that you can beat the professionals by using your own eyes and ears to find what he calls *ten-bagger stocks* (stocks that rise tenfold on the purchase price). You find ten-baggers by buying the shares of quality companies whose business you understand and, more importantly, believe in. Lynch wanted to try companies' products and services himself to get a sense of the quality of a business — he was ahead of his time in encouraging self-reliant investing.

Lynch's book sets out easy-to-follow directions for choosing stocks that can put you one-up on the market. He concentrates on the fundamentals but stresses broadening your own experience and knowledge of which products and services strike a chord with consumers. He reasons that people spend so much money and time buying products, they ought to know what others just like them want to buy! To Lynch, everyone's a sharemarket researcher.

Even with the caveat that much of the book's content can appear a bit dated — particularly with respect to the technology of the time, which may be difficult for you to experience first-hand — this book is inspirational stuff.

Value.able

Roger Montgomery, founder and chief investment officer of Montgomery Investment Management, is one of Australia's most successful value investors, and his book *Value.able: How to Value the Best Stocks and Buy Them for Less Than They're Worth* (Second Edition, 2012) distils the essence of his style. Montgomery offers an excellent framework that allows investors to analyse and value companies to decide whether they should buy them. His valuation model gives investors a simple tool for working out the price level and decide if there's a sufficient margin of safety to buy a high-quality, high return on equity (ROE) company, for less than it's worth.

The five keys to Montgomery's process are:

1. Buy shares as part-ownership stakes of a business, rather than bits of paper.
2. Look to own businesses that will grow.
3. Only buy when you have identified that a business has a competitive advantage.
4. Stick to buying businesses with a demonstrated track record of generating high rates of ROE, with little or no debt.
5. Use the intrinsic value formula and safety margin to buy these businesses for less than they're really worth.

In combining these steps, Montgomery seeks to show investors that, by doing their homework, market-beating returns are possible and within the reach of all stock market investors. *Value.able* also sets out Montgomery's simple steps to successful online trading. It's a highly readable book and you'll discover a lot.

TIP

Be sure to find the second edition to get the full benefit of reading this book.

Where Are the Customers' Yachts?

The title of this splendid book comes from a remark attributed to a Mr Travis who, one cold day in the early 1900s, was being shown around the financial district of New York. The fine yachts riding at anchor at the New York Yacht Club were pointed out to him, with the remark, 'Look, there are all the bankers' and brokers' yachts.' The famous retort by Travis (it was a cold day) was: 'Where are all the c-c-customers' yachts?'

First published in 1940, the full title of this book is *Where Are the Customers' Yachts? Or A Good Hard Look at Wall Street* (John Wiley & Sons, latest edition 2006), by Fred Schwed, Jr. Schwed had a cynical view of Wall Street, viewing it as a place where a customer could be anyone willing to put up some money. Having lost a bundle in the 1929 crash, Schwed retired from stockbroking to 'drink, play golf and write a little'. His only other published work was a children's book called *Wacky the Small Boy*. Schwed certainly had a unique style, and a major bonus of his Wall Street book is that it entertains while it educates you about the mechanics of investment.

On the practice of short selling, Schwed says, 'At the very moment when we were buying that stock, hopefully and constructively, looking forward and upward toward better things, those fellows, men without bowels, were selling it, and they didn't even have it to sell! They were looking downward and for worse things. How unnatural! How perverse! How cynical!'

Schwed published his Wall Street exposé in 1940 and it was reprinted in 1955 and 1995, when the book became part of the excellent Wiley Investment Classics series. The book is a send-up of Wall Street, so it's good for a neophyte investor to see what they're getting themselves into. Read it and you'll see why this book stands as a classic.

Common Stocks and Uncommon Profits

I wouldn't be the first to say that every investor should read Philip Fisher's *Common Stocks and Uncommon Profits*, even if the philosophy of growth investing, which he pioneered, isn't your cup of tea. First published in 1958, the Wiley Investment Classics edition (John Wiley & Sons, published in 1996 and reissued in

2003) has two additional sections: 'Conservative Investors Sleep Well' (1975) and 'Developing an Investment Philosophy' (1980). By now, the book is famous as an investment text, cited even by the great Buffett himself.

Fisher didn't see the point of value investment, which means finding companies with a share price trading at a discount to the valuation of their assets. He felt these companies had only the upside of a return to fair value; neither did he see the point in making a value investment in a company that happened to be poorly run. In seeking stand-out growth opportunities, Fisher placed a huge emphasis on a company's people, which today would be called intellectual capital. If growth companies were chosen well enough, he reasoned, an investor might never have to sell — while accruing a huge return on their initial investment.

Being a growth-oriented investor, Fisher is always peering into the future to see what products are on the drawing board that might drive revenue and earnings growth down the track. He might even have been called the first tech investor.

The Battle for Investment Survival

A friend once described his father as a big punter. I asked him how much he bet on a race day. He replied, 'Often he goes for a couple of meetings without making a bet.' That wasn't my idea of a big punter, I said. 'He's a big punter, not a habitual punter,' said my friend.

I was reminded of that story when I read Gerald M Loeb's 1935 classic *The Battle for Investment Survival*, another in the Wiley Investment Classics series (John Wiley & Sons, 2007). The advice that Gerald Loeb gives stands the test of time, although this is advice that's far from fashionable today. According to Loeb, if you invest all the time, you lose money. If you invest only when you do your homework, maybe then you can make money on the stock within six months to a year. If you're successful, keep your profit and wait until the next opportunity presents itself.

When Loeb wrote this book, investment was a battle. During the Great Depression of the 1930s, survival was about all that you could hope for. After the huge bull markets we've seen in recent years (the 1990s, the 2000s, the post-global-financial-crisis-to-COVID-crash mega-bull), reading Loeb is like reading early accounts of world exploration — you can't believe people did it that way. The book is firmly based in the psychology of a bear market. Accordingly, Loeb doesn't think much of fundamental analysis or diversification. The bear market doesn't pay any attention to fundamentals or how well your portfolio is diversified.

As soon as you buy a stock, says Loeb, you lose the power to avoid a decision about whether to hold or sell. Statistically, Loeb doesn't like your chances of a correct decision; if it goes wrong, he says, cut the loss immediately and forget that the transaction existed. Using a wartime metaphor, he advises you not to waste ammunition.

As John Rothchild, financial columnist at *Time* magazine, said in the foreword to the 1996 Wiley Investment Classics edition: 'Most of today's advisors are telling us to diversify into stocks, bonds, foreign stocks, and perhaps gold, to spread the risk; Loeb tells us to put all our eggs in one basket, and watch the basket.' Given the way that most assets fell together in the global financial crisis (GFC), and the February–March 2020 COVID crash, Loeb would have been right at home in the 21st century.

Masters of the Market

If you browse through the finance and business section of any bookstore, you come across plenty of books by and about successful fund managers — virtually all of them American. The names of Warren Buffett, Peter Lynch, John Neff, Philip Fisher, John Templeton and others fill the spines of the books on the shelves; books about their investment philosophies, processes, successes (even the odd failure because too much bragging is poor form). In particular, Buffett — along with his partner, Charlie Munger — seems to have inspired an entire publishing industry. And while a great deal of what Buffett has to say — and what is written about him — is relevant to Australian investors, the examples used and the investment philosophy still have to be translated to the Australian context.

That's why it was so important for fund managers Geoff Wilson and Matthew Kidman (of Wilson Asset Management) and Anthony Hughes (investment editor of the *Sydney Morning Herald*) to write *Masters of the Market* (originally published by Wrightbooks in 2003), which features interviews with 15 of Australia's most respected professional investors. This excellent book is a wonderful read for any-one who is interested in investing on the Australian sharemarket. Virtually every page is laden with insights of real value, but what is impressive is the consistent themes that recur: common sense, read the accounts, do your homework, seek advice but trust your judgement, don't get carried away by short-term market movements, and don't ever believe you've got the market 'sussed'.

A second edition of *Masters of the Market* followed in 2005 (republished by John Wiley & Sons in 2011), with three new 'masters' nominated by the 15 original investment heavyweights. Both editions are well worth reading.

The Ascent of Money

Eminent historian Niall Ferguson tackles money in his 2008 book *The Ascent of Money: A Financial History of the World* (Penguin), which explores the history of money, banking, credit and investing. To understand investing, I think every investor needs to understand this history. Starting from the origins of money in ancient Mesopotamia, and ranging through the lust for gold to the Medicis; the cash injection that funded the Italian Renaissance to the stock market bubble that sparked the French Revolution; the bonds that powered Britain's world war efforts to the Wall Street Crash of 1929; and the gold standard to the Great Financial Crisis meltdown, this story of boom and bust tackles a pressing question — how much does history repeat itself?

TIP

Make sure you read the paperback edition, published in 2019, which includes newer material on bitcoin and cryptocurrencies (Ferguson has subsequently admitted that he didn't properly 'get' cryptocurrency at the time), as well as the rise of China. It's concise, entertaining and informative.

I would also like to bring your attention here to a book I have not read, to be published in 2022: *Money in One Lesson: How It Works and Why*, by Gavin Jackson (Macmillan, 2022). Jackson is a lead writer for the *Financial Times*, specialising in economics, business and public policy. I gather from pre-publication reviews that Jackson also sets out to help readers understand what money is and how it shapes our societies; it sounds well and truly worth checking out.

The Mining Valuation Handbook

Mining investment expert Dr Victor Rudenno is up to the fourth edition of *The Mining Valuation Handbook: Mining and Energy Valuation for Investors and Management* (Fourth Edition, John Wiley & Sons, 2012), an essential, in-depth guide to mining investment analysis. The book is a practical guide for those who need to assess the value and investment potential of mining opportunities. The latest edition has been fully updated in its coverage of a wide range of topics, such as feasibility studies, commodity values, indicative capital and operating costs, valuation and pricing techniques, and exploration and expansion effects.

Rudenno's book deserves to be popular among Australian investors given the hefty (although diminishing) component of resources companies on the ASX lists, but also because of the dirty secret of the 'clean energy' transition — that meaningful progress to increase the proportion of what is seen as 'clean' energy in our energy mix will require a massive expansion in mining worldwide due to the essential metals required, and for which no substitutes appear to be on the horizon. Chapter 10 explores the clean energy conundrum in more detail.

Crashes

A crash is a sharp, sudden and spectacular fall in the prices on a sharemarket, or some other financial market, preceded by a long rise, culminating in a period of euphoria. How and why do crashes happen? This question is fascinating, with a simple answer — because we're human beings and we get greedy.

Behavioural finance is the name given to the study of why participants in the financial markets act the way they do. However sophisticated the sharemarket becomes as a trading platform, it is always a market. It's often said that the market is finely balanced between fear and greed but that, occasionally, one of the two firmly gains the upper hand.

Crashes by Robert Beckman (originally published by Sidgwick & Jackson in 1988) is about what happens when fear gains the ascendancy. When this happens, the market panics; that is, the human beings that use the market panic. They sell their holdings irrationally. Of course, for every share sold there is a buyer, but in a crash, liquidity dries up and buyers won't be tempted until prices are dramatically lowered. What we saw in the great market slump of 2007 to 2009 was an extreme version of a crash, but it followed the blueprint for a crash that Beckman describes.

Although behavioural finance is a relatively new field, investment writers have been thinking about this sort of thing for a long time. Other good books in a similar vein are Charles Mackay's *Extraordinary Popular Delusions and the Madness of Crowds* (originally published in 1841), Charles P. Kindleberger's *Manias, Panics & Crashes: A History of Financial Crises* (originally published in 1978) and Charles R. Morris's *Money, Greed & Risk: Why Financial Crises and Crashes Happen* (John Wiley & Sons, 1999).

TIP

For an excellent Australian perspective on behavioural finance, which explains many of the unconscious decision-making biases to which humans are prone, I highly recommend behavioural finance consultant Simon Russell's *Behavioural Finance: A Guide for Financial Advisers* (Publicious Pty. Ltd, 2019). Although Russell's book is a practical one, aimed at helping financial advisers to better serve their clients, it's full of insight into the hidden psychological traps into which investors can fall, and is thus very worthwhile cautionary reading for any investor.

Chapter **25**

Ten Great Sharemarket Crashes

Every now and then, the sharemarket experiences a *correction*, which is a sudden movement in the reverse direction to the prevailing trend. Because this trend is historically upward, a correction usually means a sudden, sharp movement downward and is normally taken to mean a 10 per cent decline in a market index. Any decline worse than that qualifies for the description of a crash. The three big crashes last century took place in 1929, 1987 and 1997. This century has seen them in 2000, 2001, 2007 and 2020.

When people talk about sharemarket crashes, they usually mean an event that precipitates a bear market, a prolonged period of falling prices, such as that experienced between November 2007 and March 2009. The loss of value in the crash itself, which occurs over a few days, is often dwarfed by the fall in prices that follows in the bear market. A 20 per cent loss in the market is the point where a correction becomes a bear market, and 30 per cent is the level where a mild bear market becomes a major bear market. The 20th century had 30 bear markets, with the average bear market resulting in a loss for the US Dow Jones Industrial Average of 27 per cent. So far this century, we've already seen the 54 per cent slump of 2007 to 2009.

The very worst bear market, during the Great Depression of 1929 to 1932, stripped 89 per cent from the notional value of the Dow Jones. The 1973 to 1974 version caused a 45 per cent loss. After a crash, the average bear market lasts about

14 months before the major sharemarket indices return to their upward trend. On six occasions last century, the Australian sharemarket suffered a loss of 30 per cent or more in a bear market.

In this chapter, I talk about ten major sharemarket crashes, including the most recent one — the 'COVID crash' of 2020.

The Tulip Mania

Although it's considered the archetype for all subsequent crashes, the Dutch tulip mania of the 17th century is no longer the historical figure of fun that it was just a few years ago. The idea that the commercially sophisticated Dutch could lose the plot in the 1630s over speculation in tulip bulbs used to be considered unbelievably daft, but who are we to laugh at them after the premature internet mania of 1999 to 2000? If the modern-day investor could take leave of his senses in such a manner, why couldn't the Dutch turn a pretty flower into the mother of all speculative vehicles?

Tulips were introduced into The Netherlands from Turkey in the mid-1500s. The Dutch loved them and they came to be in high demand. By the 1630s, people were mortgaging homes, ships and businesses to buy them and virtually the whole of the nation's capital was going into speculation in tulips. A futures market sprang up to accommodate the insatiable tulip traders. An options market followed, where tulip-struck traders could buy call and put options on their favourite tulips. Tulip analysts appeared, ready to advise the investing public on which tulips to buy.

Ordinary Dutch people traded tulips on margin. By April 1637, the end was near — the Dutch Government ruled that tulips were not a financial instrument and had to be paid for with cash, not credit. The speculative bubble burst, bankrupting The Netherlands for almost a generation.

The South Sea Bubble

A hundred years later, the equally commercially sophisticated British had their own version of a market crash. It started when a private company offered to take on £9 million of debt from the British Government for 6 per cent a year return. This was the famous South Sea Company, which did little trading in the South Seas.

In 1720, the company took on the entire national debt. It went to the public four times for new issues, each time at higher prices. It loaned investors money to buy its shares, issued instalment receipts — but it didn't actually do anything else. It was purely a speculative bubble that relied for its success on the gullibility of the public. The company bribed lawmakers and much of the nobility to cover its activities.

The South Sea Company stock soared from £100 to £1,000 in four months. Soon copycat companies were in business, so the company bribed the government to outlaw the so-called bubble companies, which it did. Stock prices for the bubble companies collapsed and, unfortunately for the South Sea Company, this had the effect of making people realise that stock prices could fall as well as rise. When the bubble burst, it burst hard. From £1,000, South Sea Company shares dropped to £896 one day and £640 the next. Two months later they were selling — if a buyer could be found — at £400. As in The Netherlands, the effects devastated the British economy for decades.

A famous anecdote from the South Sea bubble concerns the great scientist Sir Isaac Newton. He sold his stock in the company in April 1720 for £7,000, a profit of 100 per cent. Nevertheless, he went back into the market for another whirl, only to lose £20,000. His summary of the event is famous: 'I can calculate the motions of the heavenly bodies, but not the madness of people.'

October 1929

Before 1987, stories of the Great Wall Street Crash could refer to only one year — 1929. The Great Crash of 1987 was bigger in terms of percentage losses, but trading was much less efficient in 1929. In those days, you would have relied on ticker-tape for information, not computer screens, and the ticker-tape often fell many hours behind trading. In terms of effect, the 1987, global financial crisis (GFC) and COVID crash meltdowns don't even come close. The 1929 crash was followed by the Great Depression of the 1930s and put two generations off investing in the sharemarket. With World War II thrown in for good measure, the US sharemarket took 19 years to recover to its pre-crash level — a financial catastrophe with a capital C.

The crash happened the last week of October 1929 and was small bikkies compared to the bear market that followed it. Although the Dow Jones Industrial Average lost 12.8 per cent on 28 October and 11.7 per cent on 29 October for a 24.5 per cent loss over two days, the real story of the ensuing bear market was much worse. Cruelly, the Dow Jones rebounded by 12.3 per cent on 30 October and rallied again in May 1930. But these were dead-cat bounces (a Wall Street saying that refers to the fact that if you throw a dead cat out of a high-rise window, even though it bounces when it hits the footpath, it's still dead).

By the time that the bear market of 1929 to 1932 had bottomed in July 1932, the US sharemarket had plunged by almost 90 per cent. The stories of ruined stockbrokers and margin traders jumping from the balconies of the Ritz Hotel have passed into legend. However, it's not as though we don't know today what a crash feels like!

October 1987

I well remember Crash Day, 20 October 1987 (in Australia). It was a Tuesday and I was playing golf. The night before, the US Dow Jones Industrial Average had fallen by 508 points — a staggering 22.6 per cent. The Australian market, like all world markets, had already been spooked by a fall of 5.2 per cent on the US market on 16 October. On Monday 19 October, the Australian market fell another 3.7 per cent. However, nothing prepared Australian investors for what happened next. The All Ordinaries Index of the Australian sharemarket lost 400 points from its notional value, or 25 per cent. That sent $45 billion worth of market capitalisation to money heaven. The $44,000 (on paper) that I lost that day was just a drop in the ocean. Like most people, I had speculated through 1985, 1986 and 1987 thinking that I was a genius at buying stocks that went up in price.

The aftermath of the 1987 crash was not as bad as 1929; no Great Depression. However, Australia did enter a recession from 1990 through 1991. The very best stocks were back above their pre-crash highs within about 14 months. A very scary experience! During October 1987, the All Ordinaries fell by 47.4 per cent — investors thought that the earth had opened up.

The Great Japanese Crash

The Japanese escaped the crash of 1987. They avoided the crash because the Ministry of Finance called in the big broking firms and told them to buy shares. This tactic worked for about two years, but the Japanese sharemarket was so overvalued that the inevitable crash was only delayed. When the crash finally came, it was savage, but worse was to come — it turned into a 14-year bear market. The Nikkei average of the Tokyo Stock Exchange plunged from nearly 39,000 in December 1989 to 7,600 by April 2003. This loss of 80 per cent over

14 years was something of an embarrassment to those of us who advocate buy-and-hold investing. The index started to recover, but then the GFC arrived, plunging the index even lower by February 2009; Japanese investors were looking at an 81 per cent fall over 19 years.

The Nikkei is still 31 per cent lower than its peak. But, there is some humour to be drawn from the situation. On 3 January 1990, the day before share prices began collapsing, the Nikkei financial newspaper's top headline read 'Nikkei Average May Reach 44,000 at Year-End', citing 20 heads of major companies. Or not.

Sharemarket investing can be coloured by one's own personal experiences. If a Japanese investor were tempted to buy shares in February 2009, they would have seen the Nikkei rise 3.4 times in value. They would love the sharemarket — and wonder why anyone ever complained about it!

October 1997

What is it with October? Ten years after the 1987 crash came a case of déjà vu. On Monday 27 October, the US Dow Jones Industrial Average fell 554.24 points. At the time, this was the biggest one-day decline in the history of the index — but only the 12th-largest decline on a percentage basis, at a measly 7.2 per cent.

The cause for the plunge was the Asian currency crisis. From mid-1997, speculators had been attacking the currencies of the so-called tiger economies of South-East Asia, which resulted in massive currency depreciation. The subsequent capital outflows then placed the region's sharemarkets under intense pressure. Many companies in the region weren't able to repay their foreign currency-denominated debt and were technically insolvent. Chaos on the Asian financial markets caused a global sell-off of shares.

Matters came to a head on 27 October 1997, with the record fall in the Dow Jones and trading suspended twice. In Australia, the All Ordinaries sandwiched this fall with drops of 3.3 per cent and 7.2 per cent, dragged down, like all its global peers, by the stunning fall on Wall Street.

Markets were extremely nervous awaiting the US trading day of 28 October. Within minutes, the worst fears were realised when the Dow Jones fell by 180 points. However, market sentiment turned sharply in the opposite direction. Remarkably, the Dow Jones regained 337 points or 4.7 per cent, in its largest ever one-day points gain, amid the highest volume of trade in the history of the New York Stock Exchange. The Australian Securities Exchange rebounded similarly the next day (up 6.3 per cent), and it was sighs of relief all round — crash averted.

March/April 2000

The end of the 'tech boom' crept up slowly on the market. The flagship index of the boom, the Nasdaq Composite Index of the Nasdaq Stock Market in the USA, had roared into 2000, on a spree that saw it rack up 54 per cent in just four months, peaking in March 2000. However, nobody knew at the time that this would be the peak. That didn't last long! By the week of 10 to 14 April, even the most deluded of tech punters realised that the sharemarket gods were seriously peeved at the excesses of valuations that the boom had created.

In that week, the Nasdaq Composite posted three of its four worst-ever points losses. The Nasdaq was down 258.25 points on Monday (10 April) and 286.27 points on Wednesday (12 April), culminating in a 355.5-point plunge on Friday (14 April), which was its worst-ever drop in points terms. Over the month of April, the Nasdaq Composite plunged by 15.6 per cent. The battering taken by the tech stocks spooked the US Dow Jones Industrial Average to a loss on Friday 14 April, of 617.78 points, or 5.7 per cent, at the time its largest-ever loss in points terms. But the Dow Jones' loss for April was only 1.7 per cent.

Analysts point to several causes for the crash, including disappointing earnings in early April from some of the technology superstocks and tax- related selling, as investors sold shares to pay their capital gains tax bills. The Nasdaq Composite had dropped 349 points, or 7.6 per cent, on 3 April and margin calls forced more selling. At the end of April, the Nasdaq Composite Index was 34 per cent lower than its high reached on 10 March. The April crash was only the start. By October 2001, a 17-month bear market, worsened by the September 2001 crash that followed the terrorist attacks on the USA, had stripped 69 per cent from the index's high.

September 2001

The terrorist attacks on the US on 11 September 2001 certainly spooked the financial markets. Trading was suspended in the US markets for four (trading) days, the longest hiatus since the Great Depression. With the US markets closed, overseas markets bore the brunt of the selling. On the day that the planes hit, London's FTSE Index dropped 287.7 points, its record one-day points loss, or 5.7 per cent. In Germany, the DAX plunged by as much as 11.4 per cent before recovering slightly to close the day down 8.5 per cent, its then largest-ever loss. The Paris Stock Exchange's CAC 40 Index lost 7.4 per cent, and the MIB30 Index in Milan dropped 7.7 per cent.

In Tokyo, the Nikkei Index fell 6.6 per cent, crashing through the 10,000-point level to a 17-year low. In Hong Kong, the Hang Seng dropped 923.74 points, or 8.9 per cent, while Singapore's Straits Times Index surrendered 116.31 points, or 7.4 per cent. Airline stocks were particularly hard hit by the terrorist attacks, with British Airways losing 21 per cent in a day (to be outdone a fortnight later when Swissair, facing bankruptcy, lost 97 per cent in a day). Everyone waited for the reaction of the US markets.

On Monday 17 September, the Dow Jones Industrial Average suffered its worst point loss in history, losing 684.33 points, or 7.1 per cent. The Nasdaq Composite lost 115.59 points, or 6.8 per cent, while the S&P 500 sank 53.75 points, or 4.9 per cent, lower. The week of 17 to 21 September stripped a cool US$1.4 trillion from the US markets. The Dow Jones lost 14.3 per cent for the week, the Nasdaq Composite lost 16 per cent for the week, and the S&P 500 Index shed 7 per cent. At the time, it was the Dow's fourth-worst week ever, in percentage terms — the worst was recorded in 1933, when the Dow slumped 16.7 per cent in a week.

The Global Financial Crisis

By 2007, the tech bust and the September 2001 mini-crash had almost been forgotten, in the wake of four years that returned well above average results to sharemarket investors. Volatility was at historic lows and complacency was in the air. Debt flowed like wine on New Year's Eve and using it to leverage up assets was how any self-respecting master of the financial universe made his millions. Nothing could go wrong — until the US housing market turned downward.

The effect of the great bear market of 2007 to 2009 can be explained succinctly using percentages:

>> In the US, the S&P 500 Index fell 57 per cent from its all-time high in October 2007 to a low in March 2009.

>> In the UK, the FT100 Index fell 48 per cent from its all-time high in June 2007 to a low in March 2009.

>> In Japan, the Nikkei 225 Index fell 61 per cent from its high in July 2007 to a low in March 2009.

>> In Hong Kong, the Hang Seng Index fell 65 per cent from its all-time high in October 2007 to a low in October 2008.

The Australian stock market lost 54 per cent of its value — or $690 billion — between November 2007 and February 2009. According to the World Federation of Exchanges, its 53 member markets lost US$3.4 trillion in market value between November 2007 and February 2009, a fall of 54.5 per cent. It was more of a series of crashes than a crash — a bear market on a scale that investors had thought unimaginable, as individuals, companies and even countries faced the realisation that too much debt had virtually bankrupted them.

Of course, sharemarkets recovered and exceed the levels from which they tumbled in 2007 — and in fact, went much higher . . . until the next crash, in 2020.

The 2020 COVID Crash

I cover this event in more detail in Chapter 1, but the COVID-19 crash of February–March 2020 was the most amazing I've seen — for several reasons. First was its unexpected cause: the global outbreak of a mysterious disease. Second, the dizzying acceleration of the mounting panic, and the speed of the fall. Third, the equally stunning speed of the recovery. Falls are often quick, and they can immolate long periods of slow-moving gains; as the sharemarket adage puts it, 'Shares go up by the stairs, but down by the elevator.' But this was something else in its rapidity.

Even the rebound seemed to come out of nowhere. The world seemed to fear more bad news from this coronavirus, but the sharemarket started to recover in late March/early April 2020 as over-sold stocks attracted buyers. At the time, this seemed impossible, and confusing — there appeared to be a complete disconnect between the way people were looking at the global economy and the way they approached sharemarket.

Seeing the markets plunge officially into 'bear markets' in the fastest manner ever was truly spectacular. It took just 16 trading days for the Nasdaq and S&P 500 indices to fall by 20 per cent, and 19 trading sessions for the Dow Jones Industrial Average. The Australian sharemarket even beat that, dropping 20.5 per cent in just 14 days, which was the sharpest fall in Australian history.

The COVID crash included the three worst point drops in US history. On 9 March 2020, the Dow Jones slumped 2,014 points, a 7.79 per cent drop. On 12 March 2020, the Dow then set another record — falling 2,352 points to close at 21,200. That was a 9.99 per cent drop, and the sixth-worst percentage drop in history. Finally, on 16 March the Dow plummeted nearly 3,000 points to close at 20,188, losing 12.9 per cent. The plunge in stock prices was so massive that the New York Stock Exchange suspended trading several times during those tumultuous days.

As I pointed out in Chapter 1, governments and central banks around the world threw the kitchen sink at economies in response to the pandemic, bringing in stimulus measures, emergency spending and support payments. And just when things looked at their worst, in market terms, investors began to lift their eyes above the short term and regain the confidence to invest in companies.

The US markets led this resurgence, with the Dow Jones returning to its pre-'COVID crash' level by November 2020, after 193 trading days. That was the quickest recovery from a 20 per cent-plus fall in three decades, after the Dow took 191 trading days to recover in early 1991 from a bear-market drop. To put this in perspective, in all its trading history, on average it's taken 1,483 trading days for the Dow to reach a new all-time high after a 20 per cent fall.

The Australian sharemarket's S&P/ASX 200 index was a lot slower to recover its pre-'COVID crash' level, taking until May 2021 to complete the task. But it did, as the benchmark index always does — however long it takes.

Chapter **26**

Ten Great Australian Stocks

The Australian sharemarket is made up of 2,200 companies, with about 16 times that number in the corporate graveyard. That's a lot of stocks to choose from when trying to select ten great stocks in Australia. The stocks in this chapter are not necessarily the best performers — although they do feature the number-one stock on the exchange's all-time list, Westfield — but what I've tried to do in this list is assemble ten stocks that tell the story of Australian share investment. Every company has a story, and some of them have quite amazing stories to tell — with big dollops of the country's history thrown in.

Westfield Group

It's hard to go past Westfield as one of the great Australian stocks — although it doesn't exist anymore. But as I showed in Chapter 3, in its 57-year life on the Australian sharemarket, Westfield turned an original $1,000 investment in 1960 (equivalent to about $15,800 in today's dollars) into $440 million — by compounding at a rate of 25.6 per cent a year, for 57 years.

For such a globally successful Australian company, Westfield had inauspicious beginnings. And the social history aspect of Westfield's story is just as compelling as its staggering financial success.

John Saunders (born Jeno Schwarz) and Frank Lowy were just two of the many European migrants who came to Australia after World War II with not much in the way of possessions. Both Holocaust survivors, they met in Sydney and started a delicatessen in Blacktown in Sydney's western suburbs. The pair moved into residential and then retail property development, opening a small 'American-style' shopping centre in Blacktown in July 1959. Named Westfield Place, it was one of the first shopping centres to open in Australia.

When they wanted to float the business on the Sydney Stock Exchange a year later, Lowy and Saunders were told that they were crazy — Australians liked to shop in the CBD, at Myer and Grace Bros.; at David Jones and Buckley & Nunn. They weren't going to shop in big barns in the suburbs!

The Westfield float struggled to get off the ground; Lowy and Saunders relied heavily on word of mouth among family, friends and fellow migrants to bring in enough money to make it happen. But the pair had seen the future — they knew that more Australians were flocking to those suburbs, had cars to reach their shopping centre and were receptive to shopping at a range of shops under one air-conditioned roof. Westfield was listed as a public company, and from that first small shopping centre in western Sydney, Westfield built a global portfolio of shopping centres, with a list of iconic properties that included Westfield London, Westfield World Trade Centre in New York and Westfield Stratford City.

Unfortunately, December 2017 was the end of the line, as the Lowy family sold Westfield into a takeover by French–Dutch commercial real estate company Unibail-Rodamco, which added Westfield to its name. (Westfield's Australian and New Zealand shopping centre portfolio is owned and operated by Scentre Group, which was spun-off by Westfield in June 2014.) Because part of the $33 billion payment for the takeover was shares in Unibail-Rodamco, that entity still trades on the Australian Securities Exchange (ASX), where it's known as Unibail-Rodamco-Westfield (URW), so a small part of the amazing Westfield wealth creation story carries on.

CSL

Australia's home-grown biotech star, CSL, has been a huge success on the sharemarket since the Australian government privatised it through a sharemarket float in June 1994. Clearly, the government didn't have a clue what it owned; the former Commonwealth Serum Laboratories has flourished under its two modern-day chief executives, Brian McNamee (1990–2013) and Paul Perreault (since 2013).

When it floated, CSL was Australia's principal supplier of vaccines and anti-venoms (it had been since 1916) and the country's sole manufacturer of products derived from blood plasma (coagulants, immunoglobulins and albumins) for use in Australian hospitals and by doctors (the Red Cross collected the blood for free, and the government paid CSL to process it). CSL employed just over 1,300 people in Australia at the time; it earned revenue of about $170 million and made a profit of about $20 million.

Today, CSL generates annual revenue of about $13.7 billion, makes a profit of almost $3.2 billion and employs more than 25,000 people across 35 countries.

In 2000, under then-CEO Brian McNamee (who returned to CSL as its chair in 2018), CSL made its first big acquisition, buying the Swiss-based ZLB Bioplasma, the blood plasma division of the Swiss Red Cross, for more than $1 billion, which doubled the size of the company overnight and gave it major exposure to the fast-growing European and US plasma markets. That move transformed what was already a large and successful business into a healthcare heavyweight.

ZLB enabled CSL to turbocharge its business in IVIG (intravenous immunoglobulin), which is used to help treat immune deficiency disorders and inflammatory conditions. Next, in 2001, came the purchase of the bulk of the plasma collection business of US group Nabi. In 2004, CSL boosted its position even further with another $1 billion purchase of a rival plasma business, Aventis Behring of France, which was the top dog in blood products. The CSL Behring division now produces more than 80 per cent of the company's revenue, with markets in more than 100 countries across Asia–Pacific, Europe, Latin America and North America.

In 2014, CSL bought the Novartis influenza vaccine business, which is now known as Seqirus, and is the world's second-largest influenza vaccines company. Three years later, CSL picked up stem-cell therapy firm Calimmune. In 2020, it added Canadian biopharmaceutical company Vitaeris, which has developed a potential treatment option for organ transplant recipients experiencing rejection. In late 2021 came CSL's biggest deal yet, a US$12 billion ($16.7 billion) deal to acquire Swiss firm Vifor Pharma, which specialises in iron-deficiency treatments, nephrology, cardiology and rare diseases. Vifor owns a portfolio of both prescription and non-prescription medicines.

Over its almost three decades on the sharemarket, CSL has become a globally significant biotechnology company, a global leader in developing and delivering high-quality medicines that treat people with rare and serious diseases, a major contributor to the prevention of influenza globally, and a trans-continental partner in pandemic preparedness. What started out as a share floated out of government ownership, at the equivalent of 77 cents in a $300 million float, is now a $135 billion company with a share price of $300.

Although (as I discuss in Chapter 10) it has not seen a linear one-way rise in price — CSL has had a few hiccups — it has been exceptionally well-managed over a long period by a management team that has shown great discipline, commitment to the long term and vision. Quite simply, CSL is widely considered one of the best — if not the standout best — of the companies that Australia has produced. And that ties in with being a very successful wealth creator.

Cochlear

For some people, investing on the sharemarket is not only about making money, it's about making money while doing good. Ethical or 'socially responsible' investment (refer to Chapter 5) is a big growth area in Australia, worth about $160 billion at present. If actively doing good is what you want your investments to do, Cochlear is an excellent example of world-class Australian medical technology that demonstrably does good.

Cochlear has become a world leader in cochlear (inner ear) implants, which allow people with impaired hearing to receive environmental sounds and speech. Cochlear's technology originated from research at Melbourne University in the 1970s. The first successful implant was performed in 1978.

In 1981, the Cochlear company was formed. In 1985, the company's implant was cleared by the US Food and Drug Administration (FDA) for use with adults classified as profoundly hearing-impaired (PHI) — with no useful hearing. In 1990, the FDA cleared the device for use in PHI children. More than 650,000 people worldwide have now received a Cochlear implant.

In December 1995, the owner of Cochlear, the Pacific Dunlop group, floated the shares at $2.50. The share price has subsequently risen to $240, and shareholders have received a further $38.71 in dividends along the way (while Pacific Dunlop almost collapsed, before morphing into Ansell, the protective equipment maker subsidiary that generated most of its revenue).

As one of the Australian market's premier 'growth' stocks (refer to Chapter 10), Cochlear consistently rates a price/earnings ratio above that of the market — at the same time, combining an outstanding financial return with the warm inner glow of investing in a company that's brought a better quality of life to many hearing-impaired people. The company is always exposed to technological risk — hearing implants is a very competitive market, and a competitor could bring out a superior product — but then again, Cochlear has shown a pretty impressive ability to stay on the leading edge of its market through a heavy focus on research and development, and a commitment to innovation. Its global market share of about 65 per cent is testament to that.

Pro Medicus

Pro Medicus is another inspiring story of a global leader developed in Australia, this time in a significant area of medical diagnosis and communication — imaging and associated technology.

Pro Medicus was founded in 1983 by Dr Sam Hupert and Anthony Hall, a systems analyst, after the two met at a wine tasting. In the early years, Pro Medicus focused on helping medical practices do business more easily, helping them keep clinical records, as well as manage the scheduling of X-rays, through a practice management system. That led to specialising in the private diagnostic imaging market, and the company built Promedicus.net, a secure email service that enabled referring doctors located anywhere in Australia to receive encrypted patient diagnostic results via the internet.

The pair floated 20 per cent of their company in 2000, at $1.15 a share, raising $23 million, which valued Pro Medicus at $115 million. Today — despite a dip to 20 cents in 2011 — the shares trade at $60 and the company is worth $6.3 billion on the sharemarket, making both founders billionaires.

Hupert and Hall realised that radiology was moving from film to digital, so the company teamed up with Agfa in 2001, combining its informatics side with Agfa's clinical side. Over time, as their service grew from helping patients receive their radiology diagnostic results faster, Pro Medicus built a range of products designed for use by radiologists, physicians, surgeons, GPs and health professionals, including radiology information systems (RISs) and picture archiving communication systems (PACS), plus a suite of services centred on the company's product offerings. These products provided a seamless, scalable, fully integrated IT environment for healthcare professionals, enhancing workflow and increasing business efficiency.

Although the duo had realised the potential of the internet to transform medical imaging communication, Pro Medicus was still dealing in two-dimensional (2D) images. In 2007, at a Chicago exhibition, the Australians saw a company called Visage Imaging, which had three-dimensional (3D) technology. They were told by the managers that the business, which was owned by a US defence equipment company, was being sold.

Hupert and Hall let it be known that if the deal fell through, Pro Medicus would be interested in buying the company. In 2009, they received a phone call from the chief executive of Visage. Quickly, Pro Medicus stepped in and bought Visage for $4.5 million.

Visage transformed Pro Medicus. Visage's image storage and distribution technology allows doctors to instantly upload and manipulate radiology images (including using iPads and iPhones) to give instant diagnoses. Visage's technology crunches very large files into 3D images that can be streamed remotely and uploaded to mobile devices.

Pro Medicus has developed the Visage platform into a quick, all-in-one option that allows doctors to use the same screen for 2D, 3D and four-dimensional (4D) images. The speed of the system is linked to using streaming technology to transport files. The Visage RIS, the Visage 7 imaging software suite and the cloud-based solution, Visage CloudPACS, are the backbone of the system. The Visage 7 technology can handle image file sizes up to ten gigabytes per file, giving Pro Medicus a big advantage over competitors still relying on traditional 'compress and send' technology.

The company is rolling out a breast density algorithm, the first diagnostic AI (artificial intelligence) algorithm produced by Visage 7, as Pro Medicus starts to explore AI applications, such as machines identifying unusual formations in the scans and alerting doctors to them.

The company's imaging systems are conquering the US and will extend into Europe. The company is also moving into new areas such as cardiology and ophthalmology. Pro Medicus is a great Australian sharemarket story.

Washington H. Soul Pattinson

One of the oldest companies on the ASX, Washington H. Soul, Pattinson and Company Limited, was incorporated and listed on the Sydney Stock Exchange (now the Australian Securities Exchange) in January 1903. It's Australia's second-oldest listed company, behind AGL, which listed (as Australian Gas Light) on the Sydney Stock Exchange in 1871.

The business was a merger of two companies. Washington H. Soul and Co. was established by father-and-son chemists Caleb Soul and Washington Handley Soul in 1872, with the opening of a drug store and dispensary in Pitt Street, Sydney (later, the company moved into the pharmaceutical manufacturing and distribution field). Caleb Soul died in 1894, and seven years later, Washington Handley Soul merged his company with Pattinson & Co., which had been founded by Lewy Pattinson in 1886. Pattinson & Co. was a very similar business to Washington H. Soul and Co. — starting with a pharmacy in the Sydney suburb of Balmain, Pattinson & Co. had also expanded into the manufacturing and distribution areas.

Fast forward 119 years, and Washington H. Soul Pattinson is now a major investment house, with a portfolio encompassing many industries including telecommunications, resources, building products, retail, agriculture, property, financial services and other equity investments.

The company owns major stakes in telecommunications companies TPG Telecom (12.6 per cent) and Tuas (25.3 per cent); building products, property and investment firm Brickworks (43.3 per cent); and thermal (electricity) coal and agriculture company New Hope Corporation (39.9 per cent). It also holds a $1.2 billion portfolio of pharmaceutical investments and a $400 million portfolio of financial services investments, and wholly owns a copper and zinc mining and exploration company called Round Oak Minerals, which has mining operations in Queensland and Western Australia. As well, the company owns funds management businesses that hold shares, property, fixed-income and agricultural investments.

Washington H. Soul Pattinson and Brickworks are partners in the longest-lived cross-shareholding in Australian corporate history: Washington H. Soul Pattinson owns 43.3 per cent of Brickworks, which in turn owns 39 per cent of Washington H. Soul Pattinson. The cross-shareholding arrangement has been in place since 1969, but it is not allowed under the current ASX listing rules. This arrangement has been criticised by some investors; investment institution Perpetual, which has agitated against it for a long time, brought a case in the Federal Court in 2017 arguing that the cross-linkage was "oppressive" to the minority shareholders of each, but lost its case. Washington H. Soul Pattinson and Brickworks argue that the cross-shareholding makes the pair takeover-proof, and allows both companies to focus on long-term investment success.

The two companies are controlled by the Millner family, which has been involved since Jim Millner, the nephew of Lewy Pattinson's son William Frederick Pattinson, joined Washington H. Soul Pattinson as an apprentice chemist in 1938. Jim's nephew, veteran investor Robert Millner — sometimes described as 'Australia's Warren Buffett' — chairs both businesses.

But aside from the slice of history that Washington H. Soul Pattinson represents, the reason I've included it as one of Australia's great stocks is its outstanding record of paying dividends. The company has paid a dividend to shareholders every year since listing in 1903; moreover, Washington H. Soul Pattinson has increased its ordinary dividend every year since 2000. It is the only company in the S&P/ASX All Ordinaries index to have achieved this. (Brickworks has either maintained or increased its dividend every year since 1976.)

If a shareholder had invested $1,000 in Washington H. Soul Pattinson in 1981 and reinvested all dividends, the shareholding would have appreciated to $239,182 as at 31 July 2021. This equates to a compound annual growth rate of 14.7 per cent a year, for 40 years. This growth doesn't include the value of the franking credits that have been passed on to shareholders by Washington H. Soul Pattinson.

That's sustained success, in anyone's language.

Fortescue Metals Group

Fortescue Metals Group, the brainchild of Perth-based mining magnate and billionaire Andrew 'Twiggy' Forrest, is another great sharemarket success story. But it certainly didn't look that way when the company was established, in 2003.

Back then, a tiny private company known as The Metal Group, owned by Forrest, was buying unwanted iron ore tenements in the Pilbara region of Western Australia — mainly tenements that iron ore giant Rio Tinto didn't want. The reason the big miner wasn't interested in them was that they hosted iron grades between 56 and 59 per cent iron, which was well below the 'benchmark' grade of 62 per cent iron. Rio Tinto thought that it could never sell such low-grade ore. China's incredible modernisation and urbanisation process, which would prove such a voracious maw for iron ore, had not really begun. The iron ore price was around US$50 a tonne.

In 2003, The Metal Group bought a stake in the listed exploration company Allied Mining & Processing, changing its name in July 2003 to Fortescue Metals Group. Andrew Forrest was appointed executive chairman. At that point, the proposals to develop what was called the East Pilbara iron ore project began to take shape.

It was staggering stuff. Fortescue was planning to open the first major iron ore mine in the Pilbara region in 40 years, challenging the duopoly of Rio Tinto and BHP. Moreover, those incumbents owned the rail lines needed to get ore to port — and the port facilities to ship it. Fortescue proposed building a mine, a 350-kilometre rail line and a port, in a $1.2 billion plan. This from a company worth about $10 million on the sharemarket!

Aside from the challenges any businessperson would face trying to get this off the ground, Forrest was dealing with the fallout of his previous venture, the listed company Anaconda Nickel, which had tried to put into practice a revolutionary new method for treating nickel laterites (a form of ore from which nickel extraction had been notoriously difficult). After being tested successfully at pilot–plant level, the plant was upgraded to extract nickel in this way at a full commercial scale. The upgrade failed badly, with the courts later attributing the underperformance to the plant's contractors. Plagued by technical problems, Anaconda's ambitious production targets failed to materialise; its share price was slashed, and operating losses mounted. Investors lost billions of dollars. Rightly or wrongly, Forrest wore the responsibility, particularly as Anaconda Nickel's major shareholder, Glencore International, fought it out in the courts. When Forrest finally stepped down from Anaconda in 2001, his reputation was in tatters.

Yet there he was, in 2003, telling the world of his ambitious new iron ore plan. Forrest's legendary drive leached into his enthusiastic sales team, who, by 2004, had convinced China's biggest steel mill, Baosteel, to sign a memorandum of understanding to buy iron ore from Fortescue, an agreement that was later converted into a long-term offtake contract for five million tonnes a year. By the middle of 2006, more than 20 sales agreements had been signed, covering almost all of Fortescue's planned annual output of 45 million tonnes of iron ore, starting in 2008.

However, a deal for Chinese construction companies to build the mine, railway and port had collapsed in March 2005, triggering an investigation into Forrest's conduct by the Australian Securities and Investments Commission (ASIC) that went all the way to the High Court. Work had already started on the port in early 2006, funded by Fortescue, but there was no way the company could do it all on its own. Forrest and his team frantically criss-crossed the world's major capital markets and steel buyers, desperately pleading their case for funding. At the last gasp, in August 2006, the US bond market — where people vividly remembered the Anaconda Nickel debacle — came through with $2.7 billion in funding, arranged through Citigroup, and supported by US, European and Asian institutions.

Quite simply, it was a triumph for Forrest's vision and determination — and persuasiveness. But even he could not have envisaged the true scale of China's burgeoning demand for iron ore by 2006.

In October 2007, Fortescue Metals Group commenced mining iron ore at the Cloudbreak mine in the Pilbara. In April 2008, the first ore train ran on Fortescue's railway. In May 2008, the first ore ship was loaded at the company's newly commissioned Herb Elliott Port at Port Hedland. In December 2008, Fortescue became the first Pilbara railway owner to allow other miners to use its track.

In the first full financial year of mining operations, 2008–09, Fortescue produced and shipped 27.3 million tonnes of iron ore. Net profit was US$508 million. By 2020–21, production had swelled almost seven-fold, to 182.2 million tonnes, while profit had multiplied more than 20 times, to US$10.3 billion.

Fortescue has invested more than US$30 billion in its operations and infrastructure. The company's operations now comprise three mining hubs in the Pilbara region, connected to Port Hedland via 760 kilometres of the fastest heavy-haul railway in the world.

Along the way, Fortescue has been a powerful agent of social change. It employs more than 10,100 people — 954 of whom are indigenous. Over the past ten years, the company has awarded more than $3 billion in work contracts to Aboriginal-run businesses and joint ventures. More than 1,000 Aboriginal people have graduated from the company's Vocational Training and Employment Centre (VTEC) program, and 21 per cent of Fortescue's employees are female — including 25 per cent of senior leadership roles.

The shares have created massive wealth — not least for Forrest. When Forrest backed his Pilbara assets into Allied Mining & Processing to form Fortescue in 2003, the company's shares traded for less than 10 cents. By July 2021, the shares had reached $24.91 — which, given a ten-for-one share split in 2007, equates to a pre-split price of $249.10. Fortescue is a 'bagger' of staggering proportions.

Now Forrest, as non-executive chairman and Fortescue's largest shareholder, says the company will lead the way in building a steel-making industry in Australia, making 'green' steel — zero-carbon steel, using zero-carbon-dioxide-emissions energy. Fortescue has formed a new arm, Fortescue Future Industries (FFI), which will take oversight of these plans.

Forrest has also pledged that FFI will produce 15 million tonnes of green hydrogen by 2030, increasing to 50 million tonnes a year thereafter. These are ambitious plans, to put it mildly — but Forrest and Fortescue have proven many doubters wrong over the years.

Sonic Healthcare

Sonic Healthcare is yet another success story of the Australian sharemarket. The company has become a global leader in the medical diagnostics field. However, it was actually a struggling mining explorer when it listed in 1987; the company was looking for a money-making business and, under the leadership of accountant Michael Boyd, had decided to buy a pathology company, Douglass Laboratories Pty. Ltd.

That same year, a young pathologist named Colin Goldschmidt joined the company. In 1993, Boyd decided to make Goldschmidt the chief executive, even though he had no management training.

At the time, pathology was virtually a cottage industry. But Sonic Healthcare started the process of consolidating the industry, to achieve the economies of scale that were possible in what is a fixed-cost business. For the first seven years after listing, Sonic owned just one laboratory company, in Sydney. But from that base, it expanded its pathology/clinical laboratory services to become the Australian market leader, serving all states and territories. Sonic also expanded into radiology and is currently the second-largest participant in this market in Australia.

Starting with New Zealand in 1999, the company expanded its pathology laboratory operations internationally, to include significant operations in North America, the UK and Europe. Sonic is the largest private operator in Australia, Germany, Switzerland and the UK; the second-largest in Belgium and New Zealand; and the third-largest in the US. That makes it the world's third-largest provider of pathology/clinical laboratory services. It employs about 38,000 people, serving 138 million patients in the financial year 2020–21.

Sonic Healthcare has grown its pathology revenues from $146 million in 1998 to $7.7 billion in the financial year 2020–21. Its US operations are the biggest revenue generator, contributing 25 per cent of the total, ahead of Australia and Germany, each on 23 per cent.

The company is now a $21 billion global success story, and Colin Goldschmidt is still the chief executive. In tandem with Sonic's chief financial officer of more than two decades, Chris Wilks, the duo have become two of the Australian corporate scene's great leaders, and Sonic Healthcare one of the Australian sharemarket's biggest successes.

REA Group

REA Group is the greatest internet start-up the Australian sharemarket has seen. And, in keeping with the tradition of start-up companies, it was started in a garage, in 1995, in the Melbourne suburb of Doncaster East. The garage belonged to Karl Sabljak, one of the four founders. Along with his wife Carmel, brother Steve and co-founder Martin Howell, the team of four worked on creating an online solution to make it easier to search for real estate. The website realestate.com.au was born.

At the time, property listings formed one part of the famous 'rivers of gold' that flowed into the coffers of newspaper publisher Fairfax — the other components of this revenue stream were classified job and car ads. Fairfax may not have wholly realised it, but realestate.com.au — and seek.com.au and carsales.com.au — were coming for that gold.

The founders of realestate.com.au recognised the power of the online revolution and built their vision of an Australian real estate 'market space' on the internet. They envisaged this as a 'one stop shop' for home buyers, sellers, investors, tenants and real estate agents — with the most comprehensive range of properties, financial and other ancillary services for anybody interested in Australian real estate. As well as providing the essential information that home buyers, sellers, investors and tenants were looking for, the site aimed to create opportunities for its advertisers and real estate agency partners as much as it wanted to showcase real estate market information.

By 1999, with the help of major shareholder Macquarie Bank, realestate.com.au was ready to float on the sharemarket. By then, it had already captured a significant market share of Australian online real estate traffic. As well as being consistently rated as the number one Australian real estate site, realestate.com.au was consistently ranked in the top 20 of all Australian internet sites. At the time of its prospectus, realestate.com.au was recording more than five million hits a week.

But the initial public offer (IPO), in December 1999, was unfortunately timed, running headlong into the 'dotcom bust' or 'tech crash' in March 2000 (refer to Chapter 25 for more on the March 2000 tech crash). Floated at 50 cents to raise $7.65 million, the sale of 37 per cent of realestate.com.au valued the company at $13 million. However, in the wake of the global sharemarket crash that followed the September 2001 terrorist attack in New York, the stock sank to a price of just 4.9 cents. News Corporation (the newspaper publishing arch-rival of Fairfax) stepped in to save the day, injecting $2 million in cash plus $8 million of TV and print advertising, in exchange for 44 per cent of realestate.com.au. That valued the company at $23 million.

News Corporation still owns 61.4 per cent of REA Group (as the company is now named, after its ASX ticker code), which means its $10 million investment is now worth $13.2 billion, because that $13 million company floated in 1999 is now worth $21.6 billion.

As I showed in Chapter 3, at $172, shareholders in the IPO have made 344 times their money. And if you were one of the prescient investors who snapped REA up for 4.9 cents a share in September 2001, when the sharemarket in its wisdom judged that the business wasn't going so well — you've multiplied your investment by 3,510 times. To make $1 million, all you had to do was chip in $285 when the stock was going for 4.9 cents. REA Group — which now operates 16 property websites on three continents — has been a multi-decade mega-bagger, compounding on an amazing scale for investors.

TIP

Check out Chapter 5 for a description of how the REA Group achieved this mighty feat — first disrupting and stealing the 'rivers of gold', and then deploying the *network effect* (where a product or service gains additional value as more people use it) in all its glory.

Afterpay

Afterpay is one of the great stories of the Australian sharemarket — although it wasn't really on it for long. But not many companies create a new business and become a verb, while also minting the country's youngest (paper) billionaire — that is, measured on the company's market valuation if the holding were to be sold — and becoming a '100-bagger' for their float subscribers. And while it never made a profit as a listed company, it was a once-in-a-generation stock, rocketing from the depths of microcap land to the ASX Top 20 by market value in just five years.

All that looked very far off when Afterpay floated in April 2016. The company had been founded two years earlier, when Nick Molnar and Anthony Eisen, who, as the story goes, met as neighbours in the Sydney suburb of Bellevue Hill when Eisen (then chief investment officer at investment company Guinness Peat Group) was curious as to why Molnar's bedroom light was on so late most nights. Eisen remarked on this when he encountered Molnar at the post office one day; from that conversation, the relationship was born that resulted in Afterpay.

Over vegemite toast around a kitchen table, the two worked-out the business case for Afterpay — and thus, effectively invented the modern concept of buy-now-pay-later (BNPL). By shopping with participating retailers, shoppers are able to pay for individual purchases in four fortnightly payments. Afterpay pays the retailer immediately after the transaction, and the retailers pay Afterpay a fee for each transaction. In return for being paid up-front by Afterpay, and handing off the payment risk, the merchant — not the shopper — pays Afterpay a fee. After-pay bears full responsibility for recovering money from the customers on the due dates, recouping the purchase value from the shopper in four equal fortnightly payments over a maximum term of 56 days.

Although the gloss was to come off the BNPL model — and Afterpay with it, especially when store closures during COVID-19 saw it lose $156.3 million over the 2020–21 year — what investors in Afterpay were most interested in was the global growth opportunity that the BNPL market represented.

According to data from fintech giant FIS Worldpay, ecommerce transactions around the world were US$4.6 trillion ($6.3 trillion) in total in 2020, of which BNPL accounted for 2.1 per cent. FIS Worldpay forecast that global penetration to double by 2024. BNPL providers had a very big runway for growth — and Afterpay was the market leader.

Shoppers appeared to see Afterpay as a better option than a credit card. The company said it was simply empowering shoppers — particularly Millennial shoppers and those from Generation Z — to use their own money, without charging them interest or hidden fees. Afterpay anticipated that the Millennial and Generation Z share of discretionary spending would increase by 47 per cent by 2030 (from 31 per cent in 2021). These shoppers' peak earning years are still to come.

Although there were plenty of doubters during the company's time on the ASX, Afterpay pointed to the fact that its customers in Australia who had been using it for more than four years transacted 31 times a year on average, up from 25 times the year earlier. Those that had used Afterpay for more than three years used it 20 times a year; more than two years, 16 times; more than one year, 11 times; while first-year users tended to use it four times. The *customer lifetime value* (how much a single customer is worth to the business) was expanding all the time.

The other main point about Afterpay was how it worked for the retailers that signed on to use the service. First, it boosted their sales because it allowed shoppers to spend money they didn't yet have. It increased retailers' *conversion rates* (the percentage of visitors to a retail outlet who make a purchase). And when it came to online buying, it increased a shopper's 'basket' size. Finally, retailers tended to see a lower goods return rate.

Furthermore, for retailers, using Afterpay saw higher numbers of new and returning customers. Afterpay customer 'cohorts' tended to transact in greater size, and more frequently, the longer they used the platform. In the 2020–21 financial year, 93 per cent of underlying sales were coming from repeat customers.

TIP

What many investors, and critics of the company, failed to grasp was the very powerful network effect that Afterpay created. Professional investors are always looking for the network effect — where every new participant creates more value. Afterpay not only benefited its shoppers, it also massively benefited the retailers that signed on to offer the service — they saw higher numbers of new and returning customers, higher conversions, increased online 'basket sizes' and lower return rates, both online and instore. More customers led to more retailers, which led to more customers — which ultimately led to better, richer customer data for Afterpay, which helped it to improve its real-time risk assessment. Afterpay generated leads for the retailers that used it, creating a virtuous retail circle.

That's what US payments giant Block, Inc. (then called Square, Inc.) must have been thinking in August 2021 when it announced an agreed deal to acquire Afterpay in a *scrip bid* (using its own shares as the currency), in a $39 billion deal that was settled in early 2022. When the bid was announced, Square, Inc. shares were worth US$247.26, implying a transaction price of $126.21 per Afterpay share.

That was for a stock that floated in April 2016, at $1 a share. The long-term growth of the merged entity (which still trades on the ASX in the form of CHESS Depositary Interests, or CDIs — refer to Chapter 12 — of Block, Inc.) could potentially be massive. Block now operates Afterpay as its BNPL platform within its suite of payment solutions.

But whatever happens going forward, Molnar and Eisen can be credited with creating a once-in-a-lifetime moonshot of a stock — one that shook the financial services world, and quickly earned some staggering capital gains for investors.

BHP

The story of what is today the BHP Group began in 1883, when a sheep station boundary rider in north-west New South Wales, Charles Rasp, discovered a silver, zinc and lead deposit that came to be known as Broken Hill. The discovery was not wholly a fluke — Rasp had studied chemistry in his native Germany and was known as a very observant man — but it is true that when he pegged the claim, he thought he had found an outcrop of tin. What he had stumbled upon was the first indication of a massive ore body that turned out to the largest — and richest — single source of silver, lead and zinc ore ever discovered on earth.

Rasp and two partners pegged a mineral claim in September 1883. Initially, they formed a syndicate of seven members, but when they realised the enormity of their claim they formed a public company. In August 1885, the Broken Hill Proprietary Company Limited was formed, and listed on the Sydney Stock Exchange.

That was the genesis of Australia's famous BHP, which, along with its birthplace Broken Hill, played a major role in transforming Australia from an agricultural backwater and into a modern industrial nation. The minerals dug up by BHP helped to support Australia through two world wars, two global depressions and profound, prolonged social change.

BHP ceased operations at Broken Hill in 1939. Other companies kept mining the original mining leases until the early 1990s. Newer deposits of zinc, silver and lead are still mined under the city to this day.

BHP has reinvented itself several times. In 1915, the company expanded into steel manufacturing, with operations at Newcastle and Port Kembla in New South Wales, and Whyalla in South Australia — eventually spinning off its steel operations in the 2000s. In the 1950s, BHP began petroleum exploration in Bass Strait, with a major discovery there in 1965 triggering growth that would eventually see BHP Petroleum becoming one of the world's biggest oil and gas producers, with producing assets in the US Gulf of Mexico, Australia, Trinidad and Tobago, and Algeria, as well as appraisal and exploration options in Mexico, Trinidad and Tobago, the Gulf of Mexico, Eastern Canada and Barbados.

In 2001, BHP merged with the London-based (but Dutch-founded) Billiton mining company to form BHP Billiton, which was dual-listed in London and Australia, trading as two separate companies, BHP Billiton Limited in Australia and BHP Billiton Plc in London, with distinctive, different shares. Shareholders in both companies received the same dividend payments and voting rights; however, the ASX and UK-listed shares traded differently, with the Australian shares typically commanding a premium because of the franking credits available to the ASX-listed BHP Billiton Limited shareholders. In August 2021, BHP announced that it would delist from the London exchange, with all shareholders transferred to the Australia-based BHP Group Limited.

In 2015, BHP spun out South32, an Australian listed company formed to hold assets outside what were then the company's four commodity 'pillars' — iron ore, oil, copper and coal. South32 contained the commodities outside this core portfolio (mainly aluminium, manganese, nickel, silver and lead), as well as some steel-making coal mines in Australia and thermal (electricity) coal operations in South Africa. This demerger was followed in November 2018 by the dropping of the 'Billiton' name, with the UK listing changing to BHP Group Plc and the ASX listing changing to BHP Group Limited. (In January 2022, BHP relinquished its London Stock Exchange listing, becoming a solely ASX-listed company, BHP Group Limited.)

In 2019, BHP announced that it would exit the thermal (electricity) coal business, in keeping with its long-term goal to achieve net zero operational greenhouse gas emissions by 2050.

In August 2021, BHP and Australian oil and gas giant Woodside Petroleum entered into a merger commitment deed to combine their respective oil and gas portfolios by an all-stock merger, meaning it would be the largest energy company listed on the ASX, as well as becoming one of the global top ten independent energy companies by production.

At the same time, BHP also announced that it had approved US$5.7 billion of capital expenditure for the first stage of the Jansen potash project in the Canadian province of Saskatchewan. The resources giant said that this *potash* (agricultural fertiliser) investment aligned with the company's strategy of growing its exposure to 'future-facing commodities' in large, low-cost but world-class assets. Jansen is a classic BHP long-term play — the first ore is targeted for 2027, but the company says peak demand for potash is not expected for at least another 100 years.

The 'Big Australian' as BHP has been known for generations is now the world's largest diversified natural resources company by market capitalisation, with more than 80,000 employees and contractors around the world. BHP is among the world's top producers of major commodities, including iron ore, copper, nickel and metallurgical (steelmaking) coal (sometimes called coking coal). The company's revenue and earnings remain heavily skewed towards its iron ore operations in Western Australia.

These days, BHP says it is "focused on the resources the world needs to grow and decarbonise." That means copper for renewable energy; nickel for electric vehicles; potash for sustainable farming; and iron ore and metallurgical coal for the steel needed for global infrastructure and the energy transition. It says it has a "resources mix for today and for the future." Charles Rasp and his fellow visionaries of the 1880s would probably approve.

REMEMBER

For generations, BHP has been considered one of the bluest of blue-chip Australian companies, with the shares treated as family heirlooms. That is actually not the way the shares should be viewed. BHP has not always been a great investment; in fact, there have been periods in which it has been a dud. It has posted big losses at times, disappointed the market, been a middling investment performer for periods — all of which should realistically be expected of a company exposed to the vagaries of commodity prices and exchange rates. Even now, at the time of writing, its five-year total return (capital gains plus dividends) is 17.6 per cent a year — very good, in a low-interest-rate environment, but not spectacular. 2021 has seen an all-time high in the share price — above $52, as iron ore prices surged — but there have certainly been periods over the years in which the BHP share price has slid lower and underperformed the market. But as a company, a story, a piece of Australian history and a global flag-bearer for Australia, BHP has been, quite simply, an icon.

IN THIS CHAPTER

» Staying patient with your stocks

» Understanding volatility

» Staying cool and calm

» Ignoring dividends at your peril

» Knowing what you're buying into

» Letting go of lost returns

Chapter **27**

Ten Things Not To Do, Ever

When dealing with the sharemarket, you face many dos and don'ts. All the chapters in this book deal with the many dos that can guide you to making the right investments on the sharemarket. Now the time has come to give you a chapter that deals with some of the very important don'ts.

Don't Think You Can Get Rich Quick

The sharemarket is a place to get rich slowly. While the sharemarket offers the best chance for long-term wealth creation, the market can also be used for short-term speculation, which is a form of gambling. Sure, short-term killings can be made on the sharemarket but, in the main, if you try to compress the wealth-growing powers of the sharemarket into months or weeks (even days), you're asking for trouble.

It's very tempting, in boom times, to say, 'Every share that I buy goes up in price. Where has this instant wealth been all my life? I am a genius!' The reality is that the shares you bought are rising in price because the sharemarket is experiencing a boom. The shares are not going up in price because you, 'the genius', chose them. You'd be amazed how hard it is for people to face reality and rid themselves of these insidious thoughts. Conversely, in November 2007 to March 2009, or February to March 2020, your shares weren't falling because you were a 'bad' investor — the market was falling across the board.

WARNING

A corollary to this rule is: Don't sign up for an expensive share-trading course (or software program) if the promoters use the term 'millionaire' to get you in or, worse, say you'll be able to quit your day job. The way to wealth on the sharemarket is through diversification, careful stock selection and time, time, time. Investment can't be hurried and anyone who says you can get rich quick is a fraud. Don't waste time talking to them and don't waste money buying their product.

TIP

Another corollary to this rule: Don't listen to tips (except the ones in this book). If you buy shares on a tip, how can you be sure that the tip didn't originate from insiders who want to lock in a profit before the price falls? A fall they most likely know is coming.

Don't Underestimate Volatility

Yes, shares have been the best-performing asset class over long periods of time. Since 1900, according to AMP Capital, Australian shares have earned a return of approximately 11.8 per cent a year, as measured by the S&P/ASX All Ordinaries Accumulation index — which counts capital growth and dividends — and its predecessor indices.

But shares have also been the most volatile of the asset classes. In any given year, shares could be the worst-performing asset class. Over the long term, however, nothing beats shares as a wealth accumulator. The biggest mistake you can make is to leave shares out of your investment portfolio. You see more rising years than falling years, making shares a great long-term generator of wealth; statistically, however, investors can expect a negative year on the sharemarket about every five years. Since 1950, says research firm Andex Charts, which has studied 841 12-month periods of investment in the S&P/ASX All Ordinaries Accumulation index and its predecessor indices (that is, investments made at month-ends), almost one in four (23.2 per cent) of the 12-month investments in the Australian sharemarket have made a loss. The best return was 86.1 per cent (year to 31 July 1987), while the worst was minus 41.7 per cent (year to 30 November 2008). The average gain was 13.3 per cent.

The volatility in any given year can be a big problem for investors. A 54 per cent fall in the stock market index — as occurred between November 2007 and March 2009, at the height of the global financial crisis (GFC) — certainly got investors rethinking risk versus return, as did the 36.5 per cent fall in February to March 2020, the fastest slump in the market's history. These days, investors are far more attuned to volatility and the risk they're taking.

TIP

If you're a long way from retirement, the sharemarket's good long-term track record is working for you. But if you're getting close to retirement and the share-market's volatility worries you, maybe look to move to some investments that are not highly correlated to the sharemarket. Bonds have traditionally been seen as fitting the bill, but in extreme market scenarios such as February to March 2020, this correlation argument for bonds can fail.

Don't Be Panicked Out of Your Shares

You've bought your shares. You like the company's prospects for making money and paying you a dividend. But all you hear on the evening news is that no end seems to be in sight for the bear market. That's what confronted a lot of investors during the GFC, and many 'capitulated' — they sold out and moved to the per-ceived safety of cash, thinking that they could buy back in later, to participate in the recovery. The problem is that this is a difficult strategy to get right; you need well-timed selling and re-buying decisions.

Behavioural finance is a fascinating field, and superannuation funds report that many investors switch options at the worst possible time. For example, during the GFC, many switched their accounts to the most conservative options in March 2009, when markets were at their lowest ebb. In March 2020, despite warnings from the superannuation industry against locking in financial losses by selling shares into a plunging market, a significant cohort of retirees acted on impulse and shifted their super from their funds' 'balanced' or 'conservative' investment options and into the cash option. If they had remained in their original investment options, they wouldn't have missed out on the large gains made after the market hit its bottom. As Paul O'Neill, former US Treasury Secretary, once put it: 'You don't pull up your turnips to see how they're growing.' Nor can you accomplish anything useful by selling your share portfolio during a market downturn. Think of yourself as an investor for the long term and not a trader.

REMEMBER

A loss is only a loss if it's realised. If you don't have a very pressing need for money, you don't have to sell a share that you believe will eventually recover in price. Also, tax and cost considerations are involved in selling out. Finally, remember the paradox of cash; it's the safest investment option, but it won't give you the growth in capital you need over the long term.

Don't Ignore Dividends (Especially Franked Ones)

Since 1900, according to AMP Capital, Australian shares (as represented by the S&P/ASX All Ordinaries Accumulation index and predecessor indices) have earned a return of approximately 11.8 per cent a year on average — despite wars, recessions, economic crises, full-blown sharemarket crashes and a depression. Of this return, share price growth contributed 49 per cent, and dividends contributed 51 per cent.

That's right — over the (very) long term, just over half of the total return came from the humble dividend. The dividends from high-quality stocks are far less volatile than their share prices. If you're picking up the dividend income stream from this kind of stock, you don't have to worry about the share price on a day-to-day basis. Over the long term, the share price will probably benefit you, but you can afford to ignore that.

REMEMBER

The really great thing about using shares for income is that over a long holding period, the rising dividend can start to generate almost incredible yields, based on the original purchase price. Due to the benefits of franking credits, tax takes less of the return from Australian shares than from the return of any other asset class. The lower the investor's tax rate, the more the after-tax return exceeds the before-tax return. Franking credits have a value that is part of your total return as a shareholder, and these credits come in very handy at all tax rates, but they start to give huge benefits in the superannuation environment. Make sure you understand how helpful franked dividends can be.

Don't Buy a Share You Know Nothing About

I should have known that the technology stock boom was doomed in early 2000 when a work colleague boasted about the gain she'd made on a stock, which she referred to by its three-letter Australian Stock Exchange code. I asked her what the company was and what it did. She didn't know the company's name, let alone its business. As the saying goes, 'If you can't explain what a company does, don't invest in it.' When you buy a share, you're supposed to know something about the company's cash flow, how profit is made and whether money is reinvested to fund the development of the business or used to pay you a dividend.

TIP

As an investor, you should invest your time getting to know the companies that you're considering for your portfolio. Knowledgeable investing requires you to work out a few basic financial ratios, which helps you understand how well the company's managers are running the business. Being able to quote the stock exchange code won't help you evaluate a company. If you buy shares and don't do your homework, you're only a punter.

Don't Expect Things to Stay the Same

Try to avoid imagining that recent past returns will be repeated in the future — investors do this all the time. Predicting the future based on the past reflects wishful thinking, and an inability to imagine the prevailing sentiment — be it good times or bad times — ever changing. It's why Australian investors have a bad habit of getting into and out of an investment at the wrong time — either into it when it's peaking, and all the headlines make it seem you're a fool for missing out, or out of it when it's bottoming out, and no one wants to touch it with a barge pole.

REMEMBER

When you're investing on the sharemarket, it's never 'different this time'. If share prices, price/earnings (P/E) ratios and investor returns divert from long-term averages for too long, they will revert to that mean. Over the last 70 years the Australian sharemarket generated an average total return (capital growth and dividends) of 11.8 per cent a year. More recently, over the last 20 years, the share-market has delivered total return of 8.3 per cent a year (that lesser figure shows the impact of the 'tech bust' in 2000, the GFC slump in 2007 — which more than halved the value of the market index — and the COVID crash of 2020). But whether the sharemarket's running hot or running cold, rest assured the opposite state is not too far away.

Between December 2018 and what we now know to have been the February 2020 high-point before the COVID crash, the Australian sharemarket's S&P/ASX 200 index rose by 33 per cent in just 14 months. In price terms (that is, without count-ing dividends), the market usually delivers a gain of about 5.7 per cent a year. Thus, the market had, in 14 months, delivered nearly 5.8 years' worth of average annual returns. It couldn't last — and it didn't. But when the sharemarket is hav-ing a bad trot — like its two consecutive losing years in 2008 and 2009 — that can't last, either. In the 11 calendar years since 2009, the sharemarket has racked up ten positive years. Just remember that averages are averages — if you expect a smooth return of 11.8 per cent a year from your Australian share portfolio, you will be disappointed.

Don't Delay a Sale to Save Capital Gains Tax

If you own a share for less than 12 months, any capital gains you make on its sale are taxed at your marginal tax rate. When you hold shares for more than 12 months, only half of your capital gain is taxed (which means, in effect, that the rate of capital gains tax, or CGT, is halved). Good practice is to cash in a profit if your shares rise sharply in price. In such cases, you may hesitate because you haven't held the shares long enough to qualify for the discounted CGT rate. You may think that if you hold on to those shares for just a few more months, you'd save half of the capital gains tax bill.

TIP

When you find yourself thinking like this, place your face under a stream of cold water. Let the capital gain you made on the shares drive your decision, not the capital gains tax. If you decide to delay the sale to save on the tax bill, you may well lose out on the entire profit if the share price falls.

Don't Let Tax Drive Your Investment Decisions

Don't invest in a share investment mainly for tax reasons. This is particularly true in the case of a margin loan. A *margin loan* is a long-term wealth accumulation strategy that can be structured to ride out short-term market fluctuations. Margin loans are attractive to traders as leverage vehicles and because they offer a tax deduction, but you should enter into a margin loan with the intention of owning the portfolio outright, just as if you'd taken out a home loan.

With a margin loan, you're making a leveraged investment in the sharemarket, which is one of the most volatile of all asset markets. After you take out a margin loan, the sharemarket will be revaluing, every day, the portfolio that you bought. A margin call for more cash (or shares) can happen to you at the worst of times and be a nasty surprise.

WARNING

While on the subject of gearing, I want to caution you not to overdo it, particularly with one stock. A portfolio geared to 70 per cent (that is, 70 per cent of the funds are borrowed) can get into a margin call situation very easily (with a fall of only 6 per cent), but a portfolio geared to 40 per cent would need a 45 per cent fall in the market for that to happen. As was seen from 2007 to 2009, such a fall is possible — a margin loan would have had to be geared to 30 per cent to have escaped a margin call in that market rout.

Don't Fret Over Lost Profit

When you sell a share at a profit, don't follow its later progress and worry about the money you could have made. You need great mental discipline to do this, but it does help keep your stress level low.

REMEMBER

Investing in the sharemarket is not a competitive sport. The only runner you're trying to beat is inflation; you're not competing against other investors. The extra profit that another investor gets from the sale of a share at a higher exit point than you is not money that you didn't get.

If somebody delays a sale and reaps a better selling price than you did, congratulate them. Their success doesn't detract from your profit, which has been banked or put towards new entries in promising stocks. You made your profit, which took into account your needs and objectives. You set a target. You had the discipline to sell and move on. If you'd hung on another day, the risk/reward equation could have changed dramatically.

Don't Try to Time the Market

The sharemarket fluctuates — *corrections* (falls of 10 per cent or more) are reasonably common within what is an overall rising trend over long periods of time. With the benefit of hindsight, many of the big swings in the markets — like the tech boom (and bust) and the GFC — look inevitable and thus predictable. So, wouldn't it make sense to pull out of the market before a correction occurs — and get back in before the recovery begins?

Well, yes, it would, if you could do it consistently — but even the best professional investors struggle to 'time' the market with any success. Plenty of experts, whether they're using fundamental or technical analysis, give free advice on where the market is heading — but they may be wrong, and identifying when to get out and in is easier said than done. And, of course, getting it wrong can cost you a chunk of money.

At the time of the COVID crash in March 2020, Shane Oliver, head of investment strategy and chief economist at AMP Capital, brought out a timely piece of research showing that someone who had invested in Australian shares between January 1995 and February 2020 would have earned a return of 8 per cent a year (including dividends, but excluding franking credits, tax and fees). If this hypothetical investor had shown great market timing and avoided the ten worst days the sharemarket had experienced over that time — and got back into the market after each of these — they would have boosted their return to 11 per cent a year — an improvement of more than 37 per cent. If their market timing had been perfect and they had pulled out before each of the 40 worst days over that period, their return would have almost doubled, at 15.8 per cent a year.

However, some of the market's best days often follow hot on the heels of its worst days, as the index jumps around in the volatility that surrounds a big correction. Many investors only get out after the bad returns have occurred — just in time to miss some of the best days. According to Oliver, if trying to time the market caused this hypothetical investor to miss out on the ten best days, their return would have fallen to 6.1 per cent a year. And if they had missed out on the 40 best days it would have been disastrous, as their return would have dropped to just 2.2 per cent a year.

It might be a sharemarket cliché, but it's true — time in the market beats timing the market.

Glossary

accumulation index: An index that assumes all dividends are reinvested, thus it measures the total return (capital growth plus dividend income) from the index. For example, the S&P/ASX 200 Index measures capital growth from the Australian sharemarket; the S&P/ASX 200 Accumulation Index measures the total return from the Australian sharemarket.

accumulation phase: The phase of a person's superannuation fund membership during which they are contributing to the account, or during which their super balance is 'accumulating' (combining the person's contributions with the capital growth earned on the investments made by the super fund).

active management: The style of professional funds management in which the manager relies on its investment research, analysis, forecasts and its management team's own judgment and experience in making decisions on which assets to buy and sell. The active manager is seeking to leverage its skill to generate 'alpha' — that is, to make returns above the accepted benchmark return for the asset class.

administration: When ASIC appoints an accounting firm to take charge of an insolvent company's affairs, in the place of the management and board of directors.

all or none: An order placed on the basis that it's to be filled entirely, or not at all.

alpha: Returns above the accepted benchmark or index return (or average market return) for the asset class, which itself is called 'beta'. In effect, alpha measures an investment's outperformance of the index return for that asset class.

amortisation: Similar to depreciation, an annual deduction made from the book value of any goodwill held by the company, and charged against profit.

ASIC: The Australian Securities and Investments Commission, which regulates companies and the securities markets.

ask: A selling quote; the price that a particular seller is prepared to accept to sell the shares.

asset allocation: The process of apportioning an invested portfolio into a diversified variety of investments.

assets: Items an individual or company owns that may be converted to cash if sold.

ASX: The Australian Securities Exchange.

ASX Trade: The Australian Securities Exchange's trading system, on which all trading takes place.

at best: An order that tells the broker to obtain the best buying or selling price they can.

at limit: An order that stipulates to your broker the highest price you're prepared to pay, or, if selling, the lowest price you'll accept.

at market: An order placed on the basis that you will accept a price at or about the market price for the shares at that time.

averaging down: Buying more of a stock if it falls in price. Investors do this to lower the average cost per share of the holding.

backdoor listing: When a company lists on the stock exchange by acquiring (or being acquired by) a company that has been suspended by the stock exchange, but retains its listing.

balance date: The day on which a company rules off its books to balance accounts for the year (or half-year).

barrier warrant: A warrant that works in exactly the same way as a vanilla warrant, provided the closing price of the underlying share remains above a set barrier price over the life of the warrant. If the price of the underlying share closes at or below the barrier price, the barrier is breached and the warrant terminates.

bear: Investor who believes the market will fall.

bear market: The term used if the market index falls by 20 per cent or more.

beta: (1) The relative volatility of a stock, as in the amount it moves in price compared to moves in the benchmark index. For example, if a share has a beta of 1, then the stock will tend to go up and down by the same return as the market. If it has a beta of 2, then it will tend to go up by twice the market's return when the market goes up, and down twice as much as the market when the market goes down; (2) The exposure of a portfolio to market risk, which cannot be diversified away. This means that the 'beta' return is effectively the return of the market index; it can be captured through a passive fund that is structured to track the index, before fees.

bidder's statement: A company making a takeover offer for another company must prepare a bidder's statement to be sent to all shareholders of the target company. The bidder's statement is normally followed by the 'target's statement'.

bids: The prices that buyers are prepared to pay for a share at any given time.

bigger fool theory: The investment theory, prominent in a boom, that says that no matter how crazy is the price you pay for a share, a bigger fool will come along to buy it from you for more.

black box: A software system that generates buy and sell recommendations through proprietary algorithms (methods of calculation developed by the software writers).

block trade: A share parcel traded between institutions. Sometimes called a 'special'.

blue chips: The 'core stocks' of a long-term portfolio. Blue chips are considered the most reliable in terms of capital growth and dividend income, and are usually the least volatile shares on the market.

blue sky: The possibility of making very large future gains; the reason why people buy speculative stocks.

bond: A security showing that the owner has lent money to a government (or semi-government authority, or company) and is entitled to interest payments on the fixed dates, and to have the money repaid on the date of maturity of the bond.

bonus issue: An issue of shares (or options) to shareholders on a pro rata basis; for example, one free share for every five held.

bookbuild: The process by which the underwriters in an initial public offering (IPO) may call for tenders for shares from institutional investors, who may make offers for a certain number of shares at a certain price. Using this knowledge, the underwriters can delay setting the final price of the shares until they know what the demand is, so in theory the underwriters get the price close to what the market can actually bear.

bottom line: Term for a company's net profit after tax because this figure is at the bottom of the income statement.

bottom-up investing: Concentrating on the attributes of individual stocks rather than economic factors. It's the opposite of top-down investing.

brokerage: The fee that a broker charges for buying or selling shares on your behalf.

bull: An individual who expects the market to rise.

buy and write: A strategy in which the investor writes (sells) call options over shares they own, to generate extra income. Because the investor owns the shares, these are known as covered calls.

buyback: When a company offers to buy some of its shares back from the shareholders.

call option: Gives its buyer (or 'taker') the right to buy a specified number of shares on or before a specified date, at a predetermined price.

capital gain: The profit made by selling an asset for more than its purchase cost.

capital gains tax (CGT): A tax levied on a person's capital gains.

capital-guaranteed product: An investment product which, if held to maturity, guarantees that you get at least your original investment back.

capital loss: The loss made by selling an asset for less than its purchase cost.

cash burn: A negative net cash flow. Spending that is not being replaced by any inflow of cash.

cash extraction: A strategy where an investor converts his shares into instalment warrants, unlocking cash that can be used to buy other investments.

cash flow: The difference between a company's revenue and its expenses.

chart: A graph of the price of a share, usually with price represented on the vertical (y) axis and time on the horizontal (x) axis.

charting: Another term for technical analysis.

CHESS: The Clearing House Electronic Sub-register System, an electronic transfer and settlement system developed by the ASX. All shareholdings on the ASX are registered electronically on CHESS.

class: Put or call options with the same underlying shares.

closed-end fund: Investment vehicles in which, after the initial capital raising, investors have to buy the existing shares.

closing-call price (CCP): The daily closing price (or premium) established in the options market. All margin requirements are based on this price.

commodity index fund: A fund designed to track a commodity price index.

company option: A security issued by a company, which trades along with the company's shares on the ASX and carries the right to be converted into shares by a later date, for a certain price. If the options are not converted, they lapse. Option holders don't get dividends and don't have a vote.

compliance listing: When the stock exchange allows a company to list without offering new shares. Such a listing requires an information memorandum rather than a prospectus.

confession season: The period preceding each reporting season, when companies that realise they're not going to meet the market's profit expectations (or their own previously provided guidance) inform the market of this.

consensus forecasts: The collated and averaged earnings forecasts of the analysts that follow each company, considered to give the market view of likely earnings.

consolidation: When a company decreases its total number of shares on issue by parcelling (for example) four shares into one. In this case, the share price would quadruple to reflect the adjustment.

continuous disclosure: The regime under which each ASX-listed company operates, under which any news that could conceivably affect its share price must be made known to the market as soon as the company becomes aware of it.

contract for difference (CFD): An equity derivative that represents a theoretical order to buy or sell a certain number of shares. The price of a CFD is derived from the spread quoted on the ASX — the value of the CFD mirrors the share price.

contract note: A written confirmation that a share transaction took place, issued by the stockbroker to the client, giving the number of shares traded and the transaction price, the brokerage paid and the total cost of the transaction (if buying) or sum realised (if selling).

contrarian investing: Doing the opposite of what the great majority in the market seems to be doing. For example, buying in the middle of a crash, and selling when prices are skyrocketing.

contributing (or partly paid) shares: Shares issued on the understanding that at some time in the future, the company may need the rest of the money and 'make a call' on the outstanding amount.

conversion effect: When changes in the value of the A$ have a direct effect on a company's cash flow.

convertible note: A fixed-interest security issued by a company in return for cash. The security is issued for a fixed period and pays a stated rate of interest, not a dividend, then is convertible into ordinary shares at certain dates in the future. When the note expires, the note's holder can either get their money back, or convert the note into shares, at a set price (or ratio).

convertible preference share (CPS): A preference share that may be converted into ordinary shares in a specified ratio at any time, or at a later date.

core/satellite strategy: An investment strategy that typically involves a core holding (often an index fund) that functions as the stable 'core' of the portfolio, with carefully chosen 'satellite' holdings (often active fund managers or direct shares) that the investor believes will either deliver alpha (out-performance of the index) or show low correlation to the core index return.

corporate governance: The way in which a company is run, and the processes by which the company is directed.

correction: A fall of 10 per cent or more in the market's main index.

coupon: The annual interest rate at which a bond is issued. If the bond is held to maturity, this interest rate will not change.

covered call: A call option sold over shares that the writer owns.

crash: When a stock market index drops severely (more than 10 per cent) in a short period of time; in other words, a very sudden correction. Generally occurs at the end of an extended bull market.

current assets: In a company's statement of financial position (the balance sheet), assets that will be used (converted to cash) within one year.

current liabilities: In a company's statement of financial position (the balance sheet), the debts that fall due within one year.

cyclical stock: A share with sales and earnings that depend heavily on the economic cycle. An example is a discretionary retailer such as Super Retail Group, which benefits when consumers are confident in the state of the economy and feel more willing to spend on non-essential items.

data: Numerical information on shares. For a fundamental investor, the data required on a particular company are earnings, dividends, assets, liabilities and price. The data that a trader needs are price and volume.

day only: An at limit order can be lodged for the day only. If the order isn't filled, it will be purged, or cancelled, by the ASX Trade system.

debt-to-equity ratio: A ratio showing the extent to which a company is financed by debt. Also called the gearing ratio.

default option (or fund): A superannuation fund into which your super contributions will be placed by your employer if you don't choose an option or fund for yourself.

defensive share: A stock that's relatively unaffected by economic cycles because its business experiences ongoing demand; for example, a supermarket stock such as Coles or Woolworths, or a telecommunications supplier such as Telstra.

deferred dividend share: A share on which it's stipulated that dividends will not be paid until a certain date.

defined benefit fund: A type of superannuation fund that pays out a specific or defined amount of money regardless of how much has been contributed or how well the fund has performed. The fund member's retirement benefit is calculated based on annual salary and the number of years worked with the employer. Defined benefit funds are now rare, and most super funds are accumulation funds.

delisting: When suspension becomes permanent, and the company ceases to trade.

demerger: When a company carves out (or 'spins off') a business that it owns into a legally separate company, transferring a proportional number of shares in the demerged entity to its shareholders and listing it separately. The newly separate business may also be called a 'spin-off'.

demutualisation: A process by which mutually owned insurers and co-operatives have converted their structure to share-based companies and listed on the sharemarket.

depreciation: An annual deduction made from the value of real (tangible) assets to represent wear and tear, and charged against profit.

derivatives: Securities that 'derive from' other securities; for example, options and warrants, which derive from the physical market in the shares.

dilution: Adjusting a company's earnings per share, cash flow per share and NTA per share figures to take into account the actual number of shares on issue, and also the number of potential shares, such as options and convertible notes. For example, a fully diluted EPS figure assumes that all of those possible conversions into ordinary shares have taken place. Dilution can also refer to what happens when a company makes a share issue — the increased number of shares reduces the proportion of the ownership of the company by each investor (this can be unpopular with existing shareholders).

direct share investment: Buying shares in your own right.

discount: (1) The difference between a share's first price upon listing and its issue price, if it is a loss; (2) A negative difference between any of one stock's fundamental data and another's.

distribution: The equivalent of a dividend in a managed fund or a trust.

diversification: The spreading of your invested funds across a range of assets.

dividend: A portion of a company's profits distributed to its shareholders. An interim dividend is paid for the first six months of the company's financial year, and a final dividend for the second half. The two amounts make up the annual dividend.

dividend cover: The number of times that a company's dividend is covered by its net profit.

dividend imputation: System in use in Australia that allows investors who've been paid a dividend to take a personal tax credit on the tax already paid by the company. The rebate, known as the franking credit or imputation credit, can be used by a shareholder to reduce their tax liability.

dividend yield: The return in percentage terms represented by the dividend income from a share investment. The dividend yield is calculated by dividing the dividend per share by the current market price of the shares and multiplying the result by 100.

dollar-cost averaging: Making regular investments of the same amount of money in a stock (or equity fund). You buy fewer shares (or units) when the price is higher, but more when the price is lower. Over the long term, this approach smooths out peaks and troughs in the price.

dual listed company (DLC) structure: When two companies, listed on separate stock exchanges, execute a binding legal agreement to operate as though they jointly owned the combined assets of the group. The individual shares remain listed as before. For example, in 2001, BHP merged with the London-based Billiton in a DLC structure; but in January 2022, BHP relinquished its London Stock Exchange listing, becoming a solely ASX-listed company. Its fellow global miner Rio Tinto, however, remains a DLC, jointly listed in London and the ASX.

due diligence: The study of every aspect of a company and its business. It is the process by which an underwriting firm or lead manager researches a firm that is conducting an IPO, in order to set the price of the shares. Due diligence is also performed by a company that is looking to make a takeover bid for another company. (The term is also used for any situation that involves a deep and thorough analysis of a business or a proposition.)

earnings per share (EPS): Measures the portion of profit earned for every ordinary share on issue. EPS represents the E in P/E (the price/earnings ratio.

earnings yield: The inverse of the price/earnings (P/E) ratio, the earnings yield measures the yield on the company's earnings before they are split, with one portion going into retained earnings and the remainder going out to shareholders as dividends.

EBITDA: Earnings before interest, tax, depreciation and amortisation. EBITDA is a measure of a company's actual cash earnings, before money goes off to meet various commitments.

emerging market: A sharemarket in a developing country, such as those in South-East Asia, eastern Europe or Latin America.

environmental, social and governance (ESG): An investment philosophy and framework that prioritises consideration of criteria in three main areas: environmental (how a company or an investment performs as a steward of the natural environment); social (how a company or an investment manages relationships with employees, suppliers, customers and the communities where it operates); and governance (how a company or investment is operated, in terms of its leadership, executive pay, its standards in terms of reporting and auditing, its compliance with regulation, and how it deals with shareholder rights).

equities: Shares are sometimes called equities because, in law, the part of the assets of a company owned by shareholders is called equity (the shareholders' funds).

equity crowdfunding: A means by which an unlisted private company can raise money by selling shares to non-associated investors through a crowd-funding platform, subject to certain restrictions.

equity fund (or 'equity trust'): A managed fund that invests solely in shares.

equity risk premium: The difference between the risk-free return (the ten-year government bond rate) and the much riskier return on shares. The premium compensates the share investor for the added risk.

escrow: The stock exchange rule by which some shareholdings in a company about to list may be frozen — voluntarily or at the direction of the exchange — for a period of time, usually one or two years. Usually, the shares placed in escrow are those owned by the company's vendors or promoters. Escrow is sometimes called the 'patron saint of patient investors'.

ethical investment: An investment philosophy that avoids investments in companies whose activities or products the investor considers morally unacceptable; for example, uranium mining, munitions, pornography, alcohol, tobacco or gambling. Ethical investment funds are a subset of socially responsible investment (SRI) funds.

exchange-traded bond (XTB): A stock that represents a fraction of a bond, and is traded on the ASX.

exchange-traded fund (ETF): A stock that represents a portfolio or an index, and tracks its return.

exchange-traded managed fund (ETMF): A managed fund that is traded on the stock exchange. ETMFs are similar to ETFs, but they're actively managed funds. Typically, ETMFs are a unit class of an unlisted fund, but the investor can buy or sell on the ASX at any time. Because an ETMF is an open-ended fund, units are created and cancelled to meet demand; this supply and demand means that the unit price should not stray far from the fund's net tangible asset (NTA) value, solving the discount-to-NTA problem that plagues LICs. ETMFs are known as quoted managed funds (QMFs) on the Cboe Australia exchange.

exchange-traded option (ETO): What is normally meant by option. An ETO is a contract representing the right to buy or sell a parcel of the underlying shares. ETOs are not issued by the companies, but by the stock exchange. In this case, the companies over whose shares the options are issued have no connection to the options trading.

excluded fund: A former self-managed super fund that didn't have to comply with many of the requirements set for the public offer funds.

excluded offer: An offer to professional investors to take up shares in a company, by invitation, in $500,000 lots. These offers are accompanied by an information memorandum which does not have to be lodged with ASIC, and which contains far less information than a prospectus.

execution-only broker: A broker who conducts only transactions. Sometimes called discount brokers because they're significantly cheaper than full-service brokers. These days, execution-only brokers usually means internet brokers.

exercise: In the options market, the written notification by the buyer (or taker) of an option of his decision to buy or sell the underlying shares pertaining to an options contract.

exercise (or 'strike') price: In the options market, the price at which the underlying shares may be bought or sold by exercise of the option.

factor: A quantifiable characteristic of a stock that can explain differences in returns. Examples of factors are 'quality', 'low volatility', 'value' and 'momentum'.

fair-value: Some non-current assets, for example investment property, or shares or bonds held for trading, are not depreciated, but fair-valued each year. To get a fair value, the company looks at market price, or looks at prices of similar assets to infer a value, or uses some other form of valuation technique. This must be done every balance date.

fill and kill: An order placed with your broker on the basis that as much of the order is to be filled as possible, immediately, and the rest cancelled.

financing cash flow: A company's cash flow from issuing shares, borrowing from (or repaying) banks, or receiving (or paying) dividends.

float: The first time a company's shares are sold on the sharemarket. The official term is an initial public offering (IPO).

fractional shares: Portions of whole individual shares or ETFs.

franking account: An Australian company pays corporate tax at a rate of 30 per cent. When it pays tax, it builds up credits in its franking account. The company's ability to frank its dividend depends on the credit balance in this account.

franking credit: The personal tax credit received by a shareholder, attached to a company dividend, on the tax already paid by the company on its profit.

free cash flow: The cash flow available to the company after all capital expenditure and maintenance requirements have been met and the dividend paid.

full-service stockbroker: A broker who offers individual advice, research, portfolio management, access to floats and financial planning as well as execution of transactions.

fundamental analysis: Assessing the financial health of a company, using numerical data given in its regularly published accounts, to decide whether its shares are under- or overvalued.

fundamentals: A company's 'fundamentals' are hard numerical data such as earnings, dividends, assets and liabilities, given in its published accounts.

futures contract: The means by which buyers and sellers of a commodity (or financial asset) agree to buy or sell a specific amount of the commodity at a particular price on a stipulated future date.

futures market: A place where futures contracts are traded. In Australia, the futures market is operated by the ASX.

gapping: Where a share price (or index level) opens significantly higher or lower than its close of the previous day, without trading at the intervening prices or levels.

gearing: (1) The ratio of a company's borrowings to its shareholders' equity (or shareholders' funds); (2) Making an investment using borrowed funds.

goodwill: An asset that's created when one company acquires another. Goodwill represents the difference between the price paid and the value of the acquired company's assets, representing all of the intangible factors that make people do business with a company, such as brand loyalty and reputation.

greenshoe: An arrangement in an initial public offering that allows the vendor or its underwriting panel to buy in the secondary (post-listing) market more shares than were offered through the prospectus. The greenshoe is available to the underwriters for a limited period to stabilise the share price in a volatile market.

grey box: A software system that resembles a black box in that it generates trade suggestions from proprietary algorithms, but gives the user a general idea of how the formula works and may allow the user to modify the settings or parameters.

gross domestic product (GDP): The value of all goods and services produced in a nation's economy is that nation's GDP.

growth stocks: Shares with earnings that are expected to increase faster than the growth rate of the average business in their industry; or the market as a whole; or the economy (as measured by growth in GDP).

guidance: The practice by which companies seek to manage the market's expectations of their revenue or profit, either by giving specific forecasts themselves, or by commenting publicly on the forecasts posted by research analysts.

hedge fund: An aggressive trading fund.

hedging: Investing in one asset to offset the risk in another.

holder identification number (HIN): A number that registers an individual's ownership of shares in CHESS, if they're sponsored in the system by a broking firm. Shareholdings in any number of companies can be registered under an individual's HIN.

holding statement: A statement, like a bank statement, that details changes in a shareholder's holding of a particular share. A statement is issued by CHESS whenever the holding has been altered by a transaction during the month. A separate statement is issued for each security held in CHESS.

hybrid security: A security with a mix of debt and equity, paying an interest rate for a time then being convertible to shares.

imputation credit: Another term for franking credit.

income statement: One of the three main financial statements, the income statement (formerly known as a profit and loss statement, or P&L) is a summary of the company's revenue and expenses over the year. The income statement shows whether or not the company's operations for the year generated a profit.

index (plural 'indices'): A notional portfolio designed to reflect the wider sharemarket as accurately as possible. The index gives investors a means of tracking market performance.

index fund: A managed fund that replicates a particular index. The manager of an index fund constructs a portfolio that closely tracks a specific market index by holding all or, in the case of very broad indices, a representative sample of the securities in the index.

index warrant: A trading warrant giving the investor the right to buy or sell the notional basket of shares that makes up the Australian Securities Exchange's S&P/ASX 200 index.

indirect share investment: Where your investment in shares is not in your own right; for example, when you own shares in a managed fund or equity fund.

inflation: The rate of change in the cost of living, as measured by the Consumer Price Index (CPI).

information memorandum: The document that accompanies a compliance listing or an excluded offer. It is not required to contain as much information as a prospectus.

infrastructure: The huge fixed assets that provide utility and transportation services.

initial public offering (IPO): The US term for a company float, now widely used around the world.

insider trading: A criminal offence described in Section 1002G of the Corporations Law, which says that insider trading occurs when a person possesses and trades on information not generally available to the market and they know, or ought reasonably to know, that this information is not generally available to the market.

instalment receipt: A security giving evidence of ownership of a share, part of the purchase price of which has been paid. The instalment receipt may be traded up until the payment of the final instalment of the share price; on payment of the final instalment, holders of instalment receipts become the registered holders of the shares.

instalment warrant: An investment warrant in which the investor buys a share by paying some of its current value now and the rest later. The investor borrows the funds from the warrant issuer to buy the underlying shares.

institution: An organisation that invests professionally, such as a super or pension fund, insurance company, funds manager, investment company, trustee company or bank.

intangible asset: Anything that contributes to a company's value, but can't be recognised in its statement of financial position (the balance sheet). Intangible assets are those that can't be touched, for example, goodwill, media titles, brand names, broadcasting licences, management, even market share and distribution networks.

interest cover: The number of times that a company's interest payments are covered by its earnings.

in the money: An option or warrant that could be exercised now at a profit.

intrinsic value: In the options market, the difference between the market value of the underlying shares and the exercise price of the option. It cannot be less than zero.

investing cash flow: A company's cash flow from buying or selling a business, shares, intellectual property or any other asset.

investment-grade: Stocks that are considered suitable for investment by institutional investors. Just what constitutes investment-grade differs between institutions, but usually it means the stocks in the S&P/ASX 200 index (usually companies valued at $1.4 billion or more).

investment warrants: A range of investment products that are designed to allow investors to trade on their estimation on where share prices, indices, currencies and commodities are heading. Still known as warrants but are typically traded less frequently, and have longer-dated expiries. The major kind of investment warrant is the instalment warrant.

investor: A sharemarket user who invests capital in stocks for maximum capital growth over the long term.

leverage: Another term for gearing. Where borrowed money has been used in an investment, or the investment is in options and warrants, and controls a much larger number of shares than could be bought with the actual invested amount, the investment is said to be leveraged.

liabilities: Any amounts owed by an individual or a company.

liquidation: When a court appoints an accounting firm to wind up the affairs of an insolvent company, sell its assets, settle its debts (if possible) and pay out any remaining cash to the shareholders.

liquidity: (1) The ease with which an asset can be converted to cash; (2) The amount of trading in a particular share.

listed investment company (LIC): An equity fund that's itself listed on the sharemarket; in effect, a share that invests in other shares. Structured as a company, underlying assets are managed in a pooled vehicle by professional investment managers. LIC managers treat the dividends and capital gains from underlying investments as income; the LIC pays tax on its earnings and pays distributions to investors in the form of dividends, whether franked or unfranked.

listed investment trust (LIT): Similar to an LIC, but structured as a trust, LITs distribute all net income and realised capital gains to investors on a pre-tax basis — and it is the investor who is liable to pay tax. LIT income streams are more likely to be unpredictable, fluctuating with the fund manager's trading activity — to offset these fluctuations, LIT managers can pay distributions above the fund's income level, through a 'return of capital'.

managed fund (or 'unit trust'): A vehicle in which small investors pool their money to buy assets that are larger in size and more numerous in spread than they could buy individually, and which is managed on their behalf by a fund manager. A managed fund has greater buying power and can more easily diversify its assets than an individual investor.

margin: (1) The percentage of each dollar of sales revenue that is turned into profit; (2) The amount of collateral that must be lodged in some leveraged investments — for example options, warrants and margin loans — to ensure that the investor can meet their obligation in the event of a loss.

margin call: When a leveraged investment temporarily goes against the investor, the lender or the ASX may request more margin collateral be lodged. If this is not paid, the investment may be closed down. For example, in a margin loan the lender will set a loan-to-value ratio (say, 70 per cent of the portfolio's value) that it does not want the loan to exceed. If the portfolio value falls and the loan-to-value ratio rises, the lender will ask for the loan-to-value ratio to be restored by a further contribution from the borrower. If the client cannot meet a margin call, the lender will sell the shares.

margin loan: A loan for the purpose of buying shares.

market capitalisation: Total value of a company's shares on the sharemarket at any time.

market depth: At any time in any share, the list of all bids and offers.

mFunds: Unlisted managed funds that trade on the ASX's mFund platform.

MINI warrant: A type of trading warrant that offers leveraged exposure to shares, indices, commodities and currencies.

minorities: The shareholders in a company in which the majority of the shares are held by another company or single investor.

monetary policy: Alterations to official interest rates by the Reserve Bank of Australia.

MSCI: The Morgan Stanley Capital International indices, used globally as benchmarks. The absolute performance of a country's sharemarket index is often measured against one of the MSCI indices to assess how it has performed relative to the rest of the world.

naked call: A call option sold over shares that the writer doesn't actually own.

net cash flow: The sum of net operating cash flow, net investing cash flow and net financing cash flow gives net cash flow, or the net increase in cash held for the period.

net tangible asset (NTA) backing: The dollar amount of a company's real assets that stand behind each share. If you value the real assets of the company, leaving out intangible items like goodwill or brands, and divide this amount by the number of shares on issue, you have the NTA.

north: A rising share price is said to be 'heading north' (because north is at the top of a map).

offers: The prices that sellers of shares are prepared to accept for their shares at any given time.

open-end fund: As in an unlisted equity trust, investors can buy new units at any time.

operating cash flow: A company's cash flow from selling products or services.

operator: Employee of a broking firm who executes buy and sell orders on the ASX Trade screen.

option: A security that gives its holder the right to buy (or sell) a specified number of shares on or before a specified date, at a predetermined price.

order: Instructions to a stockbroker to buy or sell a particular amount of shares.

ordinary (or fully paid) shares: The basic units into which a company's equity capital — literally, its ownership — is divided.

out of the money: An option or warrant that could not be exercised now at a profit. It has no intrinsic (real) value but has time value, whereby you are buying time to be right.

owners' earnings: A concept of famed US investor Warren Buffett, this is a company's earnings (per share), minus dividends (per share) plus capital expenditure (per share). This is the cash that the business has left after all of its commitments and its required maintenance spending.

passive investing: A style of investment that involves simply buying a fund structured to follow one of the major indices (for example, the S&P/ASX 200 index) and thus generating, over the holding period, the return earned by that index, before fees.

payout ratio: The percentage of a company's net profit after tax that is paid out to shareholders in dividends (sometimes called the 'dividend payout ratio').

personal super fund: Another term for self-managed super fund or DIY super fund. Formerly known as an excluded fund.

placement: The sale of a parcel of new shares by the company, to a single investor or institution.

preference share: A form of share ranking before ordinary shares (but behind the company's creditors) in the event of the company being wound up. Preference-shareholders receive a fixed dividend rate but usually do not carry a vote at meetings.

premium: (1) The difference between a share's first price upon listing and its issue price, if it is a gain; (2) A positive difference between any of one stock's fundamental data and another's; (3) The price of an options contract, representing at any time the value of that contract in the market.

pre-open: The phase of ASX Trade between 7am and 10am, in which operators can enter buy or sell orders and amend or cancel orders left over from the previous day. These orders do not trade until the market opens at 10am.

pre-retirement phase: The phase of a person's superannuation fund membership during which they may still be working, but they have used their super to start a 'transition-to-retirement pension'.

preservation age: The age at which a person can gain access to their superannuation; at the time of writing, the preservation age depends on the person's date of birth, but ranges between the ages of 55 and 60.

price/earnings (P/E) contraction: The situation where investors detect a worsening outlook for a stock, and accept paying less for a dollar's worth of that stock's earnings, with the result that the P/E comes down. Sometimes called 'de-rating'.

price/earnings (P/E) expansion: The situation where investors believe the stock's outlook is improving, and become more willing to pay more for a dollar's worth of that stock's earnings, with the result that the P/E is pushed higher. Sometimes called 're-rating'. The opposite situation, when investors dislike the stock's outlook and become less willing to pay more for a dollar's worth of that stock's earnings, is called P/E 'contraction'.

price/earnings (P/E) ratio: The P/E is calculated by dividing the current share price in cents by the company's earnings per share figure, or EPS. The P/E thus calculated may be historical — that is, using the most recent EPS figure — or prospective, using an estimated EPS figure.

primary market: When the sharemarket is used by a company to offer its shares to investors for the first time.

private equity: An investment in a company that is not yet listed on the stock exchange, but is still 'privately owned'.

privatisation: (1) The process by which government-owned businesses have been sold through the sharemarket; (2) Confusingly, it also refers to the situation where a majority shareholder buys out the minorities and 'takes the company private' — that is, buys it off the sharemarket.

pro forma: Information being presented hypothetically. For example, two companies might have merged in order to float as a new company; the prospectus for the new company would present pro forma historic accounts that represent what would have been the accounts had the companies been merged earlier.

profit: Usually taken to mean net profit after tax (NPAT), the amount left over after all wages, operating costs, overheads, interest, taxes and allowances for the depreciation and amortisation of assets have been subtracted from revenue.

profit warning: A company announcing to the market that its next profit is likely to be reduced, or even a loss. It's a softening-up process, but it's required under the continuous disclosure regime.

prospectus: A document lodged with the ASX and ASIC containing details of the business and prospects of a company that proposes to list on the stock exchange. The prospectus must present enough information about the company's business, financial details, prospects and risk factors to allow a prospective investor to make an informed choice about whether to subscribe for the shares.

protected equity loan: A loan to buy shares where, if the value of the shares falls during the term of the loan, at the end of the loan, the lender takes back the unprofitable shares as full repayment of the loan. For this protection, borrowers pay a much higher interest rate than a normal margin loan.

public company: A company that is listed on the stock exchange is said to be a public company, because the public may invest in it.

public offer fund: A superannuation fund that accepts money from the public.

purged: The ASX Trade system purges itself of day-only orders every night, cancelling any that are unfilled.

put option: An option that gives its buyer (or 'taker') the right to sell a specified number of shares on or before a specified date, at a predetermined price.

quality of earnings: Refers to the extent to which a company's reported earnings come from actual operations; whether they are boosted (or lessened) by one-off non-operational items that will not recur, for example, if a manufacturing company were to include in its profit the profit on the sale of a surplus factory.

quote: At any time in any share, the highest bid and the lowest offer in the market.

quoted managed fund (QMF): The term by which exchange-traded managed funds (ETMFs) are known on the Cboe Australia exchange.

ramping: Boosting a company's share price by the deliberate use of false or misleading information.

real estate investment trust (REIT): An investment trust (fund) created to hold property, and allow investors to share in that ownership by buying trust units. This term has replaced 'listed property trust'.

receivership: When an accounting firm is appointed, either by a creditor or a court, to take charge of an insolvent company's affairs until its debts are paid.

recession: Two consecutive quarters of shrinking gross domestic product (GDP).

renounceable rights issue: A rights issue in which shareholders may choose to trade the rights to the shares on the stock exchange during the lifespan of the issue, typically 30 to 60 days.

reporting season: Companies report their financial results to the stock exchange at least twice a year: an interim (half-yearly) and a preliminary final result. The two main reporting dates are 31 December and 30 June. Most Australian companies use the 30 June ending date for the financial year. In January–February and July–August, the market is inundated with profit announcements. In July–August, the companies whose financial year ends on 30 June report their final results for the year, while those that use the calendar year report their interim (half-yearly) results. The reverse occurs in January–February.

reserves: (1) Capital built up by transfers from profit, or when certain types of assets are revalued; (2) The economically mineable part of a measured or indicated mineral resource. Ore reserves are subdivided into probable reserves and proved reserves.

resistance area: On a chart, this is a price level that has previously acted as a barrier. Historically, a price rise has stabilised at this level, and then reversed.

retail investor: An individual who uses the sharemarket for their own investments. Also known as private investors.

retained profit: That portion of profit not paid out to shareholders as a dividend, but reinvested in the business.

retirement phase: The phase of a person's superannuation fund membership that begins when the person starts receiving a 'super income stream' or 'pension' from the super fund.

return: The amount of income an investment earns through interest, dividends or capital gain.

return on assets (ROA): Measures the return the company's management generates on its assets, whether they were funded by debt or equity.

return on equity (ROE): Measures the return the company's management generates on its shareholders' equity.

revenue: The money that comes into the company. It's usually divided into sales revenue, generated through selling the company's products or services; and other revenue, which could be in the form of dividends, rentals, interest and the proceeds of sales of non-current assets.

rights issue: Offer of shares in which current shareholders are offered the opportunity to buy new shares at a price lower than the market price, on a pro rata basis; for example, to buy one new share for every five held. A rights issue may be 'renounceable', in which case investors can sell their rights (which trade on the ASX for a certain period), or 'non-renounceable', in which case investors cannot sell their rights, which must either be taken up or lapse.

risk: In the context of investment, risk means the possibility of losing the invested capital.

scheme of arrangement: A method by which one company can take over another through a proposal (that requires approval of the target company's shareholders and a Court) that transfers all shares in the target to the bidder, in return for consideration paid by the bidder to the target company's shareholders. Used in a 'friendly' (or 'agreed') takeover, where the target company agrees to the deal.

secondary market: Trading in a company's shares after they list for the first time.

second-liners: Stocks not yet considered investment-grade (suitable for investment) by institutional investors, but which might make the grade. Usually means those stocks outside the S&P/ASX 300, but within the S&P/ASX All Ordinaries index (the top 500 companies by market capitalisation).

securities: Shares, options, warrants and bonds are sometimes called securities, because they signify ownership with certain rights.

self-funding instalment warrants: Instalment warrants where the dividend income from the underlying shares is used to reduce the loan amount, and annual interest is capitalised (added to the loan amount).

self-managed super fund (SMSF): A personal super fund that can have up to six members. The SMSF is managed by its members, and thus can have far greater control, a wider choice of investments, increased flexibility and personally tailored circumstances than a public-offer super fund; however, in return for this freedom, many responsibilities, requirements and penalties may apply to SMSF members/trustees.

series: All options contracts of the same class having the same expiry date and exercise price. For example, all ANZ December $30 calls comprise a series.

settlement: Paying for shares you've bought, or handing over shares you've sold.

share: The basic unit of ownership into which a company's capital (or equity) is divided.

share buyback: When a company buys back and cancels a portion of its shares, to lessen the number of shares on issue.

Shareholder Registration Number (SRN): A number that registers an individual's ownership of shares in CHESS, if they are sponsored in the system by a company whose shares they buy. Only shareholdings in that company's shares can be registered under an SRN.

shareholders' equity: What the company's shareholders own. Sometimes called shareholders' funds, it is calculated by subtracting total liabilities from total assets.

shortfall: Any shares that are not bought during an IPO or rights issue.

short selling: Selling a stock that you don't own, in the expectation that by the time you have to deliver it to the buyer, its price will have fallen and you will have bought it for less on the market, thus making a profit.

sideways: A share that is neither rising nor falling in price is said to be 'trading sideways', because the only direction it is moving on a chart is along the horizontal (time) axis.

slippage: When the price at which a share order is executed does not match the price at which it was requested. Slippage usually happens in fast-moving, highly volatile markets.

socially responsible investment (SRI): An investment philosophy that invests in companies that promote sustainable economic development as well as issues of social responsibility.

sole purpose test: The requirements set out in the *Superannuation Industry (Supervision) Act* 1993 to the effect that the trustees of a self-managed super fund must ensure that the fund is maintained for the sole purpose of providing retirement benefits to members.

south: A falling share price is said to be 'heading south' (because south is at the bottom of a map).

speculative stock (or 'spec'): Once referred specifically to a minerals or petroleum explorer, but now used to refer to any stock that doesn't have a positive financial track record but which might have good prospects one day.

split: When a company makes its total number of shares on issue larger, by splitting (for example) each share into four. In this case, the share price would fall by 75 per cent to reflect the adjustment.

sponsorship: In the CHESS system, to receive a holding statement shareholders must be sponsored by (that is, registered under) a stockbroker, or the company whose shares they buy.

spot market price: In the commodities and futures markets, the term for the quoted price right now.

spread: (1) At any time in any share, the difference between the highest bid and the lowest offer quoted on the ASX (the narrower the spread, the better for the trader); (2) The number of shareholders in a company. To be traded on the ASX, a company must have a minimum of 500 shareholders.

stag: An individual who subscribes to a float through its prospectus, with the intention of selling for a quick gain. Also, the verb 'to stag'.

standard deviation: In any sample of numbers (such as a share's closing price over time) there is an average value; the standard deviation measures the extent to which each of the numbers in the sample varies from the average. The lower the standard deviation of return in a stock, the lower is its relative risk.

statement of cash flows: One of the three main financial statements, the statement of cash flows (formerly known as the cash flow statement) summarises the company's cash receipts and payments for the period.

statement of financial position: One of the three main financial statements, the statement of financial position (formerly known as the balance sheet) is a summary of the net worth of the company at balance date, recording its assets and liabilities.

statutory profit: The profit figures presented by a company in its formal company report, subject to strict requirements and accounting standards. The statutory profit figure may differ from the 'underlying' profit figure.

stop-loss: An order that tells your broker to sell a particular share you own if it falls to a certain price.

straight-through processing: When a trade is fully automated through a stockbroker's trading platform, and the investor is trading directly into the market.

sub-underwriter: A broking firm that agrees (with the underwriter) to place among its client base some of the shares being sold in an IPO.

superannuation ('super'): Long-term concessionally taxed investment vehicle for the provision of retirement savings through regular contributions from savings to be pooled into a large fund of money, which is then invested in a broad range of asset classes, including shares, property, bonds and cash deposits.

support area: Support is the opposite to resistance. On a chart, support is the price level where a price fall has historically stabilised, and then risen again.

suspension: When the stock exchange removes a company from trading, for a variety of reasons.

T+2: The settlement time frame used by the ASX; a transaction must be settled within two business days (transaction plus two).

takeover bid: When one company attempts to buy another company by making a bid for the shares.

taker: Buyer of an options contract.

target's statement: A company that has received a takeover offer from another company, and whose shareholders have received a bidder's statement, is required to send to its shareholders a 'target's statement', which must contain all the information the shareholders would reasonably require to make an informed assessment about whether to accept the offer under the bid. Usually, the target's statement will include an independent expert's report that states whether the offer is fair and reasonable. Where the target company's directors reject the bid on the basis that they believe it does not represent fair value, the reasons for this view must be disclosed in the target's statement.

technical analysis: The study of changes in the price and volume of a share, as shown on a chart, to identify a history of its behaviour in the market and predict its possible future behaviour. Sometimes called charting.

time value: In the options and warrants markets, the longer the time until expiry, the more investors are prepared to pay for the possibility of being right.

top-down investing: Taking an overview of the state of the economy, determining which sectors of it are likely to do well, and then choosing the companies in those industries for the best candidates for investment. It's the opposite of bottom-up investing.

top line: Term for a company's sales revenue, because this figure is at the top of the income statement.

trader: A sharemarket user who buys and sells blocks of shares for profit. Traders don't care how long they have owned a stock; they are simply looking to make money.

trading halt: A temporary suspension requested by a company to allow an important announcement to be made, to stop the market trading on rumour.

trading warrant: A security giving the right to buy or sell a share at some future time, at a certain price.

translation effect: When changes in the value of the A$ affect the amount of a company's foreign earnings when repatriated to Australia and reported in A$ terms (as opposed to a conversion effect).

trend: In technical analysis, the direction of the market or a share price.

trendline: A line drawn on a share chart to represent the trend.

turnover: (1) The volume of trade in a company's shares; (2) Another term for a company's revenue.

underlying profit: When presenting its profit figure, a company may, alongside its statutory profit figure, also present its 'underlying' profit figure (sometimes described as the 'normalised' or 'cash' profit), which is adjusted to remove the impact of items that the company considers to be 'one-off' or 'non-recurring'.

underwriter: The entity that brings a company to list on the market, agreeing to take the shares if they cannot be sold to the investing public — usually a stockbroking firm or an investment bank. An underwriter may also be required to support any subsequent issues of securities.

unit: The equivalent of an ordinary share in a managed fund; the smallest portion of the fund's ownership.

utility: A business that provides an essential service, such as power, telephone, natural gas, water and sewerage.

value stocks: Shares that are considered to be priced low relative to the company's earnings or assets.

value trap: A share that appears on measurements such as price/earnings (P/E) ratio or dividend yield to be trading at an attractive price, but where there are very good qualitative, operational or business reasons why that is so. Simply, it looks better on paper than in reality — the value is probably not what the investor believes it to be, and it's a potential trap.

volatility: Often confused with risk, volatility is in fact a measure of risk; it means the extent of fluctuation in prices. The higher the volatility of the price of an asset, the less certain is the return from that asset (the volatility of an investment reduces over time).

volume: The total number of shares (or other securities) traded in a given period.

warrant: A security giving the right to buy or sell a share at some future time, at a certain price. The only difference between a warrant and an exchange-traded option (ETO) is that the former lasts longer. Sometimes called a trading or vanilla warrant to distinguish it from an investment warrant.

working capital: The amount of money available to a company from liquid assets, which is current assets minus current liabilities.

write-downs: Under Australian account-ing standards, companies must revalue their assets at each balance date, and if the directors believe that the amount for which an asset could be sold is less than the value at which the asset is recorded in the statement of financial position (the balance sheet), the value of the asset must be written down to the lower amount.

writer: Seller of an options contract.

zero-sum game: A situation where if one party to a transaction makes a profit, the other party makes a loss; for example, exchange-traded options (ETOs).

Index

About the Author

Over a 33-year career, James Dunn has built a reputation as one of Australia's leading investment journalists. James was founding editor of *Shares* magazine, and oversaw one of the most successful magazine launches in Australian publishing history. He wrote for *BRW*, *Personal Investor* and *The Age*, and was subsequently personal investment editor at *The Australian* and editor of financial website investorweb.com.au. He writes for *The Australian*, *The Australian Financial Review*, *Asia Asset Management* and *Listed@ASX*. James is contributing editor at The Inside Network, publisher of *Investor Strategy News*, *The Inside Investor* and *The Inside Adviser*, and is also a sought-after speaker on investment, economic and leadership issues.

Born and raised in Ararat, western Victoria, James graduated from the University of Melbourne as Bachelor of Letters and Bachelor of Arts. He is a fellow of the Williamson Community Leadership Program, operated by Leadership Victoria.

In 1984, James won two BMWs on *Sale of the Century*. The sale of the cars financed a year of overseas travel and a substantial share portfolio, which did not survive the crash of 1987 because it was virtually all in speculative stocks. After that event, James decided on a career in financial journalism.

He has never lost his fascination with the sharemarket, and has developed a strong interest in educating people about their investments.

Dedication

Some things have not changed from the first, second and third editions of this book, when I wrote: 'This book simply would not exist without the support of and inspiration from my family.' Writing a book is a selfish thing to do, and I can't thank my wife, Jane, enough for her love and support. I dedicate this book to her and to my wonderful children, Eliza and Harry. In earlier editions, I apologised for locking myself in the study and, worse, hogging the computer; now that my children are adults, they have their own computers (indeed, the concept of one for the household now seems absurd).

Share Investing For Dummies is also dedicated to my mother and father, who made books a part of my life from my earliest memory. At long last, I was able to put my own on the other side of the ledger, a feat they never doubted.

All of the preceding still stands in this fourth edition of *Share Investing For Dummies* — quadruply so with regard to Jane, Eliza and Harry.

My thanks, once again, to Sam and Brendan, for the coffee and support.

Author's Acknowledgements

Thanks firstly to commissioning editor Lucy Raymond and developmental editor Ingrid Bond, who drove this fourth edition. Also, thanks enormously to the project editor who oversaw the process, Kerry Laundon. All three handled the delicate task of badgering and cajoling me with huge reserves of patience and understanding, and I want them to know how much I appreciate that. Thanks also to Zoë Wykes at John Wiley in the US and to the designers and everyone else at John Wiley who have helped to make this book possible.

I also want to express my appreciation to David Park, Anastasia Anagnostakos, Andrew Weaver, Graham O'Brien at ASX, Daryl Guppy at Guppytraders.com, David Reid at Andex Charts, Marc Angelovsi at FactSet Research Systems, Shane Oliver and Dermot Ryan at AMP Capital Investors, Alex Dunnin at Rainmaker Information, Jason Orthman and Julie Irwin at Hyperion Asset Management, Monik Kotecha at Insync Funds Management, Belinda Williamson and Stephen Mickenbecker at Canstar, Elizabeth Tian at Citi, Tamas Szabo at Pepperstone, Arnie Selvarajah at Bell Direct, Harrison Worley and Jacqui Coleman at Honner, Martha Wood and Robin Bowerman at Vanguard, Jeff Louie at Investment Trends, Chanuka Herath at Commonwealth Bank, Richard Burns at CommSec, Callum Thomas at Top Down Charts, Craig Badings at Senate SHJ, Sudhir Kissun at Allan Gray Australia, Ken Atchison at Atchison Consultants, Andrew Boal at Deloitte, Henry Pike at the Property Council of Australia, Jason Aravinis at IBISWorld, Nadja Jiang at Standard & Poor's, Louisza Court at Cboe Australia, Mihaela Croitoru at World Federation of Exchanges, Danielle Stitt at Bluechip, Alicia Kokocinski at Equity Trustees, and Richard Kersley at Credit Suisse. Special thanks go to Professor Elroy Dimson, Professor Paul Marsh and Dr Mike Staunton, of the London Business School.

Publisher's Acknowledgements

Some of the people who helped bring this book to market include the following:

Acquisitions, Editorial and Media Development

Project Editor: Tamilmani Varadharaj

Acquisitions Editor: Lucy Raymond

Production

Proofreader: Susan Hobbs

Editorial Manager: Ingrid Bond

Copy Editor: Kerry Laundon

Indexer: Estalita Slivoskey

The author and publisher would like to thank the following copyright holders, organisations and individuals for their permission to reproduce copyright material in this book:

>> **Cover image**: © WHYFRAME/Shutterstock

>> **Figure 1-1, Table 5-3, Table 6-2, Figure 13-1**: © ASX Limited ABN 98 008 624 691 ASX 2022. All rights reserved. This material is reproduced with the permission of ASX. This material should not be reproduced, stored in a retrieval system or transmitted in any form whether in whole or in part without the prior written permission of ASX.

>> **Figure 1-2, Figure 3-1, Table 5-1, Table 20-1, Figure 20-1, Table 20-4**: Andex Charts Pty Ltd

>> **Table 2-1**: International Federation of Stock Exchanges

>> **Figures 4-1, 4-2, 4-5**: © IRESS Market Technology

>> **Figures 4-3, 4-4, 4-6, 4-7, 4-8, 4-9, 4-10, 5-1, 5-2, 5-4, 11-2, 13-2, 13-3**: © FactSet Financial Data and Analytics

>> **Figure 5-3**: Munro Partners (Munro Asset Management Limited)

>> **Table 5-2**: Reprinted with permission of Standard & Poor's Financial Services LLC, a wholly owned subsidiary of The McGraw-Hill Companies. © 2014. All rights reserved.

>> **Figure 6-1**: CommSec

>> **Table 6-3**: CANSTAR Pty Ltd

>> **Figures 11-1, 11-3, 11-4, 11-5, 11-6, 11-7, 11-8**: AMP Capital

>> **Table 11-1**: Investors Mutual Limited

>> **Table 13-1**: OnMarket

>> **Table 13-2, Figures 13-4, 13-5**: Baby Bunting Group Limited

>> **Figures 16-1, 16-2, 16-3, 16-4, 16-4, 16-5, 16-6, 16-7, 16-8, 16-9, 16-10, 16-11, 16-12, 16-13, 16-14, 16-15, 16-16, 16-17, 16-18, 16-19A, 16-19B**: MetaStock

>> **Table 19-1**: Association of Superannuation Funds Australia

>> **Tables 20-2, 20-3**: MSCI

Every effort has been made to trace the ownership of copyright material. Information that will enable the publisher to rectify any error or omission in subsequent editions will be welcome. In such cases, please contact the Permissions Section of John Wiley & Sons Australia, Ltd.